ADULT
PSYCHOPATHOLOGY

ADULT PSYCHOPATHOLOGY

A Social Work Perspective

Edited by
Francis J. Turner

THE FREE PRESS
A Division of Macmillan, Inc.
NEW YORK

Collier Macmillan Publishers
LONDON

The Free Press
A Division of Macmillan, Inc.
866 Third Avenue, New York, N.Y. 10022

Collier Macmillan Canada, Inc.

Printed in the United States of America

printing number
1 2 3 4 5 6 7 8 9 10

Library of Congress Cataloging in Publication Data

Main entry under title:

Adult psychopathology.

  Includes index.
    1. Psychology, Pathological. 2. Psychiatric social
work.   I. Turner, Francis Joseph.   [DNLM:
1. Mental disorders—In adulthood. 2. Social work.
WM 100 A2416]
RC454.4.A38 1984   616.89′0024362   83-48127
ISBN 0-02-933000-9

To my mother, in memoriam

*"Her ways are ways of pleasantness,
and all her paths are peace."*

Proverbs III:17.

Contents

Preface _____

So great are the changes taking place in the human services that uncertainty is a common, though often hidden, characteristic of many practitioners. Two interconnected developments have contributed to this uncertainty: first, the expansion of knowledge about the human condition and how it is influenced, altered, and improved—reflected in the upsurge of new books, journals, and approaches focusing on intervention and service delivery; second, a lowering of barriers among the professions that serve people—a by-product of the expansion of knowledge. To practice responsibly in today's world, social workers need to be aware of these developments and to come to terms with them.

In spite of the best of intentions, busy practitioners are often not able to keep up with emerging ideas and therapies. Although practitioners generally do attempt to keep abreast of developments through reading, consultations, conferences, and workshops, heavy caseloads leave little time to synthesize the many trends and findings of critical importance to practice. Practitioners thus are concerned that they are not at the leading edge of their discipline.

The need for quality professional services is broadly recognized in our society, and practitioners in all settings are seeing clients with a wider range of problems than ever before. Thus, they need to be familiar with the various forms of psychopathology. This textbook brings together current developments in theory and practice to aid the clinician in the treatment of psychopathological disorders.

It is the fervent hope of the contributors that this book will help reduce the uncertainty associated with rapid changes in the field and thereby improve the services clients receive.

Acknowledgments _____

There are five groups of people to whom I wish to express my gratitude now that this project has reached its conclusion. First, there are the many patients with whom I worked in a large provincial psychiatric hospital several years ago. This group of very human people gave me the determination to learn more about ways of helping clients. I recently reread a letter to me from one of these persons in which she wrote: "yes I want you to remember the thankfulness of those too, who have no words to express their feelings, but the look in their eyes". Second, I want to thank the chapter authors, who were very supportive of the project, made excellent suggestions, and helped expand my own knowledge of the field. Third, I wish to thank the staff at The Free Press, especially Gladys Topkis, who was adamant that this book be written, and Joyce Seltzer and Laura Wolff, who saw it through to completion. Fourth, Linda Mainville and Murielle Graff at Laurentian University in Ontario were extremely helpful in the endless job of typing and editing. Last, my family encouraged me throughout. My wife, Joanne, helped keep the project in its proper perspective and Anne-Marie's, Sarah's, and Francis's enthusiasm and assistance made it worthwhile, although Duffy was no help at all.

About the Contributors _____

Peter E. Bohm completed an M.S.W. at Indiana University in 1969. After working in Indiana's family care program for several years, he joined the Addiction Research Foundation of Ontario. He received a Ph.D. from the University of Toronto in 1981. Currently, he is head of a treatment and training center in the Addiction Research Foundation's School for Addiction Studies in Toronto.

Edward J. Hart is a pediatric neurologist and assistant professor in the Department of Pediatrics and Neurology at Boston University School of Medicine. His M.D. is from New York University. His pediatric training was at Children's Hospital in Philadelphia and his neurological training at Columbia Presbyterian Medical Center in New York. He is also a clinical pediatric neurologist at Kennedy Memorial Hospital for Children in Boston, a facility for children with neurologically based handicaps.

Harriette C. Johnson is on the faculty of the Adelphi University School of Social Work in New York, where she teaches social work practice and social welfare policy. She has an extensive background both in casework and community organization and in research. She is the author of numerous articles and two books, *Behavior, Psychopathology, and the Brain,* on the physiological bases of behavior, and *Government Money for Everyday People,* a guide to income support programs, co-authored with Gertrude S. Goldberg.

Bert Kaplan is currently associate professor and director of the Division of Behavioral Sciences in the Adelphi University School of Social Work in New York. He holds a certificate from the Institute of the Study of Psychoanalytic Psychotherapy, is engaged in private practice, and is director of training at the Psychotherapy Study Center in Old Bethpage, New York.

Charlotte Kirschner is the director of Geriatric Family Service, a private consultation service in New York City, offering counseling to the aged and their families. A graduate of the Columbia University School of Social Work, she has had extensive experience both as a nursing home consultant and as a specialist in home care management. She has published several articles, has presented papers to the Gerontological Society of America and the Group for Geriatric Psychiatry in New York City, and frequently lectures on the subject of adult children and their aging parents.

Karen Kline has an M.S.W. from the Jane Addams College of Social Work in Chicago. She has worked in the adoption, child therapy, and day treatment areas of social service. She is currently at home caring for two small children while on a leave of absence from the youth services department of a mental health center in Warsaw, Indiana.

Lynn-Marie Mackay received a B.A. from the University of Toronto. Before starting graduate school, she worked in a variety of mental health settings in California. She completed an M.S.W. at the University of Toronto Faculty of Social Work in 1971. Her practice has included individual, family, and group therapy in children's and adults' psychiatric inpatient settings. She currently is a social worker in the Psychosomatic Medicine Unit of the Clarke Institute of Psychiatry in Toronto, where she combines clinical, teaching, and research duties with an emphasis on family therapy in the treatment of anorexia nervosa patients.

Donald E. Meeks earned a Ph.D. in clinical social work from Smith College. At present, he is a professor of social work at the University of Toronto and director of the School for Addiction Studies of the Addiction Research Foundation of Ontario. He also serves as a consultant on international drug dependence training projects in Thailand, Nigeria, and the Caribbean region.

Judith Mishne is a member of the faculty of the New York University School of Social Work. In addition, she is a private practitioner, agency consultant, and member of the summer faculty of Smith College. Her B.S.W. is from the University of Wisconsin, her M.S.W. from Case Western Reserve, and her Doctorate in Social Work from Hunter College, in New York City. In addition, she has a certificate in child therapy from the Chicago Institute of Psychoanalysis. She is the author of *Clinical Work with Children*.

Mary Kay O'Neil is a social work practitioner in the University Health Service Psychiatric Division of the University of Toronto. She has a B.A. from the University of Western Ontario, an M.S.W. from the University of Ottawa School of Social Welfare, and a Ph.D. from the University of Toronto. Her professional experience has included teaching, private practice, and mental health agency casework.

Enola K. Proctor received a B.A. from Butler University, an M.S.W. from the University of Texas at Arlington, and a Ph.D. from Washington University in St. Louis. Her practice interests and experience include mental retardation, mental health, and rape and abuse. She is an assistant professor in the George Warren Brown School of Social Work, Washington University, and is presently conducting research in the areas of worker–client relationship, treatment planning, and interracial therapy.

Mary Sheridan is the social work education coordinator for the Pediatric Pulmonary Center at Kapiolani–Children's Medical Center in Honolulu. She is an adjunct instructor in the University of Hawaii School of Social Work, and formerly taught at the University of Illinois in the Abraham Lincoln School of Medicine.

Terry Smolar is an associate professor in Fordham University's Graduate School of Social Services. She is also a psychoanalyst in private practice, a member of the Society for Psychoanalytic Training, a supervisor and training analyst at the New York Center for Psychoanalytic Training, and a member of the American Orthopsychiatric Association.

Herbert S. Strean is a distinguished professor of social work in the Rutgers University Graduate School of Social Work. He is also in private practice in New York City, where he is president of the Society for Psychoanalytic Training. Author of 14 books and over 60 articles, he most recently published *The Extramarital Affair* and *Freud and Women,* co-authored by Lucy Freeman.

Ray J. Thomlison is a former professor of social work at the University of Toronto and a private practitioner. He is now dean of social work at the University of Calgary. A specialist in behavior modification, he has participated in the development of behavioral techniques for marital and family therapy, as well as phobic disorders.

Francis J. Turner is executive vice-president at Laurentian University in Ontario. He is a former dean of the Faculty of Social Work at Wilfrid Laurier University, and has taught at the University of Ottawa and Memorial University of Newfoundland. He has worked in community mental health settings, family service agencies, and children's aid societies, as well as in private practice. His M.S.W. is from the University of Ottawa and his D.S.W. is from Columbia University.

Mary Woods is a full-time social work private practitioner in the New York area and a clinical consultant to agencies in the region. She has extensive experience in child protective services, as well as in family agencies, as practitioner, supervisor, consultant, and program developer. She is co-author, with Florence Hollis, of the third edition of *Casework: A Psychosocial Therapy.*

Monna Zentner is an assistant professor of social work at Renison College, University of Waterloo, Ontario. She also has taught at Wilfrid Laurier University in the Faculty of Social Work. She has extensive clinical experience and is an aging consultant and private practitioner. Her M.S.W. is from the University of Kansas.

1

Mental Disorders in Social Work Practice

Francis J. Turner

As knowledge about human behavior, healthy and problematic, becomes more and more the common base of the helping professions—and the proper domain of no one profession—all clinicians must be well informed about, and well trained to deal with, psychopathology. Social workers in clinical practice, regardless of setting, always have confronted the whole range and intensity of psychopathology; however, their recognition as equal partners with other helping professionals has been hard to win. Equality of status requires commensurate contributions to the body of therapeutic knowledge, and social work has not yet fully met this challenge. Decades of experience have yielded only a sparse and unsystematic social work literature on the development and management of various aspects of psychopathology. For example, there is a relative wealth of articles on schizophrenia but only minimal discussion about paranoia. This unevenness leaves an unclear picture of the level and extent of social workers' knowledge in these areas.

Nevertheless, for over 40 years, courses in psychopathology have been an important part of the social work curriculum. This material has figured differently in various training programs, and its utility for students planning to enter large systems practice has long been debated, but it has been required at least of students preparing for clinical careers.

1

In my view, knowledge of psychopathology is necessary for all practitioners.

At the same time that courses in psychopathology have been a part of social work training, they have not always been taught by social workers. Frequently, psychiatrists have had responsibility for this part of the curriculum. Although this practice fosters communication, understanding, and cooperation between the two professions—and therefore ought to continue—delegating the teaching of this material to another profession limits social work from developing fully a unique understanding of psychopathology.

Another factor that has discouraged social work from enriching its own knowledge base in this area is the field's long-standing concern about classification or labeling of clients. Social workers emphasize individuality and respect the idiosyncracies of human nature. They have experienced the dangers in the misuse of classification. Hence, there has been a strong reluctance to develop or use systems of diagnostic or problem classification. It is interesting that a review of the social work literature points to the need for classification of clients and problems although practice does not. Let us look more closely at this issue.

Social work offers diverse reasons in support of its anticlassification position:

> labels are unidimensional and clients are multidimensional
> labels stereotype people and minimize their individuality
> labels have a tendency to be self-fulfilling
> labels may lack adequate theoretical or empirical support and therefore give a false sense of understanding to both client and social worker
> labels stress problems rather than persons and weaknesses rather than strengths

These concerns are valid—as noted earlier, most social workers have experience with the harm a misapplied label can cause to a client—but categorization is nevertheless essential to practice. As a psychiatrist explained in reference to his field:

> Because one patient resembles many others in certain important characteristics it does not mean he loses the unique characteristics that mark him as an individual. Diagnosis is a short hand method for summarizing those characteristics which he shares with a number of other individuals of the given class at a given time, and which are relevant to etiology, the treatment chosen and prognosis. (Eron, 1966, p. 9)

Arguing against classification systems can be a way of avoiding the task of improving diagnosis. The diagnostic process is fluid—often, treatment itself will modify an initial assessment. However, the difficulty of developing and applying classifications is a poor excuse for rejecting this approach: understanding the human condition requires analysis and categorization. Behavioral phenomena are complex and can be grasped only through systematic scrutiny, which entails the creation of reliable and precise nomenclature.

In fact, social workers are not so much opposed to the use of labels as such as they are to the use or misuse of certain labels. For example, homosexuality used to be considered a form of psychopathology. Similarly, burnout is so widely diagnosed today that the term may have lost its precise meaning. Criticism also frequently concerns such diagnostic tags as schizophrenic, paranoid, antisocial, character disordered, or untreatable. These categories often carry a stigma and must be used cautiously. At the same time, by their blanket rejection, the social worker can prevent clients from obtaining the kind of help they need. Clearly, no one classification can entirely describe a client: an accurate diagnosis comprises a series of classifications and will be useful to the extent that it is precise, verifiable, and understandable. Thus, social workers must distinguish between the inadequacies of past categorizations of behavior and the potential benefits of a well-designed classificatory scheme.

Social work's acceptance of the obligation to develop a system of classification as the foundation for professional activity brings with it an awesome responsibility precisely because new categories of clients or problems have a tendency to be overused or misapplied. If the field is to foster understanding of human behavior by improving the analysis of both normal functioning and psychopathology, then the nomenclature must be responsibly developed and used. Social workers, as we have seen, are uncomfortable with labeling because they have witnessed the rise and fall of so many diagnostic terms. However, publication in 1980 of the third edition of the American Psychiatric Association's *Diagnostic and Statistical Manual* (DSM-III) may have indicated that this pattern is changing.

DSM III revised terminology and rearranged clinical entities to meet the demands of current practice. Obviously, the full impact of these changes is not yet known. Neither the literature nor the practice of social work has completely adjusted to the revisions, as the range of topics covered in this book demonstrates.* Nevertheless, it is expected that DSM III will markedly affect social work curricula, and Williams (1981), a social worker who participated in the preparation and testing of the new diag-

---

*DSM III was published as the outline for this book was being developed. Some topics were omitted, others were renamed, and still others were subdivided or rearranged to accord with the new system. However, all the sub-classifications in the new DSM system have not been fully covered as there has not as yet been sufficient experience in social work practice to assess their relevance.

nostic system, predicted that DSM III will greatly influence diagnosis in social work.

The new conceptual scheme introduced by DSM III is a multiaxial system that embraces biological, psychological, and social factors. Under this system, clients are assessed in terms of five areas, or axes: clinical syndrome; personality and developmental disorders; physical condition; stresses; and level of function over the past year. This multiaxial approach to diagnosis is extremely important for social workers because it answers the common criticism that diagnosis is unidimensional: ''The new approach represents APA's [American Psychiatric Association] acknowledgement of the importance of a holistic approach to mental illness in general. More specifically it encourages the recognition and management of certain social factors'' (Williams, p. 102). Social workers have long advocated a multidimensional approach to diagnosis. The essence of this profession is the study and management of persons in interaction with significant others and environments. The embodiment of this view in DSM III pays tribute to social work's long involvement in the field of psychopathology.

Social workers must continue to expand their knowledge base to insure that a holistic approach to clients guides both assessment and treatment. As practitioners, social workers are interested in knowledge for use. Diagnosis is important only to the extent that it leads to effective, economical, and nonharmful intervention. This book is designed to assist social workers dealing with clients who manifest some aspects of psychopathological functioning. Such clients have long been served by social workers, and it appears that this component of social work practice is expanding. The book brings together social work's wealth of knowledge and experience in this area. The social work literature on psychopathology is not easily accessible to practitioners under the pressures of day-to-day practice and this book can serve as a convenient reference. Finally, the book is designed to contribute to our understanding of human behavior. Although health professionals have long talked about the need to understand behavior from a biological-psychosocial perspective, the boundaries between disciplines have restricted progress in this direction. This pattern is starting to change as the number of theoretical orientations in the helping professions increases and as the body of research that looks at all aspects of behavior grows, forcing us to recognize the complexity of the human condition. Indeed, the extent to which pharmacological and physiological processes are discussed in this book reveals the increasingly interdisciplinary emphasis in social work—an emphasis that will be felt more and more in formal training programs, that will improve client services, and that will inevitably be reciprocated by other professions involved in health or mental health.

Note that the volume focuses on adult clients. Although a few chapters do consider some aspects of childhood, the diagnostic and therapeutic needs of children are sufficiently different to require separate treatment.

The goal of this book is to help clinicians make more precise diagnoses and thereby better to target their interventions with clients exhibiting the many forms of nonnormal behavior that cause suffering and diminish the human potential.

References

American Psychiatric Association: *Diagnostic and Statistical Manual of Mental Disorders*, ed 3. Washington, DC; American Psychiatric Association 1980.

ERON D (ed): *The Classification of Behavior Disorders.* Chicago, Aldine Publishing, 1966.

HOLLIS F: *Casework: A Psychosocial Therapy*, ed 2. New York, Random House, 1972.

LEVY S: Labeling: the social worker's responsibility. *Social Casework* 1981; 62: 332–342.

TURNER F J (ed): *Differential Diagnosis and Treatment in Social Work*, ed 3. New York, Free Press, 1983.

RAKOFF V M, STANCER H C, and KEDWARD H B (eds): *Psychiatric Diagnosis.* New York, Brimmer Mazel, 1977.

WILLIAMS J B W: DSM III: A comprehensive approach to diagnosis. *Social Work* 1981; 26: 101–106.

2

The Biological Bases of Psychopathology

HARRIETTE C. JOHNSON

The past 15 years has witnessed an explosion of knowledge in the area of the biological bases of psychopathology. Acceleration of the development of technology for studying the relationship between brain and behavior has contributed to the current revolution in knowledge. The prevailing distinction in psychopathological theory between emotional and cognitive disturbances that are "organic" in origin, as opposed to those that are "psychosocial" or "functional" in origin, appears in the light of recent research to be inaccurate. Psychopathology can seldom be considered a case of either–or.

The importance of physiological factors in psychopathology has been demonstrated dramatically in two recent studies of undiagnosed medical illness in psychiatric patients (Hall, 1981; Koranyi, 1979). Among 2,090 patients screened at a psychiatric clinic, 43% were found to be suffering from a major illness (Koranyi, 1979). Nonpsychiatric physicians had missed major illness in one-third of the patients they referred; psychiatrists had missed major illness in one-half; and social agencies and individual social workers had had no knowledge or even a suspicion of an existing major physical illness in 83% of the cases they referred! Social workers were no more knowledgeable than self-referred patients. Researchers judged that 69% of these major medical illnesses contributed significantly to the psychiatric state of the patient (Koranyi, 1979). In another study, 46 of 100 patients admitted to a state hospital were found to have previously undiagnosed medical illnesses that had either caused or exacerbated their psychiatric illnesses (Hall, 1981). Twenty-eight of the 46 patients showed rapid and dramatic diminution of psychiatric symptomatology when the underlying physical illnesses were treated.

Diseases most frequently implicated in psychiatric pathology in the Hall (1981) and Koranyi (1979) studies were endocrine dysfunction, metabolic disturbance (diabetes, hypoglycemia), nutritional deficiency, and circulatory and digestive disorders. The studies provided clinical evidence that the centers of the brain regulating the emotions are profoundly affected by the endocrine system, by processes related to carbohydrate metabolism, by deficiencies in certain vitamins and minerals, and by other bodily factors. Failure to recognize the physical bases of psychiatric conditions has resulted in several recent lawsuits against psychiatrists (Taylor, 1981).

The study of psychopathology, then, clearly requires an understanding of the physiological processes through which emotional states are mediated. Neither psychoanalytic nor behavioral theory addresses this important area of knowledge.

The originator of psychoanalytic theory was himself a neurologist. In the early years of his work, Freud sought to unravel the mysteries of the relationship between physiological factors—the function of neurons, or nerve cells—and observable behaviors and emotions. The dearth of scientific knowledge and of technologies that might allow for expanding and deepening that knowledge frustrated Freud in his search (Fisher & Greenberg, 1977). In his later works, he abandoned the search for elucidation of brain–behavior interactions. Freud's definitive theories of psychopathology attribute most psychic phenomena, both so-called normal and abnormal, to intrapsychic and interpersonal developmental processes without reference to the neurophysiological underpinnings and correlates of these processes (see Jones, 1953, on Freud's theories of psychopathology).

Present-day scholars, by contrast, have at their disposal a wealth of knowledge derived from research in many disciplines, including neuroanatomy and neurophysiology, biochemistry, molecular biology, clinical psychiatry, endocrinology, radiography, ethology, allergy, special education, and clinical and experimental psychology. Major technological developments have made it possible to break through barriers to advancement in knowledge about the relationship between observable behaviors, emotions, and cognitions, on the one hand, and the neurophysiological events that lie behind these phenomena, on the other (see *Scientific American* 1979, vol. 241, for a review of recent research in this area). It is likely that Freud, a pioneer in empirical discovery, would have revised his theories to bring them into conformity with the empirically based knowledge about neurological function that is now available.

In this chapter, I review some recent research that may be helpful in the social worker's everyday practice. Social work needs to expand the dimensions of diagnostic thinking so that practitioners develop the habit of considering a variety of possible explanations for a given clinical phenomenon, rather than assuming, as has too often been the case, that the source of emotional dysfunction lies exclusively in the breakdown of interpersonal functioning. A truly systems oriented approach to assessment requires genuine observance of, not lip service to, the biopsychosocial paradigm. Too often, social workers' diagnoses, which claim to be biopsychosocial, strongly emphasize psychological components, devote only peripheral attention to social factors, and completely ignore biological factors.

It is important to emphasize, however, that I am deeply committed to a biopsychosocial model of assessment. The importance of social conditions in generating emotional stress must not be underestimated (Johnson, 1978, 1983). According to a widely accepted view in social work, the psychosocial milieu can generate psychological events that are manifested in disturbed behavior. It is equally true, but not as widely accepted, that changes in the biochemistry of the brain, arising from physical events in the body, can generate behavioral, emotional, or cognitive disturbances. A stressor introduced at any point in the complex chain of events that constitute psychic functioning can set off reverberations throughout the entire delicate and intricate chain (for a discussion of this process see *Scientific American* 1979, vol. 241). Interpersonal and social stresses cause changes in body chemistry, which, in turn, alter functions in the brain centers that regulate emotion and thought. These functions can also be altered as a result of changes in body chemistry arising from excesses or deficiencies of certain substances in the system; ingestion of toxic substances such as lead, even in minute quantities; scar tissue from lesions in the brain; or genetically determined deficiencies in the enzymes in the brain that govern the manufacture of substances critical to the transmission of nerve impulses (Johnson, 1980).

Disturbed behaviors induced by any of these factors then have an impact on the individual's external environment. Bizarre or deviant behavior provokes responses from relatives, neighbors, friends, colleagues, employers, caretaking persons, police, judges, and social workers. Environmental responses may escalate the imbalance in the entire cycle or may defuse and deescalate the disruption, helping the individual and the environment to return to the so-called premorbid level of functioning or helping the individual and the environment to reach an accommodation at a new and possibly more satisfactory level of functioning. What is crucial to remember here is that any number of different interventions—diet, drugs, detoxification, removal from a stressful environment, or effecting change within that environment—can operate to restore equilibrium. Of course, if the disruption has been caused by a sensitivity reaction in the brain to an ingested substance, no amount of family therapy will remedy the problem. On the other hand, if the disturbance has been precipitated by an environmental event such as job loss, adherence to a nonallergenic diet cannot be expected to effect any change.

Some case examples may illustrate the importance of considering biological and socioeconomic, in addition to intrapsychic and interpersonal, factors in the diagnosis of psychological problems.*

A married mother of three in her forties was subject to severe depression. She was treated unsuccessfully with psychotherapy and finally hospitalized at the nearby state hospital, where she remained for two years. Her husband spoke with the social worker about getting a divorce, although, he said, they had been happy together before her illness. When an in-depth physical examination revealed the presence of hypoglycemia, treatment with diet was instituted. Within a few months, she was home with her family, fully recovered. Her husband appeared surprised when the worker alluded to his earlier plans for divorce, stating that the family was very happy and that separation was totally out of the question.

A group of 32 unemployed older persons (mean age 63) was interviewed. Symptoms of depression such as suicidal thoughts, sleeping and eating difficulties, self-deprecation, and nervousness were widespread. After placement of these people in CETA jobs, these symptoms vanished (Briar, 1979).

A 28-year-old woman suffering from acute postpartum depression (involving violence toward her children and slashing of her own forearms) became symptom-free after five days' fast in the hospital. When foods were reintroduced, severe reactions occurred with bacon, eggs, oatmeal, veal, tongue, instant coffee, and chocolate.

Ten foods were then tested in a double-blind technique. Five of the foods had induced severe adverse reactions in prior testing; the other foods had not caused reactions. The patient was given these foods through a tube into the stomach via the nose. The tube was covered so that neither patient nor investigator knew which food was being given. The patient reacted strongly to the five foods to which she had reacted previously, confirming the hypothesis that improvement had been due to elimination of the foods. As long as the patient continued to avoid the offending foods, she remained symptom-free without medication (Sheinkin et al., 1979).

A six-year-old boy was referred to a child psychiatric facility because of constant trouble at school, at home, and in the neighborhood. He had changeable moods, was sometimes wild and violent, punched and poked other children, knocked them down, and took their toys. He often provoked his father, who would then

*Much of the materal in this chapter has been adapted from Johnson's book *Behavior Psychopathology and the Brain*, Curriculum Concepts Inc., New York, 1980, with permission of the publisher. [Editor's note]

fly into violent rages himself and beat the boy quite mercilessly. It would have been natural to ascribe all the child's difficulties to the chaotic and punitive environment at home.

EEG abnormalities were identified and the boy was treated with methsuximide (an anticonvulsant) and amphetamine and placed in a special class for brain dysfunctional children. His behavior improved markedly. Within eight months his arithmetic and spelling performance had increased by three grade levels and his reading by four grade levels. The atmosphere at home improved considerably as the father responded to the improvement in the child. When the amphetamine was discontinued for a few days, the boy reverted to hyperactive and hyperaggressive behavior (Gross & Wilson, 1974).

In each instance, the problem was alleviated by altering either the internal environment (through diet or drugs) or the external environment (through creating jobs). In none of the examples could counseling have solved the problem since the origins of the problems were environmental (internal or external). For a social work practitioner to be effective in any of these situations, it would be necessary to know that allergy and hypoglycemia can cause emotional disturbance, that deficiencies in the labor market (lack of jobs) can cause depression, and that subtle neurologic dysfunction can cause aggressive behavior. Without this knowledge, the worker would be likely to focus almost exclusively on interpersonal transactions, which themselves might be *effects* rather than *causes*. Only when an in-depth evaluation indicates that *nothing can be done about the causes themselves* should attention be directed exclusively to effects. In the absence of such an evaluation, attention to results (interpersonal effects) may simply impede identification of causes.

The remainder of the chapter is divided into three sections: a review of research on the biological determinants of the major psychopathological states as designated by the American Psychiatric Association's (1980) latest classification (DSM III); a summary of principles of brain function that may help the practitioner see links between observable behaviors and underlying physiological processes; and a discussion of the implications for social work practice of research on biological determinants of psychic functioning.

Biological Determinants of Emotional and Cognitive Functioning in the Major Psychiatric Conditions

Disturbances of Mood: Manic-Depressive Disorder and Depression

Both "bipolar" (manic-depressive) and "unipolar" (depressive only) states have been studied extensively with reference to their biological underpinnings. The discovery of the dramatic effectiveness of lithium in the treatment of manic-depressive disorders underscored the importance of biological determinants in affective disturbances. A manic-depressive individual is subject to alternating states of hyperactivity, grandiosity, and excitement (the "manic phase") and sad, tearful, self-recriminatory lethargy (the "depressive phase"). Most studies have demonstrated that lithium is by far the most effective treatment for bipolar illness and is also effective in some unipolar disorders (Fieve, 1975). Since lithium not only calms manic states in 80–85% of patients but also prevents recurrence of both mania and depression in most of these patients, it has been described as the first truly preventative agent in psychiatry (Fieve, 1975). Although lithium has been available in America only since 1970, it was used for manic depression in ancient Greece and Rome. Mineral water prescribed by a physician named Aurelianus in the fifth century B.C. came from springs now known to contain large amounts of lithium (Fieve, 1975).

Genetic factors have recently been found to play a significant role in manic-depressive illness. The condition has been linked with color blindness, as well as with certain blood groups. Affective disorders in a family are frequently traceable over several generations, and studies of risk for contracting the disease have shown the incidence of manic-depressive illness to be much higher in relatives of manic-depressive patients than in the general population (Fieve, 1975). The probability of the monozygotic (identical)twin of a manic-depressive patient contracting the illness has been found to be 70–100%, while in dizygotic (fraternal) twins the probability is only 15–25% (Fieve, 1975). Dramatic differences also have been found in the genetic background of individuals who respond to lithium versus those who fail to respond (Fieve, 1975). A family history of bipolar illness is significantly associated with positive response, while the absence of such a history is frequent in nonresponders. This finding suggests that genetic differences may determine the amenability of a patient's illness to lithium therapy. Although the precise modes of transmission in manic-depressive illness are still unknown, observers agree that the evidence is compelling for a genetic theory of transmission.*

*Recent studies suggest that certain chemicals that transmit nerve impulses (namely, the catecholamine neurotransmitters) are important in manic-depressive states, as well as in unipolar conditions. The increased level of motor activity in mania has been found to be accompanied by very high urine levels of a product of the metabolism of norepinephrine, one of the catecholamine neurotransmitters. Since lithium is known to accelerate the presynaptic destruction of norepinephrine, to inhibit the neuronal release of norepinephrine and serotonin (another neurotransmitter), and to increase the reuptake of norepinephrine after release, it may act to reduce manifestations of mania by limiting the production and activity of norepinephrine and other catecholamines.

The picture is complicated by the finding reported in a number of studies that lithium has effectively controlled symptoms in some chronically psychotic individuals diagnosed as

Monoamine oxidase (MAO) is an enzyme (substance that facilitates chemical reactions) that acts at the synapses (spaces between nerve cells) to break down norepinephrine and dopamine, two chemicals, called *"neurotransmitters,"* that transmit nerve impulses.* Murphy and Weiss (1972) found that cellular MAO activity measured in blood platelets was 45% lower in patients with a history of manic-depression than in patients who had suffered depression only and in normal controls. Recent studies of platelet MAO levels have indicated that different types of unipolar depression may be discriminated by differences in MAO activity. High levels of platelet MAO have been associated with endogenous depression and low levels with nonendogenous depression (Schildkraut, 1983).

It is well known that clinical treatment of depression with either drugs or electroshock therapy sometimes precipitates manic episodes. Various theories have been proposed about the relationship between manic and depressive states. Factors that propel the individual into a depression, as opposed to a manic state, however, and the precise biochemistry of these states are still obscure.

Unipolar affective disorder, or depression, is the most common psychiatric diagnosis (Nielsen & Williams, 1980). In a random sample of more than a 1,000 households, the combined frequency of major and minor depression was found to be 5.7% of the general population when only definite cases were counted and 6.8% when probable cases were added to the former group (Weissman et al., 1981b).

Few investigators and practitioners dispute the thesis that external environmental stresses, in particular, loss of a loved person or a situation that diminishes an individual's self-esteem, cause depression in many people. The prevalence of depression arising from physical causes, however, appears to be significantly underestimated. Two major causes of depression have been found to be dysfunction of the endocrine system (hormonal imbalance) and metabolic imbalance (erratic levels of blood sugar, as in diabetes and hypoglycemia) (Bardwick, 1976; Carroll, 1978; Kalimo & Olsson, 1980; Pfeiffer, 1975; Phillippe & Kitzmiller, 1981; Prange & Loosen, 1980; Vandenbergh, 1980; Whybrow & Prange, 1981).

---

schizophrenic, particularly those found to be unresponsive to phenothiazines and other neuroleptics usually prescribed to treat schizophrenia (e.g., Klerman, 1982). In these patients, underlying biochemical processes may be more similar to those occurring in manic-depressive conditions than to those in most schizophrenic illnesses.

*Some readers may find the technical material in this chapter difficult to understand. For readers who wish to deepen their knowledge of such topics as the function of the neurotransmitters and the action of psychotropic drugs, careful study of the section on brain function may be useful. Texts on physiological psychology can also be found among the references at the end of the chapter. For readers who do not wish to pursue this material, it is possible to skip over the technical material and yet understand the major concepts for which it provides evidence.

Another important physiological dynamic of depression appears to be disruption of natural biological rhythms related to patterns of sleep and wakefulness (see Chapter 5; Duncan et al., 1980; Vogel et al., 1975; Wehr et al., 1979).

The development of laboratory tests for discriminating among types of depression and for predicting responsiveness to various medications has advanced our ability to treat depression clinically, even though the underlying pathophysiological mechanisms are not yet understood (Schildkraut, 1983) and even when the origin of the depression is a stressful psychosocial event. In addition to the measurement of platelet MAO, two other tests are used: the dexamethasone suppression test (DST) and tests for urine levels of a product of catecholamine metabolism referred to as MHPG (methoxyhydroxyphenylglycol). In the DST, a drug is administered that normally lowers the body's natural cortisone level. Because the body's adrenal system overfunctions in some kinds of depression, test results that fail to show reduced levels of cortisone are likely for patients suffering from a particular form of depression, melancholia (an endogenous depression). Measurements of MHPG levels have been found to be useful in discriminating among subtypes of depression and for predicting responsiveness to different medications (Schildkraut et al., 1981). MHPG appears in the urine in varying levels: low levels are associated with schizoaffective and bipolar depressive disorders, while in unipolar nonendogenous depression, urine levels of MHPG are frequently high. MHPG level has also been found to be a useful predictor of responsiveness to two tricyclic antidepressants, imipramine (called Tofranil commercially), and amitriptyline. Patients with the lowest levels of MHPG had the best response to treatment with imipramine; whereas depression with higher levels of MHPG responded most favorably to amitriptyline; patients with mid-range MHPG showed very poor response to both imipramine and maprotiline, another antidepressant (Schildkraut, 1983).

The intricate relationships among neurological, endocrine, and metabolic functions are not clearly understood; however, the fact that they are very closely related is well established. These relationships are explored in some detail in the following discussion.

Hormones and Depression

Relationships between mood and endocrine function have been studied for many years. Postpartum psychosis (a severe depression) and postpartum blues (a common mild depression) have been related to the precipitous drop after delivery in chorionic gonadotropins (one type of sex hormone) (Vandenbergh, 1980). The relationship between mood changes in woman and cyclic differences in estrogen levels led Bardwick (1976) to hypothesize that premenstrual depression is related to low levels of estrogen, which induces high levels of monoamine oxidase. Estrogen appears to be the most potent of the gonadal hormones affecting MAO levels. High levels of MAO at the synapse are associated with low levels of catecholamines, a state associated in turn with certain types of depression. Increases in estrogen, which elevate mood, may act to decrease the quantity of MAO or to increase the level of catecholamines.

Sex appears to be related to a predisposition for depression, as well as to the speed of response to tricyclic antidepressants. Women, not only become depressed more often than men but also when treated for depression with tricyclic antidepressants their response is slower (Bardwick, 1976). Whybrow and Prange (1981) and Prange and Loosen (1980) found that a small dose of thyroid hormones, given in combination with tricyclic antidepressants, speeds recovery from depression in women but not in men, thus offsetting one of the chief drawbacks of these drugs for women, the slow onset of therapeutic action. The hormones also remedy failure to respond to tricyclic antidepressants in both men and women.

In persons predisposed to bipolar affective disorder, on the other hand, thyroid hormones can precipitate mania. Lithium carbonate, the principal treatment for mania, also has antithyroid effects. One hypothesized explanation for the effects of thyroid hormones is that they modulate the receptivity of certain neurons to particular neurotransmitters—the catecholamines—thus potentiating the action of some neurotransmitters and inhibiting the action of others (Whybrow & Prange, 1981).

These activities of the brain may be secondary to earlier perturbations in the individual's steady state, induced by psychological loss, infection, or pharmacological assault, interacting with a genetic predisposition (Whybrow & Prange, 1981).

Sugar Metabolism and Depression

Both diabetes (excessive blood sugar) and hypoglycemia (insufficient blood sugar) have been related to depressive symptoms. This should not be surprising since the brain uses glucose (a simple sugar) almost exclusively for metabolism. The brain derives its energy for functioning from glucose in the blood. Either an inadequate or an overabundant blood glucose supply will cause immediate functional and metabolic disturbances and, if severe, permanent brain injury (Kalimo & Olsson, 1980).

In his study of 900 psychiatric clinic patients suffering from major medical illness, Koranyi (1979) found 57 cases of undiagnosed diabetes mellitus, in addition to cases diagnosed before the inception of psychiatric treatment. He found diabetes to be one of the most frequently overlooked diseases that is particularly prone to cause emotional disturbance. An additional psychological danger to patients from failure to diagnose diabetes is that this disorder often causes impotence. Koranyi found that many men had undergone prolonged and futile psychotherapy for impotence prior to the diagnosis of diabetes.

Hypoglycemia, a dysfunction of carbohydrate metabolism, is manifested in physical symptoms of fatigue, sweating, rapid heart rate, poor appetite, and chronic indigestion; neurologic symptoms of headache, dizziness, tremor, muscle pain, and backache; and psychological symptoms of depression, insomnia, anxiety, irritability, crying spells, phobias, lack of concentration, and confusion (Hoffer & Walker, 1978). A sufferer may have any combination of these symptoms. Hypoglycemia is aggravated by consumption of sugar, refined carbohydrates, and alcohol, a substance chemically related to sugar. In normal individuals, ingestion of sugar is followed by a rise in blood glucose, which, in turn, stimulates the pancreas to secrete insulin, necessary for metabolism of the sugar. In some persons, the pancreas overreacts, secreting more insulin than is necessary. As a result, blood glucose drops to abnormally low levels. At this point, symptoms of hypoglycemia appear.

Biorhythms and Depression

Studies of rapid eye movement (REM) sleep patterns led to experimentation with alteration of sleeping habits as a treatment for depression. Patients with melancholia were awakened at the onset of each REM period, resulting in long-lasting clinical improvement (Vogel et al., 1975). A single case study of a severely depressed person showed that by advancing bedtime by six hours, so that sleep occurred at about five or six in the evening, depression could be alleviated for a period of one to two weeks (Wehr et al., 1979). In another study, 9 of 16 depressed patients became temporarily less depressed after one night of sleep deprivation; those who responded to the sleep deprivation were significantly more depressed prior to the treatment than were nonresponders on a scale measuring degree of depression (Duncan et al., 1980). A hypothesis relating to these findings is that depression is associated with disturbed, or desynchronized, circadian rhythms; sleep deprivation is thought to alleviate depression by resynchronizing patterns of brain wave rhythms (Duncan et al., 1980).

Depression as a Reaction to Medication

As many as 20% of persons 60 years and older are thought to suffer from depression, but many fewer are treated, due to a prevalent myth that depression is an inevitable concomitant of aging (Alexopoulous, 1983). Among those elderly patients actually treated for depression, the condition is thought to be induced by medications prescribed for other conditions in about 25% of cases (see the section on dementias of old age; Alexopoulous, 1983).

Many manifestations often regarded as a natural part of the aging process are reversible, treatable symptoms of depression. Among 213 patients treated in a geriatric psychiatric unit in 1982, 60% were diagnosed as having "pseudodementia," a form of depression whose symptoms are hard to distinguish from those of senile dementias such as Alzheimer's disease. Among these patients, 80% showed marked improvement when treated for depression (Shamoian, 1983). These findings are of great importance because they indicate that failure to diagnose and treat mental problems correctly may be causing a great deal of unnecessary suffering for aging people and their families.

Treatment Considerations of the Biological Bases of Depression

The debate over the relative advantages of talk therapy and drug therapy in the treatment of depression has been raging for many years. The information now available with regard to the possible metabolic and endocrinological origins of some depressions dictates that the debate must now expand to include diet modification, hormone therapy, and other physiological treatments such as sleep deprivation.

Studies comparing nutritional and metabolic treatments with traditional treatments (psychotherapy, medication) have not yet been carried out. However, major studies have compared psychotherapy and pharmacotherapy. A one-year study of ambulatory, unipolar, nonpsychotic, acutely depressed patients who had received either interpersonal psychotherapy (IPT) antidepressant medication (amitriptyline hydrochloride, marketed as Elavil), or a combination thereof over a four-month clinical trial period found no differential effects one year after treatment (Weissman et al., 1981a). Most patients were asymptomatic and functioning reasonably well, but patients who had received interpersonal psychotherapy with or without drugs did better on measures of social functioning related to parental functioning ($P < .01$) and social leisure activities ($P < .05$). An earlier study, however, had indicated that psychotherapy was not helpful in preventing depressive relapses (see Chapter

5; Weissman, 1978). In a controlled clinical trial of 44 nonpsychotic, unipolar depressed outpatients treated with either cognitive therapy or an antidepressant medication (imipramine hydrochloride, marketed as Tofranil) over a 12-week period, both groups showed significant reduction in level of depression (Kovacs et al., 1981). The cognitive therapy group showed greater symptomatic improvement and higher treatment completion rates. At a one-year follow-up of the 35 patients in the study who could be interviewed, both treatment groups were found to have remained well. There were no significant differences between the two groups except in the patients' self-rating on level of depression; persons treated with cognitive therapy perceived greater improvement in themselves than did the drug treated group. The researchers concluded that for most ambulatory, unipolar patients there is more than one way of dealing with the depressive syndrome.*

In order to try to shed empirical light on the drug–psychotherapy debate, a group of researchers tested the common allegation made by proponents of each kind of treatment that combined use of their favorite treatment (drugs or talk therapy) and the other method is harmful. Fifty-six patients from an original group of 96 completed treatment by one or the other or both methods through random assignment to a treatment group. The results indicated that a combination of pharmacotherapy and psychotherapy was more effective than either treatment alone. Symptom reduction and maintenance in treatment was greater for the combination group than for the pharmacotherapy alone group and the superiority of combined treatment increased over time. Researchers found at follow up no early termination from medication; no negative placebo effect (reduced use of psychotherapy after the study ended) for those in the combination group; and no differences in the amount of psychotherapy used after the study ended between patients who had received psychotherapy alone and those who had had psychotherapy combined with a drug. The group that had had psychotherapy alone, however, did rely less on pharmacotherapy at follow-up.

Mattes (1981) argued that just because the combination patients fared best on outcome measures, combination is not necessarily optimal for all patients. Some patients may be responsive to medication while others are not. Some may need only medication; others may be better helped by psychotherapy alone; and patients receiving combination treatment are perhaps being helped by only one, not both, of the treatments. Mattes pointed out that the study did not show how much each patient had been

*The results of these two studies may be clouded, however, by the fact that not all patients who respond to amitriptyline also respond to imipramine, and vice versa (Kovacs et al., 1981; Weissman et al., 1981a). Therefore, nonresponsiveness to the particular medication used might not indicate that drug therapy in general is ineffective but simply that the drug choice was inappropriate.

helped, a measure that might have discriminated between the treatments' level of effectiveness. In addition, psychotherapies differ greatly from each other, so that inference about the effectiveness of psychotherapy in general is not warranted.

The complexity of the interactions between brain biochemistry and social and environmental influences on psychic states requires a study of depression that encompasses more variables than have been examined to date. Nutritional, metabolic, and hormonal factors need to be evaluated since treatment by either drugs or psychotherapy alone may mask or fail to address these other possible causes of depression. The reliance on a limited number of indicators of depression may result in specious inference. For example, the fact that a stressful event preceded an acute depression in no way precludes the possibility that a preexisting physical state, such as hypoglycemia or hormone imbalance, was the cause of the depression and that the event was merely the straw that broke the camel's back. In the absence of detailed and comprehensive patient evaluation, no meaningful determination can be made; certainly, no assumptions about causality are warranted.

Disturbances of Cognition

Biological factors have been found to play a significant role in conditions in which cognition (i.e., thought processes) deviates from the commonplace. This is true both for severe disorders (the schizophrenias, autism, or pervasive developmental disorder) and for minor disorders (specific learning disability, or specific developmental disability).

The Schizophrenias*

A great deal of evidence has now been amassed in support of the hypothesis that the origins of schizophrenia are physiological. Techniques for separating nature–nurture components, notably, adoption and twin studies, have been employed in the study of schizophrenia by various researchers. In addition, experimental manipulation of variables has produced convincing evidence that biochemical intervention, rather than psychotherapy, is the treatment of choice for schizophrenia. In ad-

---

*The condition once called "schizophrenia" is now widely believed to include several disorders (see Chapter 4). Hence, the label "schizophrenic" in this chapter refers to this cluster of illnesses.

dition to drug therapy, whose efficacy has been well established, lesser known methods of treatment for schizophrenia, such as nutritional therapy and hemodialysis, are beginning to attract support.

The advent of widespread use of psychotropic medication in the treatment of the psychoses was the most significant event in the recent history of the treatment of the mentally ill. An early study demonstrating the effectiveness of drugs was reported by Wold (1961). This study was the prototype for many succeeding studies on the responses of patients to various medications. Wold studied six chronic schizophrenic patients who had been hospitalized 1–10 years. They had made sufficient improvement on chlorpromazine to be discharged from the hospital. To test the extent to which the medication was responsible for the improvement, researchers administered placebo instead of the drug. Each time placebo was given, five of the six patients showed dramatic relapses. When chlorpromazine was reinstated, however, they returned to their previous levels of improvement. Ten relapses were observed over a 42-month follow-up, followed in all instances by return to prior level of improvement upon administration of chlorpromazine.

Greenblatt (1972) pointed out that in the early days of drug treatment, clinicians were likely to attribute patient relapses to psychosocial factors exclusively rather than to the removal of medication or inadequate dosage levels. To test the relative effectiveness of drugs versus other types of treatment, a study of chronic schizophrenics who had been hospitalized for an average of 10 years was undertaken at the Massachusetts Mental Health Center in 1956. A group of patients was transferred from a state hospital, where "poverty, lethargy, and boredom" prevailed on the wards, to the active milieu of the mental health center. A comparable group of chronic patients remained at the state hospital and served as a control. Both groups were then divided in half, so that 50% of the patients in each setting would receive tranquilizers. About 25% of the patients in both settings showed significant improvement with even moderate doses of medication. The unmedicated groups in both settings failed to show improvement during the same period of time (Greenblatt et al., 1965). The mental health center, the active milieu, had a high staff–patient ratio, many planned activities, and psychotherapeutic programs, in contrast to the state hospital. Although this part of the study indicated that drugs, not therapeutic milieu, induced positive change, 12- and 18-month follow-up studies revealed that the patients who had had the active milieu *in addition* to the drugs made further gains, while the drug treated patients in the state hospital did not. Greenblatt and associates attributed these extra gains to the efforts of social workers in resurrecting family interest in the patient and in finding transitional placement for patients well enough to leave the hospital.

Genetic Factors in Schizophrenia

Relatives of schizophrenics have a much higher incidence of the disease than does the general population, and the closer a person's relationship to a schizophrenic, the more likely he is to become schizophrenic himself. Children with a schizophrenic parent are about 15 times as likely to become afflicted as other individuals. To determine whether genetic or environmental factors are at work here, Slater and associates (1968) selected adult subjects born to schizophrenic mothers but placed in adoptive or foster homes before the age of one month. A control group, also placed in homes other than with the biological parents, was chosen from persons whose parents had no record of psychiatric disturbance. Psychiatric interviews, along with school, police, Veterans' Administration, and medical records, showed that the experimental subjects with a biological schizophrenic parent had a significantly higher incidence of schizophrenia, as well as an excessive amount of other psychiatric disorders, than did the control group.

Another study produced similar results (Rosenthal et al., 1974). The researchers coined a phrase to describe the disorders seen among the biological relatives of schizophrenics—"schizophrenic spectrum disorders," which include schizophrenia, possible schizophrenia, schizoid disorders, borderline states, and "inadequate personality." They postulated that these disorders represent different degrees of severity of the same basic disorder. They found a significantly higher incidence of schizophrenic spectrum conditions among children of schizophrenics reared in adoptive and foster homes than among children of nonschizophrenics reared by adoptive and foster parents. These researchers also observed differences in familial association between acute and chronic schizophrenia, with more evidence for genetic transmission in chronic than in acute schizophrenia. (Kety et al., 1975).

A study in Iceland of persons born to schizophrenic parents and reared in foster homes also showed evidence of genetic transmission (Karlsson, 1966). Karlsson found that 6 of the 29 developed schizophrenia, whereas none of their foster siblings, reared in the same homes, developed schizophrenia. In this study, only schizophrenia, not related disorders, was considered.

Several studies of schizophrenia in twins further support the idea that schizophrenia is biologically transmitted. In five studies, the average probability that the monozygotic twin of a schizophrenic would become schizophrenic was about .46 (Segal et al., 1976). Most of the remaining 54% of identical twins in these studies were also found to have some psychiatric abnormalities; in most instances, they were designated schizoid.* Only about 13% of the identical twins of schizophrenics were regarded as normal.

The fact that only about half the identical twins of schizophrenics develop the disease has been used to try to refute genetic theories of etiology. However, many variables interact with genetic factors to determine outcome; therefore, an identical genetic endowment will not inevitably give rise to identical expression of the genes. What needs to be explained is the very high concordance in genetically similar individuals as compared with incidence in the general population.

Since monozygotic twins of schizophrenics were found to be about as likely to be schizoid as to be schizophrenic, some theorists concluded that the inherited trait is something called "schizoidia." This suggests that the so-called schizophrenic spectrum disorders are alternative expressions of a single genotype and that variations in the *severity* of the disorders may be the result of differences in environmental factors (Segal, 1976). Klerman (1982) posited that among the schizophrenias, there is a core group of conditions with a strong genetic component, creating a vulnerability that becomes an overt psychosis in the face of environmental stress.

Schizophrenia, Disease, and Drugs

Psychotic states closely resembling and in some instances indistinguishable from certain forms of schizophrenic reaction accompany some physical diseases and can be induced by drugs, prolonged deprivation of sleep, sensory deprivation, and ingestion of substances known to be toxic. For example, Addison's disease and Cushing's disease produce cognitive and affective dysfunctions related to hyperfunction or hypofunction of the adrenal cortex, the organ that secretes cortisonelike steroids.

The parathyroid system has also been implicated in psychiatric disturbance. The predominant change occurring in disturbances of parathyroid secretion at the cellular level consist of changes in the level of the circulating, available calcium ion, a level that is easy to measure. One researcher demonstrated that the degree of psychic disturbance in hyperparathyroid patients increased with increasing serum calcium level (Petersen, 1968). Petersen established a linear relationship between impairment of cognition and concentration of serum calcium. Affective and

---

*Schizoid refers to persons whose life style has some general features of withdrawal from reality contact but not the more definitive schizophrenia symptoms.

drive disorders were found to be associated with lower levels; as levels increased, acute organic psychosis was found to occur.

Although the role of histamine in the genesis of schizophrenia is still uncertain, there are indications that histamine metabolism, also central to allergic conditions, may be significant. Schizophrenic patients have been found to have a low incidence of allergy; the onset of schizophrenia frequently coincides with remission of asthmatic symptoms; schizophrenics have shown lack of sensitivity to administered histamine; and histamine levels in the blood of schizophrenics are elevated. Abnormalities in histamine metabolism have often been linked to schizophrenia (Wyatt et al., 1971).

The hallucinogenic effects of drugs such as mescaline and LSD are well known. Similarities between this type of drug psychosis and the early stages of acute schizophrenic breakdown have been noted. Psychedelic drugs elicit feelings of heightened self-awareness, ecstasy, and increased acuity in all types of sensory perception. Patients suffering from acute schizophrenic reactions sometimes have similar experiences. Unlike chronic schizophrenics, who show flattened affect, they may experience extremes of joy or dread, similar to the extremes of ecstasy and terror seen in users of psychedelic drugs. The "psychedelic" phase of schizophrenia does not continue for a long period of time. The acute phase is either ended by return to normal mental functioning or by development of fixed delusional systems, restricted emotional interactions, flattened affect, and/or formal thought disorder (Snyder et al., 1974).

Amphetamine psychosis, currently on the increase, has also provided researchers with insight into biochemical aspects of schizophrenia. Many cases of amphetamine induced psychosis are misdiagnosed as acute paranoid schizophrenia until it is learned that the patient has a history of drug use. Amphetamine psychosis is characterized by delusions of persecution, ideas of reference,* visual and auditory hallucinations, changes in body image, and hyperactivity and excitation. Disorientation and clouding of memory, however, are not present, as they are in other toxic psychoses. Amphetamine psychoses are also like schizophrenia, and unlike other toxic psychoses, in the extent to which delusions become fixed and patterns of stereotyped, repetitive behavior are developed. This fact suggests that a similar biochemical phenomenon may take place in both types of disturbance. Stereotyped, repetitive behavior has been induced in cats by the administration of amphetamine (Ellinwood, 1976).

---

*Feelings that things that are separate from them are in fact having a direct influence on them.

Schizophrenia and Food Sensitivity

For about two decades, a few physicians have asserted that schizophrenic symptomatology can appear as a reaction to lack of certain nutrients or to irritants in certain foods. Some studies of diet related factors in schizophrenia suggested that abnormal carbohydrate metabolism, excessive or insufficient amounts of certain minerals, sensitivity to wheat gluten, or vitamin deficiency could induce or aggravate symptoms of schizophrenia. For example, Cott (1973) found that among a group of 70 chronic schizophrenic patients given a six-hour glucose tolerance test, 50% were hypoglycemic; the rate of hypoglycemia in the general population is estimated at 10%. Pfeiffer (1975) found copper excesses and zinc deficiencies in the blood of schizophrenics.

Dohan and Grasberger (1973) conducted studies with 150 hospitalized schizophrenics (mean age 38) whose symptoms were so severe as to require confinement on a locked ward. The investigators hypothesized that schizophrenics might be similar to celiac patients in having an intolerance for wheat gluten. Because celiac patients show sensitivity to milk, as well as to gluten, the investigators decided to remove both substances from the diets of the experimental patients and then to add gluten as a challenge food. Gluten is found in wheat, rye, barley, and sometimes oats. Both gluten and milk were abundant in the regular diets of the patients.

The patients and the staff responsible for their care were told that the subjects were to be randomly divided into two groups. One group was to continue receiving the regular hospital diet, while the other was to receive a diet free of both gluten and milk. Unbeknownst to patients and staff, however, a third group was selected from among the group that was to receive the gluten- and milk- free diet. Wheat gluten was secretly added to their muffins. The purpose, of course, was to set up a double-blind condition in order to mitigate the effect on outcome of patient and staff expectations. Patients who received the gluten- and milk-free diet showed sufficient improvement to be discharged significantly sooner than the controls, who received either the regular hospital diet or the diet to which gluten had secretly been added.

These results were subsequently replicated by Singh and Kay (1976). In their experiment, also conducted with schizophrenics on a locked ward, the patients were maintained on grain- and milk-free diets while continuing to receive optimal treatment with neuroleptic drugs. They were noted to make progress during the period in which their diet was free of gluten and milk. When a wheat gluten challenge was given, schizophrenic symptomatology became exacerbated. It was determined that the patients' deterioration was not due to any variations in the medication that they were receiving concurrently. Upon withdrawal of the gluten, improvement was reinstated. The results of this study and the Dohan and Grasberger (1973) study strongly support the thesis that wheat gluten has schizophrenia promoting effects in some patients.

Vitamin Therapy in Schizophrenia

In two double-blind studies of schizophrenic patients, Hoffer and Walker (1978) tested the effectiveness of vitamin B_3 (nicotinic acid) in treating schizophrenia. These studies were based on the hypothesis that a deficiency in nicotinic acid exists in at least some schizophrenics; it was presumed that the biochemical imbalance involving the deficiency arises from genetic factors.

In the first study, 30 patients were randomly assigned to one of three groups. The first group received placebo. The second group received nicotinic acid. These individuals could readily be identified since nicotinic acid produces a flush when it is first administered. The third group received nicotinamide, another form of the vitamin, which acted as a hidden control since it does not produce flushing. About half the patients, distributed among the groups, also received electric shock therapy. The patients were treated with either nicotinic acid or nicotinamide for 33 days and then discharged. After one year, they were reevaluated by a worker who did not know what treatment they had received. At follow-up, one-third of the patients who had received placebo were well, in comparison with two-thirds of the patients in both of the vitamin treatment groups. In a subsequent double-blind study with 82 patients, similar results were obtained.

Hoffer's pioneering work in the treatment of schizophrenia with nutritional substances has been further developed by Hoffer, Osmond, and others. Pfeiffer (1975) reported numerous case histories of successful treatment of schizophrenia with combinations of pyridoxine (vitamin B_6), zinc, antihypoglycemia diet, and other nutritional approaches. The dearth of well-controlled studies of these treatments has, unfortunately, provided grist for the mill of traditional psychiatrists, who denounce nutritional treatment, as well as other unorthodox treatments such as dialysis, as worthless.

Dialysis as a Treatment for Schizophrenia

Like advocates of nutritional therapy for schizophrenia, proponents of dialysis for the treatment of schizophrenia have encountered opposition from the medical establishment. Nevertheless, the reported effectiveness of hemodialysis in achieving complete or partial remission of schizophrenic symptomatology adds support to the hypothesis that a systemic chemical imbalance might cause some forms of the illness.

Dialysis is the procedure by which the blood of patients with kidney failure is washed to remove waste and toxic substances. Although recent experimentation in the use of the technique to treat schizophrenia has aroused controversy, as yet no well-controlled studies are available that could support or refute its value.

Wagemaker (1978) reported the successful use of dialysis in the treatment of chronic schizophrenic patients who had been ill for 4–14 years. They had shown marked impairment of thinking, affect, and behavior. Even when they were out of the hospital, they had functioned poorly. They were unable to work, go to school, or engage in "meaningful" relationships. The patients were dialyzed once a week for 16 weeks after having been taken off drug therapy. Each patient received a psychiatric evaluation before dialysis and weekly evaluations during the treatment through the use of two instruments (the Brief Psychiatric Rating Scale and the Clinical Global Impression Scale). At the end of the 16 weeks, 10 of the patients (all 6 females and 4 of the 9 males) were reported to have shown marked improvement. They were no longer isolated and withdrawn; were able to go to work or to school; and were reported by their families to be greatly improved. Two male patients showed moderate improvement without total remission. One of these was able to work and attend graduate school. Three male patients did not improve.

Critical responses were forthcoming from the medical establishment. One report challenged the findings on the basis of two cases (Kroll et al., 1978). These two patients, both chronic schizophrenics, had been receiving hemodialysis for renal disease with no signs of alleviation of schizophrenic symptomatology. The National Institute of Mental Health (1978) issued a policy statement declining to endorse the treatment and warning the public against false hopes. Recovered patients, however, gave television testimonials about the dramatic remission of their symptoms and the amelioration of their lives.

The apparent effectiveness of dialysis in some cases gives rise to several questions. Can the marked improvement be attributed to removal of schizophrenia inducing substances in the body? If so, what substances? Or is it a giant placebo effect? If the latter is true, how can remission of symptoms for more than one to five years be explained? The problems in conducting controlled testing of the method are considerable since the procedure of dialysis entails risks and cannot be undertaken readily. Nevertheless, despite the lack of controlled studies, it would appear to be difficult to discount the results of Wagemaker (1978). Since the function of dialysis is to remove certain substances from the blood, the reported success suggests that some chemical factors responsible for

schizophrenic symptoms may have been removed in the patients showing significant improvement.

Early Neurologic Indicators of Schizophrenia

In a longitudinal study of two cohorts of infants, Fish (1976) found
evidence of neuropathology as early as the age of one month in infants
who later became schizophrenic. She followed two groups of children.
Children from one group, randomly selected from a well baby clinic in a
lower class neighborhood, were born in 1952–1953. There was a high incidence of pregnancy and birth complications in this group. The other
cohort, born in 1959–1960, were infants of chronically ill schizophrenic
mothers. Most had been placed in adoptive or permanent foster homes.

The infants were given repeated developmental tests, including
measurement of their state of arousal. The children were evaluated independently at ages 10 and (the first group also at) 18 by psychiatrists
and psychologists who were not familiar with their history. They were
given tests of intelligence and educational achievement, as well as projective tests. Two of the 24 children were diagnosed as childhood schizophrenics, and 4 others were considered to have severe personality
disturbances resembling schizophrenia (they had disorders in thinking,
identification, and personality organization). Neurobiologic abnormalities had been identified in the preschizophrenic children as early as
one month of age in the areas of gross motor, visual-motor, and physical
development. Throughout the childhood of these children, disorders in
neurologic maturation were observed. The four other children with
severe personality disturbances also showed delayed physical and neurologic development but of a milder form. The children who had suffered
complications of pregnancy or birth showed brief lags in early development, which were compensated for later. None of the six children with
severe personality disturbances had had such complications. The incidence of severe disturbance was significantly related to a genetic
history of schizophrenia.

Other studies have confirmed the presence of early motor symptoms
and neurologic disorders in children who became schizophrenic as
adults.

Neurotransmitters and Schizophrenia

A major focus of research attention in recent years has been the different transmitter substances in the brain: how they are synthesized;
how they are released; how they interact with receptors in the postsynaptic neurons; and how they are inactivated, thereby allowing the neural

impulse transmission to reoccur. The transmitter systems are thought to be of crucial importance in many psychiatric disorders, including schizophrenia and manic-depressive psychosis (see the section on brain function). The transmitters that have been the subject of the most widespread investigation include dopamine, serotonin, norepinephrine, gamma-aminobutyric acid (GABA), and acetylcholine. While there is as yet no definitive knowledge about the biochemical events involved in the schizophrenic process,* the diverse studies reviewed in this chapter suggest strongly that genuine understanding of schizophrenia will ultimately arise in the area of biochemical research. Interactions between psychotropic drugs and neurotransmitters have proven the most fruitful area of investigation into the biochemical aspects of schizophrenia. The phenothiazines have had probably the most far-reaching effects in improving the condition of schizoprhenics. They have enabled many to leave hospitals and function almost normally within society. Prior to the advent of the phenothiazines, these patients would have been condemned to a lifetime behind institutional walls. The danger of unpleasant side effects from long-term use needs to be weighed against the danger of lifelong hospitalization.

One of the central research questions pertaining to the use of these drugs has been whether their effects are merely sedative, i.e., acting to quiet patients, or whether they help restore abnormal biochemical conditions to states approaching normal levels. Recent studies have demonstrated unequivocally that they exert a specific antischizophrenic action. Whether this is by directly reversing biochemical abnormalities or by affecting emotional functions via independent pathways is not known.**

Researchers at the National Institute of Mental Health and the Veterans' Administration compared the effectiveness of sedatives, particularly phenobarbital, with that of phenothiazines. They found that phenobarbital was no more effective than placebo in treating schizophrenia, while most phenothiazines were more effective than either phenobarbital or placebo. These findings support the hypothesis that the phenothiazines have a specific antischizophrenic effect, rather than simply a tranquilizing effect. If the phenothiazines exerted only a tranquilizing effect, one might expect them to produce effects similar to those

---

*The data suggest that an overactive dopamine system, especially in the limbic region of the brain, is present in schizophrenia and that antischizophrenic drugs act by inhibiting this system. It has also been suggested that the overactivity of the dopamine system may be the result of a dysfunction in some other system; in this case, the effect of treatment would derive not from correcting a dopamine imbalance, but rather by stimulating another system that produces effects countering the action of the dopamine system (Smythies, 1977).

**The principal theories about how drugs operate to reduce symptomatology are explained in Segal and associates (1976) and in Frazer and Winokur (1977). See also the section on brain function.

of phenobarbital since phenobarbital depresses the overall functioning of the central nervous system.

Symptoms suggested by Bleuler as the fundamental signs of schizophrenia—autism, flat affect, and thought disorder—respond extremely well to treatment with these drugs. Other symptoms, such as delusions, hallucinations, and hostility, also respond but to a lesser degree. Finally, symptoms often present in schizophrenia but common to many psychiatric conditions, such as anxiety and depression, do not show improvement with phenothiazines (Snyder et al., 1974). Sedatives such as Valium, Librium, and phenobarbital, on the other hand, relieve agitation but fail to influence thought disorder or abnormal affective responses.

Diagnosis and Treatment of Schizophrenia

As I have suggested, there are various schizophrenias with different etiologies. It would seem to follow, therefore, that a treatment method that succeeds in one case will fail in another and that no universally effective treatment will be found. Among the wide variety of approaches that have been used to treat various forms of schizophrenia, all methods except psychotherapy and milieu therapy address physiological process. Advocates of each method claim success. These methods include:

pharmacotherapy
electric shock therapy
psychosurgery
dialysis
psychotherapy (individual, family, and group)
milieu therapy
megavitamin therapy
modification of diet
other methods (insluin shock, perfusion)

While the causes of schizophrenia are still unknown, the data do appear to justify certain assertions.

1. Among the various treatment modalities, pharmacotherapy has induced significant improvements in the largest number of sufferers. Pharmacologic agents used in treating schizophrenia do not act globally to quiet patients. They have specific antischizophrenic effects related to certain biochemical processes within the brain.
2. In addition to pharmacotherapy, other methods of treatment are based on the thesis that schizophrenic symptoms arise from imbalance in the neurotransmitter systems of the brain. These approaches include diet modification (elimination of allergenic foods, reduction of carbohydrate intake, megavitamin ingestion) and dialysis to remove possible schizophrenia inducing substances from

the blood. These methods appear to be successful in some cases, but they have generated bitter opposition from the medical establishment.*

3. The importance of genetic factors in schizophrenia has been established in studies of children raised by nonbiological parents. Incidence of schizophrenia in adulthood is significantly higher among children of schizophrenics than among children of non-schizophrenics. Environmental stressors are thought to determine the severity of the disease.

4. Hypotheses of genetic origins of schizophrenia are consistent with etiological theories stressing biochemical imbalance since genetic factors express themselves through biochemical processes.

5. Conditions closely resembling schizophrenia can be induced by chemical agents (amphetamines, corticosteroids, hallucinogenic drugs such as LSD and mescaline); by physiological deprivation (sleep and sensory deprivation); by diseases related to malfunction of the adrenal cortex and the parathyroid system; and by vitamin deficiency (pellagra).

6. A relationship between schizophrenia and histamine levels has been suggested by changes in severity of asthmatic symptoms accompanying changes in histamine blood levels with the onset of schizophrenia.

7. Neuropathology has been identified as early as one month of age in infants who later became schizophrenic.

8. Abnormal levels of certain neurotransmitters have been found in body fluids of schizophrenics. Some of these neurotransmitters are known to be active in brain systems that regulate emotion, such as the limbic system. The effectiveness of pharmacologic agents is thought to be related to the ability of drugs to alter biochemical balances at the synapses and thus to change the rate of firing of neurons involved in cognitive and emotional processes (see the section on brain function).

This composite of information is consistent with theories of schizophrenia that attribute major causal significance to physiological factors. These theories do not conflict with the idea that external stress can precipitate or exacerbate underlying schizophrenic processes. However, they do raise serious question about the validity of theories of etiology that emphasize childrearing practices and mother–child relationships as the cause of schizophrenia.

*Funding for research in nontraditional methods of treatment has been negligible in comparison with the financial investment by the government and foundations in research on drug treatment and psychotherapy. It is not surprising, therefore, that there is a dearth of controlled studies, which could either support or refute claims made by advocates of these methods.

Autism

Autism is a condition that probably is present at birth even when unrecognized (Ornitz & Ritvo, 1976). Autistic individuals show symptoms that include difficulty relating to others, distorted perception, erratic developmental rate, disturbance of language and speech, and bizarre patterns of motility such as whirling and hand flapping. Many do not learn to speak. They may be impervious or hyperreactive to sensory stimuli; for example, they may show no startle response to loud noise, or they may react with catastrophic fear to the sound of a vacuum cleaner or a siren. From early infancy, they show aversion to physical contact or may be unresponsive to attention.

Bettelheim (1967) and Mahler (1949) proposed that childhood autism, as described by Kanner (1943), Rank (1949), and others, is the result of a disturbed mother-child relationship. Few observers still take psychogenic explanations of etiology in autism seriously (see the criticism of Bettelheim in Rimland, 1970). The evidence supporting physiological etiology is extensive and varied (for reviews see Campbell et al., 1981; Cohen & Young, 1977; Fish & Ritvo, 1979; Ornitz & Ritvo, 1976). The precise causal mechanisms are complex and are not yet precisely understood, but there is little doubt that physical events—biochemical, traumatic, neuroendocrine related, viral, and others—are the precursors to autism (Campbell et al., 1981; Chess et al., 1971; Stubbs, 1978; Wing et al., 1976). Specific neuropathologies (such as enlarged ventricles) are often found in autistic persons, and seizures frequently occur in late childhood or adolescence. A number of experimental studies have been conducted utilizing a variety of observational and neurophysiological techniques (Bryson, 1970; Frith, 1970; Lelord et al., 1973; Lovaas et al., 1971; MacCullogh & Williams, 1971; Ornitz et al., 1974; Ritvo et al., 1976; Yuwiler et al., 1976).

Damasio and Maurer (1978) found evidence in the literature relating autism to specific brain areas. They reviewed the reports on established neurological syndromes and found enough similarities between known disorders in particular regions of the brain and infantile autism to suggest that neurological mechanisms underlying autistic symptomatology arise in the same areas. These manifestations include disturbances of motility, communication, attention, and perception; ritualistic and compulsive behaviors; and failure to develop normal social relationships. These characteristics appear both in autistic individuals and in persons with damage to certain brain structures, particularly, the frontal lobe, or to structures closely related to the frontal lobe (e.g., the basal ganglia or the limbic system). Failure to develop normal social relationships in autistic persons was seen by Damasio and Maurer as secondary to an organized

collection of primary defects resulting in disturbances in motility, attention, and communication and in ritualistic behaviors. Because the brain
structures that seem to be implicated in these disturbances contain a
large proportion of dopaminergic neurons, they suggested that the
neural dysfunction causing autism is produced or at least accompanied
by changes in dopamine content, owing to various possible mechanisms
such as damage to the cells, genetically determined neurochemical abnormality, perinatal lack of oxygen, or infection.

Specific Learning Disabilities

Evidence for the physiologic origin of specific learning disabilities
(dyslexia, dyscalculia, and dysgraphia) is accumulating. "Dyslexia"
refers to difficulty with reading: "dyscalculia," difficulty with computa-
tion: and "dysgraphia," difficulty with writing. While poor reading or
arithmetic can arise from anxiety, limited intelligence, or deficient
schooling, children whose reading is below grade level for any of these
reasons do not as a rule show the characteristic testing patterns (e.g.,
poor decoding, inadequate comphrehension) of their peers with specific
learning disabilities.

Although learning disabilities do not, strictly speaking, constitute
psychopathology, they are important to mention because they are frequently (and erroneously) attributed to psychopathology rather than to
neurologic dysfunction. Specific learning disabilities may persist
through life in affected individuals, many of whom develop psychological problems arising from the frustrations and failures caused by the
disability itself.

Tests to identify the physiologic bases of specific learning disability
have been carried out in various studies (Gross et al., 1978; Marcel & Rajan, 1975; Marcel et al., 1974; O'Neill & Stanley, 1976; Preston et al., 1974;
Stanley & Hall, 1973). Results of several studies suggest that specific
cerebral functions involving ability to automatize simple tasks are deficient in some children with normal intelligence who are poor readers
(Drake, 1970; Mathewson, 1967; Whiting et al., 1966). There is no
evidence that anxiety of psychogenic origin can account for these deficiencies. If anxiety were the cause, higher order cognitive functions, such
as those involving comprehension or restructuring ability, should also be
affected. Moreover, microscopic examination of the brain tissue of a
dyslexic on autopsy showed difference in neuroanatomical structure
from similar tissue in a nonlearning disabled person (Geschwind, 1979).
In the dyslexic, some neurons had migrated to an outer layer of tissue,
where such cells are not ordinarily found, and the architectural arrangement of the cells differed from the normal pattern. While no firm conclu-

sions can be drawn from individual cases, this finding adds support to the thesis that specific learning disability is of neuroanatomical and/or neurophysiological origin.

Personality Disturbances

Attention Deficit Disorder, Residual Type

In DSM III, "attention deficit disorder" (ADD) in children (and its residual type in adults) replaces earlier terminology such as "minimal brain dysfunction" or "hyperkinetic syndrome" (see Johnson, 1980, for a discussion). ADD is marked by the same characteristics but the new designator avoids the causal connotation suggested by the term "brain dysfunction." This syndrome, extremely common in children, is also exhibited by many adults but its prevalence in adults has not been established.

According to DSM III inclusion criteria for adult ADD, an individual must have at least four of the following characteristics, one of which must be either the first or the second:

motor hyperactivity persisting from childhood
attentional deficits persisting from childhood
affective lability
inability to complete tasks
hot or explosive temper
impaired interpersonal relationships or inability to sustain relationships over time
impulsiveness
stress intolerance

This diagnosis cannot be applied if the individual has ever met DSM III criteria for schizophrenia, schizoaffective disorder, primary affective disorder, schizotypal personality, or borderline personality.

In a study of the effectiveness of a stimulant medication, pemoline (marketed as Cylert), in the treatment of ADD, Wender and associates (1981) found that the subgroup of patients whose parents had described them as being markedly hyperactive showed significantly greater improvement on penoline than on placebo.

The attention deficit disorder is of considerable diagnostic significance in the psychopathology of adulthood for at least two reasons. First, it appears to be the antecedent and/or concomitant of several adult syndromes, including antisocial personality, explosive personality, violent dyscontrol, early onset severe alcoholism, and personality disorders involving irritability, impulsiveness, and emotional instability. Some subgroups of schizophrenia may also be included (Wender et al., 1981). Second, among the subgroup of patients who respond to psychostimulants, dramatic improvement in functioning, and hence in quality of life, may sometimes be obtained through the use of drugs like pemoline. Social workers need to be aware that seemingly intractable characterological problems may in fact represent an attention deficit disorder that is treatable with medication.

Alcoholism

The major physiological origins of alcohol addiction appear to be genetic. Genetic factors in alcoholism have been identified by several researchers. Schuckit and associates (1972) studied persons reared apart from their biological parents who had either a biological parent or a nonbiological rearing parent with a drinking problem. Subjects were significantly more likely to have drinking problems themselves when they had an alcoholic natural parent than when they had an alcoholic surrogate parent. From a sample of 32 alcoholics and 132 nonalcoholics, 62% of the alcoholics had an alcoholic biological parent, while 20% of the nonalcoholics had an alcoholic biological parent. There did not apper to be any relationship between the amount of personal contact the individual had had with the alcoholic natural parent and subsequent development of alcoholism. Other studies have supported the hypothesis of a genetic component in alcoholism (Ewing et al., 1974; Goodwin et al., 1974; Vesell, 1972; Wolff, 1972). Evidence of genetic transmission does not, of course, detract from the importance of socioenvironmental determinants. As in many other psychopathological conditions, the disorder most probably arises from an interplay between physical and social factors.

Antisocial Behavior

Biological correlates of antisocial behavior in adults and delinquency in children have been identified. Again, psychosocial factors probably play a part in antisocial behavior, but brain dysfunction or other organic factors are also likely to be important in etiology.

Organic Origins of Antisocial Behavior

A number of observers have tested the hypothesis that the origins of the antisocial personality (formerly referred to as "psychopathic personality" or "sociopathic personality") are organic, not psychogenic (see Chapter 12). A "sociopath" was defined by Ziskind (1975) as an individual who demonstrates several characteristics, including inability to profit from adverse experience, superficiality of affect, irresponsibility, impairment of conscience, and impulsiveness. Ziskind and associates (1977) supplied data revealing the abnormally high incidence of severe enuresis, hyperkinesis, nail biting, and specific learning disabilities in the childhood histories of sociopaths seen in adulthood. Sixty individuals diagnosed as sociopathic personalities were compared with 55 controls. Hyperkinesis was found to have been present in 20% of the sociopaths, compared to 4% of the controls; reading disabilities in 26% of the sociopaths, compared to 1% of the controls; enuresis in 29% of the sociopaths, compared to 7% of the controls; and nail biting in 50% of sociopaths, compared to 27% of the controls. Ziskind and associates postulated that a specific neurologic basis for sociopathy, namely, deficits in the ability to integrate aversive conditioning, lies behind the sociopathic characteristic of failing to learn from experience. Sociopaths in whom the personality disturbance manifests itself as criminal behavior are well known to demonstrate a high degree of recidivism, a fact suggestive of the inability to learn from punishment.

To test their hypothesis, Ziskind and colleagues (1977) studied 16 sociopaths and 16 matched controls. In the study, one conditioned stimulus was presented together with a noxious unconditioned stimulus; another conditioned stimulus was presented alone. Skin conductance, heart rate, and EEG readings were recorded. In contrast to the control subjects, sociopaths demonstrated a dissociation between verbal or cognitive learning of the difference between the paired and the unpaired conditioned stimulus and physiological manifestations of that learning. That is, while sociopaths were able to distinguish verbally between the paired conditioned stimulus and the unpaired stimulus, their physiological responses, unlike those of the control group, indicated that this learning had not taken place on a physiological level.

Violence and Aggression

Patterns of behavior involving violence, rage, or aggression have been related to neurologic phenomena by a large number of researchers. Mark and Ervin (1970) found that stimulation of the amygdala, a group of tightly clustered cell bodies in the limbic region of the brain, resulted in rage reactions. Bach-y-Rita (1975) and Brown (1976) induced aggressive behaviors and rage by stimulation of the amygdala, the hypothalamus, and the reticular formation. Kluver and Bucey (1939) found removal of the amygdala in monkeys produced tranquility. Malamud (1967) found that a high proportion of patients with intracranial tumors of the limbic system had histories that included assaultiveness. Charles Whitman, who in 1966 murdered 16 people and injured 31 others in a shooting spree in Texas, was found at autopsy to have a tumor in one temporal lobe in close proximity to limbic structures (Schwartz, 1978). Finally, rabies generates rage as a result of viral insult to the brain.

Various studies linking aggressive behavior in humans with disturbed cerebral function have been reported. Of 62 habitually aggressive men studied in a large prison, a group from which all overtly psychotic individuals had been eliminated, 61% were found to have suffered a brain concussion prior to age 10; childhood histories also revealed hyperactive or stimulus seeking behavior and severe impulsiveness (Bach-y-Rita, 1975). Morrison and Minkoff (1975) reported that persons with explosive dyscontrol behavior during adulthood had histories of hyperactivity, insult to the central nervous system, or epilepsy during childhood. Early investigation, supported by subsequent studies, found a much higher incidence of EEG abnormality among convicted criminals, particularly those with a diagnosis of psychopathic personality, than in the population at large (Bach-y-Rita, 1975). In a study of 1,250 subjects in custody for crimes of violence, 62% of 333 randomly selected subjects had a history of habitual physical aggression or explosive rage (Williams, 1969). Of this group, 65% of the habitually aggressive subjects had abnormal EEGs; 24% of the subjects who had committed violent crimes but were *not* habitually aggressive had such abnormalities; but only 12% of the population at large demonstrates abnormalities on the EEG. Even if a small part of this dramatic difference could be explained by the tendency of the researcher to interpret EEGs in accordance with his wish to find significant differences, and allowing for the variability that is known to exist in the interpretations of the EEG by different neurologists, these findings provide evidence for a strong association between habitual aggression and abnormalities of brain function that is hard to refute.

Treatment of Antisocial Behavior

No drugs have been identified that selectively prevent aggressive or violent outbursts without seriously affecting other functions (Goldstein, 1974). This fact should not be surprising, however, because a variety of conditions with diverse causes are known to induce aggressiveness. Treatments specific to these conditions have been found to be effective in reducing the aggressivity associated with the particular condition. Examples include lithium for manic states; amphetamines for hyperactive aggression in children with minimal brain dysfunction; phenothiazines and butyrophenones for schizophrenia; and anticonvulsants for seizure disorders (Goldstein, 1974). Reports of efficacy vary. Medication to control aggression in the absence of specific treatable conditions, however, has been found to have only limited effectiveness (Goldstein, 1974).

Most studies concur in failing to demonstrate the effectiveness of psychotherapy in alleviating aggressive dyscontrol (Goldstein, 1974; Pincus & Tucker, 1978). Nor has milieu therapy been found to be of much value (Pincus & Tucker, 1978). In a group of juvenile delinquents (one-third of whom were violent) treated at a well-respected residential center, the recidivism rate following discharge was 75% (Hartelius, 1965). Similar rates of recidivism have been found for populations of untreated violent criminals (Gibbens et al., 1959).

Psychosurgery, involving either the stimulation or the removal of certain regions of the brain, is ethically controversial. Reports of effectiveness are mixed (Goldstein, 1974). Nevertheless, some argue that when all other treatments have proven ineffective, it is the patient's only hope for relief of distressful symptoms (e.g., Goldstein, 1974).

Dementias of Old Age

Unlike mental and emotional symptoms in most other age groups, those commonly associated with aging—such as confusion, forgetfulness, disorientation, irritability, depression, apathy, restlessness, agitation, hallucinations, delusions, incontinence, and anxiety—are frequently attributed to physiological causes by both lay and professional persons. Constellations of these symptoms are often referred to as "senility" or "senile dementia" (see Chapter 19). Recent studies of aging, however, have pointed out that many popular beliefs about mental deterioration in the elderly are false (Butler, 1975; Galton, 1979). Although these symptoms often do arise from physiological processes, the notion that such conditions are natural or usually irreversible is not borne out by evidence. Symptoms may be due to treatable physical conditions, drug reactions, or nutritional deficiency.

Various treatable physical conditions can cause symptoms of mental dysfunction. These include narrowing of blood vessels to the brain (these can be dilated biochemically); coagulation and clotting of blood cells due to slower flow through narrowed vessels (treatable with anticoagulants); thyroid malfunction; congestive heart failure (which reduces blood flow to the brain); anemia (treatable with diet modification and nutritional supplement); high blood pressure; parathyroid dysfunction; and adrenal insufficiency or overproduction.

The drugs prescribed for many illnesses in the elderly can also cause mental and emotional symptoms. A certain proportion of users of various drugs experience adverse side effects due to sensitivity to the drug, incorrect dosage, interaction of the drug with other drugs being taken concurrently, or interaction of the drug with certain foods. Galton (1979) listed possible mental side effects of about 80 medications commonly prescribed for many conditions, including high blood pressure, thyroid malfunction, peptic ulcer, angina pectoris, infections, insomnia, anxiety, depression, allergy, and arthritis. Galton enumerated ways in which these drugs can produce mental symptoms, either alone or in combination with other drugs or certain foods.

In addition to physical illness and drug effects, nutritional deficiencies have also been demonstrated to cause deterioration in mental functioning in elderly persons. Nutritional deficits can be caused not only by inadequate intake of certain nutrients but also by inability to absorb nutrients properly (even when present in the diet) or interference with the body's utilization of the nturient (even though absorbed). Aged people have frequently been found to be deficient in thiamine (vitamin B_1), riboflavin (vitamin B_2), niacin (vitamin B_3), pyridoxine (vitamin B_6), cobalamin (vitamin B_{12}), folic acid, potassium, magnesium, and zinc (Galton, 1979). Inadequacies in these substances can result in confusion, memory impairment, irritability, difficulty in concentration, depression, hallucinations, insomnia, apathy, and disorientation.

Because physicians sometimes neglect to perform exhaustive investigations of possible nutritional deficiencies, drug reactions, drug–diet interactions, or disorders in absorption, social work practitioners need to become familiar with the wide range of possible causes of mental problems in the elderly. Familiarity with these possible causes should enable the practitioner to raise questions pertinent to the care and treatment of their clients. It should enable them to assess whether or not sufficiently comprehensive evaluations have been carried out before cases of senile mental deterioration are dismissed as inevitable and untreatable.

Other Nonpsychotic Conditions: Anxiety, Phobia, and Obsessive-Compulsive Disorder

Nonpsychotic conditions subsumed in DSM III under the label "anxiety disorders" (1980) differ from psychoses in the absence of gross personality disorganization or severe misperception of reality. They include anxiety reactions, phobic reactions, and obsessive-compulsive disorders. Generally attributed to adverse parent–child interactions, these disorders may sometimes have a physiological basis.

Studies of the biochemistry of anxiety neurosis support the hypothesis that innate physiological differences are important determinants of the propensity for anxiety. The work of Pitts and McClure (1967) corroborated the results of four earlier studies showing that patients with anxiety neurosis have excessive lactate production (Miner, 1973). Pitts and McClure tested the hypothesis that the lactate ion itself could produce anxiety in susceptible persons (for an explanation of ions see the section on brain function). A double-blind experiment was conducted with 14 patients diagnosed as having anxiety neurosis and 10 controls. Experimental and control subjects were given infusions of three types of solutions containing, respectively, lactate ions, lactate ions plus calcium, and glucose (placebo). Among 13 of the 14 anxiety neurotics, anxiety attacks developed within one to two minutes after infusion of lactate, while only 2 of the 10 controls had such attacks. When calcium was added to the lactate, symptoms were largely prevented. No symptoms were induced by glucose.

Biochemical theories to explain these findings, too complex to be presented here, were developed by Pitts and McClure (1976) and by Grosz and Farmer (1972). Their explanations differ; however, both are consistent with the hypothesis that biochemical mechanisms play a significant role in the genetic–environment interactions resulting in anxiety neurosis.

Anorexia Nervosa

In anorexia nervosa, the individual eats little or nothing and develops an aversion to food (see Chapter 14). Because anorexia is seen most often in adolescent females who have gone on stringent diets in order to lose weight, it was believed to be entirely psychogenic in origin for many years. Recent studies suggest that physiological factors contribute to maintaining the condition once it is present and may even be causative. Katz and associates (1976) performed studies supporting earlier findings of abnormality in the functioning of the hypothalamus in anorexia nervosa. It could not be determined conclusively whether the hypothalamic defect predated the onset of anorexia and might thus account for the abnormal eating behavior and the cessation of menstruation that accompanies it or whether clinical changes in the endocrine system were the *consequence* of dieting and extreme weight loss. Edminson (1979) reported on experiments in which an extract of the blood from patients with anorexia nervosa was injected into laboratory animals, producing an aversion to food that lasted for several weeks. This finding seems to suggest that even if most cases of anorexia are initiated by social environmental conditions (i.e., desire to lose weight), a biochemical process is set in motion that contributes to perpetuating the condition.

Summary

Biological factors have been found to be important in disorders of mood and cognition, personality disturbances, antisocial behavior, dementias of old age, and anorexia nervosa. The complexity of psychic functioning makes determination of the precise causes or origins of psychopathology extremely difficult. There is no doubt, however, that brain function, the bodily processes that control and and regulate emotions, behavior, and cognition, can be strongly affected by any number of variables, both psychosocial and biochemical. In the following section, the reader is introduced to some fundamentals of brain structure and function (neuroanatomy and neurophysiology). This material should help readers understand and appreciate the significance of research showing the influence of biology on behavior.

Some Principles of Brain Function

The Brain as the Organ of Communication

The brain is the center of communication within the human body. It receives messages from all parts of the body, makes decisions about how to respond to these messages, and sends out commands to parts of the body capable of implementing these commands. The brain's signaling system is both chemical and electrical, as will be explained shortly. The human brain represents only about 1–3% of the total body weight but consumes about 20% of the body's oxygen when the body is in a resting state (Iversen, 1979). That is, compared with the rest of the body, it burns (metabolizes) energy at an extremely high rate.

Topology of the Brain

The human brain is divided into many parts, and different regions have specialized functions. Experiments with animals, as well as clinical observations of humans with brain injuries or illnesses known to affect particular regions of the brain, have demonstrated that different brain centers control various specific functions such as vision, memory, analytic thinking, breathing, perception, language, voluntary movement, and a variety of emotional responses. However, under certain conditions, one part of the brain may perform tasks considered to be a specialty of another part, while responses normally expected from other parts of the brain sometimes do not take place. The gross anatomic structures of the brain are extremely complex. Only a brief review is given here.

Certain regions of the brain are linked with the emotions, for example, the limbic structures and the diencephalon (Fig. 2–1). Limbic struc-

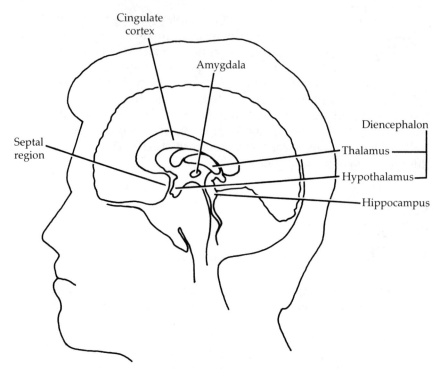

FIGURE 2–1. Schematic drawing of some structures of the limbic system and the diencephalon.

tures include the hippocampus, the septum (septal region), the amygdala, and the cingulate cortex. Diencephalic structures include the thalamus and the hypothalamus. The septum and amygdala are involved with manifestations of rage and aggression. The hippocampus appears to be related to the ability to inhibit responses. The hypothalamus is involved in rage reactions and levels of emotional responsiveness. The reticular system, of which the diencephalon is a part, is important in processes involving arousal states and is thought to be related to levels of attentiveness (Schwartz, 1978). Most of these structures are thought to serve other functions in addition to the regulation of emotions.

Structure and Function of Neurons

The brain contains billions of neurons, the cells involved in the communication process. The number of neurons in the brain is currently estimated at between 10 billion and 1 trillion, with a probable figure of 100 billion (Hubel, 1979). The neurons are surrounded and supported by another type of cell, the glial cell. Glial cells also number in the billions. They provide nutrients to neurons and help carry away the waste products of neuron metabolism. It is still not known whether glial cells also participate in the communication process. In addition to neurons and glial cells, the blood transports nutrients and oxygen to brain and spinal cord cells and takes away waste products from these cells via arteries and veins, respectively.

Of all the neurons in the central nervous system, only 2–3 million are motor neurons (neurons that transmit messages to muscles to cause them to move). Taken together, motor and sensory neurons (neurons that transmit messages from sensory organs to the brain) constitute only about 0.02% of all neurons, while the neurons of the "great intermediate net," which transmit information between some of the sensory and motor neurons and performs the brain's incredibly complex computations, represent about 99.98% of all neurons (Nauta & Feirtag, 1979).

It is believed that neurons in the central nervous system of mammals do not continue to multiply and divide for more than a short time after birth. We are born with most of the neurons we will ever have. When neurons die, they are not replaced, although they do have some ability to heal if injured.

Brain cells are very small; the cell body of a large neuron is about one-tenth of a millimeter in diameter.* However, neurons can be very long, sometimes as much as a meter in length. There is very little space between cells, which accounts for the fact that so many can be packed into the space inside the skull and the spinal column.

Because neurons come in many different sizes and shapes, it is not possible to represent all types of neurons here. Instead, a schematic representation of "typical" neurons is given in Figure 2–2. The cell body of the neuron branches out into many tiny threadlike dendrites. Dendrites pick up messages transmitted from other cells. Another extension of the cell body is the axon. This branch is usually longer than the dendrites. Unlike dendrites, it does not taper at the end into a point; it forms small end feet. An axon may itself branch out and form axon collaterals. The axon carries messages from the cell body to the end feet. The end feet are involved in transmitting messages to adjacent cells. Dendrites do not extend more than a few millimeters, while axons can extend as far as a meter or more.

Many axons are encased in a white material, the myelin sheath (Fig. 2–3). Myelin is composed of the cell bodies and membranes of a type of glial cell. Between the segments of myelin surrounding the axon are

---

*To examine neurons in detail, very high magnification is necessary, far greater than that which can be provided by ordinary microscopes. Electron microscopy is a recently developed technique by which minute objects can be photographed. Various tiny brain structures can now be seen in photographs obtained with electron microscopes.

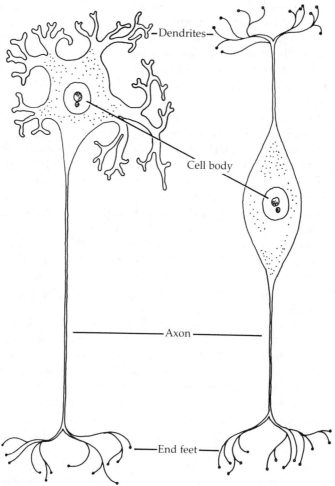

FIGURE 2–2. Two types of neurons.

gaps, the *nodes of Ranvier*, where there is little or no myelin over the axon membrane. The myelin does not extend onto either the cell body or the end feet.

Inside the cell body is a nucleus, which contains chromosomes carrying the hereditary information guiding the functioning of the cell. The nucleus is surrounded by intracellular fluid, composed of molecules of the various substances needed for the life of the cell.

The exterior surface of the neuron, the cell membrane, performs a central function in the transmission of nerve impulses. This membrane is semipermeable; that is, it has tiny pores that allow some substances to cross through it between the outside and the inside of the cell while

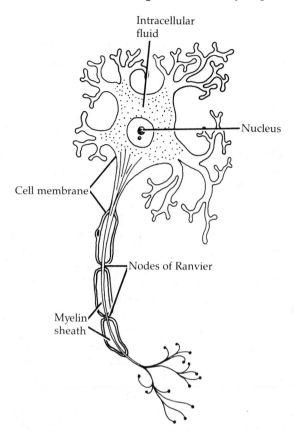

Intracellular
fluid

Nucleus

Cell membrane

Nodes of Ranvier

Myelin
sheath

FIGURE 2–3. Neuron with myelin sheath.

preventing the passage of other material. Small particles called "ions" are among the substances to which the cell membrane is differentially permeable. Thus, certain ions can cross through the membrane into and out of the interior of the cell, while other ions are blocked. An ion is an electrically charged particle. It is actually part of a molecule that has either lost or gained one or more electrons. The electron is the part of the atom carrying a negative charge. Ions are formed when certain substances are dissolved in water. Table salt, or sodium chloride, is an example of an ionizing compound. Sodium chloride (NaCl) breaks apart, or dissociates, into a sodium ion (Na^+) and a chlorine ion (Cl^-) when dissolved in water. The positive ($+$) and negative ($-$) signs indicate whether the ion carries a positive or a negative charge. Ions carrying a positive charge have lost one or more electrons during the process of dissociation. Ions carrying a negative charge have gained one or more electrons.

Since much of the brain, like all human tissue, contains water, substances that ionize in water, like NaCl, do not exist within the brain. Instead, ions like Na^+, Cl^-, and K^+ (potassium) are present. Positive ions repel each other but attract negative ions, while negative ions repel each other but attract positive ions. The fact that the brain contains these electrically charged particles is of crucial importance in understanding the operation of the nerve impulse.

Because the cell membrane allows some ions to pass through more easily than others, there is an unequal distribution of types of ions inside the neuron and outside it. K^+ ions pass more easily than Na^+ ions when the cell membrane is at rest. The intracellular fluid contains a higher concentration of K^+ ions than does the extracellular fluid but a lower concentration of Na^+ ions. The intracellular fluid also contains large organic ions (A^-), which are virtually absent outside the cell wall.

There is a slight excess of positively charged ions on the exterior side of the membrane and a slight excess of negatively charged ions on the interior. Although these excesses are small, they are sufficient to create a voltage differential, or potential, across the cell membrane. The word ''potential'' conveys the idea that differences in the degree of positive or negative charge in different areas create the possibility for movement of charged particles from one location to another.

This difference in charge between the inside and the outside of the cell, the potential, is measured in millivolts mV. When the cell is at rest, this difference is about 70 mV. The difference is usually represented as -70 mV, indicating that the inside of the membrane is always negatively charged with respect to the outside when the cell is in a resting state.

Neurons do not remain at rest. When they are stimulated, they become active and produce nerve impulses. For a fraction of a second, Na^+ ions on the outside of the cell are allowed by the stimulated cell membrane to pass through to the interior of the cell. This changes the electric charge momentarily from negative to positive. This reversal in voltage lasts only a fraction of a second. K^+ ions then pass out through the membrane, restoring the original negative charge on the inside. The neuron recovers its resting voltage and is then ready to respond to further stimulation. Meanwhile, the impulse is carried down the length of the axon. This brief event can occur many thousands of times per hour in an individual neuron.

The key to understanding neuron function, according to some theorists, is knowledge of the types and functions of proteins attached to, or embedded in, the cell membranes of the neurons (Stevens, 1979). These membrane proteins perform such functions as pumping Na^+ ions through the membrane or acting as gates that allow some types of molecular particles to pass through while blocking the passage of others. There are five classes of membrane proteins: pumps, channels, receptors, enzymes, and structural proteins. One protein may perform two or three functions. A typical small neuron may have 1 million sodium pumps with the capacity to move more than 200 million Na+ ions per second (Stevens, 1979). The channel proteins act as gates: some smaller Na+ ions can get through certain of these channels, while larger K+ ions cannot. Although the exact molecular structure of channel cells that accounts for this phenomenon is not known, the general principle is understood. Interactions take place between ions and parts of the channel molecular structure, and proteins change shape as they function, allowing this gating mechanism. A receptor is a molecule of the postsynaptic neuron with which substances from presynaptic neurons interact to form chemical reactions. An enzyme is a substance that promotes or accelerates chemical reactions.

Transmission of the Nerve Impulse

The electrical state of a nonconducting nerve is referred to today as the "membrane potential," or "resting potential," of the neuron. The resting potential is maintained by the difference in ionic concentrations in the fluid media inside and outside the cell. As explained earlier, the membrane is semipermeable; it allows some ions to pass through more easily than others. Inside the cell there is a high concentration of positive potassium ions (K+); outside, a high concentration of positive sodium ions (Na+). Because the membrane of the resting neuron blocks the inward passage of Na+ ions while it permits a high rate of passage outward of K+ ions, the inside of the nerve cell is left electrically negative relative to the outside.

The crucial event that lies behind the initiation of the nerve impulse is the increase in the permeability of the membrane to Na+ ions. Scientists have not yet discovered exactly what molecular changes allow this to happen, but these changes are believed to take place in the membrane protein molecules acting as gates or pumps. When suitable stimulation is applied to the neuron, the membrane suddenly becomes much more permeable to Na+ ions. These Na+ ions imediately rush into the interior of the cell both because ions always move from regions of greater concentration to areas of lesser concentration and because the positively charged Na+ ions are attracted to the negatively charged organic ions (A−) in the interior.

The length of time during which the membrane becomes readily permeable to Na+ ions is very short; it has been estimated to be less than 0.5 milliseconds (msec). While the number of Na+ ions that manage to cross the membrane during this time is very small, only a few electrical charges need to be moved from one side of the membrane to the other to produce the momentary change in voltage from −70 mV to some slightly positive voltage (about +30 mV). When the internal voltage reaches about +30 mV, for some reason as yet unknown the membrane loses its permeability to Na+ ions.

The return of the neuron to its resting potential is brought about mainly by a change in the permeability of the membrane to the K+ ion. The peak of the membrane's permeability to K+ (or its ability to conduct K+ from the interior through to the exterior of the cell) occurs *after* it has become impermeable to Na+ and the Na+ ions no longer can cross the membrane readily. At this point, the K+ ions move out from the interior of the cell across the membrane to the exterior because the concentration of K+ is much higher on the inside than on the outside.

Even though the negative organic ions on the inside still attract the K+ ions, there are so many K+ ions on the inside that the force pushing them out is greater than the force of attraction exerted by the negative ions inside. There is, therefore, a net outflow of positive charge as the K+ ions move to the outside. This outflow is what restores the voltage across the membrane to its resting potential of −70 mV. The inflow of Na+ ions, then, is responsible for the rapid change of inside voltage from −70 mV to +30 mV, while the subsequent outflow of K+ ions is responsible for restoring the original potential of −70 mV.

Movement of the Nerve Impulse Down the Axon

The nerve impulse usually begins near the part of the axon emerging from the cell body. In some neurons, the axon has a lower threshold at this point than at others. The threshold is the minimum depolarization, or change in potential in the direction of zero, needed to trigger a nerve impulse. It must be at least 10–15 mV. That is, if the resting potential is −70 mV, the point at which a nerve impulse will be triggered is somewhere between −60 and −55 mV.

As Na+ ions enter the neuron after the initial stimulation has caused the membrane to become permeable to Na+, the influx of positive ions changes the resting potential from −70 to −60 mV, then on to −50, −40, down to zero and past zero up to +30. The nerve impulse begins when the voltage is about −60 or −55 mV. The ionic current is now flowing in a manner similar to that described for electron current in wire conduction; that is, the motion of the ions produces a domino effect, which causes an ionic current flow much faster than the movement of the ions themselves.

This ionic current brings more positive charge into the axon. In this way, the membrane is further depolarized. This triggers an even greater inflow of Na+ ions. At the same time, this ionic current also depolarizes the next adjacent area of the membrane, just ahead of the point at which the impulse is taking place. This new part of the membrane thus is stimulated to enter the cycle of increased permeability, Na⁺ inflow, and K⁺ outflow. This is the manner in which the impulse is propagated down the axon to its end feet (Fig. 2–4).

The duration of the nerve impulse is about 1 msec. The characteristics of the nerve impulse are the same no matter what type of neuron is involved; the only aspect that varies is the rate of firing of impulses. That is, the crucial question is how many times per second a neuron fires an impulse. This is important because each impulse from a preceding neuron affects the succeeding neuron by either exciting or inhibiting it. If the first neuron fires at a rapid rate, its (exciting or inhibiting effect on the next neuron) is greater than the effect of a neuron that fires more slowly.

Any one neuron may be acted on by hundreds of other neurons, some of which excite it and others of which inhibit it. Whether or not this succeeding neuron fires depends on whether it is affected by a larger number of excitatory or of inhibitory impulses from preceding neurons. The net sum of incoming signals determines whether the neuron will or will not fire and at what rate it will fire. Therefore, if neurons generating inhibitory effects fire at a slower rate than neurons having an excitatory effect, the net effect on the receptor neuron will be to excite it and cause it to fire at a fast rate.*

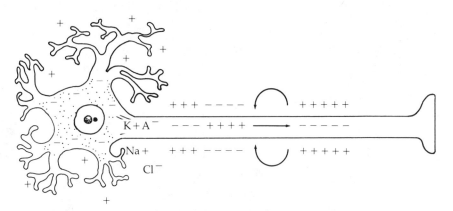

FIGURE 2–4. Transmission of electrical impulse down the axon.

*An example of the behavioral consequences of this process might be that overexcitation of neurons in parts of the limbic system results in overt behaviors of rage and aggressiveness. What is ordinarily referred to as "disturbed behavior" is believed by many observers to be an outward manifestation of an imbalance between excitatory and inhibitory operations in the brain.

The Synapse

The term "synapse" refers to points of contact between one neuron and another. The synapse includes three elements: (1) the presynaptic end foot of the axon of one neuron; (2) the synaptic cleft, or tiny space between one neuron and the next; and (3) the postsynaptic receptive site at the tip of the dendrite or on the cell body of the second neuron. (Fig. 2–5).

The synapse is of critical importance in brain function. A typical neuron is thought to have 1,000–10,000 synapses and may receive information from more than 1,000 other neurons via synaptic connections (Stevens, 1979). The total number of synapses in the brain is estimated at 100 trillion (Hubel, 1979).

To visualize the interconnections between neurons, imagine a telephone switchboard. Each incoming wire connects with 1,000–10,000 other wires, and each of these wires, in turn, connects with another set of 1,000–10,000 wires. If the total number of such connections is 100 trillion, we can begin to appreciate how amazing it is that any messages come through clearly. In comparison to the human brain, the world's most complicated computer looks like a simple toy.

When a nerve impulse arrives at the end foot of the axon of the presynaptic neuron, neurotransmitters are released into the synaptic cleft. Transmitters are manufactured either in the presynaptic end feet or in the cell body. When manufactured in the cell body, they are transported

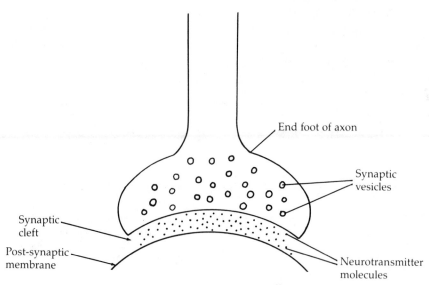

FIGURE 2–5. Synaptic transmission.

down to the end feet, where they are stored in small containers (synaptic vesicles).

Although small amounts of these transmitters are released into the synaptic cleft even when the neurons are at rest, the arrival of a nerve impulse greatly increases the rate of transmitter release. After the transmitter is released, it diffuses across the synaptic cleft and contacts receptor molecules in the postsynaptic neuron.

The Role of Neurotransmitters

It is now widely accepted that the neurotransmitters are of crucial importance in the regulation of normal behavior and in the occurrence of virtually all of the psychiatric disturbances. Presently, there are about 30 known or suspected transmitters (Iversen, 1979).

To qualify as a transmitter, a substance must meet several criteria (Frazer, 1977). Some mechanism must be available for synthesizing and storing the transmitter within the neuron; it must be released from the neuron when it receives appropriate stimuli; and some mechanism must be available to terminate the action of the transmitter at the receptor of the postsynaptic neuron membrane. While there are differences among the various transmitter systems, they all share these properties.

Transmitters are stored in the synaptic vesicles. They are released into the synaptic cleft when the neuron is stimulated and then interact with receptors on the postsynaptic membrane. The action of transmitters at the synapse is terminated in various ways. While a certain amount of the termination process is due to degradation of transmitters in the presence of specific enzymes, the primary action involved in termination is a process known as "uptake." Uptake refers to the actions of neurons in absorbing concentrations of transmitter substances from the synapses into which they have been released. Different drugs affect the uptake process in diverse ways, depending on the transmitter and the extent to which its uptake is carried out by neuronal or nonneuronal tissue.

If uptake is inhibited by chemical intervention, the existing pattern of neural transmission is drastically altered. Both tricyclic antidepressants and cocaine act to inhibit the uptake process. Differences in the actions of various drugs are illustrated by the fact that desipramine, a tricyclic antidepressant, inhibits the uptake of norepinephrine, one transmitter, 1,000 times as strongly as it inhibits the uptake of dopamine, another transmitter. Drugs of the desipramine type are effective in treating conditions in which norepinephrine imbalance is implicated. The effectiveness of desipramine in alleviating depression is highly suggestive that a malfunction of the norepinephrine transmitter system is an important cause of depression.

Neurotransmitters may produce two types of effects when they interact with postsynaptic receptor molecules: excitatory and inhibitory. When the transmitter and the receptor molecule interact in excitatory fashion, a small depolarizing current is set in motion. A depolarizing current is a flow of electrically charged particles that reduces negative potential on the inside of the neuron from -70 mV progressively toward zero and beyond. This depolarizing current is called an "excitatory postsynaptic potential" (epsp). When the effect is inhibitory, the transmitter has interacted with postsynaptic receptor molecules to produce a hyperpolarizing current. The hyperpolarizing current makes the interior of the cell even more negatively charged with respect to the exterior of the cell than when it was at rest. It therefore causes the neuron to move further away from the threshold at which a nerve impulse is generated. This is called an "inhibitory postsynaptic potential" (ipsp).

When an excitatory interaction is taking place at a synapse, the release of the transmitter substance stimulates the postsynaptic neuron to produce nerve impulses. When inhibitory interaction is taking place, transmitters react with molecules on the postsynaptic neuron to inhibit the firing of an impulse by the postsynaptic neuron. Differences in receptors are thought to be responsible for excitatory and inhibitory actions. Ahlquist (1948) termed these receptors "alpha" (responsible for most excitatory actions) and "beta" (responsible for most inhibitory actions).

Since action at some synapses is excitatory while action at other synapses on the same neuron is inhibitory, opposing forces must act on a single neuron at a given time. As we have seen, if the excitatory forces are stronger than the inhibitory ones, the neuron's rate of firing impulses will increase; if the inhibitory forces are stronger, the rate of firing will decrease; if the forces balance each other, no change in the rate of firing will take place.

The synapse thus modulates brain activity by making ongoing transmission of a nerve impulse conditional on the relationship between excitatory and inhibitory effects. Behavioral manifestations of hyperactivity, aggressiveness, rage, or lethargy are the outward, observable manifestations of these synaptic transactions. As has been pointed out, imbalances between excitatory and inhibitory actions at the synapses are thought to account for some behavioral disorders in humans that were formerly considered psychogenic in origin.

Since the transmitters are primary actors in the chemical interactions that determine whether the postsynaptic neuron will or will not fire, they are of great importance in brain function. Drugs used to treat psychiatric disorders may act either to inhibit release of a transmitter or to block its reception by the postsynaptic neuron. Researchers have been intensively involved during the past decade in studying the relationship between imbalances in some of these substances and various types of behavior.

Recent discoveries about impulse transmission have been made possible by use of the electron microscope. The theory of unidirectional transmission of impulses from axon to synapse and then to dendrites of another cell has been found to be an oversimplification. It is now known that axons may connect with other axons and dendrites with other dendrites, thus altering the direction or modifying the characteristics of impulse transmission.

Transmitters are not randomly distributed throughout the brain but are localized in clusters of neurons whose axons project to other highly specific regions of the brain; transmitters have discrete centers of origin and pathways to other brain areas (Iversen, 1979). The neurotransmitters whose routes are best known are the monoamines, a group that includes dopamine, norepinephrine, and serotonin.

Recent research has revealed that behavioral effects of drugs and of substances that are toxic to neurons arise from their ability to disrupt or modify chemical transmission between neurons (Iversen, 1979). It also seems likely that the causes of mental illness may ultimately be traced to defects in specific transmitter systems. As Iversen explained, the brain's ability to modulate and specify its responses arises from the diverse chemically coded systems of neurotransmitters that are superimposed on neuronal circuitry, or wiring, in the brain.

Recently developed techniques such as the radioactive labeling of deoxyglucose (Hubel, 1979) make it possible to detect what cells in the brain are active during a given experimental procedure. Since neurons take up more glucose when active than when at rest, accumulations of deoxyglucose, which is taken up like simple glucose but is then trapped in the cells and accumulates, indicate the activity level of those cells.

The Cycle of Neurotransmitter Synthesis and Activity

There are five major steps in transmitter activity: (1) synthesis of the substance in the neuron, (2) storage in the synaptic vesicle or cell body, (3) release of the transmitter, (4) reaction of the transmitter with receptor molecules and (5) inactivation or termination of transmitter action (Iversen, 1979). Brown (1976) outlined six ways in which drugs can modify the transmission of impulses across the synapse: (1) interference with the synthesis of the neurotransmitter, (2) interference with the release of the neurotransmitter, (3) facilitation of the release of the neurotransmitter, (4) interference with enzymatic deactivation of the neurotransmitter, (5) activation of the postsynaptic membrane, and (6) inhibition of the neurotransmitter's action on the postsynaptic membrane. Drugs can either enhance or inhibit release of a particular transmitter from the axon terminal into the synapse. They can act as substitutes for the transmitter by reacting chemically with receptor molecules in a manner similar to that of the transmitter itself, thus increasing quantities of the transmitter available in the synapse. They can combine chemically with receptor molecules in different ways from those of the transmitter, thereby preventing the transmitter from doing its work. They can potentiate the effects of transmitters by blocking enzyme action that degrades the transmitter. Finally, they can block the reuptake of the transmitter by the presynaptic neuron (Iversen, 1979).

It is commonly believed that neurons usually contain the biochemical machinery to make only one kind of transmitter, which the neuron releases from all axon terminals (Iversen, 1979). These transmitter molecules are prepared by modification of precursor molecules, usually an amino acid, through a series of enzymatic reactions. They are then stored in vesicles at the axon terminals. There may be thousands of vesicles at each terminal, each containing 10,000–100,000 transmitter molecules. These vesicles protect the transmitter molecules from enzymes in the surrounding areas that would destroy them.

The transmitter is thought to be released into the synapse by a process known as "exocytosis," in which the vesicle fuses with the presynaptic membrane and opens up into the synaptic cleft, discharging the transmitter particles. The transmitters then generate reactions at receptor sites. They can interact with receptors throughout the body. Receptors are contained in neurons, muscles, and glands. If the receptor is part of a neuron, the transmitter may react with it either to excite or to inhibit that cell. If the interaction is with a muscle cell, the transmitter may stimulate the receptors to contract the muscle. If the receptor is part of a gland, the transmitter may stimulate the gland to manufacture and secrete some kind of hormone. In each case, the receptor translates a message encoded in the molecular structure of the transmitter molecule into a specific physiological response. This response may take a fraction of a second, as in the stimulation of a muscle contraction, or it may take minutes or hours, as in the secretion of hormones.

Psychoactive Drugs and Neurotransmitters

The importance of the neurotransmitters in disorders of mood, cognition, and behavior becomes clear when their relationship to some of the psychoactive drugs is explored. For example, a wide variety of drugs known to be effective in alleviating manifestations of schizophrenia, such as chlorpromazine and haloperidol, share the property of binding tightly to dopamine receptors (Iversen, 1979). They join chemically with these receptors, thereby preventing dopamine itself from reacting chemically with the receptors. This reduces the rate of firing of the postsynaptic neuron by reducing dopamine interaction with receptors.

Schizophrenia has been associated with both overproduction of dopamine and overresponsiveness to it in certain regions of the brain. Abnormally high concentrations of dopamine and dopamine receptors have been found in the brains of deceased schizophrenics, especially in the limbic system. Therefore, it is possible that dopamine pathways in this region may be a primary target for antipsychotic drugs (Iversen, 1979).

It is noteworthy that amphetamine is known to release dopamine and that overdoses of amphetamine can induce symptoms often indistinguishable from those of schizophrenia (Angrist et al., 1971; Griffith et al., 1970; Iversen, 1979). Dopamine is also associated with pleasure and arousal systems (Crow, 1972; Hornykiewicz, 1977). Euphoria and increased alterness, the effects sought by users of stimulants such as amphetamine, are thought to be induced by enhancement of dopamine mechanisms (Hornykiewicz, 1977). The similarity in chemical structure between amphetamine and the neurotransmitters dopamine and norepinephrine can be seen in a diagram of their structures (Fig. 2–6).

Gamma-aminobutyric acid (GABA) is the most common inhibitory transmitter in the brain; it has been estimated that as many as a third of the synapses in the brain employ GABA as a transmitter (Iversen, 1979). GABA is involved in the phenomenon of anxiety; it appears that the brain may contain some substances that act on receptors sensitive to GABA either to increase or to relieve anxiety naturally (Iversen, 1979). GABA is a target for antianxiety drugs such as diazepam (marketed as Valium), which seem to increase the effectiveness of GABA at its receptor sites. The molecular structure of GABA, an inhibitory transmitter, closely resembles that of glutamic acid, thought to be a transmitter that

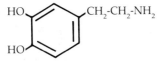

Dopamine   Norepinephrine

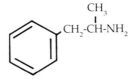

Amphetamine

FIGURE 2–6.   The chemical structures of dopamine, norepinephrine, and amphetamine.

acts in an excitatory fashion. A slight difference in molecular structure, then, can give rise to completely different physiological effects (Iversen, 1979).

Many psychoactive drugs may act by mimicking natural transmitters at receptor sites. For example, hallucinogenic drugs bear structural resemblances to natural transmitters. Mescaline resembles norepinephrine and dopamine, while LSD and psilocybin resemble serotonin. These resemblances indicate the importance of further investigation of the behaviors of these neurotransmitters and the drugs that resemble them in chemical structure.

Some drugs potentiate the effects of transmitters by blocking their degradation in the synapse. Iproniazid (marketed as Marsalid) and other drugs that inhibit the action of the enzyme monoamine oxidase in breaking down dopamine, norepinephrine, and serotonin enhance the arousing effects of these transmitters. These drugs, known as monoamine oxidase inhibitors, produce antidepressant effects by enhancing the action of these monoamine transmitters.

Still another group of drugs acts to block the reuptake from the synapse of certain transmitters (norepinephrine and serotonin). These include imipramine (marketed as Tofranil) and amitriptyline (marketed as Elavil), commonly used to treat depression. Cocaine is thought to work in similar fashion. This suggests that depression is associated with low levels of amine transmitters; mania, with high levels (Iversen, 1979).

A family of chemicals in the brain, called "neuropeptides," has recently been discovered. Neuropeptides are thought to be transmitters. In 1975, Hughes and Kosterlitz (Hughes, 1978) isolated two naturally occurring peptides that bound tightly to opiate receptors and named them "enkephalins." Related substances, later isolated from the pituitary gland, were named "endorphins." Enkephalins and endorphins are structurally very similar to the opiate morphine. Certain regions of the brain bind opiate drugs very readily. These opiate receptor areas have been identified by measuring the binding of radioactively labeled opiate compounds to fragments of neuronal membranes; the compounds were found to be concentrated in regions involving perception and integration of pain and emotional experience (Iversen, 1979).

Experiments have suggested that several procedures employed to treat chronic pain, including acupuncture, direct electrical stimulation of the brain, and hypnosis, may act by eliciting release of enkephalins or endorphins. That is, pain relieving treatments that involve no ingestion of drugs may work because they induce the release in the brain of natural pain relieving substances that resemble morphine. (It might be more apt to say that morphine, a drug, resembles the enkephalins and endorphins, which occur naturally in the brain!) This hypothesis is based on the finding that the effectiveness of all these procedures can be largely eliminated by administration of naloxone (marketed as Narcan), a drug that blocks the binding of morphine to opiate receptors (Iversen, 1979).

Many of the neuropeptides are concentrated in terminals of particular neurons and are released under certain conditions. Minute amounts have significant effects on either neuronal activity or behavior in experimental animals (Iversen, 1979). Substance P, one of the candidates for neurotransmitter status, excites neurons that respond most readily to painful stimuli, suggesting that it is a sensory transmitter associated with transmission of pain related information from peripheral pain receptors into the central nervous system (Iversen, 1979). Enkephalins, as well as opiate drugs, are known to suppress the release of substance P from sensory fibers. It appears, therefore, that enkephalin containing neurons may reduce pain by regulating the input of painful stimuli to the brain through modulating the release of substance P.

Neuropeptides have been observed to produce global effects; very small amounts can trigger highly specific behavior patterns such as intense thirst and drinking behavior or female sexual behavior (Iversen, 1979). de Wied and associates (1976) showed that administration of small amounts of the neuropeptide vasopressin markedly improves memory for learned tasks in laboratory animals.

Knowledge about the actions of neurotransmitters is expanding rapidly; new findings relevant to their role in mental illness are emerging all the time. While the precise chemical disturbances underlying such conditions as schizophrenia, depression, alcoholism, and epilepsy are still obscure, the rapidly developing body of knowledge about the role of neurotransmitters indicates that answers ultimately will be found in this area of investigation.

Implications for Practice of New Knowledge about Biological Factors in Psychopathology

It is almost inevitable that advances in knowledge bring with them implications for changes in existing approaches to practice. The current proliferation of empirically derived knowledge about physiological, institutional, and macrosystemic influences on behavior requires that we take a hard look at present-day practice and its knowledge base.

The findings reviewed earlier seem to require that practitioners look for multiple causes of psychopathology and search out specialists qualified to evaluate various possibilities. Social workers should be suspicious of professionals from any discipline who too readily prescribe one particular treatment—be it individual or family therapy, behavior modification, megavitamins, or drugs—before all possible alternative causes have been carefully evaluated.

Responsible professional behavior requires that social workers ask themselves a number of questions in a practice situation. What do I think the origin of the problem is? What else might it be? How are my own biased influencing my choice of diagnostic approach? Is referral for psychiatric consultation sufficient? Is a neurologist needed? An allergist? A learning disabilities specialist? A nutritionist? An endocrinologist? What specialists are sufficiently conversant with the latest research findings to warrant my confidence in their evaluations of the problem? These are enormously difficult questions. For the most part, social workers have not been trained to assess problems, much less to intervene, in this way. And it is difficult to evaluate the validity of assessments made by specialists who have training in areas such as the biological sciences. (Bear in mind, however, that medically trained personnel are also frequently biased, ignorant of information outside their specialties, and prone to prescribe treatments consistent with the kind of practice they are accustomed to perform.)

By no means should the difficulties facing social workers be a cause for despair. Although the task of expanding the field's knowledge base and developing new treatment resources is a large one, the familiar social work technique of "partialization," that is, dividing an overall presenting situation into its component parts and dealing with selected parts, can be helpful here. In this section, I outline some steps that can be taken to begin to integrate the new knowledge into practice. First, four paradigms of practice are described and illustrated. It will be readily evident that the paradigm I find most useful, the physiological-ecological model, relies heavily on tried-and-true social work skills. Second, I sketch a series of specific steps for expanding knowledge and developing appropriate resources.

Four Models of Practice

The beliefs that practitioners hold about the etiology of mental illness have important consequences for the treatment they provide. A case example may illustrate the relationship between theory of etiology and choice of practice approach.

George P is 30 years old, has been hospitalized twice, for several months each time, with a diagnosis of schizophrenia, chronic paranoid type, and currently lives with his parents, Mr. and Mrs. P. Mr. P works as a machinist and Mrs. P is a housewife. George is unemployed and spends his time either watching television or walking back and forth to the town center, not far from his home. George has never displayed any assaultive behavior but seems to be in his own world much of the time. He sometimes hallucinates, as evidenced by his holding conversations with nonexistent persons. The content of his hallucinations is strongly flavored with persecutory ideation. Mrs. P worries constantly about George, urging food on him, cautioning him about talking to strangers when he goes out, and insisting that he comes home before dinner. Mr. P is extremely irritated by George and snaps at him when they are together. Mostly he tries to avoid his son and leaves his care to Mrs. P.

The situation of George and his family is typical of patients and families seen in outpatient psychiatric agencies. Workers in such facilities might approach this case in different ways. I shall use this vignette to illustrate four models of practice.*

Interpersonal-Clinical Approach

Workers who believe that psychopathology is caused primarily by interpersonal factors (even when they acknowledge the existence of innate predispositions to psychopathology) stress interpersonal forms of therapy. They often regard drug therapy as a necessary evil needed to quiet patients or relieve their symptomatology in order to make them amenable to treatment. Individual or family therapy is used to approach the "real" causes of the condition, interpersonal psychogenic pathology. I call this approach "interpersonal-clinical." Worker A, using this paradigm, might work with George and his family in the following manner.

I see George once a week individually and meet with the family twice a month for family therapy. I am working with George on trying to help him express his feelings of rage toward his mother. I am trying to help Mrs. P be less controlling toward George and allow him to grow up. I am trying to engage Mr. P in a more supportive and positive interaction with his son.

Physiological-Clinical Approach

Practitioners who believe that physiological factors are the predominant cause of psychopathology (even when they acknowledge the potentiating effect of interpersonal events) interpret observable phenomena such as delusions, hallucinations, or assaultive behavior as arising from interior physiological events. They see psychotic symptomatology as the

*The purpose of models is to highlight essential features while eliminating confusing or distracting detail. Accordingly, the models of practice presented here oversimplify. In real life, the distinctions between them are by no means so clearly delineated.

outward manifestation of internal biochemical imbalance. The so-called double-bind and schizoprhenogenic patterns of communication and interaction often observed in families with schizophrenic members take place, according to this theory, either because the parent of the schizophrenic has an underlying schizophreniclike (schizophrenic spectrum) disorder (Shields et al., 1975) or because the family members have developed repertoires of atypical responses in an attempt to adapt to the pathological behaviors of the patient. In either case, the origins of schizophrenic patterns of communication are considered physiological. Hence, alteration of underlying physiological events through pharmacotherapy is the preferred treatment procedure. This approach may be called "physiological-clinical." Worker B, using this approach, might work with the family in the following way.

George is currently receiving Thorazine, which he sometimes forgets to take. I call Mrs. P to verify this when George appears agitated or more disoriented than usual. I am now asking George to call me every Friday to report on how he has been doing with his medication. He has been given a calendar to check off each time he takes his medication.

Interpersonal-Ecological Approach

In the "interpersonal-ecological" approach, an interpersonal theory of etiology leads to heavy emphasis on individual and family therapy. This is combined with such services as day treatment, contacts by the worker with income support sources (e.g., to obtain supplemental security income for disabled and elderly persons), and development of natural support systems. The worker engages in activities to promote linkage with resources, together with interpersonal therapy intended to modify what are believed to be illness generating interpersonal phenomena. Worker C, practicing in this model, might proceed as follows.

I see George once a week individually and meet with the family twice a month for family therapy. I am working with George on trying to help him express his feelings of rage toward his mother. I am trying to help Mrs. P be less controlling toward George and allow him to grow up. I am trying to engage Mr. P in a more supportive and positive interaction with his son. I am working with George toward getting him to attend a day treatment center and have also contacted the state employment service to see whether any part-time maintenance work might be available. George has done custodial work and lawn care in the past. I am also helping Mrs. P explore the possibility of joining a women's activity group, where she could socialize and find some companionship without having to travel too far. I have been in touch with the social security administration because George's supplemental security payments are often late.

Physiological-Ecological Approach

In the "physiological-ecological" model, practice behaviors are based on the same theory of etiology as in the physiological-clinical approach and stress equally the importance of careful monitoring of drug therapy as the major component of the individual directed aspect of treatment. In addition, practitioners using this paradigm emphasize enhancement of the quality of life of the patient and the family by directing a wide range of practice behaviors toward amelioration of environmental conditions. Because the theory of etiology is physiological, not psychogenic, there is less emphasis than in the interpersonal approaches on trying to promote communication and express feelings and more emphasis on husbanding resources, insuring accountability by community service providers, and looking for as many kinds of social supports as possible. Worker D, using this approach, might work with George and his family as follows.

George is currently receiving Thorazine, which he sometimes forgets to take. I call Mrs. P to verify this when George appears agitated or more disoriented than usual. I am now asking George to call me every Friday to report on how he has been doing with his medication. He has been given a calendar to check off each time he takes his medication. I am working with George toward getting him to attend a day treatment center and have also contacted the state employment service to see whether any part-time work might be available. George has done custodial work and lawn care in the past. Mrs. P feels enormous stress because of George's constant presence in the home. We are exploring the possibility of a group home for George, as well as resources for Mrs. P, where she could socialize and find some companionship without having to travel too far. Mr. P has expressed resentment at never being able to go away with his wife on a vacation because of George. The last time they left him alone for a week to go on a trip, he had an acute psychotic episode, which resulted in hospitalization. They have never left him alone since that time. We are currently exploring possibilities for overnight care for George so that his parents can get away together. There have been recurring problems with George's supplemental security payments. I have made several calls to the social security office about this and finally went there to talk with the supervisor.

A Comparison of the Four Models of Practice

The four vignettes illustrate two theories of etiology and four approaches to practice.

Workers A and C believe that damaging childrearing practices and family transactions *cause* and *maintain* mental illness. They engage in psychotherapy with patient and family directed to modifying both intrapsychic functioning (George) and behavior (parents). The parents are viewed as a primary cause of the illness; therefore, a goal of treatment is to modify their schizophrenogenic behavior even though the workers theoretical orientation is psychodynamic, not behavioral. (Ego psychologists who find behavior modification repugnant would do well to note this similarity!) While worker A limits practice interventions exclusively to this arena, worker C also engages in environment changing efforts consistent with an ecological model of practice.

Workers B and D believe that mental illness is a physiological disease that is manifested in various social behaviors and that affects interpersonal relationships. They emphasize supportive and directive measures to insure that the primary therapeutic agent, medication, is properly used. Worker D, like worker C, also engages in environment changing efforts consistent with an ecological model of practice.

In the physiological-ecological model (worker D), a behavioral theory unified around the concept of stress lies behind the combination of practice behaviors. This approach is directed toward relieving stress of both biological and environmental origin rather than toward expressing feelings or modifying behavior. It assumes that styles of interpersonal communication and behavior more favorable to promoting growth will be a by-product of alleviation of stress. While worker B is interested primarily in relieving physiologically generated stress through biochemical intervention, worker D is mounting a multifaceted campaign to improve the quality of life for all the P family. This includes pharmacotherapy as an indispensable component, as well as a search for community supports for the patient and the family.

The reader may ask at this point: "Haven't interpersonal factors been left out of the physiological-ecological model? Doesn't this model omit the most important aspect of mental or emotional illness: interpersonal relationships?" To the contrary, the physiological-ecological approach views interpersonal relationships as very important components of the total life situation of the patient and the family. However, they are seen as functions of the biological and social context in which the patient and the family are enmeshed.

While workers A and C may be quite correct in noting that Mrs. P is obsessively preoccupied with George's safety when he is out on the street, the physiological-ecological point of view interprets this in the light of environmental realities. The outside world *is* likely to perceive George as bizarre, threatening, or ridiculous. Mrs. P may recognize this and want to protect her son from rejection or ridicule. Like mothers of nonschizophrenics, she feels any pain, real or imagined, that is inflicted on her child. This is not necessarily infantilizing. Parents of so-called normal adult children do not typically stop worrying about them with they reach 21.

In order to alleviate her anxiety and lessen her hovering behavior (which workers A and C label "controlling"), worker D addresses Mrs. P's need for relief from anxiety about George when she is not present to protect him. Since workers A and C interpret the hovering behavior as one aspect of Mrs. P's schizophrenogenic personality, these workers neglect the reality based and adaptive features of the behavior. It is interpreted as arising from internal psychopathological processes rather than being viewed in its ecological context. It is important to note that worker C, who practices an ecological model of social work, gets diverted from making a really ecological assessment because of a bias arising from an interpersonal theory of etiology.

In the physiological-ecological model, then, interpersonal factors are by no means excluded. In fact, they are given a great deal of attention. What is different in this model is the interpretation of interpersonal factors. They are seen as functions of biological and environmental forces impinging on both patient and family. Intervention is geared to alleviating as many sources of stress arising from some of these forces as possible. Interpersonal tensions are expected to decrease when various stresses are alleviated. There is no expectation that either patient or family will gain significant insight into their interpersonal dynamics; nor is this seen as a necessary condition for improvement in functioning. Should family members develop more insight, this may be a by-product of relief from stress rather than a curative event.

Combined evidence from nine major studies of the outcome of social work intervention led Geismar and associates (1972) to conclude that intervention in instrumental areas of social functioning appears to be more effective than intervention in expressive areas: "Advice, guidance, and support in such areas as childrearing, health care, homemaking, house hunting, etc., had a sharper impact upon family living than interpersonal counseling or treatment of behavior problems" (p. 184). The effectiveness of casework was found to be limited in many instances by lack of decent housing, adequate medical care, nourishing diet, and other material resources. The bases for these lacks were insufficient income and absence of opportunity for steady employment. Geismar and colleagues concluded: "It is not argued here that client behavior had no need to change. Instead, we must question whether some types of behavior change are feasible in the absence of situational modifications and whether, in some instances, behavior change constitutes a poor substitute for environmental change" (p. 185). The physiological-ecological model of practice is consistent with the point of view expressed here. It does not deny the desirability of behavioral change. However, it places more emphasis, relative to the other approaches described, on the alleviation of some combination of internal and external stresses than it does either on changing client behavior or on working through feelings.

The Tavel Paradigm: A Method for Implementing a Physiological-Ecological Approach

A repertoire of techniques for serving ex-mental patients in the community, congruent with the physiological-ecological model, has been developed by Tavel (1979).* This typology is based on a physiological theory of etiology, combined with an ecological orientation to practice. This approach is ecological because practice behaviors are directed to several facets of the total life situation of the patient and family. Workers using the Tavel paradigm of practice:

1. teach clients skills for everyday coping, such as dressing, basic communication, shopping, use of mass transit, and budgeting
2. train clients how to negotiate various systems, such as social security, local mental health services, and Medicaid; clients must be provided with knowledge about their rights and must be trained to obtain and influence the services to which they are entitled (this entails training in community organization skills)
3. train clients to use medication responsibly; individual and group sessions can be used to prevent both failure to use and overuse (abuse); clients should be trained to notice side effects from medication and to report these to the prescribing physician
4. develop teams and networks of systems (e.g., day hospitals, sheltered workshops, public assistance) that impinge on clients to insure comprehensive and coordinated care
5. support and help develop natural social networks of clients for both social activities and psychological support; clients with higher levels of competence can be engaged as listeners and as bridges to professional staff

The kinds of knowledge and skills needed to practice in this paradigm include:

1. knowledge about the physiological bases of mental illness and the action of pharmacological agents in ameliorating underlying physiological imbalances; knowledge about possible side effects of medication
2. knowledge about the signs and symptoms of decompensation (lapses into more severe manifestations of a condition); workers need to know what signs are typical of what conditions and what the likely causes of deterioration may be (such as failure to take medi-

*With appropriate modifications, this paradigm can be used with clients with less severe problems in functioning.

cation or use of agents that interfere with the effectiveness of the medication)

3. knowledge of existing resources, such as supplemental security income, Medicaid, housing, transportation, legal services, job training and subsidized employment, special funding for handicapped individuals, recreational facilities, peer support groups, night and weekend crisis intervention services, and advocacy groups
4. a repertoire of techniques for negotiating and influencing these systems to make them maximally responsive to client needs
5. legal knowledge pertaining to entitlements, vehicles for appeal, and legislation pending in state and federal legislatures so that appropriate pressure can be applied when needed
6. a repertoire of interpersonal skills for working with individuals and groups, including clients, service providers and community representatives, and political figures, who vote on funding and other relevant legislation

Selecting Intervention Tasks: Some Steps for Practitioners

The point at which implementation of the physiological-ecological paradigm may appear overwhelming is perhaps in the recommendation that the social worker be knowledgeable about possible causes and available treatments in order to help clients find the most appropriate kind of assistance. Acquisition of knowledge about possible causes and treatments is, of course, an imposing prospect, given the enormity of existing research and the rapidity with which new and relevant findings are emerging. This part of the task, however, can be accomplished through the following series of steps:

1. consult published summaries of research on the biological bases of psychopathology (e.g., Johnson, 1980; Johnson et al., 1982; Sheinkin et al., 1979; Snyder, 1980)
2. form small study groups to work on these materials or invite speakers with expertise in particular areas, such as nutrition or the use of medication
3. broaden the educational process to include representatives from many different areas of practice in the community*

---

*Dissemination of information is the first necessary condition for expanding treatment options within a community. Considerable resistance to new ideas must be expected; however, it is not necessary for an entire community to accept the new knowledge in order to introduce it into practice. A videotape on techniques for promoting community participation is available by Jack Rothman, University of Michigan School of Social Work, Ann Arbor.

The second part of the task, finding the most appropriate kind of help, may be significantly more difficult than the educational part of the undertaking. Even specialists who acknowledge the importance of biological factors in psychopathology do not agree about the nature of the physiological processes themselves. Since it is often difficult to judge who is correct, the best service the practitioner can offer clients at this stage of the development of knowledge is to explain what the alternatives are; where resources for pursuing these alternatives can be found; and what possible caveats they should be aware of before embarking on a particular course of evaluation and/or treatment. The very fact that clients are forewarned about the propensity of specialists to overemphasize the value or applicability of their favorite type of treatment (i.e., advocate its use for *all* or *most*, instead of *some*, types of problems) helps protect clients against exploitation by professionals.

Few communities possess facilities that offer comprehensive services for evaluation and treatment. Even so-called holistic medical practices are only partially successful in this regard. For example, some centers offer evaluation of allergic, toxic, nutritional, neurological, and intrafamilial factors but do not evaluate organizational or other environmental factors that may be of great importance in assessing a particular problem.

Utilization of services is frequently hampered by the refusal of third-party payers, both private and public, to pay for nutritional evaluation, treatment by dietary supplement, and other nontraditional approaches. Lack of availability of third-party reimbursement results in the limitation of these treatments, no matter how potentially effective they may be for certain individuals, to persons wealthy enough to pay for evaluation and treatment out of their own pockets. Lack of availability of third-party payment should be a target for community organization and social action.

Practitioners should compile a roster of all available resources in their communities and compare this against a checklist of all types of services that are needed. For example, a community may have a neurologist, a family agency, and a nutritionally oriented physician but no qualified service for evaluating and treating learning disabilities and no laboratory for testing for the presence of heavy metals in the system or sensitivities to foods.

Once service lacks have been identified, interested consumers and practitioners can begin to develop strategies for bringing such services to the community or for bringing residents to communities in which such services already exist.

Self-help groups now exist for almost every problem. Many of these groups have national offices or central clearinghouses from which information about resources throughout the country can be obtained.* Practitioners should contact these groups for assistance in learning about services and developing resources within their own communities.

Conclusion

Rather than serve as a cause for despair, the expansion of knowledge during the past decade should give us reason for hope that increasing numbers of the emotional and behavioral problems that hamper the functioning of entire families and destroy their well-being can be alleviated. I have suggested some approaches that practitioners can take to benefit their clients.

*The National Self-help Clearing House, directed by Alan Gartner and Frank Riessman, is located at the Graduate School and University Center of the City University of New York. It permits ready access to information about various self-help groups across the country, which can save considerable expenditure of time and effort.

References

AHLQUIST RP: A study of adrenotropic receptors. *Am J Physiol* 1948; 153:586–600.

American Psychiatric Association: *Diagnostic and Statistical Manual of Mental Disorders*, ed 3. Washington, DC, American Psychiatric Association, 1980.

ANGRIST BN, Shopsin B, Gershon S: Comparative psychotomimetic effects of stereoisomers of amphetamine. *Nature* 1971; 234: 152–153.

BACH-Y-RITA G: Biological bases of aggressive behavior: clinical aspects, in Widroe H (ed): *Human Behavior and Brain Function*. Springfield, Thomas, 1975, pp 25–32.

BARDWICK J: Psychological correlates of the menstrual cycle and oral contraceptive medication, in Sachar E (ed): *Hormones, Behavior, and Psychopathology*. New York; Raven, 1976.

BETTELHEIM B: *The Empty Fortress*. New York, Free Press, 1967.

BRIAR K: The human costs of unemployment for young, middleaged, and aged workers. Read before the Annual Program Meeting of the Council on Social Work Education, Boston, Mar 5, 1979.

BROWN H: *The Brain and Behavior*. New York, Oxford University Press, 1976.

BRYSON CQ: Systematic identification of perceptual disabilities in autistic children. *Percept Mot Skills* 1970; 31:239–246.

BUTLER R: *Why Survive? Being Old in America*. New York, Harper & Row, 1975.

CAMPBELL M, COHEN IL, ANDERSON LT: Pharmacotherapy for autistic children: a summary of research. *Can J Psychiatry* 1981; 26:265–273.

CANCRO R: Schizophrenia: clinical aspects, in Frazer A, Winokur A (eds): *Biological bases of Psychiatric Disorders*. New York, Spectrum, 1977.

CARROLL BJ: Neuroendocrine procedures for the diagnosis of depression, in Garattini S (ed): *Depressive Disorders*. New York, Schattauer, 1978, pp 231–236.

CARROLL BJ, FEINBERG M, A specific laboratory test for the diagnosis of melancholia. *Arch Gen Psychiatry* 1981; 38:15–22.

CAVANAUGH JJA: Allergy, hearning loss, and learning disability in children. Read before the American College of Allergy, Denver, Mar 28, 1968.

CHESS S, KORN SJ, FERNANDEZ PB: *Psychiatric Disorders of Children with Congenital Rubella*. New York, Brunner/Mazel, 1971.

COHEN DJ, YOUNG JG: Neurochemistry and child psychiatry. *J Child Psychol Psychiatry* 1977;16:353–411.

COTT A: *Orthomolecular Treatment: A Biochemical Approach to Treatment of Schizophrenia*. New York, American Schizophrenia Association, 1973.

CROW TJ: Catecholamine-containing neurons and electrical self-stimulation: a review of some of the data. *Psychol Med* 1972; 2:414–421.

DAMASIO AR, MAURER RG: A neurological model for childhood autism. *Arch Neurol*. 1978;35:777–783.

de WIED D: Pituitary-adrenal system hormones and behavior. in F Schmitt and F. Worden, eds., *The Neurosciences: Third Study Program*. Cambridge: MIT Press, 1974.

DOHAN FC, GRASBERGER JC: Relapsed schizophrenics: earlier discharge from the hospital after cereal-free, milk-free diet. *Am J Psychiatry* 1973;130:685–688.

DRAKE CH: *The Relation of Automatization to the Reading Process in Children and Adolescents*, thesis. Harvard University School of Education, Cambridge, 1970.

DRAKE CH, SCHNALL M: Decoding problems in reading research and implications. *Pathways Child Guidance* 1966;8:1–7.

DUNCAN WC, GILLIN JC, et al: Relationship between EEG sleep patterns and clinical improvement in depressed patients treated with sleep deprivation. *Biol Psychiatry* 1980;15:879–889.

ELLINWOOD EH: Amphetamine psychosis: a multidimensional process, in Segal D, (eds): *Foundations of Biochemical Psychiatry*. Boston, Butterworth, 1976.

EWING JA, ROUSE BA, PELLIZZARI ED: Alcohol sensitivity and ethnic background. *Am J Psychiatry* 1974; 131:206–210.

EYSENCK NJ, PRELL DB: The inheritance of neuroticism: an experimental study. *J Ment Sci* 1951; 97:441–465.

FIEVE R: New developments in manic-depressive illness, in Arieti S, Chrzanowski G (eds): *New Dimensions in Psychiatry: A World View*. New York, Wiley, 1975.

FISH B: Biological disorders in infants at risk for schizophrenia, in Ritvo ER, Freeman BJ, Ornitz EM, et al (eds): *Autism: Diagnosis, Current Research, and Management*. New York, Spectrum, 1976, pp 175–184.

FISH B, RITVO ER: Psychoses of childhood, in Noshpitz JD (ed): *Basic Handbook of Child Psychiatry*. New York, Basic Books, 1979.

FISHER S, GREENBERG R: *The Scientific Credibility of Freud's Theories and Therapy*. New York, Basic Books, 1977.

FRAZER A: Neurochemistry of central monoamine neurons, in Frazer A, Winokur A (eds): *Biological Bases of Psychiatric Disorders*. New York, Spectrum, 1977.

FRAZER A, WINOKUR A (eds): *Biological Bases of Psychiatric Disorders*. New York, Spectrum, 1977.

FRITH U: Studies in pattern detection in normal and autistic children. *J Exp Child Psychol* 1970; 10:120-135.

GALTON L: *The Truth about Senility—and How to Avoid It*. New York, Crowell, 1979.

GEISMAR LL, LAGAY B, et al: *Early Supports for Family Life: A Social Work Experiment*. Metuchen, Scarecrow, 1972.

GELLER E, RITVO ER, FREEMAN BJ, et al: Preliminary observations on the effect of fenfluramine on blood serotonin and symptoms in three autistic boys. *N Engl J Med* 1982; 307:165-169.

GERMAIN CB: An ecological perspective in casework practice, *Soc Casework* 1973; 54:323-330.

GESCHWIND N: Specializations of the human brain. *Sci Am* 1979; 241:180-199.

GIBBENS TCN, POND AD, STAFFORD-CLARK D: Follow-up study of criminal psychopaths. *J Ment Sci* 1959; 105:108-115.

GITTERMAN A, GERMAIN CB: Social work practice: a life model. *Soc Serv Rev* 1976; 50:601-610.

GOLDSTEIN M: Brain research and violent behavior. *Arch Neurol* 1974; 30:1-36.

GOODWIN DW, SCHULSINGER F, et al: Alcohol problems in adoptees raised apart from alcoholic biological parents. *Arch Gen Psychiatry* 1973; 28:238-243.

GOODWIN DW, SCHULSINGER F, Drinking problems in adopted and nonadopted sons of alcoholics. *Arch Gen Psychiatry* 1974; 31:164-169.

GOTTESMAN I: Differential inheritance of the psychoneurosis. *Eugenics Q* 1962; 9:223-227.

GREENBLATT M: Foreword, in Grinspoon L, Ewalt J, Shader R, (eds): *Schizophrenia: Pharmacotherapy and Psychotherapy*. Baltimore, Williams & Wilkins, 1972, pp ii–iii.

GREENBLATT M, SOLOMON MH, et al: *Drugs and Social Therapy in Chronic Schizophrenia*. Springfield, Thomas, 1965.

GRIFFITH JJ, CAVANAUGH JH, OATES JA: Psychosis induced by the administration of d-amphetamine to human volunteers, in Efron D, (ed): *Psychotomimetic Drugs*. New York, Raven, 1970, pp 287-294.

GRINSPOON L, EWALT J, SHADER R (eds): *Schizophrenia: Pharmacotherapy and Psychotherapy*. Baltimore; Williams & Wilkins, 1972.

GROSS K, ROTHENBERG S, et al: Duration thresholds for letter identification in left and right visual fields for normal and reading-disabled children. *Neuropsychologia* 1978; 16:709-715.

GROSS JM, WILSON W: *Minimal Brain Dysfunction*. New York, Brunner/Maxel, 1974.

GROSZ HJ, FARMER BB: Pitt and McClure's lactate-anxiety study revisited. *Br J Psychiatry* 1972; 120:415-418.

HALL RCW, GARDNER ER, et al: Unrecognized physical illness prompting psychiatric admission: a prospective study. *Am J Psychiatry* 1981; 138: 629-635.

HARTELIUS H: Study of male juvenile delinquency. *Acta Psychiatr Scand* 1965; 40:7-138.

HOFFER A, WALKER M; *Orthomolecular Nutrition*. New Canaan, Keats, 1978.

HORNYKIEWICZ O: The neurochemical basis for drug therapy of behavioral disorders, in Blaw M, Rapin I, Kinsbourne M, (eds): *Topics in Child Neurology*. New York, Spectrum, 1977, pp 308-317.

HUBEL D: The brain. *Sci Am* 1979; 241:44-53.

HUGHES J ed: *Centrally Acting Peptides*. Baltimore: University Park Press, 1978.

IVERSEN LL: The chemistry of the brain. *Sci Am* 1979; 241:134-149.

JOHNSON HC: Integrating the problem-oriented record with a systems approach to case assessment. *J Educ Soc Work* 1978; 14.

JOHNSON HC: *Human Behavior and Social Environment: New Perspectives*. Vol 1: *Behavior, Psychopathology, and the Brain*. New York, Curriculum Concepts, 1980.

JOHNSON HC: *Human Behavior and Social Environment: New Perspectives*. Vol 2: *Culture, Organizations, and Macrosystems: How They Affect Behavior*. New York: Curriculum Concepts, 1983.

JOHNSON HC, GEISS G, MAKAR R, et al: *The Biological Bases of Emotional and Cognitive Disorders: A Bibliographic Bulletin*. Garden City, Adelphi University School of Social Work, 1982.

JONES E: *The Life and Work of Sigmund Freud*. New York, Basic Books, 1953.

KALIMO H and OLSSON Y: Effects of severe hypoglycemia on the human brain. *Acta Neurol Scand* 1980; 62:345-56.

KANNER L: Autistic disturbances of affective content. *Nervous Child* 1943; 2:217-250.

KARLSSON JL: *The Biologic Basis of Schizophrenia*. Springfield, Thomas, 1966.

KATZ JL, ROYAR RM, et al: Toward an elucidation of the psychoendocrinology of anorexia nervosa, in E Sachar ed., *Hormones, Behavior, and Psychopathology*. New York, Raven Press, 1976.

KETY S, WENDER P, and ROSENTHAL D: Mental illness in the biological and adoptive families of adopted individuals who have become schizophrenic, in R Fieve, ed. *Genetic Research in Psychiatry*. Baltimore: Johns Hopkins, 1976.

KLAIBER E, BROVERMAN D, and KOBAYASHI Y: The automatization of cognitive styles, androgens and monoamine oxidase *Psychopharmacologia*, 1967; 11:320-336.

KLERMAN, GL: "Defining Schizophrenia." in *Management of Schizophrenia: A Symposium*. New York, Trans, Medica, pp. 3-12.

KLUVER H and BUCEY P: Preliminary analysis of functions of temporal lobes in monkeys. *Arch Neurol Psychiatry* 1939; 42:979-1,000.

KORANYI EK Morbidity and rate of undiagnosed physical illnesses in a psychiatric clinic population. *Arch Gen Psychiatry* 1979; 36: 414-419.

KOVACS M, RUSH J, et al: Depressed outpatients treated with cognitive therapy or pharmacotherapy. *Arch Gen Psychiatry* 1981; 38:33-39.

KROLL P, PORT FK, and SILK KR: Hemodialysis and schizophrenia a negative report. *J Nerv Ment Dis* 1978; 166:291-293.

LELORD G, LAFFANT F, et al: Comparative study of conditioning of averaged evoked responses by coupling sound and light in normal and autistic children. *Psychophysiology* 1973; 10:415–425.

LOVAAS J, SCHREIBMAN L, et al: Selective responding by autistic children to multiple sensory input. *J Abnorm Psychol* 1971; 77:211–222.

MACCULLOUGH MJ, WILLIAMS C: On the nature of infantile autism. *Acta Psychiatr Scand* 1971; 47:295–314.

MAHLER M: On childhood psychosis and schizophrenia, autistic and symbiotic infantile psychosis. *Psychoanal Study Child* 1949; 7:286–305.

MALAMUD N: Psychiatric disorders with intracranial tumors of the limbic system. *Arch Neurol* 1:113–123.

MARCEL T, KATZ L, SMITH M: Laterality and reading proficiency. *Neuropsychologia* 1974; 12:131–139.

MARCEL T, RAJAN P: Lateral specialization for recognition of words and faces in good and poor readers. *Neuropsychologia* 1975; 13:489–497.

MARK V, ERVIN F: *Violence and the Brain*. New York, Harper & Row, 1970.

MASTERSON J: Treatment of borderline and narcissistic personality disorders. Read before the Second Annual Killington Psychiatry Conference, Killington, Vermont Feb. 6–11, 1983.

MATHEWSON S: *Oral Reading Problems in Children: A Cognitive Style Approach*, thesis. McGill University, Montreal, 1967.

MATTES J: Drugs and psychotherapy in acute depression. *Arch Gen Psychiatry* 1981; 38:115.

MINER GD: The evidence for genetic components in the neuroses: a review. *Arch Gen Psychiatry* 1973; 29:111–118.

MORRISON JR, MINKOFF K: Explosive personality as a sequel to hyperactive child syndrome. *Compr Psychiatry* 1975; 16:343–348.

MURPHY DL, WEISS R: Reduced monomine oxidase activity in blood platelets from bipolar depressed patients. *Am J Psychiatry* 1972; 128:11.

National Institute of Mental Health: Renal dialysis as a treatment for schizophrenics; current NIMH policy statement. *Schizophrenia Bull* 1978; 4:2.

NAUTA WJH, FEIRTAG M: The organization of the brain. *Sci Am* 1979; 241:88–111.

NIELSEN AC, WILLIAMS TA: Depression in ambulatory medical patients: prevalence by self-report questionnaire and recognition by nonpsychiatric physicians. *Arch Gen Psychiatry* 1980; 37:999–1004.

O'NEILL G, STANLEY G: Visual processing of straight lines in dyslexic and normal children. *Br J Educ Psychol* 1976; 46:323–327.

ORNITZ EM, BROWN MB, et al: Effects of visual input on vestibular nystagmus in autistic children. *Arch Gen Psychiatry* 1974; 31:369–375.

ORNITZ EM, RITVO ER: Medical assessment, in Ritvo ER, Freeman BJ, Ornitz EM, et al (eds): *Autism: Diagnosis Current Research, and Management*. New York, Spectrum, 1976, pp 7–23.

ORNITZ EM, RITVO ER: The syndrome of autism: a critical review. *Am J Psychiatry* 1976; 133:609–621.

PETERS P: Psychiatric disorders in primary hyperparathyroidism. *J Clin Endocrinol Metabol* 1968; 28:1491–1495.

PFEIFFER CC: *Mental and Elemental Nutrients*. New Canaan, Keats, 1975.

PHILLIPPE M, KITZMILLER JL: The fetal and maternal catecholamine response to insulin-induced hypoglycemia in the rat. *Am J Obstet Gynecol* 1981; 139: 407–415.

PINCUS JH, TUCKER GJ: Violence in children and adults. *J Am Acad Child Psychiatry* 1978; 17:277–288..

PITTS FN, McCLURE JN: Lactate metabolism in anxiety neurosis. *N Engl J Med* 1967; 277:1329–1336

PRANGE AJ, LOOSEN PT: Some endocrine aspects of affective disorders. *J Clin Psychiatry* 1980; 12:29–34.

PRESTON MS, GUTHRIE JT, CHILDS B: Visual and evoked responses in normal and disabled readers. *Psychophysiology* 1974; 11:452–497.

RANK B: Adaptation of the psychoanalytic techniques for the treatment of young children with atypical development. *Am J Orthopsychiatry* 1949; 19:130–139.

RIMLAND B: Freud is dead: new directions in the treatment of mentally ill children. Distinguished Lecture Series in Special Education, University of Southern California, Los Angeles, June 1970.

RITVO ER, FREEMAN BJ et al: *Autism: Diagnosis, Current Research, and Management*. New York, Spectrum, 1976.

ROSENTHAL D, WENDER P, et al: The adopted-away offspring of schizophrenics, in Mednick SA et al, eds., *Genetics, Environment, and Psychopathology*. Amsterdam, North-Holland, 1974.

RUTTER M: The development of infantile autism. *Psychol Med* 1974; 4:147–163.

SCHATZBERG AF, ORSULAK PJ, et al: Catecholamine measures for diagnosis and treatment of patients with depressive disorders. *J Clin Psychiatry* 1980; 41:12:35–38

SCHILDKRAUT JJ: Update on the pharmacology of depression. Lecture Second Annual Killington Psychiatry Conference, Killington, Vermont. Feb 6–11, 1983.

SCHILDKRAUT JJ, ORSULAK PJ, SCHATZBERG AF, COLE JO, and ROSENBAUM AH: Possible Pathophysiological mechanisms in subtypes of unipolar depressive disorders based on differences in urinary MHPG levels. *Psychopharmacol Bull* 1981; 17:90–91.

SCHUCKIT MA, GOODWIN DW, and WINOKUR G: A study of alcoholism in half siblings. *Am J Psychiatry* 1972; 128:122–126.

SCHWARTZ M: *Physiological Psychology*, ed 2. Englewood Cliffs, Prentice-Hall, 1978.

SEGAL D, YAGER J, and SULLIVAN J: *Foundations of Biochemical Psychiatry*. Boston, Butterworth, 1976.

SHEINKIN D, SCHACHTER M, HUTTON R: *The Food Connection*. Indianapolis, Bobbs-Merrill, 1979.

SHERMAN EA, NEUMAN R, and SHYNE AW: *Children Adrift in Foster Care: A Study of Alternative Approaches*. New York, Child Welfare League of America, 1973.

SHIELDS J, HESTON LL, and GOTTESMAN I: Schizophrenia and the schizoid: The problem for genetic analysis, in R. Fieve, D. Rosenthal, and H Brill, eds. *Genetic Research in Psychiatry* Baltimore, Johns Hopkins Press, 1975.

SINGH MM and KAY SR: Wheat glutens as a pathogenic factor in schizophrenia. *Science* 1976; 191:401–402.

SLATER E, ROSENTHAL D, and KETY S: *The Transmission of Schizophrenia*. Oxford, Pergamon, 1968.

SMYTHIES JR: The biochemical organization of the brain and schizophrenia, in C Shagass, S. Gershon, and A Friedhoff, eds., *Psychopathology and Brain Dysfunction*. New York: Raven, 1977, pp. 113–124.

SNYDER SH: *Biological Aspects of Psychiatric Disorders*. New York, Oxford University Press, 1980.

SNYDER S, BANERJEE S et al: Drugs, neurotransmitters, and schizophrenia. *Science* 1974; 184:1243–1253.

STANLEY G and HALL R: Short term visual information processing in dyslexics. *Child Dev* 1973; 44:841–844.

STERN D: *The First Relationship: Infant and Mother* Cambridge, Harvard University Press, 1977.

STEVENS CF: "The neuron," *Sci Am* 1979; 241:54–65.

STUBBS EG: "Autistic symptoms in a child with congenital cytomegalovirus infection," *J Autism Child Schizophr* 1978; 8:37–43.

TAVEL J (1979) Available Adelphi University School of Social Work, Garden City, N.Y.

TAYLOR W: Psychiatry on Trial- The role of Psychiatrists in the courtroom, in RCW Hall, ed. *Psychiatry in Crisis*. New York, Spectrum.

THOMPSON R: Thalamic structures critical for retention of an avoidance conditioned response in rats. *J Comp Physiol Psychol* 1963; 56:261–267.

VANDENBERGH RL: "Postpartum Depression," *Clin Obstet Gynecol* 1980; 23:1105–11.

VESELL ES: Ethanol metabolism: regulation by genetic factors in normal volunteers under a controlled environment and the effect of chronic ethanol administration. *Ann NY Acad Sci* 1972; 197:79–88.

VOGEL GW, THURMOND S, et al. REM sleep reduction; effects on depressive syndromes. *Arch Gen Psychiatry* 1975; 32:765–777.

WAGEMAKER H: The effect of hemodialysis on fifteen chronic, process schizo phrenics. *Artif Organs* 1978; 2:205–206.

WEHR T, WIRZ-JUSTICE A, et al: Phase advance of the circadian sleep-wake cycle as an antidepressant. *Science* 1979; 206:710–713.

WEINBERGER DR, TORREY EF, NEOPHYTIDES AN, and WYATT RJ. Lateral cererbal ventricular enlargement in chronic schizophrenia. *Arch Gen Psychiatry* 36: 1978, 735–9.

WEISSMAN MM: Psychotherapy and its relevance to the pharmacotherapy of affective disorders: from ideology to evidence, in *Psychopharmacology: A Generation of Progress*, M Lipton, A DiMascio, and K Killam, eds. New York, Raven, 1978 pp. 1313–1321.

WEISSMAN MM, KLERMAN GL, et al: Depressed outpatients. 1981; *Arch Gen Psychiatry* 38:51–55.

WEISSMAN MM, MYERS JK, THOMPSON D: Depression and its treatment in a U.S. urban community, 1975–1976. *Arch Gen Psychiatry* 1981; 38:417–421.

WENDER PH, REIMHERR FW, WOOD DR: Attention deficit disorder (Minimal brain dysfunction) in adults. *Arch Gen Psychiatry* 1981; 38:449–456.

WHITING D, SCHNALL M, DRAKE CH: *Automatization in Dyslexic and Normal Children.* Wellesley, Reading Research Institute, 1966.

WHYBROW PC, PRANGE AJ Jr: A hypothesis of thyroid–catecholamine receptor interaction. *Arch Gen Psychiatry* 1981; 38:106–113.

WILLIAMS D: Neural factors related to habitual aggression. *Brain* 1969; 92:503–520.

WING L, YEATES SR,: The prevalence of early childhood autism: comparison of administrative and epidemiological studies. *Psychol Med* 1967; 6:89–100.

WOLD PN: Longterm evaluation of chlorpromazine in six chronic schizophrenic patients, in Greenblatt M, (eds): *Mental Patients in Transition.* Springfield, Thomas, 1961.

WOLFF PH: Ethnic differences in alcohol sensitivity. *Science* 1975:449–450.

WYATT R, TERMINI B, DAVIS J: Biochemical and sleep studies of schizophrenia: a review of the literature, 1960–1970. *Schizophr Bull* 1971; 4:10–66.

YUWILER H, GELLER E, RITVO E: Neurobiochemical research, in Ritvo E, Freeman BJ, Ornitz EM, et al (eds): *Autism: Diagnosis, Current Research, and Management.* New York; Spectrum, 1976.

ZISKIND E; Is sociopathy a neurologic disorder? *Bull Los Angeles Neurol Soc* 1975; 40:124–128.

ZISKIND E, SYNDULKO K, MALTZMAN I: Evidence for a neurologic disorder in the sociopath syndrome: aversive conditioning and recidivism, in Shagass C, Gershon S, Friedhoff A (eds): *Psychopathology and Brain Dysfunction.* New York, Raven, 1977, pp 255–265.

3

Neurological Disorders

HARRIETTE C. JOHNSON
AND EDWARD J. HART

Readers may wonder why a chapter on neurological disorders, such as epilepsy, brain injury, Huntington's chorea, and stroke, is included in a textbook on adult psychopathology. There are at least three reasons why it is desirable to study conditions usually thought of as neurological (as contrasted with psychiatric) as part of the overall study of psychopathology.

First, diseases that affect the central nervous system often affect not just one but multiple functions controlled by the brain. Neurological symptoms that are unequivocally physical in nature, such as clumsy, irregular, or jerky movements or awkward gait, frequently appear in combination with symptoms usually thought of as psychological, such as irritability, inappropriate affect, or explosiveness. Emotional, affective, and cognitive functions, just as much as motor and sensory functions, are controlled by the brain. Impairment in the centers of the brain that control rage reactions, for instance, can as surely result in behaviors we call "psychopathological" as can frustrations building up from life with a punitive parent or an uncaring spouse. It is important for social workers to become familiar with the psychological manifestations that may arise directly from central nervous system pathology in addition to those that arise from the psychosocial stress generated by being disabled. Appropriate counseling and other treatment planning require knowledge about the nature of the illness or disability.

A second and related reason for studying neurological conditions is the frequency with which these disorders are misdiagnosed. Since some neurological diseases manifest themselves primarily in mental symptoms, they are often identified as psychiatric disorders. Common errors in diagnosis are to label Huntington's chorea or Tourette's syndrome as schizophrenia; multiple sclerosis as hysteria; brain injury as unsocialized aggressive reaction or antisocial personality; and certain kinds of stroke as manic excitement or schizophrenia. The similarity in symptomatology between various psychiatric and neurological conditions, in and of itself, is indicative of the close relationship between neurobiological processes and psychiatric symptoms.

Readers may be surprised to learn that stroke, not uncommonly, can produce a gamut of psychological symptoms in the absence of either sensory or motor symptoms (Mesulam, 1979). When the site of the stroke is a center of the brain that controls emotion, thought, perception, judgment, or attention, behavioral disorder may dominate the clinical picture or may be the only symptom. Bizarre behavior may include "funny talk, inappropriate alacrity, or unpredictable belligerence" (Mesulam, 1979, p. 815). This configuration is often incorrectly diagnosed as schizophrenia or manic excitement. Extreme apathy, sometimes seen when the frontal lobes of the brain are involved by the stroke, may be mistaken for a reactive depression. When other brain regions are affected, there may be an agitated delirium with excitement, aggressiveness, shouting, and swearing; acute onset of confusion; or severe derangement of insight, judgment, and behavior. When the right hemisphere of the brain is the site of the stroke, the patient may become brazen, impulsive, argumentative, and tactless. These conditions, designated "silent stroke," often remain undiagnosed in the absence of sensory and motor symptoms.

In certain kinds of seizure disorders, notably, temporal lobe epilepsy (also called "psychomotor" or "complex partial seizure disorder"), a major feature of the disease may be alterations in the emotional life (Geschwind et al., 1980). Both anecdotal case reports (Waxman & Geschwind, 1975) and larger surveys (Bear & Fedio, 1977) have suggested that these individuals are at greater risk than either normal individuals or those with other forms of epilepsy for the development of rather distinct behavioral changes that are seen on an ongoing basis but lack an obvious relationship to seizure episodes. Unusual or excessive philosophical or religious preoccupation, change in sexual behavior (hypersexuality or hyposexuality), and overconcern with making detailed records of their daily life experiences are traits that tend to cluster together in some of these patients.

Geschwind and colleagues (1980) reported the case of a 34-year-old mother of two, who after an uneventful and conventional life became markedly exhibitionistic. She sunbathed naked on her front porch in full view of passersby and attended a dance class partially nude. She saw nothing inappropriate about this behavior. She reported episodes of sexual arousal in church, where she experienced "vaginal tingling," culminating in orgasm while looking at a crucifix. She wrote long letters about her sexual preoccupations. Medication for temporal lobe epilepsy, which was diagnosed on the basis of extensive testing, brought about a dramatic remission of symptoms in two weeks. She gained insight into the inappropriateness of her sexual behavior, experienced mortification about it, returned to conservative dress, had fewer religious thoughts, and showed a complete cessation of letter writing. After three months, she unexpectedly stopped taking the medication. Less than a month later, her husband brought her back to the neurological service, reporting a recurrence of sexual excesses and religious fervor. Again, a dramatic improvement took place when the medication was reinstated. While most case anecdotes undoubtedly are less dramatic, this example does illustrate the importance of being aware that neurological illness can manifest itself in psychopathology.

A third reason for the inclusion of a chapter on neurological conditions is the prevalence of neurological disorders among the population. Although no precise figures on total numbers of cases in the United States are available (since many remain undiagnosed or unreported), it is possible to derive rough estimates of the total prevalence of neurological conditions by adding together the prevalence estimates for each individual disorder. When migraine headache, the most common condition, is excluded from calculation, an estimated 4% of Americans suffer from neurological disorders. When migraine is included in the estimate, the prevalence rises to about 14% (other forms of headache have been left out because so many are related to other diseases).

When the number of persons suffering from one or another disorder is added to the number of family members of the patients, the total number of individuals directly and intimately affected by neurological disease is large indeed. Social workers are likely to encounter both persons with these disorders and their family members in virtually every practice setting.

This chapter is divided into three major sections. The first summarizes the chief characteristics of the more common neurological diseases. Readers are referred to textbooks of neurology for information about less common conditions. However, the problems and needs of the sufferers of the conditions discussed in the chapter, and the variety of social work practice approaches for addressing these common problems, will be found to be applicable to most or all neurological diseases. The second section of the chapter outlines the problems, needs, feelings, and reactions common among neurological patients and families. A few case examples illustrate some of the issues with which patients and their families typically must deal. The concluding section discusses social work interventions that address the many difficulties and needs identified in the preceding section.

The Major Neurological Disorders

Cerebrovascular Disease

Apart from migraine headache, cerebrovascular disease is the most common neurological disorder in adults. In most cases, signs and symptoms of a cerebral vascular episode have a sudden onset and reach maximum intensity within minutes or hours. Symptoms and signs of stroke vary greatly depending on the location and the extent of the area(s) involved. "Symptom" refers to a subjectively experienced event, such as a headache; a "sign" can be seen by others, such as paralysis. Common symptoms and signs here are paralysis, speech and language deficits, and sensory loss, but they may range from headache and vomiting to confusion, convulsions, and coma.

Stroke occurs at the end stage of cerebrovascular disease and results from either atherosclerosis (accumulation of substances on the walls of blood vessels, ultimately causing blockage) or hypertension. Each year 275,000 Americans die and 300,000 others are disabled by cerebrovascular disease. About 2 million Americans (approximately 1%) suffer from the disease at any one time, of which 30% are under 65 years of age. Roughly 15% of admissions to institutions for chronic care in the United States result from cerebral atherosclerosis and related neurological disability. Aproximately 20% of strokes are due to hemorrhages and the remaining 80% to blockage of the veins or arteries to the brain by clots of blood, tumor, fat, or air.

Stroke patients show great variability in return of functions. About half the patients who survive stroke remain permanently disabled. Typical sequelae include difficulty walking, using the hand for skilled acts, and speaking. Recurrence is frequent; thus, patients often suffer the double burden of loss of functions and fear of a repeat (and often fatal) attack. Fear of recurrence is a major source of stress for stroke patients and their families.

Brain and Spinal Cord Injuries

Traumatic brain injury, most often resulting from automobile accidents, is a leading cause of acquired neurological disability at all ages and commonly gives rise to sequelae that significantly affect the individual's ability to function again at her previous level. Severe head injuries, with prolonged periods of coma, usually result in major handicaps in both physical and mental functioning. However, even mild head injuries carry the risk of later development of convulsive seizures and, at times, of the so-called posttraumatic syndrome.

During the period of initial hospitalization following a head injury, when the very survival of the patient may be in doubt, there is enormous stress on the family of the patient. Uncertainty about ultimate outcome does not end with the knowledge that the patient will survive the injury but extends for weeks and months while the patient slowly emerges from coma and begins the arduous process of rehabilitation.

In addition to physical disabilities, significant personality alteration, memory loss, and impairment of mental abilities are often seen, with a need, therefore, gradually to acknowledge and accept the extent of the individual's altered functioning and its implications for the future. Less severe head injuries may leave the individual unaffected physically but nonetheless significantly handicapped with regard to intellectual and emotional functioning. Transient psychotic episodes, memory loss, and confusion are often seen during the early stages of recovery, with resolution of the more severe behavioral and emotional disturbances a usual outcome. Permanent aftereffects, however, can include personality disorder, memory loss, and deterioration of mental abilities.

Posttraumatic syndrome appears in about 35%–40% of patients who sustain minor head injuries, but there is no direct relationship between the severity of the injury and the development of symptoms. Symptoms may be present for a few weeks or may persist for years. Adults experience headache, dizziness, insomnia, depression, irritability, poor power of concentration, and restlessness. Patients are bothered by noise, for example, by the presence of children or by television. They cannot enjoy themselves and have poor control of their temper and emotions. Children are likely to suffer behavioral and personality changes. Typical sources of stress for adult patients with posttraumatic syndrome are financial worries and anxiety about legal proceedings that are usually in progress with regard to insurance or other liability claims. Such external sources of stress can impede recovery and aggravate psychological symptoms. Although prognosis in posttraumatic syndrome is uncertain, usually progress is noted with the passage of time.

Convulsive seizures are the most common late complication of head injuries, but they occur in only a minority of patients. Several large studies have documented risk rates, ranging from 5% to 15% of hospitalized head injury victims, with the risk proportional to the severity of the injury. The formation of scar tissue in the brain following injury predisposes the patient to these seizures. Treatment with anticonvulsant medication has a good chance of success. The development of this complication, however, represents still another ongoing burden to the patient and his family and an impediment to rehabilitation efforts.

Cerebral Palsy

The term "cerebral palsy" refers to a variety of nonprogressive conditions involving motor and cognitive dysfunction caused by damage to the brain early in life. Many factors are thought to be causative, including genetic defects associated with chromosome abnormality or inborn errors of metabolism; head injury in infancy or early childhood (including that caused by child abuse); infectious disease such as meningitis; and difficulties arising during pregnancy or at birth, particularly, lack of oxygen to brain cells.

There are three main types of cerebral palsy. In the "spastic type," the arms and legs are stiff and movement is restricted due to the extreme tightness of the muscles. In the "athetoid type," involuntary, sudden, and uncontrolled movements are seen. In the "ataxic type," disturbance of the sense of balance is present, along with varying degrees of tremor. Common manifestations include difficulty in muscular control and coordination; awkwardness of gait; seizures; inability to see, hear, speak, or learn normally; and psychological and behavioral problems. Mental retardation is present in about half the cases.

Spina Bifida

In this condition, the spinal column fails to close properly due to a defect in early fetal development. Spina bifida is fairly common, occurring with varying degrees of severity in about 100/100,000 live births in North America. It is frequently associated with other physical anomalies and neurological defects, especially hydrocephalus and mental retardation. Direct and indirect complications of spina bifida may require numerous hospitalizations over the years for infections and orthopedic and neurological operations. Spina bifida ravages many body systems. Patients who survive into adulthood usually require lifetime supportive services.

Seizure Disorders

The term "epilepsy" refers to recurrent seizures or episodes of altered states of consciousness, often but not always accompanied by convulsive body movements. Epilepsy is extremely common. Prevalence has been estimated at 2% of the population, or about 4 million Americans (Massey et al., 1980).

Treatment of seizure disorders includes elimination of causal factors such as brain abscess or tumor or endocrine abnormality; chemotherapy with anticonvulsant drugs; surgical therapy in a small number of patients with focal epilepsy; appropriate physical care such as regular eating and sleeping, moderate exercise, and avoidance of alcohol. Long-term medication is effective in controlling or significantly reducing the occurrence of seizures in a majority of patients. In addition use is made of social measures designed to encourage the patient to live as normal a life as possible and not to lapse into a state of invalidism.

Because the term "epilepsy" refers to a variety of conditions, attempts at classification are not altogether precise. One method classifies seizures into two groups according to the presence or absence of known organic pathology (i.e., a lesion in the brain). This method of classification is thought by some neurologists to be inadequate since current methods of diagnosis do not always permit identification of existing lesions. A new international classification of epilepsy attempts to differentiate between seizures that begin in a single, or focal, area of the brain ("partial seizures") and those that begin diffusely, over all areas of the brain ("generalized seizures"). Another approach to classification divides patients into groups according to the manifestations that occur during attacks.

Grand Mal Seizures

In grand mal seizures (which account for 90% of patients with convulsions), the attack starts with an aura (described as dizziness, weakness, fear, numbness, or peculiar sensation), sometimes followed by a shrill cry. Then loss of consciousness and jerking movements of the arms and/or legs ensue. The patient may bite his tongue, have urinary or fecal incontinence, salivate at the mouth (saliva may be mixed with blood if the tongue or cheek has been bitten), and on rare occasions ejaculate. Then the patient lapses into a deep sleep, from which he awakes minutes or hours later. After awakening, the patient may have headache, stiffness in the muscles, nausea, and fatigue. The patient may be confused or may behave in an automatized fashion for hours or days after a severe attack. There may be residual paralysis or sensory disturbance. The attack itself may vary in length from less than a minute to 30 minutes or more. Frequency varies from many attacks in a day to one in several years. Grand mal seizures can be controlled by medication in 50% of cases and significantly reduced in another 35%. Petit mal seizures are controlled by medication in 60% and improved in 33% of cases.

Jacksonian Seizures

These seizures, sometimes called partial seizures, usually occur in patients with an organic lesion in the cortex. The seizure starts with convulsive twitching in a particular part of the body and may spread to involve an entire extremity. If the seizure activity involves the language area of the brain, speech may be impaired during the seizure itself. If the abnormal electrical activity caused by the seizure spreads to involve both hemispheres of the brain, the seizure becomes generalized and consciousness is lost.

Psychomotor Seizures

Also called "temporal lobe seizures" and "complex partial seizures," psychomotor seizures show enormous variability in their manifestations and may range from brief interruptions of consciousness without associated body movements to prolonged periods of confusional or dreamlike states lasting many hours. Often heralded by an aura of anxiety and visceral symptoms such as a sensation of welling up in the throat, the seizure itself may be characterized by an alteration in but not a loss of consciousness, accompanied by brief stereotyped movements such as lip smacking or manipulation of the patient's clothing. Some patients experience hallucinations (visual and auditory) and bodily delusions; others manifest affective disturbance such as expressions of anger, fear, or depression. In 28% percent of patients, the disorder can be controlled with medication; another 50% improve with medication.

Still unsettled is the question of whether there is an increased incidence of violent and aggressive behavior in temporal lobe epilepsy patients. Some studies have shown a high incidence of psychomotor epilepsy in criminal offenders (e.g., Lewis & Balla, 1976). There are two questions related to this issue: whether an episode of rage is actually an epileptic seizure and whether these individuals have a more violence-prone personality on an ongoing basis. A recent survey suggested that seizure episodes expressed as outbursts of aggression and violence do occur but are extremely rare (Delgado-Escueta et al., 1981). Stevens and Hermann (1981) reviewed much of the data bearing on the issue of personality maladjustment and, in particular, a tendency toward aggressiveness in temporal lobe epilepsy patients. They concluded that patients with both grand mal and psychomotor epilepsy are at increased risk for psychiatric disturbance. They postulated that the risk appears to reflect the site and extent of the underlying brain damage rather than the effects of the epileptic seizures themselves. The interaction of these factors with the individual's psychosocial history may account, in their opinion, for the wide variation in symptomatology seen, since the majority of patients with all types of epilepsy do not manifest these personality disorders.

Petit Mal Seizures

This form of epilepsy is a disease of childhood. Seizures may become infrequent or disappear in adult life. The typical petit mal seizure consists of transient loss of contact with the environment. In some patients, the attack may last only a second or two and may consist of a blank expression or fixed gaze, which may pass unnoticed. Longer attacks may last 15–90 seconds, during which time the patient is out of contact with the environment and may show a few jerks of the arms or the eye muscles, a drooping head, or a stagger. After the attack, the patient immediately becomes alert again and resumes activities. Patients with petit mal may have very frequent attacks, from a few daily to as many as 30 in a single hour.

Intracranial and Spinal Tumors

Intracranial tumors presently afflict the largest proportion of admissions to neurological services after cerebrovascular and infectious diseases and head trauma. Symptoms and signs of these lesions vary according to whether the tumor is benign and slow growing or malignant and fulminant, or rapid, in onset. The location of the tumor determines whether the major symptoms and signs will be those of increased intracranial pressure (headache, vomiting, blurred vision, lethargy) or of dysfunction related to a particular area of one or the other cerebral hemisphere (emotional or behavioral disorder, weakness of one side of the body, convulsive seizures). The effectiveness of surgery varies according to the location of the tumor and its type, with outcomes ranging from complete cure to rapid deterioration and death. Even when a relatively good outcome is achieved with surgery and/or radiation therapy, the individual may be left with the significant mental and physical residual deficits that characterize other forms of neurological disability.

Spinal cord tumors are uncommon. Like brain tumors, however, they vary in their presenting signs and symptoms according to location and type of tumor. As with brain tumors, the outcome varies considerably. Many survivors of spinal cord tumors sustain residual paralysis, with the complications similar to those of spinal cord injury.

Neurofibromatosis

This genetic disorder, also called "von Recklinghausen's disease", has varied manifestations. Most commonly, patients develop multiple growths (benign tumors) along nerves, including those of spinal or cranial origin, and the skin. Associated complications may include seizures, learning difficulty, and mental retardation, as well as malignant tumors. The disease may remain stationary for many years, but periods of rapid growth of lesions occasionally are experienced. The disease is quite common; prevalence has been estimated at about 50/100,000 in the United States. The majority of cases are mild, but severe disability occurs in some patients. Existence of the disease in an individual is usually indicated by excessive numbers of large, coffee-colored birthmarks. Issues relating to genetic counseling and uncertainty of progression of the disease contribute to a high level of ongoing stress and anxiety in families carrying the gene for this neurofibromatosis.

Headache

Headache is a complaint expressed by more than half the patients who seek attention from a physician. Headache can be caused by intracranial or systemic disease, a personality problem, external stressors, sensitivity to foods or chemicals, or a combination of factors. The most important tool for evaluating the source of the headache is the patient's history (Merritt, 1979). A severe headache with sudden onset may indicate a life-threatening condition, such as cerebral hemorrhage, or an infectious illness, such as meningitis or encephalitis. Headaches that first appear late in life are seldom due to migraine, tension, or psychiatric disturbance and should be investigated thoroughly by a physician.

Migraine (popularly called "sick headache") is an intensely painful headache often accompanied by nausea. Prevalence is estimated at 5–10% of the population, with 70% of the sufferers women. Migraine has been related to estrogen level; sensitivity to chemical additives and to foods such as ripened cheese, chicken liver, red wine, citrus fruits, and caffeine; sensitivity to inhaled chemicals such as perfume or natural gas; stress; and weather changes or high altitude. In most instances, however, the migraine attacks occur without obvious antecedents. Current advances in therapy have enabled the vast majority of migraine sufferers to experience significant relief from this condition. Medications are available that can help prevent the occurrence of the attacks or significantly alleviate pain at the time of an episode.

Multiple Sclerosis

Multiple sclerosis (MS) is a chronic disease with very diverse symptoms and signs. These may include muscle weakness, visual disturbance, urinary problems, pain in the legs or abdomen, speech disturbance, clumsy gait (ataxia), loss of libido, impotence in males, and mental symptoms. Studies have revealed disturbances of affect in 54% of cases, mental deterioration in 26%, and psychotic episodes in 4% (e.g., Merritt, 1979 p. 787). Peyser and associates (1980) found that about half of 55 MS subjects judged by neurologic examination to have intact mentation actually suffered cognitive impairment. Other symptoms include bizarre or transient complaints such as loss of color vision, tinnitus (buzzing in the ear), and vertigo. Because of the transient and unusual nature of some of its manifestations, MS is sometimes misdiagnosed as hysteria.

The cause or causes of MS are unknown; current research centers on theories relating to altered immunity and viral infection. It has repeatedly been verified that the incidence of the disease is much higher in countries at higher latitudes than in countries closer to the equator.

MS may follow a steadily progressive course over one or several decades; occasionally, the disease may progress rapidly to death. MS is generally not fatal. Death directly from the disease is rare; death usually occurs from other diseases such as infections of the urinary tract, respiratory infections, and septicemia and, in older patients, from the usual fatal illnesses such as heart disease, cerebrovascular disease, and cancer. Survival rates have varied in different studies. In one study, 476 men given the diagnosis of MS in army hospitals were found to have a survival rate of 76% after 20 years and 69% after 25 years following onset of MS. The study suggested that half of patients with onset at 25 years of age live about 35 years after onset.

An important concept for the social work practitioner to bear in mind is that the prognosis is not always as disastrous as it is generally thought to be. About one-third of patients continue to be able to carry on their lives without significant disability; another third have enough impairment to require altering their lifestyle; and the remaining third become severely disabled.

Most forms of treatment with drugs have not been found to be effective in MS. ACTH (adrenocorticotropic hormone) and some other corticosteroids such as prednisone and dexamethasone are commonly used and are believed by some neurologists to be effective in inducing remission. However, their effectiveness is disputed by other neurologists. Experimental therapies, including alteration of the immune response through medication or "washing out" of antibodies through plasmapheresis (a type of transfusion), are actively being investigated. Unfortunately, as with any chronic disabling condition without a known cure, patients and their families are often pressured by well-meaning family or friends to try unproven or faddist treatments.

Amyotrophic Lateral Sclerosis

Amyotrophic lateral sclerosis (ALS) is a disease of the skeletal muscle, brain, and spinal cord. Progressive muscle wasting, with weakness and atrophy, is the major sign, accompanied by diffuse twitching of muscle fibers. As the disease progresses, paralysis ultimately occurs. Pain in the extremeties occurs in about half the cases. Urinary frequency or incontinence occurs in about 15–20% of patients. Emotional lability related to the neurological dysfunction occurs in about one-third of patients at some stage of the disease: manifestations include uncontrollable laughing and/or crying. Intellectual abilities remain intact, with acute awareness of the decline in physical functioning, often resulting in significant and understandable reactive depression. In about 50% of cases, the disease progresses rapidly to death within 3 years; another 20% survive 5 years; 10% survive 10 years or more; and 20% reach a plateau as the disease ceases to progress. Prevalence is thought to be 5–7 cases per 100,000; as many as 30,000 persons are believed to have the disease at any time in the United States.

Neuromuscular Disorders

Muscular Dystrophy

There are a number of progressive muscular dystrophies of different types. These are usually inherited conditions, but the underlying mechanisms for the diseases are unknown at the present time. The age of onset and the distribution of muscle weakness vary according to the particular condition. Most common is Duchenne's muscular dystrophy, an inherited disease that affects only males and is passed on through the mother.

The disease first manifests itself as progressive muscle weakness, with waddling gait and hypertrophy (overenlargement) of the calves in the early school years. Learning disorders and mental retardation are sometimes seen. A significant minority of muscular dystrophy cases are considered to be the result of genetic mutation; maternal transmission does not apply here. Progressive muscular dystrophy occurs at a rate of about 4/100,000. An estimated 10,000 patients presently are to be found in the United States.

The course of the muscular dystrophies is variable, Duchenne's dystrophy is uniformly fatal by the late teens or early twenties. The other forms of progressive muscular dystrophy are compatible with long life, but the patient is significantly handicapped.

Myasthenia Gravis

This disease involves a defect in neuromuscular transmission. Prevalence estimates are 3–10/100,000 in the United States. Although etiology is not known, the mechanism by which the disease is activated has been found to be the presence of antibodies to the acetylcholine receptor sites at neuromuscular junctions. This defect prevents effective transmission of nerve impulses to the muscles, thereby limiting the ability of the muscle to contract. Manifestations include muscle weakness, which fluctuates within a day or even within minutes. Weakness first affects the muscles of the eye in about 40% of cases and ultimately affects these muscles in about 85% of cases. Weakness of facial muscles and muscles of the mouth and throat is also common. Limb and neck weakness also occurs frequently. Respiratory muscles are affected only when the patient is in a crisis condition such as respiratory infection.

Myasthenia is a disease of varying progression and severity. In a small number of cases (10% or less), there is rapid progression to death. The majority of cases are milder and may intermittently go into remission. The severity of the disease is usually established within weeks or months after the symptoms first appear. For example, if they are restricted to ocular muscles at that time, the disease is likely to remain restricted; only rarely will it become generalized.

Myasthenia gravis responds to cholinergic drugs so uniformly that this response is now considered one diagnostic criterion in establishing the presence of the disease. Definite diagnosis is possible with electromyography (EMG) and nerve conduction studies.

Huntington's Chorea

Huntington's chorea is a genetic disease, transmitted by a dominant gene, that affects 50% of the children of sufferers. Chronic progressive chorea, named after George Huntington, who first described this disorder in 1872, is characterized by choreiform (jerky, involuntary, and abrupt) movements and mental deterioration. These two types of signs may occur together at onset or one may appear first, to be followed years later by the other. Profound depression and/or severe emotional disturbance with hallucinations may occur years before physical symptoms appear, resulting in frequent misdiagnosis as schizophrenia.

Typically, the disease progresses over a 10–20-year period and ends in death, usually from infection, heart failure, or choking. Beginning signs and symptoms are fidgetiness, irritability, slovenliness, and neglect of responsibilities. Early manifestations also often include fits of violence, bouts of depression, or impulsive behavior. Mental deterioration is similar to that encountered in organic dementia: progressive loss of memory, loss of intellectual abilities, apathy, and failure to attend to personal hygiene. As the disease progresses, choreiform movements become more pronounced.

Huntington's disease is fairly common: recent evidence suggests that it may occur in 10/100,000 in the United States. Because of frequent misdiagnosis and because families sometimes conceal the disease, accurate prevalence estimates have been difficult to obtain. A particularly poignant aspect to this disease is the fact that its symptoms and signs do not become manifest until the early thirties, usually after the individual has decided whether or not to risk passing on the disorder by having children. Issues relating to genetic counselng, alleviation of guilt when the disease becomes manifest, and other facets of reproduction are prominent aspects of counseling of these patients and will be discussed at length later in this chapter.

Gilles de la Tourette's Disease

Onset of Tourette's syndrome (also called ''multiple tic disorder'') is between the ages of 2 and 13. Signs and symptoms include facial twitching and grimacing; abrupt, jerky movements of the neck and shoulder and, later, the limbs; explosive and often foul language; obsessional thinking; and hyperactive behavior. The disease increases in severity during childhood but sometimes spontaneously remits by adulthood. However, the disease is generally lifelong and chronic. It has been estimated that there may be as many as 50,000 patients in the United States, a prevalence of about 25/100,000.

Tourette's disease can be treated with haloperidol, a drug that has been found to be successful in controlling the severity of inappropriate verbal outbursts and involuntary movements. Because of the peculiar and often bizarre manifestations of this neurological condition, misdiagnosis is the norm rather than the exception. Most patients receive years of fruitless psychotherapy prior to accurate diagnosis.

Parkinson's Disease

Parkinson's disease, named for James Parkinson, who first described this disorder in 1817, is an extremely common disease with various manifestations; U.S. prevalence is believed to be 100–150/100,000. Manifestations include tremor (shaking), muscular rigidity, and loss of postural reflexes. Parkinsonism is a leading cause of neurologic disability in persons over the age of 60. Onset occurs most frequently between the ages of 50 and 65. Tremor is the initial symptom in 70% of cases. Patients with parkinsonism may have extreme difficulty in walking, feeding themselves, and generally in performing ordinary activities (e.g., dressing and washing). Treatment with levodopa has been effective in many cases, alone or in combination with other drugs. Surgery has also been successful in some cases.

There is a difference of opinion as to whether dementia is an intrinsic characteristic of the disease. Cognitive, memory, and perceptual deficits have frequently been found, but do not appear to be severe.

All forms of parkinsonism are progressive disorders that result in considerable motor disability. Some forms have a fatal outcome within 5 years, while other forms progress very slowly; thus, patients sometimes continue to function for 30 years or more.

Motor Disability Associated with Tranquilizer Use

Motor disability resembling Parkinson's disease is sometimes seen as a complication of treatment over an extended period of time with major tranquilizers of the phenothiazine type. Many forms of this acquired parkinsonism can be successfully treated by reduction of the tranquilizer dose or by addition of antiparkinson medication. Related motor and movement disabilities occuring as adverse reactions to these tranquilizers are not so readily treatable, however, and represent a significant problem in both psychiatric and neurological therapeutics.

The diseases and conditions described in this section share certain characteristics and differ in others. "Chronic progressive diseases" include those with progression toward death (80% of cases of amyotrophic lateral sclerosis, some brain tumors, Huntington's chorea, some types of muscular dystrophy, and a few cases of parkinsonism) and those with progression of disabling symptoms not resulting in death in most cases (multiple sclerosis, most cases of Parkinson's disease). "Chronic nonprogressive diseases" include cerebral palsy, brain and spinal cord injury, spina bifida (when victims survive childhood), epilepsy, neurofibromatosis (in most cases), and Tourette's syndrome (after initial progression in childhood).

Some diseases are characterized by remissions (multiple sclerosis, myasthenia gravis, migraine headache, some cases of Tourette's disease). Variation in symptomatology, sometimes from day to day or even from hour to hour, may occur (myasthenia gravis, sequelae of brain injury, parkinsonism). Acute onset conditions include those that result in severe, chronic disability (some strokes, some brain injuries) and those in which no serious disability results (about one-half of strokes, migraine headache, some cases of brain injury). Some conditions are characterized by sudden onset of symptoms without warning (epilepsy, stroke). The psychological factors in patients and families associated with various conditions differ according to whether the disease is progressive or nonprogressive, the predictability of its effects on a day-to-day basis, the severity of existing disabilities, and the degree to which symptoms are socially embarrassing.

Common Difficulties Faced by Patients with Neurological Disorders and by Their Families

The majority of neurologic disorders entail varying degrees of loss of both physical and mental functions. As frustrating and frightening as the loss of physical abilities is, observers tend to agree that the prospect of losing mental faculties—of becoming "crazy"—is more devastating. In progressive diseases, the pain of today's disability is made immeasurably worse by the prospect that tomorrow (or next year, or 10 years from now), impairment will be more severe than it already is.

Loss of Physical Functions

Patients with parkinsonism, multiple sclerosis, Huntington's disease, muscular dystrophy, and amyotropic lateral sclerosis face progressive worsening of symptoms such as tremor, unsteady gait, difficulty in dressing and feeding themselves, difficulty with bladder and bowel control, drooling, and inability to swallow. Fear of choking is common in advanced stages of some conditions, as is fear of falling and bumping into things. Slowness in perceiving, responding, and moving are characteristic of some diseases. Ability to follow conversations may be seriously impaired. Loss of capacity to speak, even when the intellect remains completely intact, is an enormous source of frustration.

Persons suffering with chronic nonprogressive conditions (cerebral palsy, traumatic brain injury) may experience any of the symptoms that patients with progressive disorders experience. The chief difference between the two groups is that in nonprogressive disorders, the patient does not have to fear continual worsening of an already bad situation. Adjustments that individuals have made to the condition, therefore, can be expected to continue to be appropriate. In progressive diseases, new adjustments are continuously required.

It is sometimes difficult for patients to cope with physical symptoms both because they often have very low energy levels and because they lack control of their muscles. The well spouse must often assume a parental role with the patient in relation to physical care. Breakage and spillage often result from loss of manual dexterity. Simple activities like making a cup of instant coffee or smoking a cigarette pose hazards of spilling boiling water or setting a home on fire. Hans and Koeppen (1980) recounted a case in which the wife of a Huntington's patient experienced the death of one son from disease and the destruction of her home by fire caused by another afflicted son's smoking at home unsupervised.

Psychological Distress in the Patient

Psychological reactions to the diagnosis of a progressive disease have been conceptualized in terms of stage theory, for which the Kübler-Ross (1969) model of stages toward the acceptance of impending death serves as a prototype. The Kübler-Ross progression (denial, anger, bargaining, depression, and acceptance) may be applicable to conditions expected to result in death in the near future, such as many cases of amyotrophic lateral sclerosis. Models applicable to chronic disability also have been proposed (e.g., Falek, 1979). The Falek model includes denial and shock, anxiety, anger or guilt, depression, and psychological homeostasis.

The most common initial reaction to a diagnosis of a serious progressive disorder, such as multiple sclerosis or Huntington's disease, is denial ("It can't be me. The doctor made a mistake."). The patient and/or family members may seek other medical opinions in the hope of finding someone who will give a different diagnosis. Falek (1979) pointed out that counselors often consider patients "firmly entrenched in denial" to be good clients because they "accept [the diagnosis] so well" (p. 40). This appearance of maturity, however, is misleading; the individual has avoided acknowledging the real stress at an emotional level and is therefore not motivated to make the behavioral changes necessary to deal with the new reality. For example, in some Huntington's patients, decisions to have children are made despite the knowledge that every child of a Huntington's disease patient has a 50% probability of developing the disease. During the denial phase, the individual's capacity to absorb new information about the situation may be very limited. Denial in patients with such diseases as multiple sclerosis, in which there is a fair chance that the patient may continue to live without significant disability, may not, however, be pathological. Rather, denial can be seen as an adaptive coping mechanism in the early stages of the illness, when, in fact, the individual is not disabled. Denial is likely to decrease as neurologic impairment and physical disability increase (Baldwin, 1952).

Wexler (1973) pointed out that feelings of hopelessness cement denial. Patients may be failing to perform at work, may have escalating interpersonal stresses within the family, may have withdrawn from hobbies formerly enjoyed, and may have withdrawn from social activities in which their disabilities cause embarrassment, humiliation, and avoidance by other people. Wexler reported two cases of Huntington's disease in which rigid denial, which had persisted for many years, gave way when the patients were given new hope. One patient was given a new medication, which proved effective in controlling his chorea. Another became aware of research and fund raising activities that a national advocacy group, the Committee to Combat Huntington's Disease, were carrying out. For the first time, he admitted to having the disease and began to attend meetings of the local committee chapter.

The second phase in Falek's (1979) model of the coping sequence is a period of anxiety, during which reality testing forces cognitive recognition of the illness. Bouts of anxiety may show themselves in irritability, nervousness, headaches, fatigue, insomnia, loss of appetite, and somatic complaints. The patient is still trying to retrieve the "good old days" but is finding it impossible to maintain the denial that would allow her to continue pretending that nothing has really changed.

The frustrations aroused in this phase lead to a period of anger. Patients may show resentment toward, rage at, or envy of well relatives or acquaintances and hostility even toward the people who care most about them.

Depression occurs over the loss of one's former capacities, unfulfilled hopes and desires, increasing need to be physically dependent on other people, loss of control over one's life, and deprivation of formerly enjoyable activities, which have become painful or embarrassing. Depression is a salient feature of most disabling illnesses.

The final stage, psychological homeostasis, is conceptualized as the desirable but not always achievable resolution of earlier stages. Like the Kübler-Ross (1969) model, the Falek (1979) model of stages in chronic disability does not necessarily progress in chronological order. One Huntington's patient, who appears to have reached some measure of psychological homeostasis, described his experiences as a Huntington's victim (Nee, n.d.):

My ailment seems to have two parts, the uncontrollable movement you see on the outside plus small continuous movements inside that no one can see. I can feel it, but no one can see it; others might interpret this as my being just "nervous and highstrung." I remember the inner movements began at least 10 years before the outer movements. . . . It is important for others to realize that because the disease is progressive and so much of it is not observable to the naked eye, things are constantly going on internally that are upsetting.

I am aware of the usual progression of Huntington's so I want to keep myself in as good physical condition as possible for as long as possible. I do this through extensive exercising. . . . walking was important because I would sleep better and not disturb others in the house. As beneficial as walking was, it was not without its concerns because when I walked, I staggered, and people thought I was drunk. I finally solved this by going out and telling the neighbors that I had Huntington's Disease and that I don't drink.

With the progression of the disease I sometimes act hardheaded or angry because it is so difficult for me to ask for help, and even when I ask, it is difficult for me to get the kind of help I need. It is difficult for people to understand that I can paint an entire room but be unable to remove the light switches and door knobs to begin the job.

Embarrassment or Humiliation

Many neurological diseases subject sufferers to signs that range from mildly embarrassing to repulsive. These include tremors (parkinsonism), jerky movements, drooling, bladder and bowel incontinance, speech impairment, tics, facial and other bodily distortions (present in several disorders), bizarre noises such as grunts (Tourette's syndrome, Huntington's disease), and even large, multiple, wartlike bumps (neurofibromatosis). Feelings of shame, embarrassment, and humiliation are common among patients who have outwardly visible manifestations of this nature. Individuals who have epilepsy frequently are mortified by having grand mal seizures in public. Family members are also embarrassed by patient's symptoms.

Uncertainty

Difficulty in diagnosis creates ambiguity about the status of the patient's health. In diseases such as multiple sclerosis, early manifestations are often intermittent and ambiguous. The diagnostic process can be protracted and uncertain; this causes patients and families to be apprehensive and often to fear the worst. Physicians may be unable to make a diagnosis, or, having made it, may be reluctant to tell the patient. Uncertainty is enormously anxiety provoking. Even after the diagnosis has been made, the great variability in both the rate of progression and the ultimate degree of disability makes uncertainty a prominent feature of the disease throughout most of its duration. With MS, drastic symptomatic changes occur, ranging from symptom-free periods to periods of severe disability. In myasthenia gravis, symptoms can occur and disappear within minutes.

Social work practitioners have found that discussion of the problems of adaptation to the stress of chronic uncertainty enables some patients to take positive steps in their lives that they had previously been unable to take. An example was given of a 31-year-old MS patient, an accountant (Hartings et al., 1976). He was unable to decide whether to apply for social security disability (thereby resolving the ambiguity of his health status by planning for a downhill course) or to try to retain his faltering position at the office in the hope that the disease would not get worse. Encouraged by discussions in an ongoing peer group, he came to the conclusion that "life gives no guarantees to anyone" and that "even people without MS have troubles." He decided to ask for a raise. The point of this anecdote is not to advise patients to resolve ambiguity by choosing a course of action based on a more hopeful assessment of the future course of the illness but rather to illustrate the effect of ambiguity on making life decisions.

Fear of Fatal Attack

Patients, as well as family members, may live in constant fear of a fatal attack, both when the condition is clearly life threatening, as in stroke, and when ramifications of the disease (falling, choking, losing consciousness) may result in severe physical harm or even death. Fears of the latter kind are common in epilepsy, Huntington's disease, and other disorders that disrupt motor function.

Marginality

Another issue related to physical disability is what has been called "marginality," or the "borderline phenomenon." These terms refer to people whose disability is minimal and who must live on the borderline between health and sickness. Patients are often fatigued, weak, or uncomfortable but do not as yet have outward signs of illness. They may feel ambivalent about this situation, wishing both to maintain an appearance of normalcy and to surrender to the fatigue or to other distressing symptoms. Family expectations of the patient remain the same as they were before the onset of illness, as do expectations of people outside the family. These expectations can create added stress for the patient (Hartings et al., 1976). An example was given of a 34-year-old mother of three who prior to the onset of her illness had been energetically involved in her children's extracurricular activities. On a particularly bad day she was called and asked to bake a cake for the Brownie troop. Aware that she was going to have difficulty making it through the day as it was, she declined to bake the cake. She then felt discontented with herself and worried that the other mothers would think that she was avoiding responsibility.

Redefinition of Lifelong Social Norms

Adaptation to chronic disease with physical disability requires that patients redefine their daily experiences and unlearn social norms that have been internalized since childhood (Hartings et al., 1976). An obvious example relates to loss of bladder control. Patients may have to wear diapers. The stark physical realities may occur long before the individual has made the cognitive and emotional shifts that alleviate the sense of humiliation and failure that accompanies the physical problem.

Adaptation to Physical Dependence

Asking for help in situations in which the request is entirely appropriate may represent weakness and defeat to the patient with a neurological disorder. An example was given of a middle-aged father of two children who had been in a wheelchair for more than a decade because of multiple sclerosis (Hartings et al., 1976):

> One Saturday afternoon while watching a TV football game he got thirsty for a beer. Knowing he would feel bad asking his teenage daughter, sitting nearby, to get a beer for him, he considered getting it for himself; but as the kitchen was some distance from the den, he knew it would take him several minutes to maneuver his chair through the house by himself. So he deliberated on whether he would be better off to get it himself, putting his independence "to the test" as it were, or to "just this once", ask his daughter to help out. After much deliberation he meekly, as if defeated by an internal foe, enlisted his daughter's aid, thus conceding to himself weakness and defeat. She cheerfully obliged. Dinner was ready shortly afterwards and our patient wheeled himself briskly to the table, forgetting to bring his half-full beer can along. And again, more grist for the mill: "Should I get it myself or ask Karen?" Now it seems that a person who has been confined to a chair for 10 years ought not to go through that every time he is thirsty. Yet we continually find patients immobilized for years in the lonesome job of bringing their thoughts and feelings into harmony with actual physical capability. (p. 70)

This issue was dealt with in group counseling sessions with MS patients. Group members helped the patient change his viewpoint and recognize that fetching a beer is a small task unworthy of inner turmoil. Viewing oneself as an independent adult does not have to depend on such capabilities.

The response of family members to the needs of the patient for physical assistance requires considerable sensitivity. On the one hand, it is important not to reinforce patients' feelings of inadequacy by doing for them things that they are quite capable of doing for themselves. Patients should be allowed to take as much time as they need to complete a task and should not be rushed by family members. It may be tempting to complete tasks for the patient because it saves time and may relieve the patient's (or the relative's) frustration momentarily. However, it may also decrease the patient's motivation to help himself and may compound feelings of helplessness. On the other hand, it is important that family members give help when needed or even, as in the preceding example, when not strictly needed if a small service by a family member will add to the patient's comfort.

In some conditions such as Parkinson's disease, there is extreme variability even during a day in the severity of symptoms. For example, tremor, slowness of movement, or rigidity may be more pronounced during the morning than during the afternoon. The patient may be fully capable of dressing at one time and not at another. This unpredictability and variability is extremely confusing for family members and promotes misunderstanding and frustration on the part of everyone. The family needs to be aware that the patient is most probably not malingering and that it is the variability in the disease itself that causes the fluctuation in ability to perform activities of daily living.

Expression of Aggression

Expression of aggression takes on new meaning in families with a disabled member. It is not considered acceptable to be angry at ill persons. Sick and disabled persons themselves may fear to express irritation or anger in the manner that they had done before the onset of illness because they acutely feel that they are burdens to spouse, children, or to other relatives. To give vent to anger might risk abandonment or loss of affection by the already taxed relative on whom the patient is so dependent.

Sexuality

In working with 150 MS patients in group counseling, Hartings and colleagues (1976) found that sexuality was the issue most difficult for patients to address. Difficulty in sexual function, or inability to perform, appears to be a highly charged issue for them. Although the topic of sexual functioning was raised routinely by group leaders, only 2 out of 10 groups expressed interest in exploring this area. In these two groups, attendance dropped by 50% or more when the topic was scheduled to be discussed. The subject is sometimes approached indirectly through discussion of body image. Patients talk freely about their feelings pertaining to the first experience with a cane or a wheelchair. A common attitude is bravado: "There is nothing to be ashamed about. Dammit, it doesn't bother me at all!" Once the topic of body image is opened some patients can go on and discuss aspects of the disease affecting sexual functioning.

Competence

The patient's competence is a highly emotionally charged topic that profoundly concerns the patient's sense of dignity and self-esteem. When this issue relates to physical matters, such as the ability to drive a car, patients often resent attempts by relatives or outside agents, such as licensing departments, to deter them from an activity. The issue of driving is particularly salient in epilepsy since the patient is fully capable except when having a seizure. States either stringently monitor or entirely prohibit the driving of motor vehicles by persons with epilepsy. When the issue of mental functioning arises, the question of competence is even more charged and traumatic. Doubts about the patient's mental competence, whether based in reality or not, often lead family members, physicians, and other professionals to treat the patient as a nonperson by withholding information, offering "reassuring" lies, preventing patients from participating in the process of making decisions about their own lives, or talking about them in their presence as if they were not there. Such behavior is enormously demeaning and often very frightening to patients; it reinforces their worst fears about the seriousness of their condition and the loss of their mental functions.

Psychological Distress in Family Members

In families with a physically disabled member, other members experience certain common concerns and emotions. Spouses and others close to the patient may go through similar stages in reaction to learning the diagnosis as the patient goes through. Initially, denial is common. Anger, often suppressed, may accompany realization of the meaning of the illness. Spouses may feel extremely burdened by the constant physical care necessitated by the patient's illness; round-the-clock care can become extraordinarily wearing even for healthy, energetic, and devoted relatives. When the signs of the disorder are socially embarrassing, the trauma of going out with the patient may lead the family to stay home. Entertaining in the home may also become difficult or uncomfortable. Thus, relatives may find themselves deprived of sources of enjoyment and companionship that they enjoyed prior to the onset of the illness. At the same time, spouses may have to assume new and unaccustomed responsibilities: breadwinning; childrearing; bathing, feeding, diapering, and/or lifting adult patients; management of financial affairs; and a plethora of household chores. Anger is an appropriate reaction to excessive burdens, combined with decreased pleasure and enjoyment in life. Family members need to be helped to acknowledge and accept their angry feelings when previously learned prohibitions against being angry at sick people cause them to suppress or deny these feelings. Depression is also common among spouses and other family members. The spouse (or child) may lose companionship, affection, and nurturing as the ill member's disability causes her to become more and more self-engrossed.

Loss of Mental Functions

In neurologic disease, deterioration of mental functions can take a variety of forms. Patients may become disoriented or forgetful. They may have difficulty following conversations. They may become depressed, withdrawn, and secretive or suspicious and hostile. There may be marked fluctuations in mood, with inappropriate crying or laughing. Hypochondriacal preoccupations may occur. Occasionally, overt psychosis may appear, with hallucinations or delusions. Violent or aggressive outbursts are characteristic of certain conditions, notably, Huntington's chorea. In Tourette's disorder and presenile dementias (see Chapter 19), sufferers may call out obscenities. Brain-injured persons may display characterological changes ranging from mild to severe. Many neurological conditions also cause combinations of visible physical manifestations, such as jerky movements or facial distortions.

Reactions of others to illness vary according to its manifestations. Physical sickness with no observable deformity or mannerism evokes a sense of revulsion combined with pity. Mental disorders evoke avoidance reactions, as well as a sense of embarrassment at inappropriate behaviors. Diseases that cause a combination of bodily defect and mental disturbance tend to evoke the most extreme avoidance, rejection, ridicule, or revulsion.

Falek (1979) described in stark terms the reactions to patients with Huntington's disease:

> Similar to that which occurs with elderly people, particularly with those who show signs of deterioration, individuals diagnosed with Huntington's Disease

are frequently treated as socially dead when they are still physically alive. Social death. . . . results in a mechanistic approach to health care for the diagnosed patient. This is particularly true for those with Huntington's Disease; patients show increased difficulties with speech, and exhibit grossly abnormal movement patterns. Grotesque movement patterns and long periods of muteness are considered by most medical personnel, many family members and friends as evidence of mental deterioration. Treatment for the patient is discussed with others (family and medical staff) but never with him or her. Difficulties in communication and awkward body movements produce embarrassment, frustration and distaste which are dealt with by treating the patient as a non-person. This is often done without determining his competency to understand and make decisions about his own treatment.

Similar to that found with elderly patients, the individual we are treating as socially dead may be sensitive to his or her environment and able to understand all or most of what is said and done in his presence. (p. 36)

Researchers have identified several types of characterological alterations in brain-injured persons that are likely to create problems for families. Brain-injured patients tend to have an impaired capacity for social perceptiveness. This is manifested in self-centeredness, lack of empathy, and diminished or absent capacity for self-reflective or self-critical attitudes. Impulse control is often impaired; patients are impulsive, restless, impatient, and irritable. Patients may be disorganized and unable to plan and execute activities. They may verbalize intentions that they do not carry out. They may exhibit dependence on others, overreactivity to stimuli, and a seemingly imperative need for immediate gratification. Emotional changes may include irritability, silliness, emotional overreactivity, apathy, or greatly increased or decreased interest in sex. Patients are frequently unable to learn from experience even though their intellectual ability to absorb information appears intact.

These characterological changes are often bewildering to family members, who remember the patients as they were prior to the disability. Family interactions may remain geared to the patient's previous personality for some time after the changes have occurred. That is, relatives expect the patient to be what she was before the illness or accident, not what she is now. Even small changes such as mild irritability or diminution in drive can create stress for families. Any changes may leave family members feeling cheated, angry, and probably guilty about harboring such feelings toward a disabled person.

When major changes have occurred in the patient's personality, so that he is now demanding, irresponsible, excessively dependent, or possibly violent or dangerous because of impaired judgment, stress in the family escalates. As Lezak (1978) pointed out, the burden is felt most critically by the person or persons who have assumed major responsibility for the patient's care. Caretaking relatives usually feel trapped. They may have had to give up work or hobbies or a social life because of the consuming needs of the patient.

Social isolation is a very common problem for family members, as well as patients (Bardach, 1969; Malone, 1977). Even if no trouble at home, the patient may embarrass the family in public by bizarre or loud behavior, may get lost, or may become upset in unfamiliar surroundings. Families may find the effort of going out too great and may find it less traumatic to stay home. Embarrassment arising from the patient's behavior, how- ever, may also isolate them at home since it may no longer be possible to invite friends. Lezak (1978) gave the example of a teenage girl who stopped bringing female friends to her house because her brother, who was physically fit but brain injured, could not keep his hands to himself.

Even when family members maintain their social contacts, they may feel lonely because their friends, who have not experienced similar situa- tions, lack empathy or understanding. The extended family, too, may withdraw from the immediate family both physically and emotionally as the patient's disabilities generate discomfort. Relatives who have not had to assume caretaking responsibility tend to be liberal with criticism of the caretaking relative (Buchanan, 1976). As Lezak (1978) put it:

> Without day-to-day experience of the patient's irresponsibility, impulsivity, or foolishness, or of the onerous duties, vigilance, and sacrifices undertaken by the caretaker, they can easily misperceive the caretaker as being too protective or restrictive, too neglectful or uncaring. Only relatives who have experienced the caretaker's burdens are likely to be genuinely grateful and emotionally supportive. (p. 593)

Some brain-injured patients become frankly abusive toward family members, especially spouse and children (Lezak, 1978). Patients may be frustrated by their condition, demeaned by needing care, upset at being a burden to their families, but terrified of losing their caretakers. These caretakers may become the focus of hostility because they act as constant reminders to patients of their dependence and lack of competence. Pa- tients may belittle or heap complaints, accusations, and demands upon the caretaker or even threaten physical violence such as striking with a cane, tripping with a crutch, pushing, or slapping.

Ordinarily, family members have unrealistic expectations for the pa- tient—expectations based on the person she was before onset of the dis- order. Misinterpretation of deteriorating behavior may put stress on both patient and family in the early course of a degenerative disease or during the recovery stage from a sudden onset brain condition (Trethowan, 1970). Patient and family, as well as professionals working with them, are likely to mistake irritability or childishness for a psychiatric condition. Family members may wonder what they are doing wrong and believe (sometimes with professional reinforcement) that their behavior toward the patient is causing the behavioral changes. When patients are recover- ing from a sudden onset brain condition, such as stroke or head injury, family members are likely to be solicitous and supportive initially. "Delight at his survival, however, can turn into impatience, exasperation, and ultimately anger as discrete capabilities improve but an increasingly irritable, demanding, and dissatisfied patient makes little or no effort to resume his ordinary responsibilities" (Trethowan, 1970, p. 594). Considerable time is often needed for families to realize that their loved one is not the same person he was prior to the disability. Neither counseling nor trying to reason or plead with the patient tends to improve the situation (Lezak, 1978).

Family members may provide more care than the patient actually needs due in part to the personality characteristics of the brain-injured patient (demandingness, dependence, childishness, negativism). Brain-injured patients may be overindulged, fostering the dependence and demandingness that are part of the problem to begin with. Family members may do more for a patient than is necessary in order to silence critical relatives, to give purpose to their own lives, or, they hope, to ameliorate the patient's condition. Accordingly, caretaking relatives are likely to be exhausted, resentful, and deprived of outlets of their own.

Spouses of brain-injured persons are subject to multiple stresses. The spouse may have lost a person who supplied companionship and affection and sexual gratification. Since many brain-injured patients no longer have the capacity for empathy and interpersonal sensitivity, their ability to satisfy spouses' needs is strictly curtailed. There may be a disparity between their sexual competence and their demands for sexual attention; for example, many patients make incessant demands whether or not it is realistic to expect the spouse to keep satisfying them. The sexual act may be one-sided, without regard for the partner. When a husband is impotent, he may blame his wife and pursue her all the more vigorously. And while the spouse has lost a companion, she is not free to seek another. Divorcing a handicapped spouse is often condemned by relatives and regarded as unethical by the healthy spouse. At the same time, the spouse cannot mourn the loss of a partner although the loss is real.

When there are young children in a family with a brain-injured parent, the healthy parent may lack sufficient time and energy to devote to the children because of the enormous burden of running the family single-handedly while caring for a difficult or demanding spouse. Disabled parents may "bully and belittle their children in childish competition for their spouses' attention and affections, and to recover a few shreds of self-esteem as their children's developing competencies begin to surpass their own" (Lezak, 1978, p. 594). The well parent may be faced with a painful choice: to remain with the ill parent at the expense of the children or to abandon an ill and dependent mate.

Given the stresses of living with a brain-injured person, it should not be surprising that family members sometimes become seriously depressed and occasionally seek relief in drugs or alcohol. Some degree of depression should be expected in all family members. Those who can escape or avoid the situation, finding their satisfactions elsewhere, are likely to be less prone to serious depression than are persons who are trapped with the patient.

Mental deterioration in Huntington's disease takes on a special and grotesque significance for family members. Since the illness tends to appear after the early childbearing years, families may not know whether their children will stand a 50% risk of contracting the disease until after the children are born. Children and other close relatives of Huntington's disease (HD) victims live in dread of contracting the disease. Wexler (1973) described the reactions of 35 at-risk men and women:

> For all these men and women at risk no matter how mature and well-adjusted they were to the presence of the illness in the family, the nature of HD symptomatology seemed to strike at the core of their physical and psychological self-esteem. The peculiarities caused by uncontrollable movements and mental deterioration became translated for many into a vision of a Frankensteinian monster, one who approaches others with affection but from whom others recoil in horror. Subjects spoke repeatedly of how "disgusting," "repulsive," "grotesque," "ugly and horrible" the HD patient becomes. There was a particular dread of losing bladder and bowel control. Some reported feeling nauseated at the sight of their ill parents.
>
> Most fantasize the period following diagnosis to be a prolonged wait on death row. . . . None of the at risk individuals mentioned feeling afraid of death per se. On the contrary, death is often cited as a welcome relief from life with symptoms. . . . Approximately half the sample felt that they would seriously consider suicide as an option if and when they started to deteriorate. (pp. 201–204)

Spouses of persons who contracted Huntington's chorea after their children were born experienced resentment and rage that the existence of the disease in the patient's family, known to the patient and in-laws, had in most instances been concealed from them prior to the marriage (Hans & Koeppen, 1980).

Environmental Sources of Stress

In addition to the sources of stress arising from loss of physical and mental functions, economic and social factors place a burden on patients and families. An almost universal problem is financial hardship. Income maintenance programs for the disabled provide no more than poverty level subsistence for most. Loss of earning capacity by the patient and also, possibly, by the relative who must stay home to care for the patient, enormous medical bills, and the need for expensive supportive services all contribute to making financial problems a major component of disability for both patient and family.

In order to qualify for Medicaid to finance whatever care is needed, families must often spend their life savings on medical services for the patient before they become eligible for assistance. This means, in effect, that many families lose everything they have worked for during a lifetime because of the misfortune of having an ill member.

Shortage or absence of necessary services such as home health care, transportation, socialization opportunities for the patient, and, above all, service to provide respite to the family immeasurably adds to the grief and anguish that patients and families experience. The inadequacy of treatment and care options is particularly striking in the area of part-time alternatives to home or institutional care. The all-or-nothing nature of the decision to institutionalize, with the anguish it brings to both patient and family, is a sad commentary on the dearth in our society of alternate residential and care arrangements for chronically ill and incapacitated persons (Counts, 1978). Partial hospitalization (day, night, weekday, or weekend), group homes, supervised apartments, and foster family placements are available in some areas of the country (although in insufficient quantity and quality) for psychiatric patients. Similar facilities for other disabled persons, however, are sparse or nonexistent in most locations. As a result, patients and families are often faced with two heartbreaking alternatives: total home care or total institutionalization.

We have seen that total home care can condemn caretakers to full-time and exhausting servitude with no possibility for a life of their own. The notion that the family should take total responsibility for loved ones, no matter how overwhelming the task, harks back to the individualistic ethos of American society, which dictates complete self-sufficiency on the part of individuals and families. The breakdown of the extended family system in response to changing economic conditions has made this ethos anachronistic, even assuming that it once had validity. Nuclear families simply do not have the physical, emotional, and financial resources to assume full-time care of seriously disabled persons without great sacrifice unless they happen to be both extremely wealthy and unusually strong and determined.

Total home care also limits the patient's opportunity for socialization with others with similar problems, who might constitute an invaluable source of emotional support and companionship. It intensifies the patient's feelings of being a burden on loved ones. And it generates hostilities between patient and family members due to the high level of stress inherent in the situation.

Full-time hospitalization or other institutionalization, on the other hand, deprives patients of family life; separates them from any community other than that of the institution; dehumanizes; and frequently amounts to de facto incarceration. Patients often feel that families have deserted them. Families, too, are burdened with guilt at having abandoned their family member.

Part-time out-of-home care, used creatively in cobination with home care, could do much to alleviate the adverse effects of the full-time care alternatives. Day, night, weekday, weekend, or other part-time hospitalization or inpatient nursing; group homes; foster family care; and supervised apartment living for less severely disabled persons are urgently needed. Development of such resources is a challenge to communities. It requires concerted efforts by patients, families, and professionals to demonstrate need, lobby for funding, and insure competent implementation.

Social Work Intervention with Neurologic Patients and Their Families

Various approaches have been developed by social workers and other helping professionals to try to alleviate the inevitable hardships and pain of neurological illness and its attendant disabilities.

Initial Diagnosis and Ongoing Communication

Of utmost importance is the communication of information directly to patients, as well as to their relatives. Studies have shown that the great majority of patients react positively to, and express satisfaction for, the frank information they receive but that the vast majority of physicians and related helpers withhold many important facts from patients (Oken, 1961; White, 1969). Certainty of something bad has been found to be regarded as more bearable than uncertainty (Whittier et al., 1972). Nevertheless, when a diagnosis is catastrophic—as is the case in neurologic diseases such as Huntington's chorea and multiple sclerosis—the affected individual is often deprived of the right to make decisions about the future course of her life by both family members and physicians at the time of the initial diagnosis. This is so even when the patient is still fully competent intellectually and has no impairment in ability to communicate (Falek, 1979).

Families and professionals inadvertently heighten, rather than diminish, the patient's anxiety by attempting to explain away symptoms while becoming increasingly solicitous. The patient, who is well aware that the disability is not going away (it may even be obviously progressing), worries that information is being withheld—an unmistakable signal that something too terrible to talk about is occurring. The use of euphemistic language, for example, referring to epilepsy as "seizure disorder," reinforces the stigmatization that is experienced by the patient and may prevent the patient from learning the full significance of the disease. Persons with epilepsy, for example, may unwittingly falsify insurance applications, leaving themselves open for catastrophe later, when the company refuses to pay a claim (Massey et al., 1980). Maintaining the deception over a period of time increases everyone's burden, as family members try to protect each other from the truth and carry their burdens alone. Thus, attempts at protection can actually worsen an already highly stressful situation.

Honesty is the sine qua non of a helpful relationship with a patient. Sensitive workers, of course, support denial when there is good reason to believe that the patient will be better off not knowing the whole truth, but this does not mean that workers should ever tell outright lies. Omission of devastating information is not a violation of honesty; stating falsehoods is.

Although both patient and family experience an initial shock when a diagnosis is given and its meaning explained, most people can begin to work through the feelings such information generates. Knowledge about the realities of the situation is often necessary to make realistic plans, involving care for the patient, location of new sources of income if the patient has been a breadwinner, readjustment of lifestyle, and understanding some of the most emotionally charged facets of the disability such as loss of sexual function. These issues can be dealt with only when the condition is identified and its possible course considered.

Maintaining the dignity of the patient is of utmost importance; depriving him of the truth strips the individual of one basis for a sense of dignity, i.e., knowledge about what is happening and information about possible ways of responding to the situation. Early information giving can favorably influence the course both of treatment and of the disease if positive aspects, such as things the patient can continue to do or the possibility of trying a new medication, are presented.

Ordinarily, it is the physician who communicates, or fails to communicate, with the patient and family about the diagnosis. Frequent failure by physicians to perform this responsibility (White, 1969) underscores the importance of social work intervention with patient and family. The social worker can assess the patient's and the family's readiness to know and can work with the physician in developing a plan for conveying the information in the most effective way possible. Should the physician show great unwillingness to engage in giving painful information, the worker may consider it advisable to undertake this role.

The worker should elicit feedback from patient and family to try to ascertain their understanding of the information they have received. Frequently, the shock of the initial diagnosis prevents people from absorbing all the information that has been presented. At a later time, the worker should again try to ascertain the patient's and family's level of comprehension and knowledge about the condition. The worker may reintroduce information at this time to help patient and family deal with their feelings, make realistic plans, and pursue treatment in the most efficacious manner possible. It is often extremely useful to provide written information about the condition, so that patients and relatives, who are likely to forget much of what has been told them initially, can read and reread about the disease at their leisure, in the privacy of their homes (Appolone, 1978). Advocacy and self-help organizations now exist for the majority of disorders. One of the functions of these groups is to prepare written material about the condition for the public. Practitioners should routinely send for literature from the advocacy groups pertaining to their client population and should try to have available as much of this literature as possible to distribute to clients.

When following a drug regimen is a crucial factor in the prevention of symptoms or attacks, as in epilepsy, misconceptions and fears may contribute to ''forgetting'' to take the medication.* In such situations, the information exchange process may have a decisive influence on the course of the illness. Neurologists have noted that noncompliance with a regimen of medication is the most common cause for increased frequency of epileptic seizures (Massey et al., 1980).

The type and content of counseling at the time of diagnosis depend primarily on individual needs. Shoulson (1977) outlined a series of steps for telling patients and families about Huntington's disease. His model can be adapted, as follows, to other conditions:

1. ask what the patient or the family member knows about the condition; the reply gives the counselor some indication as to where to begin
2. explain the symptoms and signs that generally occur, including motor, sensory, intellectual, and emotional aspects; explain the likely clinical course of the condition; if, as in multiple sclerosis, the future course is highly uncertain, acknowledge the unpredictability and the stress this uncertainty creates
3. explain whatever is known about the causes of the condition and how it operates in the central nervous system

---

*Appolone (1978) pointed out that patients and family members frequently do not reveal their fantasies and misconceptions about an illness to the physician and may do so to the social worker only sheepishly. He gave an example of the mother of a 14 year old who was subject to grand mal seizures. The mother revealed that she believed a blood clot was present that, she feared, would either lodge in her son's brain, making him ''crazy,'' or in his heart, killing him.

4. outline alternative available treatments and the potential benefits and hazards of each; distinction needs to be made between cure for the condition, for which in most of the conditions described in this chapter none exists, and treatments, which alleviate the condition
5. explain general approaches to care that can be carried out by patient, family, and supportive services
6. again elicit feedback to help assess the impact the information has had on the patient or the family member

Chronic illness and the life circumstances of families dealing with chronic illness are subject to vicissitudes. The communication process, therefore, needs to extend over a long period of time. Even if a situation of equilibrium results in lack of contact for months or even years between worker and clients, it is highly desirable to encourage patient and family to call whenever the need arises. Long-term stress requires long-term supportive service. Needless to say, continuity of care (contact with the same worker) is most desirable, but families also feel comforted by being able to deal with the same agency or service.

The role of the social worker as individual and family counselor can be critical throughout the duration of contact. Patients need to receive recognition of their fear, frustration, anger, and disappointment, combined with positive input pertaining to constructive actions that they can take to gain meaning in their lives. The literature on chronic neurological disease repeatedly emphasizes the importance, in order to maintain hope, of identifying positive goals and steps to take toward these goals. The crucial message is that life can still be worth living despite the pain and inconvenience associated with disability.

It is extremely important for the worker to be very knowledgeable about the particular condition that a client is suffering from, so that he can relate to realistic problems (how to get to the bathroom), as well as to feelings and attitudes. A worker who brushes aside nitty-gritty physical concerns in order to delve into feelings will quickly be perceived by patients (and families) as lacking in understanding of the very real problems encountered in getting through the day.

Peer Groups as a Major Treatment Modality

Peer support groups have been widely used both at the stage of initial diagnosis and during the course of disabling conditions for patients with a variety of neurological disorders (stroke, epilepsy, multiple sclerosis, Huntington's disease). Major purposes of these groups are to educate patients and relatives about the condition, to mobilize the kind of support that comes only from others who are suffering a similar problem, to break down the social isolation that many of these illnesses generate, to disseminate information about resources, to expose patients to a range of coping strategies being used by their peers, to enhance self-image, and to help patients redefine their lives in relation to changed abilities and opportunities. Peers may be more effective in helping each other in these areas than professionals; however, professional skills are essential in planning and convening groups; in providing structure and direction when needed; in facilitating communication; and in resolving conflict or alleviating disruption when it occurs.

Hartings and colleagues (1979) developed a model for service delivery for MS patients intended to enhance coping through education of the patient and the family and through peer contact and support. The groups were designed to provide a new reference group for persons whose lifestyles had been or would have to be significantly altered. Patients were given the opportunity to talk to other patients to "learn the ropes about how to do things, how to feel, how to reorder priorities and values, how to assert legal rights, and a whole range of vital issues" (Pavlou et al., 1979). The groups were directed at psychologically normal persons and were geared to promoting exchange of information about day-to-day coping, as well as sharing of feelings and attitudes. Professional group leaders (psychologists and psychology interns) facilitated interchanges and helped in the process of labeling and understanding feelings. Leaders emphasized that although patients have little control over the disease process itself, they do have control over their reactions to it and their means of handling it. It is the patients' responsibility to find a new lifestyle and a way of contributing to the well-being of others.

The initial meeting was more structured than subsequent meetings and included a lecture on multiple sclerosis by a neurologist. Groups contained 8–12 members and included family members. Ongoing organization of the meetings was determined by the preferences of leaders and members. Most groups were limited to 15 meetings. Topics of discussion came from members and included anger at physicians, feelings about problems with bladder and bowel control, handling employers, methods for finding financial resources, fears about welfare of children, marital and sexual problems, and ways to find meaning in life even with a disability.

Patients found the group meetings helpful in several ways. They felt less isolated and alienated. They expressed interest in learning about the symptoms and physical sensations that others experienced. Some patients stated that they now felt "a part of the human race" once more. Meaningful friendships developed between group members. After formal termination, groups often continued to meet informally to engage in activities such as playing bridge. Members called each other when the need was felt.

Patients also expressed amazement at attitudes expressed by other patients that differed markedly from their own. One man who felt isolated and stigmatized by his condition had been unable to tell anyone that he had MS. Another group member who was in the same line of business stated, "I don't worry about that. Nobody who works for me cares about my MS—they only care if they keep getting their paychecks." The first patient was then able to tell important people in his life about his condition and to begin to think differently about himself.

An important function of the group experience, exemplified by this anecdote, is to expose patients to a range of coping alternatives. Various ways of defining one's condition or disabled state are expressed. In addition, concrete assistance is often given, from advice on handling bedsores to applying for social security disability payments.

Geronemus (1980) presented a model of care based on the concept of crisis prevention and predicated on normalcy rather than pathology. In this model, chronic illness is viewed as a developmental life crisis, or a difficult stage in the life cycle. Different types of services are suggested for different degrees of disability, but individual, family, and group counseling may be indicated at any level of disability depending on the person's life situation, family dynamics, resources, and response to the disability.

For newly diagnosed, nondisabled patients and their families, a major therapeutic strategy is the use of time-limited, educationally oriented groups whose composition can vary (couples, patient or family groups, or combinations thereof). These groups focus on increasing knowledge about the disease: ways to prevent complications, possible effects of medication, introduction of patients and families to available resources, enhancing patient and family ability to negotiate the medical system, and helping to increase the patient's ability to exert control over the illness and over daily activities. These groups provide a nonthreatening, goal oriented support system.

Minimally to moderately disabled patients and their families receive individual, group, and family therapy; sexual counseling; and vocational rehabilitation counseling. Treatment is tailored to individual needs. Social workers with extensive knowledge about the disease itself act as therapists or co-therapists with nurses or rehabilitation counselors.

Group therapy for the moderately disabled population is long term and emphasizes therapeutic rather than educational goals, including relieving tension, enhancing self-esteem, helping the patient adjust to a changing self-image, developing methods for coping with stress, recognizing feelings and needs and learning ways to deal with them, understanding the effects of one's behavior, confronting one's own illness through shared experience with group members, and using group feedback and support to test newly acquired behaviors.*

Groups for family members, in the Geronemus (1980) model, serve the purposes of breaking down social isolation, relieving concern that they are too impatient with, or intolerant of, the patient's difficult behavior and symptoms, reducing the anger arising from the need to assume new roles and additional burdens, understanding changes in the patient, learning new ways of responding to the changed family member, recognizing needs of other family members despite the illness, promoting maintenance of ties with other relatives and with friends, learning to set limits on patient demands, promoting the patient's independence, and promoting constructive patterns of using medical and social support services. Individual and family therapy are proposed as alternatives for patients and families who do not appear to be able to benefit from groups.

A model has been developed for working with groups of young adult epileptic patients in order to help them reject the "sick role," often based on a lifetime of reinforcement (Appolone & Gibson, 1980). These groups have been used to reeducate patients about opportunities to assume other roles. The group process is conceptualized as a series of stages of group development.

In the first stage, a sense of identity is confirmed. Many members had never talked to other epileptics prior to the inception of the group. Some had an ever present fear of disclosure ("closet epilepsy"). One young man had never discussed his condition with his wife although she had witnessed several of his grand mal seizures. A school administrator whose seizures were well controlled kept his epilepsy a secret for fear of losing his job. Group members shared feelings of shame and mortification about having grand mal seizures in public. Development of trust is an important task of early meetings. Leaders are supportive, nonconfrontational, and active in giving encouragement and praise. Information giving is another important component of early meetings. Epileptics were found to harbor many of the same misconceptions about their illness as does the public. Accurate information was provided to groups both by leaders and by pamphlets.

Exploration of goals is the focus of the second stage. Members were asked to state what they would like to be doing five years from now and then each member was required to form a plan of action. Leaders saw passivity as epidemic in this population. They fantasized about ambi-

---

*Some observers have noted that group cohesion is much more likely to be fostered when individuals have things in common other than their illness; for example, it is preferable not to put teenage patients with elderly patients since their basis for sharing is limited (e.g., Anthony, 1960).

tions and aspirations but "waited for magic to carry them there." Confrontation may be used to get members to explore how they have been using their epilepsy as a crutch or a manipulative tool. "What can *you* do about it?" became a group litany once members had heard the leaders say this repeatedly.

Modification of behavior patterns characterizes the third stage; direct confrontation is used intensively (e.g., "If you're sleeply all the time, see your doctor about changing the medication," or "If your job counselor isn't helping you, be assertive about what you want."). At this point in the process, a single meeting was called for family members, including the extended family, to give them information about the condition; to give them the opportunity to share experiences, doubts, and feelings of guilt; and to enlist their support for changes that were occurring in the patients. Leaders recognized that it might have been desirable to offer families additional meetings.

In the final stage, assessment of progress, members evaluated their gains and the group terminated, with two follow-up meetings scheduled for 6 months and 12 months after termination.

Husbanding Resources: The Linkage Function

Throughout the course of a protracted illness or a chronic disability, the social work function of "brokerage"—linking consumers with community resources that provide financial assistance and other services—is essential. A variety of referrals may be needed to income support resources; health care services; lawyers or financial counselors for such matters as guardianship, wills, and financial concerns; educational and vocational counseling, especially for wives who may have to prepare to become breadwinners; and to daycare, sheltered workshops, homemaker services, and respite care. In order to be effective, social workers must inform themselves about available services, some of which may not be listed in official resources directories.

The Case Manager Function

A crucial additional function of the social worker, seldom mentioned in the literature on chronic disability, is the case manager, or monitoring, function. All too often, fragmentation of services, staff turnover, poor communication between agencies, and other obstacles impede use of services. The social worker is the logical professional to assume the role of monitoring the combination of services received by the patient and the family; to stay in contact with service providers to assure maximum accountability; and to serve as a coordinator of information. Changes in patient or family status or in the nature of resources available may require the case manager to help patient, family, and service providers reassess needs and service plans and to supervise implementation of new plans.

Advocacy

The social worker often will have to become an advocate for the patient or the family when bureaucratic obstacles prevent their obtaining financial entitlements, home care services, transportation, or other services. For severely disabled patients, even greater advocacy efforts are likely as the need for supportive services escalates and existing resources become inadequate. When institutional placement is decided upon, advocacy may be necessary to overcome obstacles to the patient's admission.

Family Counseling

Counseling with families can be enhanced by attention to common problems families face. Lezak (1978) outlined issues that are frequently salient for families of patients with brain injury. Many of these issues also pertain to care of physically disabled persons. When families do not raise these issues, it is desirable for the counselor to do so.

The worker should emphasize that anger and frustration, as well as grief, are natural emotions for close relatives:

> It is bad enough feeling chronically annoyed or tied down by a once-beloved person; but these feelings become harder to endure when complicated by guilt. After months of caring for an unhappy, ungrateful, difficult patient, with no end in sight, close kin are apt to be frightened or upset by their irrepressible wishes for the patient's early demise. (Lezak, 1978, p. 595)

Family members need continual reassurance that these feelings are natural.

Caretakers must attend to their own needs in order to be effective in caring for the patient. As Lezak (1978) pointed out, this issue should be brought up early and often since the notion of enlightened self-interest runs counter to moral axioms about the virtue of self-abnegation and duty. The caretaker needs to understand that the patient's well-being depends directly on his own well-being.

When patients have impaired judgment or when relatives offer well-intentioned but inappropriate advice, the caretaker may have to rely on her own judgment in opposition to the patient's or relatives' wishes and opinions. This may be extremely difficult for the caretaker since unilateral decisionmaking may be contrary to the nature of the relationship that existed prior to the disability.

The counselor needs to help patient and family members clarify and identify the type of the role changes demanded by the disability. Adult patients often become irresponsible or dependent, but assuming a parental role toward the adult patient can be very upsetting. Role changes involve reversals of patterns established over many years of interaction; complex, subtle, and often automatic behaviors are likely to be involved here. The counselor should identify these behaviors and indicate how they are being changed by the illness or need to be changed to accommodate the changed circumstances of the family.

Family members are frequently confused by shifts in the patient's behavior. Reference to developmental stages can sometimes ease their puzzlement. For example, when a patient's impulsiveness or poor judgment is likened to that of a three year old, the family may be helped by being told that a new, unfamiliar, and uncomfortable role—that of authority figure—is now necessary and appropriate. Since different family members can act at cross-purposes with each other, it is extremely important to include all the family in counseling sessions to clarify these issues.

Family members can do little or nothing to change the patient's condition; hence, they do not need to feel guilty or inadequate when their ministrations do not result in improvement. The practitioner should make sure that family members understand that trying harder cannot, in most instances, be expected to ameliorate a physiologically determined disability.

An agonizing issue for responsible relatives is that of conflict between the interests of the patient and the interests of other family members. When children are being belittled or even physically abused by a brain-injured patient, the responsible parent may have to choose between the children's welfare and the needs of the patient. Management of such behavior by the well parent requires firmness and even punitiveness at times toward the ill parent:

> For many of these childish adults, the most effective tool for gaining the patient's cooperation that the spouse has is his/her own presence or absence, judiciously applied. Just as childhood temper tantrums can be reduced and often eliminated by benign neglect, so do tantrums of adult patients tend to dissipate when the spouse leaves the room—or the house if necessary—quietly and predictably; and in turn, desired behavior, such as setting the table or picking up dirty clothes, can be fostered by the spouse's undivided attention. . . . In many ways, managing an irascible, bullying, brain injured spouse is not much different than disciplining a refractory two or three-year-old. (Lezak, 1978 p. 595)

Placing a patient in an institution, when home management becomes too difficult, is an enormously traumatic step for all concerned; however, in many situations it may be the only realistic alternative. The social worker's sensitivity to the needs and feelings of patient and family around the time such a decision is being considered may play a crucial role in their adjustment, or lack of it, to institutionalization. Alleviation of family guilt is a major task at this stage.

Natural Helping Systems

Potentially of great importance is the use or enhancement of natural and quasi-natural helping networks, in addition to the chief natural helping system of the peer group. An example of a natural helping network is a neighbor housewife who may feel isolated or unimportant; engaging such a person in helping care for the patient on a short-term basis in order to allow the caretaker to go out might meet mutual needs. An example of a quasi-natural helping system is a local organization (such as a church or fraternal organization or even school children willing to do community volunteer work). The practitioner should explore the availability of such supports to help ease the burden on the family or to provide companionship or stimulation for the patient.

Self-help and Advocacy Groups

Self-help groups and advocacy groups cannot be overstressed as a resource both for patients with all kinds of neurologic disease and for their families. A national directory of existing groups, most of which have chapters throughout the country, can be obtained from the U.S. Department of Health and Human Services.* Practitioners should obtain this directory and write to the appropriate agencies listed in it to obtain information.** Many advocacy, research, and support groups have described their functions in published material.

The goals of the Tourette Syndrome Association are typical of the purpose of such organizations:

> to help patients who have been undiagnosed and misdiagnosed by publicizing the symptomatology of this disease

---

*Voluntary Health Agencies Working to Combat Neurological and Communicative Disorders, U.S. Department of Health and Human Services publication no. 81–74 (Bethesda: National Institutes of Health, 1981).

**Information on resources can also be obtained from the National Self-help Clearing House, City University of New York, New York City.

to publish and distribute medical and nonmedical information via booklets and other media

to regularly schedule meetings of our membership to exchange information as well as to learn about the new developments in this field from informed and knowledgeable speakers

to raise funds to support research into the nature and causes of the disorder

The Committee to Combat Huntington's Disease, which has local chapters throughout the country, similarly describes its functions:

to provide a listening ear
to have regular meetings
to provide a medical advisor
to give medical and social service referrals
to publish newsletters
to raise funds to support the committee's work in research and public and professional education
to provide patient services
to promote legislative advocacy

Lack of needed services, financial resources, and job opportunities for disabled persons is critical in many parts of the United States. Community organization efforts to develop and coordinate resources on the local level can do much to promote adequacy of services. Ultimately, however, organized social action on the national and state levels will be necessary to bring about significant improvement in care.

Social Action

The final social work role to be mentioned is that of social activist. No amount of counseling and therapy, no matter how soothing or consoling, can prevent some of the serious casualties of our economic and social welfare systems, which bankrupt ordinary, hard-working families who are unlucky enough to be stricken with a chronic disability; which demand that families become destitute before financial assistance is given; which subject families to demeaning investigations before providing needed assistance; and which define the individual family as the social unit that has the sole obligation to care for disabled members, no matter what its means and no matter how devastating the effects of the illness or injury. In some other countries, such burdens are distributed throughout society by the provision of adequate and timely financial assistance, group care facilities, and respite resources for families. In the United States, the enormous responsibility of full-time care of chronically disabled persons is compounded by the gnawing and realistic fears that families have of being destroyed financially as a result of an unlucky roll of the dice. Governmental financial assistance for disabled individuals, in the absence of private wealth, condemns both patient and family to subsistence below the poverty line (Johnson & Goldberg, 1982).

Social workers must, *as part of their everyday practice*, join with advocacy groups for welfare recipients, disabled persons, the elderly, and others to lobby for more humane government policies. However, many people who became active in promoting social change devote their energies exclusively to a particular group in which they have a special interest. In today's political climate, single issue activism, if effective, may produce benefits for one group at the expense of another, equally needy group. Advocates for disabled citizens, therefore, should form coalitions with advocates for other groups in order to press for increasing the overall size of the pie, rather than simply redividing an undersized pie so that some get larger and some get smaller slices.

Conclusion

This chapter has reviewed some of the more common neurological disorders resulting from injury, infection, and genetic causes. The various conditions have differing major characteristics (e.g., progressive versus nonprogressive) that give rise to different constellations of problems that patients and families must face. The common issues that arise with neurological disorders have been discussed and illustrated with case material. Finally, approaches to social work intervention, geared to alleviating the multiple stresses and burdens created by neurological disorders, have been presented.

References

ADAMS J, LINDEMANN E: Coping with long-term disability. in Coelho G, Hamburg D, Adams J (eds): *Coping and Adaptation.* New York, Basic Books, 1974.

ANTHONY E J: Age and syndrome in group psychotherapy. *Long Island Consult Center* 1960; 1:3.

APPOLONE C: Preventive social work intervention with families of children with epilepsy. *Soc Work Health Care* 1978; 4:139–148.

APPOLONE C, GIBSON F: Group work with young adult epilepsy patients. *Soc Work Health Care* 1980; 6:23–32.

BALDWIN MC: A clinico-experimental investigation into the psychologic aspects of multiple sclerosis. *Nerv Ment Dis* 1952; 115:299–342.

BARDACH JL: Group sessions with wives of aphasic patients. *Int J Group Psychother* 1969; 19:361–465.

BARNES R, BUSSE E, DINKEN H: The alleviation of emotional problems in multiple sclerosis by group psychotherapy. *Group psychother* 1954; 6:193–200.

BEAR DM, FEDIO P: Quantitative analysis of interictal behavior in temporal lobe epilepsy. *Arch Neurol* 1977; 34:454–467.

BENNIS E, SHEPPARD H: A theory of group development. *Human Relations* 1956; 9:415–437.

BLUMER D, BENSON DF: Personality changes in frontal and temporal lobe lesions, in Benson DF, Blumer D (eds): *Psychiatric Aspects of Neurologic Disorders.* New York, Grune & Stratton, 1975.

BREGMAN A: Living with progressive childhood illness: parental management of neuromuscular disease. *Soc Work Health Care* 1980; 5:387–408.

BUCHANAN D: The usefulness of group psychotherapy with chronically ill neurology patients, in *Symposium on Treatment Techniques in Clinical Psychology.* Paper presented at the Fourth Annual Meeting of the International Neuropsychology Society, Toronto, Feb. 1976.

CAPLAN G: *Support Systems and Community Mental Health.* New York, Behavioral Publications, 1974.

CARPENTER JO: Changing roles and disagreement in families with disabled husbands. *Arch Phys Med Rehabil* 1974, 35:272–274.

CHAPMAN LF, WOLFF HG: The cerebral hemispheres and the highest integrative functions of man *Arch Neurol* 1959; 1:357–424.

COBB S: Social support as a moderator of life stress. *Psychosom Med* 1976; 38:300–314.

COGSWELL B: Conceptual model of the family as a group: family response to disability, in Albrecht G (ed): *The Sociology of Disability and Rehabiltation.* Pittsburgh, University of Pittsburgh Press, 1976.

COOPER IS: *Living with Chronic Neurologic Disease.* New York, Norton, 1976.

COUNTS R: *Independent Living Rehabilitation for Severely Handicapped People: A Preliminary Appraisal.* Washington DC, Urban Institute, 1978.

D'AFFLITTI JG, WEITZ GW: Rehabilitating the stroke patient though patient–family groups, in Moos R (ed: *Coping with Physical Illness.* New York, Plenum, 1977.

DELGADO-ESCUETA AV, MATTSON RH, KILG L, et al: Special report: the nature of aggression during epileptic seizures, *N Engl J Med* 1981; 305:711–781.

DELISA JA, MIKULIC MA, MILLER RM, et al: Amyotrophic lateral sclerosis: comprehensive management. *Fam Physician* 1979.

DEMBO T, DILLER L, GORDAN W, et al: A view of rehabilitation psychology. *Am Psychol* 1973; 28:719–722.

FALEK A: Observations on patient and family coping with Huntington's disease. *Omega* 1979; 10:35–42.

FOWLER RS, FORDYCE W: Adapting care for the brain damaged patient. *Am J Nurs* 1972; 72:2056–2059.

FREIDSON E: *Professional Dominance.* Chicago, Aldine, 1970.

GERONEMUS DF: The role of the social worker in the comprehensive long-term care of multiple sclerosis patients. *Neurology* 1980; 30:48–54.

GERONEMUS DF, HOLLAND NJ, SPRINZELES LL, et al: Chronic ambulatory care: a model. *Am Rehabil* 1980.

GESCHWIND N, SHADER RI, BEAR D, et al: Case 2: behavioral changes with temporal lobe epilepsy: assessment and treatment. *J Clin Psychiatry* 1980; 41:89–95.

GLATZER HT: The relative effectiveness of clinically homogeneous and heterogeneous psychotherapy groups. *Int J Group Psychother* 1956; 3:258.

GOFFMAN E: *Asylums.* New York, Doubleday Anchor, 1961.

GOFFMAN E: *Stigma.* Englewood Cliffs, Prentice-Hall, 1963.

HAMBURG D: Coping behavior in life threatening circumstances. *Psychother Psychosom* 1974; 23:13–25.

HANS MB, KOEPPEN AH: Huntington's chorea: its impact on the spouse *J Nerv Ment Dis* 1980; 168:209–214.

HARTINGS MF, PAVLOU MM, DAVIS FA: Group counseling of MS patients. *J Chron Dis* 1976; 29:65–73.

HEDGES C: Huntington's disease: some implications for social work, in *Huntington's Disease Handbook for Health Professionals.* New York, Committee to Combat Huntington's Disease, 1973.

JACKSON P: Chronic grief. *Am J Nurs* 1974; 74:1289–1290.

JOHNSON HC, GOLDBERG GS: *Government Money for Everyday People: A Guide to Income Support Programs.* Garden City, Adelphi University School of Social Work, 1982.

KAPLAN SR, RAZIN AM: The psychological substrate of self-help groups. *J Operat Psychiatry* 1978; 9.

KAPLAN SR, ROMAN M: Phases of development in an adult therapy group. *Int J Group Psychother* 1963; 12:10–26.

KAPLAN D, SMITH A, GROBSTEIN R, et al: Family mediation of stress. *Soc Work* 1973; 18:60–69.

KELLY WD, FRIESEN SR: Do cancer patients want to be told? *Surgery* 1950; 27:822–826.

KÜBLER-ROSS E: *On Death and Dying.* New York, Macmillan, 1969.

LEVINSON R: Resources for epilepsy: access and advocacy, in Sands H (ed): *Epilepsy: A Handbook for the Mental Health Professional.* New York, Brunner/Mazel, 1982, pp 225–263.

LEWIS D, BALLA D: *Delinquency and Psychopathology.* New York, Grune & Stratton, 1976.

LEZAK MD: *Neuropsychological Assessment.* New York, Oxford University Press, 1976.

LEZAK MD: Living with the characterologically altered brain injured patient. *J Clin Psychiatry* 1978; 39:592–598.

LEZAK MD: Subtle sequelae of brain damage: perplexity, distractibility, and fatigue. *Am J Phys Med* 1979; 57:9–15.

LISHMAN WA: The psychiatric sequelae of head injury: a review. *Psychol Med* 1973; 3:304–318.

LITWAK E: Theory of natural support systems and self-help groups. Read before the American Psychiatric Association, Atlanta, 1979.

MALAMUD N: Organic brain disease mistaken for psychiatric disorder: a clinico-pathologic study, in Benson DF, Blumer D (eds): *Psychiatric Aspects of Neurologic Disease.* New York, Grune & Stratton, 1975.

MALONE R: Expressed attitudes of families of aphasics, in Stubbins J (ed): *Social and Psychological Aspects of Disability: A Handbook for Practitioners.* Baltimore, University Park Press, 1977.

MARQUIT S: *Psychological factors in the Management of Parkinson's Disease.* Miami National Parkinson Foundation, n.d.

MASSEY EW, FOLGER WN, RILEY TL: Managing the epileptic patient. *Postgrad Med* 1980; 67:134–139.

MCCORMICK GP, WILLIAMS M: Stroke: the double crisis. *Am J Nurs* 1979; 79:1410–1411.

MERRITT HH: *A Textbook of Neurology,* 6. Philadelphia, Lea and Febiger, 1979.

MESULAM MM: Acute behavioral derangements without hemiplegia in cerebrovascular accidents. *Primary Care* 1979; 6:813–826.

National ALS Foundation: *Home Care for the Patient with Amyotrophic Lateral Sclerosis,* ed 2. New York, National ALS Foundation, 1979.

NEE LE: *Experiences of a Huntington's Disease Patient.* New York, Committee to Combat Huntington's Disease, n.d.

OKEN D: What to tell cancer patients: a study of medical attitudes. *JAMA* 1961; 175:1120–1128.

OLIN HS, WEISMAN AD: Psychiatric misdiagnosis in early neurological disease. JAMA 1964; 189:533–538.

OTA Y: Psychiatric studies on civilian head injuries, in Walker AE, Caveness WF, Critchley M (ed): *The Late Effects of Head Injury.* Springfield, Thomas, 1969.

OUNSTED C: Aggression and epilepsy: rage in children with temporal lobe epilepsy. *J Psychiatr Res* 1969; 13:237.

PAVLOU M, JOHNSON P, DAVIS FA, et al: A program of psychologic service delivery in a multiple sclerosis center. *Profess Psychol* 1979.

PEYSER JM, EDWARDS KR, POSER CM, et al: Cognitive function in patients with multiple sclerosis. *Arch Neurol* 1980; 37:577–579.

PINCUS JH, TUCKER G: *Behavioral Neurology,* ed 2. New York, Oxford University Press, 1978.

POWER PW, SAX DS: The communication of information to the neurological patient: some implications for family coping. *J Chron Dis* 1978; 31:57–65.

PRITCHARD PB, LOMBROSIS CT, MCINTYRE M: Psychological complications of temporal lobe epilepsy. *Neurology* 1980, 30:227–232.

ROBINSON MB: *Aids, Equipment, and Suggestions to Help the Patient with Parkinson's Disease in the Activities of Daily Living.* New York, American Parkinson Disease Association, n.d.

SHOULSON I: *Clinical Care of the Huntington's Disease Patient and Family*. New York, National Huntington's Disease Association, 1977.

STEVENS JR, HERMANN BP: Temporal lobe epilesy, psychopathology, and violence: the state of the evidence. *Neurology* 1981; 31:1127–1132.

SURRIDGE D: An investigation into some psychiatric aspects of multiple sclerosis. *Br Psychiatry* 1969; 115:749–764.

TRACY S, GUSSOW Z: Self-help health groups: a grassroots response to a need for services. *J Appl Behav Sci* 1976; 12:381–396.

TRETHOWAN WH: Rehabilitation of the brain injured: the psychiatric angle. *Proc Soc Med* 1970; 63:32–36.

TUCHMAN BW: Developmental sequence in small groups. *Psychol Bull* 1965; 63: 384–399.

Voluntary Health Agencies Working to Combat Neurological and Communicative Disorders, US Dept of Health and Human Services publication no. 81–74. National Institutes of Health, 1981.

WAXMAN SG, GESCHWIND N: The interictal behavior syndrome of temporal lobe epilepsy. *Arch Gen Psychiatry* 1975; 32:1580–1586.

WEXLER NS: (ed) Living out the dying: HD, grief, and death, in *Huntington's Disease Handbook for Health Professionals*. New York, Committee to Combat Huntington's Disease, 1973.

WHITE LP: The self-image of the physician and the care of dying patients. *Ann NY Acad Sci* 1969; 164:822–831.

WHITTIER JR, HEIMLER A, KORENYI C: The psychiatrist and Huntington's disease. *Am J Psychiatry* 1972; 128:12–20.

YALOM ID, RAND K: Compatibility and cohesiveness in therapy groups. *Arch Gen Psychiatry* 1966; 15:267–275.

4

Schizophrenic Disorders

Terry Smolar

Schizophrenia is a complex, baffling psychological disorder and a significant mental health problem. It is a major psychosis accounting for nearly
one-third of all patients admitted to psychiatric hospitals. Between
100,000 and 200,000 people become schizophrenic every year; it is estimated that there are 1–2 million chronic schizophrenics in our population. More than 50% of the psychiatric hospital beds are occupied by
schizophrenics (Turns, 1978).

Keith and associates (1976) reported that discharged schizophrenics
are likely to be chronically or periodically unemployed; moreover, one-
third of all schizophrenics are rehospitalized within a year of initial admission and within two years the figure increases to 50% (Gunderson,
1979). The most common age of onset is 15–35 years, an important period
in terms of education and job training. What is lost in productive years of
life is exceeded only by the cost in suffering among inflicted individuals
and their families.

Schizophrenics are hospitalized longer than any other psychiatric patients except those with depressive disorders. However, the increased
availability of alternatives to inpatient care and the high cost of hospitalization have had the result that schizophrenics often are discharged into
the community earlier than before (Keith et al., 1976).

119

The concept of schizophrenia as a unitary disease is losing favor. Studies of different groups of schizophrenics have led some investigators to suggest that schizophrenia represents several disorders having certain primary symptoms in common. Currently, process–reactive schizophrenia, true schizophrenia, schizophreniform, and acute–chronic psychosis are collectively known as the "schizophrenic disorders."

"Process patients" are people who insidiously and without unusual stress become schizophrenic. "Reactive patients" are people who become schizophrenic after severe and obvious external stress; their psychosis is considered a reaction to this stress. The process–reactive distinction is strongly related to prognosis: reactive patients are more likely to have an episodic problem and a good prognosis, while the process patient experiences a slow, insidious deterioration (Neal & Oltmans, 1980).

"True schizophrenia" applies to patients whose illness is progressively deteriorating and severe. These patients rarely, if ever, show significant recovery.

"Schizophreniform" has been characterized by Langfeldt (1960) as a psychosis that results from clear, precipitating stress, usually psychological. The patient demonstrates illusions, ideas of reference, confusion, and disorganization but has a good prognosis.

"Acute schizophrenia" differs from "chronic schizophrenia" in terms of length of onset, in other words, the period of time from the beginning of personality change to the appearance of overt psychosis. If the patient's illness takes between three and six months to manifest itself, the condition is said to be "acute"; if more than six months, it is described as "chronic."

Symptomatology and Classification of Schizophrenia

The symptoms of schizophrenia include social withdrawal, depersonalization, feelings of being controlled by outside forces, and anorexia or severe weight loss. Moreover, the illness may recur periodically or there may be one time-limited episode. The schizophrenic patient's subjective emotional experience may be diminished and flattened. He may have difficulty communicating the responses of which he is aware. Warm and positive feelings are sporadic and unreliable. It is as though the patient feared these feelings and sensed that her existence could be threatened by achieving intimacy.

Schneider (1959) included in his set of specific symptoms for schizophrenia voices commenting on the patient's actions and/or thoughts; voices arguing; interferences with thought, such as delusional perceptions; influences perceived to be playing on the body; and impulses, drives, or volitional acts that are experienced by the patient as the work or influence of others.

DSM, III (American Psychiatric Association, 1980) criteria indicate that schizophrenia always involves delusions, hallucinations, or certain disturbances of thought. During the active phase of the illness, there is decline from the patient's previous level of functioning. Although some approaches still classify schizophrenia as a deteriorating disease, DSM III includes under the rubric "schizophrenic disorders" episodes of brief duration with recovery. However, DSM III categorizes latent, borderline, and simple schizophrenia as "personality disorders" (see Chapter 7). Onset of illness after midlife also precludes a diagnosis of schizophrenia; these patients are listed under the category "atypical psychosis." Individuals who have symptoms of depressive or manic syndromes for an extended period before the appearance of psychotic features are classified "schizoaffective."

DSM III classifies schizophrenic disorders as follows:

"disorganized type"—distinguishing features include incoherence; absence of systematized delusions; and blunted or inappropriate behavior

"catatonic negativism"—distinguishing features include motiveless resistance to all instructions to move or attempts to be moved; catatonic excitement, that is, excited motor activity that is apparently without purpose and is not influenced by external stimuli; and catatonic posturing, that is, involuntary assumption of an inappropriate or bizarre posture.

"paranoid type"—distinguishing features include persecutory delusions; grandiose delusions; delusional jealousy; and hallucinations with persecutory or grandiose content (see Chapter 13)

"undifferentiated type"—distinguishing features include prominent delusions; hallucinations; and incoherent or grossly disorganized behavior

"residual type"—distinguishing features include a history of at least one previous episode of schizophrenia with prominent psychotic symptoms; a clinical picture without prominent psychotic symptoms that occasioned evaluation or admission to clinical care; and continuing evidence of schizophrenic illness such as blunted or inappropriate affect, social withdrawal, eccentric behavior, illogical thinking, or loosening of associations

Historical Development of the Concept of Schizophrenia

Descriptions of schizophrenic behavior long predate use of the term "schizophrenia." In 1856, Morel introduced the term "dementia praecox" to describe psychotic symptoms reminiscent of the features of schizophrenia. He and other early investigators believed that mental illness has an organic basis and their thrust was to identify onset, course, and outcome in order to clarify the physiological-pathological underpinnings of psychotic disorders. In 1919, Kraeplin (1971) attempted to bring order to the psychiatric nomenclature. He enlarged "dementia praecox" to include the catatonic, hebophrenic, and paranoid symptoms we now associate with schizophrenia. However, Kraeplin believed that mental pathology could be explained solely by reference to heredity and constitutional factors and, later in his writings, by metabolism. He virtually dismissed the psychological components of mental illness, with the result that his writings fostered a narrow definition of "schizophrenia" and an emphasis on description. In contrast, Bleuler's (1950) work led to a broader concept of schizophrenia and a broader theoretical base. Thus, in 1911 Bleuler published *Dementia Praecox*, wherein he suggested that schizophrenia is a group of diseases, not a unitary disorder. He differed from Kraeplin in proposing that dementia praecox is not necessarily a deteriorating disease but an illness marked by remission and exacerbation. Moreover, Bleuler introduced the term "schizophrenia", in preference to "dementia praecox," to reflect his view that there is an underlying personality split in the patient (Cancro, 1972).

In 1914, Freud (1961b) presented a dynamic theory to explain cases of schizophrenia and paranoia, a syndrome he called "paraphrenia." He argued that schizophrenic language and actions are meaningful: they can be understood according to the laws of primary process thinking and can be connected genetically to the life experiences of the patient. He viewed psychosis as a defense against traumatic experiences, in other words, as withdrawal from an unbearable reality.

Freud's reformulation in the 1920's of both libido theory and his hypothesized structure of the mind influenced his attempt to understand schizophrenia. Thereafter, he tried to differentiate between neurosis and psychosis in terms of his new structural hypothesis. He viewed the ego as an intermediary controlling defensive apparatus between the impulses derived from the id and the frustrating forces that stem from the environment. Subsequent psychoanalytic work attempted to define ego defects in schizophrenia (Freud, 1961).

Jung applied psychoanalytic concepts in the treatment of schizophrenia. Jung also believed that many symptoms of schizophrenia are reproductions of archetypes deposited in the collective unconscious. For example, what an individual feels about her mother is influenced not only by her experiences and memories but also by what the culture for generations has taught about motherhood (Arieti, 1979). Jung stressed the importance of congenital factors in schizophrenia and became increasingly pessimistic about his ability to intervene therapeutically with

schizophrenic patients. Nevertheless, he described some striking therapeutic successes (Karon & Vandenbos, 1981).

Meyer had a great impact on the evolution of American psychiatry
and its view of schizophrenia (Zilboorg, 1941). He suggested that disordered behavior is a reaction to psychological and biological stresses. Rejecting the notion that deterioration necessarily follows the onset of
schizophrenic illness, he argued that proper therapeutic intervention
could lead to eventual recovery.

Newer theories of schizophrenia are based on the recognition that the
schizophrenic develops his pathological vulnerability over an extended
period of time and under circumstances that go far beyond early parent–
child interactions. First enunciated by Sullivan (1931), this view addresses the impact of the interpersonal network and social climate within
which the individual developed beyond the first year or two of life. This
theory, first posited by Sullivan (1931), and influenced by Freud, emphasized the underlying emotional and cognitive factors that motivate
schizophrenic withdrawal from interpersonal relationships. His work
with psychotics, described as highly intuitive and apparently effective,
stimulated interest in, and optimism about, psychotherapy with schizophrenics (Boyer & Giovacchini, 1980).

In the 1930's, Fromm-Reichman began to work with psychotics, using
principles derived from her training in and experience with Freud's concept of psychoanalytic therapy. She also found Sullivan's operational
interpersonal conceptions to be of great value in the treatment of
psychotics. As both a therapist and a teacher, Fromm-Reichman influenced Wills and Searles, both of whom are prominent figures in the
theory and treatment of schizophrenia. Her work, along with Sullivan's,
encouraged psychoanalysts in the United States to use a modified
psychoanalytic method in the treatment of schizophrenics. Following
this lead, Arieti (1974), Menninger (1963), Searles (1965), and others have
taken the position that schizophrenic patients can improve and even
recover (Fine, 1979).

Nonbiological Models of Schizophrenia

Theoretical models in the last forty years have focused on the question of
whether schizophrenics suffer from a personality deficit ("deficit
theory"), reflecting inordinate ego weakness, or whether schizophrenia
can best be understood as a disorder of defense ("conflict theory"). According to the latter view, schizophrenia lies on a continuum with other
emotional states but schizophrenics use defenses other than those used
by neurotics.

The deficit theory suggests a defective process of early internalization (called "introjection") but does not intimate that this deficiency is constitutional. According to deficit theory, the core conflict in internal object images, that is the way the infant imagines external objects to be, occurs when the infant is between three and six months old and when she experiences predominantly destructive impulses toward the mother; this causes confusion between love and hate, and Freud maintained that the ego's conflict with reality, which results in the denial of reality is a central characteristic of schizophrenia. He attributed this denial to an abnormal or defective ego. Federn (1933) revised Freud's concept and postulated that the defect is not due to the ego's denial of reality but to its permeable and flexible boundaries, which allow for the creation of a false reality. The work of Freeman and associates (1964) further developed this point of view.

Freud outlined the conceptual framework later utilized by Wexler (1951), who hypothesized that the vulnerability of schizophrenics is due to loss of their ability to formulate inner representations of reality. This view states that the preschizophrenic child, because of his deficient perceptual aparatus and learning capacity, does not internalize a stable sense of himself from his early experience with his parents. In times of stress, the fragile sense of self does not endure, leaving the schizophrenic selfless and alone. This overwhelming experience leads the schizophrenic to attempt to understand objects that have been distorted (object restitution) in the ways that constitute familiar symptoms of schizophrenia (e.g., hallucinations and delusions).

Many variations of deficit theory have been advanced. Rado's (1962) view emphasizes a genetically determined inability to repress selectively. Aronson (1972) attempted to modify Wexler's (1951) view by conducting controlled animal experiments. He reported on the weakness in adaptive quality in vulnerable infants exposed to frustrating experiences and suggested that these responses become maladaptive. However, Searles (1965) cautioned that the therapist's readiness to emphasize deficits in the schizophrenic person is related both to the therapist's unresolved difficulties in dealing with her own bad mothering experiences and to her own unresolved countertransferential issues. Klein (1946) emphasized the importance of pathological splitting, that is, separating objects and persons into separate parts such as the good person and the bad person, including faulty perception of reality, ego weakening, and bizarre fantasies, in schizophrenia. However, she suggested that the anxieties of infancy are the same in schizophrenia as those reflected in other psychotic states and that the defenses are similar in both cases.

The conflict theories of schizophrenia can be divided into three models: "object relations," "ego defect," and "affect intolerance." All of these models give a much more central place to aggressive drives in the schizophrenic process than did Freud's theory of defense, which stressed only libidinal drive alteration.

Conflict theory is largely attributable to the work of Arlow and Brenner (1964). They argued that schizophrenic psychosis is a defensive effort involving regression to avoid the emergence of anxiety in regard to inner conflicts, which generally are about regressive impulses. These defenses differ from so-called normal defenses only in the degree of disruption of reality that they cause, not in any qualitative sense.

Semrod (1969) extended this view, suggesting that the schizophrenic psychosis is a defensive operation to avoid intolerable affects, including anxiety, that uses denial, projection, distortion, and identification with the perceived cause of pain, the "aggressor," to ward off the pain accompanying deprivation or overindulgence in early childhood relationships. By not allowing herself to feel the deprivation, the child prevents inner turmoil from occurring. This mechanism produces severe personality disorders, and later in life internal affect is handled by the person as if it were an external danger.

One means by which recent theorists have sought to overcome the split between conflict theory and deficit theory is to delineate the central organic issues, which may be viewed either as the cause of defective structure or as the result of (or an adjunct to) weak structure. In this perspective, self-control, or self-regulation, is either too tenuous or too rigid; thus, the person has trouble maintaining autonomous feelings.

Mahler (1968) stressed the central role of separation and individuation in normal and pathological development. She stated that there are normally occurring autistic and symbiotic phases in the infant's relationship to the mother. During such phases, the infant has a poor sense of himself as independent from the mother. It is only through a gradual process of separation that the formation of a stable sense of self is possible. This process is seen as dependent largely upon the libidinal gratification available from the mother.

According to Cameron (1963), the premorbid schizophrenic, like all other prepsychotic personalities with basic ego defects, seems especially vulnerable to five general situations: loss or threatened loss of a major source of gratification; loss or threatened loss of basic security; upsurge of erotic or hostile impulses; sudden increase in guilt (conscious, preconscious, or unconscious); and reduced general effectiveness of ego adaptation or defense. The schizophrenic person, whose conscious and preconscious are flooded with infantile impulses, fantasies, conflicts, and fears, meets adult demands with archaic forms of defense, such as massive projection, introjection, or denial. The loss of reality adaptation renders this person unable to control the environment or negotiate the various aspects of daily living.

Gunderson and Mosher (1975) described schizophrenia as a disorder of ego functioning caused by developmental parent–child experiences and possibly, too, by biological-constitutional elements. They suggested that the schizophrenic cannot develop and maintain accurate internal representations of the outside world and this causes the production of restitutional symptoms such as delusions and hallucinations. These symptoms become prominent when the individual is confronted with the stresses of developing independent, mature, and trusting relationships.

Biological Models of Schizophrenia

Investigations into the biological bases of schizophrenia have looked at the role of genetic predisposition, infectious agents, allergy, and metabolic disturbance in this disorder. Overall, the data indicate that biological factors do play a role in the genesis of schizophrenia, particularly in individuals who are highly vulnerable to environmental stress.*

Genetics and Schizophrenia

Three major lines of inquiry have focused on genetic factors in the etiology of schizophrenia: twin studies, family studies, and adoption studies. Studies on the incidence of schizophrenia among relatives of index cases, together with data from twin studies, support the thesis that genetic factors operate in the development of schizophrenia, although the findings are not accepted by all. (Kessler, 1980).

Twin Studies

Kallman (1938, 1946) reported a 73% concordance rate for schizophrenia among identical (monozygotic, or MZ) twins. Kety (1969) Shields (1968), and Slater (1968) suggested that this figure was too high, and Rosenthal (1977) pointed out that Kallman had failed to explain why such a large percentage of MZ twins are discordant for schizophrenia even though identical twins have the same genetic material and the same polygenetically determined constitution.

Tienari (1968) studied a much broader sample of twins in Scandinavia and found a 6% concordance rate among MZ twins when he used a strict definition of schizophrenia. Follow-up brought the rate to 35%.

In his discussion of the Scandinavian twin studies, Arieti (1979) noted that in over 60% of the cases, one twin was not suffering from schizophrenia; therefore, since twins are genetically equivalent, differences between them must be due to factors that are not hereditary in nature.

*Editor's note: Chapter 2 takes a much stronger position on the biological bases of schizophrenia.

Family Studies

If a disorder is genetically transmitted, then relatives of affected individuals are more likely to have the predisposing gene(s) than are persons in the general population. If the incidence of the disorder among the former is significantly higher than among the latter, a genetic contribution to the etiology is suspected. Thus, a disorder that shows a pattern of transmission from unaffected mothers to one-half of their sons suggests that an X chromosome linked mode of inheritance is involved (Karon & Vandenbos, 1981). If both parents and children manifest a disorder, the gene suspected of causing the condition must be dominant. When 25% of the progeny of unaffected parents manifest a disorder, the responsible gene is considered to be recessive. Schizophrenia does not seem to fall into any of these categories (Kessler, 1980; Lidz, 1977).

Recent studies have found that for all siblings of a schizophrenic person, the risk of schizophrenia is higher than for individuals in the general population; the rates vary from 2 and 46 times higher than the average risk for schizophrenia in the population (e.g., Rosenthal et al., 1975). Among first-degree relatives of the patient, the average risk for schizophrenia is roughly 8–10%. The risk for relatives is graded, so that relatives who share relatively fewer genes with an affected individual show a lower rate of schizophrenia than do those who have more genes in common.

An apparently consistent finding is that the siblings and children of schizophrenic patients have a higher risk of schizophrenia than do the patient's parents. Rosenthal suggested that modeling by the schizophrenic affects the total functioning, including the ability to find and hold jobs and to assume marital responsibilities, both of his siblings and of his children.

Adoption Studies

One of the methodological problems in family and twin studies of schizophrenia is that neither type of study can differentiate between biological inheritance and sociocultural and familial influences. For example, disordered environments and disordered intrafamilial communication patterns may occur concurrently with a genetic predisposition for schizophrenia. In such cases, it is not possible to separate the effects of genetics from nongenetic influences, although the genetic factor cannot be excluded (see Chapter 2).

Genetically oriented investigations have not resolved this problem. Studies of twins have indicated that heredity and environment interact in the etiology of schizophrenia but have not established the relative importance of these factors. Rosenthal (1977) noted, for example, that twin studies are problematic because the more similar siblings are, the more parents treat them alike; in addition, MZ twins tend to identify with each other often to the point of contracting the same physical illness within weeks of each other. Adoption studies are one way around the heredity–environment problem.

Rosenthal (1975) cited several critical studies that separated genetic and family environmental factors in schizophrenia. Heston compared children of schizophrenic parents adopted away at birth with other adopted children and looked at the rate of schizophrenia. He found a greater incidence of schizophrenia among biological siblings of adopted schizophrenics than among their foster siblings. Wender and associates (1968) studied the rate and form of pathology in biological and adoptive parents of schizophrenics and normals. He found that the biological parents of schizophrenics showed more pathology than did the adoptive parents of schizophrenics. Wender and associates (1974) later found that normal children adopted by families in which one parent eventually became schizophrenic did not have a statistically higher than base rate for developing schizophrenia. Rosenthal (1975) studied the rate of schizophrenia in adult adoptees whose biological parents were schizophrenic. Using a psychiatric examination, he found an insignificantly elevated incidence of schizophrenia, under a narrow definition of this disorder, and a significantly higher rate, under a broader construction. Rosenthal suggested that being reared in an adoptive home may indeed protect children of schizophrenic parents from developing the disorder themselves.

Other Proposed Biological Bases of Schizophrenia

A number of investigators have suspected that infection plays a part in the etiology of at least some cases of schizophrenia (e.g., Heath & Krupp, 1968). However, identification of an infectious agent has not been confirmed.

Metabolic or allergic factors in the etiology of schizophrenia are suspected on the basis of abnormal protein content in the blood of schizophrenics. Simopoulos and colleagues (1974) postulated that the genetically predisposed person converts tryptophan into dimethyltryptamine (DMT), a known hallucinogen. Another hypothesis is that epinephrine and/or norepinephrine is converted to adrenochrome or adrenolutin. Other suggestions implicate increased serotonin levels in the development of acute schizophrenia (See Chapter 2). On the other hand, all mental and emotional activities require that a biochemical process take place and it is logical that an abnormality in emotional functioning could be accompanied by a chemical abnormality.

Family Relationships and Schizophrenia

Early research on the relationship between upbringing and schizophrenia used retrospective accounts by schizophrenic patients and their parents or siblings. Through this research, the concept of the "schizophrenogenic mother" emerged. The basic view is that the mother of a preschizophrenic is both overprotective and rejecting of her child, so that he does not learn skills and techniques which are necessary for independent social adjustment (Fromm-Reichman, 1948). The schizophrenic reaction occurs when the need for independence arises and the mother–child bond must be broken in early adulthood.

Bateson and co-workers (1956) attempted to identify the conditions that lead schizophrenics to confound the messages from significant persons early in their lives so as to develop thought disorders. They suggested that parents often convey "double-bind messages": a communication that the child is to follow two contradictory courses of action. In this pattern, a first instruction is given at one level of abstraction and followed by another injunction, which contradicts the first. The individual is constantly in a situation in which she is punished for responding; thus, she learns not to respond, thereby removing herself from reality.

Wynne and co-workers (1958) reported that the family system associated with schizophrenia is composed of a series of rigid role relationships in which every effort is made to maintain the status quo. The family members behave as separate uninvolved units, each member following the rigid rules of the family bureaucracy. Therefore, the family is unable to adapt to the developmental needs of the children or to adjust to outside changes that might affect the family. The children may then develop disordered thought patterns and exhibit an inability to adapt to new role demands and dynamically changing situations, patterns that can evolve into schizophrenic behavior in adulthood.

Jackson (1959) found that in schizophrenia the family equilibrium often is maintained at the expense of one family member, who is labeled the sick one. If this family member improves, the family equilibrium is disturbed. According to Jackson, schizophrenia should be considered a family's pathology rather than an individual's illness.

Lidz and associates (1973) found a high level of disorganization in the families of schizophrenics. In families with a schizophrenic son, the father behaves like a jealous sibling toward his child, competing for the mother's attention and discouraging the son from achieving independence. In the families of female schizophrenics, the father tends to be hostile and aggressive toward his wife, undercutting her authority, and extremely demanding and hostile toward the daughter.

Bowen (1960), in his studies of mothers and daughters and entire families, concluded that it is necessary to include previous generations in the study of schizophrenia. Bowen suggested that schizophrenia is a process that takes at least four generations to evolve. He posited that such families have a "critical" level of immaturity and are characterized by emotional distance. Bowen pointed out that the mother's fears about how to respond appropriately are transmitted to the child, who becomes extremely sensitive to her mother's anxieties and withdraws from interpersonal contact. The functional helplessness of the preschizophrenic child, manifested in diminished demands on the mother by the child, enables the mother to become less anxious.*

Class and Psychological Impairment

A series of hypotheses has been presented to explain the clustering of psychosis, particularly schizophrenia, among the poor. Explanations include downward drift, constitutional inferiority, biochemical alteration, social selectivity, and psychiatric bias. Roman and Trice (1967) argued that evidence is lacking to support any of these hypotheses. They offered a sociopsychological account of the concentration of schizophrenia at the lowest social stratum.

Roman and Trice (1967) observed that socialization in the lowest stratum families is so structured that many children do not learn to cope adequately with the social environment; effective intervention between individuals and their environments is a function both of the individual's ability to structure reality and of the consistent structure of reality itself; and deficiencies in perceiving and adapting to reality may interact in such a way as to give rise to behavior that is labeled "schizophrenic." This formulation views schizophrenia as the end point of a series of frustrating, painful experiences in an environment that is contradictory, uncertain, and deviant from that of the dominant society. Withdrawal from a social reality with which he cannot cope is the schizophrenic's method of adaptation Becker (1963). The position that social deviance is a social phenomenon rather than an individual illness is reflected in the works of Schur (1965), Scheff (1966), Goffman (1961), and Szasz (1961).

Hollingshead and Redlich (1958), using data on incidence and prevalence, found a relationship between neurosis and social class: neurosis was concentrated in the upper social classes. A significant concentration of psychosis was found in the lowest social classes. Hollingshead and Redlich also reported on the different paths to treatment followed by patients from different classes. They suggested that the relatively limited

---

*Searles (1965) pointed out that a child who desires a less anxious mother will adjust his behavior to the mother's needs even if such behavior leads to arrest in the child's development.

choice of treatments available to the lower class person explains the preponderance of schizophrenics among the poor.

The widely reported inverse relationship between psychosis and social class bears scrutiny (Dunham, 1965; Miller et al., 1959). Is the concentration of severe mental illness in the poorest segment of society a reality? If so, what are the reasons for this phenomenon?

Investigators such as Leighton emphasize that social conditions are important determinants of whether or not individuals will suffer psychological disorder. Dohrenwend and Dohrenwend (1975) analyzed 44 studies that attempted to assess the "true prevalence" of psychological disorder in various populations. Their analysis of these studies showed that the most consistent finding was an inverse relation between social class and reported rate of psychological disorder. They noted that this relationship held not only for overall measures of disorder but also for two major subtypes, schizophrenia and personality disorder. Dohrenwend and Dohrenwend (1975) also noted that stressful events appear to be more severe for lower-class than for middle-class persons and within classes both more frequent and more severe for blacks than for whites.

Myers and co-workers (1973), investigating the link between social class and psychiatric symptoms, studied a sample of 720 adults in New Haven, Connecticut, as part of a longitudinal study on the use of a community health center. Their sample represented a cross-section of the population of metropolitan New Haven and included all ethnic, racial, and socioeconomic groups. Myers and colleagues found a significant relationship between social class and psychiatric symptomatology. In 1967, twice as many persons in the lowest class as in the highest fell into the highest symptom category (25% compared to 12%).

Two years later, when the respondents were reinterviewed, the relationship between social class and symptoms was found to be virtually unchanged. They also found a strong relationship between life events and psychological distress.

The New Haven study suggested that the greater amount of psychiatric distress found in the lower class in community studies is due to the uneven distribution of life events measured by a scale of "desirability change." Lower class individuals experience more unpleasant events that have a high readjustment or change impact than do persons higher in the social hierarchy. Such events, in turn, are related to psychiatric symptomatology:

> Thus the lower class person, confronted with a certain quantity of disturbance and living in relative economic and cultural poverty, exhibits symptoms because of the increased strain *imposed upon him*. Interpersonal relationships at this social level tend to be fragile and provide relatively minimal social support to the individual facing an undesirable crisis which requires considerable coping. (Dohrenwend and Dohrenwend, 1975, p. 202)

According to Myers, the individual, by developing this symptomatology, may be asking for the needed support that he is otherwise not getting.

Evaluating the Effectiveness of Treatment in Schizophrenia

Since 1960, six major studies have assessed the effectiveness of psychotherapy with schizophrenics.

The Pennsylvania study (Brody, 1959) attempted a rigorous evaluation of "direct analysis" (Rosen, 1953), a form of psychoanalytic psychotherapy designed to establish strong parental transference. Critics of this study pointed out that the technique produced compliance but not necessarily therapeutic results.

The California study (May, 1968) sought to find out whether the quality of the therapeutic relationship has a direct impact on treatment outcome. May evaluated treatment with and without medication and concluded that the treatment of choice is medication. Karon and Vandenbos (1981) pointed out that although medication is particularly effective in improving ward behavior, it is not highly correlated with successful real-world functioning among schizophrenics.

The Wisconsin study (Rogers et al., 1967) was the first investigation to use a control group in evaluating the effect of the patient–therapist alliance on outcome. Rogers and associates reported that the quality of the therapeutic relationship with a schizophrenic patient has a direct impact on the outcome of treatment (see Chapter 2).

The Massachusetts study (Grinspoon et al., 1972) evaluated the use of medication in the treatment of schizophrenic patients. This study has been used as evidence that medication has more value than experienced therapists for schizophrenic patients; however, many of the therapists in this research program, while experienced with other disturbances, had not worked with schizophrenic patients before and certainly not with chronically ill schizophrenics.

The Illinois project (Paul & Lentz, 1977) evaluated social treatment rather than individual therapy. Chronic, hardcore schizophrenic inpatients were randomly assigned either to routine medication or to one of two psychosocial treatments (milieu therapy or social learning therapy). The major finding was that both psychosocial treatments produced initial improvements and maintained these gains; however, the social learning treatment was more effective in the long run than either milieu treatment or medication. Thus, meaningful human intervention was more beneficial than medication, as was shown by the patients' ability to manage outside the hospital.

The Michigan study (Karon & Vandenbos, 1981) suggested that medication is more helpful for schizophrenic patients than no treatment at all; psychotherapy for schizophrenic patients by inexperienced but medically qualified therapists is not of much help; however, if careful quality control of psychotherapy is maintained, psychotherapy is beneficial for schizophrenic patients.

It appears from these studies that more important than the theory or modality of treatment is the capacity of the therapist to understand, support, and help the schizophrenic patient to understand and define herself in terms of her experiences, psychological boundaries, feelings, wishes, and goals. He must be helped to feel that there are those who care and wish to help.

Treatment of Schizophrenia

The treatment of schizophrenia depends on the stage of the disorder, the depth of the regression, the grasp on reality that remains, and the patient's desire for therapy and her ability to establish a relationship with the therapist. It is necessary from the onset to attempt to help the patient to move from his regressed state to a more integrated level of functioning. First and foremost, it is essential that the therapist establish a positive therapeutic alliance with the patient.

Emotional responses of patients are appropriate to the patient's inner experience even though this may be hidden from the therapist. It is the therapist's task to identify the thoughts that evoke these emotions, as Bateson (1974) explained in his account of a young man confined for lunacy in 1931:

> By detailing and explaining his sufferings and his complaints and his difficulties—he hopes to teach the wretched and affectionate relations of a deranged person, what may be his necessities, and how to conduct themselves toward him, so that they may avoid the errors which were unfortunately committed by the author's own family. (p. 49)

Bateson described how the hallucinatory and delusional distortions of this patient, Perceval, during his madness had definite connections with experiences in his early life. For example, Perceval explained that as a young boy working in an abbey he had been asked to kill a pig. He plunged the pig, while alive, into a huge pot of boiling water, having first bound the pig's mouth with sackcloth. During his psychotic episode, Perceval had a recurrent delusion that like the pig, he would be bound and plunged into a boiling cauldron, mouth covered:

> I actually believed that a sound I heard in the room next to mine like to boiling water, was a preparation for this awful punishment, and that my brother and one of my cousins were every moment on the verge of plunging me in and con-

demning me forever. . . . when they came into my room I saw them at times like natural men, but at times their countenances were horridly swollen and their faces darkened so they looked black. (p. 49)

Treatment of the schizophrenic individual requires considerable patience and constancy. The client's frustration tolerance is often exceedingly low; he may suspect the motives of the therapist, and he may project onto the therapist his own prejudices and fears. Since he feels incapable of dealing with real life, the patient may resent the therapist's intrusion into his fantasy life. Although he is aware that the goal of the therapist is to return him to the real world, this prospect holds untold terrors for him. Often, anxiety with a temporary return to regression may interrupt therapy (Childs-Gowell, 1979). Also, the patient may erupt with hostile or violent reactions when he feels that his retreat is being threatened by the efficiency of treatment.

Fromm-Reichman (1959) explained that the therapist must be engaged in an ongoing sympathetic and understanding relationship with the schizophrenic patient and that the intellectual comprehension of the illness is secondary. Wolberg (1954) emphasized that the therapist must analyze his own reactions all the time since his sense of frustration may arouse aggression on the part of the patient and interfere with treatment. He cautioned that the therapy must provide unlimited warmth, understanding, protection, and help:

> The chief emphasis in treatment must be on the creation of a human relationship with the patient that has pleasure value for him. Only by this means will he relinquish the safety and gratification of regression and utilizing the therapist as a bridge, return to reality. (p. 63)

Since the schizophrenic patient's ego is very immature, the patient's reactions to people are unstable and ambivalent. She feels rejected and frustrated for insufficient reasons; her concept of reality is distorted and unreliable, so that inner mental processes are often confused with outer reality. Such a patient may react with hostility if the therapist does not grant what he wishes.

The schizophrenic patient may choose to remain silent throughout the treatment hour. In such cases, when the patient feels safe and trusting enough to communicate with the therapist, she will often reveal all that she absorbed during her silence.

Case Studies in Schizophrenia

The Silent Scholar

A young man of 16 was a conscientious Orthodox Jew, studying the Talmud every evening, attending religious services regularly, and behaving like his fellow yeshiva students. One day, he brought the Bible to his father to show him where the devil had written between the lines; he said he was meant to eat pork and refused to partake of any meals that were kosher.

When I saw him at the hospital, he sat mute, not having eaten for days; he would not communicate with either the staff or his family. We met regularly. I talked while he twirled the ends of the window shades. He was observed to cry often in speaking to other voices when he thought no one could hear. I said I wished that I knew what was being said to him that made him cry very hard. He hurriedly glanced at me and looked away. I talked about what I knew of his history—he was the youngest of five boys (his parents had been disappointed that he had not been a girl) and he was different from his brothers in that he liked sports and played at every opportunity. He was looked upon as anathema in this family, in which boys studied the Talmud and did not "make trouble."

During his mother's visits, he fidgeted with his genitals and made loud gutteral noises when she tried to get him to eat kosher food. Visitation by the parents was stopped for several days. During that period, he started to relate to me. He had not eaten in several days (he drank only milk), and I began to take pastries and milk into our sessions. The first time he spoke, he said, "I want some." I gave him a bun, which he devoured. He then looked at me and asked whether I like baseball. He slowly returned to what I had spoken of in the days during which he had sat mute. What began to unfold was the enormous rage and aggression he felt toward his parents. With continued support, interest, and treatment, he improved sufficiently to be discharged eight weeks later.

It is helpful to remember that symptoms express the patient's feelings. When patients make strange gestures, they should be paid attention to since they are nonverbal communications by the patient. The first step in resolving psychotic symptoms in a patient is to establish emotional contact with her. Sometimes, making an accurate interpretation of what the patient is verbalizing will make him feel secure enough to give up some psychotic manifestations.

The Abandoned Actor

A 23-year-old man came to see me because he was confused and frightened and "did not know what to do." By that he meant that he did not know where to go when he left my office. Before coming to see me, he had begun to hallucinate but when he tried to explain this to some acquaintances, they shunned him.

He had come to New York City from the Midwest eight months earlier, after college graduation, and had had some success in dinner theaters and off Broadway shows. He had been living with a young woman, who was working full-time as a lab assistant. Recently, she had met a young doctor, fallen in love, and left the patient. A few days later, he felt that a television announcer was talking directly to him about having bad breath. He called some friends, who told him that this notion was silly. He found it difficult to eat and swallow. When he called his mother, she was "very uninterested" and refused to send him the money to come home. His sisters, to whom he also appealed for money, found him "too spoiled." His father told him he was lazy and wished he would just disappear. Subsequently, he began to hear voices, which he could not understand. Most disorienting were the figures he would see at his bedside at night when he attempted to fall asleep. Asked how the voices made him feel, he answered that they made him feel less threatened—reminding him of the singing his mother used to do when he was small, before she and his father separated. After his father left, his mother became quite distant and depressed; his sisters, disorganized and upset.

This man was able to see that he had experienced his girl friend's leaving as an abandonment for which he was ill prepared when stress over not working and general feelings of inadequacy were overwhelming him. The ability to make connections between the present trauma and the past history (abandonment by father) helped him sufficiently to cause cessation of symptoms.

The major difficulties in coping with each developmental task are of critical importance to the social worker and mental health practitioner, whose task is to strengthen the individual's capacity to deal with the exigencies of his environment. Clarifying the patient's problem and identifying special stressors related to certain events in the life cycle are of essential value in treatment.

The Young Mother

A young mother of 24 was referred to me because her baby was failing to thrive. He was underweight, irritable, and restless, and vomited after meals. The mother of the child related to the referring doctor, who thought it was unlikely that the baby's problem was due to any social or emotional reasons since the woman was of "good family" and had had a "good upbringing." She came from an upper middle-class background and had had a good education.

On her first consultation, M. brought her baby because the babysitter had failed to come. When the baby awakened and cried, she did not pick him up for about three minutes. When she did pick up the child, she held him (like a sack) a distance from her, rapidly banging the child on the back while continuing to talk as if the whimpering were not going on. Then, although the crying continued, she put the baby back in the carriage and said, He does this to annoy me when I'm busy."

According to Spitz (1965), what the mother expresses depends not on her conscious or even unconscious relations with the child but rather on her unconscious guilt feelings from the past, provoking anxiety that does not permit her truly to identify with her child. Thus, she avoids the most elementary form of identification: immediate, affective physical contact. The mother in this vignette thought that the child was purposely crying to be "mean," just as her mother had accused her of "behaving mean" when she was young. Arrangements to have the child cared for by a stable and warm person helped the child's physical symptoms to abate and did much to relieve this mother of her constant anxiety.

The Reassuring Voices

Mrs. R's daughter was admitted to the psychiatric ward of a general hospital for the fourth time. Mrs. R's husband had left her for a younger woman a year earlier, and since then her daughter had had four out-of-wedlock pregnancies and had been diagnosed schizophrenic. This was her fourth pregnancy and she was suicidal.

When the mother visited me, she spoke quite logically about how disturbed her daughter was and about how upset her son was to see his sister that way. She did not think her daughter "could make it" if it were not for the help the mother was getting. She would not reveal what this help was. It was private and it would not stop her from coming to see me. Months later, she confided to me that when her daughter had been readmitted to the hospital, the mother began to hear voices. This was reassuring because the voices told her what to do and what to say to her daughter when she visited her on the ward, so everything would be fine. Mrs. R had been brought up very strictly. For her daughter to have gotten pregnant was a "sin" but the voices told her to forgive her daughter. Later in treatment, she reported that the voices reminded her very much of her Aunt Harriet, the family oracle, to whom she always would go as a child because her parents were away from home.

Emotional responses are always appropriate to the patient's inner experience, and it is the therapist's task to identify the thoughts that evoke these emotions.

Guidelines on the Treatment of Schizophrenic Patients

Special countertransference issues arise in therapy with schizophrenics. Most notably, the basic dependence needs of the schizophrenic patient have not been adequately gratified. This is one of the reasons that the symptoms of the schizophrenic are so severe. If the therapist can gratify the patient's needs in a practical and realistic way, the results can be surprisingly positive.

Generally, patients suffering from severe forms of schizophrenia benefit most from learning basic trust and self-acceptance through the therapeutic alliance. As I noted earlier, the schizophrenic patient fears experiencing warm and positive feelings, which, in any case, are sporadic. The therapist should utilize her own optimistic and encouraging approach to generate an affective relationship with the patient.

While the schizophrenic person has a fear of becoming close, he also has a wish to become a part of others in order to make himself feel whole. Establishing and maintaining emotional support is of utmost importance in the therapeutic relationship. It is only when the schizophrenic patient is able to have a satisfying experience with someone who does not encompass and overwhelm her that she can begin to trust in and benefit from the relationship.

Arieti (1979) discovered while working in a state mental hospital that some patients considered hopeless improved enough to be discharged after years of hospitalization. These cases were deemed to be instances of spontaneous recovery. Not satisfied with this explanation, Arieti looked into the matter and found such patients had developed a warm relationship with either an attendant or a nurse.

If the patient is listless and withdrawn, the therapist should attempt to stimulate his interest in the environment. The patient's withdrawal is an attempt to deal with frustration and hopelessness and he needs great encouragement to give up this coping mechanism. While often ambivalent about giving up her isolation and social withdrawal and attempting to cope with life, the schizophrenic also wishes that someone would care enough about her to help her to do so. Withdrawal is also a way to prevent rejection, and the schizophrenic patient may make it clear that he will accept pleasant experiences only on his own terms. The therapist should accept the patient's limitations while providing consistent interest. It is of great importance to follow the lead of the patient in keeping the emotional distance with which the patient feels comfortable.

Even though the schizophrenic patient is often preoccupied with fantasy material, it is best to postpone direct exploration of this until he is better integrated. At the same time, MacKinnon and Michels (1971) suggested that the therapist pay close attention to her own responses to the distorted thinking of the schizophrenic patient. If the therapist has trouble understanding the patient, he might say that he is having difficulty following what the patient is saying. In this way, the therapist can both ascertain whether the patient is able to present material in another way and learn what the patient wishes to communicate. The therapist should also actively assist the schizophrenic patient in defining problems and focusing on issues. She should direct attention to the patient's strengths (as well as pay attention to problems), thereby furnishing positive feedback. Any advance is very significant to these patients, so the therapist should be sure to acknowledge each one.

There is agreement that rage commonly underlies the schizophrenic patient's inhibition. He withdraws from contact with the world for fear that if he expressed himself, he might lose control of his aggressive, destructive impulses.

Group Psychotherapy with Schizophrenic Patients

Group psychotherapy grew out of the awareness that patients with similar medical or psychological problems could benefit from one another, as well as from their respective therapists. The primary aim of group psychotherapy is the facilitation of insight into personal and interpersonal problems and provision of a supportive environment in which patients can develop social skills. Group work with schizophrenics helps patients develop social skills and establish friendships.

Family Therapy in Schizophrenia

Family therapy with schizophrenics focuses on correcting family role relationships and skewed and schismatic family patterns. It has become a popular treatment approach, usually involving patient, parents, and/or spouse; other relatives central in the patient's life may also be included. Family therapy can help family members understand better each other's point of view. This can modify a family's attitude and behavior, which may be related to the development and maintenance of the patient's illness.

The failure of parents to preserve appropriate age and sex boundaries between family members plays a role in the etiology of schizophrenia. Sometimes the parent turns to a child rather than the spouse to gratify emotional needs. In other cases, children are obliged to assume the parenting role. In still other families, communication is disordered. Since researchers have produced the strongest and most consistent evidence for links between patterns of maladaptive family interaction and schizophrenia, it is essential that both individual and family therapy be employed in the treatment of adolescents and young adults (Lidz, 1973).

Lidz (1973) suggested that family pathology is often extensive and forms a pathogenic environment for the patient. Therefore, it is usually unwise for the patient to return to this environment. Although making alternate living arrangements usually requires considerable work with the parents and the patient, the outcome of treatment may depend on taking this step.

Pharmacotherapy and Electroshock in Schizophrenia

Drug therapy has replaced insulin coma and psychosurgery in schizophrenia because it was found to be more effective, safer, and more economical (Fink, 1979). The tranquilizing drugs have proved valuable in the treatment of schizophrenia. They alleviate fearfulness and the more dramatic symptoms and enable patients to think more clearly and to function more appropriately. However, most authorities agree that the tranquilizing drugs should be supplemented by other forms of treatment (see Chapter 2 on research in this area).

Popular in the 1940s and 1950s, insulin shock therapy is no longer used in schizophrenia, but electroconvulsive treatment (ECT) is still occasionally administered. While ECT may give more rapid results than the neuroleptics and is considered the treatment of choice for extreme catatonic stupor, the results are temporary and maintenance is more difficult than with antipsychotic medication (Lehrman, 1975). The principal complications of ECT are brain damage, memory impairment, spontaneous seizures and death (Fink, 1979).

Hospitalization and Other Treatment Settings in Schizophrenia

The large and impersonal institutions that house the mentally ill and offer long-term hospitalization are now believed to be antitherapeutic: staffing tends to be inadequate and the patient has little contact with family or significant others, both of which increases her isolation and dependence on a fantasy world.

Chronically mentally ill persons have, as a group, been profoundly affected by deinstitutionalization, despite the need of this population for institutional care. Treatment and care are now available primarily through community mental health programs; hospital care is available to few, and in few communities is the amount of care adequate. Therefore, the chronically ill schizophrenic patient often will need to use hospital emergency rooms and walk-in clinics, as well as crisis intervention services run by family agencies to deal with episodic crises in their lives. Chronically mentally ill patients must have round-the-clock access to psychiatric services, both inpatient and outpatient. They also need referrals for vocational rehabilitation, part-time jobs and other employment opportunities, and government provided financial support. Social workers can offer counseling, make referrals, and otherwise give support to the chronically mentally ill.

Anthony and associates (1972) found that transitional living arrangements (halfway houses and daycare centers) are effective in reducing recidivism as long as the patient remains a member of the facility. Many schizophrenics can benefit from partial hospitalization in either day or night centers. Similarly, short-term care in well-staffed facilities can provide a protective environment for the troubled patient and respite for the family.

Deinstitutionalization has been severely criticized because many patients have been discharged into the community without careful planning and adequate resources. They do not eat well and often lack proper clothing. Community residents tend to be hostile to these people: they fear for their own safety and are uncomfortable having mentally ill people in their neighborhood. Professional literature of the 1970s helped highlight the numerous deficits existing in community care systems and documented the failure of community health programs to give adequate care and benefits to severely mentally ill persons.

The mental hospital or the psychiatric unit of a general hospital can be a temporary protective environment in which the patient is helped through the initial period of acute disturbance. He can then be transferred to an alternate facility in the community. However, long-term treatment hospitalization may offer the best therapeutic results in some cases and should be available.

After the patient has emerged from her initial crisis, she will need help adjusting to life in the community. Occupational therapy, vocational counseling, job training, art therapy, and social clubs are appropriate supportive programs. Community centered treatment of schizophrenic patients can provide them with the social and job skills required to lead productive and meaningful lives outside the hospital.

Meeting the Social and Psychological Needs of the Schizophrenic Person

Social work practitioners are called upon to identity high-risk populations and to offer preventive, as well as therapeutic and palliative, services. The social worker participates as part of the hospital therapeutic team in treatment and planning for the psychiatrically ill patient and is responsible for treatment and planning in outpatient and community care facilities. Schizophrenic patients require ongoing supportive help to remain in the community, and their families need help adjusting to this disorder. Social workers can develop family and patient self-help groups, set up supervised residences and sheltered workshops, and make necessary referrals.

The administrative structure of community mental health services is unwieldly and does not facilitate care of the chronic patient: responsibility for such patients is divided among state, county, and voluntary agencies. Social workers can help coordinate community facilities and evaluate both the need for care and the agencies' ability and willingness to meet the community's identified mental health needs. By initiating joint planning on the part of hospitals, public health facilities, welfare agencies, and voluntary agencies, social workers can make efficient the now fragmented mental health service system, much to the benefit of the chronically mentally ill.

Equally important, we must identify vulnerable persons and get them into treatment before they develop an illness that overwhelms both the family and the patient. To this end, it is necessary to develop new resources, organize natural helping networks, and establish linkages between people and these resources. It is also necessary to help people overcome their resistance to utilizing these resources.

Resistance to using mental health facilities and related services has several causes. First, mental illness is regarded with fear or is poorly understood by the public. To change the popular view of mental illness requires large-scale education programs that focus on symptom recognition and the value of obtaining treatment early. In addition, community leaders should be recruited to help educate their neighbors in terms meaningful to the community. Groups that underutilize health care services may be different culturally or linguistically from mental health workers and may therefore refrain from seeking help. Community leaders can do much to reverse this trend. Second, mental health facilities often are insensitive to the values, goals, and attitudes of the community they serve (e.g., by not employing bilingual workers in neighborhoods in which English is not the primary language); this discourages community utilization and results in inferior diagnosis and treatment (e.g., symptoms may be incomprehensible to a therapist unfamiliar with the cultural values of a patient). Again, community leaders can play a part here by alerting service agencies to community needs and concerns. Third, communities often lack an adequate range of services. Thus, patients who need only daycare may go untreated rather than make use of hospital inpatient facilities. Crisis intervention, partial hospitalization, and long-term care must be made available, along with the spectrum of patient and family support services.

Conclusion

Schizophrenia can be neither prevented nor cured. Nevertheless, substantial numbers of patients recover sufficiently to lead rewarding and functional lives in the community. Schizophrenics are treatable by a combination of medication, therapy, and other modalities. However, it is critical to identify the person in psychological trouble before personality change, withdrawal from friends and relatives, and interpersonal difficulties become pronounced. Effective treatment cannot be provided if necessary resources do not exist or remain underutilized by various social and ethnic groups. Social workers have an invaluable role to play in rectifying this situation.

References

American Psychiatric Association: *Diagnostic and Statistical Manual of Mental Disorders*, ed 3. Washington, DC, American Psychiatric Association, 1980.

Anthony WA, Buell GJ, Sharratt S, et al: The efficacy of psychiatric rehabilitation. *Psychol Bull* 1972; 78:447–456.

Arieti S: *Interpretation of Schizophrenia*, ed 2. New York, Basic Books, 1974.

Arieti S: From schizophrenia to creativity. *Am J Psychother* 1979; 33:83–84. (a)

Arieti S: *Understanding and Helping the Schizophrenic: A Guide for Family and Friends.* New York, Basic Books, 1979.(b)

Arlow J, Brenner C: *Psychoanalytic Concepts and the Structural Theory.* New York, International Universities Press, 1964.

Aronson G: Defense and deficit models in schizophrenia. Read before the Fall Meeting, American Psychiatric Association, 1972, New York City.

Barrett J, Kuriansky J, Gurland B: Community tenure following emergency discharge. *Am J Psychiatry* 1972; 128:958–964.

Bateson G (ed): *Perceval's Narrative: A Patient's Account of his Psychosis.* New York, Morrow, 1974.

Bateson G, Jackson D, Haley J, Weakland J: Toward a theory of schizophrenia. *Behav Sci* 1956; 1:251–264.

Becker HS: *Outsiders: Studies in the Sociology of Deviance.* New York, Free Press, 1963.

Bleuler E: *Dementia Praecox, or the Group of Schizophrenias.* New York, International Universities Press, 1950.

Bockhaven S: Moral treatment in American psychiatry. *J Nerv Ment Dis* 1956; 124: 167–194.

Bowen M: A family concept of schizophrenia, in Jackson DD (ed): *The Etiology of Schizophrenia.* New York, Basic Books, 1960, pp 346–372.

Boyer LG, Giovacchini PL: *Psychoanalytic Treatment of Schizophrenic, Borderline, and Characterological Disorders.* New York, Aronson, 1980.

Brody MW: *Observations on Direct Analysis.* New York, Vantage, 1959.

Cameron N: *Personality Development and Psychotherapy.* Boston, Houghton Mifflin, 1963.

Cancro R: The genetic studies of the schizophrenic syndrome: a review of their clinical implications in disorders of the schizophrenic syndrome, in Bellak L (ed): New York, Basic Books, 1979, pp 136–149.

Cancro R (ed): *Annual Review of the Schizophrenic Syndrome.* New York, Brunner/Mazel, 1972, vol 1.

Chiland C (ed): *Long-term Treatment of Psychotic States.* New York, Brunner/Mazel, 1977.

Childs-Gowell E: *Reparenting Schizophrenic: The Cathexis Experience.* North Quincy, Christopher Publishing, 1979.

Dohrenwend BP, and Dohrenwend BS: Sociocultural and social-psychological factors in the genesis of Mental Disorders. *Journal of Health and Social Behaviour,* 1975; 16 (4): 365–392.

Dunham HW: Social structures and mental disorders: a review of epidemiological knowledge. *Milbank Mem Fund Q* 1961; 39:259–311.

Dunham HW: *Community and Schizophrenia: An Epidemiological Analysis.* Detroit, Wayne State University Press, 1965.

FAIRBAIRN WD: *Psychoanalytic Studies of the Personality*. London, Routledge, 1952.

FEDERN P: The analysis of psychotics. *Int J Psychoanal* 1933; 15:209–215.

FINE R: *A History of Psychoanalysis*. New York, Columbia University Press, 1979.

FINK M: EST and other somatic therapies of schizophrenia, in Bellak L (ed): *The Disorders of the Schizophrenic Syndrome*. New York, Basic Books, 1978, pp 353–363.

FREEMAN H, SIMMONS O: *The Mental Patient Comes Home*. New York, Wiley, 1963.

FREEMAN T, McGHIE H, CAMERON J: *Chronic Schizophrenia*. New York, International Universities Press, 1964.

FREUD S: Mourning and melancholia, in London, Hogarth, 1961, vol 17, pp 243–258. (a)

FREUD S: *The Standard Edition of the Complete Psychological Works of Sigmund Freud*, Strachey J (ed). London, Hogarth, 1961, vol 14. (b)

FREUD S: The Standard Edition. The Ego and The Id and Other Works (1923–1925), Strachey J (ed). London, Hogarth, 1961, vol 19. (c)

FREUD S: *The Standard Edition of the Complete Psychological Works of Sigmund Freud*, Strachey J (ed). London, Hogarth, 1961, vol 20. (d)

FROMM-REICHMAN F: Notes of the development of treatment of schizophrenics by psychoanalytic psychotherapy. *Psychiatry* 1948; 11:263–273.

FROMM-REICHMAN F: Transference problems in schizophrenia, in *Psychoanalysis and Psychotherapy; Selected Papers*. Chicago, University of Chicago Press, 1959.

GOFFMAN E: *Asylums*. New York, Doubleday, 1961.

GRINKER R: Changing styles in psychosis and borderline states. *Am J Psychiatry* 1973; 130:151–152.

GRINSPOON L, EWALT JR, SHADER RI: *Schizophrenia: Pharmacotherapy and Psychotherapy*. Baltimore, Williams & Wilkins, 1972.

GUNDERSON JG: The relatedness of borderline and schizophrenic disorders. *Schizophr Bull* 1979; 5: 17–22.

GUNDERSON JG, MOSHER LR: *Psychotherapy of Schizophrenia*. New York, Aronson, 1975.

HEATH RG, KRUPP IM: Schizophrenia as a specific biologic disease. *Am J Psychiatry* 1968; 124:1019–1024.

HOCH PH, POLITAN P: Pseudoneurotic forms of schizophrenia. Psych. Q 1949; 23:248–276.

HOLLINGSHEAD AG, REDLICH FC: *Social Class and Mental Illness*. New York, Wiley, 1958.

JACKSON DO and WEAKLAND JH: Schizophrenic symptoms and family interaction. *Archives of General Psychiatry*, 1959; 1:618–621.

KALLMAN FG: *The Genetics of Schizophrenia*. Locust Valley, Augustin, 1938.

KALLMAN FG: The genetic theory of schizophrenia. *Am J Psychiatry* 1946; 103: 309–322.

KARON BP, VANDENBOS GR: *Psychotherapy of Schizophrenia: The Treatment of Choice*. New York, Aronson, 1981.

KASANIN JS (ed): *Language and Thought in Schizophrenia*. New York, Norton, 1964.

KEITH SJ, GUNDERSON JG, REIFMAN A, et al: Special report: schizophrenia. *Schizophr Bull* 1976; 2:510-565.

KESSLER S: Special report: schizophrenia. *Schizophr Bull* 1980; 6:14-26.

KETY SS: Biochemical hypothesis and studies, in Bellak L, Loeb L (eds): *The Schizophrenic Syndrome*. New York, Grune & Stratton, 1969, pp 155-171.

KLEIN M: Notes on some schizoid mechanisms. *J Psychoanal* 1946; 27:99-110.

KRAEPLIN E: Dementia praecox and paraphrenia, in Robertson GM (ed). New York, Krieger, 1971, pp 74-86.

KRAFFT-EBING R: *Psychopathia Sexualis*. New York, Pioneer, 1946.

KRINGLEN E: An epidemiological-clinical twin study of schizophrenia, in Rosenthal D, Kety S (eds): *The Transmission of Schizophrenia*. Oxford, Pergamon, 1968, pp 49-65.

LAING RD: *The Divided Self*. London, Tavistock, 1960.

LANGFELDT G: Diagnosis and prognosis of schizophrenia. *Proc R Soc Med* 1960; 53: 1047-1052.

LEHRMAN HE: Psychopharmacological treatment of schizophrenia. *Schizophr Bull* 1975; 13:27-45.

LEIGHTON S: *My Name is Legion*. New York, Basic Books, 1957.

LIDZ T: *The Origin and Treatment of Schizophrenic Disorders*. New York, Basic Books, 1973.

LIDZ T: Reply to Kety et al. *Schizophr Bull* 1977; 3:522-526.

LIDZ T, FLECK S, CORNELISON AR: *Schizophrenia and the Family*. New York, International Universities Press, 1965.

MACKINNON RA, MICHELS R: *The Psychiatric Interview in Clinical Practice*. Philadelphia, Saunders, 1971.

MAGERO PA (ed): *The Cultural Context of Madness*. New York, Pergamon, 1976.

MAHLER MS: *On Human Symbiosis and the Vicissitudes of Individuation: Infantile Psychosis*. New York, International Universities Press, 1968, vol 1.

MAY PA: *Treatment of Schizophrenia: A Comparative Study of Five Treatment Methods*. New York, Science House, 1968.

MENNINGER K: *The Vital Balance*. New York, Viking, 1963.

MILLER SM, MISHLER EG: Social class, mental illness, and American psychiatry: an expository review. *Milbank Mem Fund Q* 1959; 37:174-199.

MORRIS R (ed): *Encyclopedia of Social Work*. New York, National Association of Social Workers 1971.

MUSSEN PH, CONGER J, KAGEN J: *Child Development and Personality*. New York, Harper, 1963.

MYERS JK, LINDENTHAL JJ, PEPPER MP: Social class, life events, and psychiatric symptoms: a longitudinal study. Read before the Conference on Stressful Life Events, New York, June, 1973.

PAUL GL, LENTZ RJ: *Psychosocial Treatment of Chronic Mental Patients: Milieu versus Social Learning Programs*. Cambridge, Harvard Universities press, 1977.

RADO S: Theory and therapy: the theory of schizotypal behavior, in *Psychoanalysis of Behavior*. New York, Grune & Stratton, 1962, vol 2, pp 127-140.

ROGERS CR, GENDLIN ET, KIESLER DJ, et al: *The Therapeutic Relationship and Its Impact: A Study of Psychotherapy with Schizophrenics.* Madison, University of Wisconsin Press, 1967.

ROMAN PM, TRICE HM: *Schizophrenia and the Poor.* Ithaca, New York, New York State School of Industrial and Labor Relations, 1967.

ROSEN J: *Direct Analysis.* New York, Grune & Stratton, 1953.

ROSENTHAL D: Genetics of Schizophrenia, in Arieti S, Body E (eds): *American Handbook of Psychiatry,* ed 2. New York, Basic Books, 1974, vol 3, pp 588–600.

ROSENTHAL D: Searches for the mode of genetic transmission in schizophrenia: reflections and loose ends. *Schizophr Bull* 1977; 3:268–276.

ROSENTHAL P, WENDER PH, KETY SS, et al: Parent–child relationships and psychopathological disorder in the child. *Arch Gen Psychiatry* 1975; 32:466–476.

SCHEFF TJ: *Being Mentally Ill: A Sociological Theory.* Chicago, Aldine, 1966.

SCHNEIDER K: *Clinical Psychopathology.* New York, Grune & Stratton, 1959.

SCHUR EM: *Crimes without Victims.* Englewood Cliffs, Prentice-Hall, 1965.

SEARLES HR: *Collected Papers in Schizophrenia and Other Related Subjects.* New York, International Universities Press, 1965.

SEARS RR: *Survey of Objective Studies of Psychoanalytic Concepts.* New York, Social Science Research Council, 1943.

SEMROD E: A clinical formulation of the psychoses, in *Teaching Psychotherapy of Psychotic Patients.* Van Busherk D (ed): New York, Grune & Stratton, 1969, pp 5–17.

SHIELDS J: "Summary of genetic evidence," in Rosenthal D, Kety S (eds): *The Transmission of Schizophrenia.* Oxford, Pergamon, 1968, pp 95–129.

SIMOPOULOS RM, PINTO A, UHLENHUTH EH: Dyphenylhydantoin effectiveness in the treatment of chronic schizophrenia. *Arch Gen Psychiatry* 1974; 30:106–111.

SLATER E: "A review of earlier evidence on genetic factors in schizophrenia," in Rosenthal D, Kety S (eds): *The Transmission of Schizophrenia.* Oxford, Pergamon, 1968, pp 15–27.

SMOLAR T: *Mother's Seeking Help: Stress and Demographic Variables as Related to Mother's Referral of Children in Need of Treatment,* thesis. Columbia University, New York, 1976.

SPITZ RA: *The First Year of Life: A Psychoanalytic Study of Normal and Deviant Development of Object Relations.* New York, International Universities Press, 1965.

SULLIVAN HS: Environmental factors in the etiology and course in understanding treatment of schizophrenia. *Med J Rec* 1931; 133:19–22.

SULLIVAN HS: *Schizophrenia as a Human Process.* New York, Norton, 1962.

SZASZ TS: *The Myth of Mental Illness.* New York, Hoeber, 1961.

TIENARI P: Schizophrenia in monozygotic male twins, in Rosenthal D, Kety S (eds): *The Transmission of Schizophrenia.* Oxford, Pergamon, 1968, pp 27–37.

TAUBE CA, REDIK RW: *Provisional Data and Patient Care Episodes in Mental Health Facilities: Statistical Note 127,* US Dept of Health, Education, and Welfare publication no. (ADM) 76-158. Rockville, National Institute of Mental Health, 1976.

TURNS DM: The epidemiology of schizophrenia, in Denber HC (ed): *Schizophrenia: Theory, Diagnosis, and Treatment.* New York, Dekker, 1978.

WENDER P, ROSENTHAL D, KETY SA: Psychiatric assessment of adoptive parents, in Rosenthal D, Kety S (eds): *The Transmission of Schizophrenia.* Oxford, Pergamon, 1968, pp 235–251.

WEXLER M: The structural problem in schizophrenia: the role of the internal object. *Int J Psychiatry* 1951; 32:157–166.

WOLBERG LR: *The Technique of Psychotherapy.* New York, Grune & Stratton, 1954.

WYNNE LC: Communication disorders and the quest for relatedness in the families of schizophrenics. *Am J Psychoanal* 1970; 30:100–114.

WYNNE LC, RYCKOFF I, DAY J, HIRSH S: Pseudomutuality in family relations of schizophrenics. *Psychiatry* 1958; 21:205–220.

WYNNE LC, SINGER MT: Thought disorder and family relations of schizophrenics: a research strategy. *Arch Gen Psychiatry* 1963; 9:199–206.

ZILBOORG G: *A History of Medical Psychology.* New York, Norton, 1941.

5

Affective Disorders

MARY KAY O'NEIL

Depression is the most common form of adult psychopathology confronting mental health professionals. Since antiquity, depression has been recognized as a painful affective state associated with physical, psychological, and social distress. The extent of the problem is currently reflected in the increasing rate of depression among young adults, the spiraling number of suicide attempts, and the upsurge in suicides and accidental deaths, as well as in the recognition that depression is a potential threat at every age and phase of development. It is estimated that more than 12% of adults will at some point become sufficiently depressed to require treatment and 15–30% will suffer from less severe but nevertheless disabling symptoms; however, only 10–25% of people with depressive symptoms seek professional help for this disorder (Klerman, 1975, 1978). Thus, the majority of clinically depressed individuals, for a variety of reasons such as social and/or financial circumstances, psychological resistances, and lack of appropriate treatment resources, fail to receive needed help. These facts about depression provide a challenge to the social work practitioner.

I wish to acknowledge with thanks the help of Frederick Lowy, M.D. who provided the author with psychiatric consultation and gave critical review of this chapter.

It is important, therefore, for social workers to be able to recognize depression, especially in its early stages or when the mood disturbance is masked by other symptoms. It is also important, in the light of recent clinical and research developments, for social workers to identify those depressed persons who can be helped by modern drug treatments and who ought to be referred for psychiatric assessment. Social work practitioners will find it easier to recognize depression, make appropriate referrals, and mobilize psychosocial factors in treatment if they are familiar with the epidemiology, etiology, psychopathology, and treatment of depression.

This chapter surveys these topics, paying special attention to advances during the past two decades that have led to changes in the classification, diagnosis, and treatment of depression. These advances, especially in the area of psychosocial factors, have major implications for the social worker confronted with depressed clients.

The Nature of Depression

Use of the Term "Depression"

"Depression" is a term used in everyday language to connote a well-known dysphoric feeling state. In the medical-psychiatric literature, the word "depression" is used to refer to a mood, a symptom, or a syndrome. A "depressed mood"—the phenomenon of feeling blue, sad, unhappy in response to the difficulties and disappointments of everyday life—is experienced by all people at some point. "Depression as a symptom" is usually more intense, prolonged, varied, or inappropriate to the situation than the common dysphoric mood state. Depressive symptoms can occur in affective disorders, as well as in most other psychiatric and some medical disorders, or even without a concomitant diagnosable disorder. In contrast, a "depressive syndrome" is a cluster of symptoms and behavioral disturbances that meets criteria for a psychiatric diagnosis of one of the subtypes of clinical depression, currently referred to as "affective disorders."

Features of Depression

The signs and symptoms of a depressive syndrome include:

dysphoric mood: feeling sad, unhappy, blue, despondent; unable to enjoy life; sometimes showing irritability, anxiety, intense worry, or fear

cognitive disturbance: low self-esteem; ideas of helplessness, hope-lessness, worthlessness, failure, guilt, self-blame, at times to the point of delusional thinking; suicidal ideation, which may lead to suicide attempts (see Chapter 6); desire to be dead or recurrent thoughts about death; indecisiveness and inability to concentrate
behavioral disturbance: psychomotor retardation or agitation
disturbance in social functioning: loss of interest or pleasure in social-izing or usual activities; impaired capacity to perform work related and other tasks
disturbance in physiological functioning: loss of appetite and im-paired gastrointestinal function; menstrual disturbance or even amenorrhea; insomnia or hypersomnia; sexual disturbance, possi-bly including impotence

Classification of Depression

In recent years, several new diagnostic classifications have been intro-duced and the area is in a state of flux. DSM III (American Psychiatric As-sociation, 1980) classifies depression as shown in Table 5–1. This is likely to be the most frequently used classification for some time, at least in North America. The reason for all the activity in this area and the reason

Table 5–1 DSM III Classification of Affective Disorders

Major affective disorders
    Bipolar disorder
        Manic
        Depressed
        Mixed

    Major depression
        Single episode
        Recurrent

Other specific affective disorders
    Cyclothymic disorder
    Dysthymic disorder (or depressive neurosis)

Atypical affective disorders
    Atypical bipolar disorder
    Atypical depression

Source: American Psychiatric Association, *Diagnostic and Statistical Manual of Mental Disorders*, ed. 3 (Washington, D.C.: American Psychiatric Association, 1980), pp. 17–18.

why mental health workers need to pay attention to the subdivisions of depression is that some depressed patients (but not others) have been found consistently to respond favorably to somatic treatment—antidepressant drugs, lithium, and electroconvulsive therapy (ECT).

The symptoms of, and diagnostic criteria for, the various types of affective disorders are reviewed in the standard psychiatric textbooks (e.g., Freedman et al., 1974) and in DSM III. Essentially, the subtypes of depression are distinguished by the specific symptoms of mania and depression, as well as by the number, intensity, and duration of symptoms. For example, the DSM III diagnostic criteria for "major depressive episode" include prominent and persistent dysphoric mood and at least four symptoms of depression that have been present nearly every day for at least two weeks. In contrast, the diagnostic criteria for "dysthymic disorder" require that the person has been bothered most or all of the time for at least a two-year period by symptoms characteristic of the depressive syndrome but not of sufficient severity and duration to meet the criteria for a major depressive episode; there must be relatively persistent manifestations of the depressive syndrome, which may be separated by periods of normal mood lasting a few days to a few weeks, but no more than a few months at a time; finally, the person must exhibit prominent depressed mood during the depressive periods and at least three of the nonpsychotic symptoms of depression.

Epidemiology of Depression

Current Rates of Depression

Current epidemiological studies of affective disorders document the extent of the problem of depression. Measurement of these disorders has become more standardized, resulting in more reliable rates for the general population and for subgroups defined by sociodemographic factors such as age, sex, and social class.

The basic epidemiological technical terms are "incidence" (number of new cases per year); "point prevalence" (number of cases measured at one point in time); "period prevalence" (total cases in a specified period of time, e.g., one year—hence "annual prevalence"); and "lifetime expectance," or "morbid risk" (an individual's lifetime risk of having a first episode of illness). A recent review of English-language epidemiological studies of affective disorders summarized the current rates for the general population (Boyd & Weissman, 1981):

1. point prevalence of depressive symptoms ranges between 9% and 20%

2. annual incidence of bipolar disorder* is 0.009–.015% for men and 0.007–.03% for women; lifetime risk is less than 1% for both females and males
3. point prevalence of other nonbipolar depression is 3% for men and 4–9% for women; lifetime risk is 8–12% for men and 20–26% for women*

In the next few years, extensive epidemiological data, based on standardized diagnostic interviews, are expected to be available on depression and other psychiatric disorders from the National Institute of Mental Health (Hirschfeld & Cross, 1982).

Demographic Factors

Correlations between demographic factors and the occurrence of depression are important because they help identify subgroups at risk.

Sex

The most important demographic finding is the greater prevalence of depressive disorders among women: when all depressive disorders are considered, there is a fairly consistent female-to-male ratio of 2:1 (Weissman & Klerman, 1977b). The preponderance of women among depressed patients seems to be even higher for less severe depression (Klerman, 1978) and is found in all but two age groups: young adult university students (Golin & Hartz, 1979; Hammen & Padesky, 1977; O'Neil et al., 1982b; Parker, 1979; Radloff, 1980) and the aged (Wasylenki, 1980). It has been suggested that men and women in these two groups are equally likely to be depressed because there is less sex role differentiation among the aged and among students.

Age

The rarer and more serious first manic episode of bipolar disorder usually occurs before age 30; whereas major depression may begin at any age and the age of onset is fairly evenly distributed throughout adult life. Other affective disorders (cyclothymic disorder and dysthymic disorder) usually begin early in adult life. Although there is some controversy as to whether or not young children suffer from diagnosable depression, diag-

*Bipolar is the term used to describe the former category of manic-depressive illness, that is, depression followed quickly by a state of excitation or mania.

nosable affective disorders have a high prevalence at each stage of the life cycle from adolescence to old age. All age groups are vulnerable to some type of depressive difficulty.

Social Class and Marital Status

Social class, occupation, and education are related to psychiatric illnesses and sometimes determine their treatment. Although there is some tendency for the incidence of affective disorders to be slightly higher in higher social strata, this trend is neither strong nor constant (Klerman, 1978). In fact, depression cuts across all strata of society. The relationship between marital status and the spectrum of depressive illnesses is not clear. There is some disputed evidence that married women tend more toward depression than do single women; single men more than single women; and single men slightly more than married men. The separated, divorced, and widowed have slightly higher rates in both sexes (Radloff, 1980).

Help-seeking and Service Use

Depressed women are twice as likely as men to seek and receive help (Kessler et al., 1981).

Etiology of Depression

Biological Factors in Depression

Genetic factors in the etiology of depression were suspected for a long time, but the evidence was inconclusive until 10–20 years ago. Greater use of standardized interviewing techniques and operationally defined diagnostic categories has made it clear that in at least two subgroups of depression—bipolar disorder and the major (unipolar) depressions—there is a strong family pattern, along with higher concordance in monozygotic than in dizygotic twins and more depression in the biological than in the adoptive parents of depressed patients who were adopted shortly after birth (Nurnberger & Gershon, 1982). Recently, Weitkamp and associates (1981) reported on a deficit in a specific chromosome in depressed patients with a strong family history of bipolar disease.

Genetic factors likely operate through biochemical pathways, although the biochemical lesion has not yet been identified. A severely depressed patient has many bodily changes, but it is not clear which might play a role in the production of the depression and which are the result of the depression. At present, the evidence suggests abnormalities in the level of biogenic amines, which are a class of neurotransmitters (substances produced at the junction of nerve cells in the central nervous system that permit messages to pass from one nerve cell to another) (see Chapter 2). The principal neurotransmitters whose metabolism may be disturbed in depression are norepinephrine, serotonin, dopamine, and acetylcholine.

There is also evidence that a different biological system, the adreno-cortical steroid hormones under the control of the hypothalamus and the pituitary gland in the brain, is disturbed in depression.

Extensive investigation of these and other factors is presently under way, and it seems likely that in the next decade the biological factors that contribute to some types of depression will be identified. Already there are biological tests that promise to distinguish reliably bipolar and major depressions from neurotic characterological depressions.

Social Factors in Depression

In the past decade, there has been a resurgence of interest in the psycho-social factors related to depression. Particular attention has been paid to early loss of a parent or other nurturing person, family history of psychiatric illness (especially the effect of being raised by an emotionally ill parent or with an emotionally disturbed sibling), recent and chronic stressful life events, and presence or absence of social support.

Early Loss of a Significant Other

A relationship between the loss of a nurturing person early in life (childhood through early adolescence) and the subsequent development of depression was first postulated many years ago. This relationship has been supported by a vast clinical literature (for a review see Furman, 1974) and by some population studies. In a recent review, Lloyd (1980a & b) reported that the majority of studies found a higher incidence of early loss among depressed as compared with nondepressed controls. However, Crook and Eliot (1980), in a similar review, came to a different conclusion: "There is no sound base of empirical data to support the theorized relationship between parental death during childhood and adult depression." Most recently, Kennard and Britchnell (1982) concluded that although they had found a link between a poor relationship with mother and subsequent psychopathology, this link was independent of maternal loss. The research evidence, then, remains controversial.

There is also some evidence linking early loss of a parent by death to severity of depression (Brown & Harris, 1978; Brown et al., 1977) and to attempted suicide later in life (Adam et al., 1982). However, other investigators have failed to find an association between loss of a parent in childhood, either by death or by separation, and adult depression (O'Neil-Lowy, 1983; Tennant et al., 1980). Although these findings are forcing a reassessment of the hypothesized loss–depression relationship, the experience of loss in childhood does, of course, emerge as an important focus in the treatment of some depressed people.

There are several clinically relevant points here. First, it is reassuring to know that early loss does not inevitably lead to depression and that many people (even as children) have a remarkable capacity to handle major loss. In fact, it is well recognized that the circumstances surrounding the loss (quality of the lost parenting, type and handling of the loss, capacity and opportunity to mourn, presence and quality of substitute parenting) are major determinants of later psychological problems, including depression. Second, poor, neglectful parenting may be a greater factor in depression than is actual loss by death or separation, provided that the latter is dealt with sensitively. Third, even if loss does not necessarily predict later depression, the history of loss or recent loss in a particular depressed person may be highly relevant clinically and often constitutes an important focus of treatment.

Family History of Psychiatric Illness

There is much less inconsistency in the evidence for a relationship between family history of psychiatric illness and depression; in fact, the link has been recognized since the nineteenth century. Recent family studies and the identification of some biological indicators make it seem likely that recurrent major depression has a primarily biological basis (Nurnberger & Gershon, 1982).

For the bipolar affective disorders, there is reasonably good evidence of a genetic component. The evidence for the genetic transmission of recurrent major depression is not as strong (Kidd & Weissman, 1976), but some studies have confirmed that a family history of either depression or alcoholism increases the risk for unipolar disorder (Winokur, 1979; Winokur & Morrison, 1973). There is less evidence for a strong genetic component in chronic, or so-called characterological, depression. Rosenthal and colleagues (1981) found that when a group of characterological depressions were compared with primary unipolar controls there was a "significantly lower incidence of familial depressions, but higher frequencies of loss of a parent in childhood, familial alcoholism and parental assortative mating" (p. 183). They commented that "nature and nurture are both implicated in the stormy childhoods and adult lifestyles" of people suffering from characterological depression. Parker and colleagues (1979; Parker & Brown, 1979) also provided evidence that concurs with the findings of Rosenthal and associates.

It is increasingly evident from clinical studies that experiential, as well as genetic, factors contribute to the increased family incidence of psychiatric disorders (e.g., Bowlby, 1978; Winnicott, 1969). Experimental studies relating the psychosocial aspects of family history to depression have lagged behind, but research published in the past decade supports the clinical literature. For example, Rutter (1973) has proposed that vulnerability to psychiatric disorder in children raised by parents (especially mothers) who are emotionally disturbed is increased in several ways. These children are exposed to a distressing and disruptive home life, to the loss of adequate parenting, and to models of depressive and/or otherwise disturbed behavior. This early experience itself and the way in which the family coped with the ill member may well influence how the person deals with an episode of depression in later life.

A family history of psychiatrc illness (especially affective disorders) has both diagnostic and treatment implications. In this respect, social workers require an understanding of the genetic and experiential aspects of having had an ill parent or sibling in the family (Jackson, 1965).

Stressful Life Events

A great deal of attention has been paid to the role of stressful life events in the occurrence of depression. A recent review reported that, with few exceptions, the findings support the hypothesis that depressed subjects experience more stressful life events prior to the onset of the disorder than do normal persons (Lloyd, 1980b). Some studies have focused on the presumed causative role of life events in depression. Brown and Harris (1978), for example, placed particular emphasis on understanding the meaning of an event for the individual, given the person's current life circumstances, and pointed out the importance of identifying both chronic and recent life stresses. Other authors are beginning to identify certain life events that are high-risk factors in certain groups. For example, O'Neil-Lowy (1983) found that recent loss of parents and of close relationships, financial problems, and changes in academic or residential situation are specific events that are associated with depression in university students. While there is controversy regarding the relationship between early loss and depression, there is no question that recent loss is a risk factor for all age groups. Even though social workers have always been aware of the contribution of life stresses and strains to problems of functioning—and probably to a greater extent than other mental health professionals—these recent findings are particularly helpful in drawing attention to the effect of certain events in specific depressed populations.

Social Support

Social support has been identified consistently as an important variable in modifying the impact of life events and favorably influencing the risk for depression. For instance, Cobb (1976) reviewed a number of studies supplying evidence that social support is a moderator of life stress. He defined "internal and external social support" as those circumstances that lead the subject to believe that she is cared for and loved, is esteemed and valued, and belongs to a network of communication and mutual obligation. Cobb stated:

> The conclusion that supportive interactions among people are important is hardly new. What is new is the assembling of evidence that adequate social support can protect people in crises from a wide variety of pathological states; from low birth weight to death, from arthritis through tuberculosis to depression, alcoholism and other psychiatric illness. Furthermore, social support can reduce the amount of medication required, accelerate recovery and facilitate compliance with prescribed medical regimes. (p. 310)

Brown and Harris (1978) and O'Neil-Lowy (1983) demonstrated the positive influence of at least one confidant. Other investigators have examined the role of social networks (Meuller, 1980) and of social functioning (Weissman & Paykel, 1974) in the occurrence and course of psychiatric disorders, including depression. Henderson and associates (1981) concluded that it is not the availability but the adequacy of close affectional ties in the presence of distressing experiences that provides a buffer against emotional problems. Aneshensel and Stone (1982) recently provided evidence that "social support instead of merely protecting an individual against stress, may itself be important in ameliorating depressive symptoms" (p. 1392). That is, the absence of social support can directly cause depressive symptoms even in the absence of stressful life events. Social workers have a special contribution to make in the area of understanding and improving social support in a depressed person's life.

Psychodynamic and Personality Factors in Depression

Since the early works of Freud (1896, 1917) and Abraham (1911), psychoanalysts have been interested in the dynamic factors that play a role in episodes of depression. Psychoanalytic views have passed through several distinct phases, reflecting both clinical experience in the analysis and psychotherapy of depressed patients and the evolution of psychoanalytic theory. This development has been well described by Mendelson (1974).

Although there is no unitary psychoanalytic theory of depression, there is consensus among psychoanalysts on some important points.

1. Predisposition to depression is established in infancy and early childhood and results from the interplay between biological vulnerability and disturbances in parent–child interactions. The young child's sense of security—of being loved and wanted—can be threatened by parental rejection (influenced in part by the behavior of the child), leading to early mourning, which may be the prototype of later reactions to loss. The severe childhood depressions that result from separation from love objects are examples of this interrelationship (Bowlby, 1969, 1978, 1980; Spitz, 1946).

2. Although depression can occur in all people, certain personality types seem more prone to serious or recurrent depressions:

   a. oral-dependent personalities, who need a constant infusion of "external narcissistic supplies" to retain a sense of well-being (recognition, approval, admiration, demonstrations of love)
   b. obsessional, conscience-ridden personalities, who constantly struggle to control bottled-up aggressive impulses, which are readily turned against the self, leading to guilt, self-hate, and self-destructive fantasies
   c. cyclothymic personalities, who vacillate between periods of elation and despondence, which states are subclinical episodes of mania and depression

3. Central to the experience of depression is the psychic pain that results from disturbances in the sense of well-being (Sandler & Joffe, 1965) and self-esteem (Jacobson, 1971). Such disturbances can be provoked, especially in vulnerable people, by a variety of life events, of which losses are the most frequent. When defenses intended to protect against this pain fail, the result includes feelings of helplessness and hopelessness and the wish to give up (Engel, 1962).

4. Anger and aggression play an important part in many, though not all, depressions. The depressed person not only tortures himself but also the significant others in his life, whom he blames for having withheld the love, approval, reassurance, and admiration due him. Guilt and self-blame may also be involved here, resulting from the sense of being an unworthy and unlovable person.

5. Psychodynamic factors play an important role in all depressions, especially in determining the mental state that precedes and exists during the depression. However, there is a continuum that ranges from bipolar and psychotic unipolar depressions, in which dynamic factors

represent only the psychological dimension of a disorder caused by many factors, to neurotic depression (dysthymic disorder), wherein dynamic factors seem to play the dominant role. Klerman (1978), noting that research evidence supporting the etiological role of psychodynamic factors in depressions is limited, commented that ''at the present time, the psychodynamic hypotheses are primarily of great heuristic value, contributing to case formulation, guidance of psychotherapeutic practice, and the design of future research'' (p. 272).

Diagnosis of Depression

The diagnosis of a full-blown case of depression is not difficult. Most seriously depressed patients have symptoms in the areas of mood, cognition (thinking), and psychomotor and social behavior, as well as certain physiological functions. However, clinical skill is required to recognize depression when it is in an early stage or when it is masked by other symptoms (often called ''depressive equivalents'') and to diagnose the type of depression (this is important since, in the light of recent knowledge, the subtypes call for different treatment strategies).

Recognizing Depression

There is a need to distinguish depression from normal lowerings of mood (e.g., unhappiness, sadness, disappointment, frustration, hopelessness, or helplessness), which task is not always easy because depression is usually an accentuation in intensity or duration of these normal states. Certain symptoms suggest depression: withdrawal from or difficulty performing customary social roles; sleep and appetite disturbance; weight loss; loss of sexual interest; constipation or diarrhea; ideas of self-blame, (excessive preoccupation with one's own faults or guilt); suicidal ideas; and, sometimes, disturbance in reality testing, manifested by delusions, hallucinations, or confusion.

Depression can also be associated with some medical disorders or regimens:

side effects of certain drugs, especially those used to treat high blood pressure
endocrine disorders (e.g., hypothyroidism, Addison's disease)
neurological disorders (e.g., brain tumors, Parkinson's disease)
malignant diseases (e.g., brain tumors, cancer of the pancreas or lung)

If masked depressions are to be recognized, the clinician must investigate the possibility of depression even in clients who do not acknowledge feeling blue or show other clinical symptoms of depression. Masked depression is possible when there is evidence of one or more of the following symptoms:

uncharacteristic focus on bodily aches and pains, as well as psychosomatic disorders; the patient becomes a hypochondriac and goes from doctor to doctor, not feeling reassured by repeated physical examinations and lab tests

uncharacteristic accident proneness or risk-taking behavior, as though the patient were looking for trouble

anorexia nervosa and/or bulimia

excessive use of alcohol and/or drugs

anger, rage, and sometimes aggressive behavior

unexpected states of remission in patients with a long history of suicidal ideation and suicide attempts (Lesse, 1968)

Treatment Implications

Social workers need to be able to identify five categories of affective disorder (Lowry, 1980).

Bipolar Affective Disorders

In this category, formerly labeled "manic-depressive disorder," there is a strong likelihood of genetic vulnerability; accordingly, there is typically a family history of depression or mania in first-degree relatives. Such patients respond well to ECT and tricyclic antidepressants while depressed and to lithium when elated. Lithium is also an effective maintenance and prophylactic drug for the majority of these patients. When the drug works, it reduces the frequency not only of frank depressive and maniac attacks but also of subclinical ups and downs of mood. These patients should be referred to a general psychiatrist (not to someone who limits her practice to psychotherapy) for assessment and treatment. Psychotherapy is *not* the treatment of choice and should be offered only if there are specific indications over and above the depression. Support and explanation for the patient and family are useful adjuncts to psychiatric treatment.

Major Depressive Disorder

Patients in this category, which includes unipolar affective disorder and psychotic depression, probably have a genetic vulnerability, but the evidence is not as strong as in the bipolar affective disorders. There is often a history of depression in first-degree relatives but not of mania. There is usually a good response to ECT and tricyclic antidepressants, but lithium is not as effective here in preventing recurrences. These patients should be referred for psychiatric assessment and psychopharmacological treatment and here psychotherapy when indicated is used in combination with drugs or ECT.

Neurotic Depression

There is no good evidence of genetic vulnerability for this disorder, formerly called "reactive depression" but renamed "dysthymic disorder" in DSM III. There may be psychosocial predisposition as a result of early life experiences, and external precipitants often are clear. The treatment of choice here is psychotherapy; ECT and lithium have no place. The antidepressant drugs can be useful during periods of acute depression. Monoamine oxidase inhibitors are probably better than the tricyclic antidepressants but there is no evidence that long-term drug maintenance is useful.

Characterological Depression

This category, also called "depressive personality disorder" or "chronic dysthymic disorder," includes cyclothymic disorder (see Chapter 7). The evidence for and against genetic vulnerability in this category is inconclusive. These patients may require long-term care. If their personality deficit is not too severe, they will benefit from definitive psychotherapy. If the personality deficit is severe, they likely will not benefit from such an approach. The best strategy is to provide intervention when needed. Long-term, continuous support to patients and family should be offered only if they cannot do without it. Drugs should be used sparingly and only for brief periods in acute phases because of the high addictive potential of many patients in this group.

Depression Secondary To Other Diseases

Depression is often secondary to other major psychiatric disorders such as schizophrenia, acute and chronic brain syndromes, severe obsessive-compulsive disorder, and paranoia. Depression should be distinguished from other affective states, especially anxiety, in such patients (Roth & Mountjoy, 1982). It is not uncommon for depression to be a direct result of certain medical conditions such as endocrinological or neurological problems or to represent a drug side effect. There is, as well, a diagnosis known as "postinfluenza depression" (Sinanan & Hillary, 1981). Social workers ought to be alert to the possibility of depression secondary to these psychiatric and medical disorders so that both the primary and the secondary diagnosis can be made and appropriate treatment provided.

Medical and Psychiatric Referrals in the Diagnosis of Depression

In general, when in doubt, obtain a consultation; refer early rather than late; and prepare the patient and the family so as to get the greatest benefit from the consultation. People with the following problems should always be referred for medical or psychiatric assessment:

1. patients who are very severely depressed, irrespective of diagnosis, but especially if they are psychotic or suicidal
2. patients who become depressed for the first time after age 40 (brain tumors and other somatic illnesses are more common in this group and need to be ruled out
3. patients who request referral for another opinion or for medical assessment
4. patients with many physical complaints; these need to be evaluated to rule out treatable somatic illnesses (see Chapters 2 and 17). If on investigation the complaints are found not to be due to physical illness, the social worker will be able to concentrate on psychological and social issues without being constantly distracted by concern with the seriousness of the physical complaints. Sometimes it is best for such patients to see their family physician regularly, concomitant with the social worker's treatment.
5. patients who are taking medication on an ongoing basis, especially antihypertensive medication or steroids
6. patients with symptoms suggestive of bipolar affective disorder or major depressive disorder, especially if a strong family history of depression or alcoholism is present
7. patients with symptoms suggestive of neurotic depression or characterological depression should be considered as potential candidates for intensive psychotherapy or psychoanalysis. However, only the minority of patients within these groups is likely to be suitable candidates. If the worker is not a trained psychotherapist or analyst the patient should be assessed by a mental health worker who is so trained.

Social Work Treatment of Depression

Therapeutic Alliance between Social Worker and Depressed Client

The "therapeutic alliance," or therapist–client working relationship, is the sine qua non of all treatment. Although the nature of the relationship may vary with treatment circumstances (e.g., length, depth, purpose), the helping relationship to be established with depressed individuals has a number of elements and difficulties that apply in all cases. Bear in mind that the feelings of hopelessness, helplessness, pessimism, worthlessness, guilt, self-blame, inadequacy, and failure—the core of the depressed person's inner world and the basis of the need for help—are the very feelings that challenge the establishment of a therapeutic alliance.

All depressed patients need the social worker to convey a sense of hope, support, and qualified reassurance. These can be justifiably supplied since most depressive episodes are time-limited and even very severe depressions eventually improve.

Excessive dependence, ambivalent wishes to regress and be cared for, and manipulation represent common therapeutic problems. These can be managed through recognition of the need for respite from daily responsibility, for time to heal, and for understanding, support, and a degree of dependence. At the same time, a measure of structure (regularity and consistency) and encouragement for gradual reinvolvement in activities and social relationships do much to restore independence, as well as feelings of adequacy and self-worth.

Depressed persons' view of themselves as worthless, of the outside world as empty and rejecting, and of the future as bleak and hopeless also present difficulties in treatment. Persistent expression of these dark and hostile sentiments may evoke feelings of anger, frustration, and impotence in the worker. Yet, awareness and containment of such reactions is essential so that the patient gradually perceives the worker as trustworthy, accepting, and helpful instead of rejecting, hostile, and useless.

Suicidal thoughts, self-destructive behavior, and the possibility of successful suicide are ever present features of the treatment of depressed people (see Chapter 6). Their extremely painful expression of hopelessness and worthlessness, of anger and hostility at an uncaring world, always needs to be taken seriously. The worker must deal with these issues in a sensitive and empathic fashion but without allowing the patient to manipulate the worker into feeling guilty and unduly responsible for the patient's life. In particularly difficult cases, involving a psychiatrist or a family physician can be beneficial for both the patient and the therapist.

Social Work Roles with Depressed Patients

The nature of a social worker's involvement with depressed clients varies according to whether the patient is an outpatient or an inpatient and is receiving medication or not. Although the initial goals of treatment—reduction of symptoms; restoration of hope, a sense of adequacy, self-esteem, and social functioning; and exploration of maladaptive patterns of behavior—are the same, the conditions of treatment have important implications for the caseworker's role.

The Hospitalized Depressed Patient

The psychiatrist and ward staff have primary responsibility for the hospitalized patient; the social worker is responsible for the support of the family and the patient–family interaction. Deykin and colleagues (1971) described the differences in the caseworker's role with the hospitalized patient and the outpatient. They noted that the hospitalized person is removed from her family, the social structure of everyday life, and familiar roles. The social worker's first responsibility is to pay attention to, and mobilize support from, the patient's social situation. This is done by helping the family understand the illness, adjust to the temporary loss of a member, and maintain contact when the patient is unable to do so, and by facilitating meaningful communication between patient and family. The authors noted that maladaptive communication is often a by-product of the frustration, guilt, and anger evoked by the illness and felt on all sides. By working with the family, the social worker can help alleviate these sentiments, repair relationships, and prepare the family for the patient's reentry into the outside world.

If the hospitalized patient is receiving drug therapy, the caseworker's primary function is to interpret drug therapy to family members, to allay their anxiety when immediate improvement is not evident, to stress the need for continuing medication on home visits, and to educate the family about suicidal drug overdose in patients or dietary restrictions that must be observed with certain drugs.

Two other therapeutic issues arise with the hospitalized patient: the social worker's relationship with the patient's primary therapist (the prescribing physician) and the role of the social worker in the patient's aftercare program. The former is discussed in the following section and the latter is dealt with in the section on social environmental therapy as a treatment modality.

The Depressed Outpatient

The social worker's role with the depressed outpatient depends on who is identified as primary therapist, the quality of the patient–family relationship, and the existence of a drug regimen. The social worker as primary therapist is discussed under treatment modalities. Even though the outpatient remains within the family, the social worker still has tasks to perform with the family: to help the family perceive the patient's symptoms as part of his illness, to recognize the extra burden the family bears, and to help family members tolerate their own feelings of guilt, frustration, and fear about having a depressed person in the family and, at times, about having contributed to the patient's breakdown. Gradual resumption of the patient's social roles and duties is facilitated by having the outpatient remain in the family and the social worker encourage improved patient–family interaction.

The social worker's role with the outpatient receiving medication is crucial because medication is not as well controlled at home as in the hospital. To gain the patient's and family's confidence and cooperation with the drug regimen, the social worker should explain the expected course of drug effect, reassure patient and family about delayed effects, and encourage compliance. Equally important is communication with the physician who is prescribing the antidepressant medication. It is essential to inform her of unusual or severe side effects and of any indication of increased alcohol intake, impulsiveness, or suicidal ideation.

The professional relationship between social worker and prescribing physician is a critical part of combined drug and casework treatment. In an article on casework and pharmacotherapy in the treatment of depression, Weissman (1972a) noted that

> the problems associated with combining casework with pharmacotherapy arise out of the divergent goals of each treatment. The casework goal is improved social and interpersonal functioning and the goal of drug treatment is symptom reduction. . . . The collaboration of caseworker and psychiatrist will help to decrease misunderstanding and make casework and drug treatment more effective. . . . [This is necessary] because of the inevitable ambiguity as to what treatment is really helping, the patient's loyalties to the two therapists and the patient's variable clinical state. (p. 44)

Content and Level of Therapy in Depression

What do social workers and their depressed patients talk about during their therapeutic contacts? Weissman and Klerman (1973), in a study of psychotherapy with depressed women, identified 10 content themes: physical symptoms, mental symptoms, current treatment, practical problems, family of origin, spouse, sex, children, interpersonal relationships, and early experiences. Weissman and Paykel (1974) also reported that

> discussion of current social adjustment occupied most of the therapy and revolved around practical problems such as work, finance, recreation, as well as relationships with husband, children and close friends. Little time was spent discussing physical symptoms and current treatment. The least time was spent on discussion of early experiences or sexual problems. Therapy discussions were primarily descriptive accounts of daily life and not reflective of insights or childhood developmental material. (p. 192)

Since daily concerns, family issues, and social relationships are strongly associated with depressive illness, it should not be surprising to any therapist, regardless of orientation, that these are the main things a depressed person talks about. In fact, recent research confirming the association between depressive illness and psychosocial factors has helped to heighten awareness of the importance of these factors to the depressed person. The level at which these themes are discussed depends on the patient's primary concerns, needs, and wishes, his orientation to psychological understanding, as well as the modality of treatment. Weissman and Klerman (1973) postulated that therapist and patient may run into difficulty about the content and nature of their discussion

> where the therapist's expectations include preconceptions about what the patient should discuss. . . . most writings on psychotherapy stress the value of clarification of problems and their causes. It may be frustrating to the therapist to find that the patient spends most of the time describing everyday problems and not postulations about past experiences. We may underestimate the benefit to the patient derived from being able to share these problems with a non-judgemental and sympathetic listener. A considerable amount of sharing may be necessary to foster the patient's self-examination. The therapist's listening, rather than the search for clarification, may be the "non-specific" factor in therapy which contributes to psycho-therapeutic change. For many patients, particularly from the lower social classes, problems with housing, work and finances can be serious. The therapist should not underestimate their significance and push for what might be considered more important therapeutic topics." (pp. 59–60)

The question arises, then, as to how beneficial it is to attempt understanding of the psychodynamic meaning (conscious and unconscious) of a client's depression. I suggest that the content of the therapy should be determined by the patient and that the level at which the material is discussed (e.g., descriptive, reflective, interpretive) should be determined by the type of therapy that is appropriate and feasible for that patient. Of course, it is valuable for the therapist to gain an understanding of the dynamics of the patient and the social situation, whether or not she decides explicitly to introduce this material during the sessions.

Modalities of Treatment in Depression

The main modalities of treatment available to the social worker as the primary therapist are individual (long- and short-term) psychotherapy or casework, family and marital therapy, group therapy, and social environmental treatment.

Long-term Individual Therapy

Social workers in private practice or associated with a psychotherapy clinic may routinely provide long-term, intensive, psychodynamically oriented psychotherapy. The psychoanalytic literature abounds in information about case selection criteria and techniques and in case examples of process and outcome (Arieti, 1982; Jacobson, 1971; Winnicott, 1969; Zetzel, 1965), but reports are noticeably lacking research.

There is another type of long-term treatment that social workers may be called on to employ. Such treatment is long-term in the sense that the patient is seen for brief periods over many years, often for different bouts of depression or at times of crisis for preventive purposes. Brief psychotherapy, crisis intervention, monitoring of medication, or concrete help may be used at various times during these contacts. The unifying factor here is the reassurance of a long-term relationship, preferably with the same social worker or with someone else at the agency, where the person feels known. When a new social worker must be assigned to the client, familiarity with the patient's history of contacts is important in order to meet the patient's need for a sense of continuity between contacts. Fear of abandonment is often at the psychological core of chronic or recurring depression.

Short-term Individual Therapy

In the past decade, there has been a gradual development of short-term psychological approaches to the treatment of depression. Patient selection criteria, problem assessment, focus, goals, and techniques have been refined for several of these therapies, the main types being behavioral, cognitive, interpersonal, and psychodynamic. Clinical trials and other investigations have provided evidence for the efficacy of these treatments in depressed patients. Theory, research, and clinical applications related to these four approaches were comprehensively dealt with by Rush (1982). Since social workers are frequently employed in settings that use or investigate brief therapies, the reader is referred to Rush for further information about behavioral, cognitive, and psychodynamic brief therapy. Weissman and colleagues (Klerman & Weissman, 1977; Rounsaville et al., 1979) are at the forefront of the development and investigation of interpersonal psychotherapy, and their work is reviewed here.

Interpersonal psychotherapy (IPT) is based on the premise that depression (regardless of symptomatology, severity, biological vulnerability, or personality) occurs in a psychosocial and interpersonal context and that understanding and renegotiating the interpersonal problems associated with the onset of symptoms is important to the depressed person's recovery and possible to the prevention of further episodes. IPT is a brief (12–16 weeks), weekly psychological treatment of the ambulatory, unipolar, nonpsychotic depressed patient that focuses on improving the quality of the depressed patient's current interpersonal functioning. This approach is suitable for use, following a period of training, by experienced psychiatrists, psychologists, or social workers and it can be applied alone or in conjunction with a pharmacological approach. Two general goals are identified: alleviating depressive symptoms and helping the patient devise more effective strategies for dealing with interpersonal problems. The problem areas focused on are grief, interpersonal disputes, role transition, and interpersonal deficits. Techniques such as reassurance, clarification of emotional states, improvement of interpersonal communication, and reality testing of perceptions and performance are employed. Therapeutic work is aimed at conscious and preconscious levels; unconscious factors are recognized implicitly. Problems are defined in here-and-now terms and childhood experiences are recognized only in relation to presenting problems.

Research has demonstrated the efficacy of maintenance IPT, as compared to low contact, in helping depressived clients improve their social functioning. IPT also has been shown to be more effective than the non-scheduled treatment of acute depressives in achieving symptom reduction and later in enhancing social functioning (improvement in social functioning takes at least six to eight months to become apparent).

The use of IPT and cognitive therapy (Beck, 1976) with primary depressives will be tested in a multicenter, collaborative psychotherapy study sponsored by the National Institute of Mental Health. Clinical trials—IPT alone and in combination with antidepressants will be compared with cognitive therapy, plus antidepressant medication—will be conducted to ascertain whether the treatments are differentially applicable to, and effective with, specific subtypes of depressed patients.

Family and Marital Therapy

Family and marital problems have a cause-and-effect relationship vis-à-vis depressive disorders. The impact of depression is felt between people, as well as inside each person and is often an integral part of the family system. Therefore, family or marital therapy is frequently a treatment of choice for depressed clients. Social workers using this modality should assess and treat the interpersonal context in which the illness is experienced. Byng-Hall and Whiffen (1982) stated that family and marital therapists

> attempt to help families cope with current stress and strengthen the family by facilitating parental (or step-parental) intimacy, improving parent–child relationships, and some also aim to reduce the long-term effects of post-traumatic experiences, especially losses. [Depressive disorder seen from the family or marital perspective is] only one element in the web of emotional bonds which have been broken, are breaking or are threatening to break. The techniques for dealing with affective disorder cannot then be isolated from those which are aimed at resolving the conflicts in the regulation of distances between family members. (p. 318)

Lask (1979) and Gurman and Kriskern (1978) reviewed the research in this area. A few well-designed studies have indicated:

1. marital therapy with drugs in the depressed partner leads to greater improvement in family relationships than do drugs alone (Friedman, 1975)
2. marital therapy helps improve communication patterns between the depressed and nondepressed spouse (Hinchliffe et al., 1978)
3. depressed women with concomitant marital disputes who improve their marriage during the course of treatment also experience an improvement in depressive symptoms, while those whose marriages do not improve experience less improvement or a worsening of symptoms (Rounsaville et al., 1979)

A number of clinical papers that describe family and marital therapy with depressed clients also could be enlightening to social workers (Feldman, 1976; Hogan & Hogan, 1975).

Group Therapy

Group therapy as a specific treatment for depression has not received much attention in the literature or in research, even though Stein (1982) reported that it is an effective method with certain characterological disorders, unipolar depressive reactions, and bipolar affective disorders. The group provides some important benefits to the depressed patient: through group interaction, the members learn much about their depression and the effect it has on those around them; they give each other some dependence gratification; they provide mutual support, thus minimizing the pain and discomfort that they experience and provoke in others; and, if they are at different stages of managing their depression, they generate hope of improvement in each other. The leader, freed of some of the burden of supporting depressed clients, is able to help group members focus on strengthening individual identity, self-esteem, and coping capacity and on modifying distorted cognitions and affects, as well as on improving their interpersonal relationships (Stein, 1982).

Levin and Schild (1969) stated that "the group treatment of depressed clients has been found to be therapeutically advantageous. As the group members relate to each other, they tend to be less manipulative of and dependent on the worker." They identified three stages of treatment: mutual mourning, ego reactivation, and mastery. Case examples with the rationale for specific therapeutic interventions are provided. The reader is referred to Stein (1975) and Yalom (1975) for further information about the use of group therapy with depressed people.

Social Environmental Treatment

Treatment of a depressed person by manipulation of the social environment (an old-fashioned social work term) is an approach that should not be forgotten or underestimated by social workers (Bennett, 1982). The capacity of seriously depressed people to cope with the everyday world may be severely, and often chronically, impaired (Bothwell & Weissman, 1977; Weissman & Klerman, 1977). Provision of concrete services may be the treatment of choice for some depressed people, especially those just out of the hospital. Goering (1982), in a study of posthospital outcome in neurotic, mostly depressed women, suggested that legal aid, job counseling, housing services, assertiveness training, budgeting courses, daycare, and Parents without Partners are useful, if not essential, adjuncts to traditional psychiatric aftercare. In fact, there is a great need for more aftercare programs (Wasylenki et al., 1981) and social workers could well be leaders in this important area of care of the depressed person.

The depressed elderly are another group for whom environmental manipulation may be a very effective type of therapy. As Wetzel (1980) pointed out: "Social scientists have found institutions to be guilty of accelerating, rather than reducing, the symptoms of helplessness and hopelessness in the elderly" (p. 234). She suggested a number of interventions "for prevention and treatment of depression in aging women and men who are living in institutional settings. (p. 234)

Social Support in Depression: A Special Social Work Contribution

The treatment of depression is a vast and varied field in which social workers can make an important contribution. Developing and using social supports is a particularly appropriate area for social work efforts. Cobb (1976) stated this well:

> We should start now to teach all our patients both well and sick, how to give and receive social support. Only in rare instances of clear psychiatric disability should this instruction require a psychiatrist. It seems to me that this is the real function for which Richard Cabot designed the profession of medical social work. (p. 312)

Problems related to interpersonal relationships are a prime focus of any kind of psychotherapy for depression, but improvement in the patient's supportive, close relationships is frequently a main goal of treatment. Lack of social support is both a cause and a result of depression. Recent loss or lack of warm, dependable people, especially a confidant, increases vulnerability to depression. Moreover, the depressed person may provoke relationship problems; that is, the depressed mood may negatively affect those around her. It is difficult for family and friends to manage the hopeless withdrawal or the demanding, clinging dependence of the depressed person. Providing support for this person is always a burden, but this task is made more difficult when familial or close relationships are chronically disturbed. Fear, rejection, anger, and guilt are not uncommon reactions to another person's depression. At times, these sentiments are difficult for even a confidant to control. In a poor relationship, such reactions may compound the ill person's problems. Social workers can help improve the depressed patient's personal relationships, but different situations call for different strategies.

Supportive Relationships Are Strong and Constructive

In this situation, the social worker provides understandng and interpretation of the illness (its nature, causes, and course); helps the close person bear the pain and burden of dealing with a depressed patient and provides hope for eventual improvement; relieves the pressure upon the close person by sharing the patient's excessive dependence, hopelessness, helplessness, and suicidal ideation, which can be frightening to those around; helps the depressed patient both to moderate expectations and demands and to appreciate the good support that the close person offers; and encourages mutually dependent interaction.

Supportive Relationships Are Weak and/or Destructive

Preexisting problems in the relationship or the depression itself may seriously disturb marriage or family dynamics. In this situation, the social worker has a number of options: determine whether the partner or children themselves need help for individual problems and make appropriate referrals if necessary; relieve the close person of providing support and take responsibility for the treatment of the depression; provide concrete help (e.g., homemaker services); intervene in the destructive interaction by identifying constructive, practical, gradual ways in which at least minimal support can be given to increase the self-esteem and feelings of adequacy on the part of everyone involved; treat the destructive, maladaptive relationship separately from the depression (e.g., through family therapy); or separate the depressed patient from the family or the marriage (e.g., arrange for hospitalization or separate living arrangements).

Supportive Relationships Are No Longer Available

In this situation, the social worker should assess the nature of the recent loss to determine whether it is permanent or temporary and within or outside the patient's control; interpret the effect of the recent loss of social support and explain its association with the current depressive episode; provide transitional support; assess the patient's capacity for relationships and build on this; and, as the depression decreases, encourage reinvolvement in the former support system if possible and/or the establishment of new supports within the patient's capacity for closeness (this capacity should improve, at least to the pre-illness level, as the depression lifts).

Supportive Relationships Are Unused

Some depressed patients are characteristically socially withdrawn and when depressed become even more so. This situation is often the most difficult for the social worker to manage because these people are hard to engage. In this case, it is important to assess the patient's capacity for relationships and ability to cope on his own; respect the patient's social isolation, especially if it is evident that ordinarily the independent coping style works for this individual (some people have a well-developed capacity to be alone and prefer this state); and make it clear that the therapeutic relationship is being offered for the purpose of helping with the debilitating depression (this recognition of the patient's need for distance may decrease the fear of closeness, especially at times when help is needed).

In all four situations, the social worker's most powerful tool for helping the patient develop or maintain good social support is the helping relationship, which was discussed earlier. This relationship encourages the development of self-esteem, self-sufficiency, and individual identity. The depressed person will have learned something about give-and-take, about realistic needs and expectations, and about ways to meet these through relationships with other human beings.

Sex Differences in Depression and Help-seeking

Women are more often the focus of the literature on depression than are men. Although much of what is written about depression in women is applicable to men, in two areas—risk factors and help-seeking behavior or service use—sex differences are evident and have treatment implications.

Roy (1981) identified three vulnerability factors associated with depression in men: parental loss before 17 years of age, poor marriage, and unemployment. Similar factors were also related to depression in women, but parenting factors (the number of children under 14 at home and the woman's not working outside the home) were also significant for women (Brown & Harris, 1978; Roy, 1979; Weissman, 1972b; Weissman et al., 1973). It seems, then, that sex-specific factors in depression are very much related to sex differences in life situations and role definitions. Close attention should be given to the meaning of sex-related differences in risk factors when assessing depression in men and women.

As I noted earlier, depressed women are more likely to make use of psychiatric services than are depressed men. Kessler and associates (1981) and O'Neil and associates (1982) found that these differences are due neither to sex differences in the occurrence of depression nor to differences in symptom expression but rather to differences in attitudes toward emotional problems and help-seeking and to differential referral patterns by physicians. What all this means is that it is more difficult for men to recognize and acknowledge their depressive symptoms and that physicians tend to be less accurate in assigning psychiatric diagnoses to them. Therefore, proportionately fewer depressed men receive treatment. Social workers involved with male clients for presenting problems other than depression (eg., marital, family, or unemployment difficulties) are in a prime position not only to detect depression in men but also to help them accept treatment. Frequently, it is difficult to treat a man as the identified patient but much can be done by treating the depressive symptoms indirectly, for example, by therapy aimed at a disturbed family situation.

Conclusion

Despite the variety of treatment approaches and techniques available to social workers helping depressed people, it is not yet clear which types of depressed patients do best with which treatment modalities or whether different modalities are equally effective for the various types or subtypes of depression. For example, all four brief psychotherapies have been shown to be effective with unipolar, nonpsychotic affective disorders (Rush, 1982). Are these therapies equally effective? Is it mainly the skilled, sensitive therapist selecting a familiar, well-tested technique and working within a positive therapeutic alliance who determines a good outcome? These questions remain to be answered.

Perhaps social workers can best deal with this somewhat confusing situation by keeping up with developments in the field; by making certain that they are well trained in whatever type(s) of treatment they use; and by doing what social workers have long been known to do best—developing their skills as partners in the therapeutic alliance. Indeed, recent research provided evidence that the therapeutic alliance is one of the main variables predicting positive outcome in psychotherapy (Gomez-Schwartz, 1978; Marziali, 1982). Social workers can further contribute to the understanding and treatment of depression by identifying and researching areas that have always been of prime interest to the profession (eg., interpersonal relationships and social support). There is much for social workers to write about in this area, especially since a survey of the leading social work journals over the past decade revealed only a handful of articles on the social work treatment of depression.

Winnicott (1969) provided some food for thought for the social work practitioner:

> I suggest that our work becomes intelligible as well as rewarding if we keep in mind the heavy weight of depression which has to resolve itself inside the depressed person, while we try to help with whatever happens to be the immediate problem. There is an economics in our work and we can do what we have to do if we do the right thing at the right moment; but if we attempt the impossible the result is that we become depressed ourselves and the case remains unaltered. (p. 57)

Depression, the most common form of adult psychopathology confronting mental health practitioners, has been discussed here from the perspective of the social worker assessing and treating the depressed patient. It is important, however, not to forget that depressed mood is an inevitable part of the experience of everyday life for both social worker and client. Winnicott (1964) emphasized "the ego strength and personal maturity that is manifested in the 'purity' of the depresed mood" (pp. 56–57). He explained this well:

> Depression belongs to psychopathology. It can be severe and crippling and may last a lifetime and it is commonly a passing mood in relatively healthy individuals. At the normal end, depression which is a common almost universal, phenomenon relates to mourning, to the capacity to feel guilt and to the maturational process. Always depression implies ego strength and in this way depression tends to lift, and the depressed person tends to recover. (pp. 126–127)

Social workers assist people at each phase of the life cycle and with many depressing situations and experiences. Much can be done to help each client develop the vital capacity to bear the inevitable depressions of life (Craig, 1977; Lebow, 1976; Leonard, 1964; Macon,1979; Shepherd & Barraclough, 1979, Wallerstein & Kelly, 1980). Zetzel (1965) summed this up beautifully:

> Mature, passive acceptance of the inevitable thus remains a sustained prerequisite to the remobilization of available adaptive resources at all times. While failure in this vital area may be consistent with long periods of successful adaptation, it represents a serious potential vulnerability that becomes increasingly relevant in the later years of life, when experiences of loss, grief, and frustration are not to be avoided. In his conclusion to *Childhood and Society* (1950) Erikson said: "Healthy children will not fear life if their parents have integrity enough not to fear death." I submit that healthy children who do not fear life—in spite of subjective awareness of its limitations—will become adults with integrity enough not to fear death. (p. 273)

References

ABRAHAM K: Notes on the psychoanalytic investigation and treatment of manic-depressive insanity and allied conditions, in Jones E (ed): *Selected Papers on Psychoanalysis*. London, Hogarth, 1949, pp 248–279.

ADAMS KS, BOUCKOMS A, STREINER D: Parental loss and family stability in attempted suicide. *Arch Gen Psychiatry* 1982; 39:1081–1085.

AMERICAN PSYCHIATRIC ASSOCIATION: *Diagnostic and Statistical Manual of Mental Disorders*, ed 3. Washington, DC, American Psychiatric Association, 1980.

ANESHENSEL CS, STONE JD: Stress and depression: a test of the buffering model of social support. *Arch Gen Psychiatry* 1982; 39:1392–1396.

ARIETI S: Individual psychotherapy, in Paykel ES (ed): *Handbook of Affective Disorders*. New York, Guilford, 1982, pp 297–306.

BECK AT: *Depression: Clinical, Experimental, and Theoretical Aspects*. New York, Harper & Row, 1967.

BECK AT: *Cognitive Therapy and the Emotional Disorders*. New York, International Universities Press, 1976.

BENNETT D: Social and community approaches, in Paykel ES (ed): *Handbook of Affective Disorders*. New York, Guilford, 1982, pp 346–360.

BOTHWELL S, WEISSMAN MM: Social impairment four years after an acute depressive episode. *Am J Orthopsychiatry* 1977; 47:231–237.

BOWLBY J: *Attachment and Loss*. Vol 1: *Attachment*. New York, Basic Books, 1969.

BOWLBY J: *Attachment and Loss*. Vol 2: *Separation*. New York, Basic Books, 1978.

BOWLBY J: *Attachment and Loss*. Vol 3: *Loss*. New York, Basic Books, 1980.

BOYD JH, WEISSMAN MM: Epidemiology of affective disorders. *Arch Gen Psychiatry* 1981; 38:1039–1046.

BROWN GW, BROLCHAIN M, HARRIS T: Social class and psychiatric disturbance among women in an urban population. *Sociology* 1975; 9:225–254.

BROWN GW, HARRIS TO: *Social Origins of Depression*. New York, Free Press, 1978.

BROWN GW, HARRIS TO, COPELAND JR: Depression and loss *Br J Psychiatry* 1977; 130:1–18.

BYNG-HALL JJ, WHIFFEN R: Family and marital therapy, in Paykel ES (ed): *Handbook of Affective Disorders*. New York, Guilford, 1982, pp 318–328.

COBB S: Social support as a moderator of life stress. *Psychosom Med* 1976; 38:300–314.

CRAIG Y: The bereavement of parents and their search for meaning. *Br J Social Work* 1977; 7:41–54.

CROOK T, ELIOT J: Parental death during childhood and adult depression: a critical review of the literature. *Psychol Bull* 1980; 87:252–259.

DEYKIN E, WEISSMAN MM, KLERMAN GL: Treatment of depressed women. *Br J Soc Work* 1971; 1:278–291.

ENGEL G: Anxiety and depressive-withdrawal: the primary affects of unpleasure. *Int J Psychoanal* 1962; 43:89–97.

FELDMAN LB: Depression and marital interaction. *Fam Process* 1976; 15:389–395.

FREEDMAN AM, KAPLAN HI, SADOCK BJ (eds): *Comprehensive Textbook of Psychiatry*, ed 2. Baltimore, Williams & Wilkins Company, 1974.

FREUD S: Mourning and melancholia, in *Standard Edition* London, Hogarth, 1953, vol 14, pp 243–258.

FREUD S: Further remarks on neuropsychosis of defense, in *Standard Edition* London, Hogarth, 1953, vol 3, pp 167–189.

FRIEDMAN AS: Interaction of drug therapy with marital therapy in depressive patients. *Arch Gen Psychiatry* 1975; 32:619–637.

FURMAN E: *A Child's Parent Dies*. New Haven, Yale University Press, 1974.

GOERING P, et al.: Social support and post hospital outcome for depressed women. *Can J Psychiatry* (in press).

GOLIN S, HARTZ MA: A factor analysis of the Beck Depression Inventory in a mildly depressive population. *J Clin Psychol* 1979; 35:322–325.

GOMEZ-SCHWARTZ B: Effective ingredients in psychotherapy: prediction of outcome from process variables. *J Consult Clin Psychol* 1978; 46:1023–1035.

GURMAN AS, KNISKERN DP: Research of marital and family therapy: progress, perspective, and prospect, in Garfield SL, Bergin AE (eds): *Handbook of Psychotherapy and Behavior Change: Empirical Analyses,* ed 2. New York, Wiley, Sons, 1978, pp 817–901.

HAMMEN CL, PADESKY CA: Sex differences in the expression of depressive responses on the Beck Depression Inventory. *J Abnorm Psychol* 1977; 86:609–614.

HENDERSON S: A development in social psychiatry: the systematic study of social bonds. *Journal of Nervous and Mental Disorders* 1980; 168:63–69.

HENDERSON S, BRYNE DC, DUNCAN-JONES P: *Neurosis and the Social Environment.* Sydney: New York, Academic, 1981.

HINCHLIFFE MK, HOOPER D, ROBERTS FJ: *The Melancholy Marriage: Depression in Marriage and Psychosocial Approaches to Therapy.* New York, Wiley, 1978.

HIRSCHFELD RMA, CROSS CK: Epidemiology of affective disorders: psychosocial risk factors. *Arch Gen Psychiatry* 1982; 39:35–46.

HOGAN P, HOGAN BK: The family treatment of depression, in Flach FF, Draghi SC (eds): *The Nature and Treatment of Depression.* New York, Wiley, 1975, pp 197–228.

JACKSON G: Depression in the family. *Br J Psychiatric Soc Work* 1965; 8:32–41.

JACOBSON E: *Depression.* New York, International Universities Press, 1971.

KENNARD J, BRITCHNELL J: The mental health of early mother separated women. *Acta Psychiatr Scand* 1982; 65:388–402.

KESSLER RC, BROWN RL, BROMAN CL: Sex differences in psychiatric help seeking: evidence from four large-scale surveys. *J Health Soc Behav* 1981; 22:49–64.

KIDD KK, WEISSMAN MM: Why we do not understand the genetics of affective disorders, in Cole JO, Schatzberg AE, Frazier SH (eds): *Depression: Biology, Psychodynamics, and Treatment.* New York, Plenum, 1976, pp 107–121.

KLERMAN GL: Overview of depression, in Freedman AM, Kaplan HS, Sadock BJ (eds): *Comprehensive Textbook of Psychiatry.* Baltimore, Williams & Wilkins, 1975, vol 3.

KLERMAN GL: Affective disorder, in Nicholi AM (ed): *The Harvard Guide to Modern Psychiatry.* Cambridge, Belknap, 1978, pp 253–282.

KLERMAN GL, ROUNSAVILLE B, CHEVRON E, et al: Short-term Psychotherapies for Depression. New York, Guilford, 1982.

LASK B: Family therapy outcome research, 1972–78. *J Fam Ther* 1979; 1:87–92.

LEBOW GH: Facilitating adaptation in anticipatory mourning. *Soc Casework* 1976; 57:463–465.

LEONARD P: Depression and family failure. *Br J Psych Soc Work* 1964; 7:191–197.

LESSE S: The multivariant masks of depression. *A J Psychiatry* 1968; 124 (May suppl): 35–48.

LEVIN B, SCHILD J: Group treatment of depression. *Soc Work* 1969; 14:46–52.

LLOYD C: Life events and depressive disorder reviewed: II. Events as precipitating factors. *Arch Gen Psychiatry* 1980; 37:541–548. (a)

LLOYD C: Life events and depressive disorder reviewed: I. Events as predisposing factors. *Arch Gen Psychiatry* 1980; 37:529–535. (b)

LOWY FH: Use of drugs and other treatments in depression, in Ayd FJ (ed): Baltimore, Ayd Medical Communication, 1980, pp 179–186.

MACON LB: Help for bereaved parents. *Soc Casework* 1979; 60:558–561.

MARZIALI E: Prediction of outcome of brief psychotherapy from therapist's interpretative interventions. Read before the Annual Meeting of the American Psychiatric Association, New York, May 1983.

MENDELSON M: *Psychoanalytic Concept of Depression*, ed 2. New York, Spectrum, 1974.

MEULLER DP: Social networks: a promising direction for research on the relationship of the social environment to psychiatric disorder. *Soc Sci Med* 1980; 14A:147–161.

NURNBERGER JI, GERSHON ES: Genetics, in Paykel ES (ed): *Handbook of Affective Disorders*. New York, Guilford, 1982, pp 126–145.

O'NEIL MK, LANCEE WJ, FREEMAN SJJ: Sex differences in depressed university students. Read before the Ontario Psychiatric Association, Toronto, Jan 1982.

O'NEIL-LOWY MK: Psychosocial factors and depressive symptoms in university students. Doctoral dissertation, University of Toronto, 1983.

PAYKEL ES (ed): *Handbook of Affective Disorders*. New York, Guilford, 1982.

PARKER G: Parental characteristics in relation to depressive disorders. *Br J Psychiatry* 1979; 134:138–147.

PARKER G, BROWN LB: "Repertoires of response to potential precipitants of depression." *Aust NZ J Psychiatry* 1979; 13:327–333.

RADLOFF LS: Risk factors for depression: what do we learn from them?, in Belle D, Salasin S (eds): *Mental Health of Women: Fact and Fiction*. New York, Academic, 1980, pp 93–109.

ROSENTHAL TL, AKISKAL HS, SCOTT-STRAUSS A: Familial and developmental factors in characterological depressions. *J Affect Disord* 1981; 3:183–192.

ROTH M, MOUNTJOY CQ: The distinction between anxiety states and depressive disorders, in Paykel ES (ed): *Handbook of Affective Disorders*. New York, Guilford, 1982, pp 70–92.

ROUNSAVILLE BJ, WEISSMAN MM, PRUSOFF BA, et al: Marital disputes and treatment outcome in depressed women. *Compr Psychiatry* 1979; 20:483–490.

ROY A: Vulnerability factors and depression in women. *Br J Psychiatry* 1979; 133:106–110.

ROY A: Vulnerability factors and depression in men. *Br J Psychiatry* 1981; 138:75–77.

RUSH JA: *Short-term Psychotherapies for Depression*. New York, Guilford, 1982.

RUTTER M: *Children of Sick Parents*. London, Oxford University Press, 1973.

SANDLER J, JOFFE WG. Notes on childhood depression. *Int J Psychoanal* 1965; 46:88–96.

SHEPHERD DM, BARRACLOUGH BM: Help for those bereaved by suicide. *Br J Soc Work* 1979; 9:67–74.

SINANAN K, HILLARY I: Post influenza depression. *Br J Psychiatry* 1981; 138:131–133.

SPITZ RA: Anaclitic depression. *Psychoanal Study Child* 1946; 2:313–314.

STEIN A: Group psychotherapy in the treatment of depression, in Flach F, Draghi S (eds): *The Nature and Treatment of Depression.* New York, Wiley, 1975, pp 183–196.

STEIN A: Group therapy, in Paykel ES (ed): *Handbook of Affective Disorders.* New York, Guilford, 1982, pp 307–317.

STUART RB: Casework treatment of depression viewed as an interpersonal disturbance. *Soc Work* 1967; 9:27–36.

TENNANT C, SMITH A, BEBBINGTON P: Parental loss in childhood: relationship to adult psychiatric impairment and contact with psychiatric services. *Arch Gen Psychiatry* 1981; 38:309–314.

WALLERSTEIN JS, KELLY JB: *Surviving the Breakup: How Children and Parents Cope with Divorce.* New York, Basic Books, 1980.

WASYLENKI D: Depression in the elderly. *Can Med Assoc J* 1980; 122:525–532.

WASYLENKI D, GOERING P, LANCEE W, et al: Psychiatric aftercare: indentified need versus referral patterns. *Am J Psychiatry* 1981; 138:1228–1231.

WEISSMAN MM: Casework and pharmacotherapy in treatment of depression. *Soc Casework* 1972; 53: 38–44. (a)

WEISSMAN MM: The depressed woman and her rebellious adolescent. *Soc Casework* 1972; 53:563–570. (b)

WEISSMAN MM: The depressed woman: recent research. *Soc Casework* 1972; 53:19–25. (c)

WEISSMAN MM, KLERMAN GL: Psychotherapy with depressed women: an empirical study of content themes and reflection. *Br J Psychiatry* 1973; 123:55–61.

WEISSMAN MM, KLERMAN GL: The chronic depressive in the community: unrecognized and poorly treated. *Compr Psychiatry* 1977; 18:523–531. (a)

WEISSMAN MM, KLERMAN GL: Sex differences and the epidemiology of depression. *Arch Gen Psychiatry* 1977; 34:98–111. (b)

WEISSMAN MM, PAYKEL ES: *The Depressed Woman.* Chicago, University of Chicago Press, 1974.

WEISSMAN MM, PINCUS C, RADDING N, et al: The educated housewife: mild depression and the search for work. *Am J Orthopsychiatry* 1973; 43:565–573.

WEITKAMP LR, STANCER HC, PERSAD E, et al: A gene on chromosome 6 influencing behavior. *N Engl J Med* 1981; 305:1301–1306.

WETZEL JW: Interventions with the depressed elderly in institutions. *Soc Casework* 1980; 61:234–239.

WINNICOTT DW: The value of depression. *Br J Psych Soc Work* 1964; 7:123–127.

WINNICOTT DW: *The Family and Individual Development.* London, Tavistock, 1969.

WINOKUR G: Unipolar depression: is it divisible into autonomous subtypes?, *Arch Gen Psychiatry* 1979; 36:47–52.

Winokur G, Morrison J: The Iowa 500: follow-up of 225 depressives. *Br J Psychiatry* 1973; 123:543–548.

Yalom ID: *The Theory and Practice of Group Psychotherapy*. New York, Basic Books, 1975.

Zetzel E: Depression and the incapacity to bear it, in Shur M (ed): *Drives, Affects, and Behavior*. New York, International Universities Press, 1965, pp 243–274.

6

Suicide

Francis J. Turner

One Friday afternoon I received a call from a client, asking that I see her before the weekend. Prior to this call, we had had two or three interviews regarding her young son, who was having problems dealing with his parents' deteriorating marital situation. I agreed to see the woman for a few moments.

Although she appeared calm and controlled in discussing her son's behavior, it soon became clear she wanted to talk about herself. Some direct probing made it evident that she was actively contemplating suicide. She had collected a large supply of sleeping tablets and was on the verge of taking them. With appropriate support, she was able to get through the weekend and later to work out a satisfactory adjustment to separation from her husband.

Although I had worked with suicidal clients before, this case sharply reminded me of the need to be aware constantly of that segment of society whose life situation reaches such a point of despair that suicide is actively considered, attempted, or even committed. It also demonstrated that the cry for help from such persons is frequently disguised or hidden and can come at any time.

Social workers who practice in crisis clinics or suicide centers are cognizant of these aspects of suicide. They see suicidal clients in their day-to-day practice and have developed the skills and attitudes necessary to deal with this critical situation. However, not all suicidal clients end up at crisis services or similar facilities. Social workers and other mental health professionals meet them in all aspects of practice and, frequently, the desperation of the client can be easily missed, with deadly consequences.

During the process of treatment, clients sometimes go through suicidal periods, which because of shame or anxiety they choose not to share with the therapist. Fortunately, these instances do not always end in suicide. Not every person who thinks about suicide attempts it. Moreover, not all attempts are successful. In fact, the vast majority of people who contemplate suicide will never try to commit it. Thus, the odds are good that a missed cry for help will not end in death.

At the same time, we cannot be content to play the odds. People who think about suicide are suffering and need help even if they do not actively try to kill themselves. As I have become more alert to this reality, I have been surprised at the number of clients for whom suicide has been an active consideration. I now consider suicide a possibility in every first interview with a client and carefully watch for signs during the life of the case.

Obviously, we cannot prevent all suicides. Most practitioners will lose clients to suicide at some time, and they must be ready to accept this fact. Nevertheless, we need to strive to reduce the incidence of self-inflicted deaths by remaining alert to the nature, symptoms, and management of suicidal clients.

Suicide in Society

Suicide is not a phenomenon peculiar to our times: as long as people have been able to exercise the power of choice, they have been able to choose not to live. However, by the early nineteenth century, some consideration was being given to the concept that suicide is a form of mental illness. This idea was advanced by the work of Jean-Pierre Falret, a French physician who argued that the suicidal person is suffering and in need of help (Coleman, 1976).

Although in our times suicide is still officially considered a crime and a sin, it is popularly viewed as a sign of serious upset—a social and mental health problem rather than a legal and religious one. In the past 25 years especially, the helping professions have devoted considerable attention to the problem of suicide, which ranks among the top 10 causes of death in the Western world. In Canada there are over 3,500 suicides each year and in the United States over 20,000, with an estimated 8 to 10 times as many attempts at suicide in both countries.* In addition, hundreds of thousands of other individuals have suffered considerable anguish and terror as they have struggled with suicidal thoughts.

Suicide is of particular interest to social workers. As clinicians, they are aware of the terrible suffering that people experience when their life situation has reached a point at which death seems to be the only solution. Social workers are also familiar with the suffering that a suicide causes to the significant others of the deceased. In addition, social workers are concerned with the question of prevention. This requires identifying those conditions in society that foster suicidal behavior and seeking to eradicate them. The unnecessary loss of any member of society is a loss to the whole society.

A Sociological Perspective on Suicide

Suicide is both a personal and a societal act and needs to be studied from both perspectives. From a sociological perspective, suicide is interesting because it occurs in a highly patterned way. Thus, rates of suicide vary from country to country: Hungary has the highest world rate; Mexico and the Philippines, the lowest. Suicide also varies by sex, with four times as many men committing suicide as women; however, many more women attempt suicide than do men. Suicide varies with age; although older persons have the highest rate, the rate among 15–24 year olds is rising in an alarming manner. Suicide varies by ethnic origin. It varies, as well, by profession, with physicians and dentists standing high on the risk scale. It varies with time of day, day of the week, and season of the year. Finally, suicide varies by method: men tend to use more violent means, such as guns and hanging, whereas women use gas or drugs.

Suicide may also have something of a contagious effect in terms of either method or group. Recall the ritualistic suicides in Vietnam of Buddhist monks in the 1960s. Recently there was a series of suicides among the faculty of a small department in a university; each case was explicable in itself yet together they could be seen as a part of a pattern. By understanding the sociological components of suicide we can help alter the social causes that lead a person to take or consider that fatal step.

Durkheim's (1951) groundbreaking work on suicide pointed out that suicide varies among social groups in part in response to their societal situation; that is, rates of suicide tell us something about the place of dif-

*Statistics on suicide are probably underreported because some accidental deaths may in fact be suicides, but police lack proof thereof. Similarly, physicians are sometimes reluctant to report suicide as the cause of death both to save family feelings and to spare the family a contest with the insurance company over the payment of death benefits.

ferent groups in the social system. From this perspective, Durkheim concluded that there are three types of suicide: "egoistic suicide" is found among persons who belong to social groups that are excessively individualistically oriented and poorly integrated (e.g., people without strong religious ties); "anomic suicide" occurs among groups in which traditional norms and mores are violated or are no longer functioning (e.g., in times of intense social change or during economic depressions,); and "altruistic suicide" occurs among groups in which individuality is minimized and there is a high degree of social integration (e.g., high-status military groups or some religious groups).

Although Durkheim's (1951)* types have been criticized because they are difficult to test empirically, there is general support for the concept that variation in suicide rate among different groups in society is strongly related to status, to perceived status, and to status integration in society (Gibbs, 1966). More work needs to be done to develop a well-defined and well-tested theoretical explanation of suicide from a sociological perspective. Since rates of suicide tell us something about the place of different groups in the social system, such a model should be of critical importance to social workers as a way of identifying high-risk groups so that preventive steps can be taken.

Psychological Theories of Suicide

As therapists, social workers are also interested in the personal reasons for suicide. Freud (1959) described suicide as the act of turning against oneself hate directed at another: "It is true that we have long known that no neurotic harbours thoughts of suicide which are not murderous impulses against others redirected upon himself" (p. 162). Menniger (1966) refined Freud's ideas and postulated that in all suicides there are three principal elements: a wish to kill someone, a wish to die, and a wish to be murdered. The wish to kill arises from intense anger directed at a love object toward whom the person has ambivalent feelings. The wish to die usually includes a fantasy of escape from an intolerable life situation or, in some instances, a wish to be reborn into a new and problem-free existence. The wish to be killed is related to a sense of guilt as punishment for a perceived failure or crime (e.g., "I desired the death of someone; therefore, I need to be punished by death."). Some analysts have suggested that many suicides have a sexual component related to a distorted form of physical submission (e.g., Jackel, 1975). In any event, "suicide is not a simple act. . . . contrary to the popular tendency to assign so often the entire motivation to the immediately proceeding and obvious prob-

---

*This work was originally published in 1897.

lem situation, illness, heartbreak, or traumatic event, and so on, the roots are always deeper'' (Laughlin, 1967, p. 206). As we have seen, these roots include anger, the desire to punish oneself or significant others, and the desire to make retribution for real or imagined transgressions. Suicide may also be an attempt to become reunited with a real or fantasied lost love object. Finally, in suicide there is one further strong emotion that predominates: the sense of hopelessness, which makes the person believe that there is nothing to be done to change the situation that is causing so much suffering except to end life.

A Psychosocial Perspective on Suicide

Suicide seems best understood from a psychosocial perspective that includes multiple potential causes. In this perpective, there is no factor that inevitably leads to suicide; likewise, potential causes of suicide—revenge, philosophical or theological dictates, physical suffering, negative self-concept, feelings of hopelessness, desire for notoriety—may be present without resulting in suicide.

Suicidal potential is best seen as a continuum. Thus, the important clinical question should be: what degree of suicidal risk characterizes this client? Answering this question requires identification not only of existing risk factors but also evaluation of their strength over time. Clinical experiences shows that the state of being actively suicidal is highly transitory, lasting from a few minutes to a few days. That is, the situation leading the person to this point of desperation may not change, but the contemplation of suicide as a response to the situation may subside. It is because of this variation that potentially suicidal persons often are not taken seriously; they are perceived as seeking attention because many do not make an attempt on their lives even when it appears that they might.

Assessment and Diagnosis of Suicidal Clients

Identifying high-risk clients, involves several factors. First, the clinician must be constantly alert to the possibility of suicide. Second, many clients for whom suicide is a distinct possibility conceal or distort this information. For example, with her therapist, a suicidal client may talk about a friend who is in a desperate state; hint that something is going to happen; use language that has a final quality to it (e.g., ''Things are desperate''; ''What's the use?''; ''I can't go on''; ''I do not see any solution''; ''It would be nice to get away from it all.''); dwell inordinately on elaborate plans for a long vacation, talk about making a will, or mention wanting to disappear for a while. Obviously such expressions are found in the day-to-day conversation of most people and rarely connote suicidal thoughts. However, it is our responsibility in practice to recognize that at times such expressions may be death wish messages unconsciously distorted by ambivalence. The client might make offhand remarks about suicide that she will deny upon questioning. Moreover, the cry for help is not always directed to a professional. Often, the person hints to friends or relatives that he is contemplating suicide. Social workers must listen to what clients are saying about significant others in their lives because they unwittingly may have heard a cry for help. Third, social workers have their own fears about suicide and death, and most fear the prospect of suicide in their clients. Thus, it is understandable that they tend to minimize the seriousness of a client's concerns, preferring to focus on the less problematic aspects of clients' lives. Like everyone else, social workers often avoid coming to terms with the prospect of their own death and are frightened at the possibility that clients may want to involve them in their struggle about taking their own life.

Rating Scales on Suicide Potential

The professional literature is a valuable resource for clinicians. An impressive array of articles, monographs, and texts deals with suicide, and it is important to keep abreast of developments in the diagnosis and management of suicidal clients.

Throughout the literature on suicide, frequent reference is made to rating scales that are available to aid in determining the suicidal risk category of a client (Coleman, 1976; Kiev, 1977; Laughlin, 1967). Like all other rating scales, they do have a use, helping to reduce uncertainty about a diagnosis. However, such scales are informative only when used in conjunction with critical professional judgment.

Depression and Suicide

Depression is a critical factor in an estimated 75% of all suicides. Thus, in all depressed clients, it is important to assess the possibility of suicide. Suicidal thoughts tend to be transitory, however, and one of the frequent concomitants of depression is withdrawal from significant others, so that suicidal indicators are frequently missed. Depression also can be masked, and depressed clients may remain undiagnosed, especially in early therapy sessions, when their behavioral patterns are not as clear to the worker as they become later.

A particular aspect of depression in relation to suicide is what has come to be called the "trough syndrome" (Laughlin, 1967), in which the risk of suicide increases for a period when the worst of the depression is over and the client is beginning to feel better. This factor seems to be a question of both cause and effect. Improved spirits are an effect in people who find comfort in having made the decision to suicide. Death is seen as a way of finding relief from their suffering and in anticipating this escape they begin to feel better. On the other hand, improved spirits may play a causal role when the very intensity of the depression has been a form of protection. That is, in the depths of depression, people feel so bad that they become incapable of taking deliberate action even to find relief from their suffering. Only when they begin to feel better are they capable of action and one of the solutions open to them, especially from the restricted perspective of the depressed person, is suicide.

A 22-year-old woman suffering from Huntington's chorea entered the hospital because of depression about her deteriorating physical condition. After a few days, the depression began to lift and on Friday evening of the first week the treatment team agreed that she was doing better. Over the weekend, she maneuvered her wheelchair to a nearby lake and drowned herself.

In depression there is inevitably a breakdown in the individual's coping abilities. This frequently results in feelings of collapse and helplessness. The sense of helplessness is a critical feature of the high-risk suicidal person. A person feeling utter helplessness can envision only a narrow range of potentially remedial actions about a problematic situation. As the state of helplessness intensifies, the possibility of getting help from outside seems more and more remote. At this point, the prospect of living seems less and less attractive and the possibility of escape into death more attractive.

Alcohol Abuse and Suicide

Alcohol abuse frequently accompanies depression and/or feelings of helplessness and hopelessness in a person who attempts suicide. Obviously, everyone who drinks is not thereby potentially suicidal. Rather, alcohol seems to increase the possibility of suicide in high-risk individuals. Thus, from a diagnostic perspective, the drinking habits of a potentially suicidal client need to be assessed.

Psychotic States and Suicide

Not all suicides are related to depression or feelings of hopelessness. Persons in psychotic states may become involved in a delusional system that leads to self-destruction. In other situations, a highly elaborate fantasy life can lead a person in a schizophrenic state or under the influence of a drug to seek death as a way of achieving release and attaining paradise.

Therapist Anxiety as an Indicator of Suicidal Potential

Klugman (1976) suggested that therapists learn to trust their own anxiety as an indicator of suicidal potential in clients. Since from a psychodynamic perspective, suicide is an unconscious wish to kill and be killed, some of these feelings should be evident in the client–worker relationship even in early contacts. Thus, the worker may experience high anxiety about a client's suicidal potential before there is clear clinical evidence pointing to this possibility. Other authorities hold that reacting to one's own anxiety responses is not responsible clinical practice. Nevertheless, responses to clients should not be ignored, and if the therapist begins to get anxious about a suicidal possibility, then she has a responsibility to consider that the client may be at high risk.

Suicidal Plans

Another diagnostic indicator is the extent to which the person has made concrete plans as to how, when, and where to suicide. If asked, some persons will indicate that they have very carefully worked out plans (Jackel, 1975). This type of preparation shows that suicide is very much a part of the client's agenda.

Family History of Suicide

A predisposing factor to suicide is suicide by a parent, child, or other significant person in the client's life, especially within the year. Earlier, mention was made of patterns of suicide among people with similar characteristics. This same factor appears to operate among family members or colleagues closely linked professionally. The first suicide seems to legitimize subsequent attempts.

Personal History of Suicide Attempts

People who have tried suicide before are apt to try it again. It appears that having broken through the barrier of attempting suicide, the person is less frightened by the prospect of self-destruction.

Personality or Life Changes and Suicide

An acute personality change is another a danger signal. The usually active person becomes quiet and contemplative, or the usually passive person becomes agitated. In particular, newly emerging ruminations with a high content of self-recrimination or questioning about the worth of existence or the purpose of life are danger signals. Sometimes, a dramatic change in a person's accustomed behavior, as in depression, is a warning signal. In other clients, abrupt changes take the form of psychosomatic complaints, accompanied by a perception that something dramatic is going to occur.

A common and critical change that may increase the risk of suicide is the rapid restriction of the individual's circle of significant others or supportive social system, as in the death of a spouse in an older couple. Without alternate support, the bereaved individual may feel that suicide is the best response in the face of this loss.

Persons with few coping resources also are potentially suicidal in times of crisis, especially if no help is perceived as being available. A crisis related suicidal urge is often of very short duration, perhaps a few hours. For example, from time to time, the police report the suicide of someone arrested for such a thing as drunken driving. In many of these cases, it is impossible to find other indicators of suicide potential.

Medical Factors in Suicide

Suicidal risk is higher in older persons who have had a great deal of surgery. It appears that for some, the prospect of additional suffering is less acceptable than death. Similarly, suicide is more common in terminally ill persons even when death has been judged to be imminent. In these situations, it seems important that the person control the timing of his death rather than wait for a proximate but unknown date. Finally, some supposedly accident-prone people may have latent suicidal tendencies.

Intervention with Suicidal Clients

An important first consideration in the treatment of suicidal clients is the number of myths that still abound about suicide. That such myths exist among the general population is serious enough, but what is of particular concern is that many of these myths influence persons in the helping professions (e.g., ''People who talk about suicide will not do it.'').

The suicidal person tends to be ambivalent about this course. However, the clinician should build on the positive component of the ambivalence, the will to live, rather than misinterpret ambivalence as lack of intent. There is also an aspect of attention getting in the suicidal person's behavior, but it relates to ambivalence. Although sham suicide threats can be used to frighten or control others, the prudent route is to see any suicide threat initially as an indication of need.

According to one myth, talking about suicide will only put ideas into the client's mind. When a client has thought about suicide, talking about it with her is not going to bring her closer to the decision to suicide. The therapist's task is to help the client understand what he is really contemplating. Some people engage in magical thinking about suicide. They believe that they will not really hurt themselves because they have some type of immunity from harm or that death is only a temporary state from which they will return to life. The worker must confront the client with the reality of death.

Not talking about suicide plays into the client's denial and can strengthen her resolve by allowing the illogical or disturbed component of the personality to take over. Indeed, avoidance of this subject can be seen by clients as a form of rejection: the therapist does not care enough about them to respond to their need. Silence can also be viewed by the client as proof that this component of his person is so distasteful or so bad that the therapist cannot even talk about it.

Another myth holds that it is impossible to stop someone who is determined to kill himself. In a few cases, this is true. Some people hide all signs of suicidal thinking and insure that nothing can prevent their death. However, the vast majority of people are ambivalent about a contemplated suicide. Suicidal intent is not an omnipresent commitment; its strength expands and contracts. The therapist's task is to work toward strengthening the desire to live. Thus in clinical work with a client, as well as focusing on the suicidal material, we need to actively seek out the components of the personality where there is still a wish to live.

According to a related myth, once suicidal, a person will always be suicidal and will eventually destroy herself. In fact, most people are seriously suicidal only for brief periods even during a crisis or in a psychotic state.

There are several ways in which social workers come into contact with the suicidal client. The first contact may be through a phone call. Persons working in crisis centers or suicide prevention centers are accustomed to this kind of call. Klugman (1976) reported that the caller may begin in a joking or hostile manner as a way of disguising his suicidal struggle. Unless this tactic is understood, the worker may fail to respond appropriately. Thus, it is important to give all incoming calls sufficient time and attention.

Once a suicidal situation is identified, the initial task of the therapist is to try to establish a helping relationship as quickly as possible. It is important to convey to the person his interest, concern, availability, competence, and access to resources. Equally important, the therapist must gather as much identifying information as possible, including the place from which the person is calling and what people—friend, physician, clergyman, or employer—can be contacted if need be. This information is important in case the person hangs up unexpectedly or a subsequent crisis emerges.

A former inpatient of a psychiatric hospital telephoned, sounding distraught and confused. She had been living in a single room since discharge. The social worker quickly ascertained that she had turned on the gas in her stove. Fortunately, the case record contained the person's address and a second worker was able to call the police, who arrived in time to rescue the client.

After establishing an initial working relationship with the client and gathering information, the therapist's task is to estimate the suicidal potential of the caller. How strong are her suicidal thoughts and how close is the person to following through on them? If it is clear that the suicide attempt is imminent or that the person has already taken some suicidal steps, then emergency procedures are required such as calling the police or contacting a family member or friend. In agencies that provide crisis services, routine procedures exist for dealing with this type of critical situation. However, settings that handle crises less frequently also should establish routines for dealing with such emergencies.

These steps, as in all aspects of treatment, will not be followed in a sequential manner; rather, they are part of an ongoing process. A further component of this process is to identify the problem or situation that has brought the person to the crisis. The very task of trying to determine this can be the beginning of the reintegration to a non-suicidal stage for the patient. Throughout this process, the therapist keeps the focus of discussion on the suicidal theme and is frank with the client. This helps reduce the patient's anxiety.

The final aspect of the phone contact is to develop a plan to deal with the situation. Such a plan may entail emergency measures, discussed earlier, or long-term treatment.

Suicidal clients also may be identified by coming to a walk-in client in search of help. Obviously, this situation is much less stressful for the worker than a phone call from an unknown person. In the office, there is a chance to do a more thorough assessment; there is not the risk of having the person terminate contact abruptly by hanging up; and there is the opportunity to make use of the setting's resources, including ways to deal with emergencies if they present themselves. Still, the same steps are necessary in the first office contact as over the phone in an emergency. The patient stands in need of a therapeutic encounter in which his feelings of hopelessness are reduced, the will to live is increased, and some concrete preventative and restorative steps are taken.

In practice, social workers often see clients who do not need emergency care but for whom suicide is nevertheless a distinct possibility. Intervention will be similar to intervention in crisis situations. That is, the therapist must be available on an as needed basis. Treatment will be intensive but short-term (less than 10 sessions). The client needs help understanding what is happening to her, which includes impaired thinking and problem solving ability. The worker should be highly supportive but quite forceful as to the various steps that must be taken to restore the client's ability to manage his life. Finally, it is important to remove any obviously suicidal equipment that the client may have gathered, such as a gun or a supply of sleeping pills. Sometimes, the worker can do this directly; at other times, the client's friends or relatives must take part.

The therapist's task during the suicidal crisis is to help the client identify alternatives in her immediate situation and look ahead to an altered lifestyle. Alternatives are necessary because suicide generally is seen as the only solution by the client. To help the client expand his coping repertoire requires input from the client's present support network, which may be extended by involving significant others and professionals.

Examination of the client's current suicidal struggle should try to uncover earlier suicidal attempts and earlier unresolved problems. Such knowledge is important in assessing the seriousness of the suicidal potential. In evaluating both the seriousness of the suicidal risk and its time dimensions, the therapist should bear in mind that although crises are time-limited and will pass, the longer the client has been contemplating suicide, the more serious the situation. But during the period of crisis, however long, clients are in an emotionally vulnerable situation. One of the aspects of emotional distress is that unresolved problems and struggles from the past tend to be close to the surface and thus susceptible to influence. This inquiry is stress producing for the client but often is therapeutically useful.

Of course, suicidal thoughts do not always betoken a crisis. Such thoughts are frequently present in clients concerned about themselves, others in their lives, or problems they are encountering. The worker needs to be sensitive to this reality both from a diagnostic and from a therapeutic perspective. Suicidal thoughts are extremely frightening to most persons and the therapist should help the person talk about this anxiety and the many other emotions surrounding the suicidal ideation, such as fear, anger, and guilt. Many clients are relieved to learn that others have experienced similar feelings.

Individual Therapy with Suicidal Clients

There is an additional treatment point related to a client's suicidal thoughts. Once a high-risk period has passed, the client may feel sufficient remorse, terror, or guilt to provoke another crisis. Being aware of this kind of reaction helps the therapist respond to these feelings and assist the person achieve a clearer and more positive image of himself, which can be both therapeutic on a short-term basis and preventative over the long term. Bear in mind, however, that lack of remorse following a suicide attempt suggests a continuing high-risk situation.

Often, the clinician is so relieved that the person did not suicide that she terminates contact too soon, leaving a considerable number of problems unresolved. This is especially common in settings strongly committed to brief intervention. The relationship between the postcrisis response and the likelihood of a subsequent suicide attempt points to the need for fairly considerable follow-up.

Sometimes the therapist does not learn about the client's suicidal espsode until after it has passed and the person has regained some equilibrium. The client may say he missed an appointment because he was away or not feeling well. However, some of these absences may be related to depression with occasional suicidal content. Awareness of this possibility should make the therapist more responsive to the client's needs.

One final comment about working with suicidal clients is to avoid seeing only the suicidal possibility and forget other aspects of the client's life in which help is also needed. Suicide is a message, not an end in itself.

Joint Interviewing with Suicide Intervention

Klugman (1976) reported that joint interviews, including the patient and an important person or persons from the client's life, can be beneficial in several ways. First, this approach expands the network of persons who are actively concerned about the possibility of suicide. Such persons can be a support to the client, a resource locator, and a symbol of hope and concern. They also can inform the therapist about changes in the suicidal intent and other aspects of the client's life, including sources of stress or additional supports. Involving significant others in interviews with the client results in other persons becomming involved in seeking solutions, giving encouragement and providing understanding. Obviously, the therapist must assess the ability of the significant others to deal with the stress in the client that the suicide episode brings.

Group Therapy in Suicide Intervention

The literature on working with groups of suicidal clients is not rich. There have been reports of successful group therapy with inpatient suicidal clients (e.g., Ludin, 1966), and a strong theoretical case can be made for this type of intervention. The patient is reassured that others have felt so miserable, learns that there is ground for hope and that there are other solutions besides suicide, and expands her circle of significant others. On the other hand, there is the risk of negative contagion among group members, as well as the strain put on the therapist by working with suicidally inclined patients. Furthermore, suicidal persons may be so deficient in social skills that they have little to give to other group members. It would appear, then, that groups may be more appropriate for clients in whom suicidal risk is lower.

Family Therapy in Suicide Intervention

Family intervention has a particular role to play in the management of suicide, especially as a way of mobilizing the family around the potentially suicidal person. Often, breakdown of the family communication network is one cause of the intense feelings of abandonment and hopelessness in the client. Even if communication is open, family members may not be available but be spread across the country. Nevertheless, when possible it is useful to involve one or more family members both to aid diagnosis and to extend support to, elicit concern about, and generate alternatives for the person who perceives there is nothing further to be done.

Use of Friends and Volunteers in Suicide Intervention

Friends and volunteers can be invaluable during and following a suicidal crisis. The social worker must be frank with these persons about the suicide attempt itself and the likelihood of further attempts. Like family members; friends and volunteers strengthen the support system available to the client, providing hope, showing concern, and helping the patient identify alternative coping strategies.

Institutionalization of Suicidal Clients

In high risk situations, it is frequently essential to seek hospitalization or other forms of institutionalization for the patient. Institutionalization can protect the client from herself, remove her from a highly negative environment, and provide ready access to a rich array of therapeutic resources.

There are several points to be made here. Sometimes the person is highly resistant to hospitalization and physicians may be reluctant to use their authority or influence to have a person admitted. Moreover, the ambivalence shown by suicidal individuals may convince institutional staff that the person should not be there. Thus, the patient may not get the full attention of staff—all too often with the result that the person succeeds in killing himself.

Family members and friends are often a problem with the institutionalized patient. They may be ashamed or reluctant to have the person in the hospital and thus press for an early release. Alternatively, the family may be overjoyed to observe that the person has greatly improved and thus press for an early release. As we have seen, any improvement needs to be assessed carefully because it can foreshadow a further suicidal attempt.

Treatment Settings in Suicide Intervention

Some settings are more capable than others of providing services to the moderately and severely suicidal patient. Crisis centers, hospitals, outpatient clinics, and suicide prevention services are geared to respond quickly with a wide range of resources. This must be taken into account by the therapist making an assessment about a particular client. Every potential suicide victim need not be referred to a crisis service; such a referral may even intensify the crisis. However, the therapist must establish a working relationship with the available facilities so that help, information, consultation, and advice are readily forthcoming when needed.

Consultation with Colleagues in Suicide Intervention

Consultation and/or supervision are essential to the therapist working with suicidal clients. First, there is the sense of urgency and responsibility that accompanies this kind of case. The worker needs opportunities to explore her own reactions, fears, and concerns about particular cases with colleagues. Second, consultation insures objectivity in the client–therapist relationship and confidence in the diagnosis. It is also important from the perspective of planning treatment, locating resources, and making decisions about actions, with potential legal implications. Such consultation may be on an informal, ad hoc basis or on a regular, case-by-case basis.

Colleagues can also serve as co-therapists. This is a way of extending the resource network of the client. Co-therapy is especially important in high-risk situations since the worker cannot always be available and the need for help is unpredictable.

Finally, colleagues in other professions and in other settings can be of great assistance both by bringing their knowledge to bear in assessment and diagnosis and by providing the worker with particular resources, such as medication for the client.

Legal Assistance in Suicide Prevention

The question of how much we can intervene in a person's life even to save it is a grey area. Nevertheless, the courts and the police can be of assistance to social workers seeking a way to keep a person from self-destruction. Obviously, how and when these resources are used will vary with the client and other factors, but legal assistance may be needed in some cases.

Postsuicide Considerations

Frequently, discussions on the management of suicide seem to imply that suicide almost never occurs. As I noted earlier, suicide does occur in spite of all our efforts. When a person does kill herself, the social worker has a therapeutic responsibility both to the survivors and to his colleagues.

Persons who have lost a close friend or relative through suicide can experience a wide range of responses. They can suffer the loss of the loved one; they can feel guilt at having failed to be more helpful; they can be anxious about the reason; they can be disappointed at the waste of a life or angry at the mess that has been left behind. Some of these reactions are powerful and even incapacitating; hence, the therapist must be aware of their potential magnitude and respond as appropriate. Because of the power of this legacy of suicide, it is important to remember anniversaries of suicide in families; these can be high-risk situations for the survivors.

Colleagues who have lost a client through suicide also can have intense responses, similar to those of family and friends. It is most important that social workers be aware of the potential impact of a suicide on colleagues and indeed on themselves and, when suicide does occur, reach out to fellow workers in a supporting, understanding way (those in supervisory positions should be particularly sensitive to this issue). Certainly, if a therapist failed to observe obvious suicidal messages, she needs to acknowledge her missed diagnosis, but we cannot prevent all suicides short of locking everyone up. Therapists can only narrow the gap by being more knowledgeable and skillful.

Suicide Prevention

Society as a whole has become more sensitive to suicide (Coleman, 1976). We are more aware of its prevalence, we are more open in discussing it, and we are less prone to see it as a moral or legal wrong. We have set up crisis lines and suicide centers. Professional training programs now focus more on suicide. Practitioners are doing a better job of establishing service networks, providing round-the-clock access to care, and crossing professional boundaries to insure quality service. It is difficult to measure accurately success rates in prevention over the short run. Most practitioners—whether they work in crisis centers or not—can identify cases in which, insofar, as it is possible to judge, they prevented suicide at least temporarily. Whether, in fact, we are making progress in preventing suicide in any components of society is not yet demonstrable, but this must not deter us from continuing to try.

Conclusion

Suicide is an area in the field of psychopathology about which much is known. This high degree of interest must continue. Demographic research can reveal a great deal about rates, distribution, and patterns of suicide, but clinicians must also scrutinize each case of suicide or potential suicide with which they come in contact, identifying critical issues of prevention, management, and aftermath.

As our society changes the way it looks at death and dying, the question of rational or altruistic suicide takes on urgency. Social workers are committed to preserving life; their task is to prevent suicide. But many in society argue that people have a right to kill themselves; that there are situations where suffering is too intense, where there are no other acceptable solutions, where it is culturally condoned to "save face," or where a perceived good will result if someone suicides. Groups have been formed in several countries to encourage this alternative. A recent headline described the prohibition on publishing a book which described a series of sure and painless ways of killing oneself. (Several such books have, in fact, been published.) There have been controversial legal cases of aiding and abetting where a husband or wife helped a suffering partner to suicide.

Social workers may face clients who have reached the decision to suicide on the basis of a rational evaluation that self-destruction is the best alternative for them. My position at this time is to strive to prevent suicide whatever the client's reason. However I also know that our understanding of human behavior continues to evolve and the final word on this subject has not yet been spoken.

References

BECK AJ, RESNIK HSP, LETTIERNI DJ (eds): *The Prediction of Suicide*. Bowie, Charles, 1974.

BOCK EW, WEBER IL: Suicide among the elderly: isolating widowhood and mitigating alternatives. *J Marriage Fam* 1972;34:24–31.

BROWN JH: Reporting of suicide: Canadian statistics. *Suicide* 1975; 5:21–28.

COLEMAN JC: *Abnormal Psychology and Modern Life*, ed 5. Glenview, Scott, Foresman, 1976.

DURKHEIM E: *Suicide: A Study in Sociology*, Simpson G (ed). New York, Free Press, 1951.

FARBEROW NL: *Suicide*. Morristown, General Learning, 1974.

FARBEROW NL, et al; Suicide prevention around the clock. *Am J Orthopsychiatry* 1966; 36:551–558.

FEIDEN ES: One year's experience with a suicidal prevention service. *Soc Work* 1970; 15:26–32.

FREUD S: Mourning and melancholia, in Riviere J (ed): *Collected Papers*, New York, Basic Books, 1959, vol 4, pp 152–170.

GIBBS P: Suicide, in Merton RK, Nisbett RA (eds): *Contemporary Social Problems*. New York, Harcourt, 1966, pp 281–321.

GIBBS JP (ed): *Suicide*. New York, Harper & Row, 1968.

JACKEL M. Depressions, in Wiedeman GW, Mateson S (eds): *Personality Development and Deviation*. New York, International Universities Press, 1975, pp 401–403.

KIEV A: *The Suicidal Patient: Recognition and Management*. Chicago, Nelson-Hall, 1977.

KING M: *Evaluation and treatment of suicide prone youth. Ment Hygiene* 1971; 55:344–350.

KLUGMAN DJ, LITMAN, E, WOLD C: Suicide: answering the cry for help, in Turner FJ (ed): *Differential Diagnosis and Treatment in Social Work*. New York, Free Press, 1976, pp 749–758.

KOVACS M, BECK AJ, WEISSMAN A: Hopelessness: an indicator of suicidal risk. *Suicide* 1975;5:95–103.

LAUGHLIN HP: *The Neuroses*. Washington, DC, Butterworth, 1967.

LUDIN BM: The crisis club: a group experience for suicidal patients. *Ment Hygiene* 1966; 50:280–290.

MENNINGER KA: *Man against himself*. New York, Harcourt, 1966.

MILLER DH: Suicidal careers: case analysis of suicidal mental patients. *Soc Work* 1970; 15:27–36.

MINTZ RS: Some practical procedures in the management of suicidal persons. *Am J Orthopsychiatry* 1966;36: 896–903.

ORTEN JD: A transactional approach to suicide prevention. *Clin Soc Work J* 1974;2:57–63.

PRETZEL PW: *Understanding and Counseling the suicidal person*. Nashville, Abingdon, 1972.

REDLICH FC, FREEDMAN D: *The Theory and Practice of Psychiatry*. New York, Basic Books, 1966.

SCHNEIDMAN ES, FARBEROW NL (ed): *Clues to suicide*. New York, McGraw-Hill, 1957.

SHEPHERD DM,. BARRACLOUGH: Help for those bereaved by suicide. *Br J Soc Work* 1979; 9:67–74.

SINGER RG, BLUMENTHAL JJ: Suicide clues in psychotic patients. *Ment Hygiene* 1969; 53:346–350.

STANLEY JE; BAXTER JI: Adolescent suicidal behavior. *Am J Orthopsychiatry* 1970; 87–96.

STENGEL E: *Suicide and Attempted Suicide*. Bristol, MacGibbon and Kee, 1965.

WETHERILL PS: Predictability, farlane, and guilt in suicide: a personal account. *Fam Process* 1975; 14:339–370.

WHITIS P: The legacy of a child's suicide. *Fam Process* 1968; 7:159–169.

ZEE HJ: Blindspots in recognizing serious suicidal intentions. *Bull Menninger Clin* 1972; 36:551–554.

7

Personality Disorders

Mary Woods

The terms "personality disorder" and "character disorder" (sometimes used interchangeably) have been plagued with trouble. Over the years, for clinicians and theoreticians alike, the multifarious personality disorders have created even greater confusion and controversy than have many other diagnostic designations. Definitions, classifications, and theories about etiology and dynamics are extremely divergent. To add to the problem, in recent times there has been a tendency to equate the personality disorder and the borderline disorder. As this chapter will clarify, the borderline personality is only one of several subcategories of the personality disorders.

In spite of the usefulness of clinical diagnoses, they are—as we all know—replete with ambiguity and hazard and, at best, inadequate for understanding the complicated emotional and situational dilemmas to which clients seek solutions (Blanck & Blanck, 1974, 1979; Briar & Miller, 1971). Fundamental social work values—including commitment to approach clients from the social environmental perspective and to respect the dignity and uniqueness of each individual—can be affronted by superficial use of psychiatric classifications. There are also reasons for particular concern about the label "personality disorder."

First, more than many others, this diagnosis has often been used to describe the *total person* rather than a *condition* (e.g., "She's a borderline"; "he's a passive-aggressive"). Of course, a person is not a common cold; even if it is serious, a cold is something a person has or suffers from; the diagnosis tells us precious little about the individual except that she is sick and probably will be uncomfortable for several days. However, it is not uncommon to hear, "I have a caseload full of personality disorders," implying a homogeneous group of *people* rather than a heterogeneous assortment of *disorders*. Just as one cannot be a neurotic conflict, one also cannot be a personality disorder.

Second, a person pegged as having (or being!) a personality disorder is often viewed—either subtly or bluntly—in pejorative terms. It is true that recently clients with borderline conditions and other personality disorders are looked upon less disparagingly than before, but how often we hear, "Oh, for the good, old days when we saw mostly neurotics!" This attitude stems from a widespread, but as yet empirically unsupported, assumption that patients with personality disorders are peculiarly resistant to change.

Third, the clinical diagnosis of a personality disorder focuses on *pathological* traits—behaviors, thoughts, and feelings. For the most part, diagnostic thinkers have failed to develop a systematic means for assessing *positive* personality characteristics that bear upon the way individuals handle themselves and their lives. In spite of genuine interest in ego psychology and some tools that have been developed to assess particular ego functions (Bellak et al., 1973), we are not very far advanced in being able to describe and understand the "mature," or "healthy," personality.

In this chapter, I examine personality disorders according to a framework that incorporates several theoretical approaches, such as psychoanalytic, ego psychology, object relations, and systems theories. Because the psychosocial model is an open system of thought, it has been able to incorporate and integrate concepts from various fields, including psychology, sociology, anthropology, and education (for further elaboration see Hollis & Woods, 1981; Turner, 1978, 1979).

Personality Disorders and Diagnosis

Classification of Personality Disorders

There have been innumerable attempts to describe personality types, as well as disturbances. Theories correlating body type with character organization or style (e.g., Kretschmer, 1936; Sheldon, 1954) generally have been viewed as simplistic and therefore are not widely followed in clinical circles. Similarly, many studies have demonstrated some sex-linked personality characteristics (perhaps largely socially determined); however, there is also evidence that clear-cut differences between the sexes "are relatively slight when compared with the range of individual differences within each sex" (Stanton, 1978, p. 285).

Theories about character were not a major interest of psychoanalysts until the 1930s and 1940s. In 1908, however, Freud did develop a notion that connected certain traits—such as orderliness and obstinacy—with an anally oriented instinctual life. Subsequently, psychoanalytic thinking developed two distinct, yet interrelated approaches to the classification of personality disorders.

The first, following Freud's early identification of the anal character, classifies personality disorders according to the level of psychosexual development at which libidinal energy has been fixated. Thus, when a child fails to master the tasks of one developmental phase, he is unable to move on easily or completely to the next; energies are still invested in the earlier phase and the child continues to seek satisfactions related to that phase. As the child with the fixation moves into adulthood—still trying to gratify early needs in a repetitive and frustrating manner—dysfunctional traits and patterns develop and produce a personality disorder. Over the years, psychosocial workers have tended to use this model for the classification of oral, anal, and the less well defined urethral and phallic disorders (for further discussion see Cameron, 1963; Fenichel, 1945; Lidz, 1968; Millon, 1981; Reiner & Kaufman, 1959; Stanton, 1978). This system addresses etiological and psychodynamic issues but is limited because of lack of emphasis on interactional factors and family and social dynamics. Erikson's (1950) typology of the eight stages of man was greeted enthusiastically by many social workers because social and cultural considerations influenced his thinking.

The second system classifies personality disorders on the basis of clinical syndromes, such as paranoid, schizoid, or dependent. All three editions of the *Diagnostic and Statistical Manual of Mental Disorders* (American Psychiatric Association, 1952, 1968, 1980) have followed this approach, although each edition introduced changes in specific syndromes and categories. DSM III is the most commonly used reference today and its outline of subcategories will be followed in this chapter.

Descriptive Definitions of Personality Disorders

Personality disorders have been defined in various ways over the years. Space does not permit discussion of most of the definitions (for more detail see Cameron, 1963; Jackel, 1975; Lion, 1974; Stanton, 1978). Some related terms (such as "neurotic character" and "character neurosis") were ambiguous and have been discarded. Included here are only those descriptions that serve the purpose of this chapter. These mostly current definitions apply to the entire range of personality disorders.

Jackel (1975) said that personality disorders are manifested "primarily in the person's characteristic modes of response and behavior." Describing the history of psychoanalytic thinking on the matter, he wrote: "It became evident that patients could react *unconsciously* with repetitive patterned responses that pushed them into characteristic difficulties. These patterned responses had a marked bearing on choice of career, choice of mate, marital adjustment, and many other aspects of social conduct" (p. 287).

Millon (1981) contrasted the healthy and the unhealthy personality:

When an individual displays an ability to cope with the environment in a flexible manner, and when his or her typical perceptions and behaviors foster increments in personal satisfaction, then the person may be said to possess a normal or healthy personality. Conversely, when average or everyday responsibilities are responded to inflexibly or defectively, or when the individual's perceptions and behaviors result in increments in personal discomfort or curtail opportunities to learn and to grow, then we may speak of a pathological or maladaptive pattern. (p. 9)

Millon put normality and pathology on a continuum but identified three behavioral characteristics that distinguish pathological from normal personalities:

1. adaptive inflexibility: the individual with a pathological personality has few strategies for adapting to, or coping with, stress, and these are practiced rigidly
2. vicious circles: the maladaptive patterns themselves "generate and perpetuate existent dilemmas, provoke new predicaments, and set into motion self-defeating sequences" (p. 9)
3. tenuous stability: the individual with a pathological personality is distinguished by fragility and lack of resilience under stress; recurrent failures ultimately lead to less control and a distorted view of reality

An important distinction should be made between "maladaptive personality traits" and "symptoms." Simply put, maladaptive traits usually have existed over the course of an individual's life and have significantly affected important aspects of her functioning. Whether or not the person objects to, or complains about, a maladaptive trait, it is nevertheless seen as an integral part of the personality. A symptom, on the other hand, may be episodic or appear abruptly; it often has a beginning and an end, as many physical symptoms do. Without treatment, a symptom may last a long time or recur, but, in contrast to a trait, it is not viewed by the clinician or experienced by the suffering individual as part of the fabric of the personality. According to DSM III:

> Personality *traits* are enduring patterns of perceiving, relating to, and thinking about the environment and oneself, and are exhibited in a wide range of important social and personal contexts. It is only when *personality traits* are inflexible and maladaptive and cause either significant impairment in social and occupational functioning or subjective distress that they constitute *Personality Disorders* . . . The diagnosis of a Personality Disorder should be made only when the characteristic features are typical of the individual's long-term functioning and are not limited to discrete episodes of illness. (p. 305)

Subcategories of Personality Disorders

For the reason already explained, the DSM III subcategories of personality disorders will be employed here, except for a catchall grouping "atypical, mixed, or other," the antisocial personality (see Chapter 12), and the paranoid personality (see Chapter 13).

Schizoid Personality Disorder

The person with this disorder has some of the following qualities:

1. persistent emotional blandness and aloofness; general coldness and indifference to others and to how they feel toward him; general absence of emotional expression, either tender or hostile
2. dearth of close relationships; genuine preference to be a loner, interacting with others in a mechanical style
3. absence of severely eccentric modes of behavior or communication (in contrast to the person with a schizotypal personality disorder)

A 60-year-old man lived alone in a rented house on the edge of a small town in a dairy farming area; he worked as a mechanic at a local creamery. For as long as his neighbors could remember, he had lived this way, having only occasional contacts with others and these were brief and businesslike. Children called him "the hermit," but his demeanor was not extraordinary; he was neat in dress, well-spoken, and conscientious at work. He never would have come to the attention of the community social service agency if his home had not been sold to the state to make way for a turnpike. Once help with relocation was provided, he had no desire for service; he had no complaints in spite of his extreme social isolation.

Schizotypal Personality Disorder

The person with this disorder has some of the following qualities:

1. persistent eccentricities of thought, speech, perception, or behavior such as magical thinking (e.g., superstitiousness or clairvoyance); ideas of reference; vague, digressive, or circumstantial speech; recurrent illusions; depersonalization; social isolation; constricted or inappropriate affect; bizarre habits; and hypersensitive reactions
2. some of the characteristics of the schizoid personality disorder
3. insufficient data for a diagnosis of schizophrenia, although the condition might qualify as "ambulatory schizophrenia" (Zilboorg, 1941), "pseudoneurotic schizophrenia" (Hoch & Polatin, 1949), or "masked schizophrenia" (Strahl, 1980)

A 50-year-old woman receiving public assistance because of her psychiatric disability described herself as the "black sheep" of her upper middle-class family of origin; she spoke of her relatives with apparent indifference. Her caseworker described her small apartment as "colorful, cluttered, and bizarrely decorated." The client had many statuettes and candles, which she vaguely described as having religious significance. She often gave "readings" to neighbors, saying that she could predict the future. Despite frequent run-ins with neighbors, she insisted that she did nothing to cause the friction; sometimes, she wondered whether her troubles stemmed from some dead relative's spite work. None of the several jobs she had held over the years lasted long; she had difficulty conforming to employer expectations such as punctuality and appropriate dress. Her religious and mystical thinking were not consonant with the beliefs of any other members of her family; she had no coherent social group with which she shared her idiosyncratic beliefs or lifestyle.

Histrionic Personality Disorder

The person with this disorder has some of the following qualities:

1. persistent excitability, emotional lability, flair for the dramatic; frequently attracts an undue amount of attention to herself; all emotions may be expressed in extreme terms and may seem distorted or exaggerated; suicidal threats and gestures are not uncommon; a tendency to move from crisis to crisis
2. a tendency to be perceived as charming and the life of the party and yet as shallow, self-centered, insincere, and lacking endur-

ing interest in others; relationships are often stormy and of short duration
3. frequent feelings of helplessness and dependency; craving for reassurance but not satisfied having gotten it
4. complaints about health and uncomfortable body feelings; inability to enjoy sexual experiences, even when there is promiscuity or seductiveness (Powers, 1972)

A very attractive woman of 48—flamboyantly but meticulously groomed—was taken to the hospital by ambulance after telephoning her daughter that she had "taken some pills." This action followed her discovery that her third husband was having an extramarital affair. As it turned out, she had taken a nonlethal dose of aspirin, but she had "wanted him to know how hurt I am." Her adult daughter, who had many problems of her own, complained that her mother had always been vain, demanding, and unreliable. The woman's husband revealed that his wife was a chronic "tease," playful sexually until he became excited, at which point she "turned cold." The fact that this patient actually had had an extramarital affair before her husband did seemed to have no influence on her outrage at her husband's infidelity. Exploratory marital counseling was abandoned because of this woman's volatility and frequent outbursts of temper during sessions and because her husband of less than two years decided to terminate the marriage.

Narcissistic Personality Disorder

Although the concept of narcissism has long been discussed by psychoanalytic thinkers (Freud, 1953), recent years have seen a burst of interest in pathological narcissism (Kernberg, 1975; Kohut, 1971; Loewenstein, 1977; Masterson, 1981; Palumbo, 1976). There are various viewpoints about the narcissistic personality disorder, but the differences relate mainly to etiology and to theories about personality structure, dynamics, and treatment approaches.

The person with this disorder has some of the following qualities:

1. exaggerated sense of self-importance or uniqueness (e.g., a granidose view of his capabilities or accomplishments); a talent, difficulty, or illness that is seen as "one of a kind"; endless striving for perfection
2. preoccupation with fantasies of courageous feats or outstanding achievements; extraordinary need for adulation and attention without which depression, self-hatred, or rage may ensue
3. disturbances in close relationships with others:

   feelings for others may appear genuine but, in fact, are shallow, nonexistent, or laced with rage, envy, or contempt expectation that needs and feelings of others are the same as one's own; empathy is therefore lacking

exploitative, even parasitic, treatment of others, marked by a sense of entitlement to having her needs met, regardless of the cost to others

vacillation between extreme idealization and depreciation of others (1975)

Kernberg described patients with pathologically narcissistic personalities as presenting

an unusual degree of self-reference in their interactions with other people, a great need to be loved and admired by others, and a curious apparent contradiction between a very inflated concept of themselves and an inordinate need for tribute from others. Their emotional life is shallow. They experience little empathy for the feelings of others, they obtain very little enjoyment from life other than from the tributes they receive from others or from their own grandiose fantasies, and they feel restless and bored when external glitter wears off and no new sources feed their self-regard. They envy others, tend to idealize some people from whom they expect narcissistic supplies and to depreciate and treat with contempt those from whom they do not expect anything (often their former idols). In general, their relationships with other people are clearly exploitative and sometimes parasitic. It is as if they feel they have the right to control and possess others and to exploit them without guilt feelings—and, behind a surface which often is charming and engaging, one senses coldness and ruthlessness. Very often such patients are considered to be dependent because they need so much tribute and adoration from others, but on a deeper level they are completely unable really to depend on anybody because of their deep distrust and depreciation of others. (Pp 227–228)

The flavor of the narcissistic condition was captured by Fromm (1973):

Narcissism can . . . be described as a state of experience in which only the person himself, *his* body, *his* needs, *his* feelings, *his* thoughts, *his* property, everything and everybody pertaining to *him* are experienced as fully real, while everybody and everything that does not form part of the person or is not an object of his needs is not interesting, is not fully real, is perceived only by intellectual recognition, while affectively without weight or color. A person, to the extent to which he is narcissistic, has a double standard of perception. Only he himself and what pertains to him has significance, while the rest of the world is more or less weightless or colorless, and because of this double standard the narcissistic person shows severe defects in judgment and lacks the capacity for objectivity. (p 201)

A 30-year-old bachelor attorney, who had risen rapidly in a prestigious law firm, began treatment complaining of depression triggered by the death of his widowed mother two months earlier. He was the only surviving child (his older sister had died at age 10). His mother had had "blind" faith that he could do anything; he and she had spoken on the telephone almost every day after he had moved out of her home at age 27.

He was handsome, brilliant, and athletically and musically accomplished; he sought and was usually able to get an inordinate amount of admiration. But as talented and successful as he was, the loss of his mother's ever reliable idolization left him feeling bereft and emotionally adrift. Although his mother had been painfully ill for many months before her death, this client never expressed sympathy for her suffering; he spoke, instead, of the unfairness to him that she was gone.

He explained that he had never married because to him commitment was too intense or "sticky"; he "treasured" privacy. He had always made sure, however, to have several women interested in him at one time; he charmed and disarmed them and then did only as much for them as was necessary to keep them "on the hook," available to him for attention and reassurance. His sexual relationships were influenced by the fact that he believed his penis to be smaller than average. (During one anxious meeting with his female social worker, he considered asking whether she would examine his genitals and assure him that they were all right.) His many and frequent sexual liaisons were maintained, in part, to convince himself that his unique penis was acceptable.

After three years of intensive treatment, this man was able to commit himself to one woman and to acknowledge his grandiosity and need to be special. He and his worker agreed that his exaggerated view of himself and self-absorption covered up precarious self-esteem, which was abruptly exposed when his mother's consistent adulation stopped being available.

Borderline Personality Disorder

Like the narcissistic personality disorder, the borderline phenomenon has attracted considerable interest from mental health professionals in recent years (Blintzer, 1978; Freed, 1980; Grinker et al., 1968; Kernberg, 1975; Masterson, 1976, 1981). Again, in spite of theoretical differences, this category now gathers together a group of syndromes that in the past were given various labels.

The person with this disorder has some of the following qualities:

1. impulsiveness and unpredictability; marked instability in behavior, mood, self-image, and interpersonal relationships; tendency to commit physically or emotionally self-damaging acts;
2. intensity of affect (excitability, anger, or despair); chronic anxiety, phobias, obsessions, or other supposedly neurotic symptoms; psychosomatic complaints; extreme vulnerability to stress; emotions frequently flood the intellect, impairing rational thought and action
3. marked shifts in attitude about self and others, often within brief time spans; idealization may be followed quickly by devaluation; people and experiences are viewed in extremes, shifting between all good or all bad; difficulty grasping the concept of moderation

4. subjective feelings of emptiness or boredom; transient disturbances of consciousness (e.g., states of derealization or dissociation, that is, the separation of feelings from their cognitive context); intense dislike of being alone for more than short periods
5. history of extremely erratic, disappointing life experiences
6. identity confusion (e.g., vacillation regarding sexual preferences or life goals)
7. absence of gross psychotic symptoms such as hallucinations, delusions, severe thought disorder, or inappropriate affect, in spite of transient irrational behaviors and thoughts

According to Millon (1981), the borderline condition almost invariably overlaps with every other personality disorder except the schizoid and the antisocial disorder. More often than not, the borderline personality disorder "develops insidiously as an advanced or more dysfunctional variant of its concurrent personality types" (p. 356). Consequently, he divided the borderline personality into subtypes such as "borderline-dependent" and "borderline-histrionic." This approach may be helpful in making a differential diagnosis when the client shows traits of various personality disorders but also exhibits the extreme instability or impulsiveness characteristic of the borderline pattern.

Kernberg (1975) argued that the borderline condition is not a discrete diagnostic entity. Like Millon (1981), he suggested it is a supplementary diagnosis that expresses the degree of severity of impairment in ego function and object relations.

Grinker and associates (1968) conducted a systematic empirical study in which four characteristics common to the borderline syndrome were tested and defined: "*anger* as the main or only affect, defect in *affectional* relationships, absence of indications of *self-identity* and *depressive* loneliness" (p. 176).

A 24-year-old woman was referred to a family agency by her 7-year-old son's teacher because the boy had set fires in the school playground. The client weighed almost 300 pounds, having gained half this weight over the past two years; since the birth of her son, she had lost and regained hundreds of pounds. She "hated" her husband, whom she described as cold and uncaring; they had frequent, sometimes physically violent fights. She alternated between blaming herself for her son's problems and expressing extreme rage at him for his behavior.

This client had lived in a series of foster homes as a child; her parents were alcoholics. Pregnant at age 12, she was placed in a residential institution. She married at 17, after giving birth to her son, only to separate a few months later. She had had numerous intense but short-lived relationships with men, some of which continued after she married her present husband, a year prior to the referral to the agency. She recounted many stories of stormy friendships, most of which ended in her disillusionment.

In spite of her chaotic history, impulsiveness, and unstable behavior and emotions, this client was aware of her self-destructive patterns and said she was "desperate" for help. Her life felt meaningless and frightening. As it turned out, she came to the agency regularly (once or twice weekly) over a period of almost six years. Her relationship with her worker stimulated all of the fluctuations of feelings that she experienced with others: intense dependence and sudden outbursts of angry resentment and distrust. Slowly, erratically, with frequent reversals, this client began to feel in better control of herself and her life and to be able to maintain relationships that were still intense but also enduring and satisfying.

Avoidant Personality Disorder

The person with this disorder has some of the following qualities:

1. extraordinary sensitivity to real or potential criticism manifested in extreme feelings of anguish, humiliation, and shame
2. painful shyness; isolation and loneliness are deeply felt; close relationships are avoided unless strong assurance of acceptance is given; mistrust of friendly overtures
3. low self-esteem; extreme self-doubt and self-criticism
4. strong desire for social relationships and affection (in contrast to the person with a schizoid disorder)

A 26-year-old woman, employed as a secretary and seen by others as very competent, came from an extremely disturbed family situation. Her father and three of her four siblings had been diagnosed as schizophrenic and periodically were hospitalized. She chronically devalued herself and her achievements; she was deeply disappointed that she could not make friends or get close to a man. Evenings and weekends were spent painfully alone in her small apartment; relief came when she could return to work on Monday morning.

After a few months of treatment at a mental health clinic, this woman asked to join a therapeutic group led by her worker. She hoped to become more socially comfortable. She was well accepted by other group members, but after two meetings (with one missed in between) she did not return. She explained to her worker that she felt "ashamed" about having talked about herself; she was afraid of being belittled or humiliated. Six months later, she joined the group again, but the pattern repeated itself. Her protective withdrawal from the group paralleled her general life situation: she isolated herself from others because she could not get unconditional guarantees of total acceptance.

Dependent Personality Disorder

The person with this disorder has some of the following qualities:

1. passivity; willingness to permit others to make major decisions affecting his life, even when the decisions are to the person's detriment

2. tendency to adapt behavior to please others on whom the person feels dependent; unwillingness to express her own needs or preferences, particularly if these might conflict with the wishes of others; generally compliant and conciliatory, even to the point of being self-sacrificing or allowing abusive treatment
3. fear of being alone or self-reliant
4. self-perception as weak, helpless, and inferior to others; low self-esteem

Writing about the person with the "receptive orientation," comparable to the dependent personality, Fromm (1947) described the individual who "feels 'the source of all good' to be outside, and he believes that the only way to get what he wants—be it something material, be it affection, love, knowledge, pleasure—is to receive it from an outside source" (p. 67).

Mrs. Jensen, a 52-year-old woman, sought help because she had been "in an absolute panic" since her husband, to whom she had been married for two years, announced that he wanted a divorce.

The husband, a minister, had been her confidant and counselor when her first husband was divorcing her, also a time in which she had felt extremely frightened. During this period, the minister initiated a sexual relationship with the distraught woman, left his own wife, and persuaded Mrs. Jensen to live with him. When both were divorced, they married one another. Although extremely bright, Mrs. Jensen had never worked and did not believe she was capable of becoming self-supporting. For this reason, she said, she had allowed the minister to make decisions for her, even though she knew they were in conflict with her own wishes and values.

"How come I let everyone take advantage of me?" this client repeatedly asked during early months of treatment. Gradually, the question was reframed to help Mrs. Jensen determine what she stood for, what decisions she wanted to take, what she needed to make her life more contented, and so on. As she worked with her feelings of helplessness and fears of self-reliance, she slowly became more self-directing. She discovered that she was not incompetent after all and realized that it took less "strength" to be responsible for her own life than to accept the humiliation and pain she had endured through her two marriages, in which she had let others take charge of her.

Compulsive Personality Disorder

The person with this disorder has some of the following qualities:

1. excessive conscientiousness; drivenness; concern with cleanliness, tidiness, and right and wrong; perfectionism and concern with detail, which may result in poor productivity because of fear of making mistakes and inclination to ruminate over even minor decisions; tendency to get lost in minor issues and to lose sight of major

ones; concreteness; lack of humor; harsh self-criticism and excessive guilt
2. strong, often stubborn, desire to control or dominate others; a tendency to be moralistic
3. restricted ability to express warm feelings; emotional/or material stinginess
4. inability to enjoy free time or to take real pleasure in interpersonal relationships

A self-employed accountant came to the attention of a mental health clinic because one of his two teenage sons was severely depressed. This man, who worked for himself, had been dismissed from several accounting firms for failing to meet deadlines and for indecisiveness.

In family therapy, his wife and sons complained that he was an "autocrat" whom they could never please. Both boys were excellent students, well liked, and cooperative (to a fault, perhaps), but they could not get the approval from their father that they obviously craved. Generally, he pointed to their imperfections and rarely to their achievements. He complained about his wife's "sloppy" housekeeping and poor budgeting in spite of her apparent adequacy in these areas. Family sessions easily could be dominated by his lectures to his wife and children; he was angry when they disagreed with him or refused to do what he wished. Often, he attempted to engage the worker in a debate on the merits of therapy. Clearly, he was unable to relax and enjoy other family members, who, in fact, were prepared to be caring toward him. After a few meetings, he discontinued family sessions and only reluctantly, when given a grim prognosis about his son by the school psychologist, did he allow the depressed boy, who wanted treatment, to attend the clinic.

Passive-Aggressive Personality Disorder

The person with this disorder has some of the following qualities:

1. indirect resistance (e.g., forgetting, procrastinating, inefficiency, making irrelevant excuses) to demands or assumed demands of others even when direct challenge would be possible; oppositional and negative attitudes in all aspects of life
2. tendency to be sullen, irritable, and pessimistic; assumption that the "grass is always greener on the other side"; if recognition or praise is given, it is repudiated as "too late," "insincere," etc.; resistant behavior similar to that of the adolescent
3. attribution of power to others (including equals and sometimes subordinates) that they do not have or would not exert; assumption that direct, self-assertive behavior and communications will have either no impact or else negative consequences
4. lack of self-confidence; inability to take a stand for his own convictions or needs

Brought to a family agency by his wife (diagnosed as having a compulsive personality disorder) for marital counseling, Ed Klein sat sullenly during the first session. Although both he and his wife were in their forties, the caseworker noted to himself that Ed seemed more like the wife's son than her spouse. Even when spoken to directly, he mumbled or did not answer. His wife complained that he was "impossible"; he took no responsibility in the house or for the children, she said. Apparently, Ed had never been promoted from his position as a clerk because he was often late, dawdled, did only the bare minimum, and never took initiative.

This couple came for treatment intermittently, when Ed's wife got "fed up." Only after many sessions over several years did Ed begin to modify his oppositional stance. He began to initiate interactions with his wife and complain directly about her domineering and meddlesome ways. He even took tentative steps toward finding a more challenging job, but none he located suited him. Generally, he expressed his resentment toward others more openly, but he had little awareness of his own part in his problems at home or at work and little optimism about things changing very much for him.

Etiology of Personality Disorders

A thorough overview of the literature on the etiology of the personality disorders is beyond the limits of this chapter. A comparative analysis is complicated for many reasons. First, there is lack of agreement about personality traits and types; similarly, nomenclature, definitions, and conceptual frameworks differ considerably. Second, some behaviorists and family therapists, among others, have little interest in exploring the relationships between personality or behavior and early childhood influences; they deal only with current etiological influences. Third, the relative roles of hereditary and environmental factors continue to be a subject of disagreement and uncertainty. Fourth, within the same school of thought, a syndrome or disorder may be attributed to various combinations of influences. For example, from the psychosocial view, the suspiciousness associated with the paranoid disorder and the stubbornness found in the passive-aggressive style may have been influenced most strongly either by family interactions or by pervasive social forces (e.g., deprived or oppressive conditions such as poverty and lack of opportunity, repressive climates like that of the McCarthy era of the 1950s). Even among writers with a psychoanalytic–ego psychology–systems approach, there are many major and minor differences. Thus, significant variations in thought can be found regarding the nature of libidinal and aggressive drives, ego organization, and the interrelationships among these. For example, followers of Kernberg (1975) and Kohut (1971) disagree with each other about the developmental issues that contribute to narcissistic and borderline conditions. Object relations theory and ego psychology, on which notions about the origins of personality pathology often rest, also contain differences (see Blanck & Blanck, 1974, 1979; Guntrip, 1961, 1971).

The central interacting influences on the development of all personality disorders, from the psychosocial view, will be discussed here first. This will be followed by a review of factors that contribute to specific disorders. While influences are sometimes discussed as though they were discrete, of course each one interacts with the others and either stimulates or retards the evolution of the disorder.

Heredity and Personality Disorders

Genetic factors have been of interest to scientists studying severe psychopathology and many believe that there are genetic predispositions to psychosis (Kallman, 1946; Strahl, 1980). However, Millon (1981) cautioned that

> no systematic research in psychiatry has utilized a polygenic model of inheritance despite its appropriateness as an explanatory vehicle for such less severe and less sharply delineated pathologies as personality disorders. This reflects the preoccupation of researchers with easily diagnosed severe patients, with the dominant, if erroneous, belief that all forms of psychopathology are best conceived in a dichotomous model of health versus disease, with no intermediary steps. (p. 69)

Among lay people familiar with newborn babies, there is agreement that enormous differences among them can be seen immediately. Some babies are active or fretful while others seem passive or contented. Research supports these observations; hundreds of infants studied from birth and followed into adolescence were found to maintain many of their original characteristics over the years (Murphy and Moriarty, 1976; Thomas & Chess, 1977).

Of course, inborn factors are influenced by the interactions and systems to which an individual is exposed. For example, if, in fact, there is a genetic predisposition to the dependent personality, this tendency will be either checked or reinforced depending on the style of the child's caretakers. If they usually satisfy the child's needs before the child has had to ask, dependent tendencies will be strengthened; on the other hand, if the child's independent behaviors are encouraged, dependent qualities are less likely to become disabling. A baby with a happy temperament often provokes cheerful, loving responses; in contrast, the fretful infant tries the parents' patience or undermines confidence in their caretaking. By the same token, temperament, at least to some degree, probably can be reversed; for example, a withdrawn infant may become more active and alert in the context of a supportive, interested family.

Early Developmental Influences and Personality Disorders

In spite of differences between psychoanalytic and psychosocial thinkers, there is consensus that the child's very early years *crucially* affect subsequent development. Of course, later experiences and environmental conditions can either reinforce or reverse early influences as these interact with the personality.

Spitz (1965) discovered that babies deprived of adequate mothering developed abnormalities of functioning and anaclitic (related to a damaged dependency between mother and child) depression. Bowlby (1969, 1973) stressed the importance of physical closeness and attachment to *one* maternal figure, seeing this as necessary for healthy development. He (1973) added: "experiences of separation from attachment figures, whether of short or long duration, and experiences of loss or of being threatened with separation or abandonment—all act, we can now see, to divert development from a pathway that is within optimum limits" (pp. 369–370). Mahler and co-workers (1975) described the child's early developmental phases; many notions about the etiology of ego deficits and pathological personality development have been derived from their work.

Winnicott's (1965) familiar concept of "good enough mothering" covers the theoretical issue of overriding concern to object relations writers. Simply put, it is believed that a satisfactory relationship between the child and his parent or caretaker requires 1) *consistent* parental availability and support and 2) age-appropriate encouragement of the child's independence and self-direction. When dependence needs are not adequately filled by the parental person or when caretaking is interrupted by separations and losses, psychological damage is expected to ensue. Likewise, when a parent clings to a child or for some other reason discourages autonomous functioning, healthy growth is stunted and deviations occur.

There is sufficient evidence from experimental research and from empirical observation to claim that influences in the child's early years do, indeed, have detrimental effects on personality and adaptive functioning. But it is equally obvious that the personality system is infinitely complex and that we are a long way from being able to predict which children—on the basis of their unique endowments and early experiences—will develop specific personality strengths or disorders. It is possible, for example, that some children with "good enough" or even excellent parenting are unable to get the full benefit of it. "Contributions to the etiology may come from either or both sides of the mother–child equation—from both nature and nurture" (Masterson, 1981, p. 132).

Family Relationships and Personality Disorders

The importance of the family system to personality development has long been recognized by social workers (Richmond, 1917; Towle, 1957). Recent developments in family therapy have added sophistication to our understanding of the complexities of family relationships (Hollis & Woods, 1981). Concepts about family roles and communication have contributed to knowledge about family dynamics. Increasingly, clinical social workers are becoming experts on family, as well as personality, theory, thereby adding understanding to the nature of the reciprocal influences between them.

Just as the early parent–child dyad can affect personality development, so the entire family system can distort or promote a child's healthy growth. Writing about the pathological family triangle, Satir (1967) remarked:

> I have been repeatedly struck by how readily the [identified child patient] drops his role as intervener once family therapy is under way. Once he is assured that arguments do not bring destruction and that marital amicability lightens parental demands on him, the [patient] actively helps the therapist help his parents as *mates*, while at the same time he tries to get his parents to recognize him as a separate individual with needs of his own. (p. 56).

Concepts about differentiation have been central to family systems theories and also to ego psychology. Healthy development is presumed to be fostered by the family that helps individuals (children and adults) to see themselves as separate, self-directed people at the same time that they share close or intimate relationships with others. Difficulties arise when one assumes that one must negate one's sense of self in order to avoid abandonment by others or, conversely, when one fears that loss of autonomy stems from intimacy and therefore shies away from close relationships.

Boundaries are the means by which individuals (and family subsystems and generations) protect their separateness and sense of identity (Bowen, 1971; Minuchin, 1974). When boundaries are either too permeable or too rigid, personality problems may develop. For example, if an individual believes that family members will be accepting only if they are allowed to take responsibility for major areas of her life, low self-confidence, passivity, and subservience—traits associated with the dependent personality disorder—may be fostered. By the same token, the individual who attempts to prevent intrusiveness on the part of other family members may develop an aloof or bland style and prefer isolation to companionship—qualities found in the person with the schizoid personality disorder.

When forces in the family shift, individuals usually have to find new ways of functioning and adapting. For example, clinicians frequently see dramatic changes in the behavior or mood (e.g., a depressive reaction) of the spouse of an alcoholic when the latter stops drinking. Similarly, an apparently dependent and weak spouse may become self-reliant and even gain a new lease on life when the domineering, or strong, mate dies.

The Larger Environment and Personality Disorders

The interplay between people and their environments—including those extending beyond the family—has been a major interest of social work theory and practice. It is generally acknowledged that one cannot discuss the etiology of personality disorders without reference to their relationship to community and societal systems (Germaine, 1979; Hollis & Woods, 1981; Meyer, 1976). Reiner (1979) noted "that individualism and narcissism are defenses against the latent depression and lack of self-esteem that are fostered by many aspects of society" (p. 3). She added that a sense of personal irrelevance originating in early childhood can be

recreated or intensified in later life by the struggle to survive emotionally in a society that provides few supports in developmental crises or times of stress. A sense of personal irrelevance may include having one's needs unrecognized by others, having one's anger considered unjustified or unacceptable, or feeling unloved, isolated or abandoned, insignificant or worthless, and powerless to effect change. (p. 3)

Surely, feelings of loneliness, helplessness, and low self-esteem derived from conditions beyond the individual's control foster rigid traits associated with disorders of personality. People adapt to their environment by conforming to its demands or by attempting to change it to suit needs and goals. When changes in the larger social system are not possible—as they are not for many people living under deprived, frightening, humiliating, or other severely destructive circumstances—deep personality scars are inevitable.

Generally, the literature attributes personality disorders to influences of nature and nurture in early childhood. Without denying the importance of these factors, it is necessary to emphasize also the roles played by psychologically or physically noxious conditions at *any* stage of life. Whether one is forced to live in a concentration camp, the back ward of a mental institution, a rat infested or unheated tenement, or a community marked by terrorism, personality damage must ensue. As ego functions of adjusting to reality, mastery, and autonomy are assaulted, maladaptive reactions (that may endure even if the environment improves) are unavoidable.

Etiology and Subcategories of Personality Disorders

It should be emphasized that one of the important factors influencing the perpetuation of any personality disorder is the disorder itself. In other words, the behavior of the individual with the disorder frequently elicits reactions from others that reinforces maladaptive traits. The discussion of etiological contributions to specific disorders will elucidate this point.

Schizoid Personality

This disorder is sometimes assumed to derive from meager emotional warmth or body contact in early life (Cameron, 1963; Millon, 1981). Detached and cold parenting, on the one hand, or intrusiveness, on the other, can induce withdrawal and schizoid traits. Inborn temperamental qualities are also thought to contribute to the development of this disorder. Obviously, loners perpetuate their aloofness by failing to pursue or attract people with vitality or warmth.

Schizotypal Personality

The eccentricities manifested by the person with this disorder are presumed to have both organic and experiential roots (Millon, 1981; Strahl, 1980); but there is little consensus about the relative weight of these factors. Surely, bizarre communications and ungratifying family relationships of various sorts can create personality traits characteristic of people with this condition. Some of the pioneers of the family therapy movement, such as Jackson, Bateson, and Weakland (Jackson, 1968) stressed the relationship between schizophrenia (on which this disorder is assumed by some to border) and human communication. Frequently, individuals with schizotypal traits are unable to sustain meaningful interpersonal relationships; their isolation serves to exaggerate their peculiarities and a downward spiral is often set in motion, with the end result being hospitalization and/or deterioration of interpersonal skills.

Histrionic Personality

Individuals with this disorder (often referred to as a "hysterical disorder") are thought to come from a background in which dependence needs were unmet; such women may have had hysterical mothers themselves and emotionally distant (either passive or domineering) fathers (Powers, 1972). According to Millon, (1981) "Parents of the future histrionic rarely punish their children, they distribute rewards only for what they approve and admire, but they often fail to bestow these rewards even when the child behaves acceptably" (p. 152). Thus, recognition and approval from others become important motivators. The person is often unable to develop solid values and a robust self-definition because of inconsistency experienced in childhood. The ongoing, intense search for praise and stimulation curtails inner growth, resulting in superficiality; therefore, deeply intimate and sustaining relationships are not achieved.

Narcissistic Personality

Pathological narcissism traditionally has been viewed by psychoanalysts as a developmental arrest. Simply put, either parental inadequacy results in the very young child's failing to advance from autoeroticism ("primary narcissism") to develop attachments to particular objects or, defending herself against parental coldness or cruelty, the child regresses to an earlier, narcissistic phase. Differences about etiology among Kernberg (1975), Kohut (1971), Palumbo, (1976), and others are too abstract for this discussion. Millon (1981) used social learning theory to explain the causes of the narcissistic pattern; overvaluation by parents of a child's worth becomes internalized but cannot be sustained or validated in the real world. Horney (1939) said: "Parents who transfer their own ambitions to the child and regard the boy as an embryonic genius or the girl as a princess, thereby develop in the child the feeling that he is loved for imaginary qualities rather than for his true self" (p. 91). Since self-esteem rests on fantasy, the person is often only a breath away from depression and self-hate.

Problems for the person with a narcissistic disorder are perpetuated and reinforced. When grandiosity and other illusions cannot be externally validated and when self-centeredness and lack of interest in others leads to isolation, the person may struggle all the harder to prove that he is, in fact, special. Thus, disappointments become self-perpetuating.

Modern times may play a part in supporting the preoccupation with self. Many believe that narcissism derives from feelings of alienation, lack of opportunity, cutthroat competitiveness, or the need to retreat from the violence of our age (Lasch, 1978; Reiner, 1979). Some also think that current childrearing practices, such as reluctance to restrain children's behavior, encourage self-centeredness.

Borderline Personality

Divergent views on the etiology of the borderline condition abound. Kernberg's (1975, 1977) writings have been among the most important in bringing our attention to this disorder. From his point of view, faulty nurturing from parental figures results in the failure of some ego functions, to develop such as impairments in the capacity to sublimate primitive drives, to control or regulate impulses or affects, and to function independently. Of primary importance in the genesis of the borderline syndrome, in Kernberg's opinion, is the fixation that occurs at the stage (under one year of age) in which the ability to distinguish self from other has already developed (as may not be the case in some psychotic disorders) but in which good and bad representations of the parent and of the self have not yet been synthesized. These good and bad concepts about self and others remain separate, presumably so that the bad will not overwhelm the good. Individuals are therefore unable to develop a unified, balanced self-concept or capacity for consistency in interpersonal relationships; rapid shifts occur between overvaluation and undervaluation of oneself, others, and life events.

Inferences about the intrapsychic processes of the infant who later develops a borderline disorder are complex and abstract and have been criticized. For example, Grinker (1977) complained about Kernberg and other psychoanalysts:

> They postulate, for example, a constitutional excess of oral aggression, a deficient neutralization of aggression, a lack of anxiety tolerance with fixation at four to twelve months of age, and so on. They write of defective ego synthesis, attributing it to a rewarding and withdrawing maternal object or to an inability to internalize the representation of the maternal object. Not one indicates how many patients were investigated, by what methods, with what controls, and how reliability and validation were studied. (p. 168)

Millon (1981, p. 332) stressed the divergent backgrounds found among individuals with borderline personality disorders. Thus, he described these conditions as "advanced dysfunctional variants of the less severe dependent, histrionic, compulsive, and passive-aggressive personalities". In his view, "when these four less dysfunctional personalities prove deficient or falter under the strain of persistent environmental stress, they will frequently deteriorate into what we have labeled the 'borderline personality pattern'" (p. 332). Attributing borderline conditions to some kind of a "failed background," Millon asserted: "It is the instability of both behavior and affect, combined with their shared search for acceptance and approval, that justifies bringing these patients together into a single 'borderline' syndrome despite their divergent histories and coping styles" (p. 333). From his point of view, etiological factors cannot be specifically designated. It certainly stands to reason that *any* personality disorder that presses people into more and more futile behavior, repetitively painful failures, and disappointments in relationships will cause them to become increasingly disorganized, lonely, and hopeless and to manifest many of the qualities associated with the borderline disorder.

Avoidant Personality

The avoidant pattern is thought to derive from repeated experiences of derogation and humiliation. Whether derogation came from parents or peers (e.g., when a child is taunted for a physical handicap or for his racial, class, or ethnic background), the results can be painful sensitivity and self-doubt in social situations. Hereditary predispositions to hypersensitivity may influence the genesis of this disorder. In any event, the low self-esteem characteristic of the person with this condition often prevents her from reaching out to people; in turn, the person's frightened demeanor may cause others to retreat or reject, thus reinforcing the pattern.

Dependent Personality

When children are overprotected (for any reason), strivings for competence and individuation may be stunted. Confidence can also be undermined when circumstances force children to try to be independent before they are able to be so. In either case, the tendency to rely on others may develop. Since adults with this disorder tend to be overly cooperative and placating, they may find people to lean on; the dependent pattern is thereby perpetuated, as is low self-respect and a sense of incompetence. And, of course, when people with this pattern allow others to make detrimental decisions for them or to abuse them, the vicious cycle becomes even more serious.

Compulsive Personality

Controlling parents with high and definite expectations for their children are generally assumed to be influential in the development of the compulsive (or obsessive) personality disorder (Salzman, 1968). The "anal character," closely comparable to this condition, refers to the fixation at the phase in which bowel training is an issue. Millon (1981) quoted Rado's view of the impact of the anal pattern on obsessive traits:

> If the mother is overambitious, demanding and impatient . . . then the stage is set for the battle of the chamber pot.
>
> Irritated by the mother's interference with his bowel clock, the child responds to her entreaties with enraged defiance, to her punishments and threats of punishment with fearful obedience. The battle is a seesaw, and the mother . . . makes the disobedient child feel guilty, undergo deserved punishment and ask forgiveness. . . . It is characteristic of the type of child under consideration that his guilty fear is always somewhat stronger; sooner or later, it represses his defiant rage. Henceforth, his relationship to his mother, and soon to the father will be determined by . . . guilty fear over defiant rage or *obedience* versus *defiance*. (p. 223)

Ambivalence, Rado noted, is rooted in the underlying obedience–defiance conflict: the person "ponders unendingly: must he give in, or could he gain the upper hand without giving offense" (p. 223).

If firm and demanding parents, school teachers, or others in authority are consistently punitive when children do not meet their expectations, the child's autonomy is undermined; guilt and self-doubt are reinforced. Anxiety about not conforming begets anxiety (Cameron, 1963). Concern with perfection and sticking to the rules promotes the rigidity of the compulsive personality. Reluctance to make decisions or changes or to take risks can exacerbate the emotional constriction and other qualities associated with this disorder. Because of the tendency to comply (in spite of ambivalence or resentment), the person may receive acceptance and even praise from others, unless excessive rumination results in poor performance. Usually, however, he does not enjoy warmth and spontaneity in relationships; thus, even after sacrificing so much of his personality to be "good," he may still end up feeling alone.

Passive-Aggressive Personality

The negativism of the passive-aggressive pattern may be rooted in inconsistencies and mixed messages experienced by the child from her parents (Millon, 1981). When one parent typically sends contradictory signals or when two parents disagree with one another on a regular basis, it is difficult for the youngster to know how to achieve approval or recognition. While the person with the dependent personality usually has been able to find ways of satisfying overprotective parents (e.g., by being docile) and the person with a compulsive personality often can get some rewards from compliance and achievement, the person with the passive-aggressive style probably was unable to please his parents. For example, if a father complains to his son about the latter's lack of athletic interest but then criticizes him for preferring baseball to football, the boy must become pessimistic about pleasing his father. Family therapists often see youngsters in no-win situations with one or both parents. The "double-bind" can foster irritability and resistant behavior. Obviously, the negativism, pessimism, and stalling tactics often seen in individuals with this disorder can be annoying or even infuriating to others. Thus, behavior intended to test the sincerity of others or that which expresses disappointment and hopelessness about past relationships can serve to perpetuate the individual's no-win experiences and attitudes.

Summary

Our knowledge about the etiology of personality disorders is, for the most part, imprecise and impressionistic. However, social work clinicians who have seen large numbers of individuals and families under all kinds of conditions may be particularly well equipped to develop hypotheses about the many forces that interact to create self-defeating personality patterns.

The inflexible, maladaptive life patterns that are the hallmark of personality disorders can be viewed, in one sense or another, as defensive patterns. However dysfunctional the personality style, it seems safe to assume that *at one time* it was a safeguard against intolerable anxiety, self-hate, helplessness, or insecurity, as well as a means for warding off unacceptable sexual or hostile impulses. At the time these defensive styles are developed—to protect against inner and outer threats—they may be the *most adaptive alternatives* available to the (usually young) person creating them. While the person with a personality disorder often has forfeited some sense of autonomy or availability for interpersonal relationships, or both, it seems probable that unconsciously the vulnerable child believed the adaptation was necessary to find security in the family.

Defensive life patterns can prevent the development of healthy defense mechanisms (Lidz, 1968). For example, the individual with a dependent disorder may never have developed defenses against separation anxiety, which are necessary for autonomy, individuation, and ability to deal with reality. The therapeutic importance of understanding the function (archaic or ongoing) of defensive and adaptive patterns is discussed in the section on treatment.

It is also true that defensive personality patterns may be converted into assets. For example, many clinicians have strong caretaking qualities, which may have been defensive adaptations in early life. Perhaps the future therapist, as a young child, had to defend against feelings of insecurity by becoming protective and looking after dependent, inadequate, or ill adults in the family.

Some features of personality disorders actually may be looked upon as virtues: self-effacement, conformity, and even infantile dependence or masochistic suffering, under some circumstances, are very much admired. In my view, for the adult the issue is whether there is choice in the matter; for example, is excessive modesty or conformity felt as obligatory or is it an expression of preference under particular circumstances? Cameron (1963) discussed the matter further:

> To avoid common misunderstandings, it is essential to state here that courage, integrity, dependability, normal self-sacrifice and the ability to accept dependence upon others are not signs of character disorder. It is only when these seeming *qualities* turn out to be demands, upon a human environment which does not want them, and does not gain in warmth or understanding from them, that we call them disorders rather than virtues. (p. 640)

Social Work Treatment of Personality Disorders

Treatment and Psychosocial Diagnosis of Personality Disorders

In many instances it can take weeks or even months before the social worker has any degree of certainty about the extent or recalcitrance of a person's difficulties. One may be clear that there is a personality disorder and even know which subcategory or subcategories best describe the person's condition, but information about the complex origins of the problem or about the optimal mode of treatment often comes slowly. Diagnostic tools are not perfect. Complicated interacting and self-perpetuating influences take time to understand. Ego deficits, distortions, and defenses often are not evident right away.

Similarly, while some strengths are immediately apparent, others may be obscured from view and revealed only as treatment progresses. As discussed earlier, less attention has been given to developing tools for the assessment of positive qualities than to the diagnosis of pathological conditions. However, it is often potential strengths that determine the individual's capacity to utilize treatment and improve social functioning.

The notion that treatment determines the diagnosis (Blanck & Blanck, 1979; Boyer & Giovacchini, 1967) may be more valid for work with personality disorders than for many other forms of psychosocial treatment.

As treatment progresses, then (in individual, family, or group sessions), it is necessary continually to assess the client and her situation to discover strengths, capacities for change, and limiting influences. The therapist looks for indications of these in the quality of the client–worker relationship and the client's use of the treatment situation; the behavioral, attitudinal, or emotional shifts that occur when there are changes in the family or environmental situation (whether therapeutically induced or not); and the degree to which the environment supports the personality disorder and/or discourages change. Elaboration of these points follow.

The Client–Worker Relationship and the Client's Use of the Treatment Situation

When the worker is attuned to the client's approach to treatment and to the quality of interactions with the worker, over a period of time inferences can be made about personality structure, ego development, capacity for self-observation and self-analysis, capacity to use the therapeutic relationship, honesty, and motivation for change.

On the surface, one client may appear to be more disturbed than another but in the long run prove to be more treatable. The description of the behavior or traits of a particular client may seem to convey a poorly integrated personality structure, but the capacity for a therapeutic alliance and for change may, in fact, be better than for another client who appears to be less disturbed.

A 28-year-old woman, Sally, sought help at a mental health clinic because of extreme anxiety and episodes of disabling panic. A public relations representative for the telephone company (her seventh job in six years), she had begun to feel that the position was too much for her; she often found herself in a rage at customers. A fairly attractive and bright woman, she had no close relationships with men but instead was promiscuous in a frantic way; sometimes after drinking too much she could not remember who had come home with her. She "hated" her mother and frequently had furious arguments with her. She had two or three women friends but was feeling "fed up" with them; nevertheless, she was terrified of being alone. Except for the increased feelings of panic, her problems had not changed much over the years. Early in treatment, the caseworker diagnosed Sally as having a borderline personality with histrionic traits.

For the first two months of treatment, Sally made almost daily telephone calls to the worker. Medication prescribed by the clinic psychiatrist did not reduce anxiety. Although not suicidal, she believed she was unable to cope and would die soon. After about four months of twice weekly, primarily supportive treatment, Sally rather dramatically calmed down; now, she added, she wanted to work on "getting my act together." She had grown to trust the worker and relied on her to understand and not judge her. She could then begin to reflect on herself, on her emotional and behavioral patterns, and on her situation. After two more years of therapy, she enjoyed her job, had been promoted, and planned to stay with her company. She joined some organizations, made new friends, and was going out with a man she liked very much; she no longer drank to excess. Her anger at her mother dissipated; mostly, she felt sorry for her now. She said she was handling her life in a way she had never done before.

Phyllis, age 31, had functioned adequately as a bookkeeper at the same firm for over 10 years. She went to a clinic when her husband left her and their 10-year-old daughter to live with another woman. She was angry and depressed. Phyllis had been in therapy on two previous occasions but had never felt helped. Although she was consciously interested in making changes in her "unhappy and boring" life, very little had happened after a year of treatment. She complained about her situation and other people; she liked her worker but protested that "nothing ever helps." Intellectually, she could see that she was not working very hard to solve her problems, but she believed that she was either unwilling or unable to rally her energies to do so. In spite of the worker's interest, availability, and skilled efforts and Phyllis's general trust in the worker's goodwill, the client never developed a strong therapeutic relationship with her. Treatment terminated after the presenting depression had lifted and an afterschool play group had been located for her daughter.

As these examples illustrate, treatment uncovers prognosis. One cannot be sure how a client will use the treatment relationship and what strengths and capacities will be revealed in the process. To the layman, Phyllis might seem far less disturbed than Sally. One could describe Phyllis as a stable but cranky person leading a humdrum life. Initially, even to a clinician, Sally might seem more troubled because of the instability of her mood and her long-standing pattern of erratic behavior. As it turned out, Sally was able to make a strong connection with the worker, to be introspective, to gain some sense of mastery over her feelings and behavior, to make changes in her life, and to bolster her self-esteem. Compared to Phyllis, Sally had a greater capacity for trust, more motivation for change, a better ability to understand others and their feelings, a wider emotional range, and a greater ability to enjoy herself. Over the course of treatment, it became evident that Phyllis's defenses were more rigidly set than Sally's.

As treatment proceeds, it often becomes clear that the client who heavily uses defenses such as "splitting" (inability to integrate contradictory feelings or states of mind, in conjunction with a tendency to divide all experiences, perceptions, and affects into extremes of good and bad) and "projective identification" (projection of aggressive, negative feelings about oneself onto others as a means to reduce anxiety) and rapidly shifts from adoring to blaming the worker may actually be more available for reparative work than the client who never really engages in the treatment relationship. For example, some individuals with schizoid or narcissistic personality styles may be able to see the worker as only a shadowy figure or a pale image. Such clients may function on higher levels in certain areas of life, but they also may be less available for change than those who make strong—even if erratic—connections with others.

First meetings with clients may be misleading in various ways. For example, a client's apparent passivity may reflect initial anxiety, an attempt to conform to the presumed expectations of a person seen to be in authority, or lack of sophistication about social work treatment. Some clients either deliberately or unconsciously present themselves as dependent or deficient in coping ability, perhaps because past or present important people have been threatened by their autonomous functioning. Finally, it may not be evident immediately that a client is consciously dishonest, either to please the worker or to avoid inner anxiety.

Behavioral, Attitudinal, or Emotional Shifts that Accompany Changes in the Family or Larger Environment

The severity of a personality disorder may be revealed by the degree to which outer influences affect it. For example, suppose a mildly retarded man is moved from a punitive foster home to a halfway house that promotes self-respect and independence; if long-standing suspiciousness is diminished (at least to some degree), the worker might be more encouraged about the possibility of further change in paranoid traits than if no shift had resulted from the move. Similarly, if, in family therapy, positive changes in one family member are followed by healthy changes in the client assumed to have a personality disorder, greater flexibility may be predicted than if the reaction had been negative or dysfunctional.

Environmental Encouragement of the Personality Disorder

Obviously, if a woman with a dependent disorder is married to a domineering man, personality traits of both may be reinforced by the marital complementarity. Similarly, a paranoid disorder may be aggravated in a client whose relatives or associates behave sadistically or maliciously. By the same token, when the family system discourages differentiation of its members for any reason or requires a scapegoat to keep marital problems concealed, a personality disorder of a family member may be sustained. Under these circumstances, an individual attempting to make changes might be discouraged by the family forces mitigating against them; thus family therapy would be the treatment of choice (Hollis & Woods, 1981).

Social and economic abuses and deprivations nurture many of the traits of personality disorders. Personality changes are difficult to make (or even to consider) when one lives in any inhumane environment.

Finally, cultural or family values may discourage help-seeking (e.g., "People should solve their own problems."). Fortunately, the past decade has seen some positive shifts in attitudes about therapy; some people and groups that shied away from it formerly now view it more favorably. In many instances, men not only are willing to join their wives in therapy but more frequently than ever before are initiating contact with the agency, clinic, or social work practitioner. It is estimated that 34 million people in the United States are receiving professional psychotherapy or counseling. (*New York Times*, Oct. 28, 1981, p. C8) This wide use should help remove the stigma that has discouraged some people from seeking help in the past, rendering treatment more acceptable in years to come.

Special Characteristics of Social Work Treatment of Personality Disorders

Much has been written in recent years about the diagnosis and treatment of the so-called less than neurotically structured patient (e.g., Blanck & Blanck, 1974, 1979; Boyer & Giovacchini, 1967; Giovacchini, 1975; Kernberg, 1975, 1977, Masterson, 1976, 1981). To social workers, however, the proliferation of literature may not be very helpful for several reasons.

First, although social work papers on the subject are on the increase, much of the writing has been by psychoanalysts, who have particular methods of treatment not necessarily used by clinical social workers. Thus, social work readers may learn about diagnosis and the intrapsychic aspects of personality disorders, but they may not be sure that their training equips them to do the treatment.

Fortunately, it has been found that these conditions do yield to clinical social work treatment. Social workers are reporting more and more on successful therapy with individuals manifesting extremely severe personality disorders (Blintzer, 1978; Freed, 1980; Palumbo, 1976). The case of Mrs. Zimmer demonstrated that psychoanalysis or frequent sessions may not be necessary in order to provide a therapeutic and reparative experience that results in significant personality changes and a more fulfilling life (Hollis & Woods, 1981). Case examples included in this chapter add to the growing body of evidence that personality disorders are amenable to social work intervention. "The regressive path is an uneven one and the ego consists of various parts operating at different developmental levels" (Boyer & Giovacchini, 1967, p. 264). Social workers, who traditionally have been attuned to their clients' strengths, are demonstrating how to engage well-developed ego functions in the task of bringing the client up to a more adequate level.

Second, most writers on the subject concentrate almost exclusively on the intrapsychic issues of individuals with personality disorders and on the theoretical and technical aspects of one-to-one treatment. Psychosocial therapy draws on additional knowledge related to social, family, and environmental influences. For this reason, social workers actually are often able to engage and treat people whom other professionals do not see. Outreach, home visits, and provision of concrete services are all part of the trained social worker's armamentarium. These means can provide clients who would not ordinarily seek psychotherapy with the opportunity to make personal changes. Social workers in child welfare, probation, or other services often are able to treat clients or refer them for psychological help; some of these clients might otherwise be too uninformed or too afraid to seek treatment on their own. Even involuntary clients of protective services or prison inmates have been known to engage in treatment once they are presented with social work services.

Family or couple treatment and the provision of other environmental services can be influential in promoting change in individual clients with personality disorders. Rice (1980), a social worker, demonstrated how she has used concepts about narcissistic personality disorders in couple therapy; she quoted Ackerman, who said: "A good marriage is the most effective of all treatment relationships" (p. 271). Social workers have long known the value of working with family members and of improving the climate of family life in order to help a particular client's situation or personality problem. Systems theory now supports social work's years of experience. As Gyarfas (1980) said: "in a systems context it will be possible to examine the psychosocial proposition that there is likely to be an association between an individual's inability to meet his own and other's needs, and severely stressful events in the social systems (primary, secondary, and tertiary) on which he depends" (p. 56).

Third, the literature tends to make sharp distinctions between clients with neurotic personalities and those with personality disorders. Some clinical social workers (particularly those trained before interest in personality disorders burgeoned) may be led to believe that the therapuetic approach to clients in the latter group is so different from the methods with which they usually work that they cannot effectively treat personality disorders. It seems safe to say that in spite of variations in emphasis in the treatment of people with different clinical diagnoses, psychosocial therapy with all people has more similarities than dissimilarities (Hollis,

1981). The Hollis typology of treatment procedures (sustainment; direct influence; exploration-description-ventilation; reflective discussion of the person-situation, and of pattern-dynamic and developmental factors) pertains to every clinical condition. Of course, the actual blend is influenced strongly by the assessment of many factors, only one of which is the clinical diagnosis.

Fourth, reading the psychiatric literature, social workers might conclude that they cannot be of any help to an individual with a personality disorder unless there is motivation for basic personality change. Social workers, probably more than other professionals in the mental health field, do not expect every client to want intrapsychic therapy. Even when ego deficits, dysfunctional traits, or defenses are apparent, the social work clinician does not recklessly seek to engage the client in working on problems which he is not interested in considering. Clients come to agencies—even those equipped to provide intensive treatment—for various reasons: placement of a retarded child, vocational rehabilitation, housing problems, and family life education, to name a few. Meeting these needs is valuable in and of itself. And, of course, many such clients with personality disorders eventually do decide that they want to make changes they did not originally envision. But social workers would be patronizing clients if they underrated the importance of responding to specific requests or if they urged clinical treatment on clients who clearly did not want it.

Beginning Therapy and Establishing a Relationship with the Personality Disordered Client

Presenting Problems

Individuals later diagnosed as having personality disorders may come to the clinical social worker's attention for a multitude of reasons. Often, clients seek help in a state of crisis—when they have become excruciatingly anxious, depressed, or phobic. Such symptoms may come on the heels of drastic life changes such as marital separation, death, loss of job, or family illness. In other instances, the distress may be triggered by seemingly minor events. Obviously, the client's approach to recovery will be an important diagnostic clue; the presence of a personality problem may be revealed by the difficulties the client has in regaining equilibrium.

It is well known that people with personality disorders are not accustomed to recognizing (even intellectually) that their difficulties have any connection with their own personality or behavior. Their pain is very real and often extreme, but the cause may be seen as other people, external events, uncontrollable urges, fate, or some combination of these. Many such clients tend to be hopeless about improvement unless the factors that seem to victimize them change. Consequently, clients with personality disorders may resolutely seek environmental solutions without examining their own part in the difficulty.

As often as not, clients come to facilities in which social workers are employed for services unrelated to psychological treatment. They may come for help with employment problems, daycare, the needs of elderly relatives, temporary shelter, traveler's aid, and so on. Often, no further services are needed. In some instances, however, such inquiries rather quickly lead to treatment or referral for problems deriving from a personality disorder.

Jack contacted family court to determine whether he could take "family action" against his father for showing pornographic pictures to Jack's "girlfriend." His presenting request could not be met, but Jack's conversation with a sensitive intake supervisor brought to light considerable personal distress. Quite readily, Jack accepted a referral to a clinical social worker in private practice. He wanted help because he felt isolated and afraid of losing his relationship with the woman he loved; he was also aware that his painful sensitivity to criticism gave him problems on the job. As it turned out, he had many traits associated with avoidant and schizotypal disorders.

Jack's case also illustrates that the feelings, behaviors, or defenses of clients with personality disorders are not always as "ego syntonic," as many believe them to be. Many clients declare right away that they wish to make personality changes. Recently, a client in her mid-forties said in a first session that she was "sick and tired" of living "half a life." She believed her "entire personality" needed an "overhaul"; she hated her impulsive rages at her husband and children; she said her perfectionism gave her trouble everywhere; and she put little blame for her problems on others.

Worker Characteristics

Therapist characteristics and attitudes identified by research and clinical observation as important to successful treatment are essential in work with clients with personality disorders (e.g., Compton & Galaway, 1975; Hollis & Woods, 1981; Perlman, 1957). These include nonpossessive warmth and concern, genuineness, accurate empathy (Truax & Carkhuff, 1967), nonjudgmental acceptance, and optimism that change is possible (Hollis & Woods, 1981). Additional qualities found to take on particular importance when working with clients manifesting personality disorders are reviewed here.

Demonstration of Reliability

Consistency about appointments, punctuality, keeping promises, listening closely, and maintaining the therapeutic attitudes mentioned above are imperative with personality disordered clients. More often than not, they have had unstable parenting and (as a result of patterns that perpetuate interpersonal problems) erratic adult relationships. Such clients, who usually have not internalized a sense of confidence in others, can find it difficult to believe that the worker can be counted upon to care. People who have not had positive mothering in childhood "often not only lack the internalized 'good mother' but are incapable of feeling reassured that the therapist and/or external environment will provide what is absent" (Paolino, 1981, p. 211). Treatment begins when the reassurance is given by demonstrating reliability; aspects of the diagnosis are revealed by how quickly the client can trust in the continuity of the relationship.

Professional Security and Competence

People with personality problems often have trouble enough trusting without being faced with a worker who feels unsure. Clients who have not had satisfactory people to rely upon will want to know that their worker can understand them before they allow themselves to engage in a dependent therapeutic relationship; often, such clients intuitively perceive a worker's lack of skill or personal vulnerability. With clients with personality disorders, every effort should be made to demonstrate that the worker is not interested in exploiting them (as they often feel others are). This message can be conveyed, for example, in the course of discussing fees and acknowledging realistic needs for fee reduction; in being scrupulous in not attempting to elicit praise or gratitude to serve one's own needs; in being self-revealing *only* when it is in the interests of the client; and in avoiding unclear or evasive communications that could be interpreted by the client as dishonest or manipulative.

Capacity to Reach Out

When a reliable, professionally secure, and competent worker reaches out as a "real" person to another "real" person—by making a call to inquire about a client who has been ill, by paying a home visit, by telephoning if an appointment is missed, by providing concrete services or useful information—the probability that trust will develop (however slowly) and that the client will engage in treatment is greatly enhanced. Furthermore, as Freed (1980) said, the worker who is not passive and establishes herself as a real person will "reduce fantasies and negative transference" (p. 553).

Capacity to Maintain Respect and Empathy in the Face
of Trying Behavior and/or Lack of Progress

The worker who chooses to treat clients with personality disorders
may face clinging or distancing and rejecting behaviors, suspiciousness,
passive-aggressive attitudes, extreme mood swings, and many other
qualities that can test his patience and good humor. Even early on, the
client's repetitiveness and the tenacity of rigid defenses and self-
defeating behaviors can be frustrating to the worker. The worker can
minimize countertherapeutic reactions by remaining aware that the
disagreeable qualities are born of fear and despair and usually have little
to do with the worker as a person. With very dependent, volatile, or
otherwise difficult clients, it is often best to try to help them with short-
term goals; if these are achieved, optimism is enhanced and there is less
chance that lack of movement will result in angry or disappointed termination. Even when treatment is brief, if it has been successful in
achieving its limited purpose, the client is more likely to return if further
help is needed later on.

Family and Group Treatment

Because family interactions can support dysfunctional personality traits
or discourage positive changes in the client, either ongoing family
therapy or family meetings on behalf of the client seen in individual treatment is an effective approach to facilitating change. Also, since individuals with personality disorders frequently see their problems as
functions of the behavior or attitudes of other family members, family
treatment may be the preferred method for helping them all to sort out
whose thoughts and feelings are whose. This process of differentiation is
essential in the treatment of many clients whose self-concepts are not
well developed and of those who persistently blame others for their
troubles. Accordingly, the worker should have solid grounding in the
theory and practice of family therapy. In the initial phase of treatment,
decisions about modality are often made. If family therapy is the treatment of choice, it is usually best to begin early on. Otherwise, a client
who has been seen over a period of time in individual therapy may feel
abandoned by the shift. Family members also may doubt the worker's
impartiality if the worker has had a much longer relationship with one
member than with the others.

Group therapy has also been found to be very useful in work with
clients with personality disorders of various kinds (Freed, 1980; Yalom,
1975). In many instances, such clients are isolated and get can from the
group support and mutual understanding that exceeds anything the
worker could or should supply. Clients also get an opportunity for feed-

back and reality testing. Self-centered clients (e.g., many of those with narcissistic or histrionic traits) may begin to enhance their self-esteem when called upon to be more giving and sharing; they may learn more genuine and gratifying ways of relating to others. In my experience, it is often best to wait before suggesting a group experience. Some clients (including many with severe paranoid or avoidant traits) may not be able to tolerate a group until they have been in treatment for a long time, if ever. Some may be too impulsive or abrasive and disrupt the group process or frighten away other members. On the other hand, an occasional client—possibly with a borderline or a schizotypal disorder—is threatened by the face-to-face nature of individual treatment. Some such individuals have benefited from an initial period of group therapy (Strahl, 1980).

In any event, from the first session with a client exhibiting a personality disorder, the possibility of using family or group modalities in conjunction with (or instead of) individual treatment should be considered.

Psychopharmacologic Evaluation and Treatment

For some clients with personality disorders, medication that lifts depression or diminishes anxiety brings relief; the capacity to focus on the work of therapy is often facilitated. On the other hand, many individuals do not benefit at all from drug therapy and even seem to become more symptomatic (e.g., showing increased anxiety or extremely unpleasant side effects). The social worker needs access to a psychiatrist who is an expert in medications and with whom she can work comfortably.

Guidelines

Every person is different. The more quickly a worker finds approaches that suit a particular client, the better the chance of engaging him. For example, many clients with personality disorders (particularly when they are severe) can become very anxious and/or distrustful if the worker is extremely warm, interested, or active or appears to want to get too close to them. On the other hand, the cool, detached, passive stance can arouse feelings of rejection or abandonment. The closeness–distance, active–passive balances most comfortable for the particular client should be determined as quickly as possible.

Often, the risk that negative transference will get out of hand or that the client will sabotage the treatment process can be reduced if attention is paid to these potential problems early. For example, the worker could say, "You may find yourself getting angry or disappointed with me sometimes. It will be very important for our work together if you tell me so. The things that happen right here in the treatment hour between us can be useful in understanding problems that occur for you elsewhere.'' Resistance and opposition are diminished if the worker enlists the client as an equal in the process of searching for solutions. Clients are helped to take responsibility for any part they may play in interfering with the therapeutic relationship or process.

From the outset, various techniques can be used to establish a therapeutic climate and set the tone for the treatment process. Respect for clients with personality disorders is conveyed not only in traditional ways but also through techniques designed to promote self-awareness, mastery over life and impulses, self-esteem, self-differentiation and self-direction, self-reliance, compassion for oneself, and other ego functions. If interventions suitable to a particular client are discovered early in treatment, progress may be faster and the client's hope for change should be strengthened.

A few sample techniques are illustrated here. They are not all useful in every case, but they do serve to show that, from the start, interventions can bring focus to the work and encourage the participation of the client in the process of change:

> in the client who assumes that her thoughts or feelings force her to act in particular ways, cognitive functions and the capacity for self-direction and self-control can be promoted by saying, ''Perhaps if we both bring our good minds to the job and begin to make sense out of the irrational feelings, you will find that they will not lead you around by the nose as much as they seem to now.''
>
> in the client who has frequent rages, hope for control and respect for the client's distress can be conveyed by saying, ''We may find that your anger reflects some kind of fear or sadness about yourself or your life that we can work together to try to understand.''
>
> in the client who feels furious at, or devastated by, the disapproval or insult of another, the sense of autonomy and the development of a more consistent self-concept can be supported by saying, ''Do you ever wish you gave more credence to your own view of yourself than to the views of others?'' Or, ''Do you wish you were less sensitive to other people's opinions?''
>
> in the client who shows pessimism, distrust, or negativism; or challenges the worker or the treatment process, the fear of intrusion can be quelled and initiative encouraged by saying, ''There is no rush, but when you feel comfortable enough I would like it if you could tell me in what ways you think I can be most helpful to you.'' Or, ''In the long run, you will be the best judge of whether you are getting the help you need here.''

in the client who is harshly self-critical or who whines about never doing things right, the capacity for "self-soothing" (Blanck & Blanck, 1979) can be nurtured by saying, "You sound awfully angry at yourself about something that already hurts so much. How come?"

in the client who seems ready to begin to shed some maladaptive patterns, this readiness can be fostered by saying, "Do you think it is as important as it used to be for you to feel so diffident (distrustful, afraid of others, hard on yourself, responsible for your adult children's lives, etc.)?"

Ongoing, Intensive Treatment with the Personality Disordered Client

Setting

For some clients with personality disorders who, for various reasons, cannot or will not engage in long-term treatment, short-term or crisis intervention approaches may be beneficial. These therapies should be valued by the social worker as much as any other type of treatment. However, if clients interested in making basic changes approach an agency that is not equipped to provide intensive, ongoing treatment, appropriate referrals should be made. Personality shifts take time—often years of treatment. Unfortunately, there may be no family agencies or clinics available to serve such clients and referral to a clinical social worker in private practice will be necessary. Social work's commitment to serve all groups compels workers to press for adequate treatment facilities and to use sliding fee scales so that first-class treatment is available to everyone who wants it.

Methods and Goals

More than 20 years ago, Reiner (a social worker) and Kaufman (a psychiatrist) (Reiner & Kaufman, 1959) discussed four stages of treatment for clients with personality disorders who were parents of delinquents: establishing a relationship; ego building through identification with the caseworker; separation from the caseworker; and self-understanding of behavior and its roots in the past. Even earlier Austin (1948) had written about the "corrective" casework relationship and "experiential" treatment. Subsequently, social workers expanded on this concept. In short, the client's transference reactions and expectations of inadequate mothering are corrected in the context of the worker's acceptance and ability to understand and empathize; the worker offers explanations and interpretations that help the client reflect on his behaviors, present situation, and past life (Hollis & Woods, 1981).

Although now there is more sophisticated theory regarding the structure and organization of personality disorders, current viewpoints on treatment of clients with deficits stemming from inadequate early parenting (or parent–child incompatibility) have much in common with those social work notions of 25 years or more ago. Freed (1980) defined three phases of long-term treatment of the borderline personality: "1.) the testing phase, in which establishment of a working alliance takes place; 2.) the working-through phase (by far the longest), which includes especially resolution of the underlying depression; and 3.) the separation and establishment of a constructive life direction" (p. 554). Giovacchini (1975) said that the analyst's interpretations demonstrate her ability "to understand and pull together what to the patient was disparate, frightening and unknown. This integrative activity, analogous to the mother's understanding of the child's needs, leads to ego structuralization" (p. 276). Kernberg (1977) made similar points. Blanck and Blanck (1979) discussed the "reparative" emotional experience: "Where the patient lived, as a child, in a 'climate' that failed to encourage ego apparatuses, the therapist provides or helps the patient provide a more favorable or conducive climate. Then the cognitive and emotional capacities combine to make interpretation usable" (p. 118).

Long-term treatment, then, takes place in the context of a corrective or reparative relationship; trust is nurtured so that healing and growth can proceed. Therapy is an intricate process that varies considerably in accordance with the qualities of both client and therapist. There are no blueprints. Usually, no single interpretation or technique will produce dazzling results or even immediate effects. Rather, the accumulation of therapeutic interactions, along with the repetitiveness and consistency of the approach, slowly (but often surely) results in progress and even in substantial change. The following methods and goals have been related to the successful long-term treatment of clients with various types of personality disorders.

Promotion of Realistic Self-awareness or Self-observation

As already indicated, interventions designed to help clients reflect on themselves, their feelings, their patterns of thought and behavior, and their past lives often begin immediately. These same measures are repeated over and over throughout the treatment process. One of the first of many benefits that can come from self-observation early in treatment is the ability to begin to evaluate one's own emotional and behavioral patterns. It then becomes possible for the client to determine which are functional and which interfere with personal and interpersonal satisfaction. The notion that the client is totally at the mercy of outside forces begins to dissolve and motivation to make changes *from within* emerges. Self-awareness is encouraged by questions—sympathetically posed and sensitively timed—asked in one form or another over and over again. For example, "Are you hoping to become less frightened when your father get angry?" Or, "Do you think your daughter will feel like confiding in you, as you wish her to, when you call her names?" Gently posed inquiries gradually can have the result that dysfunctional patterns become ego alien and thus are viewed as intrusions.

Encouragement and Reinforcement of Cognitive Capacity

Throughout the treatment experience, generalizations such as "Nobody likes me," "My husband never compliments me," "If I weren't so stupid I would be making more money than I am," "The nicer I am, the more abuse I get," or, "My mother understands me better than I understand myself," are, in one way or another (with an eye to appropriate timing), questioned and examined. For many clients with personality disorders, confidence in being able to think for themselves and to figure out the world around them often needs bolstering. On one level or another, they frequently believe that *other* people are experts on their own experiences. Explanations and interpretations may be offered by the worker to help make sense out of chaotic thoughts and feelings, but every effort is made to encourage clients to begin to challenge and correct their own misconceptions and refine their own thinking.

Fostering the Capacity for Differentiation

As cognitive abilities and the relationship with the worker are strengthened, the issue of differentiation often becomes a major focus of treatment with clients with personality disorders. Frequently, such clients have difficulty distinguishing between their feelings and their thoughts or between feelings and reality. For example, a client who is rarely late for appointments may rush in five minutes after the hour and say, "I *know* you are angry that I am late," to which the worker may reply, "Are you *afraid* that I am angry or do you *think* that I am angry?" Similarly, a client may say, "If that kid disobeys me one more time, I may break his arm," to which the worker may ask, "Is it that you *feel* that you want to hurt him or that you *think* that you really will? Do you know which it is?" Techniques such as this, repeated over time, help the client learn to differentiate between feelings that are aroused by particular circumstances and what the client knows to be true. Interestingly, once better differentiation is achieved, there is greater integration between thoughts and feelings; unmanageable emotions no longer so readily flood the intellect.

Differentiating among feelings can be perplexing for many clients with borderline conditions or other personality disorders. Emotions are often experienced in amorphous, global terms. Rage, emptiness, or general depressive feelings frequently dominate the inner lives of such clients. In conjunction with increased self-esteem and self-understanding that come in other ways, techniques that help clients distinguish one feeling from another become important ego building measures. For example, "When you say you 'feel terrible,' do you mean you feel sad, scared, guilty, or what?"

Other clients—including many with paranoid disorders—tend to report and manifest predominantly irritable or hostile feelings. In the context of a solid relationship, the worker may gently probe, when indicated, for "softer" feelings: "Do you think you were disappointed when you were turned down for the job?" Or, "Were you afraid to show your wife how touched you were by her concern for you?" On the other hand, clients with avoidant or dependent personality disorders may be filled primarily with feelings of sadness or fear. In these cases, the worker can help the client search for other emotions. With a client who has been crying for hours over a friend's unfounded accusation, the worker might ask, "Do you think you were mad, as well as sad, about what happened?"

Sometimes, through identification with a worker capable of a range of emotional expression, the client begins to internalize this example and differentiate feelings more precisely. Usually, to avoid the possibility of having clients feel misunderstood, the worker recognizes that the predominant feeling states (anger, sadness, fear) are understandable outgrowths of unhappy past experiences (of which most such clients have had more than a fair share); however, clients can also be helped to realize that now more possibilities may be open to them, including the opportunity to enjoy pleasurable feelings, rarely felt by some clients.

In my experience, the encouragement of exhaustive ventilation of anger, sadness, fear, or any other characteristic emotion is usually counterproductive; more often than not, the client ends up feeling worse and becomes more regressed. While *always* acknowledging the validity of the feelings, the worker may be able to help the client use growing self-awareness and reasoning abilities to wonder, for example, why he got angry or sad in response to a loving gesture from another. Even severely impaired clients frequently can link present reactions to past (often childhood) experiences. Other sample interventions might be: "Are those tears of sadness or of pleasure?" "Do you think you have gotten into the habit of showing (feeling) anger because you are afraid you will get hurt if you express warm (or sad, frightened, disappointed, etc.) feelings?" "Do you ever wonder what would make you respond to an insult with a smile?" "Was it anger you were feeling or do you think you were feeling self-conscious about being assertive or expressing a difference of opinion to me (your husband, wife, mother, etc.)?"

Sometimes, efforts to develop a sense of identify can both outwardly and inwardly resemble anger. Just as the infant and the adolescent may seem angry and negative when they are struggling to gain independence, some aggressive feelings in adult clients reflect efforts toward growth, rather than hostility. Interpreting them in this way can be extremely helpful to the client. Family meetings also can help clients learn to differentiate one emotion from another and to develop a broader emotional range.

Distinguishing one person's feelings and thoughts from those of others can be problematic in families in which members are excessively dependent on one another. The boundaries of the individual personalities may be so diffuse that one member may say, "I know Jane's feelings better than she does," or "Joe says he is not angry but I know he is." In family therapy, the worker may suggest that family members ask one another about their feelings. By exposing and challenging projections, distortions, and inaccurate assumptions, the worker encourages individuation. In individual treatment also, as illustrated earlier, transference reactions to the worker can be helpful in differentiating the client's feelings from the worker's. When the client was five minutes late and thought the worker was angry, the worker pointed out that these were not necessarily her feelings but perhaps related to the frightened feelings of the client, who expected to be scolded for being late. Similarly, clients often believe that the worker wants either to possess and exploit them or to throw them out in the cold. Obviously, the therapeutic relationship provides the client with a nonthreatening forum in which to learn to identify unrealistic perceptions and reactions.

Nurturance of Self-Compassion

Clients with personality disorders are sometimes harshly self-critical and unforgiving about their mistakes, real or imagined. They may feel guilty about not living up to unrealistic expectations placed upon them by others; often, assumptions are made about expectations that are not true. Separation and individuation, for most clients with personality disorders, represents a major area of unfinished business. Frequently, therefore, there is a tendency to assume (not always consciously) that others will resent, be hurt by, or ridicule their assertive or independent moves. In the treatment relationship, then, self-criticism or guilt about not living up to the projected expectations of the worker can be exposed and clients often begin to be gentler with themselves. A worker may ask,

"Can you think about ways in which you may want to change without being so intolerant of your past or present behavior (feelings, thoughts, etc.)?" Even when interventions are not immediately successful in helping a client become self-comforting, an accumulation of such experiences eventually may be internalized.

Not only is self-compassion in the here and now beneficial, but also it is often helpful to clients who are self-critical about current behavior to begin to cultivate sympathy for themselves regarding past events. For example, "Do you ever feel sad for that little girl who had to spend so much time alone?" Or, "Can you be more understanding of the child who felt confused for so many of those years?" As Blanck & Blanck (1979) noted: "Self esteem can probably never be created by means of external confrontation" This is not entirely true in my view. We are in agreement, however, that "when the angry and provocative behavior can be understood and explained in its very formative processes, retrospective self empathy will produce a more positively cathected sense of self" (p. 251).

It should be emphasized that I do *not* recommend encouragement of feelings of helplessness and self-pity. Nor do I suggest that clients be urged to blame their parents; actually, when clients can feel more compassion toward themselves, they can bring more understanding (and sometimes even deeply loving feelings) to their relationships with their parents. The purpose of this approach is to facilitate the development of self-nurturing mechanisms, which can help eliminate the client's negative self-image; as self-esteem increases, the heavy reliance on external diminishes.

Healing the Split

As discussed earlier, clients with personality disorders often divide their thoughts and feelings about external events, other people, and themselves into all good and all bad compartments; there are often rapid shifts from one extreme to the other and what was all good can become all bad in a matter of moments. This separation of affects and attitudes requires constant attention in treatment sessions. For example, a man may rant about hating his son and have to be reminded that only the other day (or a few minutes earlier) he spoke very proudly and warmly about the boy. The worker might ask whether it is possible that he is very annoyed by the boy but cares about him at the same time. "Good and bad feelings can coexist" is a reminder that may startle some clients and initially make them very anxious. However, when confronted over and over again with the safety of the merger, they often learn to synthesize extremes.

Clients differ in the tenacity of their denial of the emotional connection between good and bad (or libidinal and aggressive) ego states. For some, the ability to integrate positive and negative feelings and experiences seems to be just below the surface, and tolerance for their coexistence can be achieved relatively quickly. For others, the splitting process is so entrenched that even years of treatment will fail to produce a truly comfortable synthesis.

Two notes of caution might be added here regarding the treatment relationship and the splitting mechanism.

First, for some clients, the worker may be a frequent target of bad feelings. The management of countertransference complications evoked by the client's angry attitudes and projections can become an important aspect of work with clients with personality disorders. Usually, but not always, empathic understanding of the client's defense against anxiety can prevent the worker from feeling like counterattacking or withdrawing concern. When clients are particularly difficult or when the worker for one reason or another feels vulnerable, supervision or consultation with colleagues can help the therapist regain his lost perspective. Even the most skilled and experienced workers can be provoked to react negatively under certain conditions.

Second, it is not as unusual for clients with severe personality disorders consistently to idealize or adore the worker even when they manifest extreme fluctuations of feelings in other areas of life. For many months or longer, the all good feeling for the worker seems to be necessary; this unrealistic but positive attachment may nurture some clients during the early phases of treatment, in some way making up for deficits derived from faulty parent–child connections. Of course, it is always wise to let the client know that there is a possibility that she may feel—possibly suddenly—angered by or disappointed in the worker at some time; these potential reactions should be seen by worker and client alike as providing grist for the mill in treatment. In some instances, however, it may be counterproductive to treatment to press too hard to disabuse the client of idealized feelings for the worker. In due time, as treatment progresses, realistic and balanced reactions will replace the exaggerated attachment.

Support of a Sense of Continuity

Closely connected to the often prolonged process of mending the split is the reinforcement of a sense of continuity in feelings, attitudes, and experiences. In the benign, reliable climate of the therapeutic relationship, the client with impaired object relations may begin to bring into awareness the memory that a caring person is available—even when that person is absent. Clients can be helped to develop the capacity for trust or optimism, even in the face of minor upsets, by being confronted with their overdetermined reactions. For example, ''Because your boss was angry with you, you were convinced you were going to be fired even though the day before he praised your work and recommended you for a raise." Or to a man who says he fears that his wife will leave him, "It seems hard for you to get the benefit of the fact that only last week your wife said that the best move she ever made was to marry you. How do you account for such a short emotional memory?"

Encouragement of Individuation

Strong defenses against separation and individuation have been powerful influences in the lives of many people with personality disorders (Masterson, 1976). For example, an adult living with parents or with siblings may function reasonably well until there is some forced disruption. Certain well-structured and secure employment situations can conceal a person's underlying fear of autonomy. Many clients first come into treatment when there has been a shift in the external situation: the parents die or the factory relocates, generating anxiety or depression. By the same token, during the course of treatment, as clients move toward independent goals of their own choosing, separation fears and abandonment depression may emerge. As defenses (e.g., schizoid or compulsive patterns, splitting, denial, projection) weaken and moves are made toward independence and more satisfying (either less clinging or less remote) relationships, some clients may seem to regress. Even after a period of apparent progress, such reversals can occur. (On the other hand, some clients are able to shed maladaptive patterns with few, if any, interim negative consequences.) When depression or anxiety do occur, gentle and consistent understanding and reassurance are required. Explanations about what is happening are essential and can be greatly comforting. For example, to a young woman who recently moved from her parents' home, the worker might say, "It's no wonder that you are feeling scared now. Even though you and your mother fought a lot, you two lived as though you were one. It's probably going to feel frighteningly lonely sometimes for a while until you begin to enjoy your new freedom."

Some clients will react to their moves forward by trying to cling to the worker; frequent telephone calls, requests for additional appointments, and difficulty leaving at the end of a session are familiar clinging behaviors. Patience is necessary, of course, but so is individual assessment of the client's need for additional support; either too much or too little can hamper progress.

Repetitive Positive Reinforcement

When clients develop greater self-understanding, make significant (even if not always immediately successful) efforts toward change, reach

important decisions, or provide themselves with new or more constructive life experiences, reinforcement is essential. Statements of general
support—"You seem to be feeling better recently," or "You certainly
look well," or "You have many fine qualities"—are of limited value, at
best, but remarks that are specifically directed to the person and the
situation can be extremely bolstering. For example, to a woman who
knows she is working below capacity because of fear of greater responsibility and autonomy and yet wants to make changes, the worker might
say, "It must have taken a lot of courage to apply for that promotion
when it could mean being transferred to a new and unfamiliar department. Good for you!" Or to a woman who was feeling like a prisoner in
her own home because her mother insisted on visiting every day and the
daughter was too afraid of her mother's anger to set limits, "You must
have been feeling more confident about yourself when you told your
mother you wouldn't be at home as often this summer." Over and over
again, appropriately timed comments such as "You really did a good job
on that, didn't you?" or "Are you proud of yourself for working out that
problem so well?" contribute to positive self-esteem and encourage
clients to begin to reinforce their own choices and changes.

Leaving Room for Disagreement

Explanations, suggestions, or interpretations offered by the worker
are often best framed in a way that makes disagreement possible and
shows that it is encouraged. This does not mean that the worker negates
her expertise or objectivity about a particular situation. For clients with
personality disorders, there must be confidence that the worker knows
what he is doing. However, therapeutic goals are supported if the
worker offers ideas with a built-in opportunity for the client to refute
them. This is so for several interrelated reasons: client autonomy is
fostered by the worker's expectation that the client may have a different
or better notion; the client is not encouraged to be dependent on the
worker for the last word; the client is encouraged to search for insight
and understanding from within; the worker may be under a misappre-
hension that only the client can correct; and the tendency of some clients
to get stuck in oppositional resistance is neutralized.

Conclusion

This chapter may best be concluded with the reminder that individuals
with personality disorders—even those with similar clinical
diagnoses—are very much different from one another. Intelligence;
motivation and capacity for self-awareness and change; creativity;

talents; values; and sense of humor are among the strengths that vary from person to person and appear in countless combinations. Similarly, maladaptive patterns or defenses vary both in degree and in flexibility.

Broadly speaking, psychosocial treatment is designed to build self-esteem, to repair developmental deficits, to promote self-differentiation, and to help clients learn new ways of mastering their lives. In some cases, the worker may have to be extremely active and reach out; in other instances, clients do a great deal of their own work in the context of a caring relationship. Some make remarkable progress; others—including some who try hard to change—seem tragically stuck and make only modest improvements. Perhaps as our knowledge about the treatment of personality disorders expands, the size of this latter group will shrink.

References

American Psychiatric Association: *Diagnostic and Statistical Manual of Mental Disorders*, ed 1. Washington, DC, American Psychiatric Association, 1952.

American Psychiatric Association: *Diagnostic and Statistical Mannal of Mental Disorders*, ed 2. Washington, DC, American Psychiatric Association, 1968.

American Psychiatric Association: *Diagnostic and Statistical Manual of Mental Disorders*, ed 3. Washington, DC, American Psychiatric Association, 1980.

Austin L: Trends in differential treatment in social casework. *J Soc Casework* 1948; 29:203–211.

Bellak L, et al., *Ego Functions in Schizophrenics, Neurotics, and Normals*. New York; Wiley, 1973.

Blanck G, Blanck R: *Ego Psychology*. New York, Columbia University Press, 1974.

Blanck G, Blanck R: *Ego Psychology, II*. New York, Columbia University Press, 1979.

Blintzer J: Diagnosis and treatment of borderline personality organization. *Clin Soc Work J* 1978; 6: 100–107.

Bowen M: The use of family theory in clinical practice, in Haley J (ed): *Changing Families: A Family Therapy Reader*. New York, Grune & Stratton, 1971.

Bowlby J: *Attachment and Loss*. Vol 1: New York, Basic Books, 1969.

Bowlby J: *Attachment and Loss*. Vol 2: New York, Basic Books, 1973.

Boyer LB, Giovacchini PL: *Psychoanalytic Treatment of Characterological and Schizophrenic Disorders*. New York, Science House, 1967.

Briar S, Miller H: *Problems and Issues in Social Casework*. New York, Columbia University Press, 1971.

Cameron N: *Personality Development and Psychopathology*. Boston, Houghton Mifflin. 1963.

Compton BR, Galaway B: *Social Work Processes*. Homewood, Dorsey, 1975.

Erikson EH: *Childhood and Society*. New York, Norton, 1950.

FENICHEL O: *The Psychoanalytic Theory of Neurosis.* New York, Norton, 1945.

FINESTONE S: Issues involved in developing diagnostic classifications for casework, in *Casework Papers.* New York, Family Service Association of America, 1960.

FREED AO: The borderline personality. *Soc Casework,* 1980, 61:548–558.

FREEMAN H, HILDEBRAND C, AYRE DA: A classification system that prescribes treatment. *Soc Casework* 1965; 46:423–429.

FREUD S: Character and anal eroticism, in Strachey J (ed): *Standard Edition,* London, Hogarth, 1953, vol 9.

FREUD S: On narcissism: an introduction, in Strachey J (ed): *Standard Edition* London, Hogarth, 1953, vol 14.

FROMM E: *Man for Himself.* New York, Holt, Rinehart & Winston, 1947.

FROMM E: *The Anatomy of Human Destructiveness.* New York, Holt, Rinehart & Winston, 1973.

GERMAINE CB (ed): *Social Work Practice.* New York, Columbia University Press, 1979.

GIOVACCHINI P (ed): *Psychoanalysis of Character Disorders.* New York, Aronson, 1975.

GRINKER RR: The borderline syndrome: a phenomenological view, in Hartocollis P (ed): *Borderline Personality Disorders.* New York, International Universities Press, 1977.

GRINKER R, *The Borderline Syndrome.* New York, Basic Books, 1968.

GUNTRIP H: *Personality Structure and Human Interaction.* New York, International Universities Press, 1961.

GUNTRIP H: *Psychoanalytic Theory, Therapy, and the Self.* New York, Basic Books, 1971.

GYARFAS MG: A systems approach to diagnosis, in Mishne J (ed): *Psychotherapy and Training in Clinical Social Work.* New York, Gardner, 1980.

HOCH P, POLATIN P: Pseudoneurotic form of Schizophrenia. *Psychiatric Q* 1949; 23: 248–276.

HOLLIS F, WOODS ME: *Casework: A Psychosocial Therapy.* New York, Random House, 1981.

HORWITZ L: Group psychotherapy of the borderline patient, in Hartocollis P (ed): *Borderline Personality Disorders.* New York, International Universities Press, 1977.

HORNEY K: *New Ways in Psychoanalysis.* New York, Norton, 1939.

JACKEL MM: Personality disorders, in Wiedeman GH (ed): *Personality Development and Deviation.* New York, International Universities Press, 1975.

JACKSON DD: (ed) *Human Communication,* 2 vols. Palo Alto, Science and Behavior Books, 1968.

KALLMAN FJ: The genetic theory of schizophrenia: an analysis of 691 schizophrenic twin index families. *Am J Psychiatry* 98: 544–550.

KERNBERG O: *Borderline Conditions and Pathological Narcissism.* New York, Aronson, 1975.

KERNBERG O: Structural change, in Hartocollis P (ed): *Borderline Personality Disorders.* New York, International Universities Press, 1977.

Kohut H: *The Analysis of the Self*. New York, International Universities Press, 1971.

Kretschmer E: *Physique and Character*. London, Miller, 1936.

Lasch C: *The Culture of Narcissism*. New York, Norton, 1978.

Lidz T: *The Person: His Development throughout the Life Cycle*. New York, Basic Books, 1968.

Lion JR: *Personality Disorders*. Baltimore, Williams & Wilkins, 1974.

Loewenstein S: An overview of the concept of narcissism. *Soc Casework* 58: 136–142.

Mahler MS, *The Psychological Birth of the Human Infant*. New York, Basic Books, 1975.

Masterson JF: *Psychology of the Borderline Adult*. New York, Brunner/Mazel, 1976.

Masterson JF: *The Narcissistic and Borderline Disorders*. New York, Brunner/Mazel, 1981.

Meyer C: *Social Work Practice*. New York, Free Press, 1976.

Millon T: *Disorders of Personality DSM-III: Axis II*. New York, Wiley, 1981.

Minuchin S: *Families and Family Therapy*. Cambridge Harvard University Press, 1974.

Murphy LB, Moriarty AE: *Vulnerability, Coping, and Growth*. New Haven, Yale University Press, 1976.

Palumbo J: Theories of narcissism and the practice of clinical social work. *Clin Soc Work J*, 1976; 4:147–161.

Paolino TJ: Jr: *Psychoanalytic Psychotherapy*. New York, Brunner/Mazel, 1981.

Perlman HH: *Social Casework: A Problem-solving Process*. Chicago, University of Chicago Press, 1957.

Powers HP: Psychotherapy for hysterical individuals. *Soc Casework* 1972; 53:435–440.

Reiner BS: A feeling of irrelevance: the effects of a nonsupportive society. Soc Casework 1979; 60:3–10.

Reiner BS, Kaufman I: *Character Disorders in Parents of Delinquents*. New York, Family Service Association, of America, 1959.

Rice CF: Marital treatment with narcissistic character disorders, in Mishne J (ed): *Psychotherapy and Training in Clinical Social Work*. New York, Gardner, 1980.

Richmond M: *Social Diagnosis*. New York, Russell Sage, 1917.

Salomon EL: Humanistic values and social casework. *Soc Casework* 1967; 48:26–32.

Salzman L: *The Obsessive Personality*. New York, Science House, 1968.

Satir V: *Conjoint Family Therapy*. Palo Alto, Science and Behavior Books, 1967.

Sheldon WH: *Atlas of Men: A Guide for Somatotyping the Adult Male of All Ages*. New York, Harper, 1954.

Spitz RA: *The First Year of Life*. New York, International Universities Press, 1965.

Stanton AH: Personality disorders, in Nicholi AM Jr (ed): *The Harvard Guide to Modern Psychiatry*. Cambridge, Belknap, 1978.

Strahl MO: *Masked Schizophrenia*. New York, Springer, 1980.

Strean HS: *Clinical Social Work*. New York, Free Press, 1978.

Thomas A, Chess S: *Temperament and Development*. New York, Brunner/Mazel, 1977.

Towle C: *Common Human Needs*. New York, National Association of Social Workers. 1957.

Truax CB, Carkhuff RR: *Toward Effective Counseling and Psychotherapy: Training and Practice*. Chicago, Aldine, 1967.

Turner FJ: *Psychosocial Therapy*. New York, Free Press, 1978.

Turner FJ (ed): *Social Work Treatment: Interlocking Theoretical Approaches*. New York, Free Press, 1979.

Williams JBW: DSM-III: a comprehensive approach to diagnosis. *Soc Work* 1981; 26:101–106.

Winnicott DW: Clinical study of the failure of an average expectable environment on the child's mental functioning. *Int J Psychoanal* 1965; 46:81–87.(a)

Winnicott DW: The theory of parent–infant relationships. *Int J Psychoanal* 1965; 46:235–236.(b)

Wynne LC: Some indications and contraindications for exploratory family therapy, in Boszormenyi-Nagy I, Framo JL (eds): *Intensive Family Therapy*. New York. Basic Books, pp 289–322.

Yalom ID: *The Theory and Practice of Group Psychotherapy*. New York, Basic Books, 1975.

Zentner M: The paranoid client. *Soc Casework* 1980; 61:138–145.

Zilboorg G: Ambulatory schizophrenia. *Psychiatry* 1941, 4:149:155.

8

Adjustment Disorders

Judith Mishne

The new American Psychiatric Association (1980) classification of mental disorders (DSM III) characterizes the adjustment disorder of adulthood as a residual category of maladaptive reactions to psychosocial stressors. This category embraces responses to identifiable life events that are expected to remit when either the stressful situation ceases or a new level of adaptation and coping is achieved. DSM III emphasizes that the disorder is not an exacerbation of one of the other mental disorders. The maladaptive reaction is to a clearly identified problematic event or set of adverse circumstances within the range of ordinary human experience. The response is disproportionately intense, but short-lived because the impairment is relatively temporary: "The basis of the disorder lies in the concept of trauma as psychic overload, with a subsequent partial or complete feeling of helplessness, accompanied by regression and inhibitions" (Kaplan & Sadock, 1981, p. 579). A concurrent personality disturbance or a developmental or physical impairment may cause an individual to be more vulnerable to adjustment disorders and, thus, some clients meet the criteria for both adjustment disorder and personality disorder (see Chapter 7). By itself, the term "adjustment disorder" means that a specific stressor has found the point of vulnerability in a person of otherwise considerable ego strength.

Diagnostic Criteria
of Adjustment Disorders

By definition, an adjustment disorder must follow stress, but symptoms do not always begin immediately, nor do they necessarily subside as soon as the stress ceases. However, the maladaptive reaction must, by definition, occur within three months of the onset of the stress. The severity of the stress is not always predictive of the extent of the regression and temporary impairment because group norms, cultural expectations and values, and basic personality organization always play a major role in responses to the vicissitudes of life. An adjustment disorder can occur at any age, with wide variation in manifest symptomatology. "Depressive, anxious and mixed features [are] most common in adults. Physical symptoms are most common in children and the elderly but may occur in any age group" (Kaplan & Sadock, 1981, p. 580). DSM III noted the following diagnostic criteria:

1. The maladaptive reaction is to an identifiable psychosocial stressor that occurs within three months of the onset of the stressor.
2. The maladaptive nature of the reaction is indicated by either of the following:
   a. impairment in social or occupational functioning;
   b. symptoms that are in excess of a normal and expectable reaction to the stressor. (p. 167)

As I noted earlier, an adjustment disorder is not an exacerbation of another, more fixed mental disorder. Additionally, the disturbance is expected to cease or gradually to remit either when the stress ceases or when a new level of coping is achieved.

Diagnosis of Adjustment Disorders

Adjustment Disorder with Depressed Mood

This subtype indicates that the predominant manifestations are depressed mood, hopelessness, and tearfulness. It is essential to distinguish this subtype from similar entities, most notably, "major depression" and "uncomplicated bereavement" (see Chapter 5). Major depression refers either to a single episode or to recurrent episodes marked by profound depression but without any manic or hypomanic features. Additionally present are feelings of worthlessness, prolonged or marked functional impairment, and marked psychomotor retardation. Uncomplicated bereavement is the category for normal reactions to the death of a loved one. The symptomatology encompasses normal feelings of loss related to the death, depression, poor appetite, weight loss, and insomnia. The classification "adjustment disorder with depressed mood" replaces the category "neurotic depression" in DSM III. The new category is analogous to "situational depression," or "reactive depression," because a stressor is the immediate or contributing cause and "has temporarily overwhelmed the previously normal individual's capacity to cope and adapt" (Klerman et al., 1979, p. 58).

His physician referred Mr. B to the local family service agency when she noted helplessness and depressed mood in this successful, middle-aged executive who had recently lost his job because of a company reorganization and merger. A month after demotion to an ambiguous position at work, Mr. B was noticeably withdrawn and asocial, avoiding friends and social gatherings. He showed an atypical paralysis in considering a new position or in responding to overtures and inquiries from companies interested in hiring him. He and his wife reported that his tearfulness and apathy were in contrast to his typical enthusiasm and pattern of successful coping and adaptation.

Adjustment Disorder with Anxious Mood

This category is used when the major symptoms include jitteriness, worry, and nervousness. This subtype is differentiated from "anxiety disorders" (see Chapters 9 and 10), which entail panic and generalized anxiety, with symptoms of motor tension, shakiness, jumpiness, tension, inability to relax, hyperactivity, apprehensive expectations, hyperattentiveness, distractibility, insomnia, irritability, and impatience. The similarity of symptoms between these disorders is marked; existence of a specific precipitant in adjustment disorder is the major variable to distinguish the two.

Ms. S, a 39-year-old legal secretary–administrator, sought help at a mental health clinic after successfully institutionalizing her older brother, who required nursing home care following an auto accident. Ms. S had moved across the country to help her brother immediately after the accident. She had attempted to care for him herself and had had a most frustrating, exhausting time dealing with physicians, nursing homes, and other care providers. Her brother's placement and the strain of the past year finally produced worry, nervousness, and anxiety. Ms. S found herself atypically frightened by the prospect of securing a new job and starting her life afresh.

Adjustment Disorder
with Mixed Emotional Features

This category is applied when the presenting symptoms involve a combination of anxiety and depression or other emotions and affects. The mix of emotional features might be seen in late adolescence, when a teenager moves away from home and parental supervision and support and, in college, reacts with ambivalence, anger, depression, anxiety, and increased dependencey. This same constellation of emotions might be seen in response to marriage, marital disturbance, or birth of a first child. The adjustment disorder in response to the birth of a child is correlated by some authors with life stress and absence of social support (Paykel et al., 1980).

Ms. B, age 29, gave birth to her first child. Within weeks of the delivery, she experienced anxiety, depression, and nervousness. She felt inept at handling her infant, and she realized that she worried excessively over minutia. In general, Ms. B felt overwhelmed by motherhood and a sense of loneliness. She and her husband had just moved to a new community because of her husband's graduate studies. They had no circle of familiar friends or relatives and Mr. B was in school full-time and working part-time. Finances were adequate, though tight, and Ms. B felt imprisoned at home with a demanding baby, unsure whether she could afford regular babysitting to assist her. She sought help at the counseling service of her husband's university.

Adjustment Disorder
with Disturbance of Conduct

This disorder is frequently seen in adolescence and "involves conduct in which the rights of others are violated, or age-appropriate societal norms and rules are disregarded" (Kaplan & Sadock, 1981, p. 580). This category commonly is exemplified by relatively short-lived truancy, fighting, vandalism, reckless driving, or defaulting on legal responsibilities. The major differential that must be delineated is "conduct disorder" and "antisocial personality disorder" (see Chapter 12). Conduct disorders fall into two types: the "undersocialized, aggressive" subdivision refers to a repetitive, persistent pattern of *aggressive* conduct in which the basic rights of others are violated by means of physical assaults on persons or property and in which there has been a failure to establish normal bonds of affection and empathy; the "undersocialized, nonaggressive" subdivision entails the same failure in bonding, but the repetitive, persistent pattern is nonaggressive conduct that violates the rights of others or societal norms (e.g., substance abuse, lying, stealing without confrontation with a victim, violation of rules of home and school). Both aggressive and nonaggressive conduct disorders can be classified as Socialized and Antisocial Personality Disorders. Socialized disorders refer to social attachments to gangs or peer groups if there is a demonstrated concern for friends and companions. Antisocial personality disorder requires that the individual be at least 18 and have a history since 15 of such behaviors or experiences as truancy, school suspension or expulsion, delinquency, running away, lying, substance abuse, inadequate school work, and violation of home and school rules. Manifestation after age 18 include inability to exhibit consistent work behavior, to meet parental responsibilities, and to show an enduring attachment to a sexual partner. Additional features include irritability and aggressiveness, manipulation, impulsivity, and failure to honor financial obligations.

Steven, age 17, was referred to a private therapist because of a pattern of misusing his parents' credit cards, driving the family car despite parental objections, and being arrested for speeding. Steven also argued vociferously with both parents and with teachers and guidance counselors. At the time of referral, he was abdicating responsibility for completing his college applications. The parents connected Steven's behavior with the father's recent diagnosis of multiple sclerosis. They themselves were struggling to cope with this severe illness and the lifestyle changes that would be necessary.

Adjustment Disorder with Mixed Disturbance of Emotions and Conduct

This category is used when the major manifestations are "both emotional, such as depression and anxiety, and disturbances of conduct, such as truancy, vandalism, reckless driving and fighting" (Kaplan & Sadock, 1981, p. 581).

Robert, age 21, a recent college graduate, sought help privately, complaining of feeling both depressed and anxious about his parents' recent decision to divorce. When sad and depressed, Robert drank excessively. After his drinking bouts, he stayed home from his accounting job and neglected his graduate school classes. Whether drinking or not, Robert also drove his car fast and had gotten several speeding tickets; he reported increasingly abusive and argumentative behavior toward his work superiors and his parents.

Adjustment Disorder with Work Disturbance or Academic Inhibition

This category is applicable when an individual has previously functioned adequately in school and at work and is apparently reacting to a relatively recent set of stressors.

Mr. K, an attorney in practice for five years, was doing exceptionally well in his law firm and in his community leadership position in a small eastern town. He was married and the father of two small boys. Mr. K indicated great satisfaction with his personal and professional life, but in the past three months he had been experiencing disturbance in his professional functioning and consulted a private therapist. He reported feelings of apathy, disinterest, and apprehension at the office. He described problems in concentrating and and overall disengagement from work demands and from collegial relationships. Mr. K related that the disturbance seemed to have begun with the news that his father had terminal cancer and with his wife's recent miscarriage.

Adjustment Disorder with Withdrawal

This category refers to social withdrawal in a previously well socialized individual who currently is not manifesting significant depression or anxiety.

Mrs. W reported to the intake worker at a mental health clinic that she was seeking an evaluation or consultation at the insistence of her husband. She did not feel anxious or depressed but acknowledged a relatively recent change in her lifestyle. She described a new disinclination to socialize or to participate in routine community volunteer activities since her last child had departed for college. This event coincided with her own mother's stroke, which required Mrs. W to shop for her mother and frequently visit although her mother's debilitation was not severe. At the same time, Mrs. W described a sense of loss of her mother's companionship; previously, they had participated together in community activities and had taken classes and hikes together.

Differential Diagnosis of Adjustment Disorders

In summary, in adjustment disorder proper the disturbance is not attributable to a preexisting mental disorder and the individual shows symptoms within three months of a stressful event that are in excess of a normal and expectable reaction. ''Because no absolute criteria are available to aid in the distinction between a condition not attributable to a mental disorder and adjustment disorder, clinical judgement is often necessary" (Kaplan & Sadock, 1981, p. 581).

DSM III provides useful guidelines to distinguish between reactive and long-standing psychopathologic symptomatology. However, the practitioner must bear in mind that in many instances there is no one-to-one correlation between objective events, on the one hand, and unconscious responses and manifest symptomatology, on the other. Symptoms are simply symbols that indicate that mental turmoil is taking place. If a symptom is perceived as purely reactive to stress, the professional may conclude that psychotherapy is not indicated. However, this view "neglects the fact that most persons exposed to the same stressor would not develop similar symptoms, [and] that it is a pathological response"

Freud and associates (1977) emphasized the misleading quality of manifest symptomatology:

Symptoms may be no more than the individual's answer to some developmental stress and as such transitory, or symptoms may represent a permanent countercathexis against some threatening drive derivative and as such be crippling to further development. Or symptoms though pathologic in origin may nevertheless be ego-syntonic and merged with the structure of the personality . . . to a degree which makes it difficult to distinguish between such manifestations as outward evidence of ongoing pathological involvement or as more or less normal, stable features of the individual's character. There is no doubt that in any classification system based on phenomenology, these widely different classes of symptoms appear as if on a par. (p. 33)

When one scans clinic and agency intake for referral symptoms and clients' explanations for seeking help, one can be easily misled. A child may begin lying after parental separation or divorce; this behavior may be a reactive adjustment disorder or it "may be rooted in the child's stage of ego development, i.e., [expressing] the immature individual's inability to distinguish between reality and fantasy, or may signify a delay in acquiring and perfecting this important ego function" (Freud et al., 1977, p. 34). Similarly, a seemingly well functioning adolescent may perform poorly at college. If this pattern is seen as an adjustment disorder, the youth may be prescribed minor tranquilizers. However, further assessment may indicate that the adolescent's prior adjustment was in fact fragile and that the student is experiencing separation disturbances.

In summary, manifest symptoms and external events may appear identical. In reality, however, one set of symptoms can have a wide range or possible latent meaning and pathological significance; thus, different types of interventions will be required. Accordingly, the clinician must make a thorough investigation of the client, studying symptomatology, precipitants, and the symptoms' relevance with "regard to developmental level, structure, dynamic significance, etc." (Freud et al., 1977, p. 35).

In distinguishing between patients with adjustment disorder proper and those with a personality disorder, a thorough evaluation is crucial. The Personality Assessment (Eissler et al., 1977) follows a developmental perspective by which drive development, ego and superego development, and adaptation to the environment are determined. Internal structures and pathology are evaluated in terms of inadequate mastery of the developmental tasks of adulthood, namely, the quality of functioning "in sexual relations, work, and sublimations, the pleasure in life derived from it, and by the quality of the individual's object and community relations" (Freud et al., 1977).

The assessment first identifies reasons for referral, significant environmental conditions, timing of the referral, and other variables to identify precipitants and possible reactive distress. Conflicts must be examined to distinguish external, internal, and internalized factors. This approach clarifies whether the person is manifesting indications of earlier conflict and/or fixation or whether the client is free of such conflicts and is simply temporarily debilitated by understandable clashes between the total personality and the environment.

Treatment of Adjustment Disorders

DSM III raised questions among professionals about the relationship between diagnosis and treatment. Some clinicians argue that the diagnostic discriminations needed to plan psychotherapy are absent from DSM III's multiaxial system (Karasu & Skodol, 1979). Karasu and Skodol emphasized that patients' original and present conflicts, life history, relations with others, defenses and coping styles, dream lives, needs, weaknesses, and assets require a comprehensive psychodynamic evaluation to judge

> (1) the suitability and appropriateness of psychotherapy, . . . (2) the indicated therapeutic approach influencing the prognosis of the treatment, (3) the nature of the implicit or explicit contract one may draw with these patients, (4) the required frequency of their visits and the duration of recommended treatment, (5) the goals and purpose of the psychotherapy, (6) the anticipated nature of the therapeutic relationship and its complications, and (7) the potential dispositions of the transference and countertransference. (p. 610)

and suggested that Profile Assessment can reveal the "patient's conflicts, object relations, defenses, coping mechanism and mental structure'' (p. 610). Freud and associates (1977) recommended that the clinician assess general characteristics with a bearing on the need for treatment and the ability to profit from it. The analysis must consider

> whether ego mastery over the impulses is weakened for other than defensive reasons (ego defects, psychotic core, etc.) . . . whether there is insight into the detrimental nature of the pathology, including the desire to be cured, whether there is ability for self observation, self criticism and capacity to think and verbalize . . . whether there is enough frustration tolerance to cope with the necessary restrictions on wish fulfillment in the transference setting; whether the patient has on previous occasions shown ability to persevere in the face of difficulty. (pp. 91–92)

Kaplan and Sadock (1981) argued that psychotherapy is the treatment of choice in adjustment disorders and that group therapy for patients experiencing similar difficulty can be useful; for example, recently retired people, families forced by environmental disasters to relocate, or renal dialysis patients. Medication may be briefly used with adjustment disordered patients provided that a careful assessment is done to avoid masking relevant symptoms, affects, moods, or underlying disturbances. Individual treatment also is commonly offered; sessions deeply explore the meaning of the distress.

Patients often emerge from an adjustment disorder stronger than they were in the precrisis period. Treatment approaches should be based on the clinician's assessment of the degree to which the adjustment disorder is related to the patient's earlier attempts to cope and adapt. Intensive treatment would be indicated in individuals with recurrent adjustment disorders or prolonged impairment. If the patient has sufficient ego strength to tolerate anxiety and frustration and demonstrates insight (Freud et al., 1977; Karasu & Skodol, 1979), treatment would exclude goals of identifying ''the stressors' preconscious and unconscious meanings'' (Kaplan & Sadock, 1981, p. 581).

Kaplan and Sadock (1981) cautioned about problems of secondary gain in adjustment disorder. Some highly competent and well-functioning individuals experiencing adjustment disorders may enjoy a bout of incapacitation and relative freedom from responsibility and therefore resist interventions. If this resistance is protracted, it undoubtably indicates a deeper level of disturbance—possibly, unrecognized dependence longings or internal (e.g., active-passive) or internalized (e.g., need for punishment) conflicts. Likewise, if the adjustment disorder includes conduct disturbances, with resultant difficulties with the law, school, or community authorities, ''it is inadvisable for the [therapist] to attempt to rescue the patient from the consequences of his action. Too often such 'kindness' only reinforces socially unacceptable means of tension reduction and stands in the way of the acquisition of insight and subsequent emotional growth" (p. 582).

Patients suffering adjustment disorder proper receive treatment in a range of clinical settings. Mental health clinics, family service agencies, and private practices are the settings commonly used by relatively well functioning adults who are aware of the impact of specific problematic events. Some people have considerable self-awareness and are able to appraise the decline in their coping due to relatively recent life stressors. Initially, this group may prefer to rely on old, successful coping patterns and may oppose a well-meant referral. With considerable ego strength, insight, and sound reality assessment, such individuals will eventually recognize the magnitude of their maladaptive response and its impact on family and professional functioning. At this point, they often will contact a mental health worker. Children and adolescents with adjustment disorders are likely to be referred by parents, physicians, or school personnel, rather than to be self-referred. Not uncommonly, children and adolescents who experience adjustment disorders later succumb to adult life stress-producing situations in a similar fashion. Earlier life failure at coping may portend adult fragility; that is, the adult's maladaptive responses to stressors may be a culmination of repeated, disproportionately intense life responses and vulnerability to stressors that are within the range of ordinary experience.

Conclusion

Adjustment disorder frequently occurs in highly competent, well-functioning individuals. While it is assumed that the disturbance will lessen when the source of stress disappears or that a new level of adaptation will soon be reached, psychotherapeutic help nevertheless can be invaluable in the readjustment process. Early intervention at the onset of stress offers preventative possibilities. Moreover, throughout the crisis other services and referrals may be useful adjuncts to psychotherapy. For instance, legal services and child care references may be invaluable to a couple undergoing divorce. Determining which services to provide and selecting the type of therapy best suited to the client both rest on the assessment made by the clinician at the beginning of, and throughout, the helping process.

References

AMERICAN PSYCHIATRIC ASSOCIATION : Quick Reference to the Diagnostic Criteria from Diagnostic and Statistical Manual of Mental Disorders, Third Edition. Washington, DC, American Psychiatric Association, 1980.

Eissler R, Freud A, Kris M, et al (eds): *The Anthology of the Psychoanalytic Study of the Child—Psychoanalytic Assessment: The Diagnostic Profile*. New Haven, Yale University Press, 1977.

Freud A: The concept of developmental lines, in Eissler R, Freud A, Kris M, et al (eds): *The Anthology of the Psychoanalytic Study of the Child—Psychoanalytic Assessment: The Diagnostic Profile*, New Haven, Yale University Press, 1977, pp 11–30.

Freud A: The symptomatology of childhood: a preliminary attempt at classification, in Eissler R, Freud A, Kris M, et al (eds): *The Anthology of the Psychoanalytic Study of the Child—Psychoanalytic Assessment: The Diagnostic Profile*. New Haven, Yale University Press, 1977, pp 31–53.

Freud A, Nagera H, Freud WE: Metapsychological assessment of the adult personality: the adult profile, in Eissler R, Freud A, Kris M, et al (eds): *The Anthology of the Psychoanalytic Study of the Child—Psychoanalytic Assessment: The Diagnostic Profile*. New Haven, Yale University Press, 1977, pp 82–114.

Kaplan HI, Sadock BJ: *Modern Synopsis of Comprehensive Textbook of Psychiatry*, ed 3. Baltimore, Williams & Wilkins, 1981, vol 3.

Karasu T, Skodol AE: VI axis for DSM III: psychodynamic evaluation. *Am J Psychiatry* 1979; 136.

Kessler E: Reactive disorders, in Noshpitz J (ed): *Basic Handbook of Child Psychiatry*. New York, Basic Books, 1979.

Klerman GL, Endicott J, Spitzer R, et al: Neurotic depressions: a systematic analysis of multiple criteria and meanings. *Am J Psychiatry* 1979; 136.

Paykel ES, Emms EM, Fletcher J, et al: Life events and social support in puerperal depression. *Br J Psychiatry* 1980; 136:339–346.

9

Anxiety States

BERT KAPLAN

Anxiety as a Subjective Experience

Her hands were sweating. She did not understand what was happening to her, but thoughts were racing through her mind with unbelievable speed. It was as though a locomotive had been let loose in her head and was running wild. She dimly felt the blood pounding at her temples, surging to break through her skin. Her stomach was writhing, and the sweat was pouring down her head. She gasped for breath. "Oh God, why isn't he here yet?" she thought.

Quickly she reviewed past events in her mind. He had promised to come. He swore nothing would keep him away. In the deep mist of the night, he had mouthed words of love to her. "Why isn't he here?' The words raced through her head. She had visions of him lying in a ditch, body broken, smashed beyond recognition. The next flash saw him being attacked and beaten to a pulp. She forced herself to stop.

"He said he would come!" she screamed hysterically to nobody in particular. She did not realize she had spoken the words aloud until several people around her looked up in astonishment. "Are you all right?" a faceless voice asked. She felt her head nod assent, yet she knew she was not all right. She was getting sick and would not be able to help herself. If only she were home, she would know what to do, but waiting in a strange, new place left her helpless. She felt herself beginning to gag and forced herself to stop. She had to gain control of herself. She could not let all these people see her like this.

260

Even as she fought for control, she began to feel her eyes cloud over and the room begin to spin. Her nausea got worse and the sweating was unbearable. She felt that her heart was about to burst. "If only I could breathe!" she thought, and her mind raced. "He can't be dead. He just can't be."

At that moment, the door opened and footsteps approached. Her eyes could not focus but she recognized the walk and the way he tilted his head to one side. And the voice had its usual ring. "Sorry I'm late," he said.

Psychological Aspects of Anxiety

The anxiety experience can occur anywhere and anytime. The young woman in the vignette was obviously waiting for someone whose arrival was important to her. We can imagine the possible circumstances—a concert, a wedding, a dinner appointment. Her reaction was a subjective experience of stress and apprehension in relation to an event that was about to occur, and her specific mental state was that something terrible was about to happen: in her mind, she would soon find out that her date was dead.

In anticipating disaster, the woman found that her thoughts flowed into one another, her capacity to understand what was going on around her was diminished, and her body seemed to function in atypical and almost uncontrollable ways. Most significant, she was acutely aware of herself and the way she was feeling. She was so uncomfortable, confused, and out of control that she felt herself foundering but unable to help herself. In short, this woman was experiencing an anxiety attack. While any of us may undergo such an experience on occasion, most of us are not generally subject to such extreme feelings of anxiety and are more used to the kind of apprehension experienced before taking a test, consulting a physician, or waiting for a job interview. We wonder about what could go wrong, anticipate that it might, worry about it even to the point of feeling some of the physical reactions described in the vignette, but basically retain a sense of control about ourselves and are able to attend to the business at hand despite a sense of distress.

Physiological Aspects of Anxiety

As was indicated in the vignette, physiological correlates of the anxiety experience may include sweating, increased heart rate, heightened blood pressure, rapid and shallow breathing, nausea, chest pain, choking sensations, dizziness, hot and cold flashes, faintness, and trembling or shakiness (American Psychiatric Association, 1980). All of these indicators may not be present, but several usually occur in combination. However, some form of motor tension and autonomic hyperactivity is always present, so that the person inevitably experiences a sense of jumpiness, increased heart and breathing rates, and heightened blood pressure.

Of major interest with respect to the physiological correlates of the anxiety experience is that these physical reactions are not specific to anxiety per se. A person experiencing anger, fear, or excitement may demonstrate similar physical reactions. If one were to monitor physiological responses to anger, fear, anxiety, or excitement, one would not be able to distinguish among the states without knowledge of the person's mental state. In other words, the physiological correlates of anxiety can be ascribed to anxiety only if they are accompanied by the psychological experience of apprehension with respect to impending doom. Mental ideation and physiological process cannot be conceived of separately; neither by itself defines the anxiety condition.

Basic Concepts of Anxiety

Anxiety is an affect that occurs in all individuals. Like joy, sadness, bemusement, and even grief, anxiety arises and diminishes at various times and under various circumstances. The hallmark of anxiety is a feeling of apprehension, accompanied by the idea that something bad is about to happen.

For Brenner (1974a, b) the distinction between anxiety and depression is that anxiety is an anticipatory feeling of tension, whereas depression is a feeling of tension associated with the idea that something bad has already happened. The essential distinction is that anxiety serves as a warning about whatever doom is supposed to come; depression is felt after disaster has occurred. Thus, anxiety can function as a signal that motivates.

When anxiety is anticipatory and motivating, it can be understood as a way of preparing to deal with debilitating aspects of anxiety. And when defenses are working, anxiety is diminished and the ability to go about normal, daily business remains intact even though some apprehension or worry is felt. When defenses are not working, however, anxiety does not decrease and an anxiety state (panic) occurs, during which it is not possible to continue normal routines. Thus, there are two basic types of anxiety, "signal anxiety" and a "state of anxiety." The first is a normal part of daily living, such as occurs during preparation for a job interview or an examination; in this case, apprehension serves as a motivator of activity whose purpose is to diminish apprehension. The second is more problematic since constructive functioning is not possible so long as a state of anxiety is felt.

Because correlates of anxiety can be observed in a person, it is possible to overemphasize them and designate the anxiety as the problem rather than a possible motivating force. However, maintaining a focus on the role of anxiety as a motivating force, in contradistinction to a state of anxiety, permits the inference that anxiety occurs when the person is not able to protect herself from it. In other words, even if the anticipatory function accompanies anxiety (signal anxiety), defenses may not be adequate, resulting in an outbreak of the anxious condition. Within this context, anxiety is diminished when the person becomes able to protect himself from it. Thus, it is not the presence of anxiety that is problematic but the absence of working defenses that causes difficulty.

Disorders Associated with Anxiety

As mentioned, anxiety is frequently experienced in a relatively mild form in a number of everyday situations such as taking a test or visiting a physician. Anxiety in such situations is generally advantageous, requiring us to marshal our protective forces in anticipation of what is to come. However, anxiety often plays a major role in certain defined psychological disorders: "phobic disorders," "anxiety states," and, to some extent, "somatoform disorders."

Phobic Disorders

Many individuals experience apprehension or even panic when faced with certain objects (see Chapters 10 and 17). Insects, snakes, and mice are three sources of distress that are common enough rarely to be thought of as being related to phobias. However, "phobia" is defined in DSM III (American Psychiatric Association, 1980) as a persistent, irrational, excessive fear of a specific object, activity, or situation that results in a compelling desire to avoid it. In this view, even the most common of specific fears constitutes a phobia. However, the diagnosis of a phobic disorder is rarely considered unless the nature of the phobia is such as to cause the person some role dysfunction in his daily life. Thus, a phobic condition may be evident but remain undiagnosed unless it causes the person significant distress.

Anxiety is the central experience in phobic disorders and the individual must avoid this anxiety at all costs. By associating the onset of anxiety with a specific object, the person can avoid the experience of anxiety by avoiding the object. Nothing could be more simple and nothing could be, in some instances, more effective. The etiology, symptoms, and treatment of phobias are discussed at greater length in Chapter 10.

Anxiety States

Panic Disorder

The vignette presented at the beginning of the chapter illustrated a "panic disorder," with its constellation of psychological and physiological characteristics. Criteria for this diagnosis require that at least three such attacks occur within a three-week period and that at least four of the physiologic symptoms of anxiety be present. However, the attack need not be precipitated *only* by exposure to a specific phobic stimulus.

Certainly, an individual may experience a panic attack on occasion. Such attacks are generally of no concern unless they occur frequently enough to cause disruption in everyday living. The person who reacts with panic at the slightest provocation, perhaps several times daily, is certainly in a much different category. Thus, it is not the reaction of anxiety alone that warrants concern but its frequency of occurrence, in combination with the person's capacity to cope, that is significant.

Generalized Anxiety Disorder

Chronic anxiety, accompanied by the psychological and physical characteristics described earlier and lasting continuously for at least one month, falls into this category. Once again, this is not an experience unfamiliar to most people except with respect to duration.

We all can sympathize with the anxious person who is constantly on guard, for each of us has had periods of ongoing anticipation of a dreaded outcome. However, for most of us anxiety rarely lasts more than a few days, easing as the dreaded situation passes or loses its meaning.

For the person experiencing a "generalized anxiety disorder," however, the dread does not diminish because new situations of danger are perceived as soon as the earlier ones ease. At least three of the following features must be present: motor tension, autonomic hyperactivity, apprehensive expectation, and an attitude of vigilance and scanning (possibly, too, insomnia or edginess).

There has been controversy over the concept of generalized anxiety because some theorists argue that no experience of anxiety ever exists without becoming connected to specified stimuli that are seen to cause the anxiety (Beck, 1976). In other words, the person experiencing anxiety is always able to identify the impending doom that is the reason for the anxiety. Such a view is, of course, accurate but overlooks the reality that some individuals demonstrate ongoing anxiety with changing stimuli, meaning that there is no consistent cause for anxiety. In such instances, one must look beyond rationality for the reason that anxiety persists. Certainly, ongoing anxiety does not appear without a reason, but the reason may be related more to the individual's incapacity to maintain a stable sense of identity and/or being than to specific, identifiable impending doom. For such individuals, almost anything can signify internal disorganization, with the resulting subjective experience of anxiety. This point will be discussed further in the section dealing with the conditions under which anxiety occurs.

Obsessive-Compulsive Disorder

Of the disorders mentioned thus far, the "obsessive-compulsive disorder" is probably the most confusing with respect to anxiety since if obsessive-compulsive rituals are effective, little anxiety is observed. Like phobic symptoms, obsessive-compulsive characteristics protect the person from the experience of overwhelming anxiety. Indeed, anxiety remains the central and motivating force in the development of obsessive-compulsive symptoms.

Why some individuals develop phobic mechanisms and others obsessive-compulsive ones in response to similar feelings of distress and ideas of impending doom remains uncertain. The reason may have to do with both constitutional endowment and environment or experience.

Persons suffering from obsessive-compulsive disorder display "obsessions" (recurrent and persistent thoughts, ideas, images, or impulses), "compulsions" (repetitive behaviors performed in a stereotyped manner), or both. Characteristically, the thoughts and/or behaviors occur involuntarily, and the individual feels he cannot control them. In fact, she feels helpless in the face of them. Usually, the thoughts are felt to be intrusive and the individual attempts to overlook or ignore them; however, to do so invites the experience of intense and persistent distress. The only solution, then, is to follow the dictates of the obsessive or compulsive imperatives.

Very often, the obsessive-compulsive symptom may not appear unusual to an observer. It can consist of something as simple as locking up the house or apartment in a particular sequence or dressing according to a specific routine. Once done for the day, the ritual may not have to be repeated until the next day. In more severe instances, the sense of intrusion may occur many times daily and may require significant behavioral compliance before a feeling of peace is attained. Classical examples of obsessive thinking involve thoughts of killing someone, becoming infected through handshaking, and continuous doubting. Typical compulsions are hand washing, counting, and touching.

Obsessions and/or compulsions make no sense to the person who feels forced to comply with them, nor do they make particular sense with respect to everyday living activities. Once again, the particular symptom has no a-priori meaning and its specific significance can be unearthed only as part of a developing process of increased understanding. While the generic concept that the disorder serves to allay anxiety is true, as with phobia the conditions that provoke the obsessive-compulsive experience vary with each individual.

A young woman with serious problems of self-esteem, filled with confusion over her anger toward her husband, and unable to become pregnant found herself obsessed with the idea that the plants in her house might become infected and die. She found that the only way she could help ease her tension was by examining the plants carefully each morning and evening to be sure none was infected.

When she found possible illness or damage, she immediately had to clean and repot the plant. She did not understand her behavior, which she tried to control with little or no success, worrying that it meant she was crazy. She held a responsible job, which she performed well, and was considered a valuable employee. She talked of having several close friends in whom she could confide. In many ways, she appeared to be a sensitive, thoughtful, and considerate person.

Posttraumatic Stress Disorder (Acute and Chronic)

The concept of trauma, traditionally part of psychological theory, has undergone some revision in the light of developmental theory to focus on cumulative and ongoing experience, rather than on single events (Spitz, 1965). Nevertheless, the concept has been retained with the recognition that some people undergo experiences outside the usual that leave them psychologically numb or emotionally anesthetized (Krystal, 1978). Such people report flashbacks of these experiences, finding themselves in a state of hyperalertness to their possible recurrence and prone to exaggerated startle responses and/or insomnia.

Experiences associated with "posttraumatic stress disorder" may be primarily psychological or primarily physical (e.g., sensory deprivation, mental torture, rape, military combat, accidents, death camps). While it is clear that the sense of numbness or anesthesia must follow the atypical stressful experience for the diagnosis to be made, what remains unclear is why some individuals react to atypical stress with posttraumatic stress disorder and others do not. Often, it is assumed that the person who develops this disorder was predisposed to do so. However, since we are talking about atypical stressors and must remain aware that each person has a breaking point beyond which normal functioning cannot be maintained, such an assumption is hardly warranted.

The difference between the acute and the chronic form of this disorder is whether the symptoms appear within six months of the stressor or last less than six months after its occurrence. Symptoms lasting longer than six months warrant a diagnosis of chronic.

Atypical Anxiety Disorder

This is a catchall category used when the symptom of anxiety is a central feature of the person's functioning. However, "atypical anxiety disorder" does not fit the diagnostic requirements of those conditions already discussed.

Somatoform Disorders

It is to be specifically noted that somatoform disorders constitute a distinct category of illness in DSM III (see Chapter 17). However, anxiety is so often a part of the somatoform condition that it can be difficult to determine the significance of this symptom for diagnostic purposes.

Somatoform disorders are closely associated with psychological conditions of stress and are often thought to be the outcome of an inability otherwise to process anxiety-provoking experience. Whereas the phobic or obsessive-compulsive person has found a means to allay anxiety (albeit not necessarily the most adaptive means), the person demonstrating a somatoform disorder experiences anxiety in its full physical manifestations, expressing this response as physical rather than psychological distress (Schur, 1955). In some instances, the person may be aware that his anxious condition is gradually giving way to physical discomfort. In other instances, she may be aware only of pain. It must be emphasized that the pain is quite real, and prolonged physical stress can lead to permanent and irreversible bodily change (e.g., an ulcer). However, it must also be emphasized that the same condition can occur for purely physical reasons; thus, the diagnosis of somatoform disorder is used only when no organic problem can be found.

Anxiety States: The Problem of Differential Diagnosis

From the brief summaries of the diagnostic categories associated with anxiety, it would appear that differential diagnosis would be a relatively simple matter: all one needs to know is the symptomatology in order for diagnosis to follow. However, real people do not neatly fit categories of disorder. For instance, the young woman in the example of obsessional-compulsive disorder also suffered from severe stomach problems and frequent colitis. Obviously, her obsessive-compulsive manifestations, while they helped her contain some anxiety, did not do so to the extent that somatic problems could be avoided. Clearly, under such circumstances, a choice of diagnosis must be made, a choice that rarely paints a full picture. The same is basically true, for instance, with phobic patients. Few patients evidence relatively fixed and specific phobias with little other evidence of complications. Indeed, transient and varied phobic manifestations are common in individuals diagnosed as belonging to the borderline category (see Chapter 7; Kernberg, 1975), nor is it unusual for people with chronic and generalized anxiety to evidence a number of phobias. Thus, the experience of anxiety is present in almost all categories of psychological disorder, except when it is noted by its absense, as in some cases of pathological gambling or kleptomania. This being the case, a diagnosis based primarily on symptomatology may overlook the significant role that anxiety is playing. In this situation, behaviors that are needed by the individual for protection against anxiety may become the therapeutic target, although the person needs these behaviors in order to function until her anxiety can be otherwise managed.

In other clients, anxiety may appear to be the central and most significant symptom. However, it is still necessary to note other aspects of the person's functioning since some psychotic conditions are accompanied by significant manifest and pervasive anxiety. While experience usually makes it possible for clinicians to know how to order the information they collect about a client, it must be emphasized that such ordering should always be subject to ongoing review, particularly with respect to anxiety conditions.

Perhaps the most meaningful errors in diagnosis occur with people who under the stress of intense anxiety lose rationality for a brief period of time. If seen in such circumstances, they may be diagnosed psychotic even though rapid recovery is evidenced. A more accurate assessment would distinguish between people who regress temporarily under significant stress but recover quickly and those who regress and remain regressed for long periods. Unfortunately, such a distinction may be forgotten when a person is seen at the height of an anxiety experience.

In summary, the pitfalls of diagnostic error are many and the likelihood of never making such an error is low, given the current state of knowledge. Nevertheless, clinical judgment can be improved by recognizing that anxiety is present in almost all categories of psychological disorder and by paying attention to how this affect is experienced and understood by the client.

Changing Perspectives on Anxiety States

When Freud first developed his psychodynamic model around the turn of the century, there was a strong tendency to relate cause and effect in a fairly linear manner. As a result, terms like "energy," "repression," "cathexis," and "discharge," which reflect force and motion, were used to explain what takes place in the mind.

As Freud saw it, there is a biological force, "libido" (sexuality), that requires expression and that because of a variety of reasons related to experiential factors can be subject to repression (a term used at that time to refer to all mental operations that relegate impulses to the "unconscious," where they will continue to seek expression). Since Freud's early patients demonstrated anxiety, and their problems appeared to be related to material of a sexual nature that was unacceptable to them, Freud concluded that their symptomatology was the outcome of their repressed sexuality, which was being expressed in disguised form. For Freud, then, anxiety consisted of "transformed sexuality" caused by repression, which did not permit sexual expression in its original state. Therefore, it was only natural that treatment should focus on fostering expression of the unexpressed, and the idea that repressed energy has to be discharged in order for cure to be achieved became a central theme in treatment. Left unexpressed, or repressed, the accumulated sexual energy would, in this view, eventually find itself a means of disguised expression through either physical symptoms ("conversion hysteria") or phobias ("anxiety hysteria").

This formulation, an essential component of Freud's early model of the mind, remained evident in his writings throughout the first two decades of this century. And while Freud gradually became aware of difficulties with this view, he made no formal changes until 1926, when he wrote *Inhibitions, Symptoms, and Anxiety* (Freud, 1936). By that time, he had evolved several more models of the mind, notably, the topographic and the structural, and had clarified his meaning of terms like "ego," "id," and "superego," which had previously been used without much specificity. *Inhibitions, Symptoms, and Anxiety* examined the relationship between repression and anxiety, as well as with its signal function, its expression as a state or a condition, and its relationship to defense. Most notably, Freud revised his earlier concept of anxiety as transformed sexuality caused by repression. Instead, he developed the idea that anxiety is a function of the ego that is activated whenever the ego is faced with a threat it cannot manage. Since anxiety can be overwhelming and disintegrating to whatever degree of ego organization exists, the ego invokes repression (defense) to protect itself. Thus, the ego function of anxiety became the cause of repression (defense) rather than the other way around and a new era of psychodynamic formulation dawned in which ego functions were emphasized instead of drives (see Freud, 1937, for further discussion of this issue).

In summary, Freud (1936) broke new ground by distinguishing between anxiety as a signal (a motivating force) and anxiety as a state. Both responses represent apprehension in the face of anticipated unpleasantness or danger, but the former signifies an adaptive response whereas the latter entails helplessness and psychic collapse.

Developmental Aspects of Anxiety

We are prone for diagnostic purposes to think of anxiety as a correlate of psychological distress; consequently, we often forget that the anxiety response is evident in the newborn (e.g., the startle reflex). Since it is impossible to describe the nature of mental activity in newborns, it is more accurate to state that the startle reflex is evidence of the capacity for physical responsiveness without anticipatory ideation, reserving the term "anxiety" for the response that is evident once anticipatory ideation can be reasonably determined to exist. In this context, it is interesting to note that while Freud referred to the birth experience as prototypical of the anxiety response, meaning that physiological reactions may be similar in both situations, he was quite opposed to the idea that birth itself is the initial trauma of life (Freud, 1936).

There is much evidence that anxiety as an anticipatory experience develops during the first months of life and much speculation that the nature of anticipated unpleasantness changes as children grow. Since the newborn is considered to be attuned primarily to internal biologic stimuli, any experience of anxiety that is hypothesized at that stage has to be viewed as a function of physiological stimulation. However, by definition, anxiety requires awareness of anticipated danger. Therefore, the first level of anxiety can be said to occur only after the infant becomes aware that physiological tension can be distressful enough to hurt and he is able to recognize its onset. If such is the case, and observation indicates that it is, then one can speak of "anxiety with respect to physiological tension" as the most primitive form of this affect. Indeed, there are situations wherein both children and adults have been observed to become terrified over the feeling that they may lose control of themselves and express rage that can only be hurtful. In such instances, anxiety can be quite pronounced.

Moving up the developmental ladder, anxiety can be seen to occur in response to awareness that the caretaking person (object) may become unavailable to the infant. At this point, the infant recognizes that her needs are fulfilled by someone or something "out there," and danger is anticipated when that person or object is absent. Such anxiety is referred to as "anxiety with respect to loss of the object (person)." It must be emphasized that the object is not yet specific; thus, the infant will generally accept gratification from any object that fulfills his need.

Subsequently, the infant recognizes that a specific object is the one that provides. The infant begins to value this object and assumes that her own needs are met because she is valued. Thus, concern emerges over loss of value in the eyes of the provider and "anxiety with respect to loss of love of the object (person)" emerges.

The next level of anxiety that has been hypothesized and observed relates to the oedipal phase and was originally termed "castration anxiety." However, the concept of castration anxiety reflects a perpetuation of Freud's orientation to a male dominated society, and recent research indicates that children of both sexes become concerned with punishment around the same time that they seem to become more cognizant of themselves as sexual beings. Thus, it is probably more accurate to refer to "anxiety with respect to retribution" than to "castration anxiety" at this stage. Such anxiety is evident when an individual feels he will be taken to task or punished for something he has done, felt, or thought. "My husband/wife will kill me if he/she finds out" is common enough in this vein.

The highest level of anxiety, which relates to the most complex level of development, occurs after the resolution of the oedipal conflict and is termed "anxiety with respect to the superego." Most commonly, we refer to this as "conscience."

Thus, a developmental perspective identifies a hierarchy of levels of anxiety corresponding to various developmental stages. More evidence exists for some types of anxiety than for others, but all seem to have clinical utility and are observable in practice. Knowledge of the ideation of the individual evidencing anxiety can help identify what kind (level) of anxiety is being experienced and serve as a diagnostic clue for treatment direction. In summary, five developmental levels of anxiety have been proposed:

anxiety with respect to physiological tension
anxiety with respect to loss of the object (person)
anxiety with respect to loss of love of the object (person)
anxiety with respect to retribution
anxiety with respect to the superego

Anxiety As a Diagnostic Indicator in Practice

Many people who fall into a category of psychopathology do not feel upset with themselves. The hospital patient who is so out of touch with reality as to be oblivious to her condition demonstrates little personal distress. The character disordered patient typically experiences little or no distress. And the antisocial personality may be noted by his lack of concern over the grief he causes others. Indeed, the presence or absence of anxiety, i.e., affective distress as a function of anticipated danger, may or may not serve as a diagnostic indicator.

At the same time, anxiety is not without meaning to the clinician. On the contrary, this response has a great deal of meaning to a clinician who knows how to evaluate it. The first determination to be made relates to whether or not the anxiety represents signal anxiety or a state of anxiety. Signal anxiety, as I have said, is often adaptive, meaning that defenses are usually working and that functioning is still possible. As a state, anxiety is overwhelming and helpless panic is experienced.

A client demonstrated intense agitation. He had something to talk about but could not because a cab was waiting and he was afraid it would leave without him, leaving him stranded. Of course, he could easily call another cab, but the idea that this cab might leave terrified him. I asked him whether he felt it would be easier for him to talk if he found out whether or not the cab would wait. He was afraid the driver would not be honest with him. I then offered to ask the driver myself and wondered whether he could accept the driver's answer to me. He agreed, the driver consented to wait, the client's agitation diminished, and we spent the next hour talking.

Anxiety as a state prevents people from testing reality, using their own judgment, or taking steps to correct the conditions causing the anxiety. Signal anxiety manifests itself differently.

A client called and asked for an appointment because he had beaten his wife on several occasions and was becoming aware that he could not stop himself. He wanted help so that no more incidents of wife abuse occurred.

Were I to ask which client evidenced more intense anxiety, there would be little question that the first client was the more agitated. Were I to ask which demonstrated more severe psychopathology, agreement would not be so readily forthcoming.

Thus, type of anxiety reveals what parts of the mind are working; however, it tells us little with respect to severity of the problem. Likewise, level of anxiety has limited diagnostic utility. The first client was preoccupied with object loss and abandonment; the second, with the strength of his anger or his inability to control it. The latter developmentally precedes anxiety with respect to object loss, yet the client in the second example seemed better able to prepare himself for the possibility of future danger. Obviously, assessment of anxiety is complex, but whatever determinations are possible can help with treatment direction.

Once it is established that anxiety is functioning as a signal, the next most useful assessment concerns not the level of anxiety but whether the client has any awareness of its reason. In this case, further exploration is readily possible. However, if the client believes the source of anxiety is husband/wife, job, etc., meaning that the problem is located outside the individual, then exploration into the workings of the mind must be postponed in favor of developing the capacity for self-observation. For instance, the client who was concerned about the cab had to experience conditions of greater ease before he could make use of reason and judgment. Such a detour is a detour only with respect to self-exploration, not with respect to the course of treatment since a working relationship could not otherwise be established.

One last comment about anxiety and diagnosis. Everyday living is filled with anxiety-provoking situations. Hardly a day goes by without some significant experience of internal distress or conflict. In 1939, Hartman (1958) cautioned that conflict and pathology are not to be equated. Nor are health and freedom from conflict to be considered synonymous. Usual living includes conflict and conflict-free experiences. As Hartmann noted, it is useful to consider how conflict experiences and nonconflict experiences are processed in the same person at the same time. In effect, it is not how much conflict exists or how much anxiety is experienced, but how much capacity to cope remains available in spite of the experience of conflict and anxiety.

Treatment Considerations in Anxiety

The anxious patient needs to be helped to become less anxious before functioning can be improved. This requires accurate assessment of her subjective experience of anxiety and stress. Consider the client who expressed concern about beating his wife. What information would be helpful? It is already known that he is anxious in ancitipation that he might once again lose control. Would it be helpful to know how anxious? Could it be determined whether he felt under control or whether his control was slipping? Certainly, one would want to know all of the above. The clinician might ask, ''How are you managing now? Would it be O.K. if we arranged an appointment next week or do you want to come in right away?'' This gives the client an opportunity to consider for himself just how he is coping. If he has not lost control and if his anxiety tolerance is high, he might well decide to wait. However, if physical danger were present, it would behoove the clinician to suggest an immediate appointment.

In the example of the abusive husband, issues of anxiety tolerance and internal versus external structure are evident. Generally, there is some relationship among these variables such that if anxiety tolerance is high, a reasonable degree of internal structure is probably available to the client and she can cope relatively well with her experience of anxiety. If anxiety tolerance is low, however, internal structure is usually not available and must be brought into the situation from outside. To offer structure to a client who does not need it can be infantilizing and disrespectful of his autonomy. Not to offer structure when it is needed can be devastating.

Deciding how to intervene is another exercise in clinical judgment. Does the therapist offer her services? Does he solicit support from family and/or friends? Are they available? To what extent does the therapist involve herself with a client to effect immediate change? These questions have less to do with issues of anxiety than with the clinician's overall assessment of which intervention will promote more adaptive functioning in the client regardless of the presence or absence of anxiety. Which approach will help the client feel and function better? While answers to these questions can be gained during the initial interview, this requires time and experience, and it is unlikely that a beginner will be able to answer such questions without supervisory help for quite some time.

As I indicated previously, the client's apparent anxiety or lack thereof can be misleading.

A middle-aged client came to the office and requested immediate help in getting some material for his wife. He felt he had to have the material for her that very day, but he was not sure where to get it and had driven himself to distraction trying to find out where it was available. He was rapidly approaching a panic state. I commented on his sense of urgency and wondered how crucial it was to solve the problem immediately. With almost a bewildered look, he replied that there really was no emergency and was suddenly dumbfounded that he had experienced one. The rest of our session was spent exploring what had happened to him.

Both beginning and experienced workers might find themselves influenced by the client's anxiety in such an instance, unknowingly responding to his feelings with anxiety of their own. For example, client anxiety might cause the worker to offer precipitous help, convince the worker to involve a family member in therapy, or even provoke the worker to dismiss the client. When client anxiety arouses worker anxiety that remains outside the worker's awareness and, therefore, unmanaged, a cycle is initiated in which the client arouses the worker, who further arouses the client, etc. Obviously, such a cycle is not helpful to either client or worker. However, supervision can bring such problems to the worker's attention, allowing her to examine the effect of unconscious processes on her performance and to tailor the intervention so as to support the client's capacity to cope.

Theoretical Orientations and Treatment Approaches to Anxiety

One of the most crucial concerns with respect to psychopathology is the recognition that every treatment approach to, or definition of, "pathology" has attached to it a theoretical orientation with regard to causality that supports the particular treatment approach under consideration. This is particularly noteworthy because DSM III claims to be atheoretical, offering only descriptive statements about various categories of pathology. The rationale for this approach is that no one current theoretical stance can account for the range and complexity of human behavior. Similarly, since different theories of pathology lend themselves to different foci in treatment, some practitioners have fallen into the trap of considering themselves eclectic in that they use all theories and methods of practice in accordance with their perceptions of client need, completely overlooking the problem that constructs inherent in one school of thought may well be antagonistic to constructs in another. Clients have a right to intellectual honesty that is not met by eclecticism. This trend must be replaced by a commitment to building an adequate theory of behavior.

Presently, there are several major orientations to treatment that need some discussion with respect to problems of anxiety. It should have been obvious that the section on changing perspectives on anxiety states reviewed these orientations from the "psychodynamic developmental model." I selected that model primarily because anxiety is an inner experience that can be defined and reported only subjectively. In this vein, it must be recognized that the psychodynamic model is the only one that offers an explanatory theory regarding inner experience.* Thus, the psychodynamic developmental view of anxiety emphasizes the internal workings of the mind and supports a treatment approach that sees pathology with respect to anxiety as a function of mental activity. This view, of course, does not deny that external pressures have significant impact on internal reactions, but the focus of the psychodynamically oriented practitioner would be on furthering understanding and skills within the person, thereby enabling her to cope better with the problematic anxiety expeience. According to this model, anxiety states occur when ego functions are incapacitated. Treatment would be aimed at enabling the person to develop skills to sustain these functions even under stress. Obsessive-compulsive disorders, a particular form of anxiety state, are seen as symptoms brought into play to prevent the experience of overwhelming anxiety and treatment focus would be on understanding their place within the total workings of the mind. Treatment in this model is usually offered in a dyadic or group arrangement; intellectual capacity, as well as ability for self-reflection, is a necessary client attribute for this model. Obviously, a theory that offers a model of mind and revolves around the way in which the mind works is going to lead to a therapeutic mode that explores these workings.

---

*While the humanistic and existential orientations do take steps in this direction, they do not offer a developmental approach that attempts to explain the purpose of anxiety within the frame of reference of a model of the mind.

In contrast to the psychodynamic developmental view, which emphasizes inner processes, other orientations see the reason for behavior as primarily a function of occurrences outside the individual. The "behavioral model," resting on learning theory, views behavior as a function of learned responses that have accrued as a result of a combination of rewards and punishments. In effect, sequences of behavior that are rewarded remain part of the repertoire of the individual. Inherent in this orientation is the emphasis on external factors as causally related to behavior; thus, little attention is paid to the workings of the mind. Some classical behaviorists completely dismiss concepts like mind, affect, and thought because they cannot be observed and/or measured. Attention is paid only to those aspects of functioning that can be quantified. Other behaviorists are more moderate and recognize that thoughts and feelings are components of the human condition. Nevertheless, their emphasis is that behaviors and even ways of thinking and feeling are learned and can be unlearned subject only to the influence of the proper combination of rewards and punishments. Obviously, such an orientation will develop therapies in which the therapist is in charge, rewarding and punishing, as seems fit, those behaviors that are to be changed (Ullman & Krasner, 1965). Since clients literally place themselves in the hands of the behavior therapist, such an approach can easily lend itself to abuse and, indeed, examples of such abuse are a matter of record (Milgram, 1974). More important for purposes of this chapter, behaviorists view anxiety as a learned response that can be unlearned. The usual method of treatment, following the principles of behavioral theory, is referred to as "systematic desensitization." In this approach, the client builds up tolerance to anxiety through a series of graduated exposures to anxiety-provoking stimuli. Once again, no attention is given to client understanding or self-reflection.

The "systems model" represents a third major orientation to human behavior. It tends to coincide with an "interactional model," wherein, as in the behavioral view, emphasis is placed on factors external to the individual as a way of explaining human behavior. Thus, individual pathology may be viewed as an expression of conflict within the family or even as the entire family's symptom; accordingly, therapy may focus on external influences in order to change existing family interaction patterns. A disorder involving anxiety attacks, phobic symptoms, or obsessive-compulsive behaviors can be interpreted as an interactional problem; for example, a child may protect his mother by evidencing the anxiety the mother disowns. Notably, in this orientation, terms relating to inner functioning of the mind have no utility since no concept of mind is offered. Ironically, many interactional therapists committed to a systems orientation do make use of terms like "ego" and "unconscious" even though they otherwise negate the psychodynamic model from which these terms derive. Of course, an orientation that views pathology as an outcome of interaction patterns will foster an interactional therapy and indeed, the systems model favors marital and family sessions.

The "psychopharmacological model" sees pathology as a function of biological factors, either organic or hormonal; medication is considered necessary to correct the problem. Disorders related to anxiety states presently lack a biological explanation; however, therapists who view psychopathology as the result of physiological factors believe that eventually an appropriate biological explanation will be found. They argue that since drugs do alleviate anxiety symptoms, there must be a close relationship between cause and symptom and view medication as the treatment of choice. The pure physiologist sees no value in any other explanation for psychopathology.

Finally, a new and rapidly growing approach to the problem of anxiety is "stress management." Biofeedback is a popular form of stress management based on principles of operant conditioning. The client performs a series of exercises in which she learns to attend to, and discriminate among, various physiologic reactions, which she then becomes capable of controlling. Such phenomena as heart rate, blood pressure, and muscle tension have proved responsive to this approach. Moreover, clients suffering from anxiety have benefited from training in another means of stress management, progressive relaxation, which focuses on enhancing the client's awareness of his own bodily state.

Admittedly, stress management is primarily educative and symptom oriented. Its sole purpose is to alleviate symptomatology regardless of origins. With respect to conditions associated with anxiety, stress management seeks to enable clients to master the appearance of anxiety and to keep this response within manageable limits. Stress management techniques make use of the client's cognitive capacity to develop information processing systems that are able to control functions not usually accessible to cognitive control. Interestingly enough, while this approach includes significant input from outside the client and seems to rest on external influence, its thrust is to provide the client with the necessary skills to manage her own responses. In this regard, the goals of stress management are not terribly distant from psychotherapeutic goals. At the same time, stress management does not attend to the initial causes of problem behaviors. Only further research in this area will demonstrate the clinical utility of biofeedback, progresive relaxation, and related methods.

Interdisciplinary Cooperation in the Management of Anxiety

Clients experiencing anxiety often present themselves to clinics or family service agencies for treatment. Typically, the treatment process begins with an intake and assessment procedure involving social worker, psychologist, and psychiatrist. Each is involved with the client until a treatment plan is worked out, at which time the client may be assigned to one of the three for treatment. It is common practice for the psychiatrist to function primarily as consultant, the psychologist as diagnostician, and the social worker as therapist. The social worker typically functions as a member of a treatment team, regularly reporting to the team on the client's progress. If the social worker knows how to use the other team members as resources, the client will benefit from input from several disciplines.

Mrs. G came to a family service agency in an extremely agitated state; she was distressed that her son was homosexual and blamed herself for his "failure." She was almost incoherent as she described how she had failed as a mother and was worthless as a person. Mrs. G entertained thoughts of killing herself. The worker was unsure about Mrs. G's capacity to tolerate the level of anxiety she was experiencing and worried that Mrs. G might commit suicide. Arrangements were made for Mrs. G to see the psychologist for testing to evaluate the intensity of her suicidal ideation. Mrs. G was also seen by the psychiatrist to determine how to alleviate some of her immediate agitation so that she could discuss her concerns more calmly.

In this case, interdisciplinary teamwork proved beneficial to the client, but even when the social worker is not employed by an agency, such cooperation is necessary. For example, social workers cannot hospitalize a client and remain the therapist of record; therefore, cooperation with psychiatrists is mandatory when the worker is involved with a client requiring hospital care. The same is true with respect to the need for medication and/or psychological testing, particularly with clients demonstrating phobias and/or obsessive-compulsive symptoms with accompanying somatic complaints.

Research Issues for Social Work

Social work's unique position as a primarily agency-oriented profession offers many opportunities for ongoing research that can contribute to its knowledge base. Aside from obvious projects such as case studies, which can serve to expand knowledge of theory and practice, social work's emphasis on family orientation, structure, and functioning lends itself naturally to investigating such areas as the impact of client anxiety on other family members, the relationship of phobic behavior to family interaction patterns, the impact of phobic behavior on child-rearing, and the meaning of obsessive-compulsive symptoms to other family members.

We should also consider the relationships between various case management techniques and symptoms associated with anxiety. For instance, do workers really respond with anxiety to clients in acute states of anxiety? Are more experienced or older workers less affected by client anxiety? Are clients manifesting symptoms of acute anxiety referred for testing and/or medication more frequently than other clients?

Because group theory and organizational processes are part of social work's knowledge base, social workers are in a unique position to develop studies of agency attitudes toward the anxiety-ridden client, the availability of resources for individuals requiring frequent contact, and, of course, the impact of worker anxiety on the client. While it may appear that agency procedures often increase client distress, we have little empirical evidence to support this contention. Finally, the predominance of social workers on the staffs of most crisis centers should allow them to accumulate significant data on how anxiety actually effects all aspects of client, family, and agency functioning.

References

ALEXANDER F, FRENCH T: *Studies in Psychosomatic Medicine*. New York, Ronald, 1948.

American Psychiatric Association: *Diagnostic and Statistical Manual of Mental Disorders*, ed 3. Washington, DC, American Psychiatric Association, 1980.

BECK A: *Cognitive Therapy and Emotional Disorders*. New York, International Universities Press, 1976.

BRENNER C: Depression, anxiety, and affect theory. *Int J Psychoanal* 1974; 55:25–36.(a)

BRENNER C: On the nature and development of affects: a unified theory. *Psychoanal Q* 1974; 43:532–556.(b)

COMPTON A: Developments in the psychoanalytic theory of anxiety, in Kutash Land Schlesinger R (eds): *Handbood on Stress and Anxiety*. San Francisco, Jossey-Bass, 1980, pp 81–132.

FREUD A: *The Ego and the Mechanisms of Defense*. New York, International Universities Press, 1946.

FREUD S: *Inhibitions, Symptoms, and Anxiety*. London, Hogarth, 1936.

GRINKER R: *Psychosomatic Concepts*. New York, Aaronson, 1973.

HARTMAN H: *Ego Psychology and the Problem of Adaptation*. New York, International Universities Press, 1958.

KERNBERG O: *Borderline Conditions and Pathological Narcissism*. New York, Aronson, 1975.

KRYSTAL H: Trauma and affect. *Psychoanal Study Child* 1978; 33:81–116.

MILGRAM S: *Obedience to Authority*. New York, Harper & Row, 1974.

SCHUR M: Comments on the metapsychology of somatization. *Psychoanal Study Child* 1955; 10:119–164.

SPITZ R: *The First Year of Life*. New York, International Universities Press, 1965.

ULMAN L, KRASNER L: *Case Studies in Behavior Modification*. New York, Holt, Rinehart & Winston, 1965.

10

Phobic Disorders

RAY J. THOMLISON

The hotel elevator stops at the fifth floor, momentarily interrupting its descent to the lobby. A group of people enter the already crowded car as one of the party inquires, ''Is there room for us?'' Suddenly, from the back of the car a woman, with a sense of urgency in her voice, demands that she be let out of the elevator. As she forcefully moves past the other passengers, she attempts to justify her behavior by stating, ''I hate crowded elevators!'' The look of fear on her face and the haste with which she exits causes one of the remaining passengers to observe that ''she must have claustrophobia.'' The remaining passengers smile, some perhaps with a degree of understanding, hoping that the doors will soon reopen to free them from this otherwise socially inappropriate physical closeness.

Many of us have been in a crowded elevator and have found ourselves in various degrees of discomfort as a result. However, the person described in this vignette apparently felt that she had to act (escape) in order to reduce her level of discomfort. The manner in which she acted was observed by some of the passengers to be sufficiently different from the behavior of the others to identify her as having a phobia. That is, while others in the car may have felt uncomfortable being in a relatively confined space, they did not act on the urge to escape or avoid the confinement.

This chapter examines reasons why some people experience high levels of anxiety or fear in situations in which most people experience lower levels of discomfort. Furthermore, why I consider this anxiety causes these people to act in a manner that in some instances results in a complete lifestyle change, for example, inability to leave home unaccompanied. Specifically, this chapter explores the concept of phobia, a term that has to some extent become popular psychology jargon; identifies various types of phobic disorders and their characteristics; examines the etiology of phobic disorders; and draws specific conclusions regarding the implications of phobic disorders for social work intervention.

Characteristics of Phobic Disorders

What Is a Phobia?

The term "phobia" is not new to the psychopathology literature. According to Marks (1969): "The word phobia was first used in a medical context by Celsus, the Roman encyclopaedist, in the first century when he coined the term hydrophobia" (p. 7). Descriptions of morbid fears and their accompanying behaviors have appeared in the works of Hippocrates, Shakespeare and Descartes, with more complete clinical descriptions appearing in the seventeenth and eighteenth centuries (Marks, 1969). Most writers agree that Westphal introduced the modern term "agoraphobia" in his 1871 description of three patients who were afraid of going into wide streets and open squares (Laughlin, 1967; Lewin, 1972).

The word "phobia" derives from the Greek *phobeio* ("I fear"). As Lewin (1972) pointed out: "Greek words can be readily used in compounds, -phobo and -phobia were used as combining forms. Hence, -phobia easily became one of a large class of suffixes (including -mania, -philia, -pathy, etc.) that were adopted by medical and psychological writers" (p. 81). The practice of coining descriptive labels for every feared object or situation can be carried to extremes; thus, by 1914 Hall had compiled a list of 135 phobias (Levitt, 1967). Contemporary clinical usage has tended to be more restrictive: five categories of phobia are emphasized. For interest, however, a contemporary listing of phobias is offered in Table 10–1.

Regardless of the object of fear, phobic patients share a great many characteristics and the definitions of "phobia" are rather consistent irrespective of the theoretical perspective adopted by the investigator. Consider, for example, the definitions on page 283.

TABLE 10–1. The More Common Phobic Reactions

A. *Technically Named Phobias*

Types of Phobic Reaction classified by their technical names, with their objects and derivations indicated. The type is determined and named according to the phobic object.

1. *Acrophobia.* Height. (Gr., *acra,* heights or summits.)
2. *Agoraphobia.* Open spaces. (Gr., *agora,* market place, the place of assembly.)
3. *Ailurophobia.* Cats. (Gr., *ailouros,* cat.)
4. *Anthophobia.* Flowers. (Gr., *anthos,* flower.)
5. *Anthropophobia.* People. (Gr., *anthropos,* man, generically.)
6. *Aquaphobia.* Water. (Lat., *aqua,* water.)
7. *Astraphobia.* Lightning. (Gr., *asterope,* lightning.)
8. *Bacteriophobia.* Bacteria. (Gr., *bacter,* small rod.)
9. *Brontophobia.* Thunder. (Gr., *bronte,* thunder.)
10. *Claustrophobia.* Closed spaces. (Lat, *claustrum,* bar, bolt, or lock.)
11. *Cynophobia.* Dogs. (Gr., *cynas,* dog.)
12. *Demonophobia.* Demons. (Lat., *daemon,* demon.)
13. *Equinophobia.* Horses. (Lat., *equinis,* horse.)
14. *Herpetophobia.* Lizards or reptiles. (Gr., *herpetos,* a creeping or crawling thing.)
15. *Keraunophobia.* Thunder. (Gr., *Leraunos, thunderbolt.)*
16. *Mysophobia.* Dirt, germs, contamination. (Gr., *mysos,* uncleanliness of body or mind: abomination or defilement.)
17. *Numerophobia.* A number, or numbers. (Lat., *numero,* number.)
18. *Nyctophobia.* Darkness or night. (Gr., *nyx,* night.)
19. *Ophidiophobia.* Snakes. (Gr., *ophis,* snake or serpent.)
20. *Pyrophobia.* Fire. (Gr., *pyr,* fire.)
21. *Spatiophobia.* Self-confining phobia. (Laughlin) Phobically imposed area or spatial restrictions: often gradually, occasionally rapidly progressive (pp. 121–122).
22. *Zoophobia.* Animals. (Gr., *zoos,* animal.)

B. *Phobias by Phobic Object*

Types of Phobic Reaction classified and named on a descriptive, empire basis, alphabetically and according to the phobic object. Technical name by usage, or as assigned on the basis of etymology and preference, follow

1. Air (*aerophobia*)
2. Airplanes (*flienophobia*)
3. Aloneness (*solicitudophobia*)
4. Anger (*angrophobia*)
5. Animals (*zoophobia*)
6. Arguments (*argumentophobia*)
7. Atomic explosions (*atomosophobia*)
8. Birds (*avisophobia*)
9. Blood (*hemophobia*)
10. Boats (*boatophobia*)
11. Cancer (*cancerophobia*)
12. Cats (*ailurophobia*)
13. Childbirth (*byrthophobia*)
14. Closed spaces (*claustrophobia*)
15. Confinement (*confinophobia*)
16. Cosmic phenomena (*planetary collision, etc.*) (*kosmikophobia*)
17. Crowds (*crudanophobia*)
18. Dark (*nyctophobia*)
19. Death (*thanatophobia*)

20. Demons	(*demonophobia*)	50. People	(*anthropophobia*)
21. Dependence	(*soteriophobia*)	51. Phobias	(*phobosophobia*)
22. Dirt	(*mysophobia*)	52. Poison	(*toxicophobia*)
23. Disease		53. Poliomyelitis	(*poliosophobia*)
24. Doctors	(*medicophobia*)	54. Races or racial	groups (*razza-*
25. Dogs	(*cynophobia*)	*phobia*)
26. Drugs	(*drogophobia*)	55. Rats	(*rattephobia*)
27. Fights	(*fechtenophobia*)	56. Rodents	(*rodentophobia*)
28. Fire	(*pyrophobia*)	57. Satan	(*satanophobia*)
29. Flowers	(*anthophobia*)	58. Senility	(*senilisophobia*)
30. Genitals	(*genitophobia*)	59. Sex	(*sexesophobia*)
31. Germs	(*mikrophobia*)	60. Sharp objects	(*scharfophobia*)
32. Hair	(*trichophobia*)	61. Skin	(*dermatophobia*)
33. Heights	(*acrophobia*)	62. Snakes	(*ophidiophobia*)
34. Horses	(*equinophobia*)	63. Snow	(*blanchophobia*)
35. Hospitals	(*hospitalophobia*)	64. Solitude	(*desererephobia*)
36. Illness	(*illrophobia*)	65. Soteria (*sotcriophobia;* fear of so-
37. Insanity	(*dementophobia*)	terial dependence, dread of
38. Insects	(*insectophobia*)	dependency)
39. Knives	(*knifrphobia*)	66. Spiders	(*arachnophobia*)
40. Light	(*luxophobia*)	67. Strangers	(*etrangerophobia*)
41. Lightning	(*lichtophobia*)	68. Syphilis	(*syphilophobia*)
42. Lizards	(*lacertophobia*)	69. Thunderstorms	(*brontophobia*)
43. Medicine	(*medicinaphobia*)	70. Trains	(*traherophobia*)
44. Men	(*hominophobia*)	71. Travel	(*travelophobia*)
45. Mice	(*musophobia*)	72. Veneral disease	(*venerophobia*)
46. Night	(*nyctophobia*)	73. Vermin	(*venerophobia*)
47. Occupations	(*occupatiophobia*)	74. War	(*werrephobia*)
48. Old age	(*senilophobia*)	75. Water	(*aquaphobia*)
49. Open spaces	(*agoraphobia*)	76. Women	(*femellaphobia*)

Source: Reprinted by permission of the publisher from H. Laughlin, *The Neuroses*, 1st ed. (Woburn, MA: Butterworths, 1967), pp. 553–55.

[Phobia means] a special kind of fear which is out of proportion to the demands of the situation, can't be explained or reasoned away, is beyond voluntary control, and leads to avoidance of the feared situation. (Marks, 1978b, p. 15)

[A phobia is] a specific pathological fear which is out of proportion to the apparent stimulus. The painful affect has been automatically and unconsciously displaced from its original internal object, to become attached to a specific external object or situation. The phobia is an obsessively persistent kind of unrealistic fear which is inappropriate and unreasoning. The phobia seeks to defend the unconscious and the repressed. It is a defence against anxiety which is thereby displaced externally. (Laughlin, 1967a, p. 547)

There are specific relationships, objects and situations to which the person responds with feelings of discomfort, inability, and anticipation of aversive consequences. These situations are not ones an "objective" observer would consider fear-provoking, and the person himself is very likely to report that his responses are "wrong" or "irrational". If such reactions are not socially debilitating, however, they are not considered phobias. . . . To be considered phobic the fear must be elevated as disproportionate to the situation and socially disturbing by some observer, including the person himself. That is, the response deviates from what is expected in the culture and is disruptive. (Ullman & Krasner, 1969, p. 293)

Although subtle differences among these definitions reflect the authors' theoretical biases (examined in the section on etiology), three common components of phobic disorder are identified: an excessive level of anxiety or fear; (see Chapter 9) an identified situation(s) or object(s) to which this fear may be attributed; and excessive avoidance or escape behavior on the part of the person who is confronted, or anticipates being confronted, by the fear-provoking situation or object.

Anxiety, Fear, Situation, and Avoidance in Phobic Disorders

"Anxiety" and "fear" are terms that refer to normal psychophysiological responses. Unfortunately, the literature is unclear as to whether these terms embrace different levels of emotional discomfort (Marks, 1978b) or are synonymous (Levitt, 1967) in regard to phobic disorders. Confusion stems from the tendency to use the term "anxiety" in reference to relatively low levels of emotional discomfort and "fear" in reference to high emotional arousal tending toward physical immobilization. Such a distinction would be useful if authors did not also speak about high levels of anxiety that inhibit individual performance. For this discussion at least, these terms are considered synonymous.

Anxiety is useful to the individual insofar as it promotes action in response to a challenge or threat. Anxiety mobilizes physiological responses, creating a sharpness of perception that enhances individual performance. In addition, success in meeting the challenge or staving off the threat enhances self-esteem by increasing the individual's sense of competence. Alternatively, all people have an optimal level beyond which the psychophysiological responses of anxiety lead to diminished individual performance. In this case, anxiety is dysfunctional, immobilizing the individual.

To this point, phobic anxiety and nonphobic anxiety do not qualitatively differ (Mavissakalian & Barlow, 1981a). Both the phobic and the nonphobic individual confronted with a fear-provoking stimulus will manifest one or more psychophysiological responses: increased heart rate, perspiration, shaky hands, rapid breathing, desire to urinate, feeling of dizziness or faintness, feeling of suffocation, and sometimes a feeling of dying (perhaps of a heart attack). At an extreme level, some or all of these responses can constitute "panic attacks." Panic attacks may result in temporary immobilization and a strong desire to escape the situation in which the attack has occurred. Panic attacks are very often obvious to others; to the individual, the attack represents a loss of self-control.

The difference between the phobic and the nonphobic individual lies not only in psychophysiological response potential but rather in the connection of a constellation of anxiety responses to a specific situation or object. That is, the person experiencing a phobic disorder will manifest phobic anxiety in association with specific situations and objects whether these stimuli are actually encountered or only imagined. Furthermore, because of the level of the anxiety experienced, the individual's natural inclination will be to escape the situation or object. In the future, the person will attempt to avoid the situation or object in order to minimize the chance of having a phobic response. This avoidance behavior is strengthened by the tendency of phobic individuals to think about or rehearse "their frightening experiences in their minds until they are in an agony of fearful anticipation about the next time they will meet their phobic object" (Marks, 1969, p. 4).

Thus, avoidance or escape behavior is the other major characteristic of a phobic disorder. Most phobic stimuli are an ever present element of the individual's world. Avoidance of the fear-producing situation becomes an energy-consuming exercise and for some the fear becomes so inhibiting that the individual is unable to leave the confines of his own home. The consequences of such strong avoidance behavior are severe, ranging from job loss to curtailment of most social interactions.

Phobic individuals are well aware of the unrealistic level of their feeling of fear. The recognition of this deviance further complicates life for the phobic. "What's happening to me?" "Why can't I deal with this problem?" "Am I going crazy?"—these questions are repeatedly asked by the phobic individual but the answers only exacerbate the person's confusion and anxiety.

Although anxiety, fear, situation or object, and avoidance are the central elements of all phobic disorders, these elements are more or less important in each phobia. For example, Goldstein and Chambless (1978) suggested that the fear element in agoraphobia relates not to the external situation but rather to internal fear of the person's own reaction in other phobic anxieties, the individual fears external harm: "I am afraid of dogs because I fear dogs might bite me" (Mavissakalin & Barlow, 1981a, p. 5).

Prevalence of Phobic Disorders

The fact that many people hide their phobias prevents accurate estimates of how many people are afflicted. An often cited 1969 study of Burlington, Vermont, an area representative of a medium-sized city, provided some indication of the prevalence of phobic disorders: "The total prevalence of phobia was estimated at 76.9/1000 population. Of these 74.7/1000 were considered to be mildly disabling and 2.2/1000 severely disabling. Severely disabling was defined as absence from work for an employed person, and inability to manage the common household tasks for a housewife" (Agras et al., 1969, p. 153). Marks (1969) concluded his examination of the prevalance of phobias by observing that "though phobic symptoms may be present in 20% of psychiatric patients, phobic disorders are found in fewer than 3% of all cases seen in psychiatric practice in America and England" (p. 77).

Most practitioners would agree that the number of phobic persons who seek formal help is well below the number who experience phobic disorders. For example, in a recent social work follow-up survey of individuals who had made telephone contact with a phobia treatment program, more than half the respondents stated that they had had no further contact with any professional helping resource, although the majority of these people continued to experience the problem that had prompted the initial telephone call (James Quinn, Director of SE-CURE, Ministry of Health Mental Health Services, Vancouver, B.C., conversation, March 1981).

An additional difficulty in assessing the prevalence of phobic disorder is related to the diversity of its triggers and manifestations. Phobic anxiety may be precipitated by a range of stimuli from the specific to the general. For example, a person who experiences phobic anxiety at the sight of horses is less likely to experience the debilitating effects characteristic of more severe phobias and is consequently less likely to be identified in the phobic population.

Taking into account these constraints on data collection, one is probably safe in estimating that phobic disordered people represent no more than 5% of the population.

Classification of Phobic Disorders

While the number of objects or situations that can arouse phobic anxiety is virtually unlimited, classification of phobic disorders has imposed some order in this area. After an extensive review of the literature, Marks (1969) sorted phobias into two major classes those linked to: phobias associated with external stimuli and those linked to internal stimuli. The former group of phobic disorders includes agoraphobia, social phobias, animal phobias, and miscellaneous specific phobias. Only two phobic disorders fall into the internal stimuli group: illness phobias and obsessive phobias.

The strength of this classification lies in its specific labeling of the most prevalent phobic anxieties in relation to their perceived stimuli. However, work done in the next decade, particularly in cognitive research, called into question the internal–external dichotomy. For example, there is building evidence that one of the significant stimuli in agoraphobia anxiety is, in fact, the internal thought mechanisms of the individual irrespective of the presence of an external stimulus (e.g., Goldstein & Chambless, 1978). Accordingly, the classification offered here is an amalgam of current approaches.

Agoraphobia: Simple and Complex

The most important category of phobic disorders is agoraphobia, with an estimated prevalence of 6.3/1000 (Agras et al., 1969). This condition accounts for more than 60% of all phobic disorders (Marks, 1969; Mavissakalian & Barlow, 1981) and is by far the most debilitating. The greatest number of agoraphobic individuals are women; Marks (1969) estimated a proportion of 75%. This figure is supported to some degree by the 95% female sample in a 1970 survey of 1,200 agoraphobics (Marks & Herst, 1970). Of further interest is the fact that the majority of agoraphobic women are married. The predominance of married women in the agoraphobic population has led to the coining of a popular phrase—"housebound housewife" (Roberts, 1964).

Derived from the Greek *agora* ("marketplace" or "place of assembly") the term "agoraphobia" has been used widely to refer to fear of open spaces or public places, whether crowded or relatively empty (Marks, 1969). Others have suggested that the fear arises as a result of being away from a situation of familiarity and safety (Hallam, 1978; Snaith, 1968).

The major distinguishing feature of agoraphobia is the individual's extreme feeling of fear or threat to the self if she is required to leave the house. If the person must leave the home, she usually insists on the company of another adult. The phobic anxiety may be attributed to a single object or situation, such as riding on a bus, or to a multiplicity of stimuli, with an exhaustive list of common and uncommon environmental situations and objects. The phobic anxiety stimuli most commonly identified are public transit, shopping areas, open spaces, theaters or other crowded public places, and social situations. (Hallam, 1978; Marks & Herst, 1970). Depression, depersonalization, claustrophobia, high levels of free-floating anxiety, and panic attacks are also experienced by many agoraphobic individuals (Goldstein & Chambless, 1978; Marks, 1978a; Schapira et al., 1970; Snaith, 1968).

Although it is unclear whether all agoraphobics are able to identify the onset of the phobic anxiety, most clients do report that the anxiety first manifested itself after some upset in their life, for example, a panic attack occurring either in a public location or at home. The panic attack may have occurred for no apparent reason or it may have occurred when the individual felt his performance was under scrutiny by others.

Edna, a 53-year-old married woman, had successfully raised three children and was a new grandmother. She had had no incapacitating physical or psychological problems until she began to experience excessive fear at the thought of leaving her home. At the point at which she made contact with a social worker, she had to be accompanied by her husband whenever she left the house. She recognized that her fear was unrealistic and yet she could not overcome it. Furthermore, her husband was expressing considerable impatience with her.

Assessment indicated that two years previously Edna had been waiting at a bus stop when a man standing behind her fell to the ground, apparently having had a heart attack. Edna wanted to come to the man's assistance but froze and stood watching as others offered help. Edna was extremely upset by this incident and by her inability to be helpful. She attributed her fear to this anxiety-provoking situation and although she rationally understood that the likelihood of her being faced with a similar life-or-death situation was remote, this recognition did not make leaving the home any easier.

Like Edna, many agoraphobics fear not a specific situation but the possibility of panicking, losing control, or generally underperforming if confronted with the fear-provoking stimulis or one similar to it. This fear of underperformance, of losing self-control, or of panicking, has led some researchers to identify two categories of agoraphobia (Goldstein & Chambless, 1978; Mavissakalian & Barlow, 1981a). Goldstein and Chambless posited that within the classification of agoraphobia there are individuals whose fears are associated with "various external stimuli such as attack or being hit by a car" and that these should not be designated agoraphobic. Rather, they should be identified by clear reference to the external stimulus that produces the anxiety. By withdrawing this group from the agoraphobic category, it is then possible to identify two new categories of agoraphobia: simple and complex.

"Simple agoraphobia" refers to "those clients whose symptoms are precipitated by panic attacks produced by drug experiences or physical disorders such as hypoglycemia. They do not necessarily present the same personality characteristics as other agoraphobics and usually recover more quickly when any contributing physical disorder is controlled" (Goldstein & Chambless, 1978, p. 50).

"Complex agoraphobia" has four elements, with the "fear of fear" central (Goldstein & Chambless, 1978). The phrase "fear of fear" refers to the phobic individual's fear of his own reaction or performance within a specific situation. This fear is in contrast to the phobic reactions to a particular thing or situation. The second element in complex agoraphobia is "low levels of self-sufficiency whether due to anxiety, a lack of skills, or both." Third is "a tendency to misapprehend the causal antecedents of uncomfortable feelings" Goldstein and Chambless gave the example of a person who feels anxiety following an interpersonal conflict but inter-prets this feeling as a fear of being on the street alone. The fourth element speaks to the observation of the "onset of symptoms in a climate of not-able conflict" (p. 51). Presumably, this conflict can be intrapersonal as well as interpersonal, that is, can result from inner stress as well as outer conflict.

While this classification is in the early stages of formulation, it does seem to clarify the roles of individual competence, cognition, and conflict in the creation of high-level anxiety. Furthermore, it explains why agora-phobics may fear either one or many objects, as well as why some clients respond relatively quickly to intervention while others remain un-changed.

It is also important to note that most agoraphobics do fluctuate in terms of the severity of their phobic symptoms. Some days the individual may feel less anxiety than on other days and may be able to face the phobic situation with some degree of strength. Likewise, an agoraphobic person may report feeling more tense and fearful in the morning, an-ticipating the day's activities, and less anxious in the evening. For that matter, some agoraphobics report feeling more comfortable at night due to the darkness, which gives them some anonymity and, therefore, some freedom to walk outdoors.

Understandably, family members are affected by the behavior of the agoraphobic. The restrictions on mobility, the inadequate role perfor-mance, and the demands placed on other family members create tension in the family system. When an agoraphobic is virtually housebound, other family members must perform the tasks that would otherwise be performed by the agoraphobic. Family members have difficulty knowing how to react to the affected member. They have feelings of anger and confusion—anger because of the loss of the family member and confu-sion as to whether the symptoms are real, particularly if the agoraphobic fluctuates in any noticeable way. Of course, the agoraphobic individual is cognizant of this family stress and this awareness is both an added burden and a further confirmation of an already poor self-image.

Social Phobias

Some people exhibit fear in relation to eating in public places (e.g., restaurants, cafeterias); speaking before groups, large or small; using public washrooms; or being in other situations wherein people might be scrutinizing each other's behavior. Typically, social phobics report excessive feelings of fear when a perceived authority figure is watching their performance. Even walking into a crowded room becomes a difficult task for the social phobic, who is excessively sensitive to people's glances.

Although social phobias are often part of the agoraphobic's inventory of fears, the agoraphobic tends to be more restricted than the social phobic. Furthermore, while women tend to predominate in the agoraphobic group, social phobias are equally prevalent among men and women (Marks, 1969).

Animal Phobias

It is difficult to know how many people suffer from fear of a specific animal to the degree that the condition might be labeled a phobia. Most people do not seek help for a fear of an object that they are not likely to encounter, e.g., snakes. Marks (1969), for example, noted that only 24 animal phobics presented themselves for treatment at the Maudsley Hospital in England the 1960s.

Animal phobias are more common in children than adults, but for many children animal phobias, which may start well before the age of six years, continue to adulthood. While good research data are lacking in this area, it does appear that animal phobias affect equal numbers of boys and girls; however, by far the greatest number of adult animal phobics are women (Marks & Gelder, 1966).

Other Specific Phobias

Fear of flying, heights, elevators, storms, wind, vomiting, illness, blood, death, contamination, or the possibility of harming others may produce specific phobias, all of which may lack the general fearfulness associated with agoraphobia (for examples see Alperson, 1976; Elmore et al., 1980; Murray & Foote, 1979; Nimmer & Kapp, 1974; Reeves & Mealiea, 1975; Wijesinghe, 1974). For instance, an individual who experiences fear of flying does not necessarily experience other excessive fears. Unfortunately, however, this fear may prevent the individual from traveling for business or pleasure (Reeves & Mealiea, 1975). If travel is unavoidable, the phobic flyer may, with considerable difficulty and the use of alcohol or tranquilizers, board the airplane.

Although other specific phobias are much less common than flight phobia, they are no less debilitating.

Etiology of Phobic Disorders

There is general agreement among those in the field that phobic disorders represent a fairly clear and consistent set of behaviors or symptoms that are associated with excessive, or unrealistic, levels of anxiety or fear about one or more objects or situations in the person's environment. In turn, the fear level is such that the individual must in some manner escape or avoid the feared object(s) or situation(s). There is also agreement in regard to the clinical descriptions of the different types of phobic disorder.

However, the questions of why people become phobic or how phobias can be explained elicit a wide range of answers. To date, three major theoretical models have guided the study and treatment of phobic disorders. If successful outcome of treatment is used as the criterion for acceptance or rejection of a particular theoretical model, then each model must be considered in its own right because no treatment has proven completely effective. Three theoretical models are considered here: the psychoanalytic, the biological (medical), and the behavioral.

The Psychoanalytic Model

Every student of psychoanalytic theory is familiar with Freud's well-known case of Little Hans, a five-year-old boy who was afraid of horses:

> Little Hans . . . had a phobia of horses. He feared they would bite him. Aggressive impulses toward his father had become intolerably dangerous because of the threat of possible retaliation. Hans' unconscious undeavour was to exclude the unbearable ideas from all conscious awareness. The threat and danger came to be displaced from the now internal fear of father, to an external one of horses. The danger then appeared in disguised form to be that "the horse will or may bite me." The horse thus had become a substituted, more bearable external object. It symbolically "stood for" the feared retaliatory part of father. The basis for this phobia (and for others) was assumed by Freud to lie in the Oedipus Complex. The horse could be avoided; father could not. "Flight" as an avoidance response to the object of danger was now possible. (Laughlin, 1967a, p. 551)

For Freud, a phobic reaction occurred when a person displaced a frightening or unacceptable aspect of himself onto some aspect of his reality. Thus, in the future this situation had to be avoided in order to suppress the unacceptable subjective factor. In the simplest sense, repressed instinctual desires gain expression through the functioning of the ego by displacement onto another object.

In the psychoanalytic model, the phobia is at the same time both the repression of anxiety (or pathological fear) and a defense against the anxiety (Laughlin, 1976b). That is, the anxiety results from an unconscious conflict, usually of a sexual nature. This conflict and the resultant anxiety are automatically repressed, or hidden, from the individual's awareness and unconsciously displaced from the original, internal object of conflict onto an external object or situation. In the case of Little Hans, the internal object was his father and the external (displaced) object was horses. In this manner, the original, more threatening source of anxiety is kept from the conscious mind. The defense is strengthened by displacing the anxiety onto a more manageable (less threatening) external object or situation. Arguing that the function of the phobia is to escape the anxiety, Freud suggested that by externalizing the phobic object, the individual has a greater chance of successfully escaping. After all, it is easier to escape an external danger than an internal one. To help a phobic client, according to this model, the unconscious conflict must be brought into consciousness so that the real source of anxiety can be discovered and dealt with.

Interestingly, Freud himself was the victim of agoraphobia and his own inability to resolve completely this problem may have prevented him, according to Laughlin (1976a), from interpreting the complexities of the phobic defense more. Further development in this area has been the focus of some contemporary psychoanalytic theorists (Deutsch, 1951; Laughlin, 1967b; Stamm, 1972; Weiss, 1964.)

In his study of agoraphobics, Weiss (1964) described the ego conflict facing the agoraphobic individual:

> On the one hand, the ego feels an uncontrollable urge to open a gate for the emotional relief of some repressed, but steadily increasing, drive-tension; on the other hand, the ego does not dare to have the internal, dynamic barrier removed, for this barrier secures the defensive repression of unacceptable drives. (p. 4)

Some analysts suggest that agoraphobic women have strong but ambivalent feelings toward their mother. In order to insure the well-being of their mother, who is a protector, agoraphobics must keep their mothers ever present. According to Weiss (1964): "Most analysts believe that agoraphobic patients regress to a state of dependent attachment on the mother [which] is due primarily to the feeling of helplessness which originates in specific dynamic factors" (p. 29). These dynamic factors are theoretically complex elements that range from the repression of the oedipal conflict to compensation for a missing functional part of the ego. Moreover, as is to be expected, different phobic reactions have different psychodynamic factors operating. For example, extreme feelings of hostility toward a parental figure (e.g., a death wish) may be experienced by the phobic patient as fear of his own death.

An additional point must be made with reference to agoraphobia. Weiss (1964) and Stamm (1972) both pointed to the significance of the loss of self-identity in the creation of agoraphobic anxiety. Weiss suggested that the self-identity factor may account for the depersonalization experienced by some agoraphobic individuals.

The psychoanalytic model has contributed much to the understanding of phobic disorders. However, the outcomes of treatment based on this model have been inadequately measured and this approach has been deemphasized by clinicians of late.

The Biological Model

It is premature to refer to a biological model in discussing the etiology of phobic disorders because a unitary model does not exist. What does exist, however, is an ever increasing body of knowledge about psychopharmacological approaches to the treatment of phobias (Barlow & Mavissakalian, 1981; Solyom et al., 1973; Spitzer & Klein, 1976); hereditary or biological predispositions to fears and phobias (Delprato, 1980; Shields, 1978; Slater & Cowie, 1971; Slater & Shields, 1969); physiological differences between phobics and nonphobics (Lader, 1978; Lader & Mathews, 1968; Marks, 1969); and the relationship between phobic disorders and such conditions as hypoglycemia (Chambless & Goldstein, 1981).

Research in this area has tended to focus on the cause and control of the anxiety response. Therefore, advances in pharmacological treatment have largely involved the amelioration of anxiety and panic responses. Interestingly, there is growing evidence that the antidepressants are most effective in this regard. Just how antidepressants act as antianxiety or antipanic medication is not clear, but their effect has lent strength to the view that some phobias, such as agoraphobia, are actually two independent but interacting processes: an affective disorder and an anxiety-phobic disorder. (Barlow & Mavissakalian, 1981).

The heredity–environment debate, which figures in most discussions of human behavior, also enlivens the discussion of phobic disorders. It seems likely that some biological predisposition does influence the individual's anxiety reactions. However, the research in support of so-called anxiety proneness (Slater & Cowie, 1971; Slater & Shields, 1969) remains inconclusive. After a comprehensive review of the research in this area, Delprato (1980) concluded that "no body of research that was considered is so free of methodological and/or conceptual problems that it can be presented as corroboration of the hypothesis of innate fear predispositions without qualification'' (p. 98).

Looking at physiological differences between phobic and nonphobic clients, Lader and his colleagues (1978; Lader & Mathews, 1968) verified differences in autonomic activity. Certainly the early work of Marks (1969) uncovered differences in spontaneous fluctuations in galvanic skin response among various phobic types. For example, phobic patients showed more spontaneous fluctuations in skin conductance than did normals; agoraphobic patients had more spontaneous fluctuations than did patients with specific or simple phobias; and agoraphobic patients habituated more slowly than did controls. The implications of these data for the etiology and treatment of phobic anxiety are not clear at this point, but these findings do suggest that phobic disorders differ qualitatively and that treatment approaches must take these differences into account.

A final focus of the biological approach to understanding phobic disorders is what Chambless and Goldstein (1981) labeled ''physical trauma.'' They observed that

> in a substantial minority of cases, panic attacks begin in response to physiological upheaval. The most common in our experience have been childbirth, adverse reactions to drugs (prescribed or illicitly obtained), hypoglycemia, and a major illness or surgery. We have found that the first three may set off agoraphobia in otherwise normal individuals. (p. 107)

More information is needed in this area, particularly on hypoglycemia (low blood sugar), a condition that is purportedly easy to alter through diet.

The biological model will undoubtedly have a considerable impact on our understanding of phobic disorders in the decades to come, particularly in identifying different phobic anxiety processes, as well as in inhibiting or arresting certain aspects of phobic anxiety in order to facilitate psychosocial treatment.

The Behavioral Model

Although the behavioral literature refers to the behavioral model, there is more than one such model. The two behavioral frameworks that have been most influential thus far in explaining phobic disorders are the operant and the classical (respondent). These models agree that problematic behaviors are learned through interaction between the individual and the environment. Thus, phobic anxiety and phobic avoidance, the major elements of phobic disorder, are considered to be behaviors that have been learned in response to environmental stimuli. Just how this learning is postulated to take place is where the operant and the classical model diverge. In addition there is the cognitive model. The three models will be discussed below.

The Operant Model

According to the operant theory of learning, behaviors that are freely performed by the person are subject to increases or decreases in frequency of occurrence as a result of the consequences that follow the behaviors. Simply speaking, positive consequences increase the frequency of a behavior while negative consequences decrease its frequency. Phobic behaviors, according to this paradigm, will increase or decrease in frequency in relation to the consequences that follow.

This model emphasizes phobic avoidance rather than phobic anxiety. Avoidance behavior is strengthened in at least two ways. First, the sympathetic attention of significant others can be seen as "positive (social) reinforcement" for avoidance behavior. Second, the successful escape from, or avoidance of, the anxiety-provoking object or situation has the same effect as positive reinforcement, although this process is referred to as "negative reinforcement".

The operant model not only emphasizes avoidance responses but also examines behaviors that would be either more acceptable than, or incompatible with, the avoidance behavior. In this regard, the agoraphobic client often has had a limited history of positive reinforcement for skill development. In fact, many such persons report that their attempts to assert themselves and bring about changes in their life have been punished by significant others.

Since, according to this model, problematic behavior and desired behavior are both learned in accordance with the same principles, treatment uses the positive reinforcement of approach behavior and/or the withdrawal of positive reinforcement for avoidance behavior. In addition, interventions usually include the development of other social behaviors, e.g., assertiveness training or social skills training, to expand the individual's response repertoire.

The Classical Conditioning Model

The classical conditioning paradigm has had a most significant impact on the current understanding and treatment of phobic disorders. In the simplest sense, this model postulates that behavior that is elicited by one stimulus can be brought under the control of another stimulus if both are presented together. Insofar as the learning of phobic anxiety is concerned, this model has strong historical roots in the famous case of Little Albert.

Little Albert was allowed to play with a small rabbit until he became quite relaxed and comfortable with the animal. At a later time, the rabbit was presented to Albert but simultaneously a metal object was struck behind the child, startling him. Having been startled in the presence of the rabbit, Albert now experienced a fear reaction each time the rabbit was produced.

While subsequent studies of this type failed to condition phobias (Emmelkamp, 1979), the stage was set for many years of exploration of phobic anxiety in terms of this early classical conditioning model.

The contemporary conditiong model emphasizes anxiety but also incorporates the phobic avoidance response. This is commonly called the "two-factor theory" (Mowrer, 1939). First, phobic anxiety is said to be a "conditioned response," i.e., it is learned. This phobic anxiety (response) is elicited by the "conditioned stimulus," i.e., the phobic object or situation. In other words, the phobic object takes on the power to elicit the anxiety response because this phobic object was present at the same time as some other object that naturally elicited anxiety from the individual.

The greatest impetus to the treatment of phobias, a method known as "systematic desensitization," came from this theoretical model and although contemporary investigators have been critical of the classical conditioning model, it has served as the framework for a great deal of research into the treatment of phobias.

The Cognitive Model

Not as thoroughly researched as either the operant or the classical conditioning model, the cognitive model is nevertheless having a significant impact on phobia treatment procedures. Cognitive theory stresses the statements individual's make to themselves. In this model, anxiety is assumed to result from statements of a fear-inducing nature that individuals communicate to themselves. For example, when one gets to a party, a potentially anxiety-provoking situation, one can say to oneself, "I'm going to enjoy this evening and I know people like me because I add a good deal to get-togethers," or one can say, "I'm going to have a miserable time here. I hate these functions. I never know what to talk about and people think I'm dumb." Cognitive theorists argue that such statements are reflected in behavior.

At a more complex level, the cognitive model posits that the phobic's processing of a threatening situation and how to escape from it is faulty.

Some investigators have produced data supporting Ellis's (1962) view that phobic patients think more irrationally than do comparison individuals (Rimm et al., 1977). Ellis suggested that irrational thoughts and beliefs produce the phobic anxiety in the person.

Certainly, there is ample reason to incorporate cognitive behavioral theory into the behavioral model, as some recent investigators have done (Chambless & Goldstein, 1981; Mahoney, 1974; Meichenbaum, 1974), but considerably more research is needed to clarify the presently conflicting findings on the role of cognition in phobic anxiety (Emmelkamp, 1979).

Toward a Unifying Model

Recent theoretical explorations have drawn heavily from the operant, classical conditioning, and cognitive models and have recognized the need to explain the various phobic disorders differently. What is required now is a model that incorporates the relevant, empirically supported contributions of each of the existing models but gives greater recognition to the social (interactional) aspects of phobic disorders. For social work, the most appropriate model would be the "social systems framework." This perspective can accommodate both individual causal explanations for phobic disorders (e.g., physiological predispositions toward panic attacks, differences in cognitive processing, and differences in stress tolerance) and social or environmental explanations (e.g., spouse, family, and community subsystems). The quality and quantity of interactions between the individual and each relevant subsystem can either foster or alleviate phobic anxiety.

Interestingly, although most phobic individuals are married and most have families, little is known about the role of the spouse and children in the phobic disorder. The few reports available to date have focused on the spouse as a contributor to the disorder and have examined her response to the phobic's treatment. Buglass and associates (1977) compared the husbands of 30 agoraphobic women with controls matched for age, sex, social class, and marital status. They found that "on most measures of attitudes, behavior, domestic organization and marital interaction, the two groups were strikingly similar" (p. 73). However, when the marital satisfaction level of phobic clients is examined, an association seems to exist between marital conflict and some phobic disorders (Barlow & Mavissakalian, 1981; Emmelkamp, 1974; Hafner, 1977; Torpy & Measy, 1974). One study of 21 married agoraphobics found that approximately two-thirds rated their marriage as unsatisfactory (Hand et al., 1974). Milton and Hafner (1979) evaluated the effects of treatment on 18 agoraphobics and their spouses. Not only did they observe less improvement among agoraphobics whose pretreatment marriages were rated unsatisfactory, but also they noted that treatment resulted in increased marital dissatisfaction in 9 of 15 subjects for whom there were reliable data. It is probable that further exploration of the marital relationship will clarify the association between marital discord and phobic disorders.

Chambless and Goldstein (1981) postulated that the agoraphobic and her spouse are in a mutually dependent relationship:

> Agoraphobics tend to select partners who are willing to function as caretakers. Obviously the converse is also the case; in choosing a dependent person as a partner, one has someone to take care of. Within the caretaker role, we have observed two styles. One is the emotionally detached spouse, the other the anxiously solicitous spouse. Both interact with the agoraphobic in a parent–child fashion. . . . The greatest deterrent to change . . . is both partners' fear that there will be no basis for the relationship if these roles are abandoned. (p. 135)

Although Chambless and Goldstein have yet to offer empirical support for their clinical observations, such hypotheses are consistent with social systems formulations in family treatment generally and it is surprising that more research is not available in this area.

A final area of focus from a social systems perspective would be on the interaction between the individual and his community system. These systems act as supportive resources for the individual from which she draws energy for problemsolving and stress management. As some investigators have pointed out, many phobic individuals appear to lack the coping skills to interact with these external systems. Avoiding interaction with these systems is the path of least resistance for the phobic person and yet the avoidance exacerbates the anxiety as the individual further damages his self-esteem. Little is known about the sociocultural causes of phobic disorders but such factors as feelings of being alone, age, income, and community size were all correlates with agoraphobia in the Marks and Herst (1970) survey of 1,200 agoraphobics. Lack of assertiveness, lack of social skills, and fear of disapproval from peers are also mentioned by phobic individuals as social causative factors and although the relative importance of these variables is yet to be determined, the need for the phobic individual to establish a social support system is recognized as an integral part of treatment for many.

In conclusion, while the three main etiological models have been presented here as distinct from one another, there is growing awareness that each is relevant to our understanding of different aspects of phobic disorders. What is needed now is framework that incorporates the strengths of each model and stimulates investigation of phobic disorders.

For the professional social worker, the proposed organizing model is that of social systems.

Treatment Approaches to Phobic Disorders

From a social work practitioner's perspective, two issues arise in discussing the treatment of phobic disorders. First, review of the major social work practice textbooks and journals reveals a dearth of publications in this area, even though social workers deal extensively with phobic clients. Second, models of intervention derived from other disciplines must be evaluated by the social worker for their applicability to his own practice. This section examines three major approaches to the treatment of phobic disorders, each of which has relevance to social work practice: the psychoanalytic, the behavioral, and the pharmacological. Familiarity with these approaches should help the social worker tailor his interventions with phobic clients.

The Psychoanalytic Approach

The psychoanalytic approach has been particularly helpful in providing theoretical understanding of the development and maintenance of phobic disorders. According to psychoanalytic theory, phobias result from unconscious conflicts that are repressed and displaced onto other objects or situations. The therapeutic goal is to bring the conflict into consciousness so that it can be resolved. The therapeutic goal is accomplished through client self-exploration, guided by the therapist, that is intended to uncover the unconscious conflict that gave rise to the phobic symptom. The process through which therapist and client proceed is complex and lengthy.

Laughlin (1976b) described the prolonged analysis and treatment of a young journalist who had a phobia of theaters. According to Laughlin, the patient had experienced an emotional upset as a result of not being chosen editor of his college newspaper, a position he felt should have been awarded to him. In an effort to understand the decision, he contacted the professor in charge of the newspaper. This meeting apparently was unsatisfactory and the young man focused his feelings of anger on the professor. Sometime later he attended a play at a theater, wherein he encountered the professor. According to Laughlin:

> His state of disturbance had reached a peak and he fled the theater. However, about this time his disturbing feelings were repressed and lost to consciousness. As a consequence, the conflicts and his desperate feelings in response to

them no longer threatened him. The danger was henceforth displaced to the theater. (p. 1085)

Analysis showed that the anger directed at the professor was rooted in the man's anger toward his mother, "who had constantly set impossible standards of achievement for him" (p. 1085). Not receiving the editorship symbolically represented his earlier lack of success in trying to meet his mother's standards and thereby secure her love. "In this failure he must face helplessness, nonacceptance and murderous rage over his frustration to make the parent-object 'come across'" (p. 1085). Treatment required the patient to surrender his

> basic underlying capacity for the development of the phobic pattern of phobic defense. Ultimately also the patient came to understand and to accept his helplessness and his ability to gain the fantastic mother of his unconscious wishes and longings. Only then could he accept failure to succeed. Only then could he give up compulsive working. (p. 1085).

A number of issues for social workers arise in consideration of the psychoanalytic approach. Most important is the length of time needed to treat the phobic person. Contemporary psychoanalysts require that treatment be relatively indirect, nonconfrontational, and long-term. Weiss (1964), for example, cautioned therapists against confronting the agoraphobic with the phobic situation by reminding them "that agoraphobic anxiety is a defense against more severe mental disturbances. The therapist must be warned against using direct suggestions for freeing an agoraphobic patient from his anxiety-defense, short of a therapeutically induced structural change in his ego" (p. 6). This position appears to be at odds with Freud's own observation that "one can hardly ever master a phobia if one waits till the patient lets the analysis influence him to give it up. . . . One succeeds only when one can induce them . . . to go about alone and to struggle with their anxiety while they make the attempt" (quoted in Mavissakalian & Barlow, 1981, p. 13).

Laughlin (1967) acknowledged that some phobic reactions may respond rapidly to therapuetic intervention, but he argued that "such a result should be clearly seen as a limited therapeutic goal. For lasting, healthful characterologic change, the therapeutic clarification and resolution of underlying conflicts is a prerequisite" (p. 1085). The work of one psychoanalyst who has produced data indicating that brief psychotherapy does alleviate phobic disorders (Malan, 1976) has not had much impact on mainstream psychoanalysis.

A final issue in the appraisal of the psychoanalytic approach is the lack of empirically based outcome studies. The reports on the successful treatment of phobic patients through psychoanalysis tend to be case reports with no follow-up data. While these case descriptions do provide clearly presented analyses of each phobia, there are no data regarding the percentages of successful and unsuccessful outcomes. The absence of such information makes it difficult to assess the relative efficacy of the psychoanalytic approach.

The Behavioral Approaches

Rogers was once reported to have stated that "he had never learned much from controlled studies and that his insights had come from clinical work" (Malan, 1973, p. 726). This comment appears to be consistent with the attitude of many clinicians. However, the application of the behavioral approaches to phobic disorders has demonstrated how feedback from controlled clinical studies can improve interventions.

During the later 1950s and well into the 1960s, it appeared that behavior therapy could alleviate most phobic disorders through use of systematic desensitization, a technique based on the learning theory principle of reciprocal inhibition. The reported success rate—90% with mixed phobic patients—was an impressive outcome figure, particularly since phobias had previously been thought to require years of intensive therapy. While systematic desensitization remains a central feature in consideration of the behavioral approaches to phobic disorders, further exploration of its efficacy led to the development and refinement of other behavioral techniques, some of which appear to be more effective than the original procedure.

The reports on empirical research evaluating the effects of the behavioral approaches in general and phobias in particular have outnumbered published studies which deal with other approaches. The three approaches with the strongest empirical support are briefly discussed here.

Systematic Desensitization

For a number of years, Wolpe's (1958, 1973) systematic desensitization was the treatment of choice for many professionals working with phobic clients. The approach seemed compatible with social work practice, and in later years some leading social work textbooks recommended its use (Fischer, 1978; Schwartz & Goldiamond, 1975).

Systematic desensitization is based on the hypothesis that phobic anxiety is an autonomic response learned in a situation perceived by the individual to have been anxiety provoking. To alleviate the phobic anxiety, in this view, the individual must learn a new response to the situation that provokes the phobic anxiety. In order to achieve this goal, the person must learn to inhibit her anxiety reaction when she is confronted with the anxiety-provoking stimulus. A logical alternative to an anxiety response is relaxation. Therefore, the procedure of desensitization requires that the individual learn relaxation techniques (e.g., deep muscle relaxation or imagery).

During the assessment, the individual's phobic reactions are explored with a view to compiling a list of anxiety-provoking situations. The list is divided into categories, and the situations in each category are arranged in a hierarchy so that the least anxiety provoking stimuli can be presented to the person in graded fashion until the most anxiety provoking situation is encountered. Under the direction of the therapist, the individual is helped to imagine each situation while she is in a relaxed state. The individual works through each hierarchy systematically, nonverbally signaling to the therapist if any scene arouses anxiety of an uncomfortable level. In this case, the image of the scene is withdrawn and the individual is instructed to return to the state of relaxation.

Having successfully completed a program of systematic desensitization, the individual is able without feeling the phobic anxiety to approach each imagined scene and to confront the actual phobic situation or object.

Ann, a 53-year-old woman, was referred to the social worker by a psychiatrist whom Ann had consulted regarding her fear of elevators and restaurants. Early in therapy Ann had mentioned that her ultimate goal was to have dinner with her husband in the revolving restaurant atop an extraordinarily high local tower.

Ann dated the onset of her problem to an episode that had occurred some eight years earlier, when she was living on a West Indian island. Ann's husband had achieved a high social status on this island and was regularly entertained by business leaders and political dignitaries. At one function, Ann found herself in a crowded, warm room with many persons to whom she felt quite inferior. Sometime during the evening, she was asked to join a group of people at a table; her husband was to be seated at another table. She sat down at the table but midway through dinner Ann suffered a panic attack. She abruptly left the table with no explanation. Later, she was severely criticized by her husband. The problem continued over the next few years, but Ann managed to avoid most potentially problematic situations by feigning illness or otherwise excusing herself.

When Ann and her husband moved to a large metropolitan area in Canada, her phobic anxiety increased dramatically. Her husband insisted that she secure help because Ann would not accompany him to any social engagements.

Assessment indicated that Ann's phobic anxiety was associated with three major situational themes: restaurants, elevators, and social situations (e.g., cocktail parties). Ann's hierarchy for the restaurant phobia began with a scene in which her husband would telephone to say he was entertaining an associate and would like her to join them. The hierarchy moved through a scene in which Ann was in a restaurant near an exit door, to a scene in a crowded restaurant, and to the most anxiety provoking scene—a very noisy, crowded restaurant with no visible exit and Ann's husband not available. Similar hierarchies were compiled for the elevator phobia and the social situation phobia.

Ann was seen weekly over a three-month period. Ann's first recognition of her beginning improvement came when she was able to take the elevator to the fifth-floor office of the therapist. This event took place at the sixth week of intervention. At the point of termination Ann had encountered each of the hierarchy situations and was planning the dinner at the revolving restaurant.

The behavioral literature shows positive outcome results in many cases similar to Ann's. In early comparative outcome studies, systematic desensitization also appeared to do well. For example, in comparisons between systematic desensitization and psychotherapy, the former was judged the more effective approach (Brady, 1972; Gelder & Marks, 1968; Gelder et al., 1967; Gillian & Rachman, 1974). Certainly, by the 1970s systematic desensitization was the most widely used intervention with phobic clients (Marks, 1969). However, as other behavioral approaches were developed and then compared to systematic desensitization, questions began to be raised about the efficacy and the mechanisms of systematic desensitization. Treatment was taking longer than with other methods and when follow-up data were collected the differences between psychotherapy and desensitization did not appear as great as they had seemed to be at treatment termination (Gelder, 1979). Moreover, the research evidence was calling into question the role of relaxation training in the desensitization procedure (Marks, 1978a). As one investigator concluded: "Relaxation training is redundant to the systematic desensitization procedure" (Emmelkamp, 1979, p. 71). Lastly, questions began to emerge regarding the necessity gradually to expose the individual, under a state of relaxation, to the anxiety-provoking stimulus. In some studies, the behavioral approach known as "flooding," when compared to systematic desensitization, was producing reductions in phobic anxiety at a level comparable to that of desensitization. Moreover, flooding required significantly less therapeutic time (Boulougouris et al., 1971; Hussain, 1971). While these issues did not lead to the abandonment of systematic desensitization, they did cause researchers to investigate the clinical appropriateness of other behavioral approaches.

Flooding (Implosion)

Flooding is almost the opposite of desensitization and at first this procedure appears to be more aversive than its predecessor. The development of this technique is generally attributed to Stampfl and Levis (1967), who first reported presenting fantasies to phobic clients regarding their phobic situations. The procedure requires the therapist to describe in the most vivid detail the phobic situation or object; during this session (30 minutes or longer), the client is not allowed to withdraw from the therapist's input. With this prolonged imaginal exposure to the anxiety-provoking stimulus, the individual is helped to experience the fear without escaping but rather confronting it.

Consider how Ann's elevator phobia would be treated by flooding. Ann would be instructed to imagine scenes involving particularly threatening elevators in high-rise buildings. The therapist would describe these scenes in vivid detail, including all the sensations, affects, and projected consequences associated with a real-life encounter of this nature for Ann. The session would proceed for the length of time it took to move Ann through the imagined encounter with the high-rise building's elevator. Once these scenes no longer elicited anxiety, Ann would be instructed to rest. After her rest, time permitting, she would repeat the process. Repetitions would continue in subsequent sessions until the scenes no longer caused Ann any discomfort and the anxiety response was totally extinguished.

While flooding and systematic desensitization produced impressive clinical results, studies assessing both approaches in actual phobic situations pointed to the superiority of in vivo treatment. (Emmelkamp, 1979; Marks, 1978). Several researchers concluded that manipulation of anxiety during either desensitization or flooding does not affect treatment outcome and that exposure to actual phobic stimuli appears to be the essential ingredient in successful anxiety management through both approaches (Emmelkamp, 1979; Gelder, 1979; Marks, 1978). These conclusions encouraged a shift in the treatment setting from the office to the natural environment and helped to resurrect an operant approach that had been available since the 1960s but had received relatively little attention. This approach is called either "operant shaping" or "reinforced practice."

Reinforced Practice

Systematic desensitization and, to a degree, flooding are based on classical conditioning theory and focus on the alleviation of the individual's anxiety in order to improve performance. The reinforced practice approach, however, is based on operant conditioning theory, using the principle of positive reinforcement for increments of successful behavior. This approach identifies behavioral deficits that if corrected will allow the individual to overcome her phobic anxiety. The goal of therapy, then, is not to reduce anxiety but rather to "shape" appropriate approach behavior toward the phobic situation or object. Reinforced practice uses graded exposure to the fear-producing stimulus and performance feedback to the individual, a feature that has proven most helpful in initiating change. The positive reinforcement aspect of this approach is particularly attractive from the patient's perspective (Mathews et al., 1976).

In the treatment procedure, therapist and client identify the phobic situation or object and each of the steps that the client must move through in confronting this phobic stimulus. From beginning to end, a series of goal lines is identified; these serve as achievement markers for the client. The steps needed to achieve each goal are ordered from the least to the most difficult. Instructions to the client require him actually to move through each step; the accompanying therapist will give praise for client achievement and precise feedback on the client's performance. This feedback facilitates the client's self-correction in the actual situation and as the client improves the feedback should demonstrate the degree of improvement session by session.

Studies on reinforced practice have demonstrated that treatment focusing on behaviors of the phobic individual, rather than on reduction of her anxiety level, can lead to alleviation of phobic anxiety (Crowe et al., 1972; Leitenberg, 1976). Most important, perhaps, outcome research on this approach has lent support to the view that effective therapy with the phobic client is provided not in the therapist's office but in real-life environments.

Cognitive Modification

The cognitive behavior therapist assumes that the individual's cognitive processes can mediate anxiety reactions. These cognitive processes are thoughts, mental images, beliefs, and expectancies—all of which are known to affect behavior in some fashion (Bandura, 1977). However, until relatively recently these aspects of human behavior were considered to be out of reach of the behavior analyst and therefore received little attention in the behavioral literature. Assuming the role of cognition in causally mediating both adaptive and maladaptive behavior, the cognitive approach to treating phobic disorders focuses on altering the faulty cognitions. If the cognitions that are maintaining the phobic anxiety can be altered, anxiety will be reduced and the individual will be able to approach the phobic stimulus.

The cognitive approach requires that client and therapist identify both the negative self-statements that the client makes to himself regarding the phobic stimulus and the way in which these statements maintain the phobic anxiety. The therapist then helps the client relabel the anxiety-producing aspects of the phobic situation and discover a "rational explanation" for the development of the fear response. Finally, the client learns how to use positive self-statements by giving himself encouragement as various goals are achieved.

Reports on the effectiveness of cognitive behavior modification with phobic disorders began to appear only recently. Although early results are contradictory (Emmelkamp et al., 1978), this approach appears to represent a means to alter the phobic client's all too familiar self-condemning statements.

The Pharmacological Approach

The use of drugs in the treatment of many human problems has become widely accepted and in many cases pharmacotherapy has had most impressive results. The research on the use of drugs in treating phobics has been extensive. Some studies have reported successful treatment with benzodiazepines, monoamine oxidase inhibitors, tricyclic antidepressants, or beta blockers (Stern, 1978). Overall, however, it appears that medication has only a minimal impact on the client during treatment in vivo (Emmelkamp, 1979), and at best certain psychotropic drugs may reduce anxiety to permit the initiation of structured psychosocial approaches. Citing the reviews of others, Gelder (1972) concluded:

> Although anxiolytic drugs improve results to some extent . . . the benefit is not sufficient to justify their regular use. Beta-adrenergic blockers also have been tested and also failed to improve results of exposure treatment: indeed, patients who received these drugs did rather worse during exposure treatment than did controls, who received a placebo. (p. 472)

Social Work Practice with Phobic Clients

As I mentioned earlier, the social work literature contains surprisingly few reports on practice with phobic individuals. Therefore, this section draws on my own clinical experience, as well as on published studies.

A Social Systems Perspective for Practice with the Phobic Client

The Family

With some notable exceptions (Barlow & Mavissakalian, 1981; Chambless & Goldstein, 1981; Hand, Spoehring, and Stanik, 1977), the investigators of phobic disorders have neglected the interpersonal functioning of the phobic client. The clinician is well aware of the need to have as clear a picture as possible of the client's relationships with significant others, as well as with the community at large. These subsystems represent both potential causes of the phobia and resources to assist the treatment process. In addition, a systems perspective gives the therapist greater understanding of who in the client's network of relationships is being negatively affected by the client's phobic anxiety.

In most cases, the phobic client has a spouse and children. Early research on the marital dyad showed that the spouse is actively involved in the client's phobic disturbance. At one level, this involvement may appear quite innocent; for example, the sympathetic spouse may be attempting to hide some of the role deficits of his partner. However, this helpfulness may be one of the factors maintaining the phobic avoidance. In some cases, the spouse may be content with the dyadic balance and purposefully inhibit or resist the partner's efforts at change (Emmelkamp, 1974). This resistance often comes to the attention of the therapist through client reports about the lack of support the spouse is giving or about increased ridicule, particularly during at-home practice sessions. On occasion, the therapist may receive a call from the spouse, complaining about changes in the client that "have nothing to do with the phobia." It is most advisable to involve the spouse in some joint sessions at least to help her understand their role. These sessions often evolve into marital therapy, indicating that the phobic anxiety was associated with marital conflict.

The incidence of marital conflict among phobic individuals is difficult to ascertain, but some researchers suggest it is higher than was once thought. Conflict between spouses is viewed as one of the major stressors contributing to the panic attacks experienced by agoraphobics (Chambless & Goldstein, 1981; Goldstein & Chambless, 1978). The data do not establish a causal connection but do suggest the need for spousal involvement in the treatment of phobic clients.

The role of children in maintaining or alleviating phobic behavior is almost an unknown. However, the family is a social system important to the client and clinical assessment of the children vis-à-vis the phobic parent is necessary. My experience suggests that children take on increased responsibility for family tasks, particularly when it is the mother who is phobic. Children also have great difficulty explaining the frequent unavailability of their parent at school and community functions and are confused or fearful about what is really wrong with their parent.

Therefore, even though the role of children in the onset and maintenance of phobic anxiety is unclear, the family should be seen for assessment and perhaps periodically during treatment for the purpose of information sharing.

When marital and/or family conflict does not exist, family members can play an important role by supporting the phobic client during and after the treatment process. The means by which this therapeutic resource can be strengthened needs further investigation. At present, the therapist can best use the family by involving members from the beginning and keeping them abreast of the client's progress and its meaning to them.

The Community

By the time many phobic individuals enter treatment, they have become isolated from their community and their peer group. This is particularly true of the agoraphobic client, for whom visits outside the home are extremely anxiety provoking. For these people, the community should be a treatment resource and reinvolvement of the client in the community should be a therapeutic objective.

Hand and associates (1974) and Teasdale and associates (1977) reported favorably on the development and use of "cohesive groups" in the treatment of phobics. In this type of group therapy, participants support one another in practice efforts at approaching their phobic stimuli. Not only has the outcome research provided support for the utility of this approach, but also there is some evidence for the continued progress of group members even after termination (Hand et al., 1974).

Findings of this nature should give impetus to the development of self-help groups as adjuncts to the formal treatment of phobics. One such self-help group, which was set up in Vancouver by a social worker in 1967 is known as SE-CURE (Self-cure).* The group's success prompted the establishment of branches in various parts of Canada and the United States. While no data exist on treatment effectiveness, Secure's longevity indicates that phobic individuals respond positively to self-help groups. Moreover, there is some empirical support that this type of peer group treatment can be successful in the alleviation of phobias (Hand et al., 1974).

Secure groups meet once a week and group membership is open. The emphasis in meetings is on peer group sharing and support. The experience is both educative and anxiety reducing. People find out that they are not alone in their suffering and, for that matter, that they are not mentally ill, a concern of many phobics. Tips for coping are shared and personal projects for overcoming specific fears are established. Relaxation exercises are learned and practiced. Most important, interpersonal networks are established by requiring the members to contact one another between meetings.

*I would like to express my appreciation to James Quinn, director of SE-CURE, for providing information on this self-help organization.

Social Work Intervention with the Phobic Client

Assessment of the phobic client must yield information both on the client's functioning as a member of a larger system and on the phobic disorder itself. Several scales can help social worker and client identify the anxiety-provoking situations that inhibit the client's freedom; for example, the Fear Survey Schedule, the Willoughby Questionnaire, and the Bernreuter Self-sufficiency Inventory (Wolpe, 1973). Once the assessment of the phobic anxiety has been completed, the social worker must select the most appropriate means by which to help the client confront these situations. To reach this decision, the worker must determine whether the phobic anxiety should be focused on directly or whether behavioral deficits should be the focus of treatment. Next, a decision must be made as to how much of the exposure to the anxiety-provoking situations will be accomplished through imagery and how much through direct confrontation with the phobic object or situation. Empirically based criteria for determining the most appropriate approach are only just beginning to appear and the data are somewhat contradictory. However, the following treatment considerations, based on current research and clinical findings, should inform the social worker's decisions.

If there is identified marital conflict, marital therapy should be offered concurrently with individual treatment focused on the phobic disorder.

Although relaxation training is not a requirement for modification of phobic anxiety, many clients report feeling significantly more relaxed after such sessions. Therefore, it is suggested that relaxation training be retained as a technique for clients who are highly anxious and respond to the relaxation instructions.

Systematic desensitization in vivo is useful for certain specific phobias such as fear of flying, fear of animals, and fear of particular objects or situations (e.g., elevators). While the research has favored some other approaches over desensitization with agoraphobics, I find the results equivocal and would recommend desensitization for certain agoraphobics even though this approach may take longer than flooding.

Flooding in vivo appears to be a most effective technique for situational phobics and agoraphobics. Data are lacking, however, as to the relative effectiveness of reinforced practice for phobias. Many social workers find that intense exposure through either imagery or actual contact is an unsatisfactory means to facilitate change.

There is some evidence that reinforced practice in the natural environment is useful with agoraphobics and social phobics. The stepwise approach to expanding the client's behavioral repertoire should make this technique of reinforced practice particularly attractive for the treatment of those agoraphobics who have been isolated to the point that they have lost many of their interactional skills.

Cognitive approaches have a particular appeal in that they facilitate relabeling of the phobic anxiety. To date, however, the effectiveness of cognitive treatments for phobic clients is unclear. Future research may indicate that the cognitive techniques best serve the individual by restructuring her view of the problem and thereby establishing a base upon which actual exposure to the phobic stimuli may take place.

There is reason to use family and peer group in the treatment of the phobic client. Both subsystems provide natural support for the phobic client during therapy and continued posttreatment improvement of clients with such support suggests the need for expanded efforts in this area.

It must be underlined that while the social work treatment approach suggested here requires client exposure to the phobic stimulus, this must take place within a positive therapeutic relationship. In vivo exposure must be agreed to by the client and carried out sequentially. Finally, the exposure must be accompanied by supportive feedback from the therapist.

Conclusion

Knowledge about and treatment of phobic disorders have progressed significantly in the past 20 years. While there is not complete agreement on why phobic disorders arise, the progress in treatment approaches has led to a most optimistic conclusion that "successful treatment of moderately to severely disabling phobias . . . is a goal that may be attainable within the next ten years" (Barlow & Mavissakalian, 1981, p. 199). Whether this goal will be accomplished within the next decade will depend upon the continued, concentrated efforts to accumulate research data.

Most social workers who have phobic clients are in an excellent position to contribute to this research endeavor. This is particularly true in relation to the role of family members, both in terms of their contribution to the maintenance of the phobia and in terms of their supporting the treatment process.

One area of much needed research is the function of self-help groups in the treatment of phobias. The social work profession has a long standing commitment to the use of self-help groups and yet little is known about the role they might play in the treatment of the phobic individual.

Further research is needed on the most appropriate interventions for each phobic type.

Last, there is little, if any, research on the prevention of phobic disorders. This is a particularly challenging area because it demands a clear understanding of etiology.

In conclusion, the past two decades of work with phobic disorders have yielded knowledge that, if incorporated into social work practice, will permit the successful and short-term treatment of many people who suffer the debilitating anxiety of a phobic disorder.

References

AGRAS S, SYLVESTER D, OLIVEAU D: The epidemiology of common fears and phobia. *Compr Psychiatry* 1969; 10:151–156.

AGRAS W, CHAPIN H, OLIVEAU D: The natural history of phobia. *Arch Gen Psychiatry* 1972;26:315–317.

ALPERSON J: Gone with the wind: role-reversed desensitization for a wind phobic client. *Behav Ther* 1976;7:405–407.

American Psychiatric Association: *Diagnostic and Statistical Mannal of Mental Disorders*, ed 3. Washington, DC, American Psychiatric Association, 1980.

ANDREWS J: Psychotherapy of phobias. *Psychol Bull* 1966; 66:455–480.

BANDURA A: *Social Learning Theory*. Englewood Cliffs, Prentice-Hall, 1977.

BARLOW D; MAVISSAKALIAN M: Directions in the assessment and treatment of phobia: the next decade, in Mavissakalian M, Barlow D (eds): *Phobia: Psychological and Pharmacological Treatment*. New York, Guilford, 1981; pp 199–245.

BOULOUGOURIS J, MARKS I, MARSET P: Superiority of flooding (implosion) to desensitization for reducing pathological fear. *Behav Res Ther* 1971; 9:7–16.

BOULOUGOURIS J, RABAVILAIS A (eds): *The Treatment of Phobic and Obsessive Compulsive Disorders*. Toronto, Pergamon, 1977.

BRADY J: Systematic desensitization, in Agras W (ed): *Behavior Modification: Principles and Clinical Applications*. Boston, Little, Brown, 1972.

BUGLASS D, CLARKE J, HENDERSON A, et al: A study of agoraphobic housewives. *Psychol Med* 1977; 7:73–86.

CHAMBLESS D, GOLDSTEIN A: Clinical treatment of agoraphobia, in Mavissakalian M, Barlow D (eds): *Phobia: Psychological and Pharmacological Treatment*. New York, Guilford, 1981, pp 103–144.

COSTELLO CG: Dissimilarities between conditioned avoidance responses and phobias. *Psychol Rev* 1970; 7:250–254.

CROWE M, MARKS I, AGRAS W, et al: Time-limited desensitization, implosion, and shaping for phobic patients: a crossover study. *Behav Res Ther* 1972; 10:319–328.

DELPRATO D: Hereditary determinants of fears and phobias: a critical review. *Behav Ther* 1980; 11:79–103.

DEUTSCH H: *Psycho-analysis of the Neuroses*. London, Hogarth, 1951.

ELLIS A: *Reason and Emotion in Psychotherapy*. New York, Lyle Stuart, 1962.

ELMORE R, WILDMAN R, WESTEFELD J: The use of systematic desensitization in the treatment of blood phobia. *Behav Ther Exp Psychiatry* 1980; 11:277-279.

EMMELKAMP P: Self-observation versus flooding in the treatment of agoraphobia. *Behav Res Ther* 1974; 12:229-237.

EMMELKAMP P: The behavioral study of clinical phobias. *Prog Behav Modif* 1979; 8:55-125.

EMMELKAMP P, KUIPERS A, EGGERAAT J: Cognitive modification versus prolonged exposure in vivo: a comparison with agoraphobics. *Behav Res Ther* 1978; 16:33-41.

ERRERA P, COLEMAN J: A long-term follow-up study of neurotic phobic patients in a psychiatric clinic. *J Nerv Ment Dis* 1963; 136:267-271.

FISCHER J: *Effective Casework Practice*. Toronto, McGraw-Hill, 1978.

FRANKEL AS: Treatment of a multisymptomatic phobic by a self-directed, self-reinforced imagery technique: a case study. *J Abnorm Psychol* 1970; 76:496-499.

FRAZIER S, CARR A: Phobic reaction, in Freedman A, Kaplan H (eds): *Comprehensive Textbook of Psychiatry*. Baltimore, Williams & Wilkins, 1967, pp 899-911.

GELDER M: Behavior therapy for neurotic disorders. *Behav Modif* 1979; 3:469-495.

GELDER M, MARKS I: Desensitization and phobias: a crossover study. *Br J Psychiatry* 1968; 114:323-328.

GELDER M, MARKS I, WOLFF H: Desensitization and psychotherapy in the treatment of phobic states: a controlled enquiry. *Br J Psychiatry* 1967; 113:53-73.

GILLIAN P, RACHMAN S: An experimental investigation of desensitization in phobic patients. *Br J Psychiatry* 1974; 124:392-401.

GILMORE W: Diagnostic and treatment considerations with phobic symptomed clients. *Smith Coll Stud Soc Work* 1971; 41:93-102.

GOLDSTEIN A, CHAMBLESS D: A reanalysis of agoraphobia. *Behav Ther* 1978; 9:47-59.

HAFNER J: The husbands of agoraphobic women and their influence on treatment outcome. *Br J Psychiatry* 1977; 131:289-294.

HALLMAN RS: Agoraphobia: a critical review of the concept. *Br J Psychiatry* 1978; 133:314-319.

HAND I, LAMONTAGNE Y: The exacerbation of interpersonal problems after rapid phobia-removal. *Psychotherapy* 1976; 13:405-411.

HAND I, LAMONTAGNE Y, MARKS I: Group exposure (flooding) in vivo for agoraphobics. *Br J Psychiatry* 1974; 124:588-602.

HAND I, SPOEHRING B, STANIK E: Treatment of obsessions, compulsions, and phobias as hidden couple-counselling, in Boulougouris J, Rabavilais A (eds): *The Treatment of Phobic and Obsessive Compulsive Disorders*. Toronto, Pergamon, 1977, pp 105-115.

HUSSAIN M: Desensitization and flooding (implosion) in treatment of phobias. *Am J Psychiatry* 1971; 127:1509-1514.

LADER MH: Physiological research in anxiety. *Res Neurosis* 1978.

LADER MH, MATHEWS AM: A physiological model of phobic anxiety an desensitization. *Behav Res Ther* 1968; 6:411-421.

LAUGHLIN H: *The Neuroses in Clinical Practice*. Philadelphia, Saunders, 1956.

LAUGHLIN H: *The Neuroses*. London, Butterworth, 1967. (a)

LAUGHLIN H: Unraveling the phobic defense. *Am J Psychiatry* 1967; 123:1081–1086. (b)

LEITENBERG H: *Handbook of Behavior Modification and Behavior Therapy*. Englewood Cliffs, Prentice-Hall, 1976.

LEVITT E: *The Psychology of Anxiety*. Indianapolis, Bobbs-Merrill, 1967.

LEWIN B: Phobias. *International Encyclopedia of the Social Sciences*. New York, Macmillan, 1972; vol 11, pp 81–84.

MAHONEY M: *Cognition and Behavior Modification*. Cambridge, Ballinger, 1974.

MALAN D: The outcome problem in psychotherapy research. *Arch Gen Psychiatry* 1973; 29:726.

MALAN D: The Frontier of Brief Psychotherapy. New York, Plenum, 1976.

MARKS I: *Fears and Phobias*. New York, Academic, 1969.

MARKS I: Behavioral psychotherapy of adult neurosis, in Garfield S, Bergin A (eds): *Handbook of Psychotherapy and Behaviour Change: An Empirical Analysis*, ed 2. Toronto, Wiley, 1978, pp 493–547. (a)

MARKS I: *Living with Fear*. Toronto, McGraw-Hill, 1978. (b)

MARKS I, GELDER M: Different onset ages in varieties of phobia. *Am J Psychiatry* 1966; 123:218–221.

MARKS I, HERST E: A survey of 1200 agoraphobics in Britain. *Soc Psychiatry* 1970; 5:16–24.

MATHEWS A: Behavioral treatment of agoraphobia: new findings, new problems, in Boulougouris J, Rabavilais A (eds): *The Treatment of Phobic and Obsessive Compulsive Disorders*. Toronto, Pergamon, 1977, pp 1–5.

MATHEWS A: Recent developments in the treatment of agoraphobia. *Behav Anal Modif* 1977; 2:64–75. (b)

MATHEWS A, JOHNSON D, LANCASHIRE M, et al: Imaginal flooding and exposure to real phobic situations: treatment outcome with agoraphobic patients. *Br J Psychiatry* 1976; 129:362–371.

MAVISSAKALIAN M, BARLOW D: Phobia: an overview, in Mavissakalian M, Barlow D (eds): *Phobia: Psychological and Pharmacological Treatment*. New York, Guilford, 1981, pp 1–33. (a)

MAVISSAKALIAN M, BARLOW D (eds):*Phobia: Psychological and Pharmacological Treatment*. New York, Guilford, 1981. (b)

MEICHENBAUM D: *Cognitive Behavior Modification*. New York, Plenum Press, 1977.

MILTON F, HAFNER J: The outcome of behavior therapy for agoraphobics in relation to marital adjustment. *Arch Gen Psychiatry* 1979; 36:807–811.

MOWRER O: A stimulus–response analysis of anxiety and its role as a reinforcing agent. *Psychol Rev* 1939; 46:553–565.

MURRAY E, FOOTE F: The origins of fear of snakes. *Behav Res Ther* 1979; 17:489–493.

NIMMER W, KAPP R: A multiple impact program for the treatment of injection phobias. *J Behav ther Exp Psychiatry*. 1974; 5:257–258.

O'BRIEN G: Chemical treatment of specific phobias, in Mavissakalian M, Barlow D (eds): *Phobia: Psychological and Pharmacological Treatment*. New York, Guilford, 1981, pp 63–102.

PARRINO J: Effect of pretherapy information on learning in psychotherapy. *J Abnorm Psychol*. 1971; 77:17–24.

PERMAN JM: Phobia as a determinant of single-room occupancy. *Am J Psychiatry* 1966; 123:609–613.

RACHMAN S: *Phobias: Their Nature and Control*. Springfield, Thomas, 1968.

RACHMAN S: *Fear and Courage*. San Francisco, Freeman, 1978.

REEVES J, MEALIEA W: Biofeedback-assisted cue-controlled relaxation for the treatment of flight phobias. *J Behav Ther Exp Psychiatry* 1975; 6:105–109.

RIMM D, JANDA L, LANCASTER D, et al: An exploratory investigation of the origin and maintenance of phobias. *Behav Res Ther* 1977; 15:231–238.

ROBERTS A: Housebound housewives: a follow-up study of a phobic anxiety state. *Br J Psychiatry* 1964; 110:191–197.

SALZMAN L: Obsessions and phobias. *Contemp Psychoanal* 1965; 2:1–25.

SALZMAN L: Obsessions and phobias. *Int J Psychiatry* 1968: 6:451–468.

SANK LI: Counterconditioning for a flight phobia. *Soc Work* 1976; 21:318–319.

SCHAPIRA K, KERR T, ROTH M: Phobias and affective illness. *Br J Psychiatry* 1970; 117: 25–32.

SCHWARTZ A, GOLDIAMOND I: *Social Casework: A Behavior Approach*. New York, Columbia University Press, 1975.

SHIELDS J: Genetic factors in neurosis. *Res Neurosis* 1978.

SLATER E, COWIE V: *The Genetics of Mental Disorders*. London, Oxford University Press, 1971.

SLATER E, SHIELDS J: Genetical aspects of anxiety. *Br J Psychol* (special issue), 1969.

SLUCKIN W (ed): *Fear in Animals and Man*. Toronto, Van Nostrand Reinhold, 1979.

SNAITH RP: A clinical investigation of phobias. *Br J Psychiatry* 1968; 114:673–679.

SOLYOM L, HESELTINE G, McCLURE D, et al: Behavior therapy versus drug therapy in the treatment of phobic neurosis. *Can Psychiatr Assoc J* 1973; 18:25–29.

SPITZER R, KLEIN D (eds): *Evaluation of Psychological Therapies*. Baltimore, Johns Hopkins Press, 1976, pp 233–255.

STAMM J: Infantile trauma, narcissistic injury, and agoraphobia. *Psychiatr Q* 1972; 46:254–272.

STAMPFL T, LEVIS D: Essentials of implosion therapy: a learning theory based psychodynamic behavioral therapy. *J Abnorm Psychol* 1967; 72:496–503.

STERN R: Behavior therapy and psychotropic medication, in Hersen M, Bellack A (eds): *Behavioral Therapy in the Psychiatric Setting*. Baltimore, Williams & Wilkins, 1978, pp 40–57.

TEASDALE J, WALSH P, LANCASHIRE M, et al: Group exposure for agoraphobics: a replication study. *Br J Psychiatry* 1977; 130:186–193.

TORPY D, MEASY L: Marital interaction in agoraphobia. *J Clin Psychol* 1974; 30:351–354.

ULLMANN L, KRASNER L: *A Psychological Approach to Abnormal Behavior.* Englewood Cliffs, N.J., Prentice-Hall, 1969.

WATSON G: *Nutrition and Your Mind.* Toronto, Bantam Books, 1974.

WEISS E: *Agoraphobia in the Light of Ego Psychology.* New York, Grune & Stratton, 1964.

WIJESINGHE B: A vomiting phobia overcome by one session of flooding with hypnosis. *J Behav Ther and Exper Psychol* 1974; 5:169–179.

WOLPE J: *The Practice of Behavior Therapy.* 2nd ed. New York, Pergamon, 1973.

WOLPE J: *Psychotherapy by Reciprocal Inhibition.* Palo Alto, Stanford University Press, 1958.

11

Psychosexual Disorders

Herbert S. Strean

The sexual dimension of clients' lives has received limited attention in the social work literature. In practice, too, social workers frequently overlook clients' sexual practices, problems in sexual identity, disturbing sexual fantasies, and crippling sexual inhibitions. A most serious omission in much social work treatment is the worker's failure to help the client confront and discuss directly his sexual fantasies toward the social worker when this is needed. Although social workers usually have little difficulty helping clients resolve their resistance to expressing anger toward the therapist, they are frequently most reluctant to help clients experience themselves as sexual beings in the treatment relationship.

During the past few years, social work clinicians and academicians have begun to include sexuality in both practice and teaching. Two major perspectives toward sexuality and the treatment of sexual disorders have emerged. One is the behavioral approach introduced by Masters and Johnson (1966, 1970) and the other is a psychosocial approach based largely on psychoanalytic theory and ego psychology. This chapter emphasizes the latter perspective, but a review and critique of the Masters and Johnson approach and of programs similar to theirs will be presented first.

The Masters and Johnson Program
for Sexual Dysfunction

When Masters and Johnson (1966) completed their study of the physiology of the human sexual response, they (1970) embarked on an 11-year controlled investigation that aimed to develop a rapid treatment for human sexual dysfunction. The Masters and Johnson program assumes:

1. a sexual dysfunction in a couple is the responsibility of both partners; consequently, both partners have to be seen in therapy and to take responsibility for the sexual problem and the treatment, regardless of who is suffering from a lack of sexual satisfaction and what form the problem takes
2. sexual problems are not always the result of psychic conflict; they are frequently the consequence of faulty learning and therapy, therefore, should emphasize education and information
3. sexual disorders have "superficial causes" (performance anxiety, fear of failure, and excessive need to please others) that need to be addressed in therapy
4. enjoyable sexual interaction depends on the capacity to communicate; consequently, therapy should enhance communication between partners
5. a male and female therapy team gives each patient a suitable role model
6. a behaviorally oriented graded intervention is most appropriate in the treatment of sexual dysfunction

The sexual problems that Masters and Johnson (1970) treat are premature ejaculation, impotence, frigidity and orgasmic dysfunction, vaginismus, and painful intercourse in the female. In addition to the behavioral tasks performed by all patients, specific techniques are used for specific dysfunctions. For example, in the treatment of premature ejaculation, the "squeeze technique" (Semans, 1956) is used; for vaginismus, dilators of gradually increasing size are employed.

The Masters and Johnson (1970) program consists of a two-week session of education and treatment. All couples are seen daily. Inasmuch as 90% of them live outside the St. Louis area, where the program is offered, the therapy requires a two-week "vacation" for most clients. This removal from everyday demands is considered advantageous in that it provides the opportunity for reviving communication between the partners without external distractions. An advantage of the daily conference, according to Masters and Johnson, is that it allows for immediate discussion of sexual events and feelings instead of permitting mistakes to go uncorrected or fears to intensify. An important technique used by the sex therapy team is "reflective teaching," in which the therapists restate in objective terms what the problems are and how the partners are failing to communicate with each other.

Recognizing that performance fears cannot be removed by mere exhortation, Masters and Johnson (1970) developed a highly structured behavioral conditioning approach called "sensate focus." Sensate focus exercises are designed to facilitate a gradual learning or relearning of sensual and sexual feelings under authoritative direction. Sensate focus involves a hierarchy of behavioral prescriptions in the form of body exercises performed by the partners together. First, the partners are instructed to take turns "pleasuring each other" by caressing, touching, and massaging each other's bodies but avoiding the genital area. The focus is continually on the process and not on the goal. Next, the partners are instructed to give feedback to each other and to indicate their preferences about the kind and location of touch. Experiences, mistakes, feelings, and reactions are discussed in detail during the sessions with the therapists the following day. When one step has been successfully negotiated, the next step is introduced. Gradually, as the partners progress, they move into genital stimulation.

According to Masters and Johnson (1970), their program has been extremely successful. They reported that over 80% of their subjects sustain considerable improvement over five or more years.

Modifications of the Masters and Johnson Program for Sexual Dysfunction

Because these results were considered very impressive, the Masters and Johnson methods (1970) were quickly adopted by hundreds of practitioners in clinics, agencies, and private practice. As the program moved into various settings, modifications took place. Karasu and associates (1979) summarized the most important modifications:

1. shortening or extending the time allotted for therapy to fit the clients' needs
2. making the therapy available to patients in their home community, which allows for continuous integration of the treatment experience with the everyday life of the clients
3. developing methods for working with single patients
4. using a single therapist instead of the two-member sex therapy team
5. making the therapy available to low-income and special client populations

6. integrating the specific sex therapy techniques with other forms of therapy

Hartman and Fithian (1974) are representative of the many sex therapists who have modified the Masters and Johnson (1970) approach in many ways. First, they themselves or therapists using their program actively participate in the sexual training procedures. During the "sexological" examination given to all patients at the onset of therapy, the therapists stimulate the patient's body parts, specifically the genitals. Then, the patients are requested to carry out foot, face, and body caressing exercises in the presence of the therapists. The rationale is that the therapists can observe the partners' physical interactions, instead of relying solely on their verbal reports. In addition, this method allows the therapists to teach the couple more effective techniques by direct coaching.

LoPiccolo and Lobitz (1972) fused the general program of Masters and Johnson (1970) with behavioral techniques developed by Wolpe and others. In addition to giving homework assignments, as in Masters and Johnson, they prescribe a nine-step masturbation program designed to enhance the partner's arousal toward each other, building on progressively more comfortable autoerotic experiences. Just prior to orgasm by masturbation, the patient is instructed to switch her focus to fantasies of sexual activity with the partner.

Kaplan (1974) also expanded on the Masters and Johnson (1970) method. Her approach involves a combination of prescribed sexual exercises and psychotherapeutic sessions. According to Kaplan, this new sex therapy is a "task-centered form of crisis intervention which presents an opportunity for rapid conflict resolution. Toward this end the various sexual tasks are employed, as well as the methods of insight therapy, supportive therapy, marital therapy, and other psychiatric techniques as indicated" (p. 199).

In the area of behavior modification, desensitization techniques have been reported to be successful for premature ejaculation (Dengrove, 1967; Ince, 1973), frigidity (Brady, 1975; Glick, 1975), and impotence (Dengrove, 1973). A modified systematic desensitization technique was described by Obler (1975). Because it was found that some patients are unable to imagine situations that cause extreme anxiety, as is usually done in a desensitization approach, Obler substituted erotic films and slides portraying intense anxiety experiences for the imagined sequences.

Integrating behavioral with cognitive and emotive methods in a single framework, Ellis (1975) described the rational-emotional approach (RET) to sex therapy. The main premise of RET is that people feel disturbed and act dysfunctionally in sexual, as well as other, areas when they escalate any desire or wish into an absolute—"should," "ought," or "must." As Ellis explained, every emotional disturbance consists of "A," an activating experience (e.g., a sexual failure); "C," an emotional consequence (e.g, feelings of shame or guilt); and "B," a system of rational and irrational beliefs (e.g., "How awful that I failed!"). The aim of RET is to challenge these irrational beliefs and to remove the individual's guilt about sex. The cognitive aspect of RET is designed to change the individual's "awfulizing" and "absolutizing" philosophies so that he can think and act differently. The emotive aspect of RET seeks to change irrational beliefs by altering emotions. This is accomplished by unconditional acceptance by the therapist, shame-attacking exercises, risk-taking exercises, and emotive feedback. The behavior component includes assertiveness training, homework assignments in which the client is to try out new behaviors, and operant conditioning.

A Critique of the Masters and Johnson Program and Its Variants

There is now a vast literature cricital of the Masters and Johnson's (1979) program and its variants. Criticism has been directed at research methodology, therapeutic procedures, theoretical underpinnings, and conceptions of the human being (Fine, 1981; Hogan, 1978; Karusu & Socarides, 1979; Karusu et al., 1979; Levay & Kagle, 1977; Strean, 1980; Wright et al., 1977; Zilbergeld & Evans, 1980). This section will summarize the major questions raised about the sex therapies just reviewed.

Karusu and associates (1979) criticized the Masters and Johnson (1970) program:

1. the expense of spending two weeks in St. Louis and paying for the services of two therapists denies this particular treatment to all but affluent clients
2. the impressive results may reflect sampling bias: patients have to be highly motivated to comply with the program
3. the program is designed for married couples who have relatively stable and secure relationships and who are willing to work together; it is unavailable to single individuals with sexual problems and to married people whose partners refuse to participate
4. the results achieved during the two-week vacationlike program may not carry over into everyday life
5. the need for two therapists has not been established
6. the program does not allow time for the assimilation of character or intrapsychic change; to the extent that a client has neurotic or char-

acterological problems, backsliding may occur when the co-therapists are no longer present

7. program evaluation by Masters and Johnson (1970) showed a lack of careful controls in investigating the efficacy of the method, a lack of clear statements about the degree of improvement among non-failures, and a lack of information about treatment failures

Zilbergeld and Evans (1980) pointed out that "Masters and Johnson's sex-therapy research is so flawed by methodological errors and slipshod reporting that it fails to meet customary standards—and their own—for evaluation. This raises serious questions about the effectiveness of the 10-year-old discipline they created" (p. 29). The authors further noted that although the claims of Masters and Johnson (1970) have gone virtually unchallenged, no one can replicate their findings. Zilbergeld and Evans concluded that "sex therapy is still uncritically accepted for the most part, but the fact is that the evidence for the effectiveness of Masters and Johnson's therapy—and therefore that of almost all sex therapy—is less solid than has generally been believed" (p. 43).

Masters and Johnson (1970) and their modifiers have failed to take into consideration what many experienced social work clinicians understand: the person who cannot spontaneously, warmly, comfortably, enjoyably, and successfully have a sustained sexual relationship with a member of the opposite sex is frequently full of feelings of hatred, fear, and revenge outside conscious awareness or control. These feelings are part of a personality that fears intimacy because the individual is not able to trust, to be autonomous, or to take initiative (Erikson, 1950). Social workers recognize that a sexual dysfunction is a sign of internal distress and that a happy person is a sexually free person, while a sexually dys-functioning person is an unhappy person.

Social work clinicians whose major concern is the person–situation constellation would agree with Masters and Johnson (1970) that it is frequently advisable to focus therapy on the interaction of the marital pair. However, clinical experiences have led many to believe that most chronic marital complaints are unconscious wishes. The man who complains that his wife is frigid and cold unconsciously wants the spouse to be that way; her warmth and sexual spontaneity would frighten him. Similarly, the wife who complains that her husband is weak and fragile needs this kind of husband to protect her; his potency would frighten her (Eisenstein, 1956; Strean, 1980). Moreover, the wife in the first example and the husband in the second are unconsciously conforming to the spouses' labels of them. If therapists do not take sides in a marital conflict, they eventually will be experienced by the client the same way the spouse is experienced (Strean, 1980).

When social workers utilize social systems theory, role theory, ego psychology, and psychoanalysis to buttress their clinical observations, they often recognize the ever present unconscious collusion between spouses in a sexually conflicted marriage (Strean, 1978). The masochist unconsciously cooperates with the sadist; the suffering spouse of the alcoholic client unconsciously aids and abets the alcoholic sprees; and the deceiver and deceived almost always unconsciously complement each other. What Masters and Johnson (1970) and the other behavioral therapists fail to understand is that a sexual conflict is always a manifestation of a psychosocial conflict that has its roots in the client's life story. People with sexual conflicts react as frightened, angry, or inhibited children, and it is their unresolved childhood conflicts that must be addressed in sexual therapy.

A social worker who relates to the complete person–situation constellation and utilizes the insights from systems theory, role theory, and dynamic psychology will observe that clients with sexual conflicts will relate to the therapist with the same sexual fears, anxieties, and inhibitions that they experience every day. As clients are helped to see the parallels between the therapeutic relationship and their sexual relationship, they may realize that they are writing their own self-destructive scripts for sexual unhappiness.

It can be anticipated that as behavior therapists who subscribe to the practices of Masters and Johnson (1970) become more experienced with the practical problems of handling clients, they will recognize the significance of transference, will deal with resistances, and will pay much more attention to assessment of clients' psychosocial development in order to understand their sexual conflicts (Fine, 1981). Furthermore, as they learn that transference and countertransference are ever present variables in any treatment relationship, they will be better able to evaluate objectively the results of the interpersonal experience that sexual therapy always is.

Psychosexual Development*

Freud (1957) demonstrated convincingly in his *Three Essays on the Theory of Sexuality* that the sexuality of adult men and women is strongly influenced by their experiences as children. Whether or not adults are able to enjoy a sustained and loving sexual relationship depends on how well they have resolved the psychosexual tasks appropriate to the various stages of childhood. In this section, I review the stages of human growth and suggest how failure to cope with the demands of any of these matu-

*Some of the discussion in this section is drawn from Chapter 2 of this writer's book, *The Extramarital Affair*, New York, The Free Press, 1980.

The adult who was overindulged in early childhood will tend to approach sexual relationships in the manner of a demanding baby. Narcissistic and egocentric, such a person is unable to empathize with his partner. When he or she is not catered to, she has temper tantrums, strikes out, and may even physically hurt the partner.

When the normally developing child begins to realize that he is not omnipotent and cannot control his universe, he tends to project his desires onto his parents and to believe that they have the power to do amost anything. This conviction may persist into adulthood, so that the sexual partner is believed to be an all-powerful god. When the adult ascribes unrealistic power to a sexual partner, he/she begins to feel powerless, is easily intimidated, often feels hurt and criticized, and is baffled when the partner is unable or unwilling to gratify every whim and ease every frustration. Because such a person feels like a powerless child in a sexual relationship, the adult may avoid sex, be sadistic in order to overpower the ''powerful'' sexual partner, or submit masochistically to appease his ''god.''

Couples must constantly deal with coming together and being apart, situations that involve their identity, autonomy, interdependence, separation, and mutuality. The interplay of these variables can be seen in the sexual act. Coming together sexually should provide gratification, but for an individual who has not successfuly separated from the mother, sexual union may provoke anxiety and fear of being consumed by or merging with the partner (Ables, 1977; Blanck & Blanck, 1968).

The Anal Stage

If the infant has received adequate emotional and physical gratification in the first year, he is ready during the second year of life to leave one level of adjustment and explore a higher one. During the second year, the child is ready to take on more frustrations such as toilet training. It is difficult for the child to mature: she has been the recipient of bounties for a whole year and then suddenly, during her second year of life, a dramatic change occurs in the environment. Instead of being a receiver, the child is asked to be a giver. Instead of being completely irresponsible, she is asked to take on some responsibility.

A great deal of ambivalence is characteristic of the child during the second year. Learning to met the environment's demands for cleanliness is not an easy process. It is very frustrating for the child to learn to regulate his bowel movements and excrete them in a toilet. Thus, power struggles often occur at this time between the parent, who wants the child to be toilet trained, and the child, who wants freedom of expression. The power struggles that characterize many relationships derive in large part from unresolved difficulties in the anal period. Many a partner experiences giving love or pleasing the partner as "doing one's duty," feels humiliated by this task, and, like the child who resents feeling subordinate to a seemingly tyrannical parent, wishes to defy and rebel. Many adults hate a sexual relationship because they experience sexual activity in the way that a young child experiences toilet training—as an obligation. Many impotent men and anorgastic women will not give to the partner in the same way that the constipated child refuses to present his parents with his valuable feces.

In contrast to the individual who was harshly and prematurely toilet trained, the adult who was indulged as a child and not expected to master toilet training and other learning situations in effect defecates all over others and rarely is mature enough to cooperate with a partner. She expects the partner to cater to her and submit to her narcissistic wishes. Such a person finds it difficult to empathize with a sexual partner and does little or nothing to bring the partner pleasure. Sex is all for him; in his mind, the partner, like the mother of the past, has no needs of her own except the obligation to minister to him. If the partner does not meet this person's expectations, another partner may be sought.

Many of the distortions of sex evolve from the anal period. As mentioned earlier, not only do some adults experience sex as if they were submitting to an arbitrary parent but also their notion that sex is dirty emanates from the toilet training period. The organs of excretion are the same as or close to the sexual organs, and many people are brought up with the idea that sex is a form of evacuation. As adults, such individuals may associate the feelings of shame and guilt connected with the toilet to the sexual act.

The Phallic-Oedipal Stage

At about the age of three, the youngster should begin to give love as well as to receive it. While at first the child loves both parents indiscriminately, between the ages of three and six the child turns her affection with greater intensity to the parent of the opposite sex. If the phallic-oedipal period is essentially conflict-free,* the individual will be able to enjoy achieving and loving—to form an enjoyable, trusting attachment as a carry-over from the oral stage, to be cooperative and yet feel autonomous because the anal stage was successful, and to admire the loved one

---

*There is ongoing debate as to whether the oedipal conflict is a biological phenomenon or evolves because of familial and social arrangements.

and take initiative with this person without feelings of guilt (Erikson, 1950).

Oedipal Conflict in Boys

From birth the boy has been dependent primarily on his mother for comfort and security. While the object of love, the mother, does not change during the oedipal period, the nature of her relationship to the child does. The boy continues to value his mother as a source of security, but he now begins to feel wishes toward her of a romantic and sexual nature. In much the same way that his father loves his mother, the boy between three and six years of age wants to be his mother's lover. As he competes with his father, the father becomes a dangerous rival for the mother's affection. The boy fears his father's disapproval, anger, and punishment because of his competitive fantasies toward him and, also, he usually feels guilty about his sexual wishes toward his mother. The boy fears castration by the father because of his wish to supplant him and this fear becomes reinforced when he notices the absence of a penis in his mother, sister, or girl friends. Often, the boy reasons that these females have been castrated and that the same catastrophe may befall him.

Retaliation for his hostile feelings is only one part of the oedipal conflict that creates anxiety for the boy. Because the boy needs and loves his father, he often feels like a bad boy for wishing to displace him. This is why Freud spoke of an "inverted Oedipus complex" as part of the maturational process. Inasmuch as the boy fears his father's retaliation and concomitantly loves him, he submits to the father for a while and psychologically imagines himself as the father's lover. He becomes ingratiatory and compliant with him. Unless he is helped to feel less guilt and less fear of punishment for his oedipal wishes, he can remain fixated in this position and may later become a latent or overt homosexual.

Many men experience problems with relationships because of their unresolved oedipal conflicts. Inasmuch as they often fantasize the wife as the incestuous mother, sex becomes forbidden and inability to function sexually may result. A man may experience getting married as a hostile triumph over his father and unconsciously provoke punishment for himself. He may make his wife his punitive superego and feel that she will punish him for the libidinal pleasure he has with her. Or he may renounce his wife as he renounced his mother during the stressful oedipal period of his boyhood, form an inverted oedipus complex, and go out with male friends and join them in blasting their wives. These residues of an unresolved oedipal conflict can lead to extramarital affairs because the man may feel sexually free only with a woman who is away from home and therefore does not appear to be a mother.

Oedipal Conflict in Girls

Although there are many similarities in the oedipal conflicts that boys and girls experience, there are differences as well. The girl's oedipal conflict is usually more difficult for her than the boy's is for him. In contrast to the boy, who continues to rely on his mother as a source of love and security, the girl, in directing her libido toward her father, becomes a rival with the parent who has been her main emotional provider, the mother.

Unresolved oedipal conflicts in a woman create conflicts in relationships. If the woman unconscously is still seeking her father, she may experience sex and intimacy as incestuous and forbidden. She may repudiate her partner for not being her unconscious ideal, i.e., her fantasized father. The oedipal woman may experience marriage and motherhood as a victory over her mother, feel guilty about her fantasized triumphs, and regress to an inverted Oedipus complex, spending her time with other women and enjoying being derogatory toward her husband and other men.

All children have omnipotent fantasies and want what they want when they want it. Therefore, some boys fantasize about having the privileges and pleasures of women. They want babies, breasts, vaginas, etc. Similarly, when a girl turns toward her father, she has fantasies about having a penis, which is a part of her father, whom she treasures, and, like other children, she wants to own everything in sight. Penis envy is usually buried in the unconscious and becomes manifest only through its derivatives—low self-esteem or lack of self-assertiveness. A woman with unresolved problems of penis envy may take a very subordinate, masochistic position with her partner in and out of bed.* Or, feeling competitive, she may wish to deride him and make him uncomfortable both in and away from the bedroom (Marasse & Hart, 1975).

The Latency Stage

If a child has resolved most of her oedipal conflicts, she will be able to move from the close and intense ties of the family toward the social world of her peers for many of her emotional investments and outlets. While he

---

*Editor's note: Another viewpoint suggests that the concept of penis envy need not be understood only in anatomical terms but rather reflects envy of the social status and economic powers and prerogatives of men. Indeed, some therapists consider the importance of the concept to be highly exaggerated and a further example of a masculine viewpoint of the world.

cannot feel secure in the school, neighborhood, club, or gang without the continued protection and guidance of his parents, the child between the ages of 6 and 10 should gradually become part of a peer group.

As the Oedipus complex is resolved, early in the latency period (age six or seven) the child often has her first love affair with a youngster of the opposite sex. It seems that few, if any, human beings can give up an important love object except by substitution of another.

Marriage, like the latency period, requires the individual to take on many new responsibilities. Just as the six-year-old child is required to adapt to a host of new rules and regulations in school and elsewhere, the adult who enters marriage has to share more than he did before, rather than be concerned almost exclusively with his own interests. Like marriage, school and club affiliation in latency requires frustration tolerance, compromise, negotiation, and problemsolving. Many adults handle their marital frustrations in the same way that the latency child deals with her now unacceptable impulses—by "squealing" on others who are doing the very thing she wishes to do but finds forbidden. Thus, many husbands and wives enjoy collecting injustices and relish pointing out that their partners are "unfair," "not playing the game," or "not doing their share." A favorite preoccupation of some married individuals is to find out who is the "cheater" among them and gossip about this person. This achieves the same psychological purpose for adults that similar activity does for latency children. Discussion of somebody else's sexual or aggressive activity is stimulating for the discussants, and because someone else is the culprit the superego is undisturbed. The same dynamics can be found in many intimate relationships between adults.

Adolescence

After a period of relative quiescence, the child moves into puberty and adolescence. "Puberty" refers to the glandular changes that take place from about age 11 or 12 to about age 15. "Adolescence" connotes a phase of development beginning approximately at the time puberty commences and lasting until age 18 or 19. Adolescence, although a social and cultural construct in part, is always characterized by psychological changes manifested, for example, in modified relationships with parents and other significant adults.

Adolescents are usually quite egoistic and yet at no time in later life are people capable of so much altruism and devotion. Adolescents form the most passionate love relationships only to break them off as abruptly as they began them. While they can throw themselves enthusiastically into the life of the community, they also have an overpowering longing for solitude. They may oscillate between blind submission to some self-chosen leader and defiant rebellion against any and every authority figure (Freud, 1937).

Because of the biological urge to establish herself sexually and the wish to free herself of childish feelings activated by instinctual sensations, the teenager has a strong desire to emancipate herself from subjection to childhood affectional ties and from the domination and protection of the parents. Because in his mind to agree with his parents signifies submitting to a childhood status, he is frequently argumentative. Yet the adolescent simultaneously fears complete independence, with all of the attendant tasks that are assigned to an adult. Hence, the adolescent by definition is ambivalent and vacillates about decisions and opinions, reflecting basic indecision about dependence and independence (Cameron, 1963). In her rebellion, the young person may appear to her parents to be ungrateful and callous. To the adolescent himself, his behavior seems justified. Although eventual emancipation is necessary in our culture, the fantasies attached to this goal by both parents and offspring— fear of abandonment and loss of love—complicate the maturation process.

Inasmuch as adolescence recapitulates all of the previous stages of psychosexual growth, if the young person does not resolve the conflicts and face the tasks of this period, she will find it difficult to function in a relationship. He will feel rebellious when he is asked to cooperate, he will assume a pseudo-independent facade to deny his dependence, and he will be unable to cope with a sexual partner if he has not resolved his oedipal rivalries and incestuous wishes. As Erikson (1950) pointed out, the person who has not mastered the tasks of identity versus identity diffusion and intimacy versus isolation will not be able to enjoy sex and marriage.

Mature Love and Sexuality

By the time an individual has reached the age of 18 or 19, she should be able to enjoy a mutually gratifying relationship with a member of the opposite sex. This rests on the satisfactory resolution of the stages of development just reviewed.

In any sexual relationship, the history of psychosexual development is recapitulated in condensed form. Each person follows an inner script, and that is why handbooks on sexual technique or sexual therapy utilizing behavioral prescriptions are not always helpful. If the individual as a child successfully progressed through the various psychosexual stages, he will be able to form an attachment and trust himself and his partner in it. The mature person will want to cooperate with her partner and feel autonomous as she does so. He will admire his sexual partner without feeling any loss of self-esteem. She will initiate love making without feeling uncomfortable, because she has a sense of identity. The mature person can allow passivity in himself without feeling threatened and can enjoy intimacy and devotion without feeling self-sacrificial about it. The mature person enjoys giving and receiving because symbiotic wishes, hostility, and destructive competition are all at a minimum (Fine, 1975).

Many individuals cannot engage in a devoted, intimate sexual relationship in which they freely admire the loved one and in which the attachment is not threatening. That is why so many clients have sexual problems. When people are overdependent or fearful of dependence, burdened by sadistic or masochistic fantasies, or unsure about their sexual identity, sexual disorders are inevitable.

Sexual Disorders

Because so many patterns of unconventional behavior have gained wide acceptance in recent years, many therapists have been reluctant to examine their dynamic meaning. Some social work clinicians seem to think that seeking to examine unconscious aspects of homosexuality, celibacy, extramarital affairs, impotence, or anorgasmia is evidence of arrogance, intolerance, or lack of empathy. A psychosocial approach to the client implies that behavior by itself does not convey much meaning to the diagnostician. It is much more revealing, in understanding a client's functioning, to place behavior into a metapsychological context, scrutinizing the client's instinctual wishes (the id), judgment, reality testing, object relations, and defenses (the ego), and inner standards, prohibitions, and ideals (the superego); the recapitulation of the past in the present; unconscious fantasies; use of psychic energy; and effects of the social context on interpersonal behavior. Therefore, sexual activity outside the marital bedroom can be either neurotic or adaptive and healthy; likewise, homosexuality practiced in a prison can mean something quite different from homosexuality practiced at a heterosexual social club. To the psychosocially oriented practitioner, the client's overt sexual behavior is much less crucial than how he experiences himself and his partner while engaging in sex. What fantasies are operative? What defenses are at work? What impulses stimulate anxiety? What is the client's capacity for empathy? The answers to these questions are more important diagnostically than the behavior itself (Strean, 1979).

In the psychosocial view, sex is much more than a bodily experience. It is an interpersonal transaction. In sex, the individual expresses her deepest feelings and fantasies, defenses, conflicts, body image, self-esteem, and capacity for intimacy and empathy—the complete personality is at work. Therefore, it should come as no surprise that when a couple reports that they are not enjoying each other sexually, they are also implying that they both have intrapsychic, as well as interpersonal, conflicts.

Mr. and Mrs. Cain, a couple in their early thirties, sought therapeutic help because neither of them could enjoy themselves or each other in sex. Both frequently felt nausea, depression, or extreme anxiety when they were confronted by just the idea of sex. As their histories unfolded and their fantasies were examined, it became clear that both the Cains had many unresolved infantile wishes that frightened them. Each of them unconsciously wanted to be a child, ministered to and nurtured by the other, but each unconsciously ascribed to the other an image of an omnipotent parent. In effect, they felt like helpless, weak, and vulnerable babies in the hands of a powerful parent who could devour them. It was not until after their mutual wishes for symbiosis and their cannibalistic fantasies became conscious that they were able to understand why they felt compelled to avoid a sexual relationship.

A psychosocial approach takes the position that sexual difficulties, if they are to be resolved, require the client and the therapist to get in touch with the client's feelings and fantasies about himself and his partner, particularly those unconscious feelings and fantasies that distort the meaning of sexual activity. Because sex is not a mechanical, bodily experience but an interpersonal one, it requires an interpersonal experience to modify the client's difficulties.

Sexual disorders abound and their dynamic explanation could fill numerous textbooks. In this section, I discuss only those disorders that are frequently met in social work practice. Bear in mind that for many such disorders, oral, anal, and oedipal difficulties may all be operative. In the following section, I discuss some of the therapeutic principles involved in helping a client resolve these problems.

Impotence

Many men who consult or are referred to a social worker are sexually impotent. Like other clients with sexual dysfunctions, they often do not consciously seek out a therapist for treatment of their sexual problem, but the problem invariably emerges during the treatment contact.

The impotent man may be totally unable to have an erection, or he may not be able to sustain one long enough to satisfy either himself or his partner. He may ejaculate prematurely or take an unusually long time to do so. Finally, he may be able to have an erection and an ejaculation but derive little or no pleasure from his orgasm.

The impotent man may be inundated by feelings of distrust and rage and, therefore, will not want to have contact with a sexual partner. He may also unconsciously equate the sexual discharge with anal or urinary discharge and consequently feel that sex is something dirty. Often, when a man suffers from premature ejaculation or has an ejaculation without orgasm (i.e., without pleasure), he is experiencing sex as if he were urinating or defecating on or in his partner or his partner were urinating or defecating on him.

The impotent man frequently equates his sexual partner with his mother and wants to compete aggressively with his father. The incestuous fantasies recapitulated in his relationship with his sexual partner and the murderous thoughts that he unconsciously entertains toward a father figure create enormous anxiety. To avoid this unbearable anxiety, he withdraws psychologically from sex. Often, the man's oedipal fantasies are so distasteful that he defends himself by regressing to the fantasy of being a woman, which implies that he will have sex with a man. Conscious recognition of such homosexual wishes is also very anxiety provoking, so he avoids sex altogether.

Mr. Bales, aged 35, was frequently impotent with his wife. Although he felt quite comfortable with her as a nonsexual partner, he often experienced acute anxiety, which took the form of headaches, perspiration, and impotence, when his wife approached him sexually.

It turned out that when Mr. Bales was a young boy, his mother had been very seductive with him and frequently had avoided his father. Mr. Bales began to feel quite competitive with his father and often entertained fantasies of "wiping him out." Mr. Bales's oedipal fantasies posed an enormous problem for him. His wish to defeat his father was in conflict with his strong desire to have his father's love. He attempted to resolve the conflict by submitting to his father in an inverted oedipal, or homosexual, manner. In sex with his wife, Mr. Bales fantasied himself as a woman having sex with a man. By psychologically castrating himself, Mr. Bales could avoid the threat of an oedipal victory.

It took over a year of twice-a-week therapeutic work with Mr. Bales before he could emotionally perceive that his impotence was a defense against experiencing intense sexual and aggressive fantasies.

Orgasmic Dysfunction

Some women are unable to feel any enjoyable sensations in the vagina and/or clitoris, and to experience orgasm. In vaginismus, a woman's fears cause her to tense her muscles so that penetration by the penis is impossible or very difficult.

The woman who is unable to derive satisfaction from sex with a man, like her male counterpart who is impotent, may be suffering from distrust, fear of dependence, or sadomasochistic fantasies deriving from the anal period. She may be unconsciously equating her sexual partner with the parent of the opposite sex and then punishing herself for rivalry with her mother. In some cases, the woman does not enjoy sex with a man because she is in competition with him and would like to castrate him. Feeling envious of her partner, she cannot enjoy him.

Miss Coyle, a 24-year-old single woman, found herself unable to get any sexual satisfaction in her contacts with men. Most of her relationships were with married men. With them, she initially would feel extreme excitement and elation, but this subsided after a few weeks. Then she would become very hostile to her partner and quite unresponsive sexually.

In her work with a male therapist, she recapitulated in the transference her sexual conflicts. It turned out that the men who attracted her were always unavailable (i.e., married men like her father). She derived most of her sexual satisfaction from the unconscious fight with her mother rather than from genuinely loving and appreciating her partner. A very important element in her sexual conflict was anger at her father for not succumbing to her charms; consequently, she wanted to hurt and eventually to destroy him. She acted out her revengeful feelings toward her father with her sexual partners and because she felt so much contempt for them she could not enjoy either herself or her partner very much.

Homosexuality*

In the process of growing up, everyone develops sexual feelings indiscriminately and retains a certain amount of sexual feeling toward his own sex. In situations in which there are no members of the opposite sex, such as in the military, individuals who have previously been heterosexual may turn toward homosexual relationships. This is what Fenichel (1945) called ''accidental homosexuality.''

There is no doubt that biological factors such as hormonal balance contribute to a particular sexual predisposition. However, in any discussion of homosexuality it is important to remember that what is termed ''masculine'' or ''feminine'' depends more on social and cultural than on biological factors. The roles of woman and man are based on a host of fac-

*Editor's note: Of all the topics included in a discussion of sexual disorders, homosexuality is most contentious in current practice. On the one hand, there is the position presented in this chapter that the homosexual person is experiencing psychodynamic conflict due to developmental scars. Only when such conflicts are identified, addressed, and resolved in therapy will maturity be achieved and, thereby, the preference for heterosexual relationships. A different position holds that sexual preference is a highly complex area for which we do not have all the data. This view makes a distinction between gender identity and love object choice. It also holds that homosexual persons are as diverse in personality characteristics, dynamic histories, and relationship patterns as are heterosexual adults. Therapy with homosexual clients needs, therefore, to focus on the individual dynamics of each relationship, as in therapy with heterosexual clients.

tors—economic arrangements, status assignments, arbitrary role requirements, traditional mores, and so on. Inasmuch as so many elements are
operative in the etiology of homosexuality and because it is now considered an acceptable way of life by many individuals, organizations like
the American Psychiatric Association and the National Association of
Social Workers are reluctant to study the psychodynamics of homosexual
men and women, contending that this is a disservice to them. The psychosocially oriented theorist or practitioner takes the position that if a
person is understood in depth, she will be enhanced, not demeaned.
Whether clients wish to be heterosexual or homosexual is their own decision and that decision should never curtail their civil rights. However, a
client's life may become more enjoyable when maladaptive defenses are
given up, anxiety is reduced, and more tolerance of instincts is developed. Some homosexual men and women learn in psychotherapy that
their sexual behavior has served a defensive function and with lessened
anxiety move to full heterosexuality (Bieber, 1962; Socarides, 1978).

Because of the political, ethical, and social dimensions of the subject,
some crucial psychological questions often are neglected in discussions
of homosexuality. One question that should be confronted is: when
members of both sexes are available, why does an individual choose
same-sex partners for sexual gratification?

From a psychoanalytic perspective, one of the prime etiological factors in male homosexuality appears to be castration anxiety. The man,
usually because of strong incestuous fantasies, would rather submit to
his father and be his lover than oppose him and compete with him. To
the homosexual man, the sight of anyone without a penis is so terrifying
that he avoids it by rejecting all sexual contact with women. Recognition
that there are human beings without a penis leads to the conclusion that
one might oneself become such a being. Frequently, male homosexuals
have an exaggerated love for their mothers (Socarides, 1978), and homosexuality can express itself not only as submitting to the father but also as
mothering oneself. The homosexual man gives to his partner as he would
have liked to have received from his mother. He may choose as love objects young men or boys, whom he treats with the tenderness he desired
from his mother (Fenichel, 1945). More recently, psychoanalysts have
placed great emphasis on the oral factor in homosexuality, viewing the
homosexual pair as generally a mother–child pair in fantasy (Fine, 1980).

In female homosexuality, the etiological factors are quite similar to
those in the male. In addition, some female homosexuals suffer from unconscious penis envy. Many women respond to disappointment over
their oedipal wishes by an identification with their father. In their anger
toward their father for not loving them the way they desired, they incorporate him in fantasy and become him, thus assuming an active masculine relation to women. For a woman, this inverted oedipal identification

with the parent of the opposite sex wards off the mother's disapproval and possible abandonment. Usually, the female homosexual regresses to an early mother–daughter relationship; the activities of homosexual women consist mainly of the mutual playing of mother and child. Frequently, the sight of a penis for a homosexual woman creates a fear of impending violation, but more often it mobilizes thoughts and feelings about the difference in appearance between men and women. The female homosexual, in effect, is saying to the man, "I hate you for the pleasure you can have with your penis. I will have nothing to do with it. I will relate to women sexually and do a better job than you can."

Fine (1981) points out that exclusive homosexuality is never found among persons who had gratifying love experiences with their parents for this pattern involves a total denial of the opposite sex, which can come only out of a background of severe childhood frustration (see Bieber, 1962; Socarides, 1978). When the homosexual pair is examined more closely, an enormous amount of hatred becomes manifest; one unconscious aim in homosexuality is to deprive the partner of normal outlets for heterosexual pleasure.

Critics of a psychosexual approach to homosexuality have pointed out that many homosexuals are not in distress and therefore should be considered normal. These critics, however, fail to acknowledge studies of Rorschach protocols in which overt homosexuals had consistently different dynamic patterns from those of heterosexuals (e.g., Stone & Schneider, 1975). Moreover, the notion that only distress is pathological is untenable. Lack of distress may represent repression or denial, and many homosexuals utilize denial as a defense, as is illustrated in the following vignette.

Mr. Denton, a 30-year old man, came to treatment because of depression, nightmares, psychosomatic complaints, and suicidal fantasies. For several sessions he pointed out that his life was fine—he liked his job and had many friends and enjoyable interests. Although it was clear that his symptoms had appeared right after his abandonment by a homosexual lover, Mr. Denton found it very difficult to acknowledge the connection. In his transference relationship with his male therapist, he was polite, guarded, and very distant. When this was pointed out to him, he denied the validity of the therapist's observations.

After many months of therapeutic work, Mr. Denton was able to tell the therapist how much the latter reminded him of his distant father. Slowly, the yearning for a father evolved and gradually Mr. Denton could talk about missing his lover and wanting more contact with the therapist. Once Mr. Denton had looked at his strong wishes to be his father's wife and his competition with his mother for the father, he began to recall seductive scenes with his mother. While it took him two years to do so, he became convinced that one important dynamic in his homosexuality was his tremendous fear of his incestuous wishes and of aggression toward father figures.

Extramarital Sex

Our society is an affluent one and opportunities for "expansion" of our income, status, and psyches always exist. Our appetites are constantly being whetted and new excitement is always around the corner. We live in a society that is continually inviting us to enjoy new pleasures—massages, pornographic movies, and erotic literature, to name but a few. When appeals to our narcissism, grandiosity, and omnipotent fantasies are ubiquitous, our frustration tolerance tends to decline. It is more difficult for spouse's to remain faithful in marriage today than it was 50 years ago now that more loving communication, more attentive comfort, and more exciting sexual possibilities seem readily available. The extramarital rendezvous takes the lover away from the realities of frustrating routine, delibidinized interaction, and adult work and into an arena that champions the pleasure principle (Strean, 1980).

Because the extramarital affair is now a common practice, with over 50% of married people involved in prolonged affairs (Spotnitz & Freeman, 1964), it is often considered, like homosexuality, a lifestyle whose psychodynamics should not be questioned. Many clients and social workers fail to understand that the married person involved in an affair in an unhappy person who cannot cope with the demands and frustrations of a sustained, one-to-one, intimate relationship. It is often overlooked that the person in a prolonged extramarital affair may need two part-time relationships because one relationship is frightening and anxiety provoking. Although persons having affairs, like homosexuals, rationalize their activity, repress their conflicts, and deny their childish cravings, research has documented that marital infidelity frequently has a neurotic origin and that it is not a sign of liberty and potency but of the opposite (Bergler, 1960; Caprio, 1953; Fenichel, 1945; Spotnitz & Freeman, 1964; Strean, 1980).

In order to understand the dynamics of the wandering husband or wife, it is necessary to understand what makes such people anxious in marriage. Many married people create a great deal of stress by their unconscious tendency to make the spouse a parent. Once the spouse is cast as a parental figure, marital conflict is inevitable. One feels small next to a big parent and must fight; one feels controlled by a mother or father figure and must rebel; one feels punished by a punitive conscience and therefore has to cope with a great deal of guilt. The extramarital affair is a convenient means to move away from a spouse who is experienced as demanding, controlling, and punishing.

One of the major etiological factors contributing to sexual problems in marriage is the incest taboo. When the spouse is unconsciously made a parental figure, sex is experienced as incest and pleasure must be inhibited. In this situation, the spouse can enjoy sex out of the marital bed rather than at home because the extramarital partner is not experienced as a parental figure.

Mr. Ender, a 35-year-old man, sought treatment for several reasons. He was dissatisfied with his poor performance as a stockbroker, suffered from insomnia, frequently felt depressed, had difficulty in most relationships because he tended to get involved in power struggles, and had several psychosomatic complaints.

Fairly early in treatment, Mr. Ender complained about his wife. He described her as warm, pleasant, kind, good to the children, but unexciting. He felt that marriage was like "having a noose tied around the neck" and that he had to break out of his marriage. He blamed his sexual impotence with his wife on her "unexcited" behavior in bed. He found her statements of love to him "abominable." According to Mr. Ender, his wife "sounds just like my mother, who wants to envelop me." To prove that his impotence was his wife's problem, Mr. Ender boasted of his big erections and sustained potency with another woman, who was "exciting," "stimulating," and "never controls me."

During the course of treatment, Mr. Ender reported that he had decided to take this woman away on vacation. However, she was to cook and perform other chores that his wife routinely handled. While the first day or two of the vacation were blissful, Mr. Ender, to his surprise and indignation, became impotent. As he later said in treatment, "As soon as a broad becomes like a wife, I make her into a controlling mother. She even begins to smell like my mother and I want to run."

Because Mr. Ender had a strong oedipal attachment ot his internalized idea of mothers (and, in fact, unconsciously wanted to have incestuous sex with her), he had to split women into two: the virginal mother and the whore (Eidelberg, 1956; Freud, 1953). As long as he did not have a day-to-day relationship with a woman, he was comfortable. Living with a woman and then making her into a mother stimulated a feeling in him of being controlled and attached by a noose.

A female client had a similar problem.

Mrs. Flint, aged 40, came for treatment for several reasons. She had difficulty getting along with an aged mother and wondered how much time she should give her; she had identity problems and felt insecure in her job as a librarian; and in social or professional relationships, she often got involved in sadomasochistic quarrels. In her marriage, she had a lot of resentment toward her husband, who acted like a "know-it-all," "considers me beneath him," and "screws like a naive boy."

In treatment, as Mrs. Flint began to voice more resentment toward her husband, she moved into an affair with a married man. In contrast to her husband, this man was a "man of the world" a "great lover." While Mr. Flint's statements of love made her "sick" and "engulfed" her, her lover's cool detachment "turned me on."

When Mrs. Flint and this man went on a camping trip for several days, the relationship cooled. The couple engaged in Virginia Woolf dialogues and power struggles, and the love and bliss that previously had characterized the relationship vanished. Mrs. Flint ambivalently declared upon her return, "When I was with him over time, everything lost its glamor. We fought and never got anything settled."

Mr. Ender and Mrs. Flint needed their marriages. Like young children, they wanted the ministrations of parental figures but could not tolerate sexual expression with their spouses. Sexuality was experienced as overwhelming, controlling, and debilitating—much as a child would experience sex with a parent. Extramarital partners for both Mr. Ender and Mrs. Flint were experienced as love objects whom they could enjoy as long as they were *not* together on a sustained basis; in the latter event, their incestuous wishes were activated and the bliss of the extramarital affairs could not be sustained. One of the reasons, no doubt, that open marriage or no marriage at all can be helpful to many people is that these individuals thereby avoid the ongoing, day-to-day relationship inherent in traditional marriage.

Celibacy

Increasingly, the media are reporting that large numbers of men and woman have no sex life at all. Many of these people, like homosexuals or adulterers, view their asexuality as a lifestyle and not as an expression of conflict. A psychosocial perspective would conclude that the man or woman who does not have a sexual life fears intimacy.* Asexual men and woman have strong dependence wishes that they must deny, hostility that they must repress, and incestuous and homosexual desires that they must inhibit. While asexual individuals constantly rationalize their position, it is important for the clinician to recognize that such clients are frightened and feel very vulnerable.

Mr. Gold, age 30, came for treatment because he was very depressed, received little satisfaction from his work as a teacher, and was friendless. As treatment moved on, it turned out that he had never had a sexual experience. Although initially embarrassed to report his sexual inactivity, Mr. Gold raged about men and women who wanted to devour him if they became intimate with him. His rage was a cover for his intense feeling of vulnerability when with another person, whom he unconsciously made a parent.

As Mr. Gold recalled strong incestuous fantasies and rivalrous feelings toward his father and lived these feelings out in the transference, he moved sexually first

---

*Editor's note: This position presumes that the person has access to social contacts and chooses not to become involved in relationships for conflictual reasons. Also, this view does not allow for the possibility of a value based decision to select a celibate life, as in some religious or philosophical systems.

toward men and then toward women. It was clear that his asexual life had been a protection against the expression of distrust, rage, and incestuous and homosexual feelings—all of which were entirely unacceptible to him.

Treatment of Sexual Disorders

While marital therapy or group treatment can help the client with sexual problems get in touch with some of interpersonal conflicts, one-to-one treatment appears to be the best therapeutic modality for the resolution of sexual problems. First, in individual treatment, the client has the exclusive attention of one therapist and does not need to share the therapist with the partner. Second, individual treatment offers the best opportunity for releasing forbidden fantasies—childish wishes, hatreds, and inhibitions—without having to worry about what others are thinking of such wishes. Third, the client's past can be scrutinized and its influence on the present traced. The client's history is assessed to learn what specific psychosocial tasks have not been resolved and what specific conflicts still exist. Finally, one-to-one treatment affords clients the opportunity to study their transference reactions: as clients examine their complaints about the therapist and their means of resisting the therapeutic relationship, they gain insight into how they write their own self-destructive scripts.

One of the best ways to show clients with sexual problems that they are contributing to their sexual distress is by studying their transference reactions.

Mrs. Henkin, a 35-year-old woman, was in treatment because she was unable to achieve orgasm in sex. She projected most of the sexual difficulty onto her husband, whom she called "completely unloving and unromantic."

Mrs. Henkin had been in treatment for about a year when she blurted out in a session that her husband, Joe, was "a cold, insensitive, unfeeling ox who is afraid of intimacy." On her birthday, she complained, "All Joe got me was some stinky perfume. He's afraid to have me smell nice cause then he'll feel close and that scares him!" After discharging a great deal of anger, Mrs. Henkin began to cry. In between her sobs, she said that she was very capable of an intimate relationship with a man but Joe would not or could not reciprocate her wishes for "closeness, tenderness, and warm sex." Then Mrs. Henkin fell silent for several minutes. When she was asked by her male therapist what she had been thinking about during the silence, Mrs. Henkin said, "I'm feeling very close to you now. I feel you understand me. I feel warm inside. . . . I'm fantasizing that your arm is around me and that you are lying with me on a bed." Then, after a brief silence, Mrs. Henkin exclaimed, "Now I have a fantasy of throwing a chair at you. You affect me too much, you bastard! Go away!"

Mrs. Henkin was afraid to feel close to her therapist. She protected herself from warm, sexual feelings toward him by fantasizing that she would hurt him with a chair. Psychologically, this was precisely how Mrs. Henkin coped with her husband; she attacked him in order to ward off sexual feelings toward him. When, later in treatment, Mrs. Henkin expressed the wish to seek out another therapist, she was able to understand some of her motives for arranging the extramarital affair in which she had been involved for several months. This case illustrates a point made earlier: a client's complaints about the partner express unconscious wishes that will also manifest themselves in the relationship with the therapist.

As I suggested earlier, symptoms such as impotence or anorgasmia are a protection from childish fantasies that are unbearable—sadistic cravings, masochistic yearnings, homosexual urges, etc. Defensive operations used in day-to-day life appear as resistances in the treatment situation and must be addressed by the clinician. If a man or woman routinely handles sexual anxiety by flight or fight, this maneuver will also be used in treatment.

Mr. Isaac, a 30-year-old single man, came for treatment because he found himself unable to stay in any relationship if he felt positively toward the person. As treatment moved on and he began to have warm feelings toward his female therapist, he started to come late for sessions, cancel appointments, and fail to pay his bill. When the therapist confronted Mr. Isaac with his evasive patterns, he avoided her interpretations. When this avoidance was interpreted, he became very angry and told the therapist, ''I resent you if you come too close. I must defy you when I think you are influencing me. You remind me of my mother, who smothered me.''

Mr. Isaac defended himself against closeness in order to protect himself from his wish to be a little boy with a big parent. Wanting to be a little boy inevitably made him feel smothered and vulnerable. As the therapist helped him see how he defended himself in the therapeutic situation by avoidance and withdrawal, he began to face the origin of his resistance to relationships: fear of his wish to be an infant.

A psychosocial perspective to sexual problems necessitates that client and therapist identify those psychosocial tasks that have been left incomplete. More specifically, it requires adult clients to get emotionally in touch with the part of the self that is keeping them children and perpetuating old battles.

Mr. Jones, a 30-year old man who practiced homosexuality exclusively, sought therapy for depression, loneliness, work problems, and many psychosomatic complaints. He became emotionally involved quite early in the treatment; he ''liked the idea of just talking about whatever comes to my mind.'' The ventilation of aggressive feelings toward his parents, his complaints about the therapist for not loving him enough, and ''the attention I get from you sometimes'' reduced his sense of loneliness and depression and his psychosomatic complaints after just a couple of months of twice-a-week treatment.

When the client's wishes to have a homosexual affair with the therapist became the focus of treatment and the therapist explored the client's fantasies toward him, the client told the therapist that he abhorred him in much the same way that he abhorred his parents. The therapist, like Mr. Jones's parents, never fondled him, fed him, or "tickled him" and this proved that they hated him.

Upon the release of bottled-up aggression, the client's ego functions began to emerge in a more mature fashion. After a year of treatment, referring to his homosexuality, Mr. Jones remarked, "Isn't it crazy to want to punish my parents by being a 'pervert'?" As Mr. Jones psychologically gained some separation from his introjected parents, he felt less afraid of his assertiveness. Once he needed to be less of an angry child, he was able to develop more autonomy and maturity and to think about the meaning of heterosexual relationships.

Mr. Jones's therapist did not focus directly on the client's overt sexual problem. Rather, he helped the client resolve some of his resistances to expressing his murderous feelings toward his parents and, through transference, toward the therapist. As Mr. Jones felt freer with the therapist, his depression lifted and his psychosomatic complaints diminished; he could then begin to explore with the therapist some of the dynamics of his homosexuality.

A social work clinician with a psychodynamic orientation studies the client's conflicts, fantasies, and life story, focusing on points in the client's psychosexual development at which maturation halted and offering an appropriate maturational experience based on the client's needs.

References

ABLES B: *Therapy for Couples.* San Francisco, Jossey-Bass, 1977.

BERGLER E: *Divorce Won't Help.* New York, Liveright, 1960.

BIEBER I: *Homosexuality.* New York, Basic Books, 1962.

BLANCK R, BLANCK G: *Marriage and Personal Development.* New York, Columbia University Press, 1968.

BRADY J: Behavior therapy of sexual disorders, in Freedman AM (ed): *Comprehensive Textbook of Psychiatry.* Baltimore, Williams & Wilkins, 1975, vol 2, pp 1824–1831.

CAMERON N: *Personality Development and Psychopathology,* New York, Houghton Mifflin, 1963.

CAPRIO F: *Marital Infidelity.* New York, Citadel, 1953.

DENGROVE E: Behavior therapy of sexual disorders. *J Sex Res* 1967; 3:49–61.

DENGROVE E: The mechanotherapy of sexual disorders. *Curr Psychiatr Ther* 1973;13: 131–140.

EIDELBERG L: Neurotic choice of mate, in Eisenstein V (ed): *Neurotic Interaction in Marriage.* New York, Basic Books, 1956, pp 57–64.

EISENSTEIN V: Sexual problems in marriage, in Eisenstein V (ed): *Neurotic Interaction in Marriage*. New York, Basic Books, 1956, pp 101–124.

ELLIS A: The rational-emotive approach to sex therapy. *Counsel Psychol* 1975; 5: 9–13.

ENGLISH O, PEARSON G: *Emotional Problems of Living*. New York, Norton, 1945.

ERIKSON E: *Childhood and Society*. New York, Norton, 1950.

FENICHEL O: *The Psychoanalytic Theory of Neurosis*. New York, Norton, 1945.

FINE R: *Psychoanalytic Psychology*. New York, Aronson, 1975.

FINE R: *The History of Psychoanalysis*. New York, Columbia University Press, 1980.

FINE R: *Psychoanalytic Vision*. New York, Free Press, 1981.

FREUD A: *The Ego and Mechanisms of Defense*. London, Hogarth, 1937.

FREUD S: The interpretation of dreams, in Strachey J (ed): Standard Edition, London, Hogarth, 1953, vols 4, 5.

FREUD S: Three essays on the theory of sexuality, in Strachey J (ed): Edition, London, Hogarth, 1957, vol 7, pp 125–230.

GLICK B: Desensitization therapy in impotence and frigidity: review of the literature and report of a case. *Am J Psychiatry* 1975; 132: 169–171.

HARTMAN W, FITHIAN M: *Treatment of Sexual Dysfunction*. New York, Aronson, 1974.

HOGAN D: The effectiveness of sex therapy: a review of the literature, in LoPiccolo J, LoPiccolo L (eds): *Handbook of Sex Therapy*. New York, Plenum, 1978, pp 443–452.

INCE L: Behavior modification of sexual disorders. *Am J Psychother* 1973; 27:446–451.

KAPLAN J: *The New Sex Therapy*. New York, Brunner Mazel, 1974.

KARASU T, ROSENBAUM M, JERRETT I: Overview of new sex therapies, in Karasu T, Socarides C (eds): *On Sexuality*. New York, International Universities Press, 1979, pp 345–370.

KARUSUT, SOCARIDES C (eds): *On Sexuality*. New York, International Universities Press, 1979.

LEVAY A, KAGLE A: 1977. A study of treatment needs following sex therapy. *Am J Psychiatry* 134: 970–973.

LOPICCOLO J, LOBITZ W: The role of masturbation in the treatment of sexual dysfunction. *Arch Sex Behav* 1972; 2:163–171.

MALINOWSKI M: Psychoanalysis and anthropology. *Psyche* 1923; 4.

MARASSE H, HART M: The oedipal period, in Wiedeman G (ed): *Personality Development and Deviation*. New York, International Universities Press, 1975, pp 110–122.

MASTERS W, JOHNSON V: *The Human Sexual Response*. Boston, Little, Brown, 1966.

MASTERS W, JOHNSON V: *Human Sexual Inadequacy*. Boston, Little, Brown, 1970.

OBLER M: Multivariate approaches to psychotherapy with sexual dysfunction. *Counsel Psychol* 1975; 5:55–60.

SEMANS J: Premature ejaculation: a new approach. *South Med J* 1956; 49:353–357.

SOCARIDES C: *Homosexuality*. New York, Aronson, 1978.

SPOTNITZ H, FREEMAN L: *The Wandering Husband*. Englewood Cliffs, Prentice-Hall, 1964.

STONE N, SCHNEIDER R: Concurrent validity of the Wheeler signs of homosexuality in the Rorschach. *J Pers Dev* 1975; 39:573–579.

STREAN H: *Clinical Social Work*. New York, Free Press, 1978.

STREAN H: *Psychoanalytic Theory and Social Work Practice*. New York, Free Press, 1979.

STREAN H: *The Extramarital Affair*. New York, Free Press, 1980.

WRIGHT J, PERREAULT R, MATHIEU M: The treatment of sexual dysfunction: a review. *Gen Psychiatry* 1977, 34:881–890.

ZILBERGELD B, EVANS M: The inadequacy of Masters and Johnson. *Psychol Today* 1980:29–43.

12

Antisocial Personalities

Monna Zentner

The term "antisocial personality" is used to describe those whose personality characteristics and behavioral patterns mitigate against successful interpersonal relationships, those who are in repeated conflict with society's values, and those who need to gratify impulses immediately to the detriment of other concerns.* Although the term usually refers to "a wide variety of clinical symptoms, and is used to refer to both psycho-pathological and psychodynamic features" (MacKinnon & Michels, 1971, p. 298), antisocial individuals generally show a lack of ethical development and an inability to conform to those models of behavior society deems appropriate. They are considered undependable, unable to feel guilt, and less able than others to benefit from past experience. Their antisocial behaviors range from the irresponsible to the seriously criminal offense. Their need to discharge impulse is emphasized in almost all descriptions.

*The terms "psychopathic," "antisocial," and "sociopathic" have been used more or less interchangeably to describe this pattern, but "antisocial is presently favored.

345

Etiology of the Antisocial Personality

The etiology of this disorder remains uncertain. There has been no dearth of theories, but each needs additional study. Genetic, sociocultural, interactional, and physiological explanations have been advanced and examined over a period of time, but each theory seems incomplete and is contradicted by other theories.

Many of the genetic studies have been done on antisocial persons who have run afoul of the law since they are a ready population. Crowe's (1974) adoption studies suggested that this condition has a strong genetic basis; however, they also provided evidence that the environment has an impact on antisocial patterns.

EEG abnormalities have been investigated on the hypothesis that the socially immature behavior of the antisocial person may be a correlate of developmental immaturity. There do seem to be more EEG anomalies in this group than one would expect in the normal population, but Hare (1970) pointed out that EEG abnormalities are not synonymous with brain abnormalities; nor do normal brain waves indicate the absence of antisocial propensities. Furthermore, the environment affects the EEG.

Environmental influences provide the basis for many theories explaining the origins of the antisocial personality. Cameron (1963) pointed to inconsistent parenting as a probable factor in the development of the antisocial personality: the child's needs are ignored on some occasions; on others, she is overindulged. He also focused on the probability that the child is unconsciously selected to act out forbidden impulses for the family while being punished for doing so.

Some clinicians have suggested that trust development is a troubled area for those with antisocial personalities. MacKinnon and Michels (1971) pointed out that abandoned children who live in a series of foster homes or institutions often develop syndromes that closely resemble the adult antisocial pattern; they easily extract attention from adults but have little faith or ability in sustaining relationships.

Characteristics of the Antisocial Personality

The social worker can anticipate a wide variety of clients with antisocial features. Indeed, some may fall into other categories of psychopathology (e.g., borderline personality). The very diversity of individuals who might be diagnosed antisocial has long puzzled practitioners. Nevertheless, despite apparent diversity a common style of functioning, including interests, subjective experiences, motivations, and actions, characterizes the antisocial personality whatever the degree of pathology.

The style of functioning of antisocial persons has been given little emphasis in the social work literature. Case examples, references to treatment issues, concerns about antisocial behavior, and so on, make it clear that social workers have experience with anti-social personalities, but they have not addressed the issue of characterology based on mode. The focus of social workers, as well as of most other clinicians, has been on such clients' need for immediate gratification, conflicts with the law, lack of guilt, and so forth. There has been no social work literature outlining the characterological style of antisocial personalities, and treatment methodology based on the study of this particular style. In this section, I look at both neglected and traditionally emphasized features of the antisocial personality.

Lack of Impulse Control

There is little disagreement in the clinical literature that the form of action of the antisocial person is an impulsive one. Antisocial persons act as though they were capable neither of familiarizing themselves with their own motivations nor of deciding which impulse to follow by carefully evaluating both its underlying motivation and its potential consequences. Frequently, the subject of impulsiveness has given rise to impassioned harangues about morality—from Pinel to D. H. Lawrence to Jung. This is not to suggest that there is not an important connection between morality and impulsiveness, but too often this behavior pattern has been either overidealized or excessively feared. Kubie's (1954) comments about normality suggest a perspective that enables us to view impulsiveness in clients in a more useful manner: "The essence of normality is flexibility." In short, impulsiveness per se is to be neither valued nor disdained; impulsiveness that allows for no choice, however, must invite scrutiny.

Subjectively Experienced Lack of Choice

Antisocial persons seem subjectively to experience much of their own behavior as if it were not purposive. Some of them describe their own actions as a giving in to temptation. Others explain their behavior as the result of a sudden wish inexplicably interfering with their normal functioning. Yet another group may explain their actions as a response to the wishes or pressures of others.

The client who steals a sweater may explain, "It just happened. I can't imagine why." Such an explanation reflects the idea that the evil we do is less harmful if it is unplanned. Often, it appears as though the client were not even fully aware of having wished to behave in a particular manner. Thus, the client who steals a sweater may report that she did not need a sweater, was not looking for a sweater, and did not even suspect that she might desire a sweater. The particular sweater suddenly seemed so attractive that she felt she must take it. Even after an action is taken, the antisocial person may have the bewildering feeling that it was not what he meant to do. Others may report that they acted to please someone else but are unable to explain why they felt they had to behave in a particular way to please another person.

With some antisocial clients, one gets the feeling that what they are communicating is both a sense of bewilderment and a plea that their behavior might be discounted. They seem to be saying that their own behavior does not make sense to them, that they would never plan to act in such a manner, but how can they be blamed if something not within their control forces them to behave in an undesirable way. The implicit message that if the client has not acted of her full volition then she is not responsible for her behavior (Shapiro, 1965), is not simply an appeal to external authority but also the way in which the client perceives her own behavior.

Impulsive behavior is inconsistent with long-term planning. It is directed toward the moment, with no preparations made for the future. It also is very fast action, unhampered either by any assessment of the motivation to behave in a particular way or by any conscious tendency to postpone reactions.

Antisocial personalities often seem to lack deep-seated interests; their values do not seem to extend beyond an immediate interest in their own life. When they experience an impulse, they seem to lack long-term goals that could give the immediate impulse some context. An impulse that is not incorporated into a framework of values and plans is not likely to be transformed into a deliberate choice of behaviors. It is as though the object of the impulse did not hold interest for the antisocial person, but only the individual's need for satisfaction, reminiscent of Fromm's (1973) description of narcissism, in which "only the person himself, . . . his needs . . . are experienced as fully real" (p. 201).

Defective Planning and Judgment

When most of us make a deliberate decision, we go through a process of active critical evaluation. We gather, analyze, organize, and reanalyze data and then make a judgment. Antisocial individuals may have all the necessary information but pay no attention to it. The antisocial person may even go through a travesty of deliberate decision making but, like the alcoholic who seems to be weighing the benefits of continued drinking, he is concerned only with how fully his perceived needs will be met.

The client, a young woman, was asked to share an apartment with a female class-mate. The client needed to move. The room in which she was living by herself was far too small and she found it unpleasant. Therefore, the offer was attractive to her, as it would have been to anyone else in that position. Unfortunately, the apartment was situated in a part of town not easily reached from the university that the client attended. Furthermore, the roommate did not seem to be the kind of person with whom the client would find herself compatible. The client was not unaware of some of the flaws inherent in the offer, but she seemed unable to pay attention to them and had no sense of proportion that could allow her to measure the seriousness of the drawbacks. She was overwhelmingly interested in relieving her immediate situation, so she moved into the apartment with her classmate. A short time later, when the inconveniences of this arrangement became over-whelming, she moved out.

As this case shows, the antisocial person is not inattentive; she is sim-ply attentive only to that which at the moment captures her interest be-cause it promises immediate satisfaction of some need. The initial im-pression then becomes the final judgment.

Lack of Orientation to the Future

As we have seen, the impulses of antisocial persons are not incorporated into a context of broader values, goals, or interests. Such people, in fact, have few long-range interests or desires, although they may discuss future wishes in vague terms. For example, behaviors indicating long-lasting emotional involvements are not often observed. In the absence of long-range purposes and stable values, the impulsive translation of wish into action ensues.

Piaget (1962) suggested that most of us can tolerate the frustration of not giving way to our impulses because of the greater investment we have in satisfying long-range interests and values: "Having will is to possess a permanent scale of values. . . . And conversely, not having will, means knowing only unstable and momentary values, not being able to rely upon a permanent scale of values" (p. 144). Others have sug-gested that the ability to orient oneself to long-range, future values, and thus one's ability to tolerate frustration, depends on having had suc-cesses in the past (Silber et al., 1961; Tooley, 1978).

Often sociopathic personalities will explain, quite sincerely, that they simply cannot help their behavior, that they have little control over it, that they feel like puppets with strings of chance controlling them. They may indicate that their own behavior worries them; they may wish to act in a more thoughtful manner. In this respect they resemble certain heavy smokers who acknowledge that smoking is bad for them—citing health statistics and probability tables, decrying the cost of their habit, expres-sing concern about their pollution of the environment, and complaining about the physiological effects of smoking. However, the heavy smoker does not necessarily wish to stop smoking but simply that his chest would stop hurting or that cigarettes were less costly. Similarly, while the antisocial personality may feel helpless in the face of impulses, this does not imply that he wishes or intends to behave in a different manner. He may be vaguely aware that in the long run he will suffer from his behavior but is unwilling or unable to be concerned with his future welfare.

Superego Deficits

The antisocial person is an "operator," a skilled manipulator whose constant goal seems to be immediate, measurable gain and who seems inevitably to act upon impulse. His manipulations are usually quite skilled (Bursten, 1972). From the point of view of achieving immediate aims, antisocial behaviors are not chaotic. From the point of view of long-term gains, such actions usually appear to be erratic, as well as self-defeating. Moral values are based on highly abstract principles; the gain to be derived from them is not easily measured and certainly is long-range; and the satisfaction to be derived from them is often incomplete (Piaget, 1962). Accordingly, moral values are not compatible with an antisocial personality.

Our subjective experience of conscience is a message of "I should" (Shapiro, 1965). One cannot feel that one should or should not do something if one is not capable of paying attention to and critically examining one's own behavior either from the perspective of a general principle or with the eyes of the authority figures who have been introjected. That entails looking beyond the immediate pleasures of a contemplated act to anticipate its results for oneself, important others, and society as a whole. The antisocial person, unable to attend to other than the most pressing needs of the moment, will therefore experience her conscience in a rather limited way.

To attend to the conscience implies that one is capable of anticipating and evaluating consequences before acting on one's impulse. Furthermore, to heed one's conscience, one must feel that one has a range of alternative behaviors at one's disposal, a choice of action. As has been discussed, antisocial persons do not have long-range interests or values; thus, they lack a context for action that could reveal alternative courses.

A male client picked up a woman in a tavern and went back to her house. The woman was married but she assured the client that her husband planned to be out late that evening. The client and his partner had completed their sexual activities and had gotten dressed when the woman's husband walked in. The client, saying nothing, attacked the husband and beat him quite severely. When the client was asked why he had attacked the husband, he said, ''Why, you know, I mean, you know how it is. He was coming towards me, he was a real big guy and he was probably a tough guy, and I did what any guy would have done. Nobody would have waited for him to begin the beating, so I just started it first to make sure that I would win.'' When the caseworker suggested alternative behaviors that he might have considered—explanation, cajoling, threats, withdrawal, and so on—he responded as though these were not possibilities at all. He did not so much disparage these alternatives as ignored them. Furthermore, he seemed to have a firm conviction that anyone else would have done the same thing, it was the natural thing to have done, and it could have been expected.

This client was not totally lacking in moral values; however, his moral values seemed not to influence his behavior. He was simply not interested in the morality of his action. This does not imply that he would have been unable to act in keeping with moral values had doing so been in his immediately perceived interests. From his perspective, however, his behavior was appropriate and he had no need to consider its moral implications.

Lack of Sincerity and Honesty

The capacity for spontaneity is not to be spurned. It is essential for creativity and, if we attend to Kubie (1958), a flexibility derived from a sense of mastery and competence. The difficulty for those with antisocial personalities is that their spontaneity is unremitting and, therefore, not a sign of flexibility. Such individuals may be charming—they may be delightfully playful and are often found to be humorous. However, their social skills revolve around immediate self-interest. Thus, their insight into others may be considerable, but it is inevitably used for purposes of exploitation and manipulation. Therefore, the antisocial individual seems to lack both sincerity and truthfulness.

The lack of genuineness and honesty associated with the antisocial personality seems to be present even in situations that would not suggest to others the need to be insincere or dishonest (Bursten, 1973). Moreover, the antisocial is not uncomfortable being insincere or telling lies. Such behaviors are used to gain immediate ends. For example, the antisocial person may accurately conclude that it is necessary in a given situation to impress others, to get around them, to please them, or to disarm them (Greenacre, 1945). He has little interest in what he says to people; his interest is riveted on the opportunities of the moment, and so he concentrates on saying that which he believes will work to give him satisfaction (Kernberg, 1967). This does not seem to be a conscious choice of ignoring scruples or of deciding to lie.

Whether the antisocial individual is lying or telling the truth, her fluency and apparent self-assurance give us the feeling that this is not really what she thinks or means. The antisocial person is apt to state a hunch as if it were a well-researched and long deliberated opinion. Again, this does not imply a rejection of morality. Rather, the antisocial individual is uninterested in conveying the truth when he speaks; all of his efforts are concentrated on what he must do in order to influence people or circumstances so that his immediate, short-range goals are met satisfactorily.

The antisocial person hears people in much the same way. She is not interested in the content of what is communicated so much as in the opportunities offered by particular exchanges.

Thus, for those with antisocial personalities, anticipated satisfaction through relationships with others is not a powerful motivator. Indeed, there is some agreement that even the more mundane pleasures that most of us receive through relationships are absent for these people (Kipnes, 1971). With only the immediate present as an arena in which to seek satisfaction, they seem driven to find short-range, dramatic forms of pleasure.

Passivity

Shapiro (1965) made an interesting point in discussing passive individuals. He contended that impulsiveness which characterizes the antisocial personality, is very closely related to extreme passivity. Certainly, much of the behavior of those who might be considered either antisocial or passive might as easily fit under one class as under the other. For example, one might wonder whether the drinking of an alcoholic is passive or impulsive. More important, those who fall under either description will describe their own behavior as unintentional or involuntary.

Passive people, compared to the general class of those with antisocial personalities, seem to have more of a sense of direction about their lives; they do hold vague plans for the future. They drift, as it were, but between vague parameters and not radically like those with antisocial personalities. However, a passive person in her drifting resembles nothing so much as someone searching for an impulse to follow.

A young woman who was supposedly trying to give up drinking went to a bar with a friend. Once at the bar she drank. Explaining this behavior, she said that she had had some drinks because her friend did not wish to drink alone and it seemed so important to the friend that they share some liquor together.

A young man who thought that perhaps he should stop gambling spent an evening with friends. The friends began to play cards and the young man joined in. He later explained that the men with whom he had played had thought it would be more fun if he entered the game. He had little conscious awareness that he had wished to enter the game; his subjective experience was that he had entered it in order to please his friends. He explained that he was "easily influenced."

Everybody, at one time or another, has made a choice based on a feeling of being urged by circumstances. But most of the pressures to which passive people succumb do not seem to be overwhelming; moreover, these people frequently succumb to outside influences. I suggested earlier that passive people seem to wait for situations that will make choices for them. They may have a vague idea of what their choice will be, or some may propel themselves into particular circumstances that seem for them to make a certain choice inevitable. The person who wishes to give up drinking and visits a bar seems to be seeking a particular situation in which, according to her, she will have no choice but to take a drink. The antisocial person does not have a context of long-held values and interests in which to gauge an immediate impulse. Passive people also lack such a context, except in very vague terms, and are, therefore, as vulnerable to momentary urges as is the antisocial person.

Although the passive individual chooses courses of action presumably to please others, he often shows little interest in the well-being of family and friends; his interest seems to focus on their potential to make him feel compelled to satisfy their needs. Often, a passive client will explain her behavior by saying that her friends would be disappointed if she did not act in a specific way. This does not seem to reflect concern with whether the friends would be disappointed; rather, the passive person has made a choice of behaviors, does not consciously think that he has made a choice, and is often surprised to learn that other people would not mind "disappointing" their friends. Again, there is a striking similarity between those who are passive and those who have antisocial personalities: lack of long-range perspective and little measurement of the implications and consequences of behavior.

The antisocial person's feelings of being helpless in the face of his impulses could be described more fairly as an experience in which the person has no interest in not succumbing to his impulses. Certainly, the same may be said for people described as passive. However, the passive person feels compelled by external pressure; the antisocial person, by internal pressure or impulse. Neither has a subjective feeling of making a conscious choice among alternatives; indeed, there is usually no conscious feeling of choice at all. In neither is there a sense that she may have wished to behave in a certain way but, rather, that what she consciously wishes is irrelevant for there is no choice of action.

Treatment of the Antisocial Client

Examination of the mode of functioning of the antisocial person supports the general view that individuals with this disorder suffer a multilevel, psychosexual developmental failure (Lowe, 1972). The manner of functioning of the antisocial client must also be examined for its treatment implications.

Fear of Abandonment

This type of client attributes to the worker the same incapacity to develop a trusting, intimate relationship that he has. One soon discovers in the treatment situation that the fear of abandonment, whether literal or psychological, has helped to forge the style of the antisocial person, which, in turn, helps to maintain this fear. Fear of abandonment is not consciously recognized by the client, in part because of the frenzied nature of her style.

The fear of abandonment is fed by the antisocial person's difficulty maintaining a clear internal image of the worker when not in the worker's presence. Such a client assumes that she also ceases to exist for the clinician when out of sight. Furthermore, the antisocial client sees things as extremes of good and bad. Thus, if he develops negative feelings toward the worker, these will obliterate any positive feelings that came earlier. This process is known as "splitting."

Because the possibility of abandonment so thoroughly determines the manner of functioning of the antisocial person, this issue must never be overlooked by the worker. It will become prominent quickly in the transference management, which I discuss later.

Trust and Trustworthiness

There seem to be grave deficiencies in the ability of the antisocial person to trust and hope, for without a well-defined context of past and future values and interests, there will of necessity be a curtailment of hope; moreover, lack of hope is not compatible with the establishment of trust (Erikson, 1959). To trust requires the belief that a relationship might offer more than immediate gain. An attitude of trust also suggests that certain behaviors can be relied upon. Isaacs and associates (1963) traced the sense of trust to infancy; through the parent–child relationship the person who becomes trusting learns that others are dependable and consistent in their responses. Finally, trust is based on realistic assessment; thus, most of us are willing to entertain a variety of explanations before deciding that a person with whom trust has been established is no longer worthy of that trust.

The antisocial person lacks trust in others. Reliability and consistency have not been part of the antisocial person's experiences. Thus, she has not been able to identify with trustworthy people. These deficits preclude the testing of others for trusthworthiness. Therefore, such clients view the worker only in terms of gratifying immediate needs and fail to judge the worker as either trustworthy or not.

Too frequently, clinicians simplify the problem of trust and trustworthiness. The worker may think that should he demonstrate his faith in the client, the client will eventually behave in a trustworthy manner. This is a conceit based on a romantic wish. Blind faith in the antisocial client is doomed to failure. Moreover, faith does not depend on reality assessment and therefore is not a useful perspective to hold before the antisocial client. A realistic evaluation of the client's trusthworthiness is essential to the eventual establishment of trust on the part of the antisocial individual. The treatment of antisocial clients also calls for active intervention by the caseworker in any attempts by the client to prove the worker untrustworthy. This is a complex task because the antisocial person will not consciously test the worker's trusthworthiness until the relationship is fairly well established and, consequently, of some immediate concern.

As I said earlier, the antisocial client attributes to the worker his own inability to establish a trusting, intimate relationship. Such clients will lie unnecessarily, manipulate, and so forth. The worker must be cognizant of these behaviors because if she can be easily manipulated, the client will not come to trust her.

> CLIENT: I really like your office now. That picture brightens everything. I heard from Eddy [a former client] that you loved paintings. I wish I had one like that.
>
> SOCIAL WORKER: Thanks, I do like paintings.
>
> CLIENT: You really have an eye for decorating, don't you?
>
> SOCIAL WORKER: I wonder if you're still worried about your presentation?
>
> CLIENT: That's not why I'm telling you this. I love your furniture and paintings.
>
> SOCIAL WORKER: I'm not suggesting that you don't, but maybe talking about them helps you to feel that I'll send a note to your teacher.
>
> CLIENT: I'll never understand why you won't help me. Damn it, why do I bother to come here?

The client had been attempting for some time to get a note from the worker that would excuse her from an important classroom exercise. Some hours later, the subject was raised again.

CLIENT: What I like about you is that you're so kind. Everyone who knows you says that you're gentle and nice.

SOCIAL WORKER: I wonder if you're worrying about your presentation again?

CLIENT: You're smart. You always see right through me, don't you?

SOCIAL WORKER: You may be sincere in your flattery. I can't always tell. But I think that the important issue is that you seem to feel that you have to take care of me in special ways in order to get what you think you need.

CLIENT: I need that note.

SOCIAL WORKER: I think what you really need is much more important than a note. I think that you would like to trust me and be close to me.

CLIENT: You don't give me what I need [crying].

Passive acceptance of insincere, glib, or untrue remarks serves no client. This worker did not attempt to argue with the client about the flattery; she just concentrated on the more important treatment issue.

Intensive, long-term casework is the treatment of choice for antisocial clients. Generally, this implies twice weekly appointments, evenly spaced throughout the week. This arrangement is not always possible; however, the twice weekly visits are very useful because these clients tend to lose their internal image of the worker quite easily until treatment is extremely well established and twice weekly appointments provide a greater sense of continuity than weekly ones. Thrice weekly sessions encourage too rapid a transference, and the fragile organization of the antisocial client makes her vulnerable to a intense transference, which is more likely with more frequent appointments.

Treatment Parameters

The issue of trust frequently arises around treatment parameters. These parameters and their maintenance offer an opportunity for the worker to demonstrate consistency, an important aspect of trustworthiness. The antisocial client may attempt to manipulate these parameters by missing appointments, requesting extra sessions, suggesting indirectly that payments be dispensed with, and so forth. The worker must be careful not to enter inadvertently into a silent agreement with the client that the client is special with either more or fewer privileges than others. The client most certainly should pay for her hours: the clinician works for money, as well as for other satisfactions, and should make no pretense about it. If he does, the client will recognize his hypocrisy, which does not lead to trust. Extra appointments should be granted only for emergencies since the worker already will have determined the time schedule most suitable for herself and the client. Missed appointments should not be passively accepted by the worker. It should be made clear that the client cannot be treated unless she comes for treatment. The worker and client must see each other frequently enough to get to know each other well and then to maintain their relationship. The loneliness of the antisocial client can be emphasized here. The client needs to know with no uncertainty that the worker will do all in her power to interfere with that loneliness—including actively interfering with the client's tendency to miss appointments.

Active Intervention

The glibness of the antisocial person has been mentioned. This goes hand in hand with shallow affect. Both call for active intervention, rather than passive observation, on the part of the clinician. To permit glibness is inadvertently to let the client know superficial interchange is acceptable. All of us resort to glibness and superficiality at times; certain social occasions, such as cocktail parties, automatically evoke these patterns, and they may feel comfortable when we are weary. However, most of us make choices about how to behave and are capable of sincere, thoughtful interaction with others. The style of the antisocial client, especially the lack of trust and trustworthiness, negates such decision making. The worker who intends to be of use to the antisocial client should attempt to forge such choices for him. Glibness and shallow affect deserve specific responses. The worker should point out that it seems that the client is not truly considering her feelings and responses but saying whatever is easiest. The worker should make clear that he is interested not in immediate responses but in what the client is really experiencing. The caseworker should acknowledge that the client may not recognize what she feels. She should also point out that the client is treating himself carelessly. The worker should make clear that he would rather have sincere responses, both positive and negative. This is not an issue for contention but an active attempt to help the client to be more trusting of herself as well as of the worker. The person who neglects to attend to his own responses and is unable to share them is a lonely person.

The issue of loneliness should be addressed once treatment is well established. The deprivation that occurs when one cannot trust others is debilitating. This may be unrecognized by the worker, who is repulsed by the antisocial client's cold attempts to use other people. Lack of familiarity with the far richer rewards accruing from genuine closeness can be seen in one client's attitude toward women.

> CLIENT: That's all they're good for. I can't even stand to be with them too long after we get out of bed.
>
> SOCIAL WORKER: It sounds as though you're cheating yourself of the pleasures you could have with a woman friend.
>
> CLIENT: What pleasures? I like them if they're good looking with great bodies. Who wants to talk to them?
>
> SOCIAL WORKER: You seem to concentrate so hard on getting women into bed that you overlook everything else.
>
> CLIENT: Yeah, like what? What else are they good for?
>
> SOCIAL WORKER: You've been lonely for so long. Have you given up one-half of the population?
>
> CLIENT: What good are they? [The client's voice is raised and agitated.]
>
> SOCIAL WORKER: I think you'd like it if you knew how to be close to a woman.
>
> CLIENT: Maybe I am lonely. I know I am.

The worker did not touch upon the exploitive nature of the client's relationship with women. Nor did she suggest that the client had tried to set up an exploitive relationship with her. He responded to the issue that was raised because it underlay his sense of himself: he was lonely and deprived. Viewing women solely as sexual objects deprives the viewer as much as the one viewed. Other aspects of intimacy are lost.

Identification

A stable identity has not been integrated by the antisocial person. Superego formation has been faulty. The inability to trust interferes with the identification process and identifications remain transitory. The child often identifies with the superego weaknesses of the patient, but she does not have a firm sense of self. Because the style of the antisocial client negates the establishment of a nonconflictual identify, the worker needs to provide active interventions, as well as education. The worker who does not permit the client to exploit him and who scrupulously makes clear that he will not settle for the superficial has a good chance of engaging the client in an active identification process. The worker must be certain to reinforce reality aspects for the antisocial client, as she would do with a person with a borderline personality organization. For instance, the client may suggest that she has access to real estate information of value to the worker. The worker may acknowledge that such information is advantageous to have, but he should refuse to act on it; furthermore, he must bring to the client's awareness her anticipation that the worker will act on the information although doing so would be harmful to the treatment process. The worker in a clear manner, put the treatment relationship first. This will eventually support the process of identification as the client learns that she cannot manipulate the worker but must accept her as she is. This in turn helps the client better understand her own limitations and the manner in which she deals with others, that is, to get a clearer picture of her own identity. The worker also must point out superego anomalies in the client's family. Antisocial individuals tend to assume that they and their families are representative of the greater culture. They are not, and the client must be so educated. This will also eventually help the identification process with the worker.

Autonomy

The area of autonomy is a troubled one for the antisocial person. The lack of subjective experiences of choice, the lack of subjective experiences of deliberation, and the lack of a well-defined context to modify behavior in the interest of future well-being all raise issues about self-control and self-esteem. The antisocial person uses people, and her expectation is that she will be used. In fact, he tends to feel most vulnerable when he is not using others. She also has little sense of self-control. What choices are available in a world perceived as inconsistent and unreliable? One cannot experience mastery in a chaotic world. The clinician must insist upon choice: glibness or an attempt at sincerity; exploitation or exploration of relationships; and so forth. When the client experiences some beginning success in his relationship with the caseworker, he will begin to develop, albeit slowly, a sense of responsibility.

Transference and Countertransference

The handling of transference should follow the model established for clients with borderline personality organizations. Positive transference must be carefully examined by the worker because the client will attribute omnipotence to her. This overidealization will eventually feed the negative transference unless the worker ferrets it out early in the establishment of positive feelings. This is not to suggest that the worker deny omnipotence: the antisocial client needs to view the worker as omnipotent for many months into the treatment. However, some of the idealization must be dealt with; for instance, antisocial clients often entertain the fantasy that the worker can recognize each time they lie. The worker must both acknowledge that he cannot and explain that he can usually recognize when the client is cheating herself by avoiding a topic or concentrating on getting something special rather than on more important feelings. The negative transference may show transient psychotic features, as one would expect in clients with borderline personalities. The antisocial person poses no direct threat to the clinician. The greatest problem for the worker may be her own countertransference. The worker may feel tempted to assume a moralistic attitude or be stimulated by the client's attempts to ignore the confines of society, parental pressures, and so forth. Supervisory help is strongly recommended for those practitioners who are inexperienced with borderline personality organizations, in general, and with the antisocial personality, in particular.

The perfunctory and limited conscience of the antisocial client has already been noted. The superego of the antisocial person is not just perfunctory but, when attended to, may be brutal. The worker should recall that an infantile superego is harsh and unmodified and that much of the behavior of the antisocial individual is an attempt to ward off a primitive superego.

The treatment process may be injured if the worker regards all behavior of the client as being transferentially based. The active interventions of the worker should help in making her a real person to the client. The client, in turn, is not a simple vehicle for countertransference feelings. The worker must view the client in the present as a total person, or there will be no establishment of trust. The client has difficulty viewing himself as a whole person, and for many months the caseworker will be the only one in the process capable of viewing the client as other than a series of pressing needs.

Depression

The successful treatment of the antisocial person requires the client and the worker to deal with the depression uncovered in treatment. The client has been deprived in many ways and his depression will be a response to that deprivation. The worker must sustain the client because treatment will not have been useful without a depressive reaction. Depression is the inevitable result of the worker's intervention in the antisocial client's tendency to split. The worker should attend carefully to the transference because it demonstrates the splitting process: if the client begins to view the worker as wonderful, she may be experiencing herself as terrible; on the other hand, if she views the worker as terrific, she may be splitting off all of the worker's weaknesses, treatment errors, and so forth. The worker should also search for other polarizations. Often, the antisocial client will present one parent as warm but ineffectual and the other as cold and brutalizing. According to E. Zentner (MSW) the client must be helped to acknowledge his unconscious positive feelings toward his less favored parent. In the negative transference, the client should be confronted as frequently as necessary with her tendency to use splitting techniques. The beginnings of anger toward the worker must be examined because the antisocial client will frequently admit that she is angry because she feels abandoned. Generally, the client feels that the worker is leaving him, which may be literally so or may represent an attempt by the worker to allow the client autonomy. Usually, the client becomes hurt and angry and her internal representation of the worker as trustworthy begins to waver. Again, this is a result of polarization: one's self and others are either completely good or completely bad. The client seems to lose the worker when the client has negative feelings toward her. Whenever the client's splitting techniques are interfered with, depression is the result. In this context, depression is a positive sign.

Conclusion

The style of the antisocial person precludes the easy establishment of trust between client and social worker. His style also precludes the achievement of a feeling of self-mastery, a sense of competence based on the realization of long-range goals, as well as a nonconflictual identity. A more thorough understanding of the relationship between depression and this disorder is indicated; comparison of the characteristic styles of depressed and antisocial people promises to be useful for the treatment of each. The role of the superego in the psychopathology of the antisocial personality remains a controversial issue and should be more thoroughly researched. Study of the narcissistic strivings of the antisocial personality—the search for omnipotence, the seeming deficiency of hopefulness—would enrich our theoretical knowledge. Finally, a better understanding of the integrative processes necessary to the establishment of a stable identity promises to be useful in treating clients with this disorder.

There is no professional group with a particularly sound mastery or understanding of the antisocial personality. More detailed studies of the style of functioning of antisocial personalities promise to be helpful to the treatment process of these clients.

References

BURSTEN B: The manipulative personality. *Arch Gen Psychiatry* 1972; 26:318–321.
BURSTEN B: *The Manipulator*. New Haven, Yale University Press, 1973.

CAMERON N: *Personality Development and Psychopathology*. Boston, Houghton Mifflin, 1963.

CROWE RR: An adoption study of antisocial personality. *Arch Gen Psychiatry* 1974; 6:785–791.

ERIKSON E: Identity and the life cycle. *Psychol Issues* 1959; 1.

ERIKSON E: *Childhood and Society*. N.Y.: Boston, 1950.

ESCALONA SK: HEIDER G: *Prediction and Outcome*. New York, Basic Books, 1959.

FAIRBAIRN R: *An Object-Relations Theory of Personality*. New York, Basic Books, 1952.

FENICHEL O: *The Psychoanalytic Theory of Neurosis*. New York, Norton, 1945.

FREUD S: Analysis terminable and interminable, in Ernest Jones (ed): Sigmund Freud: *Collected Papers* New York, Basic Books, 1959, Vol V pp 316–357.

FROMM E: *The Anatomy of Human Destructiveness*. New York, Holt, Rinehart & Winston, 1973.

GREENACRE P: Conscience in the psychopath. *Am J Orthopsychiatry* 1945; 15:495–509.

HARE RD: *Psychopathy: Theory and Research*. Toronto, Wiley, 1970.

HARTMANN H: *Ego Psychology and the Problem of Adaptation*. New York, International Universities Press, 1958.

ISAACS K, ALEXANDER J, HAGGARD E: Faith, trust, and gullibility. *Int J Psychoanal* 1963; 44:461–469.

JUNG C: *Basic Writings of Carl Jung*. New York, Modern Library, 1959.

KAISER H: The problem of responsibility in psychotherapy. *Psychiatry* 1955; 18:205–211.

KARDINER A, LINTON R, *et al. The Psychological Frontiers of Society*. New York, Columbia University Press, 1945.

KERNBERG O: Borderline personality organization. *J Am Psychoanal Assoc* 1967; 15:641–685.

KERNBERG O: *Borderline Conditions and Pathological Narcissism*. New York, Aronson, 1975.

KIPNIS D: *Character Structure and Impulsiveness*. New York, Academic, 1971.

KLEIN GS: Cognitive control and motivation, in Lindzey G (ed): *Assessment of Motives*. New York, Rinehart, 1959, pp 87–118.

KUBIE LS: The fundamental nature of the distinction between normality and neurosis. *Psychoanal Q* 1954; 23:182–185.

KUBIE LS: *Neurotic Distortions of the Creative Process*. Lawrence, University of Kansas Press, 1958.

LAWRENCE DH: *Psychoanalysis and the Unconscious*. New York, Viking, 1960.

LOWE G: *The Growth of Personality*. Baltimore, Pelican, 1972.

MACKINNON R, MICHELS R. *The Psychiatric Interview in Clinical Practice*. Philadelphia, Saunders, 1971.

MAUGHS S: Concept of psychopathy and psychopathic personality: its evolution and historical judgement. *J Crim Psychopathol* 1941; 2:329–465.

PIAGET J: *The Moral Judgement of the Child*. London, Routledge & Kegan Paul, 1932.

Piaget J. Will and action. *Bull Menninger Clin* 1962;26.

Reich W: *Character Analysis*. New York, Orgone Institute Press, 1949.

Shapiro D: *Neurotic Styles*. New York, Basic Books, 1965.

Silber E, *et al.*, Adaptive behavior in competent adolescents. *Arch Gen Psychiatry* 1961; 5:354–365.

Tooley KM: The remembrance of things past. *Am J Orthopsychiatry* 1978; 48:174–182.

13

Paranoia

MONNA ZENTNER

Paranoia, in its more dramatic manifestations, involves a serious deviation from reality. Those in whom paranoid functioning is most pervasive
and intense may be so severely impaired that they function on a psychotic level. Nonetheless, although paranoid behavior may be psychotic,
it is not inevitably so, nor is it necessarily apt even to border on psychotic
behavior. Paranoid styles of functioning, manners of thinking, types of
subjective experiences, and so forth appear in many degrees of severity
and may be modulated by a host of other tendencies. Shapiro (1965)
delineated two groups of people who fall within the general category of
the paranoid style. One group might be described as secretive, constricted, and fearfully suspicious; the other appears to be more openly
megalomanic, more abrasively suspicious, and rather rigidly arrogant.
Such categories are not mutually exclusive since they emphasize only
particular aspects of a more general style. A typical caseload includes
clients ranging from those with a paranoid mode of functioning of extreme severity in both categories to those whose style appears moderate
in both categories.

There is little written work on paranoia by social workers, with few exceptions (e.g., Zentner, 1980). However, there is some mention of paranoid problems in the literature that describes psychological processes of
particular importance to understanding the paranoid client (e.g.,

Loewenstein, 1977). This relative dearth is unfortunate because many social workers have extensive clinical experience with these clients and might be able to contribute from a unique perspective. Thus, the substance, this chapter is based upon the experience of the author in her practice and the writings of the authors cited.

Origins of Paranoia

There seems to be general agreement that the paranoid person has had particular difficulties during the establishment of autonomy. The clinical literature includes many reports by paranoid clients of sadistic treatment in early childhood, with repeated experiences of humiliation and shame in interaction with parents and parental figures (Cameron, 1959; MacKinnon & Michels, 1971). There is some agreement also that paranoia is intimately connected with a failure of trust, which can be traced to the oral period of development. The commonly held view that depression and a poorly established identity are underlying dynamics in paranoia strengthens the belief that both the oral and the anal period were fraught with difficulty for those with persistent paranoid behavior. Infantile narcissism, coupled with the attribution of malice to others, is another characteristic of paranoid behavior that is also linked to difficulties in the oral and anal stages.

A paranoid style of functioning may be taught by the family. In particular, fused or enmeshed families, that is, families where individual identities are blurred, often reinforce family closeness by insistence that only those within the family can be trusted (Kantor & Lehr, 1976). In such families, loyalty to the family is measured by the degree of mistrust of those outside the family experienced by each family member.

The classical psychoanalytic view of the etiological significance in paranoia of unconscious homosexuality is not universally accepted. Freud (1958) postulated that the significant drives projected by the paranoid patient relate to homosexuality. Through denial, reaction formation, and projection, a loved object is transformed into a persecutor. Although some paranoid clients have homosexual conflicts and concerns, it is widely held that paranoid people in general feel uncertainty about their sexual development and performance (Cameron, 1959). However, this is likely to be the result of developmental difficulties in establishing trust, autonomy, and intimacy.

Modes of Functioning in Paranoid Individuals

Descriptions of paranoid behavior often center on the content of interaction, rather than on the style, as though paranoid behavior were composed of finite parts. Most clinicians may tentatively diagnose as paranoid those clients who seem to experience suspiciousness, apprehension, and a lack of trust not supported by reality. When one observes projection coupled with unwarranted fears, one is apt with more certainty to categorize the client as paranoid. Yet the continual expectation of trickery or harm from others on the part of a client is not necessarily observable from the content of the client's concerns.

To understand paranoia through the examination of content, and content only, poses some difficulties. The paranoid person may be described as "tense, anxious and basically unsure of himself. He is mistrustful of others and suspicious of their intentions, and looks for hidden meanings and motives in their behavior" (MacKinnon & Michels, 1971), pp. 259–260). If the client were a young woman entering a highly competitive field that did not welcome women, she might be justified both in her uncertainty and in her suspiciousness. However, the justification of her suspiciousness would not be sufficient to preclude the possibility of paranoia. Conversely, we have all felt unwarranted mistrust in others, yet we are not, therefore, paranoid even if we have used the mechanisms of paranoia. Thus, to focus on the substance of what a person thinks or feels may cause the clinician to overlook more important aspects of the client and to make an incorrect diagnosis.

Paranoia, when prolonged beyond a single incident, may be understood as a style, or manner, of functioning. Shapiro (1965) posited that there is a paranoid style of experience, thought, and behavior that is characteristic. The acceptance of paranoid functioning as an ongoing pattern gives the social worker a clearer understanding of paranoid behavior and ideation. Shapiro insisted that it is only in the context of the mode of functioning

> that the individual significance of any given mental content can be clearly understood. A mental content or an item of manifest behavior—a fantasy or a symptom, for instance—not only reflects the content of an instinctual impulse or counterimpulse, but also it is a product of a style of functioning. It is only when we understand the style and the general tendency of the individual's mind and interest that we can reconstruct the subjective meaning of the content of an item of behavior or thought. (p. 18).

Selective Attention and Biased Assessment

Paranoid clients focus exclusively on data that will confirm their views which are usually of a suspicious nature. A law student who had been receiving excellent grades was very disappointed in her professor's response to one of her presentations. She became convinced that the professor was acting in a less friendly manner than he had previously. It was suggested to her that she discuss his reaction to her report with him.

CLIENT: Well, he said that my work wasn't as careful as usual. I did leave out one case that he thought was important. I asked him about my other work and he said that it was still excellent.

SOCIAL WORKER: Do you still feel that he's less friendly?

CLIENT: Yes, I know he is. Just because he didn't like one lousy presentation.

SOCIAL WORKER: Why do you feel that he's unfriendly? It sounds as though he considers your work generally acceptable.

CLIENT: He doesn't think I'm as bright now. I can tell.

SOCIAL WORKER: But that's not what he said, is it?

CLIENT: I could tell before I even spoke to him.

SOCIAL WORKER: But his behavior toward you was different from what you had anticipated. It sounds as though he took time to discuss your presentation. He pointed out what you had omitted and he told you that he still considers your work to be excellent.

CLIENT: You don't understand. I can tell that he doesn't like me. He only chatted with me for a few minutes.

SOCIAL WORKER: But didn't he have another class to teach?

CLIENT: Yeah, but if he liked me, he would have stayed with me a little longer. Anyway, he didn't act as warm as usual.

This client searched for clues to confirm her suspicion that her professor no longer liked her. Rational explanations by the worker did nothing to alter her conviction; for example, although she did not deny that the professor had had little time to chat, she maintained that he would have stayed with her longer had he liked her.

During the same hour, another interchange occurred.

SOCIAL WORKER: Perhaps you judge yourself harshly when you make a mistake.

CLIENT: What do you mean?

SOCIAL WORKER: I was thinking of your presentation.

CLIENT: Oh, God! I hate myself for being so stupid.

SOCIAL WORKER: You may be assuming that your professor is judging you as harshly as you are judging yourself.

CLIENT: I know I'm hard on myself. But he just doesn't like me. Sometimes, you seem to feel the same way, so how can you help me?

When the social worker attempted to modify the client's suspiciousness, the worker became a target for suspicion. This is a typical paranoid reaction toward those who try to influence the content of the suspicion. The client views such efforts as confirmation of the originally perceived threat.

Suspicious people negate that which does not confirm their suspicious idea and give credence only to supporting data. They seem to believe that what other people regard as real is only a cover for what the clients believe to be real. Paranoid individuals may be difficult to work with because their views, while biased, contain aspects of reality, their observations are occasionally brilliant, and they can direct their attention with unusual acuteness.

Vigilance and Scrutiny

Paranoid people seem to be constantly on the alert, actively anticipating attack. Their body posture itself indicates this attitude. However, the state of readiness can take various forms—some paranoid clients appear remarkably controlled; others seem quite irritable. One has the general impression with paranoid clients that their muscles and their attention are perpetually mobilized in the event that defense is necessary. Their behavior seems rigidly purposive and directed, as though such persons were under the authority of a hidden command center. The more severe the paranoia, the less spontaneity the client exhibits. He appears to be watchful of both himself and others. A client was convinced that the caseworker found him physically repulsive.

CLIENT: You feel better with your other clients.
SOCIAL WORKER: What do you mean?
CLIENT: Don't you sometimes sit in that chair when you see other clients?
SOCIAL WORKER: Yes.
CLIENT: Well, it's closer to my chair than the one you're sitting on.
SOCIAL WORKER: Yes, it is.
CLIENT: You usually keep all the chairs at the same distance. I bet you've started to sit closer to your other clients.
SOCIAL WORKER: Why would I do that?
CLIENT: Just because. I know it's closer. You just admitted it.

This client noticed that the chair had been moved by about six inches; the worker had not noticed the change at all. The client observed accurately but misinterpreted what he saw.

The intense scrutiny of the paranoid client often enables her to detect unconscious hostility in others, although she may become confused between her own unconscious feelings and those of others. The paranoid person's observations are skewed because he dismisses contradictory data. A 30-year-old psychologist had this particular difficulty.

CLIENT: My wife is so greedy. She makes me feel like she only cares about my money.

SOCIAL WORKER: How does she do that?

CLIENT: If we go anywhere near a store I can just see it in her eyes. She's just measuring. Can she get that dress? Will I buy her a bracelet? I've never met a woman who was satisfied with what she had. They act like men are born to serve them.

SOCIAL WORKER: I thought you felt that your wife was not overly interested in material goods.

CLIENT: Well, maybe she's not, compared to her friends: But I've never had a woman friend yet who wasn't greedy. You can just feel how much she wants to go on a shopping spree sometimes.

SOCIAL WORKER: Does she say that she needs new clothes?

CLIENT: No, but she says how much fun it would be to win the lottery and go shopping.

This client had probably perceived his wife's wishes correctly, at least in part. Many of us window-shop and imagine how we would look in the merchandise on display. All of us harbor greedy wishes and occasionally we act upon them. We sometimes feel annoyed because the people we love do not provide us with more luxuries. These feelings may or may not be unconscious. The client probably detected at least some of his wife's feelings quite accurately. However, he responded as though they were the only feelings his wife had toward him.

This type of scrutiny can be understood as a response to potential danger. The paranoid client uses her powers of observation as a means of protecting herself. In intensive, prolonged treatment, the clinician will observe that relentless scrutiny and inflexibly directed attention are not a response to specific threats but a primary mode of operation for the paranoid client. In other words, the paranoid client is not responding to a particular external stress. He is a person with an aim: his vigilance is maintained no matter what the external situation. The paranoid individual's intensity will not waver whether she is listening to a musical composition, evaluating a mathematical process, or assessing a competitor.

Rigidity of Thought

The parameters of the paranoid client's vision are so narrow that she misses the significance of her observations. A client may report that a mother hit her youngster. He will be able to describe in detail the child's anger, his hurt, the look on the mother's face, the force with which she hit the child, and the embarrassment of both mother and child. What the client may omit—because it is not significant to him—is that the mother was hitting the child for having run into the street. A 40-year-old musician, Mrs. B, provides us with an example

Mrs. B had been in treatment for a few months when Mrs. Y joined the orchestra in which Mrs. B played. Mrs. B admired Mrs. Y and took a very proprietary attitude toward her. Mrs. B seemed to want Mrs. Y for herself alone and deeply resented any move toward independence by the other woman. On the other hand, although Mrs. B did not want Mrs. Y to make other friends in the orchestra, Mrs. B had no intention of confining her own social life.

CLIENT: I don't know if I can still be friends with Mrs. Y. I can't really trust her not to hurt me. You know all the things she told me?

SOCIAL WORKER: What things are you referring to?

CLIENT: Well, all her confidences. She told me their financial problems, and she always tells me what she thinks of everyone. She acts nice to everyone, but sometimes she doesn't really like somebody and she always tells me.

SOCIAL WORKER: What's bothering you about that?

CLIENT: Who knows how trustworthy she is?

SOCIAL WORKER: Has she done anything to hurt you?

CLIENT: No, not directly anyway. But who knows if she still likes me?

SOCIAL WORKER: What's making you worried?

CLIENT: I thought she was just telling me her opinions. She's told them to some of the other women, too. Do you understand?

SOCIAL WORKER: Why does that worry you?

CLIENT: I thought I was her closest friend. How can I be if she tells everyone the same things she tells me?

SOCIAL WORKER: Has she done that?

CLIENT: Maybe not everything, but she tells them her opinions. I really felt embarrassed when I found out. The women thought she had made a fool out of me, acting as if I were her best friend when I'm not.

SOCIAL WORKER: How could you tell what the women thought? Did they tell you?

CLIENT: No, maybe they didn't think that.

SOCIAL WORKER: Did you think she had made a fool out of you?

CLIENT: Sure, wouldn't you?

Mrs. B probably had assessed her new friend with some degree of accuracy. Mrs. Y was unusually well regarded for a newcomer to the orchestra and she was sought out by a number of the women in Mrs. B's social circle because she, Mrs. Y, was considered to be a very candid person. In fact, Mrs. B, a secretive, constricted woman, was attracted to Mrs. Y because of her openness. Mrs. Y may have been the type of person who tries to make people feel that she is sharing her opinions with them because she values them above others, but that is very different from trying to make a fool of a friend. Mrs. B could not concentrate on any of these issues. Her chagrin at being unable to control Mrs. Y's relationships with others forced her attention to only certain aspects of reality.

Hyperalertness adds another dimension to the rigidity of the paranoid client's thinking. Life demands of us the ability to abide uncertainty or suspense. Although the unanticipated may surprise or even startle us, most of us have little need to examine closely an unexpected element. For instance, a loud noise, unanticipated though it may be, does not usually demand our scrutiny. We do not have to acquaint ourselves with the unusual stimulus in order that it cease to be a source of surprise.

An ophthalmologist had been in treatment for several months. He was unable to tolerate anything out of the ordinary and needed to bring his complete attention to any unusual item, no matter how unimportant it might be deemed by others.

CLIENT: I hear a funny buzzing. What is it?
SOCIAL WORKER: I hear it, too. It may be coming from the light tubes.
CLIENT: I'll just have a look. I wonder what it is?
SOCIAL WORKER: The sound is very faint. The maintenance crew can fix it later.
CLIENT: I think I'll just have a fast look at it. Maybe it's that light.

The client may have had some fantasies about the noise. For instance, he may have imagined that he was being taped, but the issue of danger did not seem to be paramount. It was the unexpected that claimed his scrutiny. The scrutiny of the unexpected is an attempt at mastery. By keeping himself in readiness for the unanticipated, the paranoid individual seems to achieve a measure of control over the environment. However, she is not at liberty either to direct her attention to certain stimuli or to relax it and is, accordingly, uniquely vulnerable to external influences. This, in turn, renders hyperalertness, scrutiny, etc., necessary as self-protective measures.

Projection

"Projection," or the attribution to external objects of feelings, motives, impulses, tensions, and so forth, unacceptable to oneself, is a defense mechanism common to most of us. Even the use of projection, coupled with denial and splitting, is not sufficient basis upon which to rest a diagnosis of paranoia, although this pattern is an essential characteristic of paranoid persons (Lowe, 1972).

Projection is an empathic distortion. We all view the world from a subjective stance and easily may incorrectly impute motivation to others. Nonetheless, most of us do not use projection as a basic process. Paranoid clients are unusually unaware of many of their own attitudes but exquisitively sensitive to mere traces of hostility, indifference, resentment, and so on, in others. This encourages their use of projection.

A young man was being treated for a sexual dysfunction. He had been impotent for two years, following a very abrasive marriage and a bitter divorce. He had a great deal of self-contempt and very little confidence in heterosexual relationships.

> CLIENT: I have trouble attracting girls. No wonder they don't want me. I'm short and ugly. Look at those big guys out there.
> SOCIAL WORKER: Other people may not see you as you see yourself.
> CLIENT: They sure don't. They must think I'm gay.
> SOCIAL WORKER: Why would they think that?
> CLIENT: They laugh when I walk into the bar. Whenever I ask a girl to dance, she gets the giggles. I'm not stupid.

This man not severely disturbed. After six sessions, he was no longer impotent, nor was he still concerned about being thought homosexual. However, there probably had been some truth in his cognitions: he was very unsure of himself and had a great deal of difficulty approaching women; moreover, although attractive, he looked bizarre and unkempt. His projection was a prejudiced interpretation of body postures, glances, and words. The explanation of how he made the leap from his observations to his interpretation lies in the rigidity of the paranoid style. All of us gloss over what we consider to be unimportant and we are all biased in that we view the world with a particular anticipatory set. Yet, our views are open to influence; our opinions can change in light of contradictory data. The paranoid client lacks such flexibility.

Mrs. A was jealous of another client. She was convinced that the worker gave the other client more time and attention. She suspected that the social worker saw the other client socially, although she knew intellectually that this was not so.

> CLIENT: Why did you say only five more minutes?
> SOCIAL WORKER: Because it's three o'clock and your hour ends in five minutes.
> CLIENT: You're letting me go early today. I bet you have an appointment with Mrs. J.
> SOCIAL WORKER: This is the same time you always go.
> CLIENT: Well, I just bet you're going to see your favorite client next.

The following case demonstrates in greater detail the inability of the paranoid client to be influenced by alternative explanations of phenomena. A psychiatrist who had been in treatment for a few months brought in a letter he had received from his supervisor. The psychiatrist's probationary period at work was almost over, and the supervisor reminded him in the letter that he had not yet begun the research project he had agreed to do when hired. The supervisor suggested that the client not start treatment with a new group of patients; instead, the client should devote part of his time to setting up the research project.

CLIENT: Well, how do you like this? I can recognize a setup when I see one [referring to the letter].

SOCIAL WORKER: Why do you think it's a setup?

CLIENT: C'mon. What else would it be? He wrote this so I could be fired at my probationary review.

SOCIAL WORKER: Why would he want you to be fired?

CLIENT: I don't know. Maybe because I don't suck up to him.

SOCIAL WORKER: I thought you had the impression that he likes you.

CLIENT: Yeah, but he obviously doesn't.

SOCIAL WORKER: Why do you think the letter is a setup?

CLIENT: Well, now, if I don't start the research, he can say he warned me but I didn't listen.

SOCIAL WORKER: But you were hired with the understanding that you would set up the research project.

CLIENT: Yeah, but maybe he's jealous because I do well with patients.

SOCIAL WORKER: The letter sounds as if he's trying to help you to keep your job.

CLIENT: I just knew he'd get me. I've wondered all along if he's jealous.

The client was unable to shift focus for a few weeks. Finally, after he had set up the research in time to save his job, he was able to explore alternative explanations for the letter.

Constriction of Emotion

The paranoid person does not act on whim. Everything has a purpose since casual actions are not consistent with vigilance. Positive sentiments—in particular, feelings of concern or tenderness—are treated with suspiciousness or disdain if they appear in others. If they are experienced by the paranoid person herself, they are responded to as though the person were being betrayed by her own feelings.

As Lynd (1961) pointed out, "Even more than the uncovering of weakness or ineptness, exposure of misplaced confidence can be shameful—happiness, love, anticipation of response that is not there, something personally momentous received as inconsequential. The greater the expectation, the more acute the shame" (pp. 43–44). This sense of shame operates in two spheres for the paranoid client: he is on the alert lest others shame him and lest his own tender feelings expose him to the feeling of shame he so dreads.

Constriction is not an episode for the paranoid client but a constant state. Her behavior consistently lacks spontaneity; she is always watching herself and others, ever vigilant to avert self-betrayal as well as danger from others. This person may be unaware that others more freely show their feelings because he tends to assume that everyone shares his highly purposive mode of functioning.

The conscious direction of behavior may allow a paranoid person to appear spontaneous or relaxed, but this is a facade. Alertness to her own behavior, as well as to the behavior of others, and deliberateness of gesture and expression go along with a severe loss of feelings. What happens to the affective experience of the paranoid person? Feelings cannot be commanded to disappear, but clinicians who have worked with sexually dysfunctional people often observe how successfully people ignore one set of feelings. The impotent young man discussed previously is a good example.

CLIENT: Don't get mad. I tried it. I couldn't help it.

SOCIAL WORKER: What did you try?

CLIENT: You don't want me to go to bed with anyone, but I can't help it. I gotta try it when I get the chance. You know I don't get the chance that often.

SOCIAL WORKER: What happened?

CLIENT: Linda wanted to come home with me from work. She's pretty, and she wanted to. What could I do?

SOCIAL WORKER: How was it for you?

CLIENT: Damn it. I just couldn't do it. Oh, I don't know why I did it.

SOCIAL WORKER: What went wrong?

CLIENT: I was so worried. The minute she asked if she could come over, I started to worry. What if I couldn't get an erection? Would she laugh at me? Why would she want me with all those other guys around?

SOCIAL WORKER: Were you able to enjoy being with her at all?

CLIENT: Yeah, I guess. But the minute it started, I kept thinking. What if I couldn't function?

SOCIAL WORKER: How did it feel when you were together?

CLIENT: O.K., I guess. I don't know. I just kept worrying.

It became clear once this client's erectile failure had been cured that he was a sensual person, capable of enjoying himself and his partner. Yet in this vignette, his behavior was so purposive and his concentration on it so keen that he was unable to attend to feelings of enjoyment, pleasure, tenderness, and so forth.

Autonomy and Subjugation

The vigilant, rigid mode of functioning of the paranoid person suggests that her sense of autonomy is weak and that she feels she has neither the choice nor the competence to do what she wishes. A sense of internal mastery allows one to feel some freedom in one's choice of behavior and makes one feel competent to behave in a variety of ways (Erikson, 1968). Paranoid clients may have a facade of arrogance that only thinly disguises their underlying sense of shame and vulnerability.

Most people can be guided by the wishes of others without feeling that they have lost a contest of wills. Most of us also can behave spontaneously, acceding to our own wishes without feeling either humiliated or threatened. The rigid intentionality of the behavior of the paranoid person serves to defend his sense of autonomy against his fear of subjugation. She defends herself against her own subversive feelings, as well as against the fear that her tenuous sense of self-mastery will be attacked by external forces. An extremely disturbed man serves as an example.

CLIENT: God has commanded me to die. This morning he spoke to me. I can still feel his power in my hands.

SOCIAL WORKER: What did you hear this morning?

CLIENT: He said that it's time for me to go to him. Everyone has a special time, and my time is now.

SOCIAL WORKER: Do you want to die?

CLIENT: No, I'll miss my son. But I can't help it. He has the power. He has commanded me this day. I said I don't want to, but he spoke to me and made me see his way. I have to do what he tells me.

Less disturbed paranoid clients reflect the same preoccupation with submission but in a less pathological manner. They worry lest someone exploit or trick them into giving up control over themselves.

Paranoid individuals manifest great concern about authority and power. Their lack of self-respect puts them in the uncomfortable position of feeling that persons in authority are superior: Any sign of rebuff from those in power is very threatening to the paranoid person. This becomes a complicated problem because paranoid people are apt to search for signs of rejection from authority figures; at the same time, they engage constantly in verbal combat with those in authority. Their fear seems to be that they might have to surrender intentionality. This fear is aggravated by positive feelings.

A social work student, with a borderline personality organization and a distinctly paranoid manner of functioning, had spent several months in a very negative transference to her caseworker. Finally, after several tentative attempts to do so, she let the caseworker know that the she sometimes had very loving feelings toward her. She confessed that her school performance had improved some months prior to this period, as had her placement performance. She had not told the social worker previously because she "didn't want to be expected to show feelings of gratitude." Following her admission of loving feelings and acknowledgment of improvement, she became preoccupied with being "used." According to the client, the social worker would now feel free to do as she wished with her. In the client's opinion, the caseworker would disdain her now that she knew she was a "suck." The client felt that the caseworker was now laughing at her; anyone would laugh at a woman who was stupid enough to feel affection for someone who was making a fool of herself.

This client perceived her affection as a serious weakness, a self-betrayal. She seemed to feel humiliated and weak, as though she had given permission to the worker to take control of her. For those who suffer more serious paranoid pathology, such a feeling of vulnerability would be likely to result in a more marked suspiciousness.

> A nurse, who had always been concerned that taking orders from her superiors might put her in a humiliating position, had a new supervisor whom she admired. The new supervisor was well thought of in hospital circles, and the nurse wished to impress her. She was very careful to make clear to the supervisor that she would follow her orders, simply because she liked her and she wanted to, rather than as an "underling." While the supervisor seemed to have positive feelings for the nurse, she obviously did not single her out . . . and, despite the nurse's wishes, it was clear that she was not a special favorite of the supervisor. At this point the nurse began to get very concerned that perhaps the supervisor might be taking advantage of [her compliance]. . . . She . . . began to look for signs that the supervisor was taking advantage of her and did not care for her. . . . Within a relatively short time the client changed from . . . longing for this supervisor's approval [to suspecting] the supervisor. The nurse became angrier and angrier. . . . she began to refuse [routine assignments] feeling that she now had proof that the supervisor was trying to "reduce" her in some way. (Zentner, 1980, pp. 144–145)

The fear of subjugation in this client seems to have been evoked by her admiration for a person in authority, the new supervisor. Because such admiration is experienced as vulnerability, the admired person is perceived as a dangerous. It is likely, of course, that the client's behavior toward the supervisor, who was now seen as threatening, would evoke a negative response, which would sustain the client's suspiciousness. This case exemplifies the transformation of an internal concern to an external one: the nurse felt betrayed by her feelings of admiration and, in turn, feared betrayal by the supervisor.

Treatment of Paranoia

Caseworkers who are not familiar with the style of functioning of paranoid individuals will have no clear understanding of the subjective experiences of such clients. This lack is critical because it is with the style of functioning that workers must interfere.

The treatment of paranoid clients poses special problems. If the caseworker is seeing an individual, rather than a family, long-term, intensive casework is recommended. The fear of vulnerability in the client, will not be touched in short-term contact. The client's vigilance will not relax enough to allow feelings of affection toward the worker in short-term treatment. The characteristic use of denial also takes time to alter. Most important, without the development over time of both negative and positive transference, the underlying sense of shame will remain unchanged and the style of functioning will not be altered.

There is a distortion of reality in the most moderate of paranoid people, and such deviations call for active intervention on the worker's part. Confrontation is not advocated until the treatment process is well established; however, the worker must scrupulously reinforce any realistic components of the material presented by the client and address the underlying feelings of vulnerability. At the same time, he must question clients closely to uncover their characteristic difficulties. For instance, a client may report that her dentist is always late for appointments and takes advantage of her by keeping her waiting. The caseworker should ask the client how she is being taken advantage of. She should point out that we all feel helpless when we have to wait, particularly when we think that canceling an appointment is not a suitable alternative. She should explain the difficulty of adhering to a strict schedule—the dentist cannot anticipate emergencies—but this explanation should not be used to justify the client's wait or to "correct" the client's feelings. After exploring the client's feelings further, she should inquire whether the client has had the same feelings waiting for her. Without attempting to justify any latenesses, the worker might point out how hard waiting is for some people. Justifications, unlike simple explanations, make it difficult for clients to expose their negative feelings. In addition, the worker might acknowledge how hard it is to enter into a relationship if one is not sure that one will not be hurt by it. She can then try to determine whether the client believes that her lateness has ulterior or malicious motives.

Note that the worker is not challenging the client's interpretation. She is bypassing it, addressing issues that have to do with vulnerability and mastery. She is acknowledging the distress caused by the client's feelings, but until the treatment is firmly established she will leave relatively untouched the issue of whether or not such feelings are warranted. She is extracting information: does the client feel helpless when she needs someone; does she feel helpless in the face of another's expertise; and so forth. Active involvement is called for because one cannot passively reflect reality to a client who has distorted it. Furthermore, it is too easy for paranoid clients to use projection during prolonged silences. They will project at any rate, but active verbal participation by the worker provides a structure for the therapeutic encounter that minimizes the use of projection.

Projective material should not be interpreted too literally. If a client claims that his mother wants to kill him, the clinician should not assume that the converse is true, although the client may have many negative feelings for his mother. In many ways, the content of a projection is not as important as the fact that the client is trying to deal with excessive tension, often unsuccessfully.

James was very contemptuous of others. He ridiculed his friends unmercifully. Several times he reported that people had been laughing at him, and he was very ashamed of this. Finally, the caseworker pointed out that usually when James felt that other people were ridiculing him, there was an unconscious precursor of self-belittlement. The worker wondered whether this were happening now. James responded with a sense of relief because he had not noticed the connection before. The content of the projection was left untouched, except for reality support (i.e., "Most of use feel embarrassed when people burst out laughing just as we approach them."). However, the next time James ridiculed his friends, the worker pointed out how self-destructive this behavior was: "Your harshness toward others may make you afraid that they will respond to you in the same way." Finally, James's harshness toward himself was explored. No direct challenge was used. The projective maneuvers were dealt with as separate parts, each of which the client could grapple with.

Occasionally, the content of a projection can be dealt with more directly, particularly when the client is well into the middle phase of treatment. By that time, the client will have some familiarity with observing her own feelings because the worker will have been pointing out each instance of projection onto the worker of the client's feelings.

A client told the worker that "for several hours, you've cheated by letting me go a few minutes early." The worker admitted that she had let the client go two minutes early for three hours but had stayed with her an an extra ten minutes for one hour. The two of them had discussed this previously and had decided that the time would be made up in subsequent sessions. The client was chagrined and could not imagine why she had forgotten that discussion. The caseworker wondered whether the client was cheating the worker in some way. Had she mailed her check? Was she accurately reporting during the sessions? It turned out that the client had not told the worker that she had started a new affair.

This example introduces another treatment issue. The worker must adhere as closely to schedule as possible with the paranoid client. The worker must give neither less nor more time than promised nor appear to be so doing. The paranoid person is unable to deal with the unanticipated. The worker should discuss time problems realistically and then help the client explore his responses. The worker should be careful not to grant special treatment to the paranoid person. The client enters treatment with feelings of shame. Her demand for privileged status is a denial of her lack of self-esteem and trust. The client may want extra hours, extra time following an hour, phone calls on a nonemergency basis, and so forth. Should the clinician grant these wishes, she would be reinforcing the client's fear that he is basically unworthy: neither self-esteem nor the feeling that one is valuable to others is gained by extracting special status. Should the worker grant favors, he might have a difficult time managing the negative transference when the favors are withdrawn. Of course, the worker should not be rigid. Occasionally, clients require more hours or other extras. But, the worker shoul make it clear why she is altering the treatment parameters.

The transference of the paranoid client must be carefully managed by the worker. The paranoid person tends to attribute a great deal of power to those in authority, and in the positive transference the client is apt to attribute omnipotence to the worker, which view must be moderated, if possible (Kernberg, 1975). Checking this tendency makes the negative transference more manageable. The worker should point out the unrealistic assessment the client is making. The client's inability to recognize flaws in the worker reflects her inability to accept them in herself. The correction of the more unrealistic aspects of the positive transference helps ultimately to build self-tolerance.

Bruce was experiencing a positive transference. He viewed the clinician as all-powerful. About 10 minutes into one hour, he announced that the worker was angry at him: "You're really mad at me. I can tell by your voice." The worker admitted that she was angry but not at Bruce. Furthermore, she acknowledged that the anger had no place in the hour and wondered why Bruce felt that he was the cause. After some discussion, Bruce talked about how terrific the worker was—how fair, how smart, and so forth. The worker reminded him of her earlier anger, which did not belong in the hour. Finally, she pointed out that it seemed difficult for Bruce to acknowledge that the worker had faults.

This example demonstrates the need for the worker to affirm reality components, as well as the need to check the overidealization of the worker.

It also illustrates how a worker can discuss himself in a manner appropriate to the treatment context.

The negative transference must be prepared for as much as possible. Individuals with borderline personality organizations where paranoid features predominate will have a negative transference early in treatment. The clinician should encourage verbalization of negative feelings. It is important to try to minimize this transference and not let it become too intense. Again, the clinician should acknowledge the reality components of the transference. The clinician can anticipate this phase with the client: ''Have you noticed that you eventually mistrust the motives of those whom you admire?'' The worker should tease out unspoken interpretations by the client. One example has been given by Zentner (1979).

A client informed the worker that she could not tell him what had happened with her new boy friend. According to the client, the worker would no longer admire her if he knew what she had done. The worker reminded the client that earlier in the hour she had mentioned the boy friend and then changed the subject. After some probing by the worker, the client acknowledged that when she had changed the subject and the worker had not responded, she assumed that they both felt that she had acted in a shameful manner and it was better not to discuss her behavior. Her family had always dealt with her in this way when they disapproved of her behavior. The client felt that the worker would treat her as did her family and experienced the same negative feelings towards the worker as she did towards her family when they disapproved of the behavior.

One difficulty that paranoid clients have in a negative transference is the fear of passive surrender to the worker; their negative feelings are often a defense against this possibility. This issue can be addressed once the client is well established in the treatment process. The same fear of opening herself up underlies the problem of closeness. The more disturbed or the more regressed the client, the greater difficulty he has keeping psychological boundaries between himself and the worker; the more intimate he feels with the worker, the harder it is for him not to feel too vulnerable. This issue is paramount, and it must be handled carefully. Too often, the clinician fears the suspiciousness of the client and avoids closeness.

The anger and suspiciousness of paranoid clients must be dealt with following the principles of scrupulous honesty and support of reality whenever possible, without necessarily challenging the content. For instance, new clients often behave suspiciously or indicate verbally that they are suspicious and angry. They may berate other mental health personnel, or they may challenge the social worker in particular. The worker can point out that it is difficult to talk about personal matters with someone one does not know well; it is particularly difficult when one has had some unfavorable experiences in this area; some people might feel resentful under these circumstances; and so forth. The appropriate expression of feelings of anger should be encouraged. The caseworker should accept such expressions matter-of-factly. This helps to reduce the client's omnipotent fantasies of harming others with her rage. Suspiciousness and anger should not be permitted as a weapon to enforce too much distance from the worker. The worker might acknowledge the client's suspicious feelings but ask why they are stopping the client from making use of the hour. Anger should be acknowledged, but the worker must not allow a flow of angry words or an angry silence to cut off emotional contact. The worker can point out that the client's anger is not sufficient reason to waste the hour. The client may have to be reassured that people can work together even if one is angry at the other.

The severely paranoid person may pose a danger to the clinician. The beginning practitioner should schedule appointments with such clients so as not to be physically isolated from other treatment personnel. Such danger is usually the result of a strong negative transference that the clinician has allowed the client to hide for several sessions.

Throughout the course of treatment, the worker should intervene in the client's style. For instance, one client with a sexual dysfunction was sure that it was the result of masturbation during adolescence. A few sessions later, the worker spoke about masturbation, the number of people who practiced it, its effect, and so forth. When the worker began to say that sexual functioning will proceed smoothly unless people stifle their feelings, the client interrupted: ''I bet I know what you mean. You mean I'd be alright now if I hadn't masturbated.'' The worker pointed out that she had not meant that and that, furthermore, the client was so intent on his bad feelings about masturbation that he was missing important contradictory material.

The issue of omnipotence cannot be overlooked. The worker can approach this problem by being firm and definite about the conditions of treatment. For instance, the client may say whatever she wishes, but if she yells she should be stopped. He can express himself freely but not interfere with others. For more disturbed clients, omnipotence may have to be handled creatively. The client who reported that God wished him to die was told by the worker that her God would not permit that and that her God was more powerful than his. Of course, when one uses omnipotence, one must be careful later to undo that image.*

---

*This example raises the issue of treatment for the paranoid psychotic client. Workers must insure that they are thoroughly familiar with the treatment of those with a primitive personality organization. Treatment of this problem should be followed until the psychotic or schizophrenic reaction has abated somewhat. The paranoid style should initially be disregarded for it may serve as an organizing factor to the client. Once the client shows some ego strength and the treatment tie is established, the paranoia can be fruitfully explored.

Conclusion

The paranoid person is ever alert to anticipated threats. Surprise or change is very difficult for her, so she remains prepared to respond actively to the unanticipated. Paranoid persons are seemingly incapable of being passive or casual. This effort to control the environment results in inattentiveness to any stimuli but those that serve to justify the paranoid individual's suspicions and in biased interpretations of reality.

The fear of being controlled by others and of being exposed by his own feelings is paramount to the paranoid client. Trust in the worker and in the self is the final outcome of successful treatment.

A clearer understanding of the normal and abnormal development of narcissism, with its relationship to vulnerability and autonomy, would be useful in expanding our understanding of paranoia. A careful study of the relationship between the paranoid style and the depressive mode also would be useful. Hope and omnipotence, as correlates of the development of trust, and autonomy and competence should be examined in an effort to expand our perspective on paranoia.

References

CAMERON N: Paranoid conditions and paranoia, in Arieti S (ed): *American Handbook of Psychiatry*. New York, Basic Books, 1959, vol 1, pp 508–539.

ERIKSON E: *Childhood and Society*. New York, Norton, 1950.

ERIKSON E: *Identity: Youth and Crisis*. New York, Norton, 1968.

ESCALONA SK, HEIDER G: *Prediction and Outcome*. New York, Basic Books, 1959.

FREUD S: Some neurotic mechanisms in jealousy, paranoia, and homosexuality, in Strachey L (ed): *Standard Edition of Complete Psychological Works of Sigmund Freud*. London, Hogarth, 1955, vol 18, pp 221–232.

FREUD S: Psychoanalytic notes on an autobiographical account of a case of paranoia (dementia paranoides), in Strachey L (ed): *Standard Edition of Complete Psychological Works of Sigmund Freud*. London, Hogarth, 1958, vol 12, pp 3–82.

FROMM E: *The Anatomy of Human Destructiveness*. New York, Holt, Rinehart & Winston, 1973.

HARTMANN H: *Ego Psychology and the Problem of Adaptation*. New York, International Universities Pres, 1958.

KANTOR D, LEHR W: *Inside the Family*. New York, Harper & Row, 1976.

KERNBERG O: *Borderline Conditions and Pathological Narcissism*. New York, Aronson, 1975.

LOEWENSTEIN S: An overview of the concept of narcissism. *Soc Casework* 1977: 58:136–142.

Lowe G R: *The Growth of Personality*. London, Pelican, 1972.

Lynd HM: *On Shame and the Search for Identity*. New York, Science Editions, 1961.

MacKinnon R, Michels R: *The Psychiatric Interview in Clinical Practice*. Philadelphia. Saunders, 1971.

Reich W: *Character Analysis*. New York, Orgone Institute Press, 1949.

Shapiro D: *Neurotic Styles*. New York, Basic Books, 1965.

Shapiro D: *Autonomy and Rigid Character*. New York, Basic Books, 1981.

Zenter E: Seminar, Wilfrid Laurier University, Waterloo, Ontario, March 1979.

Zenter M: The paranoid client. *Soc Casework* 1980; 61:138–145.

14

Eating Disorders: Anorexia Nervosa and Obesity

Lynn-Marie Mackay

Anorexia nervosa is a serious and enigmatic disorder characterized by a relentless pursuit of thinness leading to self-imposed starvation. This complex illness has important physical and psychological consequences and may progress to the point of life-threatening low weight. Mortality is reported to be in the 5–20% range (Bemis, 1978).

Anorexia nervosa is considered a disorder of adolescents and women, but the age of onset ranges from 10 to 30, with cases reported up to the fifties (Kellett et al. 1976); men account for 5–10% of all cases (Beumont et al., 1972). Although the illness tends to occur disproportionately in the middle and upper classes, there is some evidence that this social class skewing has diminished since the mid-1970s (Garfinkel & Garner, 1982). Once considered rare, anorexia nervosa appears to be increasing over the past 20 years. A recent estimate in London found 1 severe case for every 250 adolescent girls in high school (Crisp et al., 1976).

"Anorexia nervosa" is a misleading name since the term "anorexia" means loss of appetite. Anorectic individuals are very hungry, and it is only through the exercise of a prodigiously strong will that they manage to curb their eating. Only in the late stages of starvation does the appetite wane. A substantial proportion of patients alternate between periods of abstention from food and periods of "bulimia", the rapid consumption

384

of unusually large amounts of food with a sense of being out of control. Episodes of bulimia may be followed by self-induced vomiting and/or laxative abuse to prevent weight gain.

Central to the illness is the desire for thinness at any cost (Bruch, 1973, 1978; Selvini-Palazzoli, 1974). The German term for anorexia nervosa— *Pubertatsmagersucht* ("compulsive pubertal emaciation")—is more to the point; *Magersucht* refers to the mania to be thin. Crisp's (1970, 1977) characterization of the disorder as a weight phobia highlights the fear of weight gain as the primary concern, as opposed to food and its symbolic meanings.

Anorexia Nervosa

Historical Perspective on Anorexia Nervosa

The history of anorexia nervosa may date to ancient times and was possibly quite common in the Middle Ages among witches and pseudomystics (Selvini-Palazzoli, 1974). The English physician Richard Morton published the first documented account of anorexia nervosa in 1689. He described the illness as a "nervous atrophy" distinguished from the fever and shortness of breath of tubercular consumption. Morton believed the origins to be predominantly mental and the distinguishing symptoms to be amenorrhea, lack of appetite, constipation, and extreme emaciation ("like a skeleton only clad with skin").

Amost 200 years later, in 1868, the eminent English surgeon Sir William Gull made reference to the syndrome in an address at Oxford University. He described a case of "apepsia hysterica." In 1873, Gull (1964) renamed the disorder "anorexia nervosa" due to the presence of pepsin in the stomach and to the occurrence of the syndrome in men. He also stressed the psychological origin of the malady, drawing particular attention to the "morbid mental state" and "perversions of the ego." Gull's clinical picture of Miss A refers to the characteristic features of bulimia and hyperactivity: "Occasionally for a day or two the appetite was voracious. . . . it hardly seemed possible that a body so wasted could undergo the exercise which seemed agreeable" (p. 133).

Writing at the same time in Paris, C. Lasegue (1964) independently and similarly depicted the disorder, calling it "anorexia hysterica." Again, Lasegue attributed the disorder to psychological causes. He portrayed the pathological mental state as an "intellectual perversion." His patient's self-satisfied attitude and denial of her illness amazed him: "Not only does she not sigh for recovery, but she is not ill-pleased with her condition, not withstanding all the unpleasantness it is attended with" (p. 151).

This initial period in the history of anorexia nervosa clearly established a psychological etiology to the disorder. However, the understanding of the syndrome was thrown into confusion in 1914, when the pathologist Morris Simmonds published a report on the death of an emaciated woman whose autopsy demonstrated destruction of the anterior lobe of the pituitary. Over the next 20 years, many cases of anorexia nervosa were misdiagnosed as Simmond's disease, or pituitary insufficiency. Finally, a series of papers by Ryle (1939), Richardson (1939), and Sheldon (1939) late in the 1930s differentiated the two disorders and the psychological origin of the anorexia nervosa syndrome was reestablished.

Diagnostic Criteria for Anorexia Nervosa

Various frameworks for a diagnosis of primary anorexia nervosa have been devised using positive criteria. Bruch (1973) insisted that the following characteristics must be present in addition to the pursuit of thinness: (1) a distorted body image and a body concept of delusional proportions; (2) perceptual and cognitive disturbances in the recognition of internal states, both visceral (hunger, fatigue) and emotional; and (3) a paralyzing sense of ineffectiveness and lack of personal identity. Bruch's diagnostic criteria present difficulties in that body image and perceptual and cognitive distortions are neither universally present in, nor unique to, anorexia nervosa, nor is the sense of ineffectiveness and lack of identity.

Recently, Garrow and associates (1975) gave a succinct and precise review of the essential criteria in a diagnosis of anorexia nervosa:

1. self-inflicted, severe loss of weight, using one or more of the following devices: avoidance of foods considered to be fattening, self-induced vomiting, abuse of purgatives, and excessive exercise
2. a secondary endocrine disorder (of the hypothalamic–anterior pituitary–gonodal axis) manifest as amenorrhea in women and as diminution of sexual interest and activity in men
3. a psychological disorder that has as its central theme a morbid fear of being unable to control eating and hence of becoming too fat

These are very similar to the useful criteria established by DSM III (American Psychiatric Association, 1980).

For a discussion of the differentiation of primary anorexia nervosa from primary affective illness, schizophrenia, and obsessive-compulsive and hysterical conversion disorders, the reader may consult Garfinkel and Garner (1982). In addition to these functional disorders, several endocrinological disturbances may be confused with anorexia nervosa, including Addison's disease, hyperthyroidism, Simmond's disease, and diabetes. The differentiation of these from anorexia nervosa is based on a combination of historical information and findings from physical and laboratory examinations.

Clinical Features of Anorexia Nervosa

Anorexia nervosa is a syndrome characterized by both physical and psychological symptoms. The psychopathology of the anorectic individual tends to be interwoven with both her drive for thinness and the manifestations of starvation.

Starvation Symptoms

Important physical signs are loss of body weight, often to the point of severe "cachexia," amenorrhea, hyperactivity, and constipation. Abnormally slow heart rate, low blood pressure, and low body temperature are usually present and may be indicative of the body's tendency partially to shut down in order to adapt to semistarvation. Patients may develop "lanugo," a fine downy growth, over the cheeks, neck, arms, and thighs, possibly as a primitive mechanism of preserving body heat. There may be swelling of the feet and hands, which may also extend to the nose and ears. The skin may be dry and cracking and the nails brittle. There may be some hair loss from the scalp. Carotene pigmentation is present in some patients, possibly due to overingestion of carrots and spinach. Patients who vomit frequently may develop serious dental problems. Patients who binge on high carbohydrate foods or who drink large quantities of coffee may develop facial edema. Peripheral edema or swelling may ensue subsequent to rapid refeeding.

Amenorrhea and loss of sexual interest are related at least partially to descent below a critical fat-to-weight ratio (Frisch & McArthur, 1974). However, emotional factors are also known to make an important contribution to these signs in some cases. Sleep disturbance is a result of the starvation state. Many of the bizarre behaviors and thinking patterns of anorexia nervosa, secondary to the state of starvation, were manifest in the volunteers who participated in the Minnesota experiment in semistarvation (Keys et al., 1950).

Psychopathologic Features

The anorectic individual's overriding pursuit of thinness and morbid fear of fatness and weight gain, motivated by fears of loss of control, is generally considered to be the core psychopathology in this syndrome. The patient's preoccupation with food, due to the state of starvation, intensifies fears of being out of control. This contributes to increased dieting, ultimately trapping the patient in a vicious circle.

As noted earlier, Crisp (1970) described anorexia nervosa as a weight phobia, an avoidance of normal body and weight proportions and psychosexual maturity. The patient unconsciously sets a weight limit that is subpubertal. Problems associated with sexual and aggressive drives are concretized to a body size, that is, ''If I can achieve a particular body size, my other problems will disappear.

Selvini-Palazzoli (1974) argued that to interpret these individuals as ''refusing to grow up'' is an oversimplification. She noted that in part they want to become autonomous adults, albeit in a distorted sense. She agreed with Bruch that they have basic ego deficits and a pervasive sense of ineffectiveness. Selvini-Palazzoli discussed the feature of ''personal mistrust,'' or ''intrapsychic paranoia,'' which corresponds to Bruch's concept of defects in perception and cognition. The anorectic individual turns to control of weight to enhance self-control and ultimately self-esteem.

Anorexia nervosa is a psychosomatic disorder in which the split between mind and body is sharp. The patient attempts to demonstrate that the mind can subdue and control the body. As Selvini-Palazzoli (1974) explained: ''Every victory over the flesh is a sign of greater control over one's biological impulses'' (p. 74). She strongly argued that such extreme actions should be regarded as statements about autonomy, not as attempts at self-destruction.

The patient's delusional denial of her illness and apparent indifference to her grossly emaciated state is striking. This stubborn and defiant behavior tends to mask underlying feelings of helplessness. The patient's body image disturbance may manifest itself either as a generalized distortion of total body image or as a focus on a particular body part. For instance, a 60-pound teenager may vehemently protest that she is too fat, or while admitting her overall emaciated state, she may insist that her abdomen protrudes.

Subgroups of Anorectic Patients

Restrictors and Bulimic-Vomiters

Several subtypes of anorexia nervosa have been differentiated (Dally, 1969; Janet, 1903). Garfinkel and associates (1980) proposed two major subgroups: ''restrictors,'' who lose weight primarily by abstaining, and ''bulimic-vomiters,'' who tend to alternate between periods of overeating and periods of abstaining. Self-induced vomiting is a frequent but not constant feature in the latter group. Weight control for them is achieved primarily by means of vomiting, laxative abuse, or diuretics. Garfinkel and colleagues noted that bulimics display a number of impulse related problems, including stealing, abuse of alcohol and street drugs, self-mutilation, and suicide attempts. The bulimic subgroup has been identified by a variety of terms. Thus, Beumont and associates (1976) distinguished between "dieters" and "vomiters and purgers"; Russell (1979) discussed the metabolic and emotional consequences of "bulimia nervosa"; and Boskind-Lodahl (1976) coined the term "bulimarexic."

Male Patients

Men and boys with anorexia nervosa are often described as a separate subgroup, although their clinical picture resembles that of female patients in most ways. However, the middle-class or upper class bias is not observed to the same degree in male patients (Palmer, 1980). Some investigators have suggested a somewhat earlier age of onset; a more disturbed underlying pathology, with more marked schizoid and obsessive features; and a more guarded prognosis (Kay & Leigh, 1954). Bulimia and vomiting are noted to be more common in men than in women (Sours, 1974).

Etiological Theories of Anorexia Nervosa

Psychoanalytic Models

Thoma's (1967) view of anorexia nervosa is representative of the older psychoanalytic, drive oriented approach. He emphasized the oral-aggressive and libidinal drive fixation. There is an abandonment of the genital stage of development due to the arousal of inadmissible sexual impulses. The patient's flight from the genital stage is seen on both a subjective and an objective level by the disappearance of conscious impulses, on the one hand, and by the presence of amenorrhea, on the other.

Ego Psychology and Object Relations Approaches

The drive oriented focus has given way to the broader conceptual approach of ego psychology and object relations theory. Bruch (1962) elaborated a developmental model in which faulty learning experiences are thought to result in major ego deficits that predispose to anorexia nervosa. As noted earlier, she stressed perceptual and conceptual disturbances. Bruch hypothesized that these develop in response to maladaptive mother–child interactions in which the child is seen as an "active participant" capable of emitting signs and clues of her inner needs and feelings. Drawing on Piaget's theory of cognitive development, Bruch (1977) concluded that two forms of behavior are necessary in the child's development, those initiated by the child and those made by the child in response to others. Bruch focused on the early feeding relationship between mother and child as the prototype of learning experiences and later relationships. For her, hunger awareness is not an innate process but must be learned through appropriate response on the part of the mother to the child's signs of food deprivation. If the mother's responses are inappropriate or inconsistent or if she superimposes her own needs on the child, the child will develop a "faulty hunger awareness," unable to distinguish nutritional demands from other needs and feelings.

Bruch (1977) noted corresponding difficulties in the child's progress in conceptual development. She described the anorectic individual as stuck in what Piaget termed the "preconceptual concrete operations of early childhood," characterized by egocentrism, literal mindedness, and rigid morality. These children present no particular difficulties during the latency period, when accommodating behavior, robotlike compliance, obedience, and studiousness fit in well with the family's emphasis on achievement and external appearances. Parents in such families present a facade of marital harmony, but they compete with each other as to who has made the greatest sacrifices for the child and, in turn, expect the child to meet their demands for perfection. It is during the crisis of puberty that the child feels helpless and lacking in "internal guideposts." The child may then search for a sense of self-mastery and control through the maladaptive manipulation and control of her body. Selvini-Palazzoli (1974) described how early parent–child interactions may lead to severe difficulties in intrapersonal and interpersonal trust and control in later life. These formulations, while derived independently from Bruch's writings, closely correspond with her beliefs about the psychology and pathogenesis of anorexia nervosa (Bruch, 1977).

Masterson (1977) proposed a developmental object relations approach to anorexia nervosa based on Mahler's theories of development and on his own work with borderline individuals. He hypothesized a developmental arrest at the symbiotic and separation-individuation phases due to the mother's withdrawal of nurturance in the face of the child's efforts to separate. The result is a failure of ego development, in which self and object are not adequately differentiated and positive and negative characteristics are not integrated and recognized as coexisting in self or object.

Masterson (1977) identified puberty as a crisis for the child that renews anxiety and separation fears in the context of demands for autonomy. He postulated that at this point the anorexia nervosa symptoms serve a number of adaptive and defensive purposes. The avoidance of physical, sexual, and emotional growth relieves the individual's separation anxieties and abandonment fears. The obsessive control mechanisms around food and weight substitute for individuative feelings. Finally, there is a discharge of emotion to the ambivalently regarded object, both provoking the mother's attention and expressing the daughter's hostility.

Sours's (1969, 1974) views on the etiology of anorexia nervosa reflect a combination of the traditional psychoanalytic approach and the later approaches of ego psychology and object relations theory. His findings support those of both Bruch and Selvini-Palazzoli (1974).

Psychosexual Regression

Crisp (1965, 1980) defined the central psychological issue in anorexia nervosa as conflict over body weight and shape, representing concerns about psychosexual maturity. Crisp (1980) placed particular emphasis on the biological regression of the anorectic patient to a subpubertal weight, which he viewed as basically an avoidance or a defensive posture. He suggested that other investigators attribute undue significance to self-control and increased autonomy that the individual experiences as a result of initial success in weight control and have accordingly mistakenly considered the disorder as rooted primarily in this experience. Palmer (1980) basically adopted Crisp's view of anorexia nervosa as a "psychobiological regression."

In general, Crisp and collegues (Kalucy et al., 1977) concluded that some families are ill equipped for, and prepare their children inadequately for, the adolescent phase of development. Family members share an unusual preoccupation with weight, shape, and eating behavior. There is an emphasis on oral-dependent aspects of development rather than on aggressive, sexual, and independent strivings. The result is a narrow range of coping mechanisms for the child and restricted ego growth. Families tend to emphasize good nutrition and physical fitness as evidence of family cohesiveness and personal stability. There may be a history of weight pathology in the parents. Crisp reported that the anorectic individual tends to have been premorbidly obese, with a history of childhood overfeeding, fast growth, and early puberty. The child tends to adopt the parental value that weight control is tantamount to self-control and impulse control.

Sociocultural Factors

Sociocultural factors are considered to play a key role in the etiology of anorexia nervosa. The alarming increase in the frequency of the disorder may be related to the recent cultural emphasis on thinness, health, fitness, and good nutrition. It has been suggested that the media convey the message that weight control brings self-control, beauty, and success (e.g., Bruch, 1978; Garner et al., 1980).

As noted earlier, although anorexia nervosa has long been associated with higher social classes, some investigators have observed that the disorder is now more evenly distributed among all classes, suggesting the widespread impact of the media in the spread of common values (Garner & Garfinkel 1980; Theander, 1970). Garner and Garfinkel noted the recent increased incidence of the disorder among dance and modeling students, among whom there is an explicit emphasis on physical appearance.

Selvini-Palazzoli (1974) pointed out that women are increasingly exposed to social pressures as a result of the transition from agrarian to modern industrial society. According to her, modern women encounter contradictory and irreconcilable role models, expected, on the one hand, to be successful and competitive with men and, on the other, to maintain the more traditional values of femininity, passivity, and beauty.

Family Factors

Minuchin and associates (1978) advocated a systems approach to anorexia nervosa in which the child is seen "in context" as a member of her family: "Anorexia is defined therefore not only by the behavior of one family member, but also by the interrelationship of all family members" (p. 21). Minuchin and colleagues contrasted this approach to the linear model of illness, in which many factors are considered to be relevant but ultimately they all converge on the individual, who is considered to be the passive recipient of their effects. By way of contrast, in the systems model, illness operates in the "feedback processes" among the child, the family, and the extrafamilial environment. The family programs the child's behavior but the child, in turn, controls the family behavior.

Minuchin and associates (1978) postulated that families in which a member has a psychosomatic illness have characteristic transactional patterns that predispose to the development of somatic symptoms. They presented a nonspecific model of families with a child suffering from a variety of psychosomatic illnesses including diabetes, asthma, and anorexia nervosa. The following characteristics were noted:

enmeshment:* family relationships are intense; weak boundaries between members result in intrusion into each other's thoughts and feelings; autonomy and self-realization are sacrificed for family loyalty and protectiveness

overprotectiveness: family members are overly concerned with each other's welfare and sensitive to high levels of stress or tension; parents demonstrate an intrusive concern in the child's psychobiological needs, resulting in hypervigilance on the part of the child, who becomes a "parent watcher"; this restricts the child's development of autonomy and involvement outside the family

rigidity: families are committed to maintaining the status quo and have difficulty relinquishing accustomed patterns during such periods as adolescence, when there is a need for increased age-appropriate autonomy

lack of conflict resolution: the family's ability to engage in conflict resolution is very low and disagreement is diffused for the sake of harmony or closeness.

Minuchin and co-workers (1978) concluded that the child's involvement in parental conflict is a key factor in the development and maintenance of psychosomatic symptoms. The child's illness functions to diffuse or regulate marital conflict in several ways. In "triangulation," the child may be openly pressed to side with one parent against the other or may switch sides depending on the circumstances. An alternate arrangement is the child's entering a "stable coalition" with one parent against the other. A third pattern, "detouring" occurs when parents submerge their conflict in a united posture of blaming or protecting their sick child.

Minuchin and associates' (1978) systems approach places less emphasis on etiology than on the maintenance of the illness. The focus in treatment is on current pathological patterns that reinforce the symptoms (Minuchin & Fishman, 1979).

Selvini-Palazzoli (1974) gradually moved from a more traditional psychoanalytic point of view to a family systems orientation. In 1965, she and her colleagues at the Milan Center of Family Studies became interested in Haley's work with families of schizophrenics and began to examine family systems that resulted in the development of anorexia nervosa symptoms in children. Selvini-Palazzoli reported that these families communicated in a coherent manner, unlike families with a schizophrenic member; rejection of messages among family members was prevalent; all family members had difficulty assuming leadership or stat-

* See the excellent commentary by Aponte and Hoffman (1973), which described Minuchin's portrayal of "open doors" as a metaphor for the concept of enmeshment.

ing what they wanted in the first person; and "covert coalitions" were the central problem. Since an open alliance between any two family members would not be permitted, "perverse triangles" emerge. Frequently, the patient is invited to be a "secret ally" by both parents and in effect to make up to each parent for the shortcomings of the other. Consequently, the patient is put in the position of having to divide her resources between the two parents, with little means or energy left to build an autonomous life. Selvini-Palazzoli noted that a "spirit of self-sacrifice" characterized such families, with the result that no one was prepared to assume responsibility when anything went wrong. Finally, parents maintained a facade of respectability and unity that concealed an underlying deep disillusionment in their marriage; the patient served as the go-between in this unhappy situation.

Trigger Events

Just as there is no single predisposing factor to anorexia nervosa, there is no single precipitant. As in other psychiatric disorders, a number of events ranging from separation, loss, or death of a family member to disruption of family homeostasis through a parent's loss of a job, new adolescent demands, or perceived academic or social failure may trigger the illness. Occasionally, a physical illness with loss of weight may antedate the anorexia nervosa. Common to all these events is the threat to the individual's sense of self-worth or control over the environment (Garfinkel & Garner, 1982). The result is an intense preoccupation with the body and the belief that by losing weight all problems will be solved. Not every individual who is exposed to the various risk factors will develop the illness. It is the combination of individual, familial, and sociocultural vulnerabilities arising within the context of the individual's life at critical points that renders the individual unable to cope at that particular moment and therefore susceptible to developing the syndrome of anorexia nervosa (Garfinkel & Garner, 1982).

Treatment Issues and Approaches in Anorexia Nervosa

Once anorexia nervosa is set in motion, various factors sustain it (Garfinkel & Garner, 1982). Starvation symptoms and gastrointestinal difficulties such as an altered sense of satiety or bloating after meals may heighten fear of loss of self-control. The resolve to cut back further on eating may ensue. Vomiting entrenches the syndrome by providing a partial solution to the patient's dilemma. Various prescribed procedures, such as force feeding, also may intensify the patient's fears. And as with other illnesses, secondary gain may be a sustaining factor.

Treatment in the history of anorexia nervosa has ranged from a variety of hormonal preparations (thyroid extract, calf pituitary hormone implants, testosterone) to force feeding, electroconvulsive therapy, and even leucotomy. The reader is referred to Garfinkel and Garner (1982) for a discussion of the different pharmacotherapies in anorexia nervosa.

Initial Contact

Social workers and other mental health practitioners increasingly encounter anorexia nervosa in a wide variety of settings. Because the illness has very serious physical manifestations and sequelae, a nonmedical therapist treating an anorectic patient must have the full support of a physician with access to inpatient facilities. A patient suspected of suffering from anorexia nervosa should be medically examined and should undergo certain routine laboratory tests to eliminate the possibility of any organic cause for the illness.

Anorectic patients often are referred for help by family or friends. The parents are frequently in an uproar, having experienced intense feelings of rage and impotence at seeing their daughter starving herself. Family power struggles become commonplace. It is difficult to determine whether these are more the consequence or the cause of the illness. The therapist must avoid an attitude of blame or censure and endeavour to form a working alliance with *all* family members. Nonetheless, it is crucial to separate out individual issues with the identified patient to gain her trust and cooperation. Most important, the individual or family therapist should use a flexible approach that can readily be adapted to meet the needs in each case.

Weight Restoration

In both outpatient and inpatient treatment situations, it is essential that both weight restoration and underlying psychological and family issues be addressed. The physiological effects of a very low weight must be corrected before any meaningful psychotherapy can proceed (Bruch, 1978; Garfinkel & Garner, 1982).

A target weight within the normal range should be established to permit an eventual return of menses (Garner et al., 1981). This target weight should include a range of several pounds to allow for normal daily fluctuations. At the same time, the patient must be reassured that the purpose of the treatment is not simply to "fatten her up" and that she will not be allowed to become obese. Therefore, certain external controls must be provided. The various methods for safely restoring weight within the context of a therapeutic relationship have been discussed in detail elsewhere (Crisp, 1965; Garner et al., 1981; Russell, 1977) and will not be reviewed here.

Psychoanalytic Treatment

While psychoanalysis has been advocated (Sours, 1974; Thoma, 1967), certain features of both the patient and the technique mitigate its general usefulness in anorexia nervosa. Bruch (1973, 1978) faulted the psychoanalytic approach for re-creating the patient's original life situation, in which so-called interpretations are handed down, creating the impression that the person does not really know herself. Bruch recommended a fact finding approach in which patients are allowed to discover their own feelings, sensations, and impulses.

Individual Psychotherapy

Bruch (1977) argued that the crux of treatment for the anorectic patient must be individual therapy. Focus is on correcting the individual's distortions in cognition and perception and her underlying ineffectiveness. Bruch stressed the patient's being an active participant in this process. The goal of treatment is the establishment of a sense of autonomy and a self-directed identity. Although the restitution of normal nutrition is a requisite for effective psychotherapy, Bruch (1977) warned that this goal must be approached cautiously to avoid psychic damage to the patient. Selvini-Palazzoli's (1974) approach to individual psychotherapy in anorexia nervosa agrees essentially with Bruch's. Masterson (1977), using object relations theory, took Bruch's and Selvini-Palazzoli's approaches in a different direction by focusing on separation and individuation. He suggested that rage and depression are central issues to tackle in therapy.

Integrated Approach to Therapy

Garfinkel and Garner (1982) advocated a multidimensional psychotherapy in which individual, family, behavioral, and drug approaches are combined to create a synergistic effect. The cornerstone of their approach is a relationship type of psychotherapy that integrates concepts from several models.

Crisp (1980) advocated an inpatient program that emphasizes weight control, social skills training, and individual and family therapy. He stressed the patient's need to face her weight phobia through confrontation with normal pubertal weight. The patient is informed that this will help her in becoming more aware of her underlying sexual fears so that meaningful therapy can proceed. Sours (1980) criticized this approach as too direct, reinforcing feelings of ineffectiveness and helplessness, rather than strengthening the ego.

Behavioral Therapy

In recent years, behavioral therapies have been increasingly popular in the treatment of anorexia nervosa. Minuchin and associates (1978) however, specified that behavioral therapies remain in the tradition of the linear cause–effect approach, in which the target of intervention is the maladaptive learning "within" the individual. Thus, even when interventions are directed at other family members, they are aimed at changing the behaviors toward the patient that reinforce the inappropriate behavior.

The reader may consult Bemis (1978) or Garfinkel and associates (1977a,b) for reviews of the literature on behavior modification in the treatment of anorexia nervosa. Operant techniques, based on Skinnerian principles of positive reinforcement, have frequently been employed in the context of hospitalization. They have been lauded as successfully achieving rapid weight gain and avoiding the adverse effects of somatic therapy. On the other hand, these techniques have elicited much criticism. Bruch (1974) dismissed behavioral techniques as psychologically damaging and potentially dangerous in inducing suicidal behavior. She cautioned that forcing the patient to eat in spite of intense fears about weight gain will exacerbate the patient's profound sense of helplessness and ineffectiveness. In general, behavioral techniques have been criticized for placing undue emphasis on rapid weight gain: the patient may eat to get out of the hospital but not maintain the gain. Eating large amounts to achieve a target weight gain of one-half pound per day was criticized by Bemis (1978) as an "official endorsement of bulimia."

Family Therapy

Selvini-Palazzoli (1974) and Minuchin and associates (1978) both advocated a family therapy approach to the treatment of anorexia nervosa.

Redefining the nature of pathology, they shifted the focus of therapy from the sick individual to the sick individual in the family. The goal is to challenge the dysfunctional patterns that maintain the symptomatic behavior, that is, to develop more effective transactional patterns that encourage healthier, more adaptive family interaction.

At the same time, these clinicians would implement change in the family system in different ways.

In the approach followed by Minuchin and associates (1978), the therapist "joins" the family and forms a new "therapeutic system" of which she is the leader. A number of maneuvers are used to challenge enmeshment, overprotectiveness, rigidity, and lack of ability to resolve conflict. One of these techniques, called "enactment" requires the creation of interpersonal scenarios in which family members are asked to play out their problems in the present. The "family lunch session" explores firsthand the crucial family context. The underlying aims of the session are to change the status of the patient with the family (i.e., from sick child to disobedient child), to translate an eating problem into a problem of interpersonal relationships, and to disengage parents from using the child's eating behaviors as a conflict detouring device. Various techniques of "boundary making" are used to support the individual's autonomy. For example, everyone must speak for himself. Boundaries are not compatible with conflict avoidance, so family members are forced to resolve their disputes.

Minuchin and associates (1978) reported an 86% success rate in their survey of 53 cases of anorexia nervosa. Treatment consisted of short-term hospitalization in a behaviorally oriented program for the purpose of weight gain, in conjunction with family therapy sessions and follow-up ranging from three months to four years. Minuchin and associates have tended to treat younger anorectic patients, which may partially explain their statistical success.

In Selvini-Palazzoli's (1974) approach to family therapy, sessions are highly structured. A contract of 10 or 20 sessions with the family is usual. The interval between sessions is approximately four weeks. Frequently, four therapists participate in a session, two directly with the family and two observing behind a one-way screen. The family is informed that they will receive a number of "directives" throughout the treatment and that the success of the therapy is dependent upon their implementation. The family sessions are primarily to help the therapists gather information and devise appropriate interventions for the family to perform at home. The therapists deliver their messages in a cryptic manner and generally appear to maintain a great deal of distance from family members. This mode contrasts sharply with the "experiential approach" of Munichin and associates (1978) in which the therapist is very involved, at times forming a coalition with one individual against another.

The method of "positive connotation" is pivotal to Selvini-Palazzoli's (1974) approach. She argued that it is essential to adopt this stance in order to gain entry into the family system. The therapists reframe any actions of family members in a positive fashion to demonstrate family members' love and desire for family unity and cohesion. Frequently, the patient is prescribed the very symptom she presents. The patient is advised not to attempt to gain weight too quickly and reassured that the therapists are most sympathetic to the dangers she envisions. The parents are also advised not to change any of their usual behaviors for the time being. This puts the patient in a therapeutic double bind: the symptoms she claimed to be involuntary are the very ones that the therapists prescribe; the only way out for the patient is to rebel against the therapists, which means, paradoxically, to abandon her symptoms.

Group Therapy

Group therapy has received relatively little attention in the literature on anorexia nervosa. Polivy (1981) suggested that negative attributes of these patients such as their narcissism, manipulativeness, and obsessive self-concern have raised questions on the part of clinicians as to the appropriateness of group work. Drawing on her experience with a small group of more verbal and psychologically minded anorectic individuals, Polivy concluded that these patients can function as a supportive, cohesive group. However, Polivy cautioned that such groups can also teach symptoms and foster an anorectic identity. The reader can consult Crisp (1980), Grossniklaus (1980), Schmitt (1980), and Sclare (1977) for further discussion of the use of peer groups in the treatment of anorexia nervosa.

Rose and Garfinkel (1980) described the use of a parents' group in the management of anorexia nervosa for parents for whom family therapy was contraindicated. The group was largely educational and supportive in focus and was considered successful in achieving these aims. The group functioned to minimize unfortunate sequelae in parents and siblings and at times facilitated a family's entrance into family therapy. The major limitations of the group were the lack of development of insight around family maladaptive functioning and the lack of acceptance of parental responsibility in the disorder. Piazza and associates (1980) also discussed the use of a parents' group designed to foster cooperation between parents and inpatient staff.

Inpatient Treatment

Hospitalization is frequently a necessary phase in the overall management of anorexia nervosa. It may be essential for weight restoration in an emaciated patient and is occasionally dictated as a lifesaving measure. Hospitalization also can be helpful in disengaging patient and family from the futile struggle over control centered on food. Thus, weight restoration and stabilization of eating patterns can proceed along with exploration of the psychological and family factors underlying the illness.

A specific treatment approach to anorexia nervosa has been developed by the psychosomatic medicine unit of the Clarke Institute of Psychiatry in Toronto. Modified bed rest, high caloric intake, and supportive nursing care are the foundation upon which the program is built. Bed rest with a graduated level of activity and privileges based on weight gain serves serveral purposes. Putting the patient to bed breaks through the strong denial and underlines the nature of the illness. It also keeps patients from excessive exercise and demonstrates that they will not be allowed to be out of control. Meals are supervised by trained nursing staff, who provide on-the-spot emotional support to patients as they begin to confront their weight phobia. Nursing staff are familiar with the various subterfuges patients employ to get rid of food (e.g., hiding it in bedclothes or pillows) and are able to confront such self-defeating actions in a nonthreatening manner. Staff are aware that these behaviors are not signs of maliciousness but reflections of intense anxiety and fear associated with the consequences of eating.

Patients are started on a 1,200–1,500-calorie daily diet, which is gradually increased to 3,000–3,600 after one to two weeks. This stepwise increase in calories tends to avoid the complication of gastric dilatation, which may result from rapid refeeding of extremely emaciated patients (Garfinkel & Garner, 1982).

In group and, sometimes, in individual sessions, the dietician teaches patients about nutrition and helps them plan well-balanced meals. The patient is encouraged to confront and overcome her anxieties about feared foods. The underlying rationale is that experiencing anxiety is a necessary step to overcoming a phobia. The patient is put on a maintenance diet after attaining responsibility for her food intake prior to discharge. Since feedback is considered the most important variable in patients' success in gaining weight (Agras et al., 1974), they are made aware of the correlation between weight gain or weight maintenance and caloric intake.

Patients are gradually introduced into a variety of therapeutic groups and activities on the ward. Discussion groups and life skills training provide opportunities to deal with interpersonal problems, self-assertion, and decisionmaking. Nursing staff and an occupational therapist offer psychocalisthenics, music and movement therapy, and supervised gym periods to encourage awareness of the body and moderation in exercise. Craft activities permit exploration of individual interests and self-expression. Free time and relaxation time are important for the anorectic individual, who has long held to a rigid schedule of frantic activity.

Reintegration into the community through increasingly long leaves and job and school planning are part of the preparation for discharge. Daycare for some patients facilitates the transition from hospital to community. Length of hospitalization varies from two to four months and should allow for attainment of a healthy weight followed by a period of maintenance. Occasionally, a day program offers a means of dealing with a crisis that occurs after discharge and avoiding rehospitalization.

Individual and family therapy begin during the hospital stay. Long-term follow-up—whether individual, family, or both—is important to the maintenance of the individual's well-being. As part of the follow-up, weight is checked at regular intervals.

The Social Worker as a Member of a Multidisciplinary Team

Social work intervention in the treatment of anorexia nervosa covers the spectrum of services from individual, group, and family therapy to vocational rehabilitation, community liaison work, group home placement, teaching, and research. In my experience, it is in the area of family treatment for anorexia nervosa that the social worker can make the most significant contribution.

The opens systems model, outlined by Minuchin and associates (1978) and Selvini-Palazzoli (1974), offers the clinician a practical framework within which the patient and her family may be viewed in terms of reciprocal transactions. Behavior is simultaneously caused and causative. In viewing the family as the patient, there is greater likelihood that the family will be understood and respected, whatever its weaknesses, defenses, and resistances. An important function of the family therapist on a multidisciplinary team is to share insights into the family dynamics. The goal is to minimize scapegoating attitudes toward the family and to reduce the likelihood that similar distortions will be perpetuated in the individual therapy.

Families vary in their willingness to assume the patient role. The therapist must adopt a flexible approach. At times, it is not possible for the family to participate in ongoing therapy because of constraints like physical distance. Nonetheless, it is crucial to secure their minimal commitment to a family assessment.

Family sessions may include all family members, parents only, or siblings only, as appropriate. If the patient is married, there will also be marital therapy. The role of family therapy in the treatment of anorexia nervosa is exemplified in the following case vignettes.

Nancy, age 18, one of five siblings, had a 2-year history of anorexia nervosa. Nancy had assumed the familiar anorectic role of taking charge of the kitchen and feeding others while starving herself. A most striking feature of this family was pervasive depression. Nancy's anorexia nervosa appeared to be symbolic of the emotional starvation of the family. This case is reminiscent of Conrad's (1977) discussion of "a starving family."

The mother was encouraged to exercise her authority and reclaim her role in the kitchen; Nancy was discouraged from playing the role of substitute spouse to her mother, then directed to a more appropriate alliance with her sibling subgroup; the father' was to resume his rightful place as companion and spouse to his wife. Total family sessions freed up blocked affective expression. Focus was cast on the marital couple's inability to express anger and affection, which reflected underlying fears of abandonment and engulfment. The parent's commitment to resolve their emotional estrangement not only emancipated Nancy, the identified patient, but also safeguarded against the possibility that a sibling would move into a similar role.

Susan, the second of three sisters, developed anorexia nervosa at age 17. She was caught in the role of the "good girl" and was closely allied to both parents in a situation akin to Selvini-Palazzoli's (1974) "three-way matrimony." The older sister was equally stuck in her role as family rebel and scapegoat. The younger sister, more independent and outgoing, maintained a somewhat distant stance but secretly resented being overlooked at home. Family sessions explored the mutual resentment and tested out new behaviors and expanded roles. Marital therapy relieved Susan of her overinvolvement in the parents' relationship.

Judy was a 35-year-old married patient. She had a four-year history of anorexia nervosa, with bulimia and vomiting. In the marital sessions, it was apparent that the symptoms were related to serious dissatisfaction with the marriage. Negative feelings were not allowed expression due to a strong conflict avoidance posture on the part of both partners. Conjoint marital therapy allowed the couple to address their conflicts in a more direct and open fashion.

Prognosis in Anorexia Nervosa

Anorexia nervosa varies from an acute self-limiting disorder to a chronic debilitating illness with significant morbidity and mortality (Crisp, 1965b; Garfinkel & Garner, 1982; Morgan & Russell, 1975; Russell, 1977). Garfinkel and Darby (1981) concluded that at the present time approximately 70% of treated patients are totally relieved of their symptoms or are improved to the extent that they can lead normal lives. Criteria for successful outcome include resumption of menses, normal fertility, and normal capacity for relationships, intimacy, and work adjustment. Approximately 20% of patients develop a chronic illness in which there are repeated episodes of weight loss, bulimia and vomiting, social isolation, and depression. Garfinkel and Darby reported a mortality of 5–10%, associated with starvation, complications of refeeding, and, occasionally, suicide. A more favorable prognosis is indicated by the following factors: earlier onset; absence of bulimia, vomiting, and laxative abuse; good premorbid educational and vocational adjustment; less body image disturbance; less obsessional personality; and less severe family pathology (Garfinkel & Darby, 1981).

Research Questions in Anorexia Nervosa

The field of anorexia nervosa presents a wide scope for investigation on the part of social workers. The paucity of social work contributions is surprising given the profession's commitment to working with families. The role of the family has long been acknowledged as significant in the syndrome, but studies to date have included inadequate controls. Comments about typical family attributes and relationship patterns tend to be anecdotal in nature. Furthermore, the studies that have been conducted have been retrospective, making it difficult to distinguish predisposing factors from current patterns.

Large-scale prospective studies, though methodologically difficult, could shed light on risk factors in anorexia nervosa. Investigation of the subtypes of anorectics also could prove fruitful. Future research might compare family communication patterns in restricting, bulimic, schizophrenic, and nonpsychiatric populations. Well-controlled studies measuring the relative effectiveness of the various psychotherapies (individual, family, group) in anorexia nervosa would enhance the therapeutic armamentarium of clinicians.

Obesity

Obesity is often veiwed as the counterpart of anorexia nervosa. In both conditions, the eating function may be misused in an effort to solve or camouflage problems of living. In both conditions, afflicted individuals are conspicuous by their appearance (Bruch, 1973). However, in contrast to anorexia nervosa, obesity is not a psychiatric condition per se. And just as anorexia nervosa is not a uniform syndrome with a single pathogen, there is even more evidence that obesity is a complex disorder with multiple predisposing factors.

Bruch (1973) recommended adopting a systems point of view when examining the etiology of obesity: physiological, psychological, and environmental factors must be seen in interaction rather than opposition. She further distinguished between predisposing (primary) factors in the development of obesity and ramifications of the obese state (secondary factors) caused by social stigma and rejection. These factors should not be confused with conflicts precipitated by the active state of dieting.

Types of Obesity

Bruch (1973) developed a tripartite classification of obesity. The first group includes "many competent people who are heavy, probably in accordance with their constitutional make-up, whose weight excess is not related to abnormal psychological functioning" (p. 124). Weight excess in this group tends to be moderate and fairly stable. Reducing efforts may prove successful or the person may come to accept the excess weight as appropriate to his body build. Individuals in this group may or may not suffer from a variety of psychiatric difficulties that are not directly related to their weight. Bruch directed her attention to the other two groups, "developmental obesity" and "reactive obesity."

Developmental obesity, with childhood onset, is intimately involved in the whole personaltiy and associated with many types of disturbance. Bruch (1973) drew parallels between this disorder and anorexia nervosa, explaining both conditions as the result of faulty mother–child interactions in which the child ultimately fails to distinguish hunger needs from other physical needs or emotional states. Thus, food might either be used as an all-purpose pacifier or reward or be withheld as a punishment. According to Bruch, the obese child is often dominated by a possessive, clinging mother, who discourages any self-initiated behavior and exploration outside the family orbit. The child is accordingly isolated and her inactivity is significant. In both anorexia nervosa and developmental obesity, faulty family transactions result in distortions in body image, disturbances in cognition of internal states (hunger, satiety, fatigue, etc.), feelings of ineffectiveness, and unstable personal identity.

Bruch (1973) acknowledged the genetic potential for obesity, which has been elaborated by Hirsch and Gallian (1968), that is, the high adipose cell count in obese infants. However, Bruch emphasized that it is the interaction of the high adipose count with such environmental factors as overfeeding and inactivity that results in lasting obesity.

Reactive obesity generally occurs suddenly in adults not previously overweight. This disorder follows a traumatic event such as the death of, or separation from, a close person. The obesity serves a defensive or protective function in individuals who might otherwise succumb to deep depression, suicidal despair, or psychotic breakdown. Individuals with reactive obesity are described as more mature and better integrated than individuals with developmental obesity. They do not demonstrate the extreme disturbance in body image and such pronounced perceptual and conceptual distortions.

Obesity is usually classified by degree of severity. "Mild obesity" means 20–30% overweight; obesity in this group is likely to be of adult onset. "Moderate obesity" means 30–100% overweight. "Severe obesity,'' or ''superobesity,'' means more than 100% above ideal weight; this category would likely include those individuals with developmental obesity.

Treatment of Obesity

Treatment of obese persons includes a wide range of interventions determined by thorough assessment of each case. Bruch (1973) recommended a simple fact finding, noninterpretive psychotherapeutic approach to treat individuals with developmental and reactive obesity; this method is similar to the one she would use with anorectic patients. However, she stressed that the therapy is not directed to weight loss per se and that only after the individual has acquired some insight into her self-defeating patterns will she be ready to diet under medical supervision.

The discouraging results with traditional medical treatment of obesity have prompted the development of behavioral therapies and self-help approaches (Schachter & Rodin, 1974). These may be appropriate for mild to moderate obesity. The reader is directed to Mahoney and Mahoney (1976) for a review of behavioral techniques. The relative success of self-help groups such as TOPS (Take Off Pounds Successfully) and Weight Watchers was reviewed by Stuart and Mitchell (1979) and by Stunkard (1972). Orbach (1978) described a self-help group approach with a feminist orientation that incorporates various psychotherapeutic and behavioral principles and exercises to promote self-acceptance and responsibility for one's body. Therapy is directed toward breaking the addictive quality of eating rather than losing weight per se. Garner and associates (1978) speculated on the way in which self-help groups strengthen awareness of inappropriate eating patterns.

Jejunoileal bypass surgery (Bray, 1978) and, more recently, gastric stapling have been recommended for certain severely obese individuals with whom a traditional methods have proven ineffective. In spite of potential complications, surgery offers promising results: permanent weight loss, increased assertiveness, enhanced self-esteem, increased social activity, and improved vocational adjustment. The gastric stapling procedure seems to offer the same benefits as bypass surgery but has fewer complications. Marshall and Neill (1977), in a discussion of a group of 12 massively obese individuals who had undergone bypass surgery, noted the above mentioned individual improvements; however, they also discussed the effects of the surgery on the marital system of the patients and observed increased conflict within the marriage and a striking pattern of reciprocal changes in the areas of sexuality and dependence–independence parameters. They suggested that better understanding of the protective function of massive obesity within the marital system would yield information useful in determining more appropriate selection criteria for surgery, in obtaining a broader informed consent, and in providing more effective postoperative mananagement.

Obesity is a complex phenomenon, and each case must be thoroughly evaluated to determine the treatment of choice. Although psychosocial approaches have not proven effective for weight loss, psychotherapy may be invaluable as an indirect approach to obesity. The need for marital and family therapies, which have not been described, should also be assessed with respect to each client. Behavioral and self-help therapies appear to offer the most promising results in terms of short-term weight loss. Surgery may be an appropriate alternative for massively obese individuals who have not responded to traditional approaches.

References

AGRAS WS, BARLOW DH, CHAPLIN HN, et al: Behavior modification of anorexia nervosa. *Arch Gen Psychiatry* 1974; 30:279–286.

American Psychiatric Association: *Diagnostic and Statistical Manual of Mental Disorders*, ed 3. Washington, DC, American Psychiatric Association, 1980.

APONTE H, HOFFMAN L: The open door: a structural approach to a family with an a anorectic child. *Fam Process* 1973; 12:1–44.

BEMIS KM: Current approaches to the etiology and treatment of anorexia nervosa. *Psychol Bull* 1978; 85:593–617.

BEUMONT PJV, BEARDWOOD CJ, RUSSELL GFM: The occurrence of the syndrome of anorexia nervosa in male subjects. *Psychol Med* 1972; 2:216–231.

BEUMONT PJV, GEORGE GCW, SMART DE: "Dieters" and "vomiters and purgers" in anorexia nervosa. *Psychol Med* 1976; 6:617–622.

BOSKIND–LODAHL M: Cinderella's step-sisters: a feminist perspective on anorexia nervosa and bulimia. *Signs* 1976; 2:342–356.

BRAY GA: Intestinal bypass surgery for obese patients: behavioral and metabolic considerations. *Psychiatr Clin North Am* 1978; 1:673–689.

BRUCH H: Perceptual and conceptual disturbances in anorexia nervosa. *Psychosom Med* 1962; 24:187–194.

BRUCH H: *Eating Disorders: Obesity, Anorexia Nervosa, and the Person Within*. New York, Basic Books, 1973.

BRUCH H: Perils of behavior modification in treatment of anorexia nervosa. *JAMA* 1974; 230:1419–1422.

BRUCH H: Psychological antecedents of anorexia nervosa, in Vigersky RA (ed): *Anorexia Nervosa*. New York, Raven, 1977.

BRUCH H: *The Golden Cage: The Enigma of Anorexia Nervosa*. Cambridge, Harvard University Press, 1978.

CONRAD DE: A starving family: an interactional view of anorexia nervosa. *Bull Menninger Clin* 1977; 41:487–495.

CRISP AH: Clinical and therapeutic aspects of anorexia nervosa: a study of 30 cases. *J Psychosom Res* 1965; 9:67–68. (a)

CRISP AH: Some aspects of the evolution, presentation, and follow-up of anorexia nervosa. *Proc Soc Med* 1965; 58:814–820. (b)

CRISP AH: Anorexia nervosa: "feeding disorder," "nervous malnutrition," or "weight phobia"?. *World Rev Nutr Diet* 1970; 12:452–504.

CRISP AH: The differential diagnosis of anorexia nervosa. *Proc R Soc Med* 1977; 70:686–690.

CRISP AH: *Anorexia Nervosa: Let Me Be.* New York, Grune & Stratton, 1980.

CRISP AH, PALMER RL, KALUCY RS: How common is anorexia nervosa: a prevalence study. *Br J Psychiatry* 1976; 218:549–554.

DALLY P: *Anorexia Nervosa.* London, Heineman, 1969.

FRISCH RE, MCARTHUR JW: Menstrual cycles: fatness as a determinant of minimum weight for height necessary for their maintenance or onset. *Science* 1974; 185:949–951.

GARFINKEL PE, DARBY PL: Anorexia nervosa. *Med Clin North Am* 1981; 12:1263–1269.

GARFINKEL PE, GARNER DM: Anorexia nervosa: A multidimensional perspective, in Barrows S (ed): New York, Brunner/Mazel, 1982.

GARFINKEL PE, MOLDOFSKY H, GARNER DM: The outcome of anorexia nervosa: significance of clinical features, body image, and behavior modification, in Vigersky RA (ed): *Anorexia Nervosa.* New York, Raven, 1977. (a)

GARFINKEL PE, MOLDOFSKY H, GARNER DM: The role of behaviour modification in the treatment of anorexia nervosa. *J Pediatr Psychol* 1977. 2:113–121. (b)

GARFINKEL PE, MOLDOFSKY H, GARNER DM: The heterogeneity of anorexia nervosa: bulimia as a distinct subgroup. *Arch Gen Psychiatry* 1980; 37:1036–1040.

GARNER DM, GARFINKEL PE: Socio-cultural factors in the development of anorexia nervosa. *Psychol Med* 1980; 10:647–656.

GARNER DM, GARFINKEL PE, BEMIS KM: A multidimensional psychotherapy for anorexia nervosa. *Int J Eating Disorders* 1981; 1.

GARNER DM, GARFINKEL PE, MOLDOFSKY H: Perceptual experiences in anorexia nervosa and obesity. *Can Psychiatr Assoc J* 1978; 23:249–263.

GARNER DM, GARFINKEL PE, SCHWARTZ, D, et al: Cultural expectations of thinness in women. *Psychol Rep* 1980; 47:483–491.

GARROW JS, CRISP AH, JORDAN HA, et al: Pathology of eating, in Silverstone T (ed): *Dahlem Conferences: Life Sciences Research Report.* Berlin, 1975, vol 2.

GROSSNIKLAUS DM: Nursing interventions in anorexia nervosa. *Perspect Psychiatr Care* 1980; 18:11–16.

GULL WW: Anorexia nervosa, in Kaufman RM, Heiman M (ed): *Evolution of Psychosomatic Concepts: Anorexia Nervosa, A Paradigm.* New York, International Universities Press, 1964.

HIRSCH J, GALLIAN E: Methods for the determination of adipose cell size in man and animals. *J Lipid Res* 1968; 9:110–119.

JANET P: *Les obsessions et la psychasthenie.* Paris, Alcan, 1903.

JONES DJ, FOX MM, BABIGAN HM, et al: Epidemiology of anorexia nervosa in Monroe County, New York, 1960–1976. *Psychosom Med* 1980; 42:551–558.

KALUCY RS, CRISP AH, HARDING B: A study of 56 families with anorexia nervosa. *Br J Med Psychol* 1977; 50:381–395.

KAY DWK, LEIGH D: Natural history, treatment, and prognosis of anorexia nervosa, based on study of 38 patients. *J Ment Sci* 1954; 100:411–431.

KELLETT J, TRIMBLE M, THORLEY A: Anorexia nervosa after the menopause. *Br J Psychiatry* 1976; 128:555–558.

KEYS A, BROZEK J, HENSCHEL A, et al: *The Biology of Human Starvation.* Minneapolis, University of Minnesota Press, 1950, vol 1.

LASEGUE C: , in Kaufman RM, Heiman M (eds): *Evolution of Psychosomatic Concepts: Anorexia Nervosa, a Paradigm.* New York, International Universities Press, 1964.

MAHONEY MJ, MAHONEY K: *Permanent Weight Control: A Total Solution to the Dieter's Dilemma.* New York, Norton, 1976.

MARSHALL JR, NEIL J: The removal of a psychosomatic symptom: effects on the marriage. *Fam Process* 1977; 16:273–280.

MASTERSON JF: Primary anorexia nervosa in the borderline adolescent: an object-relations view, in Hartocollis P (ed): *Borderline Personality Disorders.* New York, International Universities Press, 1977.

MEISSNER WW: Family dynamics and psychosomatic processes. *Fam Process* 1966; 5:142–161.

MINUCHIN S, FISHMAN HC: The psychosomatic family in child psychiatry. *J Am Acad Child Psychiatry* 1979; 18: 76–90.

MINUCHIN S, ROSMAN BL, BAKER L: *Psychosomatic Families: Anorexia Nervosa in Context.* Cambridge, Harvard University Press, 1978.

MORGAN HG, RUSSELL GFM: Value of family background and clinical features as predictors of long-term outcome in anorexia nervosa: four-year follow-up study of 41 patients. *Psychol Med* 1975; 5:355–371.

MORTON R: *Phthisiologica: or a Treatise of Consumptions.* London, 1689.

ORBACH S: *Fat Is a Feminist Issue.* London, Paddington, 1978.

PALMER RL: *Anorexia Nervosa: A Guide for Sufferers and Their Families.* New York, Penguin, 1980.

PIAZZA E, PIAZZA N, ROLLINS N: Anorexia nervosa: controversial aspects of therapy. *Compr Psychiatry* 1980; 21:177–189.

POLIVY J: Group therapy for anorexia nervosa. *J Psychiatr Res Eval* 1981.

RICHARDSON BD: Simmonds' disease and anorexia nervosa. *Arch Int Med* 1939; 63:1–28.

ROSE J, GARFINKEL PE: A parents' group in the management of anorexia nervosa. *Can J Psychiatry* 1980; 25:228–233.

RUSSELL GFM: General management of anorexia nervosa and difficulties in assessing the efficacy of treatment, in Vigersky RA (ed): *Anorexia Nervosa.* New York. Raven, 1977, pp 277–289.

RUSSELL GFM: Bulimia nervosa: an ominous variant of anorexia nervosa. *Psychol Med* 1979; 9:429–448.

RYLE JA: "Discussions on anorexia nervosa." *Proc R Soc Med* 1939; 32:735–737.

SCHACTER S, RODIN J: *Obese Humans and Rats.* Erlbaum, 1974.

SCHMITT GM: *Client-Centered Group Psychotherapy in the Treatment of Anorexia Nervosa.* Göttingen, Jahrang, 1980, pp 479–551.

SCLARE AB: "Group therapy for specific psychosomatic problems," in Wittkower ED, Warnes H (ed): *Psychosomatic Medicine in Clinical Applications.* New York, Harper & Row, 1977, pp 107–115.

SELVINI-PALAZZOLI M: *Self-starvation.* London, Chaucer, 1974.

SHELDON JH: Anorexia nervosa. *Proc R Soc Med* 1939; 32:738–741.

SOURS JA: Anorexia nervosa: nosology, diagnosis, developmental patterns, and power-control dynamics, in Caplan G, Lebovici S (eds): *Adolescence: Psychosocial Perspectives.* New York, Basic Books, 1969.

SOURS JA: The anorexia nervosa syndrome. *Int J Psychoanal* 1974; 55:567–576.

SOURS JA: *Starving to Death in a Sea of Objects: The Anorexia Nervosa Syndrome.* New York, Aronson, 1980.

STUART RB, MITCHELL C: Self-help weight control groups: a professional and a consumer perspective in *Psychiatr Clin North Am* 1978; 1:697–711.

STUNKARD AJ: The success of TOPS, a self-help group. *Postgrad Med* 1972; 51:143–147.

THEANDER S: Anorexia nervosa. *Acta Psychiatr Scand Suppl* 1970; suppl 214.

THOMA H: *Anorexia Nervosa.* New York, International Universities Press, 1967.

15

Alcohol Addiction

Donald E. Meeks

Alcoholism is a multifaceted problem involving many issues, processes, and transactions. These include societal and individual attitudes toward alcohol use and abuse; the mechanisms through which alcohol is marketed and made available in a society; medical, psychological, and social problems associated with alcohol use; and massive costs to industry, to law enforcement, and to health and social agencies (Addiction Research Foundation, 1981c; *Third Special Report to the U.S. Congress*, 1978). The various dimensions of these problems require diverse interventions. In broad terms, interventions may be directed toward controlling supply, reducing demand, and treating those who have problems associated with alcohol use. This chapter briefly looks at alcohol's effects, alcoholism, theories on the cause of alcoholism, and major preventive approaches before focussing on treatment.

Alcohol's Effects and Alcoholism

The active ingredient in beverage alcohol is ethyl alcohol, or ethanol, a depressant drug. Alcohol decreases the activity of parts of the brain and the spinal cord in proportion to the amount of alcohol in the blood stream. Short-term effects appear rapidly after a single dose and disappear within a few hours or days. Long-term effects appear following repeated use over an extended period. Many heavy drinkers suffer loss of appetite, vitamin deficiencies, stomach inflammation, infections, skin problems, and sexual impotence. Some individuals may develop damage to the liver and central nervous system, as well as disorders of the heart and blood vessels (Addiction Research Foundation, 1980). Psychological and social problems, sometimes severe, are also associated with heavy use over time. In many cases, there may be confusion and/or loss of memory and blackouts. In extreme cases, the individual may suffer mental disorders such as alcoholic hallucinosis, Wernicke's encephalopathy, Korsakoff's psychosis, or nonspecific dementia (Freund, 1976). Finally, role performance and interpersonal functioning are impaired as a consequence of problem drinking. Problems may occur in all areas of social functioning. These include family dysfunction and breakdown, stress in other interpersonal spheres, and reduced productivity or difficulty holding employment.

While there has been a tendency for investigators to focus on severe alcohol dependence, alcohol related problems range widely in severity. Indeed, some consider alcoholism to be "any use of alcohol beverages that causes any damage to the individual or society or both" (Jellinek, 1960, p. 35). Others identify a range of drinking problems, putting alcoholism at the extreme end of the spectrum:

> Alcoholism is . . . a condition in which the individual has lost control over his alcohol intake in the sense that he is consistently unable to refrain from drinking or to stop drinking before getting intoxicated. (Plaut, 1967)

Jellinek (1960), who popularized the disease concept of alcoholism, conceived of loss of control as either a physiological or a psychopathological condition. The physiological view is analogous to the Alcoholics Anonymous conception of alcoholics as persons "allergic" to alcohol, i.e., constitutionally incapable of handling it. Jellinek considered loss of control to be a disease condition found only in a certain subgroup of alcoholics (he labeled them "gamma"), not occurring, as he put it, in nonaddictive alcoholics.* The logical extension of the Jellinek premise is that gamma alcoholics cannot drink in moderation: he postulated that they will eventually move toward uncontrolled drinking if drinking is not discontinued.

As I discuss later, the ability of alcoholics to drink in a controlled fashion is the subject of considerable controversy. Studies attempting experimentally to induce loss of control have not established that small

---

*Jellinek's (1960) gamma alcoholics are characterized by craving for alcohol, increased (and later decreased) tolerance, physical dependence, and alcohol withdrawal symptoms.

quantities of alcohol induce a craving for larger amounts (e.g., Paredes et al., 1973). At the same time, it is clear from clinical reports and other studies that the vast majority of severely dependent alcoholics seem unable to engage in moderate drinking.

More recent definitions and descriptions of alcoholism and alcohol problems place less emphasis on distinctions between physical and psychological dependence. In addition, there is a greater tendency to consider the health and social consequences of many patterns of consumption, not just of those at the extreme end of the spectrum. Many of the health, social, and economic problems attributable to alcohol are not caused by persons who can be described as alcoholics.

From the perspective of sociobehavioral therapists, treatment decisions do not hinge upon the presence or absence of physical dependence. In persons physically dependent on alcohol, psychological dependence is also presumed to exist. Moreover, psychological dependence continues to be an issue in treatment long after the individual is withdrawn from alcohol. Nevertheless, the terms "psychic dependence" and "physical dependence" have often been used interchangeably in the literature, causing considerable confusion. In an effort to reduce the confusion surrounding terminology, the World Health Organization (1969) defined "drug dependence" (including dependence on alcohol) thus:

> A state, psychic and sometimes also physical, resulting from the interaction between a living organism and a drug, characterized by behavioural and other responses that always include a compulsion to take the drug on a continuous basis in order to experience its psychic effects, and sometimes to avoid the discomfort of its absence. Tolerance* may or may not be present. A person may be dependent on more than one drug. (p. 6)

Whether or not this definition eases the controversy over types of dependence, it has serious deficits for the sociobehavioral therapist. Most notably, it fails to take into account the important role of social factors in addictive behaviors.

It is interesting that in 1952, the World Health Organization's Expert Committee on Mental Health defined "alcoholism" as "any form of drinking which in its extent goes beyond the traditional and customary dietary use, or the ordinary compliance with the social drinking customs of the whole community concerned, irrespective of the etiological factors leading to such behaviours." The violation of drinking codes can create both interpersonal and intrapsychic conflicts, exacerbating the effects of drinking problems. On the other hand, in cultures that accept and sup-

---

*"Tolerance" refers to a decreased effect over time of the same dose of a drug, requiring more of the drug to get the same effect. In later stages of alcoholism, smaller doses may be required to produce drug effects.

port heavy drinking, drinking norms may contribute to hazardous levels of consumption (Pittman & Snyder, 1962).

Orthodox disease concepts tend to focus on the interaction of a person with a drug. Such an emphasis ignores the fact that alcohol problems exist as much in social situations and processes as in people. Environmental factors influence attitudes toward drinking, the availability of alcohol, patterns of consumption, and societal views and self-concepts of alcoholics. Thus, they may reinforce problem drinking behavior. The disease concept of alcoholism is nevertheless useful to combat moralistic views held by drinkers, family, friends, and therapists. Many alcoholics engaged in treatment would remain untreated if the moral view on alcoholism still held sway. At the same time, a narrow disease concept is limiting: while the alcoholic may be regarded as ill, alcohol problems must be viewed from a comprehensive perspective that takes social, medical, psychological, and other factors into account.

A Sociological Perspective on Alcoholism

Whether a particular pathology is conceived to inhere in an individual or in a situation determines the locus and mode of the attempted interventions. Psychotherapeutic intervention has traditionally located pathology within the individual and has focused its attention on the management of intrapsychic variables. (Lennard & Berstein, 1969, pp 2–3)

An interactional perspective leads us to examine the dynamic interplay of individuals with other persons and with social systems. As previously stated, drinking codes in a given culture may contribute to abstinence, to moderate drinking, or to hazardous levels of consumption. In France, which has the highest incidence of alcoholism in the world, it is acceptable regularly to imbibe large quantities of alcohol (France has the highest incidence of liver cirrhosis in the world). On the other hand, the violation of social norms proscribing heavy drinking can create both interpersonal and intrapsychic conflicts, as I noted earlier, that exacerbate the effects of a drinking problem.

At least one large study suggested that most people regard alcoholics not only as sick but also as morally weak (Muford & Miller, 1964). Unlike the case with other behavior disorders, in alcoholism what is perceived to be basically wrong with the heavy drinker is the drinking itself (Trice & Roman, 1975). Yet, labeling the individual "deviant" sets in motion social processes that may hinder recovery and rehabilitation. Therefore, treatment must address the client's transactions with people and systems in the environment, as well as consumption patterns. Social work intervention is located at the interface between person and environment (Hearn, 1969). This dual focus is a unique and critical contribution made by social work to alcoholism treatment.

Theories on the Cause of Alcoholism

Many formulations have been advanced to describe the etiology of alcohol problems (McCord & McCord, 1960). Efforts over the years to isolate a single causal factor have proved fruitless. A comprehensive view considers many factors, including the perspectives reviewed here.

"Learning theory models" arise out of the conception that the administration of alcohol is a learned behavior maintained both by the depressant and anesthetic qualities of the drug and by environmental reinforcers (Rankin, 1978). Alcoholic behavior is seen as caused and maintained by the association of alcohol ingestion with positive, rewarding experiences (Armor, Polich & Stambul, 1978).

"Psychodynamic models" conceive drinking problems to be symptomatic of underlying emotional conflict or pathology. Dependence on the substance is believed to provide pleasure, on the one hand, and relief from psychic pain, on the other. Such dependence is conceived as resulting from developmental failure. Addiction, as a compromise solution, is seen as protecting the individual from graver consequences of this failure (Blum, 1966).

"Transactional models" as advanced by Steiner (1969), consider alcoholics as "engaging in repetitive, interpersonal behavior sequences involving alcohol, with the production of interpersonal pay-offs as the covert motive". In these games, the alcoholic is able to elicit disapproval from others to affirm his inadequacy. Family, friends, and therapists may unwittingly get caught up in these games.

"Physical-medical models" emphasize biomedical or biochemical factors in the etiology of alcoholism (Rankin, 1978). More recent attention to this area has been stimulated by the studies of Goodwin and associates (1973). They found that offspring of alcoholic parents raised apart from their natural parents had nearly twice the number of alcohol problems as did children of parents never hospitalized for alcoholism. These findings are not conclusive but do raise the possibility that some alcoholics may be constitutionally predisposed to problems with alcohol if it is used.

"Microsocial models" and "Macrosocial models" assign causal factors to the intense interaction of small groups (e.g., family, peer) and to broader social influences, respectively. The latter include sociocultural factors (Pittman & Snyder, 1962), alcohol availability (Popham & Schmidt, 1976), and social status and social deviance processes (Goldstein & Goldstein, 1975). Bales (1946) described three general conditions in a society that might contribute to the incidence of alcoholism: the degree of stress and tension produced by the culture, popular attitudes toward drinking, and the degree to which substitute means for gaining satisfaction and coping with stress were available.

"Moral views" have traditionally regarded alcoholism as a sign of moral decay. However, many contemporary theologians focus on the promotion of growth, self-esteem, and autonomy in alcoholics (Clinebell, 1968). Moralistic views that are to be discouraged should be distinguished from the spiritual perspectives that may play an important role in treatment for some alcoholics.

Clearly, there is no single cause for alcoholism and alcohol problems. The models surveyed here have been unevenly researched and some clearly not amenable to empirical investigation. Plaut (1967) offered an integrative model to describe the various factors that may interact to produce a drinking problem:

> An individual who 1) responds to beverage alcohol in a certain way, perhaps physiologically determined, by experiencing internal relief and relaxation, and who 2) has certain personality characteristics such as difficulty in dealing with an overcoming depression, frustration, and anxiety, and who 3) is a member of a culture in which there is both pressure to drink and culturally induced guilt and confusion regarding what kinds of behaviour are appropriate, is more likely to develop trouble than will most other persons. An intermingling of certain factors may be necessary for the development of problem drinking, and the relative importance of the differential causal factors no doubt varies from one individual to another. (p. 49)

Major Interventions for Alcoholism Prevention

Prevention of Alcoholism through Broad Social Measures

Bruun and associates (1975) described preventive strategies that have been used in attempts to reduce the prevalence of alcohol problems:

promotion and development of alternatives to alcohol use like recreational facilities

alleviation of social conditions presumed to be responsible for alcohol problems

organization of social movements to mobilize public sentiment or stimulate action against drinking

law enforcement to deter alcohol related behaviors such as public drunkenness or drunken driving

separation of alcohol consumption from its potentially harmful consequences, for example, by preventing persons who have been drinking from driving controlling the availability of alcohol

education to persuade people not to engage in harmful drinking

identification, treatment, and rehabilitation of problem drinkers (pp. 65–88)

Preventive approaches that may be of greatest interest to the helping professions are social policy measures (e.g., alcohol control) and education programs aimed at young people.

Alcohol Consumption Control Policies

Alcohol control policies are based on increasing evidence that a large proportion of alcohol related health problems are attributable to nonalcoholic populations. Lower levels of alcohol consumption than previously suspected have been associated with health risks (Pequignot, 1974). Some studies have found that the higher the overall per capita consumption in a society, the larger the number of heavy consumers and health problems associated with alcohol use (Bruun et al., 1975, Popham et al., 1975).

Policies directed toward reducing per capita consumption focus primarily on curtailing availability. While price is the central concern, other alcohol control policies seek to regulate drinking age; type and distribution of alcoholic beverage outlets; hours of sale; alcohol content; and advertising and marketing practices (Addiction Research Foundation, 1978).

Preventive Education about Alcoholism

Alcohol education programs have received increased attention in recent years. Such programs have variously sought to promote responsible drinking, reduce the adverse health effects of alcohol consumption, reduce the occurrence of alcohol related driving accidents, and urge problem drinkers to seek treatment (Moser, 1980). In the past, education programs directed toward young people focused on the evils of alcohol and drugs; such scare tactics were often perceived as biased and were rejected by young people. Contemporary programs emphasize facts about potential hazards (e.g., Sheppard et al., 1978).

Research has not yet shown that alcohol education significantly influences drinking behavior (Addiction Research Foundation, 1981a). Moreover, evaluation of alcohol education programs presents particular problems:

Evaluation studies of the educational enterprise are difficult for two reasons. First, there is a general inability to obtain widespread consensus on what should be the ultimate aim of alcohol education. Goals range from an emphasis on abstinence to a stress on decision-making and formation of values. . . . Second, the methodological considerations required to detect changes in behaviour and attitudes are difficult to approximate in real life situations. . . . An adequate evaluation procedure would have to be longitudinal in nature. (Globetti, 1978, p. 97)

It is important to note that research in this area is inconclusive, rather than condemnatory of alcohol education programs. Education programs should be carefully evaluated with respect to short-term effects. Longitudinal studies clear about their objectives and procedures should provide the evidence needed to judge the efficacy of alcohol education programs.

Guidelines for the Treatment of Alcoholism

Flexibility in Alcoholism Treatment Programs

In recent years, penetrating questions have been raised about the efficacy of alcoholism treatment. These concerns were given impetus by the work of Edwards and Orford (1977), who found no difference in treatment outcome between individuals provided an "average package of care" and those provided simple advice. From these findings, the authors concluded that until evidence to the contrary is forthcoming, the emphasis in treatment should be on low-cost, low-key programs.

In a rejoinder to Edwards and Orford (1977), Glaser (1980) cited studies (Emrick, 1975; Luborsky et al., 1975) showing that whenever two or more interventions for alcoholism are compared, outcomes tend to be equivalent. When client populations are assumed to be homogeneous and are not carefully matched to particular treatments, the results of different treatment programs are likely to be the same. Because client populations are, in fact, heterogeneous, variables important to successful client–treatment interactions will tend to be uniformly distributed in the experiment and the results in each condition will be the same for that reason (Glaser, 1978). Thus, client characteristics and treatment must accord on several dimensions:

- matching attributes of clients and attributes of therapists;
- matching attributes of clients and treatment goals;
- seeking complementarity between problems of clients and specific capabilities of treatments (Glaser, 1980).

Alcoholics differ by age, sex, social class, occupation, drinking pattern, drinking history, personality, and other factors (Lizansky, 1967). Programs providing a single treatment for all alcoholic clients assume homegeneity of the client population. Recognizing the heterogeneity of alcoholic clients is a key to the development of effective treatment programs.

Choosing Goals, Settings, and Approaches in the Treatment of Alcoholism

Goals

From a comprehensive perspective, the general goals of treatment are:

- to identify individuals who have an alcohol problem;
- to provide any necessary emergency care;
- to ensure that the individual is safely detoxified;
- to conduct a comprehensive assessment;
- to match the individual with services and treatment relevant to his/her needs;
- to assist the individual to develop an altered lifestyle, including altered drinking behaviour;
- to provide a systematic program of aftercare. (Marshman et al., 1978)

Settings

Alcoholism treatment can be carried out in a variety of medical and nonmedical specialized and general settings. Emrick (1975) found that outcomes did not differ between socially deteriorated alcoholics provided one month of inpatient treatment and those provided outpatient treatment. Edwards and Guthrie (1966) found no significant difference in treatment outcome between a residential treatment program and outpatient treatment. Similar results were reported by Baekland and colleagues (1975). These findings suggest that the traditional reliance on expensive inpatient treatments may not be well placed. A careful assessment could identify clients requiring an initial period of separation from their environments for medical or psychosocial therapies. Glaser and Skinner (1981) observed that one could expect an employed individual in stable living quarters and with strong social support to fare better in an outpatient program than an individual with little social stability. Social, psychological, health, and other factors should inform treatment decisions. Residential treatments may be less appropriate for many clients than intermediate settings such as halfway houses and daycare programs.

Approaches

A wide variety of treatment approaches have been employed with alcoholics: psychodynamically oriented psychotherapies, reality therapy, problemsolving techniques, drug therapies, behavioral approaches, marital and family therapies, group therapies, transactional analysis, and psychodrama. There is no evidence that a particular therapeutic approach is superior to all others when applied to a general population of alcoholics. In a comprehensive survey of outcomes of different treatment approaches, Emrick (1975) found outcomes to be essentially the same. It has been estimated that abstinence and improvement rates for most approaches are less than 50% (Hill & Blane, 1967).

The research evidence also fails to support the commonly held belief that intensive treatment is necessarily superior to less intensive programs (Edwards & Orford, 1977). Orford and associates (1976) found that less severely dependent alcoholics fared better with minimal treatment, while severely dependent alcoholics fared better with more intensive treatment. Clare (1977), in an analysis of treatment outcome reviews, found little difference in outcome when different approaches were used. As I suggested earlier, effective alcoholism treatment requires the careful matching of clients with interventions suited to their attributes and needs.

Matching Clients to Treatments for Alcoholism

A highly sophisticated application of the matching hypothesis awaits the development of profiles of client responses to particular treatment conditions (Skinner, 1980). At present, several basic principles can guide treatment selection:

> principle 1: alcoholics constitute a heterogeneous population, each client presenting with a mix of psychological, social, and perhaps other problems (e.g., medical, economic, legal)
> principle 2: careful assessment will identify the currently most serious problems
> principle 3: no single treatment will be equally effective for all alcoholic clients
> principle 4: treatment settings should provide treatment options; additional required services must be sought elsewhere through linkages with other agencies in the community
> principle 5: the treatment system should take into account the need systematically to provide mechanisms to match clients with needed services and to coordinate helping activities
> principle 6: whatever the treatments and services provided, aftercare is essential

The choice of treatment methods must take into account, at the least, the client's presenting problems; present alcohol and other drug use patterns; behaviors when abstinent; behaviors when drinking; relationships with family, friends, and associates; education, employment, and financial status; leisure activities; and legal entanglements (Addiction Research Foundation, 1981b). Medical assessment by a physician must also inform the treatment choice.

Various guides are available to help match patients with treatments (e.g., Glaser & Skinner, 1981). The Michigan Alcoholism Screening Test (MAST) can be used to develop a quantitative index of consequences of alcohol ingestion (Skinner, 1979). The Sociability Index (Fig. 15-1) can assist in determining the appropriateness of residential, outpatient, and other treatment settings. Decisions about specific therapies can also be approached systematically. For example, Figure 15-2 shows a schema for

1. Present Accommodation (Item 13)
   Code 2   if   Own house (4) or apt./house (3)
   Code 1   if   Room (2)
   Code 0   if   None (1), institution (5), other (6)

2. Family Contact (Items 14–17)
   Code 2   if   Daily (4) contact with either parents,
                 spouse, children, or relatives
   Code 1   if   Weekly (3) contact with either
   Code 0   if   Monthly (2), less (1), none (0)

3. Return to Live with Family (Item 19)
   Code 2   if   Yes (3)
   Code 1   if   Maybe (2) or does not apply (4)
   Code 0   if   No (1)

4. Regular Employment (Items 46 and 47)
   Code 2   if   Employed full-time for 12 months
   Code 1   if   Employed for 6 to 11 months or
                 part-time for 12 months
   Code 0   if   Otherwise

5. Job at Present (Item 49)
   Code 2   if   Yes (3)
   Code 1   if   Maybe (2) or does not apply (4)
   Code 0   if   No (1)

6. Job Changes (Item 50)
   Code 2   if   No job changes or housewife, student,
                 retired (89)
   Code 1   if   One job change
   Code 0   if   More than one change or has not worked (88)

7. Legal Status (Item 86)
   Code 2   if   No legal problems (2)
   Code 0   if   On probation, parole, or awaiting trial (1)

FIGURE 15–1. Sociability index to assist in the selection of treatment settings for alcoholic clients. Reprinted from F. Glaser and H. Skinner, ''Matching in the Real World,'' in E. Gottheil, A. McLellan, and K. Druley (eds.), *Matching Patient Needs and Treatment Methods in Alcoholism and Drug Abuse* **(Springfield: Thomas, 1981, p. 310), with permission.**

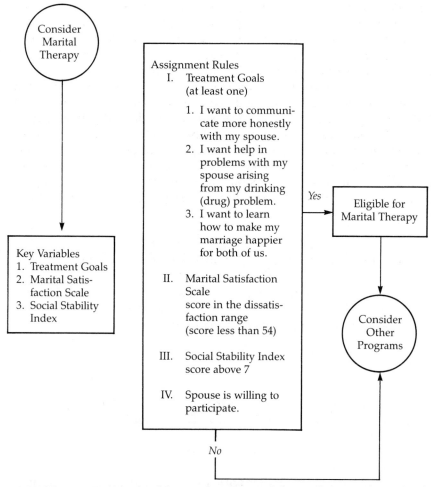

FIGURE 15–2. Instrument for assessing the need for, and appropriateness of, marital therapy with alcoholic clients. Reprinted from F. Glaser and H. Skinner, "Matching in the Real World," in E. Gottheil, A. McLellan, and K. Druley (eds.), *Matching Patient Needs and Treatment Methods in Alcoholism and Drug Abuse* (Springfield: Thomas, 1981, p. 319), with permission.

determining the relative need for, and appropriateness of, marital therapy. Similar frameworks can guide the selection of other therapeutic and supportive services.

Social Work Roles in the Treatment of Alcoholism

Social workers in virtually all settings and fields of practice come into contact with alcohol problems. It was estimated some years ago that

15–20% of applications to family service agencies involved a drinking problem (Bailey, 1963). Drinking problems may contribute to legal entanglements, separation and divorce, financial distress, delinquent behavior, wife abuse, child abuse, underachievement in school, and other problems on the part of the drinker and the family.

Efforts by social workers in the late nineteenth century were directed toward reform of alcoholics and were supportive of the temperance movement. The alcoholic was regarded as a villain and helping efforts generally were directed toward the children (Bailey, 1961). In the 1920s, with the advent of psychoanalytic concepts in social work, unconscious determinants of problem drinking became the focal point for treatment (Whalen, 1953). The contemporary literature reveals a wide range of social work approaches to alcoholism. This section looks briefly at a selection.

Individual Counseling for Alcohol Related Problems

Initial treatment encounters are often characterized by client denial and lack of motivation for treatment. These factors, along with goal setting and controlled drinking, require special attention.

Denial

The client may deny either the existence or the severity of the drinking problem. One study found that only 9% of clients later identified as having drinking problems had acknowledged the drinking problem at the outset; a variety of other problems were presented as the presenting problem (Demone et al., 1974).

The label "alcoholic" carries with it fears of stigmatization, hospitalization, loss of employment, and loss of respect. The client may refuse to accept that some of these consequences are imminent or have already come to pass. Effective counseling to deal with drinking problems cannot proceed in the face of denial. Initially, the worker may focus on other health and social problems experienced by the client and their relationship to the drinking. Connections are made between drinking and the problems acknowledged by the client or identified through available records. This approach stresses the use, whenever possible, of fact and objectivity to counter the denial.

Jacobs (1981) stressed the establishment of a therapeutic alliance in the early sessions. He advised against early confrontation, which may entrench the denial. He emphasized that the therapist must differentiate between clients who genuinely do not believe that they have a problem and those who privately fear that they can no longer control their drinking.

Actually, what is referred to as "denial" in the alcoholic usually is a combination of avoidance, rationalization, and projection, rather than denial in the psychoanalytic sense (Gaertner, 1939). The worker must attempt to distinguish between (unconscious) denial and (conscious) avoidance. Aggressive approaches to confrontation are based on the belief that the denial is a conscious process (Maxwell, 1976). Of course, the worker must make judgments about the manner and the timing of confrontation. Confrontation is best dealt with in a context of mutual trust. With alcoholic clients, such a climate may be slow to evolve. In making this decision, the worker may be well advised to err on the side of delayed confrontation.

Motivation

One large-scale study attributed 70% of treatment failures to poor motivation (Moore, 1971). Denial is one factor contributing to poor motivation: if the problem does not exist in the client's view, then treatment is not necessary.

Traditionally, clinicians conceive of motivation as something that the client must possess as a prerequisite to successful treatment. An alternative view of motivation in the treatment of drug dependent individuals was presented by Rossi (1978):

> The narrow view of motivation takes the position that it exists within the skin, intrapsychically if you will, and that the success of a treatment venture is related to high motivation for success.
>
> There are not data to support such a position, although there is strong evidence that the narrow view is a reworking of a moralistic . . . view of human behaviour. (p. 25)

Alcoholics are motivated to drink; however, this motivation exists side by side with the wish to improve health or social functioning. Dealing with this ambivalence to reinforce the thrust toward health and well-being is a central goal of treatment. It is not reasonable to expect the client to solve this dilemma before coming for treatment. This is, in large measure, what treatment is about.

Chafetz and colleagues (1962a,b) provided an example of a program designed to instill motivation. This program, located in a large general hospital in Boston, successfully identified persons with alcohol related health problems and engaged them in treatment. Employee assistance programs that base continued employment on successful treatment of the worker's alcoholism use another approach and tap another source of motivation.

Many alcoholics applying for treatment do so because of coercion from health officials, family, courts, and employers. Even in these cases, the motivation to restore health, avoid legal pitfalls, sustain respect, regain marital stability, and maintain employment may be used in treatment to counter the motivation to drink. In the initial stages, the worker must realize the significance attached by the client to giving up alcohol. Many clients, for example, initially perceive treatment to be a form of deprivation.

Goal Setting

The basic principles of goal setting with alcoholic clients were described by Edwards and Grant (1980):

> Goals have to be agreed on rather than imposed and this implies due attention to the process of decision-making. The goals should be explicit and should be worked out practically and in detail, both for the long and short term. Short-term goals should be attainable and immediately rewarding. (p. 317)

Long-term goals provide a framework for the setting of realistic, time-limited, short-term goals. Professionals are indebted to Alcoholics Anonymous for the realization that manageable short-term goals "partialize" the overwhelming challenges confronting the alcoholic. The actual attainment of goals provides a needed backdrop of success. Empirical support for the efficacy of short-term goals in behavior modification came from another context: Bandura and Simon (1977) found that overeating in weight loss subjects was best controlled by focusing on short-term goals; subjects focusing on long-term goals fared no better than members of the control group.

In treatment, the goal of abstinence should be mutually agreed upon by worker and client rather than imposed by the worker. The decision on when to suggest abstinence as a treatment goal will be dictated by early explorations. When abstinence is mutually agreed upon, a relapse is less likely to be used as a weapon against the therapist or as an excuse to abandon treatment. A drinking relapse and the circumstances surrounding it should serve as grist for the therapeutic mill. Relapse is not unusual and should not be regarded as a sign of therapeutic failure. Indeed, remaining sober for six months is a considerable achievement for a client with a 20-year drinking problem.

Controlled Drinking

Over the years, considerable controversy has raged about the appropriateness of controlled drinking as a treatment goal. Several studies found that some alcoholics were able to maintain various degrees of stability while continuing to drink decreased amounts (Davies, 1962; Gerard & Saenger, 1965; Gillis & Keet, 1969; Mayer & Myerson, 1971; Sobell & Sobell, 1973). Interest in the subject was spurred by a large-scale study popularly referred to as the "Rand report" (Armor & Polich, 1978). The Rand report found from reports of the subjects that 70% of subjects completing treatment in 44 alcoholism treatment centers were in remission at 6- and 18-month follow-ups. The remission category included abstinent and controlled drinking subjects in roughly equal numbers. In a four-year follow-up of these subjects, Polich and colleagues (1979) found that 46% of those who could be located were in remission ; and a further 18% were drinking without obvious problems. The authors did not contend that controlled drinkers will remain stable over longer time intervals.

Critics of the original Rand report have expressed concern about the reliability of self-reports, the fact that 79% of subjects were lost to follow-up at the 6-month interval and 38% at the 18-month interval, the possibility that patients who were found represented more stable segments of the original cohort, and a number of other methodological issues. Some of these concerns were dealt with in the four-year follow-up (Polich et al., 1979). Nonetheless, the issue of controlled drinking is far from resolved insofar as clinical applications are concerned. As Armor and Polich (1976) said:

> We are by no means advocating that alcoholics should attempt moderate drinking after treatment. . . . the current state of knowledge in this area is still inadequate to serve as a basis for recommending treatment goals for individual alcoholics. Moreover, we have no evidence whatsoever, nor is there any method at present, that enables us to identify those alcoholics who might safely return to drinking and those who cannot. (p. 295)

Group Therapy for Alcohol Related Problems

Many approaches to group counseling and group psychotherapy have been applied in work with alcoholics. Although there is scant evidence to support the superiority, of group therapy many clinicians regard it as the treatment of choice (Cahn, 1970). In any event, group therapy has the apparent advantage of being economical. Other advantages attributed to group therapy are the nurturance of interpersonal relationships in a population characterized by social isolation; the diffusion among members of the dependence normally directed toward a therapist; group support in helping individual's identify with the role of recovering alcoholic and with typical problems; direct observation of interpersonal behaviors; and peer modeling by successful members (Blume, 1978; Forrest, 1975; Gliedman et al., 1963).

There is wide diversity in group therapy approaches for alcoholics.* Rossi (1978) described three such approaches:

The Guidance Model generally involves lectures, videotapes or film providing information about, for example, a treatment program for alcohol effects. While the immediate aim is information provision, discussion is triggered by the relationship of the information to the situations of individual members. The objectives of guidance groups, while important are delimited. Offered as an orientation to treatment, or at intervals during the treatment process they may provide an added dimension.

The Counselling Model employs the group as a context for focusing on the problems of individual members. The shared experience, fears, and aspirations of members promote the development of new understandings, coping mechanisms, and supports. Themes derive from the interpersonal and other social problems confronting members. The interpersonal context of the group itself provides a framework for working on solutions that can be applied in the real world.

Interactional Group Therapy Models employ the group as both a means and a context. The primary focus is on interpersonal processes within the group and individual functioning within that framework. Changing dysfunctional aspects of the group process is viewed as a means of changing individual behaviours. (p. 48–51)

Family Therapy for Alcohol Related Problems

Problem drinking affects, and is affected by, family relationships and behaviors. Family interaction can either assist the alcoholic in recovery or make recovery difficult. For example, denial of the problem may be supported by the entire family. Social workers should routinely explore potential relationships between family problems and drinking behaviors. On that basis, appropriate interventions can be initiated.

In families of alcoholics, many of the family behaviors are organized to deal with the drinking problem. Jackson (1954) described seven stages of family adjustment to alcoholism: attempts to deny the problem; attempts to eliminate the problem; attempts to reorganize in spite of the problem; efforts to escape the problem; reorganization of part of the family; and recovery and reorganization of the whole family. Jackson's early formulations were based on stress theory, which saw drinking as the root cause of family problems. Contemporary family theorists conceptualize the family as a system with multiple behaviors and reciprocal effects contributing to problems in family interaction:

A central concept of systems theory is that, in order to understand individual behavior, it is essential to understand the significant group in which the per-

---

*The group therapy provided by Alcoholics Anonymous is discussed on pp. 428–429.

son lives, the relationships within that group, and the importance of any individual's behavior to maintaining the group, or system. Therefore, the target for change is the whole system, not any individual member. (Paolino & McCrady, 1977, p. 111)

As with other alcoholism treatments, there is no single approach to family therapy. Paolino and McCrady (1977) described psychoanalytic, learning theory, and systems based approaches to work with families.

In a review of family treatment of alcoholism, Janzen (1978) identified four separate but interrelated views of the spouse's relationship to the problem of alcoholism. The first emphasizes the spouse's need to have the alcoholic continue drinking in order to maintain the spouse's stability or adjustment. The second suggests that the spouse's disturbance and other family problems are attributable to the drinking. The third postulates that even if the drinking were not present, the marriage is of the sort in which serious problems are inevitable. The fourth views the husband and wife in families of alcoholics as more competitive than spouses in other marriages; each partner is perceived as seeking to gain control of the relationship. From a systems perspective, family interaction, rather than individual pathology, becomes the focal point for treatment whatever the dynamics of the couple.

Studies of family therapy are marked by the absence of a unifying model that would permit replication or accurate comparison of findings. Most promising are the systems based approaches that combine knowledge from such fields as sociology, biology, and psychology (Steinglass, 1976).

Systems approaches take the family as the unit of treatment. Meeks and Kelly (1970) advanced eight principles to be considered in systems based therapy with families of alcoholics:

- Initial attention must be given to helping the family consider why the entire family is in treatment and not just the problem-drinking member. The expectations of therapy by family and therapist should be discussed in this context.
- With the families of recovering alcoholics, the wish to maintain a present superficial harmony based on the containment of negative feelings (resistance) may defeat the constructive goals of the family as a unit. The therapist must help the family to recognize this goal conflict and its sources.
- The intrusive role of alcohol should not be negated, but put into perspective along with other behaviors which affect the relationships of family members to each other and to the family as a whole.
- "Games" that occur in treatment and mask real conflicts should be related to those that are played at home which distort reality and sustain conflict. The therapist should intervene in such behaviors and help family members become objective spectators of their own role playing and the rules underlying such interactions.

- Individual behaviors (extensions of individual needs) that reinforce family problems (e.g., drinking) should be opened up and explored. Likewise the family should be aware of its interaction in relation to the alcoholic member's fears and urges around sobriety and drinking.
- The therapist should recognize with the family that shifts in equilibrium (around for example, dependence, dominance, support, withdrawal) disturbs the established patterns of behaving and relating among family members.
- Periodically these shifts in family equilibrium and their meanings and implications should be reviewed (e.g., need for new sources of gratification, role relinquishment).
- The family should be helped to apply the problem-solving approaches employed in family therapy to their interaction outside treatment. (pp. 410–411)

While additional research is needed to examine the relative effectiveness of family therapy approaches to alcoholism, the need to provide assistance to families is not in question: Changing a family member in isolation from the family system may be ineffectual. To consolidate gains made in the individual treatment of the drinker and to minimize the risk of relapse, the family system must be helped to change'' (Meeks, 1976, p. 850).

Alcoholics Anonymous

Alcoholics Anonymous (AA) may be the world's leading example of a successful self-help group. Founded in 1935, AA has helped countless alcoholics achieve sobriety. Alcoholics Anonymous is a fellowship of men and women who provide group support within a particular framework of beliefs and philosophies (Alcoholics Anonymous, 1955).* Alanon and Alateen are recent offshoots designed to help families and the teenage children of alcoholics.

AA regards alcoholics as people who have lost control over their drinking. The twelve steps of AA invoke the role of a higher power, not intended to convey a specific concept of God. Its twelve traditions eschew promotion of the organization while affirming the importance of anonymity of its members and the primacy of its helping mission.

AA's contention "once an alcoholic, always an alcoholic" is controversial among many professionals. AA rejects the concept of a recovered alcoholic. The individual's adjustment as a dry alcoholic must always be organized around the label "alcoholic." This posture is interesting in the light of AA's major role in destigmatizing alcoholism. A recovered alcoholic, in this view, is a person who cannot handle alcohol and can never drink again.

Many professionals find little or no conflict between AA's positions and their own. In any case, a focus on ideological differences, where they exist, distorts the issue. AA should be considered as an excellent resource for alcoholics who find its approach congenial. Nonetheless, it is underutilized by professionals in many locations. Treatment may be further enhanced if AA involvement is combined with participation in a professional treatment program (Armor, 1978).

Special Issues in the Treatment of Alcoholism

Aftercare

One essential component of any treatment program is aftercare. Often, it is the expectation that when the drinking stops, all other problems will magically disappear. In fact, fundamental problems in such areas as childrearing and sexual relations may be unmasked (Cohen, 1966). With sobriety, these problems can no longer be blamed on the drinking. The recovery period is a critical time to deal with these issues and to consolidate the gains made in treatment.

Another dimension of the recovery phase is the client's need to alter lifestyle or to disassociate from drinking subcultures. Alcoholics spend many of their waking hours consuming alcohol, experiencing its effects, and dealing with its aftereffects alone or with drinking companions. Alcoholic drinking becomes a way of life. To consolidate recovery, new patterns must be developed to deal with life without alcohol. Leisure counseling (Girling, 1979) helps recovering alcoholics find new ways to fill their vacant hours and to work through impediments to social reintegration.

Alcoholics Anonymous, halfway houses, support groups, and professional counseling are among the approaches employed in aftercare. Aftercare is not an add-on. It should be carefully incorporated into any treatment program.

Children of Alcoholics

Maternal drinking has serious negative effects on newborns. The characteristic effects, which differ in nature and severity from infant to infant, are referred to as "fetal alcohol syndrome." Among the defects found in such children are limb malformations, cleft palate, a protruding forehead, a sunken nasal bridge, a short, upturned nose, a retracted upper lip, a receding chin, and deformed ears. Such infants may fail to thrive and to develop normally. In later years, they may have difficulties in sustaining activities and in intellectual performance (Rosett, 1980).

Smart (1980) surveyed the literature on the psychosocial effects of parental alcoholism on children. Children of alcoholics:

- experience a variety of family conflicts including quarrelling, economic hardships, separations and divorce;
- may develop low impulse and aggression control or may be over-assertive;
- are at high risk for developing drinking problems, problems with the law, emotional disturbances, low self-concepts and difficulties making friends. (p. 51)

Cork (1969) was a pioneer in advocating programs for children of alcoholics that combine counseling and preventive measures. Special programs may be designed for spouses and children whether or not the drinker is involved in treatment. To the extent possible, children should be involved in family therapy to work through their problems in the context of family interactions.

Adolescent Drinkers

Few special treatment programs have been developed for youthful drinkers, and most programs that do exist have not been the subject of systematic study. Smart (1979) compared treatment outcomes of youthful drinkers and adults in the same treatment facility. Youthful subjects showed fewer resources and less social stability. Nonetheless, their treatment outcomes were comparable to those of adults. The author believes that more success may be realized with young people by taking their age, values, and special needs into account.

Women and Alcohol

Kalant and associates (1980) provided a comprehensive analysis of alcohol and drug problems in women that reviewed sex differences in problem prevalence; biological influences on alcoholism; etiology; morbidity and mortaility; and treatment concerns. Annis and Liban (1979) reviewed 23 studies presenting male and female outcome information. In a report on this research, Annis (1980) concluded:

- Most studies of treatment outcome do not take sex differences into account;
- Of reports available, fifteen failed to find a relationship between remission rates and sex differences, five found evidence of better improvement rates among females, three reported greater improvement among males;

- Type of treatment (hospital alone or in conjunction with out-patient) did not account for sex differences in treatment outcome;
- Existing evidence fails to support the argument that individual counselling is superior to group techniques for women. Some studies found that women fared very well in professional group and AA programs;
- Of the few studies available for analysis, remission rates for males and females were unaffected by the sex of the therapist. (pp. 128–130)

Annis acknowledged that the number of studies was small. Moreover, many yielding relevant information had not been designed to examine sex differences. The studies also lacked uniform data sets. Reflecting on these limitations, Annis observed:

What is needed to advance knowledge on the treatment of the female alcoholic is the systematic study of the response of different types of female alcoholics to a range of specific interventions. . . . Since the female alcoholic population is not homogeneous, it is extremely unlikely that a single form of treatment will be equally efficacious for all. (p. 136)

Gomberg (1976) also described differences between male and female alcoholics that bear consideration in treatment. There may be differences in the goals of therapy (e.g., reconstituting the family may be more significant for women). Stigma and rejection are greater for alcoholic women. Loneliness and isolation seem to be more widespread and deeper among women. Depressive neurosis is a more frequent diagnosis among alcoholic women. Women more frequently cite a specific traumatic event as a reason for drinking. The percentage of women alcoholics separated or divorced is higher. Women begin to drink later and tend to use drug substances other than alcohol more often. Clinicians also report more quilt and self-condemnation among women.

There is considerable controversy over the extent to which women require separate treatment. Gomberg (1976) suggested that while some separate facilities and modalities should be available, segregation of therapy by sex seems unnecessary. At the same time, treatment should take into account the special needs of women: heavier social condemnation; dearth of marketable skills and greater need for vocational training; importance of supportive social networks in treatment; and concerns about children.

Conclusion

Alcohol problems are multifaceted, involving complex interactions among a person, a drug or drugs, and an environment. The multiple interventions required may be grouped under the general headings of prevention and treatment.

A suitable definition of "alcohol problems" is any use of alcohol causing damage to the individual or society or both. Alcoholism may be said to exist when the drinker loses control over when and how much to drink. Understanding of alcohol problems and alcoholism requires a simultaneous focus on the drinker and her interaction with relevant social systems.

There is no single cause for alcoholism. The etiology of alcoholism has been viewed from many perspectives. It is generally agreed that the interaction of a number of factors may be causative under certain conditions.

In recent years, serious questions have been raised about the effectiveness of alcoholism treatment. It is likely that deficits lie not so much in the technologies themselves—most seem to help some people—but in the failure to match patients with programs suitable to their needs. The first step in the matching process is to develop treatment alternatives as opposed to single treatment formats. A careful assessment will indicate the problems that predominate in a given patient at a given time. Planning on this basis should point the way toward appropriate treatments. For some clients, minimal care (supportive counseling) may be as effective as long-term, intensive treatment. Both teenage and female alcoholics have special needs that must be addressed in treatment.

Controlled drinking as a treatment goal has been the subject of controversy for many years. Recent studies have rivived the debate. The Rand report (Armor, 1976) found a relatively large proportion of post-treatment patients drinking moderately without serious consequences. However, no guidelines exist for identifying alcoholics able to drink moderately. Therefore, controlled drinking as a treatment goal is not generally advocated.

Problem drinking must be seen in the context of family behaviors and relationships. Accordingly, treatment that includes the family helps to consolidate gains made in individual therapy and to lessen the likelihood of relapse.

Social work's traditional focus on both person and environment provides a unique basis for intervening in the complex of psychological and social problems presented by alcoholics and problem drinkers. Social work treatment is enhanced if the social worker views problems from an interactional perspective, perceiving part of his role as active intervention in the environment.

References

Addiction Research Foundation *A Strategy for the Prevention of Alcohol Problems.* Toronto, Addiction Research Foundation, 1978.

Addiction Research Foundation: *Facts about Drugs*. Toronto, Addiction Research Foundation, 1980.

Addiction Research Foundation: *Alcohol, Public Education, and Social Policy*. Toronto, Addiction Research Foundation, 1981. (a)

Addiction Research Foundation: *An Initial Interview for Clients with Alcohol- and/or Drug-Related Problems (ICAP)*. Toronto, Addiction Research Foundation, 1981. (b)

Addiction Research Foundation: *Statistical Supplement to the 1979–80 Annual Report*. Toronto, Addiction Research Foundation, 1981. (c)

Alcoholics Anonymous, 2nd ed. New York, AA Publishing Co., 1955.

ANNIS HM: Treatment of alcoholic women, in Edwards G, Grant M (eds): *Alcoholism Treatment in Transition*. Baltimore, University Park Press, 1980, pp 385–422.

ANNIS HM, LIBAN C: Alcoholism in women: treatment modalities and outcomes. *Res Adv Alcohol Drug Prob* 1979; 5:128–139.

ARMOR DJ, POLICH JM, STAMBUL HB: *Alcoholism and Treatment*. Santa Monica, Rand, 1976.

ARMOR DJ, POLICH JM, STAMBUL HB: *Alcoholism and Treatment*. New York, Wiley, 1978.

BAEKLAND F, et al. Methods for the treatment of chronic alcoholism: a critical appraisal. *Adv Alcohol Drug Prob* 1975; 2:247–328.

BAEKLAND F, LUNDWALL L: Dropping out of treatment: a critical review. *Psychol Bull* 1975; 82:738–783.

BAILEY MB: Alcoholism and marriage: a review of the research and professional literature. *Q J Stud Alcohol* 1961; 22:81–97.

BAILEY MB: The family agency's role in treating the wife of an alcoholic. *Soc Casework* 1963; 44:273–279.

BALES RF: Cultural differences in the rates of alcoholism. *Q J Stud Alcohol* 1946; 6:480–499.

BANDURA A, SIMON KM: The role of proximal intentions in self-regulation of refractory behaviour. *Cognitive Ther Res* 1977; 1:177–193.

BLUM EM: Psychoanalytic views of alcoholism. *Q J Stud Alcohol* 1966; 27:259–299.

BLUME SB: Group psychotherapy in the treatment of alcoholism, in Zimberg S, Wallace S, Blume SB (eds): *Practical Approaches to Alcoholism Psychotherapy*. New York, Plenum, 1978, pp 63–76.

BRUUN K, GRIFFITH E, LUMIO M: *Alcohol Control Policies in Public Health Perspective*. Helsinki, Finnish Foundation for Alcohol Studies, WHO (Europe), and the Addiction Research Foundation, 1975; vol 25.

CAHN S: *The Treatment of Alcoholics: An Evaluative Study*. New York, Oxford University Press, 1970.

CHAFETZ ME, et al. Establishing treatment relations with alcoholics. *J Nerv Ment Dis* 1962; 134:395–409.

CHAFETZ ME, DEMONE HW Jr, SOLOMON HC: Alcoholism: its cause and prevention. *NY State J Med* 1962; 62:1614–1625.

CLARE A: How good is treatment, in Edwards G, Grant M (eds): *Alcoholism: New Knowledge and New Responses*. London, Croom Helm, 1977, pp 279–289.

CLINEBELL HJ Jr: *Understanding and Counselling the Alcoholic*. New York, Abington, 1968.

COHEN PA: New approach to the treatment of male alcoholics and their families. Available Family Services of Cincinnati Area, Cincinnati, 1966.

CORK MR: *The Forgotten Children*. Toronto, Paperjacks, 1969.

DAVIES DL: Normal drinking in recovered alcoholics. *Q J Stud Alcohol* 1962; 23:94–104.

DEMONE HW, MENDELSON J, BLACKER E: *Alcoholism: An Evaluation of Intervention Strategies in Family Agencies*. Boston, United Community Planning Corporation, 1974.

EDWARDS G: Alcoholism treatment: between guesswork and certainty, in Edwards G, Grant M (eds): *Alcoholism Treatment in Transition*. Baltimore, University Park Press, 1980, pp 307–320.

EWARDS G, GUTHRIE S: A comparison on in-patient and out-patient treatment of alcohol dependence. *Lancet* 1966; 1:467–468.

EDWARDS G, ORFORD JA: Plain treatment for alcoholism. *Proc R Soc Med* 1977; 70:344–348.

EMRICK CD: A review of psychologically oriented treatment of alcoholism. *Q J Stud Alcohol*, 1975; 36:88–108.

ERICKSON K: Notes on the sociology of deviance, in Becker HS (ed): *The Other Side*. New York, Free Press, 1964, pp 9–22.

FORREST GG: *The Diagnosis and Treatment of Alcoholism*. Springfield, Thomas, 1975.

FREUND G: Diseases of the nervous system associated with alcoholism, in Tarter RE, Sugerman AA (eds): *Alcoholism: Interdisciplinary Approaches to an Enduring Problem*. Reading, Addison-Wesley, 1976, pp 171–202.

GAERTNER ML: *The Alcoholic Marriage: A Study of 15 Case Records and Pertinent Psychoanalytic Writings*, thesis, New York School of Social Work, New York, 1939.

GERARD DL, SAENGER G: *Out-patient Treatment of Alcoholism: A Study of Outcome and Its Determinants*. Toronto, University of Toronto Press, 1966.

GILLIS LS, KEET M: Prognostic factors and treatment results in hospitalized alcoholics. *Q J Stud Alcohol* 1969; 30:426–437.

GIRLING KL: Leisure counselling. *Can J Occupational Ther* 1979; 6:155–158.

GLASER F: *The Phase Zero Report of the Core–Shell Treatment System*. Toronto, Addiction Research Foundation, 1978.

GLASER F: Anybody got a match: treatment research and the matching hypothesis, in Edwards G, Grant M (eds): *Alcoholism Treatment in Transition*. Baltimore, University Park Press, 1980, pp 178–196.

GLASER F, SKINNER H: Matching in the real world, in Gottheil E, McLellan A, Druley K (eds): *Matching Patient Needs and Treatment Methods in Alcoholism and Drug Abuse*. Springfield, Thomas, 1981, pp 295–324.

GLIEDMAN LH, ROSENTHAL D, FRANK JD, et al: Group therapy of alcoholics with concurrent group meetings of their wives, in Rosenbaum M, Berger M (eds): *Group Psychotherapy and Group Function.* New York, Basic Books, 1963, pp 510–524.

GLOBETTI G: A conceptual analysis of the effectiveness of alcohol education programs, in Goodstadt M (ed): *Research on Methods and Programs of Drug Education.* Toronto, Addiction Research Foundation, 1974, pp 97–112.

GOLDSTEIN H, GOLDSTEIN L: The concept of deviancy revisited. *Can Ment Health* 1975; 23:10–14.

GOMBERG ES: The female alcoholic, in Tarter R.E. Sugerman A (eds): *Alcoholism: Interdisciplinary Approaches to an Enduring Problem.* Reading, Addison-Wesley, 1976, pp 603–636.

GOODWIN DW, et al. Alcohol problems in adoptees raised apart from alcoholic biological parents. *Arch Gen Psychiatry* 1973; 28:238–243.

HEARN G: *The General Systems Approach: Contributions toward an Holistic Conception of Social Work.* New York, Council on Social Work Education, 1969.

HILL MI, BLANE HT: Evaluation of psychotherapy with alcoholics: a critical review. *Q J Stud Alcohol* 1967; 28:76–104.

JACKSON JK: The adjustment of the family to the crisis of alcoholism. *Q J Stud Alcohol* 1954; 15:562–586.

JACOBS M: *Problems Presented by Alcoholic Clients: A Handbook of Counselling Strategies.* Toronto, Addiction Research Foundation, 1981.

JANZEN C: Family treatment for alcoholism: a review. *Soc Work* 1978; 23:127–134.

JELLINEK EM: *The Disease Concept of Alcoholism.* New Haven, Hillhouse, 1960.

KALANT OJ (ed): *Alcohol and Drug Problems in Women.* New York, Plenum, 1980.

LENNARD HL, BERNSTEIN A: *Patterns in Human Interaction.* San Francisco, Jossey-Bass, 1969.

LIZANSKY E: Clinical research in alcoholism in the use of psychological tests: a re-evaluation, in Fox R (ed): *Alcoholism: Behavioral Research, Therapeutic Approaches.* New York, Springer, 1967, pp 3–15.

LUBORSKY L, SINGER B, LUBORSKY L: Comparative studies of psychotherapies: is it true that everyone has won and all must have prizes?. *Arch Gen Psychiatry* 1975; 32:995–1008.

MARSHMAN J, FRASER RD, HUMPHRIES PW: *The Treatment of Alcoholics: An Ontario Perspective.* Toronto, Addiction Research Foundation, 1978.

MAXWELL R: *The Booze Battle.* New York, Praeger, 1976.

MAYER J, MYERSON DJ: Out-patient treatment of alcoholics: effects of status stability and nature of treatment. *Q J Stud Alcohol* 1971; 32:620–627.

McCORD W, McCORD J, GUDEMAN J: *Origins of Alcoholism.* Stanford, Stanford University Press, 1960.

MEEKS DE: Family therapy, in Tarter RE, Sugerman AA (eds): *Alcoholism: Interdisciplinary Approaches to an Enduring Problem.* Reading, Addison-Wesley, 1976, pp 839–852.

MEEKS DE, KELLEY C: Family therapy with the families of recovering alcoholics. *Q J Stud Alcohol* 1970; 31:399–413.

MOORE RA: Alcoholism treatment in private psychiatric hospitals. *Q J Stud Alcohol* 1971; 32:1038–1045.

MOSER J: *Prevention of Alcohol-Related Problems: An International Review of Preventive Measures, Policies, and Programs..* Toronto, WHO and the Addiction Research Foundation, 1980.

MUFORD H, MILLER L: Measuring public acceptance of the alcoholic as a sick person. *Q J Stud Alcohol* 1964; 25:634–650.

NIELSEN J: Delirium tremens in Copenhagen. *Acta Psychiatr Scand Suppl* 1965; suppl 17.

ORFORD J, OPPENHEIMER E, EDWARDS G: Abstinence or control: the outcome of excessive drinking two years after consultation. *Behav Res Ther* 1976; 14:409–418.

PAOLINO TJ Jr, McCRADY BS: *The Alcoholic Marriage: Alternative Perspectives.* New York, Grune & Stratton, 1977.

PAREDES A, HOOD WR, SEYMOUR H: Loss of control in alcoholism: an investigation of the hypothesis with experimental findings. *Q J Stud Alcohol* 1973; 34: 1146–1161.

PEQUIGNOT G: Nutritional problems in industrial societies. *Vie Med Can Française* 1974; 3:216–225.

PITTMAN DJ, SNYDER CR: *Society, Culture, and Drinking Patterns.* New York, Wiley, 1962.

PLAUT TFA: *Alcohol Problems: A Report to the Nation.* New York, Oxford University Press, 1967.

POLICH JM, ARMOR DJ, BRAIKER HD: *The Course of Alcoholism: Four Years after Treatment.* Santa Monica, Rand, 1979.

POPHAM E, SCHMIDT W: The effectiveness of legal measures in the prevention of alcohol problems. *Addic Dis* 1976; 2:497–513.

POPHAM R, SCHMIDT W, DELINT J: The prevention of alcoholism: epidemiological studies of the effects of government control measures. *Br J Addic* 1975; 70:125–144.

RANKIN J: Etiology, in Phillips L, et al (eds): *Core Knowledge in the Drug Field*, National Health and Welfare, Supply and Services, Ottawa, 1978, 8:1–46.

ROSSETT HL: The effects of alcohol on the fetus and offspring, in Kalant OJ (ed): *Alcohol and Drug Problems in Women.* New York, Plenum, 1980, pp 595–652.

ROSSI JJ. Treatment, in Phillips L, et al (eds): *Core Knowledge in the Drug Field*, National Health and Welfare, Supply and Services, Ottawa, 1978.

SHEPPARD M, et al. *Alcohol Education Lesson Plans for Grades 7, 8, 9, 10.* Toronto, Addiction Research Foundation, 1978.

SKINNER HA: Profiles of treatment seeking populations, in Edwards G, Grant M (eds): *Alcoholism Treatment in Transition.* Baltimore, University Park Press, 1980, pp 248–263.

SKINNER HA: A multivariate evaluation of the Michigan Alcoholism Screening Test. *QJ Stud Alcohol* 1979; 40:831–844.

SMART RG: Young alcoholics in treatment: their characteristics and recovery rates at follow-up. *Alcoholism* 1979; 3:19–23.

SMART RG: *The New Drinkers*, Toronto, Addiction Research Foundation, 1980.

SOBELL MB, SOBELL LC: Alcoholics treated by individualized behaviour therapy: one year treatment outcome. *Behav Res Ther* 1973; 11:599–618.

STEINER C: The alcoholic game. *Q J Stud Alcohol* 1969; 30:920–938.

STEINGLASS P: Experimenting with family treatment approaches to alcoholism, 1950–1975: a review. *Fam Process* 1976; 15:97–123.

Third Special Report to the U.S. Congress on Alcohol and Health from the Secretary, Health, Education, and Welfare. Government Printing Office, 1978.

TRICE M, ROMAN PM: Delabelling, Relabelling, and Alcoholics Anonymous, in Davis FJ, Stivers R (eds): *The Collective Definition of Deviance*. New York, Free Press, 1975, pp 360–371.

WHALEN T: Wives of alcoholics: four types observed in a family service agency. *Q J Stud Alcohol* 1953; 14:632–641.

World Health Organization Expert Committee on Drug Dependence: *Sixteenth Report*, WHO Technical Report Series, no. 407. Geneva, World Health Organization, 1969.

World Health Organization Expert Committee on Mental Health, Alcoholism Sub-committee: *Second Report*, World Health Organization, Geneva, 1952.

ZWEBEN A: The efficacy of role induction in preventing early drop-out from out-patient treatment of drug dependence. *Am J Drug Alcohol Abuse* 1981; 8:171–183.

16

Drug Addiction

Peter E. Bohm

"Drug addiction" is a broad term. Its contemporary definition includes dependence upon readily available legal drugs,* such as alcohol (see Chapter 15), as well as upon prescription drugs and numerous illegal substances. In light of recent research generated knowledge, the expression "drug addiction" appears to be less useful than its equivalent "drug dependence." This is because "addiction" and related terms, such as "habituation," tend to limit the focus of study more than is appropriate. That is, drug dependence is most accurately seen on a continuum from nonuse to obsessive use of drugs. The World Health Organization defined "drug dependence" as "self-administration to the detriment of self and the society in which the individual lives, and a tendency to increase the dosage" (p. 9). For purposes of this chapter, the terms "drug

* The term "drug," as used here, refers to "any substance, other than those required for the maintenance of normal health (as opposed to the correction of a disease), which by its chemical nature alters the structure or function of a living organism" (Kalant & Kalant, 1971, p. 14).

I wish to thank Dr. S. Treilons, of the Addiction Research Foundation, Toronto, for assistance in the preparation of the material on drug classifications and their effects.

dependence," "drug addiction," and "drug abuse" will be used interchangeably.

Ungerleider and Beigel (1980) proposed a useful classification of drug taking patterns:

1. "experimental drug use": participated in primarily by youth and motivated by curiosity
2. "recreational drug use": indulged in by many for pleasure with one or more drugs.
3. "situational or circumstantial drug use": ingestion of drugs for specific effects, e.g., use of stimulants to improve short-term study effectiveness or athletic performance
4. "intensified drug use": regular drug use that interferes with one's behavior and one's relationships at home, at work, and/or at play
5. "compulsive drug use": obtaining drugs ("copping," "scoring," "shooting up") becomes the overriding concern of daily life (National Commission on Marijuana and Drug Abuse, 1973)

Ungerleider and Beigel pointed out that while the first three patterns represent the least serious problems, they nevertheless attract the bulk of funding and service attention, primarily in response to criminal arrest and prosecution activities. For example, marijuana possession and use has led to a tremendous amount of criminal justice activity. On the other hand, more serious drug abuse behaviors may often meet with social acceptance and even encouragement, as exemplified by our society's attitudes toward alcohol. This inconsistency is a major social issue in the drug abuse field. Accordingly, this chapter focuses on the fourth and fifth forms of drug abuse, which have the most pervasive personal and social effects.

Drug Types

A convenient framework for viewing drug types and effects from a clinical point of view is presented in this section. However, keep in mind that drug effects vary both from person to person and from one occasion to the next in a given individual depending upon biological, social, and psychological factors.

"Depressants" diminish brain functions. That is, they make one feel more relaxed, less conscious of events around one, and less inhibited.*

---

* The degree of disinhibition resulting from drugs such as alcohol is probably not as great as previously thought. Sociocultural expectations of drug effect are likely to be the more powerful influence.

On the negative side, the user feels listless or drowsy, is unable to concentrate, and in general (with increasing doses) is less competent physically and socially. Depressants include alcohol, opiates and nonopiate narcotics, barbiturate and nonbarbiturate sedatives, and minor tranquilizers (marketed as Meprobamate, Valium, Librium, and Serax, for example.) Antihistamines are also depressants but are often used by persons unaware of their psychotropic effects.

"Stimulants" heighten awareness, enabling the brain to receive more information at any one time and to process it faster (but not necessarily more effectively!). The person feels more alert but is not necessarily more productive. People who use these drugs are also inclined to feel overly excited, jittery, irritable, suspicious, and paranoid, particularly with high doses. Stimulants include amphetamines, cocaine, caffeine (found in coffee, tea, chocolate, and cola drinks), and nicotine.

"Hallucinogens" distort perception and thought; the individual experiences a change in sensations. These drugs either slow down or speed up brain functions. The term "expand the mind" translates in everyday terms into feeling different, having more intense feelings, and, on the negative side, feeling confusion, anxiety, acute panic, and a variety of unpredictable responses. Halluciongens include such substances as LSD, mescaline, MDA, PCP, DMT, and DOM.

From a clinical point of view, some drugs full into more than one type. For example, MDA appears to have both stimulant and hallucinogenic effects. Various solvents that are sniffed often produce a combination of depression and distortion of perception. Cannabis (marijuana) has both hallucinogenic and depressant effects (Addiction Research Foundation, 1980; Kalant & Kalant 1971; Treilons, 1980.

Of the drugs listed above, other than alcohol, those that generate the highest level of social concern are the barbiturates, the minor tranquilizers, and the opiate and nonopiate narcotics. There is also rising concern about illegal use of stimulants (such as amphetamines and cocaine), as well as about ingestion of legal stimulants (such as caffeine). The most widely used hallucinogenic drug of concern at this time is cannabis.

Theories of Drug Abuse

A wide range of models and theories to explain drug abuse has developed over the years, but no single theory explains drug dependence. Many of the theories focus upon character pathology in addicts and consider addiction as one form of character disorder (McKenna, 1979). However, it is currently fairly well accepted that "drug use and drug dependence is a multi-etiological phenomenon which includes social, economic, psychological, and physiological factors. Although there is a high incidence of psychiatric problems in drug dependent populations, and specific psychiatric syndromes may lead an individual to become drug dependent'' (McKenna, 1979, p. 197), ''the precise relationship between drug use and psychopathology is an open question'' (Satinder, 1980, p. 88). It is from this perspective that drug dependence as a form of adult psychopathology is discussed here.

Moral and Spiritual Theories of Drug Addiction

Although it may be intellectually tempting to disregard morally and spiritually based theories of drug addiction, use, nonuse, and abuse of drugs have a long-standing connection with numerous religious rituals and spiritual beliefs. Therefore, it is important to include this perspective in any review of explanatory theories for drug use. Depending on the group in question, particular forms of drug use may be seen as wrong, right, spiritually debilitating, or mandatory. This perspective includes the view that drug addiction reflects a moral flaw in the individual; consequently, abuse represents a moral crisis. ''Since the early part of this century, society has identified heroin and other drug 'abuse' as one of its major evils'' (Lidz et al., 1980, p. 37). Within this perspective, law enforcement is deemed essential to prevent the spread of drug abuse. This notion has encouraged the development of connections between the courts and treatment facilities and a move toward mandatory treatment (Lidz et al., 1980).

The moral and spiritual theories of addiction have also contributed to the emergence of self-help groups based largely (or partly) on religious beliefs. Programs such as Exodus House, the Salvation Army, and Teen Challenge are treatment approaches that stress the spiritual aspect of recovery from drug dependence (Langrod et al., 1972).

Biomedical Theories of Drug Addiction

Biomedical theories of drug addiction generally begin with the assumption that drug abuse is a symptom of an underlying genetic predisposition or pathology in the abuser. For example, Dole and Nyswander (1965) conceptualized heroin addiction as a metabolic disease that originates from changes in the user's nervous system as a result of single or multiple administrations of the drug. The recent discovery of endorphins (Goldstein & Cox, 1977), which are naturally occurring opiatelike substances in the body, has added some support to this theory (Callahan, 1980). Further weight is added to this theoretical position by the consistent and steadily growing body of evidence that genetic endowment is an important factor in alcohol addiction (Schuckit, 1980). Although similar findings have not yet been generated for other forms of drug addiction, it is safe to assume that genetics contributes in some degree to the development of addictive behaviors.

Naturally enough, the biomedical theories of drug addiction have led to treatments based on the medical model. These approaches focus on medical treatment for the physical and psychiatric consequences of drug use and are extremely expensive to provide.

Sociological Theories of Drug Addiction

Sociological theories of drug addiction are based mainly on the observation that ''not only is there a vast array of substances people use, there is also a very marked selectivity as to who uses which kinds of substances.'' Patterns of drug use are not random (Lukoff, 1980). In other words, distinct social groups tend to use different drugs, depending upon such factors as locale, class structure, socialization, lifestyle, and drug availability.

Becker (1980) stressed that social influences, particularly as they relate to the user's knowledge about drug use, are key variables in determining what drug is used and how it is used. Social sanctions, social expectations, product availability, and environmental stress are major sociocultural factors in drug use or addiction (Huba et al., 1980). This position argues for viewing drug addiction as part of the larger social fabric; thus, treatment aims at the alteration of lifestyle in a socioenvironmental sense (Lukoff, 1980).

Psychological Theories of Drug Addiction

Early psychological theories of addiction derived from the medical model, in which drug abuse is seen as a symptom of an underlying pathology; developmental trauma and/or a body chemistry that predisposes some persons to becoming addicted to certain substances are cited as key factors (Khantzian, 1980). Psychodynamic theories focus upon the addict's use of drugs to deal with otherwise unmanageable feelings of anger toward herself and others (Khantzian, 1980).

Personality traits were long thought to play an important role in determining whether a person becomes addicted to a drug, but research has not supported this view (Ausubel, 1980). The complexity of personality, social, and physiological variables makes predictive statements unreliable when based on personality traits alone. Multivariate analyses to identify the relationship between personality factors and treatment outcome are hampered by the absence of uniform recordkeeping and measurement methods in the drug abuse field (Ogborne, 1978). In recent years, psychological theories have broadened to emphasize the context of drug dependence—social interaction generally and family or peer interaction, more specifically (Coleman, 1978, 1981).

A useful development in psychological theories of drug use has been the conceptualization of drug dependence as learned behavior. Within this behavioral-pharmacologic view of addiction, the effects of commonly used drugs are conceived of as powerful reinforcers for drug taking behavior. In simple terms, drug use often results in feeling good or feeling less bad. Research has demonstrated that this perspective accords in a number of ways with clinical observation. Although "reinforcing functions of drugs cannot account completely for all drug-taking in humans" (Downs et al., 1975, p. 63), this theoretical position has helped substantially in refining the treatment of drug dependence.*

A Multivariate Perspective on Drug Addiction

A host of so-called theories currently exists to explain why people initially take drugs; why they continue to take them; how drug use escalates to abuse; what stops drug abuse; and how relapse occurs (Lettieri et al., 1980). This proliferation of theories suggests the need for a multivariate perspective that takes into account the most substantial evidence available. A practical, research based orientation to treating drug addiction should incorporate at least the following assumptions.

1. some individuals are biologically predisposed to drug dependence
2. some drugs are more likely to be addicting than are others
3. drug taking behavior is acquired and maintained through learning

These assumptions require the clinician to examine clients' views of how and why they use drugs. Because drug use is a behavior, a behavioral analysis is obviously helpful to this understanding. However, the clinician also must understand the phenomenological world of the client as he experiences it (Abrahms, 1979; Bohm, 1981; Pittell et al., 1979). Finally, specialized knowledge of drug problems and treatments increases the social worker's self-confidence, as well as the client's confidence in the worker's expertise (Kadushin, 1972; Matarazzo, 1978).

---

* Early behavioral treatment and research was overly simplistic in that it concentrated solely on the act of drug ingestion (Callahan, 1980).

Trends in Drug Taking and in Responses to Drug Use

"The proliferation of available addictive drugs world-wide and the increasingly wide-spread use of these drugs by persons of all ages and all strata of society constitutes one of the major societal and health problems of our time" (Ferrer, 1981, p. xvii).

Between 1962 and 1979, the prevalence of marijuana use in the United States increased from 1% of the 12-17 age group to 31%. The percentage of marijuana users in the 18-25 age group rose from 4% to 68% during this same period. Use of other drugs such as hallucinogens, inhalants, cocaine, and heroin also rose steeply during these years, from less than 0.5% to 9% of 12-17 year olds and from 4% to 33% of 18-25 year olds (Dupont, 1981).

One might ask, "Does an increased prevalence of drug use necessarily imply increased problems?" Recent research suggests that the answer is yes. As with alcohol use, "It is very likely that when drug use increases so will heavy use and problems" (Smart, 1981, p. 275). Not surprisingly, problem drug users are appearing with increasing frequency in hospitals and mental health clinics (McLellan et al., 1981), family physicians' offices (Cohen, 1981), public schools (Johnston et al., 1981), family agencies (Stanton, 1979, 1980), athletic arenas (Burks, 1981), the workplace (Wiencek, 1981), and the criminal justice system (Pittel et al., 1979).

In spite of the widespread use and abuse of drugs, little literature exists on the social work treatment of drug related problems. This is somewhat surprising because both human services agencies and drug abuse treatment programs are staffed largely by social workers. One explanation has to do with "attitudinal barriers to clinical involvement with drug abusers" (Chappel, 1973, p. 1011; Heiman, 1979, p. 87). For example, the often desperate emotional and situational problems of heroin addicts who are in methadone treatment programs may contribute to the negative stereotype of the drug addict as untreatable (Brill, 1977; Heiman, 1979). Illicit drug users, particularly heroin users, are unable to pay for their drugs through ordinary income sources. As a result, many "are guilty of theft, fraud, prostitution and related crimes committed in an effort to obtain enough money to continue their drug use at the desired level" (Kalant & Kalant, 1971, p. 94). Professionals often are unaware that this pattern describes only a small percentage of the total drug dependent population. Similarly, although some drug addiction may be too entrenched to reverse, intervention in other areas of addicts' lives can be beneficial. Furthermore, a large (but as yet difficult to predict) portion of the addict population can reduce or eliminate their harmful dependence on drugs (Harding et al., 1980).

A major assumption that is helpful in treating drug dependence was succinctly stated by Kalant and Kalant (1971): "It is not the presence of dependence itself which is the problem; it is the severity and consequences of that dependence which are important" (p. 80). Acceptance of this assumption leads to a treatment orientation that places drug dependence in a balanced perspective, forcing the clinician to set aside many ill-conceived and/or preconceived notions about drug addicts in favor of a careful analysis of specific factors that contribute to, or mitigate against, drug abuse. Society's response to drug addicts has emphasized criminal justice and social control. As social work and other professions involved in the treatment of addiction adopt the multivariate perspective advocated here, a shift in public attitudes and measures in the area of drug dependence is likely.

Treatment Modalities in Drug Addiction

Historically, the treatment of drug addiction has included the use of psychoanalysis, controlled drug maintenance, imprisonment, religious conversion, substitute drugs, hypnosis, surgery, shock treatment, pharmacologic blockage, coercion, group therapy, aversive conditioning, social support, sleep, education, isolation, and lifestyle counseling (Henry, 1974). No single modality has demonstrated clear superiority, nor is this likely to occur.

Treatment of Opiate Abuse

Three issues stand out as particularly important in the treatment of opiate abuse: the compelling nature of narcotic drugs and the notorious difficulty encountered in achieving abstinence from narcotics following a severe dependence; the role of drug maintenance, substitute narcotics, and narcotic antagonists in treatment; and the frequent involvement of the criminal justice system in treatment.

The dependence potential of the opiate drugs (particularly heroin) is perhaps best illustrated by users' notorious reputation for relapse. Rasor (1972), in his review of the treatment of narcotic abuse, reported relapse rates following treatment of 90–96% at one to five years' follow-up. In a more recent review, Callahan (1980) commented that "traditionally, the treatment of heroin addiction has been singularly unsuccessful" (p. 147). In the early 1960s, some research had suggested that most addicts "mature out" by the age of 40; however, a recent study that followed 51 addicts for 20 years found only 1 of these individuals to be drug-free (Harrington & Cox, 1979). This grim view is tempered by the findings of Harding and associates (1980) that controlled narcotic use is apparently feasible for some persons.

Heroin addiction traditionally has been treated pharmacologically. Dole and Nyswander (1965) resurrected Bishop's (1976) view that heroin addiction is a metabolic disease brought about by the use of the narcotic. Early treatment based on this view had disappointing results (Callahan, 1980; Vaillant, 1966) and a second approach to treatment, also based on the metabolic disease notion of opiate dependence, was introduced. Assuming that these patients are "metabolically 'normal' only with a narcotic in their system" (Callahan, 1980), some investigators proposed long-term maintenance on the synthetic opiate methadone; others argued for the use of morphine (or other opiates) in combination with personal and job placement counseling (Henry, 1974). Although the notion of "change from dependence on one drug to dependence on another equally addicting drug" was controversial, patients reportedly benefited in terms of improved social adjustment, educational gains, employment stability, and reduced criminal involvement (Callahan, 1980; Dole & Nyswander, 1965).

There are distinct problems inherent in opioid maintenance by means of methadone: a high death rate (30/2500); patients' decreased levels of responsiveness to a variety of stimuli; potential for abuse and diversion of the substitute drug into the illicit market; development of tolerance to the maintenance drug, which requires increasing dosage to potentially dangerous levels; addiction and potentially long-range risks in babies born to women on methadone maintenance; and ethical complications of institutionalized drug dependence (Henry, 1974).

A relatively recent advance in treating opiate addiction is the use of opiate antagonists (e.g., nalorphine and naloxone). The administration of an antagonist can reveal opiate dependence by producing abstinence symptoms (virtually immediately) in persons who have become tolerant to this class of drug. Antagonists also can be used to treat acute symptoms of opiate overdose and to facilitate behavioral treatment of opiate dependence by blocking opiates' primary, or reinforcing, effects, as well as their withdrawal supressant effects (Henry, 1974).

In large cities, where opiate addiction rates are highest, it is estimated that half of all serious property crimes are committed by addicts attempting to support the cost of their drug use. In 1965, this translated into more than $1 billion (Goode, 1972). These figures merely serve to emphasize that many severely addicted opiate users become defined as criminals through their illegal activities and subsequent convictions. The alienation associated with this pattern of living can be both a cause and an effect of drug addiction. However, for the clinician a practical consideration is the clash of institutional values brought about by treating the addict within two distinct systems: health services and criminal justice. At the very least, "this quasi-oppositional relationship of values suggests that there will be problems in integrating the activities of people maintaining allegiance to these ideologies, since they will have trouble agreeing on the appropriate goals of their venture" (Lidz et al., 1980, p. 233). Here social work has much to contribute, drawing on the considerable experience many practitioners have in negotiating between institutional differences.

Treatment of Nonopiate Abuse

Other than alcohol (which is dealt with in Chapter 15), the major nonopiate drugs are the barbiturate sedatives and the nonbarbiturate sedative-hypnotics; the minor tranquilizers; and amphetamines and other stimulants. Multiple drug use is also examined in this section.

The possibility of sudden death is a principal concern with barbiturate sedative-hypnotic and nonbarbiturate sedative abusers. Abrupt withdrawal or rapid reduction of dosage often triggers a fatal withdrawal syndrome. Coma and death are common problems associated with accidental overdose of these drugs. Fatal overdoses (suicidal and accidental) are particularly common when these drugs are used in combination with alcohol. For these reasons, social workers and other nonmedical practitioners should seriously consider medical consultation when dealing with such cases (Addiction Research Foundation, 1980; Chambers & Brill, 1972).

Minor tranquilizers such as chlordiazepoxide (marketed as Librium) and diazepam (marketed as Valium) are much less likely than the preceding groups of drugs to result in death; other tranquilizers are much more dangerous (Table 16–1). Although many of these drugs are often considered safe by professionals and lay persons,

> Minor tranquilizers have become a major cause of poisoning. . . . Their margin of safety is so wide that death rarely results from tranquilizer use alone. However, many deaths result from taking these drugs together with alcohol or other drugs. A combination of factors is probably at work: direct toxicity, drug-induced confusion, depression, the large number of doses available per prescription, and the personality characteristics of the person involved. Accumulation of the drug in body tissues as a result of prolonged use may also be a contributing factor. (Addiction Research Foundation, 1980, pp. 40–41)

The use of minor tranquilizers within the general population is widespread. A Canadian survey in 1977 indicated that "minor tranquilizers accounted for 45% of all psychotropic drug prescriptions or approximately 7% of all prescriptions sampled" (Addiction Research Foundation, 1980, p. 41). This clearly makes the use of these drugs an issue in a very large proportion of the clients seen by social workers. Knowledge of the medical risks noted in Table 16–1 can only benefit the social work

Table 16–1 Serious Physical Consequences of Nonbarbiturate Sedative Drugs and Tranquilizers

| DRUGS | | | | |
Generic	Brand	Intoxication	Dependence	Coma or Death
Meprobamate*	Miltown Equanil, etc.	Yes	Yes	Yes
Glutethimide**	Doriden	Yes	Yes	Yes
Ethinamate**	Valmid	Yes	Yes	Yes
Ethclorvynol**	Placidyl	Yes	Yes	Yes
Methyprylon**	Noludar	Yes	Yes	Yes
Chlordiazepoxide*	Librium	Yes	Yes	—
Diazepam*	Valium	Yes	Yes	—
Oxazepam*	Serax	Yes	—	—

Source: Reprinted with permission from C. Chambers and L. Brill, "The Treatment of Non-narcotic Drug Abusers," in L. Brill and L. Lieberman (eds.), *Major Modalities in the Treatment of Drug Abuse* (New York: Behavioral Publications, 1972), p. 212.
*Tranquilizers.
**Nonbarbiturate sedatives.

treatment of these clients. Furthermore, social work collaboration with medical personnel in assessment and follow-up can help identify or moderate crucial environmental elements impinging upon and perhaps endangering clients who use these drugs, thereby maximizing the benefits of prescribed use and reducing the risk of fatal overdose.

Amphetamine use is often associated with high demand situations, such as professional sports competition's or test taking. In large and repeated doses, these drugs produce hyperactivity, paranoid ideation, aggressiveness, and hostility (Addiction Research Foundation, 1980). Typically, the symptoms of heavy amphetamine use vary with the user's state (Chambers & Brill, 1972). Thus, during the withdrawal ("down") phase, users are prone initially to violent episodes; in a later stage of withdrawal, severe depression and suicide are common. Chronic heavy users sometimes develop amphetamine psychosis, which takes the form of exaggerated short-term symptoms of high doses. This syndrome may persist for days or weeks after use of the drug is stopped. In one study,

> violence (accidental and self-inflicted, and that administered by others) was the leading cause of amphetamine-related deaths. Violent death was at least four times as common among regular users of amphetamines as among nonusers of the same age and sex. (Addiction Research Foundation, 1980, p. 14)

Although it is not clear yet whether permanent brain damage can occur as a result of heavy amphetamine use, impurities in the drug can lead to problems with the kidneys, lungs, brain, or other organs. Moreover, "a generally run-down condition, lack of proper diet, lack of sleep and a frequently unhealthy environment may contribute to increased susceptibility to disease among regular users'' (Addiction Research Foundation, 1980, p. 14). Again, these are key considerations that should be taken into account by the social work practitioner.

An increasingly important issue in drug abuse is the potential interaction effect of the simultaneous or sequential ingestion of a variety of drugs. As more and more drug preparations become available legally and illegally, it is increasingly common for users to combine several drugs to obtain a particular effect or to alleviate the negative effects of other drugs. Although not discussed in this section, hallucinogenic drugs, inhalants, and cocaine can seriously complicate multiple drug use patterns. It is important to note in this regard that multiple drug users apparently tended to be more psychiatrically disturbed in several studies reviewed by Satinder (1980).

The Unit of Treatment in Drug Abuse

The "unit of treatment" (e.g., individual, family, peer group) is often confused with the "method of treatment" (set of techniques) in social work interventions. In some instances, methods may be designed for use with specific units. However, most methods or combinations of methods can be used with virtually any unit of treatment (Table 16–2).

As in virtually all clinical problems, hope and optimism on the part of the therapist is an essential ingredient in successful treatment, whatever the method or unit. This attitude can be fostered by careful selection and training of clinical personnel.

As Table 16–2 indicates, only psychosocial treatment methods are suitable with all units of treatment.

Table 16–2 Possible Combinations of Drug Addiction Treatment Units and Methods

Treatment Methods	TREATMENT UNITS				
	Individual	Family	Group	Network	Social System
Behavioral	X	X	X	X	
Cognitive	X	X	X	X	
Medical	X	X		X	
Psychodynamic	X	X	X		
Psychosocial	X	X	X	X	X
Therapeutic* community	X		X		

* Therapeutic community refers to situations of group living where the focus of the group program is to reduce drug dependency. The programs involve combinations of individual and group treatment.

Individual

While an exclusive focus on the individual as the unit of concern is clearly inadequate with drug problems, a one-to-one client–worker relationship is indispensable. For example, in a study of addicted patients' self-perceived factors responsible for successful treatment, relationship and interpersonal variables were most often linked with positive outcome: "A supportive relationship, particularly with a drug-free person, a satisfying job, and personal attributes or skills were the most frequently mentioned factors, while the absence or withdrawal of these events was associated with subsequent reinvolvement with excessive drug use" (Abrahms, 1979, p. 1079). This is consistent with some of Orford and Edwards's (1977) findings in treating alcohol dependence and it is clearly in line with social work treatment methods (Shulman, 1977).

In the drug treatment literature, numerous studies have indicated the importance of supportive counseling and coordinated services aimed at individual client goals such as job placement, use of leisure time, social skills training, and relaxation; such efforts improve the client's self-image and help to remove environmental supports of drug dependence (Commission of Inquiry into the Non-medical Use of Drugs, 1972; Pittel et al., 1979; Rush et al., 1981).

Perhaps the most compelling argument for not losing sight of the individual in the treatment of drug abuse is the substantial research evidence, reviewed by Ogborne (1978), that patient characteristics appear to account for most of the treatment outcome variance. A treatment stratgegy that identifies and builds on client's strengths is therefore warranted (Bohm, 1976).

Family

Although the family has been seen as an important unit of treatment with numerous problems (including alcohol abuse) for many years, family treatment of drug abuse has been prominent only since the early 1970s in North America. Stanton (1979), in the first review paper on the family treatment of drug addiction, discussed over 80 reports dealing with this area (more than half of them published since 1975).

The family treatment of drug abuse is based upon several plausible assumptions for which there is a growing body of empirical support. First, drug use can serve an adaptive function by maintaining the family equilibrium. Second, the label "addict" can serve as an acceptable reason for preventing a member of the family from leaving home; such a person is considered helpless and in need of protection. Third, drug abuse can function as a crisis that unifies the family and keeps it intact. Thus, although cultural and other psychosocial factors also play an important part in drug abuse, this pattern of behavior is sometimes a means of controlling family transactions. Numerous authors have reported that relatives (consciously and/or unconsciously, overtly and/or covertly) encourage a family member's drug use. This can sabotage treatment efforts with the individual.

A family oriented approach to treatment can use family influences to overcome drug problems. Numerous variations on this treatment approach have been reported in the literature, including marital groups for parents; parent–groups; family sessions; sibling oriented groups and; multiple family groups (Stanton, 1979a,c, 1980).

It is important to note that there is no set way of organizing and conducting family therapy in the case of drug addiction (Rossi et al., 1978). Obviously, many social work methods lend themselves to a family oriented approach, and this family orientation often appears to be a critical factor in positive treatment outcomes.

Network

A logical extension of focusing on the immediate family has been the move, in recent years, toward expanding the unit of treatment to include the client's social network (Speck & Attneave, 1973); including the total group of important others is seen as increasing the power of therapeutic intervention by broadening the scope and number of influential family members, friends, neighbors, employers, etc., who can help the client overcome dependence on drugs. Successful case outcomes using this approach were reported by Speck and Attneave for outpatient treatment of amphetamine abuse and by Callan and associates (1975) in the context of a therapeutic community program. Although it is hard to work with so large a treatment unit, this approach offers the potential advantages of involving a wide range of systems in the attempt to reverse or arrest serious drug dependence. This perspective, like family treatment, is consistent with contemporary social work theory and practice. Therefore, recourse to the client's social network deserves serious consideration, particularly in very difficult cases.

Small Group

Prior to the widespread use of natural family groups in the treatment process, small groups were employed to create a context that promoted drug (and other) problemsolving on the part of the client. Encounter groups became quite popular in treating drug abusers during the 1960s, especially clients who had become disconnected from their families. The group unit of treatment brings peer pressure for change, an increased array of psychosocial experiences and resources with which to address drug problems, and the potential for collective alternative activities to drug abuse (Commission of Inquiry into the Non-medical Use of Drugs, 1972). At the same time, the small group presents some risks: exchange or reinforcement of drug problems and unpredictability of interpersonal processes (Malcolm, n.d.).

Social System

A comprehensive view of drug abuse takes into account the reality that successful treatment must address the transactions that the user has with "the various social systems with which he is in contact" (Meeks, 1973, p. 27):

> Unlike other health related problems, the treatment and rehabilitation of drug users has to be viewed as a continuum and must be coordinated to the maximum extent.
>
> We have to be very cautious in adopting various modes of treatment. It would not be possible to apply a single treatment mode to a very large group because we already have empirical evidence to show that different treatments are effective with different groups of drug users. (Satinder, 1980, p. 155)

Adequate treatment planning and delivery requires a clear psychosocial understanding of how the individual's drug abuse behavior is initiated and maintained by both antecedent events and the consequences of use (Bohm, 1981). A social systems perspective highlights important links between clinical treatment and social or community treatment. Social work can assist here by acknowledging and implementing the view that institutions, individuals, families, networks, and small groups, require change with respect to drug abuse.

Contemporary Social Work Treatment of Drug Addiction

Interdisciplinary Issues

Social work treatment of drug abuse draws heavily on contributions from biomedical research and other interdisciplinary research. Drug action, tolerance, dependence, and withdrawal cannot be understood outside a biomedical perspective. Behavioral research has improved assessment, sociobehavioral interventions, and even compliance with pharmacologic treatments. The need for "making things happen" between and inter-disciplinary cooperation is also essential in coordinating community based services to insure that clients receive comprehensive assessment, treatment, support, and follow-up.

A Social Work Model for the Treatment of Drug Addiction

Social work theory and practice are well suited in many ways to the treatment of drug abuse. From a psychosocial perspective, in particular, a problem such as drug use can be viewed in its full complexity, rather than oversimplified, and the benefits of interdisciplinary thinking and collaboration can be secured:

> Psychosocial therapy has shown itself to be highly effective with a wide range of emotional, personal, interpersonal, situational and intersituational problems. Although there has been a tradition to see this approach as being highly problem—and pathology—focused, in current practice a growing emphasis can be observed on strengths, potential and healthy functioning. (Turner, 1974, p. 106)

Table 16–3 outlines a way of viewing the psychosocial treatment of drug abuse. Five sets of phases and supportive resources are identified in relation to 10 critical components of individualized treatment. These phases and components of the social work treatment process are neither unique to treating drug abuse nor mutually exclusive. Virtually all psychosocial problems require:

preparation: the practitioner needs to develop special knowledge, attitudes, and skills

induction: through the therapeutic relationship, motivational techniques, and information, the practitioner involves the client in treatment

Table 16–3 A Social Work Model for Treating Drug Abuse

PHASES OF PSYCHOSOCIAL TREATMENT				
Preparation	*Induction*	*Negotiation*	*Intervention*	*Evaluation*
Knowledge	Relationship	Assessment	Treatment	Follow-up
Attitudes	Motivational Counseling	Selection of Treatment	Primary care	Relapse Prevention
Supervision	*Information*	*Consultation*	*Collaboration*	*Corroboration*

SUPPORTIVE RESOURCES FOR PSYCHOSOCIAL TREATMENT

negotiation: the practitioner and the client arrive at a mutual understanding of, and a proposed solution to, the problem through assessment, selection of a treatment approach, and consultation

intervention: specific treatments and supportive case management
are brought to bear on the client's problem

evaluation: the results of treatment are assessed through systematic
follow-up procedures that attempt both to maintain and assess improvements through community contacts

However, there are some important differences in the content and interrelationships of these factors in the treatment of drug abuse. In particular, two central questions stand out:

how can clients be motivated to change their drug use?
how can relapse be prevented?

These may be the most important practice questions because it is widely
agreed that although *stopping* drug use is relatively easy to achieve, motivating a client to want change and maintaining change are very difficult.

Before going to the trouble of motivating the client and planning treatment, it is important to establish whether treatment is appropriate for
this particular person at this particular time. Early assessment interview
with the client should answer the following questions. (1) Is there a drug
related problem in the client's view? If yes, then the worker moves
toward the intervention phase. If no, then the negotiation phase continues. (2) Does the client want to change? If yes, then specific plans can
be made within the intervention phase. If no, then the negotiation phase
continues. (3) Can an agreement be reached on how and what the client
wants to change? If yes, then the intervention phase can begin. If no,
then the negotiation phase continues. Moving to the intervention phase
without affirmative answers to these three questions is likely to result in
wasted efforts at implementing specific treatments and in tremendous
frustration for everybody involved. A case example illustrates the application of this model.

The client was a 25-year-old man who had been using heroin intravenously three
times a day for almost two years, at a cost of almost $100 per day, along with many
other drugs (amphetamines, alcohol, cannabis). He had frequently relied on
burglary and shoplifting to support drug expenses; he was living with an emotionally disturbed female heroin addict, who worked as a prostitute to support her
drug use. Initially, the client's verbal behavior was characterized by a pessimistic
and sarcastic attitude, intellectualization, and preoccupation with violence. On
the positive side, the client was reasonable successful in his job as a band
manager; he had no physical dysfunctions, no criminal record, an IQ of 145, supportive parents, adequate housing, and an interest in pursuing medical and psychosocial treatment (Bohm, 1976).

The preparation phase (Table 16-4) involved selecting a therapist who would not be distressed by the negative aspects of the client's drug use behavior pattern and who was willing to learn about heroin addiction and treatment. The induction phase involved orienting the client to the treatment services available (medical and psychosocial) while developing a constructive relationship through effective communication. Motivational counseling involved a thorough examination of drug versus drug-free lifestyles, which identified the pros and cons of continuing heroin use; these sessions were videotaped and replayed. The negotiation phase included a careful assessment of the drug use pattern (using a comprehensive framework such as the one outlined in Tables 16-4 and 16-5). In addition to fact gathering, this phase stressed the notion of gaining a phenomenological picture of how the client saw the problem, which turned out to be in highly intellectual and medical terms. Negotiation was structured around the following questions: was there a problem in the client's view; did the client want change; what and how did he want to change? At the same time, medical evaluation and psychological testing were done to help identify risks and strengths. The intervention phase—treatment and primary care—included short-term inpatient withdrawal and outpatient (long-term, decreasing dosage) methadone maintenance, along with individual and couple counseling. During this time, collaboration with an occupational therapist was employed, leading to retraining. The couple also chose to move out of the city in which they had been living. Evaluation consisted of weekly follow-up by telephone and periodic contact with some of the client's new acquaintances in the setting in which he worked part-time as a volunteer. Relapse prevention involved deciding where he would go for local treatment if he reinitiated heroin use. Multiple criteria were used to measure the client's improvement; these criteria concerned what drugs were being used, how they were being used, and what consequences they were having in terms of physical, as well as psychosocial, functioning. From this perspective, the client maintained substantial improvement for at least five years.

Assessment

Amid the competing theories on drug use, some useful consensus is beginning to emerge. For example, learning theory and research provides a conceptual framework for some important aspects of assessment that cuts across theories (Bohm, 1981). From this perspective, client assessment for intervention planning

> focuses on four sequential and functionally related events. These are: (1) stimulus factors (i.e., antecedent cues); (2) mediational variables (i.e., attitudes and expectations); (3) consumption patterns, per se; and (4) outcome variables (consequences). Habitual substance abuse is explained on the basis of the relationship among these variables at any one point in time. Thus, a detailed description of the antecedent events, cognitive expectations, and consequent events could lead to an understanding of the mechanisms controlling addictive behaviors. (P. Miller, 1980, p. 274)

Table 16–4 Psychoactive Drug Use History. Reprinted with permission of Addiction Research Foundation.

Note to Assessment Workers re: Item No. 1
*The following are examples of specific drugs in each of the categories.**

Caffeine
Chocolate
Coffee
Cola
Tea
Sedative-Hypnotics
amobarbital – e.g. Amytal®
chloral hydrate – e.g. Noctec®
ethchlorvynol – e.g. Placidy 1®
flurazepam – e.g. Dalmane®
glutethimide – e.g. Doriden®
methaqualone – e.g. Mandrax®,
   Quaalude®
pentobarbital – e.g. Nembutal®
secobarbital – e.g. Seconal®

Stimulants
amphetamine
chlorphentermine – e.g. Pre-Sale®
methamphetamine – "speed"
methylphenidate – e.g. Ritalin®
phenmetrazine – e.g. Preludin®
phentermine – e.g. Tenuate®
Glue/Solvents/Aerosols
gasoline; lacquer thinner
Tranquillizers
chlordiazepoxide – e.g. Librium®
chlorpromazine – e.g. Largactil®
diazepam – e.g. Vivol® Valium®
haloperidol – e.g. Haldol®
meprobamate – e.g. Equanil®

Narcotic Drugs
codeine – e.g. 222's®
dihydromorphone – e.g.
   Dilaudid®
heroin
meperidine – e.g. Demerol®
methadone
oxycodone – e.g. Percodan®
pentazocine – e.g. Talwin®
propoxyphene – e.g. Darvon®
Cannabis
marihuana; hashish; hash oil
Hallucinogens
L.S.D., M.D.A.; mescaline;
phencyclidine – P.C.P.,
Angel's Dust; psilocybin
Volatile Nitrites
amyl nitrite–"poppers"
isobutyl nitrite – e.g.
Locker Room® Rush®

1. Have you used any of the following kinds of substances	Past Month	Past (12) Months
Caffeine	☐	☐
Tranquillizers	☐	☐
Sedative-Hypnotics/ Sleeping Pills	☐	☐
Narcotic Drugs	☐	☐
Stimulants	☐	☐
Cocaine	☐	☐
Cannabis	☐	☐
Hallucinogens	☐	☐
Glue/Solvents/Aerosols	☐	☐
Volatile Nitrites	☐	☐

	**Past Month	Past (12) Months
2. Have you used any other psychoactive drugs on a self-medication basis?	_____	_____
	_____	_____
	_____	_____
3. Have you used any other psychoactive drugs as prescribed by a physician?	**Past Month	Past (12) Months
	_____	_____
	_____	_____
	_____	_____

Notes to Assessment Worker re: Psychoactive Drug Use History
*(The following questions are to be asked for each category of drugs identified as being used during the past month. ***Answers are to be recorded on the Pages following.)*
Usual Drug: What particular type of (this category of) drugs do you usually use?
Time Elapsed: When did you have your last dose of (this category of drugs)?
Frequency: On how many days during the last month did you use (this category of drugs)?
Dose: On a typical day when you are using (your usual drugs of this category) how much would you take/drink/smoke? (In the case of legal drugs attempt to determine the dosage in mg, ml, oz. and record in these units. In the case of illicit drugs, report in the most accurate units possible.)
Mode of Administration: How do you usually take/administer (drugs of this category)?
Source: How do you usually obtain (drugs of this category)?
Problem Status: Do you consider your use of (this type of drugs) to be a problem?
Combination with Alcohol: Do you ever use alcohol at the same time as you are using (drugs of this category) to increase/decrease/change the effects of the drugs?
Combination with Other Drugs of this Category: Do you often use other drugs (of this drug category) at the same time as you use your usual drug to increase/decrease/change the effects of the drugs?

---

*A comprehensive list of prescription drugs can be found in the Compendium of Pharmaceutical and Specialties (CPS) published by the Canadian Pharmaceutical Association, Ottawa, Ontario and an analogous listing of non-prescription medication can be found in Canadian Self-Medication also published by the Canadian Pharmaceutical Association, Ottawa, Ontario.
**Individual has been abstinent or using drugs in an atypical manner during the past month (as a result of incarceration, hospitalization, etc.)
Complete this section with respect to most recent four week period of typical drug use.
***Refers to kinds of drugs as listed in No. 1.

Table 16–5 Health Screening. Reprinted with permission of Addiction Research Foundation.

Note to Assessment Workers
re: Items Health Screening—Guidelines for Medical/Psychiatric Referral

The purpose of this section is to provide a framework within which non-medical personnel, while assessing patients with a chemical dependence, may decide with increased confidence and precision when such patients should be referred for medical investigation, examination and treatment. The intent is not to provide the assessment worker with a comprehensive picture of the client's health status, but to provide guidelines for deciding upon the appropriateness and/or urgency of a medical referral. Before making a medical referral the assessment worker should consider the questions:
Is there any indication/suspicion that there may be a medical/psychiatric problem present? If so, how urgent is it? (Listed below are a number of areas for recording of observations or impressions which may assist in resolving doubt.)

N.B. THIS SECTION IS FOR NOTATION OF OBSERVATION AND APPRAISAL BY THE ASSESS-MENT WORKER—DO NOT ASK THE CLIENT THESE QUESTIONS.

In considering whether a medical problem exists, due either to the ingestion of alcohol/drugs or to some complicating condition, the factors listed below may indicate high risk and can be weighed according to the individual's age and apparent physical condition.

☐ *Client is not able to follow the interview.*

☐ *Client is impaired to the point of needing assistance to walk.*

☐ *Impairment appears to be the result of intoxication.*

☐ *Impairment appears to be the result of withdrawal.*

☐ *Impairment appears to be due to one of the above plus pain, injury, weakness, infection or coexisting disease disorder.*

☐ *Client appears emotionally upset (or inappropriate) beyond the circumstances of the immediate situation. This state may be indicative of potentially serious consequences.*

☐ *severe withdrawal reaction*

☐ *seizure, fit, convulsions*

☐ *suicide*

☐ *violence*

Also, a referral is likely indicated if any of the following is observed or reported

☐ *Unusual skin colour: jaundice, cyanosis, severe pallor, deep red flushing.*

☐ *Jerky eye movements, difficulty focusing (not due to lack of glasses).*

☐ *Breathing distress or difficulty.*

☐ *Breath odour: acetone, foul, bitter almond, etc.*

☐ *Gross tremor of head, hands or body, or inability to stand with feet together.*

☐ *Delinum (confusion and hallucinations—visual, auditory, olfactory or ideational): delusions.*

☐ *Stupor (somnolent and aroused only by shaking or painful stimuli).*

☐ *Disorientation to time, place or person.*

☐ *Grossly inappropriate emotion/mood/affect.*

☐ *Appears severely depressed (withdrawn, sad, despairing), expresses suicidal ideas.*

☐ *Admits to being violent or behaves with hostility.*

☐ *Exhibits marked memory loss or changes history repeatedly on requestioning—confabulation.*

☐ *Reports vomiting blood.*

☐ *Reports passing black tarry stools.*

☐ *Difficulty sleeping/change in sleep pattern.*

☐ *Difficulty eating/change in eating pattern.*

When there is doubt about the urgency of referral, it may be helpful to the assessment worker to ask or determine

1. *Has the client had a similar problem in the past?*
2. *Has he/she previously dealt with the problem successfully?*
3. *Could the condition be life-threatening?*
4. *How long has the condition been present?*
5. *Is the condition likely to have any long-term adverse consequences if attention is delayed or deferred?*

Obvious conditions present few problems in making decisions. It is the borderline situations that present difficulties. Until experience provides a firm level of confidence it is best to refer or consult when in doubt.

This kind of framework can help the worker understand what came before (early history); what happened (precipitating expectations and events related to the drug use); and what resulted (problems and benefits) from particular drug use patterns.

> Effectiveness of any treatment and rehabilitation program will depend on a reasonable understanding of the causes of the problem. If the underlying causes of drug use are not clear, the drug user is likely to return to the habit even if he or she has been without drugs for a long period. Treatment should aim at the sources of drug use, that is, psychopathology, a family situation, etc. And for rehabilitation either the causes must be known and removed or an effective substitute provided. (Satinder, 1980, p. 157)

Completing this kind of analysis requires detailed and accurate knowledge about drugs and drug abuse etiology. The worker also will make general inquiries (e.g., "What has happened normally before you use this drug?") Information about antecedents gives a clearer picture of how prior events relate to drug use. Behavioral information concerning drug administration describes obstacles and triggers to drug use itself. A description of drug use consequences indicates what rewards and punishments result (if any) from use. This information yields a clearer picture of possible historical, situational, and consequential causes of the client's drug taking; a measure of how severe the condition is; and a map of drug related variables from which a client-specific course of treatment can be developed.

Selection of Treatment

The social worker's understanding of the client's drug use in particular and of addiction in general is critical both to the therapeutic relationship and to the selection of treatment unit and method. The relationship is obviously important in negotiating any form of treatment, and when you ask clients what helped them most in counseling, they most commonly answer, "I felt understood" (Kagan, 1979). However, feeling understood is not sufficient for treatment of a severe drug dependence pattern. Thus, the therapeutic relationship must be more than empathically supportive; it must also be directive and lead to the choice of appropriate treatment units and methods. Tables 16–3 and 4 can guide the selection of treatment.

The items in Table 16–3 help identify current drug problems and past patterns of abuse. Next, the interpersonal impact of drug use or abstinence from use should be determined; the worker will need to look at the client's relationships with spouse, children, parents, siblings, and other important persons. Table 16–4 gives guidelines for appraising clients' health. The answers to these key questions should make causal factors and treatment requirements much clearer, helping the clinician choose from among behavioral, cognitive, psychodynamic, and/or immediate medical treatments.

Primary Care/Case Management

In the context of drug problems, " primary care" refers to the provision and management of long-term services. The primary care worker makes referrals; provides aftercare and follow-up; is available at times of crisis; offers psychosocial support, information, and advocacy; coordinates services; keeps records; and facilitates communication among service providers (Addiction Research Foundation, 1981b). In the absence of research establishing what combination of methods is appropriate for which client situations, the primary care function is vital in treating drug addiction because it insures that the client receives timely and necessary services.

Motivational Counseling

A careful assessment should identify a clear set of drug use consequences. Some of these will be desirable; others will not. A frank, attitudinally neutral discussion of both immediate and long-range consequences allows clients to decide what they want to do. It is fairly unusual for a client to opt for seriously harmful consequences. The counselor's job is to understand the client's reasons for drug use and to make absolutely certain that the client realizes the possible harmful consequences of continued drug taking. Adequately done (and with alternative choices given), this will very often motivate a client to decide to change (Cohen, 1981). In general, do not argue; give advice in the spirit of offering both another perspective and permission to change; and help clients see the possible damage to themselves, as well as others (children are often an issue in this regard). This approach not only may increase motivation with clients who are already seeking change but also may motivate reluctant or court referred clients to want to change.

Relapse Prevention

Relapse is not evidence of failure. It is more correctly seen as the major target for change. Cummings and associates (1980) developed some useful methods for relapse prevention and their guidelines are selectively presented here:

1. cognitive antecedents: teach clients to recognize warning signals such as making plans to visit drug users; identify high-risk lifestyles
2. coping responses: teach alternative ways of dealing with stress (e.g., relaxation); teach assertiveness skills for preventing stress; desensitize clients to stressful situations
3. self-efficacy: develop "positive addictions" such as exercise programs; increase client knowledge about drugs and their effects
4. controlled use: determine whether controlled drug use is feasible; monitor use to determine acceptable levels
5. abstinence violation: practice relapse by having the client use the drug under controlled conditions and then rehearsing helpful responses to the results; cognitively restructure clients' perception of relapse as a problem amenable to solution rather than an inevitable outcome; prepare family members to help prevent and to deal constructively with relapse

It is important to stress with clients that one drug use episode does not constitute a relapse and that drug taking can stop at that point.

Conclusion

A comprehensive psychosocial approach to the social work treatment of drug addiction has been described. I outlined an individual treatment model that takes into account multiple phases, components, and resources. This model relies heavily upon therapist skill in applying the best available knowledge, resources, and methods. Although empirical research has not yet demonstrated the utility of this approach, it has been effective in many practice settings.

References

ABRAHMS JL: Methadone maintenance patients' self-perceived factors responsible for successful rehabilitation. *Int J Addict* 1979; 14:1075–1081.

ADDICTION RESEARCH FOUNDATION: *Facts about Drugs*, rev ed. Toronto, Addiction Research Foundation, 1980.

ADDICTION RESEARCH FOUNDATION: *An Initial Interview for Clients with Alcohol and/or Drug Related Problems.* Toronto, Addiction Research Foundation, 1981. (a)

ADDICTION RESEARCH FOUNDATION: *Primary Care in Community-Based Health Care Delivery. A Sourcebook for the Community Professional.* Toronto, Addiction Research Foundation, 1981. (b)

AUSUBEL DP: An interactional approach to narcotic addiction, in Letteri DJ, Sayers

M, Pearson HW (eds): *Theories on Drug Abuse: Selected Contemporary Perspectives.* Rockville, National Institute on Drug Abuse, 1980, pp. 4–7.

BECKER HS: The social bases of drug-induced experiences, in Lettieri DJ, Sayers M, Pearson HW (eds): *Theories on Drug Abuse. Selected Contemporary Perspectives.* Rockville, National Institute on Drug Abuse, 1980, pp. 180–190.

BISHOP ES: *The Narcotic Drug Problem.* New York, Arno Press, 1920, reprinted in 1976.

BOHM PE: Accentuating the positive: strength-oriented treatment. *Addictions* 1976; 23:22–29.

BOHM PE: *Central Issues and Common Elements in Alcohol (and Other Drug) Treatment and Training.* Toronto, Addiction Research Foundation, 1981.

BRILL L: The treatment of drug abuse: evolution of a perspective. *Am J Psychiatry* 1977; 134:157–160.

BURKS TF: Drug use by athletes, in Nahas GG, Frick HC (eds): *Drug Abuse in the Modern World: A Perspective for the Eighties.* New York, Pergamon, 1981, pp. 112–120.

CALLAHAN EJ: Alternative strategies in the treatment of narcotic addiction: a review, in Miller W (ed): *The Addictive Behaviors: Treatment of Alcoholism, Drug Abuse, Smoking, and Obesity.* New York, Pergamon, 1980, pp. 143–167.

CALLAN D, GARRISON J, ZERGER F: Working with families and social networks of drug abusers. *J Psychedel Drugs* 1975; 7:19–25.

CAPPELL HD, LEBLANC AE (eds): *Biological and Behavioural Approaches to Drug Dependence.* Toronto, Alcoholism and Drug Addiction Research Foundation, 1975.

CHAMBERS C, BRILL L: The treatment of non-narcotic drug abusers, in Brill L, Lieberman L (eds): *Major Modalities in the Treatment of Drug Abuse.* New York, Behavioral Publications, 1972, pp. 203–236.

CHAPPEL JN: Attitudinal barriers to physician involvement with drug abusers. *JAMA* 1973; 224:1011–1013.

CHAUDRON CD: Theories of drug abuse. Available Addiction Research Foundation, Toronto, 1981.

COHEN S: Medical and non-medical use of psychotropic drugs: the Anxiolytics, in Nahas GG, Frick HC (eds): *Drug Abuse in the Modern World: A Perspective for the Eighties.* New York, Pergamon, 1981, pp. 62–67.

COHEN S: *The Substance Abuse Problems.* New York, Haworth, 1981.

COLEMAN SB: Family therapy and drug abuse: a national survey. *Fam Process* 1978; 107:21–29.

COLEMAN SB: An endangered species: the female as addict or member of an addict family. *Fam Process* 1981; 20:171–180.

Commission of Inquiry into the Non-medical Use of Drugs. *Information Canada,* 1972.

CUMMINGS C, GORDON JR, MARLATT GA: Relapse: prevention and prediction, in Miller W (ed.): *The Addictive Behaviors: Treatment of Alcoholism, Drug Abuse, Smoking, and Obesity.* New York, Pergamon, 1980, pp. 291–321.

DOLE VP, NYSWANDER MA: Medical treatment for diacetyl morphine (heroin) addiction. *JAMA* 1965; 193:645–656.

DOWNS DA, WOODS JH, LLEWELLYN ME: The behavioral pharmacology of addiction: some conceptual and methodological foci, in Cappell HD, LeBlanc AE (eds): *Biological and Behavioural Approaches to Addiction.* Toronto, Addiction Research Foundation, 1975, pp 53–72.

DUPONT RL: Learning from the past to cope with the future, in Nahas GG, Frick HC (eds): *Drug Abuse in the Modern World: A Perspective for the Eighties.* New York, Pergamon, 1981, pp. 267–271.

FERRER JM: Introduction, in Nahas GG, Frick HC (eds): *Drug Abuse in the Modern World: A Perspective for the Eighties.* New York, Pergamon, 1981. p xvii.

FISCHER J, GOCHROS HL: *Planned Behavior Change: Behavior Modification in Social Work.* New York, Free Press, 1975.

FORT J: The treatment of sedative, stimulant, marijuana, and LSD Abuse, in Brill L, Lieberman L (eds): *Major Modalities in the Treatment of Drug Abuse.* New York, Behavioral Publications, 1972, pp 237–256.

GILBERT R: Forty-three theories of drug abuse. *J Addict Res Found* 1981; 10:5.

GOLDSTEIN A, COX BM: Opioid peptides (endorphins) in pituitary and brain. *Psychoneuroendocrinology* 1977; 2:11–16.

GOODE E: *Drugs in American Society.* New York, Knopf, 1972.

GOTTSCHALK LA, MCGUIRE FL, HELSER JF, et al: A review of psychoactive drug-involved deaths in nine major United States cities. *Int J Addict* 1979; 14:735–758.

HARDING WM, ZINBERG NE, STELMACK SM, et al: Formerly addicted–now controlled opiate users. *Int J Addict* 1980; 15:47–60.

HARRINGTON P, COX TJ: A twenty-year follow-up of narcotic addicts in Tuscon, Arizona. *Am J Drug Alcohol Abuse* 1979; 6:25–37.

HEIMAN EM: Attitudinal issues in methadone maintenance programs. *Int J Addict* 1979; 14:77–82.

HENRY GM: Treatment and rehabilitation of narcotic addiction. *Res Adv Alcohol Drug Probl* 1974; 1:267–299.

HOLLIS F: The psychosocial approach to the practice of casework, In Roberts RW, Nee RH (eds.): *Theories of Social Casework.* Chicago, University of Chicago Press, 1970, pp 33–75.

HUBA GJ, WINGARD JA, BENTLER PM: Framework for an interactive theory of drug use, in Lettieri DJ, Sayers M, Pearson HW (eds): *Theories on Drug Abuse: Selected Contemporary Perspectives.* Rockville, National Institute on Drug Abuse, 1980, pp. 95–101.

JACOBS PE: Epidemiological and psychosocial models of drug abuse. *J Drug Issues* 1976; 6:113–122.

JEHU D: *Learning Theory and Social Work.* London, Routledge & Kegan Paul, 1967.

JEHU D, HARDIKER P, YELLOLY M, et al: *Behaviour Modification in Social Work.* London, Wiley-Interscience, 1972.

JOHNSTON LD, BACHMAN JG., O'MALLEY PM: Drugs and the nation's high school students, in Nahas GG, Frick HC (eds): *Drug Abuse in the Modern World: A Perspective for the Eighties.* New York, Pergamon, 1981, pp. 87–98.

KADUSHIN A: *The Social Work Interview.* New York, Columbia University Press, 1972.

KAGAN N: Counseling psychology, interpersonal skills, and health care, in Stone GG, Cohen F, Adlor NF, et al (eds): *Heath Psychology: A Handbook.* San Francisco, Jossey-Bass, 1979, pp. 465–497.

KALANT H, KALANT OJ: *Drugs, Society, and Personal Choice.* Toronto, Addiction Research Foundation, 1971.

KHANTZIAN EJ: An ego/self theory of substance dependence: a contemporary psycho-analytic perspective, in Lettieri DJ, Sayers M, Pearson HW (eds): *Theories on Drug Abuse: Selected Contemporary Perspectives.* Rockville, National Institute on Drug Abuse, 1980, pp. 29–33.

LANGROD MA, JOSEPH H, VALDES K: The role of religion in the treatment of opiate addiction, in Brill L, Lieberman L (eds): *Major Modalities in the Treatment of Drug Abuse.* New York, Behavioral Publications, 1972, pp. 167–189.

LETTIERI DJ, SAYERS M, PEARSON HW (eds): *Theories on Drug Abuse: Selected Contemporary Perspectives.* Rockville, National Institute on Drug Abuse, 1980.

LIDZ CW, WALKER AL, GOULD LC: *Heroin, Deviance, and Morality.* Beverly Hills, Sage, 1980.

LUKOFF IF: Toward a sociology of drug abuse, in Lettieri DJ, Sayers M, Pearson HW, (eds): *Theories on Drug Abuse: Selected Contemporary Perspectives.* Rockville, National Institute on Drug Abuse, 1980, pp. 201–211.

MALCOM AI: The tyranny of the group. Available Addiction Research Foundation, Toronto, nd.

MATARAZZO RG: Research on the teaching and learning of psychotherapeutic skills, in Garfield SL, Bergin AF (eds): *Handbook of Psychotherapy and Behavior Change: An Empirical Analysis.* New York, Wiley, 1978, pp. 941–966.

McAULIFFE WE, GORDON RA: Reinforcement and the combination of effects: summary of a theory of opiate addiction, in Lettieri DJ, Sayers M, Pearson HW (eds): *Theories on Drug Abuse: Selected Contemporary Perspectives.* Rockville, National Institute on Drug Abuse, 1980, pp. 137–141.

McKENNA GJ: Psychopathology in drug dependent individuals: a clinical review. *J Drug Issues* 1979; 9:197–204.

McLELLAN AT, WOODY GE, O'BRIEN CP: Drug abuse and psychiatric disorders: Examinations of some specific relationships, in Nahas GG, Frick HC (eds): *Drug Abuse in the Modern World: A Perspective for the Eighties.* New York, Pergamon, 1981, pp. 27–46.

MEEKS DE: Therapy and the problem of values. *Addictions* 1973; 20:20–27.

MILLER PM: Theoretical and practical issues in substance abuse assessment and treatment, in Miller W (ed): *The Addictive Behaviors: Treatment of Alcoholism, Drug Abuse, Smoking, and Obesity.* New York, Pergamon, 1980, pp 265–290.

MILLER W: The addictive behaviors, in Miller W (ed): *The Addictive Behaviors: Treatment of Alcoholism, Drug Abuse, Smoking, and Obesity.* New York, Pergamon, 1980.

NAHAS GG, FRICK HC (eds): *Drug Abuse in the Modern World: A Perspective for the Eighties.* New York, Pergamon, 1981.

NATIONAL ASSOCIATION OF SOCIAL WORKERS. Call for papers. *Health Soc Work* 1976; 1:6.

NATIONAL COMMISSION ON MARIJUANA AND DRUG ABUSE. *Drug Use in America: Problem in Perspective.* Government Printing Office, 1973.

OGBORNE AC: Patient characteristics as predictors of treatment outcomes for alcohol and drug abusers. *Res Adv Alcohol Drug Probl* 1978; 4:177–224.

ORFORD J, EDWARDS G: *Alcoholism: A Comparison of Treatment and Advice.* Oxford, Oxford University Press, 1977.

PITTELL SM, DAKOF G, FOSTER TL et al: Reentry concerns of incarcerated substance abusers. *Am J Drug Abuse* 1979; 6:59–71.

RASOR RW: The United States Public Health Service institutional treatment program for narcotics addicts at Lexington, Kentucky, in Brill L, Lieberman L (eds): *Major Modalities in the Treatment of Drug Abuse.* New York, Behavioral Publications, 1972, pp 1–121.

REID WJ, EPSTEIN L: *Task Centered Casework.* New York, Columbia University Press, 1972.

REID WJ, SHYNE AW: *Brief and Extended Casework.* New York, Columbia University Press, 1969.

ROSSI JJ, PHILLIPS LA, RAMSEY GR, et al (eds): *Core Knowledge in the Drug Field: Nonmedical use of Drugs Directorate.* Ottawa, National Health and Welfare, 1978.

RUSH AJ, SHAW, BRIAN F: Psychotherapeutic treatment of opiate addiction. *Am J Psychother* 1981; 35:61–75.

SATINDER KP: *Drug Use: Criminal, Sick, or Cultural?.* New York, Libra, 1980.

SCHUCKIT MA: A theory of alcohol and drug abuse: a genetic approach, in Lettieri DJ, Sayers M, Pearson HW (eds): *Theories on Drug Abuse: Selected Contemporary Perspectives.* Rockville, National Institute on Drug Abuse, 1980, pp. 297–302.

SHULMAN L: *A Study of the Helping Process.* Vancouver, University of British Columbia, School of Social Work, 1977.

SMART RG: Drug use and drug abuse: a statistical correlation with implications for preventions, in Nahas GG, Frick HC (eds): *Drug Abuse in the Modern World: A Perspective for the Eighties.* New York, Pergamon, 1981, pp. 272–276.

SPECK RV, ATTNEAVE CL: *Family Network.* Pantheon, 1973.

STANTON MD: Family treatment approaches to drug abuse problems: a review. *Fam Process* 1979; 18:251–279.

STANTON MD: Drug abuse and the family, in Andolfi M, Zwerling I (eds): *Dimensions of Family Therapy.* New York, Guilford, 1980, pp 29–46.(a)

STANTON MD: A family theory of drug abuse, in Lettieri DJ, Sayers, M, Pearson HW, (eds): *Theories on Drug Abuse: Selected Contemporary Perspectives.* Rockville, National Institute on Drug Abuse, 1980, pp. 147–156. (b)

THOMAS EJ: *Behavioral Science for Social Workers.* New York, Free Press, 1967.

THOMLISON RJ: *A Behavioural Model for Social Work Intervention with the Marital Dyad,* thesis. University of Toronto, Toronto, 1972.

Treilons S: Medical aspects of drug use. Available Addiction Research Foundation, 1980.

Turner FJ (ed): *Social Work Treatment: Interlocking Approaches.* New York, Free Press, 1974.

Ungerleider JR, Beigel A: Drug abuse: crisis in the treatment arena. *J Drug Educ* 1980; 10:279–288.

Vaillant GE: A twelve-year follow-up of New York narcotic addicts: I. The relation of treatment to outcome. *Am J Psychiatr* 1966; 122:717–737.

Wiencek RG: Drugs in the workplace: retrospective and prospective, in Nahas GG, Frick HC (eds): *Drug Abuse in the Modern World: A Perspective for the Eighties.* New York, Pergamon, 1981, pp. 121–126.

World Health Organization Expert Committee on Addiction-Producing Drugs. *Terminology in Regard to Drug Abuse.* W.H.O. Technical Report, series No. 273, 9, 1964.

17

Psychogenic and Psychophysiologic Disorders

Mary Sheridan
Karen Kline

Psychosomatic illnesses raise the most fundamental questions. Why do people become sick? What does their sickness mean? What can be done about it? While clinicians are used to a straight-line medical model of dysfunction generating symptoms and diagnosis directing treatment, attempts to understand psychosomatic illness lead into a labyrinth. Scientific knowledge and ignorance and ideas about self, others, religion, philosophy, ethics, and even reality itself must be explored. The simple becomes so complex that we cannot speak about it authoritatively. Nor are the issues limited to the body and mind of the sick person. Family, cultural, and social issues are involved. And beneath the theoretical formulations lies the certainty that no one can escape a personal encounter with sickness and death.

To approach an understanding of psychosomatic illness, it is necessary to know a little about the history of medical thought. In prehistoric times, illness and disease were seen as existing outside the person. Spiritual forces such as ghosts would attack the individual and be dispelled through purging or exorcism. Remnants of these ideas are still widespread. Plato hypothesized about the split between mind and body. Hippocrates is credited with introducing the hypothesis that disease originates within the body due to an imbalance of fluid matter; this imbalance could be related to, or even caused by, an imbalance in the patient's external environment and it could be studied by the scientific means available at the time. In the Middle Ages, these observations were replaced by a return to the belief in malevolent powers and sin as the origin of illness. Such evil was seen as both inside and outside the sufferer and as a province of the church. The Renaissance brought renewed interest in the scientific study of medicine. Henceforth, the study of the body was the province of science and the study of the soul was the province of religion. Psychic influences were discounted as unscientific. The triumph of the scientific approach was the discovery of germs as the cause of disease and the eradication of epidemics through the application of this knowledge. In this framework, mental processes were seen as a product of physical processes (Kaplan, 1975).

In the late 1800s, Freud brought mind and body together again. His earliest work focused on locating the physical site of mental dysfunction. Later he detailed the role of emotions in somatic conversion reactions, and ultimately his study of emotions gave birth to psychiatry. Psychoanalytic formulations about the effect of conflict, repression, and symbolic behavior were used to explain illness, particularly illnesses related to stress. Some researchers influenced by Freud tried to explain all illness as an expression of specific repressed ideas or fantasies (Singer, 1977).

In the late 1930s and early 1940s, Alexander brought a new dimension to psychosomatic research. He separated conversion symptoms from "stress reactions," with the latter seen as the response of the body to a long and painful effort to cope with unresolved emotional conflict. He concentrated his formulations on seven diseases (asthma, rheumatoid arthritis, ulcerative colitis, essential hypertension, neurodermatitis, thyrotoxicosis, and peptic ulcer), which became identified as psychosomatic illnesses. Research was then focused on finding personality traits that distinguised one group of patients from those with a different disease. Efforts in this area (and controversy over this approach) continue.

Over the years, the field of psychosomatic illness has broadened until now it includes all illness. Etiology of each differing symptom is not considered as important, since it is recognized that psychological features influence the development, course of, and adjustment to all illnesses. Currently, many efforts are under way to look at the interaction between personal and social factors that results in a person's becoming ill. There is a new emphasis on psychological care of the physically ill and on physical treatments for mental illness.

From this complex history, we are left with a number of ideas that continue to influence our thoughts about illness and medical care. One is the mind–body duality. We perceive a basic split between mind (will, spirit, feelings) and body. Although some Eastern philosophies such as yoga strive to bring mind and body into harmony, much of the Western world sees not only separation but war. It is no wonder that approaches to ill-ness have looked to either the mental or the physical but not in any systematic way to both.

The question of reality and unreality is also important in psychoso-matic illness. To the average person, professional as well as lay, the term still connotes an illness that is imaginary ("all in the head"). The as-sumption is that only symptoms traceable to an organic cause are valid; pain from nonphysical causes may be given lip service but is clearly perceived as less valid and even as a sign of personal weakness.

Throughout history, there has been ambivalence over what is often called the "locus of control." A person who believes in possession by spirits or invasion by germs sees himself as the victim of outside forces. Cure is also generally seen as coming from the outside, and professionals such as physicians or spiritual healers have a strong vested interest in this system. Patient education movements, on the other hand, attempt to change the locus of control from external to internal both to counter the feeling of helplessness experienced by many patients and to take into ac-count the mounting evidence that lifestyle affects the risk of becoming sick. Patients are taught to think of themselves as consumers—shopping wisely for medical services. Such an approach can easily bring a patient into conflict with her source of medical care and may also create a model of severe conflict.

The field of psychosomatic illness has traditionally sought causes, and in our society cause and blame are often equated. A more useful, and less simplistic, approach is to view psychosomatic illness as a range of possi-bilities and not a question of either–or and fault–innocence (Fig. 17–1).* In this chapter, we look at the spectrum of psychosomatic manifestations and review their implications for social work. We separate reactions that appear to be "psychogenic" those that appear to be "somatogenic," and those that Alexander called "stress reactions." This separation, how-ever, is merely a matter of convenience; no clear-cut distinctions exist in the realm of psychosomatic illness.

Psychogenic Disease

Psychogenic diseases, the prototypical psychosomatic illness, are the dis-orders most often dismissed as unreal. There are no organic findings *and* there is strong evidence that the symptoms are linked to psychological factors or conflicts (Spitzer, 1980). It is important to remember that these illnesses are not under the voluntary control of the patient; the conflicts

---

* For an excellent discussion of the topic of psychosomatic illness as it relates to menstrual cramps see Budoff (1980).

Psychogenic					Somatogenic
Internal conflict causes symptoms	Family systems conflict or project- ion causes symptoms	Learned responses to past physical symptoms persist even though symptoms are gone	Physical predispo- sition & stress cause symptoms	Multiple factors increase risk of disease	Physical illness causes emotional problems

FIGURE 17–1. Some approaches to psychosomatic disease

or the mechanism behind the disease are not conscious. "Malingering" (voluntary symptom production or exaggeration) and "factitious" (self-induced) symptoms" have obvious, conscious goals in relation to the individual's environment. These goals frequently involve the prospect of material gain or the avoidance of unwanted responsibility, though factitious illnesses may have less obvious secondary gain and are, therefore, more pathological: thus, a worker who fakes a back injury in order to escape from a disliked boss and collect compensation is not suffering from psychogenic illness; a worker who believes that she is happy at work but wakes up one morning totally paralyzed (without organic cause) is.

DSM III (American Psychiatric Association, 1980) uses the term "somatoform disorder" in preference to "psychogenic disease" and divides this category into four subtypes: "somatization disorder," "conversion disorder," "psychogenic pain disorder," and "hypochondriasis."

An individual with a somatization disorder manifests recurrent and multiple symptoms over the course of several years. The condition may fluctuate over time, and medical treatment is often pursued relentlessly. Thorough examinations find no organic pathology, but the individual continues to feel ill. Such a person may go from one specialist to another, often frustrating and alienating the caregivers, who are unable to offer relief or cure. Over time, the patient may receive numerous medications and undergo sophisticated tests (some for the purpose of communicating that "everything is being done," some to protect the physician from malpractice claims in case anything is discovered later). Exploratory surgery may be undertaken. At the end of this process, the patient has spent a great deal of time, energy, and money and is no nearer a solution to his problems. Along the way, "iatrogenic problems" like adverse drug reactions or surgical complications may have arisen.

Conversion disorders are seen far less frequently today than in Freud's time. It has been alleged that this is due to the lessening of sexual repression, which Freud saw as crucial to the conversion reaction process. The individual with a conversion reaction shows a loss or alteration in physical functioning that suggests a physical problem but for which there is no organic pathology. As in all psychogenic diseases, the symptoms are not under voluntary control. Moreover, conversion reaction symptoms may be anomalous; for example, psychogenic paralysis may not follow neurological pathways, as in "glove effect numbness," confined to the hand.

A conversion reaction is likely to involve the sudden appearance of a single, often dramatic symptom during a time of extreme emotional stress. The patient may show a lack of concern (*la belle indifference*) strikingly out of keeping with the impairment and its disruption of normal activities. Conversion symptoms themselves can cause physical consequences, especially if they are prolonged. For example, paralyzed muscles may atrophy; alternatively, patients may have adverse responses to diagnostic or therapeutic procedures undertaken before their dysfunction is determined to be a conversion reaction.

Several explanations have been advanced for conversion symptoms. The "specificity theory" explains the choice of symptom as a predisposition toward the affected area (Kimball, 1978). Thus, the affected area may have been the site of a past, perhaps forgotten, trauma; it may be symbolic of current conflicts; or it may be constitutionally weak.

Two mechanisms have been suggested to explain the gains from conversion symptoms (Spitzer, 1980). The individual first achieves the primary gain of keeping the internal conflict out of conscious awareness. Since the symptom itself is symbolic of the internal conflict, it functions as a partial solution. Second, the individual avoids an activity or responsibility that is upsetting or receives environmental supports that would ordinarily not be forthcoming.

In psychogenic pain disorder, the patient feels pain for which there is no organic cause. The individual often has a history of conversion-type symptoms but is unable to consider the possible role of psychological factors in the pain. She may rely heavily on pain medication and may even request palliative surgery. The pain can be so severe as to require hospitalization. The person may become an invalid and suffer the consequent impairment in lifestyle, with inappropriate or excessive behaviors that block recovery and resumption of normal life (Pankratz & Glaudin, 1980).

In hypochondriasis, the patient unrealistically interprets physical signs or sensations in light of the obsessive preoccupation that he has a serious disease. If a physical problem is actually present, it is not sufficient to account for the conviction of serious illness. Medical reassurance does not relieve the anxiety. The predisposing factor seems to be past experience with organic disease either in the patient or in a family member, along with psychosocial stressors. A generally mild, but classic, example of hypochondriasis is "medical student disease": the conviction in the student that she has signs of whatever she is studying at the time. This response is probably related to the stresses of medical school and its concentration of physical pathology (Mechanic, 1972).

An 18-year-old single woman, Ms. V, came to a community mental health center and was seen by a social worker. She spoke of depression, extreme anxiety, and numerous somatic conditions from which she had suffered for the past two years. She had severe headaches, heart palpitations, nausea, and sleep disturbance. Her family physician found no organic reason for the difficulties. The social worker asked Ms. V to see the clinic psychiatrist for further discussion of the physical complaints and for evaluation of the need for antidepressant medication.

In therapy with the social worker, Ms. V was able to talk about her depression. In time, she was able to recognize that her headaches were worse during periods of tension in the family. She acknowledged her low self-esteem and/constant need for demonstrations of caring by people close to her. She could transfer some of her needs to the social worker and could learn better ways to relate to her family. In time, Ms. V's symptoms diminished. When she understood them to be a learned reaction to stress, she was less frightened and was able to put more energy into understanding the reasons for her symptoms.

Psychogenic diseases may present themselves dramatically or, as in this case, take the form of headaches or stomachaches, experienced by everyone. Ms. V's difficulty functioning in everyday roles and her degree of distress marked this case as a situation for intervention. In this instance, the worker made sure that physical factors had been ruled out. The importance of this step cannot be overstated, even for symptoms that appear to be clearly emotional in origin, since many disorders have vague and insidious initial courses. Once the worker had received this assurance, she was able to engage Ms. V in a reflective consideration of her life situation, which included a look at her symptoms to see what they could tell her about herself. The reflective discussion—the exploration of life issues and their relation to medical symptoms—was not very different from what it would have been if Ms. V had presented with a chronic illness. In either instance, the focus is on the whole situation, the here and now, rather than on etiology.

Psychophysiologic Disease

The attempt to give meaning to symptoms has extended far beyond the psychogenic disorders. In many conditions, particularly those that Alexander called "stress reactions," physical changes are far more marked than in psychogenic disease, yet we have an enduring suspicion that there is a tie to the emotions. There has been much debate about whether these illnesses are purely psychogenic, purely somatogenic, or a combination of the two. If a combination, how does the model work? The current consensus is that both stress and underlying physical predispositions contribute to psychophysiologic disease and that there is a strong element of chronicity in most conditions. This suggests new roles for social workers, but applying mental health insights to the control of a chronic condition is far more challenging than simply applying a unitary etiological theory. Several frequently encountered psychophysiological conditions are discussed in this section.

High Blood Pressure

It is well known that blood pressure rises with strong emotion, with physical demands, and with increasing age in Western society, but the exact mechanism of "essential hypertension" (sustained, elevated blood pressure in the absence of other dysfunction) is still unknown. The suspected interplay of genetic, dietary, psychological, and physiological factors in hypertension makes research difficult. For example, black Americans have higher rates than do whites of hypertension, but they share a common inheritance, frequently eat a diet high in salt, and as a group suffer from the stress occasioned by discrimination and poverty. On an international level, hypertension has been linked to rapid sociocultural change; it is alleged that uncertainty over one's social role in a changing society is the specific stress leading to hypertension. Jenkins and colleagues found a strong association between death from hypertensive related diseases and such social factors as low education and low occupational status. However, Ostfeld and D'Atri (1977) suggested that the intervening mechanism in hypertension is diet: in poor countries, obesity is a disease of the rich; in the developed countries, however, obesity is a disease of the poor because fatty and starchy foods are relatively inexpensive.

Hypertension may or may not have symptoms. It is a lucky patient who has headaches or blurred vision in the early stages or who is identified by mass screening. Such patients require a thorough medical evaluation to determine whether the condition is chronic and whether additional physiological problems exist.

Treatment for hypertension is usually extended, often lifelong. It has been found within the past few years that lowering of even mildly elevated blood pressure is beneficial. The elimination of salt is frequently the first step, followed by diuretic medication if further control measures are needed. Weight loss is recommended for the obese. The patient will be asked to return to the physician for frequent checks of blood pressure and may be taught to take her blood pressure at home (a simple procedure). For the difficult-to-control patient, there may be a long period of trial and error before an effective regimen is discovered. It is not uncommon for the patient to become discouraged, to feel that the physician does not know what she is doing, or to resent the outlay of time and money. Patient education is imporant for all hypertensives, who tend to discontinue treatment when a prescription expires or adverse side effects, such as impotence or weakness appear.

Heart Disease

Over the past decade, research has proliferated linking coronary heart disease and heart attacks to certain personal and environmental phenomena. One of the best-known investigations was popularized by Friedman and Roseman (1974) as the "type A" and "type B" personalities. In brief, type A patients exhibit a chronic sense of time urgency, always trying to get more and more done in less time. Presence of type A behavior has been correlated with such physiological indicators as elevated serum cholesterol, a well-established risk factor for heart attack. Type Bs may have similar—or higher—levels of ambition, intelligence, and drive but a type B's "character is such that it seems to steady him, give confidence and security to him, rather than to goad, irritate, and infuriate, as with the Type A man (p. 68). The authors stated that most people are basically either type A or type B, with type A slightly more common in our society. It is important to note that social status, occupation, or other such externals do not make a type A. In fact, a type B might possess characteristics such as an ability to cooperate or to focus on essentials that make socioeconomic success more likely.

The type A–type B formulation has been widely researched and in general the distinction has been found accurate when applied to American or Westernized men. Minimal work has been done with women, although it is reported that their rate of heart attacks is rising, and this is popularly associated with women's entry into the labor force. Some researchers think that the link between type A behavior and heart disease is through serum cholesterol. Others suspect hyperreactivity to the environment and suggest that type As are less able to deal with frustration (Sparacino, 1979). Friedman and Rosenman (1974) reported that behavioral interventions can modify the type A pattern.

Lynch (1977), using broad demographic statistics, correlated the risk of death from heart disease with social isolation. He recognized explicitly that work needs to be done on distinguishing between well-adjusted and poorly adjusted single and widowed persons, but these data clearly showed an elevated risk of death among the unmarried, particularly men. Lynch further explored interactions between critically ill hospitalized patients and their nurses, finding that heart rates dropped when pulses were taken, hands held, or words of comfort spoken.

It is well accepted today that diet, exercise, smoking, and stress affect one's risk of heart disease. Modifying any one of these factors calls for a serious change in lifestyle. A number of programs have been undertaken to try to avert heart attacks in high-risk people or to rehabilitate those who have already had a heart attack. While these do call for a serious commitment from the individual, it is no longer necessary for most heart attack patients to resign themselves to sedentary, sexless lives.

Asthma

For many years, asthma was believed to be related to conflicts over dependence on the mother. This view suggested that children with asthma constituted a homogenous group whose symptoms reflected psychopathology and whose personality type could be specified. A number of studies were undertaken to explore this hypothesis. Evaluating these studies, Creer (1979) concluded that specific personality differences could not be found between asthmatics and other children, particularly other children with chronic illness. There was, however, some association between overall life adjustment and severity of symptoms. The question then becomes whether the increased dependence, guardedness, "neurotic traits," and overprotection previously associated with asthmatics are not the consequence of a frightening, unpredictable, and potentially life-threatening illness. Efforts to isolate a particular mother–child pathology have been equally unavailing. "Cure" of asthma by "parentectomy" has been widely publicized, but it is difficult to isolate the effect of removal per se from the parental home and the absolute number of children supposedly cured in this way is probably small.

It is now known that asthmatics have hyperreactive air passages whether or not they are currently having attacks. Smoke, dust, or changes in temperature that do not affect nonasthmatics will cause measurable changes in the lungs of asthmatics. It is unknown what causes this hyperreactivity or what determines whether or not a patient will have an attack. The role of genetic, allergic, and learning factors in this disorder is still unclear. It has been alleged that asthmatics will wheeze when viewing a picture of a known attack precipitant, but replication of such studies has not confirmed this finding.

In asthma, medication achieves control rather than cure. Thus, the asthmatic must form a new self-concept around the disease and learn new coping mechanisms. Modern asthma care, which is by no means universally followed, involves the regular administration of drugs (pills or inhalants). These medications often have side effects: patient on antihistamines may feel drowsy; a patient on some bronchodilators or epinephrine (often used in emergencies) may have nervousness or difficulty concentrating. Moreover, attitudes that the patient, family, or community have about drug use (specifically, illicit drugs) often are applied to the asthmatic, particularly the young adult.

Particular lifestyle adaptations may be used to control asthma. Physicians who believe that asthma is largely allergic may ban pets, wool rugs, or other suspected allergens from the home. Other physicians believe in advancing drug dosage until a patient can carry out even such extremes of exercise as long-distance running. The more modern approach to asthma is to try to help the patient live as normal a life as possible, without rigid restrictions on activity.

Clinicians working with asthmatics have found that in some clients emotional factors appear to play a major part and in others physical symptoms appear to predominate. Some asthmatics may wheeze after family arguments; others, only when they breathe cold air. For all asthmatics, a program of relaxation techniques and breathing exercises to be carried out during an attack appears warranted. Such measures may not be effective in individual cases, but in many cases they offer a measure of relief and control. These methods can be learned from a physician or a respiratory therapist, but it must be emphasized that they do not address the question or etiology.

Ulcer

There has been an exhaustive effort to find the link between ulcers and life stresses. Air traffic controllers, foremen, and other groups have higher rates of ulcers than do workers in related but less stressful occupations. Ulcer symptoms are supposed to be related to conflicts over dependence or to vacillation between active and passive behaviors in order to obtain love (Wolf et al., 1979).

A number of factors increase the risk of ulcer. Being male, having relatives with ulcers, smoking, and intake of irritants such as caffeine or alcohol (in susceptible people) may be associated with the development of ulcers. Some people are hypersecretors of stomach acid. It is not known why some of these develop ulcers, but those who do tend to have recurrences of the disease throughout life.

Since the time of Pavlov it has been known that psychic factors can influence gastric secretion and that these secretions play some role in the development of ulcers. However, methodological and definitional problems make this one of the few conclusive statements that can be made about ulcer disease. Luckily, advances have been made recently in ulcer treatment. The traditional bland diet has been replaced with permission for the patient to eat whatever does not cause distress (coffee, alcohol, and spices are generally restricted in the early recovery phase, and aspirin is always contraindicated unless prescribed by a physician). Antacid therapy has been supplemented by cimetidine, a specific acid inhibitor that allows many patients to heal their ulcers and avoid surgery. Finally, fiberoptic devices permit more accurate diagnosis without surgery and with minimal risk.

The social worker can help ulcer patients identify specific patterns that seem to aggravate their symptoms. Seasonal variations, emotional changes, mild illnesses such as colds, and other factors may form a pattern calling for extra vigilance on the part of the patient in order to prevent recurrence of symptoms.

Lower Back Pain

Lower back pain can be caused by a number of factors, some of them purely physical, some purely emotional, and some probably mixed. X-rays may demonstrate spinal anomalies or disc problems, but not everyone with such findings has pain. Muscles may go into spasm from such causes as tension, discrepant leg lengths, or poor posture. Lower back pain, like any other pain, is a subjective symptom. Only the patient can say where or how much he is hurting. The popular image of the back patient as a malingerer interested only in compensation has forced greater efforts to gain recognition that the pain is legitimate, and these efforts are sometimes perceived as further evidence against the patient (Fagerhaugh & Strauss, 1977).

In a number of patients without organic findings, lower back pain serves as an honorable escape from an overwhelming life experience. Frequently, men complain of work related pain, which appears to worsen when they feel particularly unappreciated by their company or boss. A team approach to evaluation and treatment is appropriate for such patients since no surgical relief can be provided (in the absence of a deformity) and since the long-term use of pain medication has so many problems associated with it.

Adjustment to a lower back problem, especially if it is physically based, calls for the patient to adopt lifelong restrictions (such as the lifting of heavy weights) and programs of exercise. At the same time, the patient must try to carry on a normal life, resisting the temptation to exploit the condition for its secondary gains. This is a difficult compromise for a person in pain.

Cancer

In recent years, research has suggested that cancer is related to psychological variables such as extremes in emotional expression or repression and serious loss through disappointment or bereavement (Henry & Stephens, 1977; Klerman & Izen, 1977). Particular attention has been paid to breast, cervical, and other women's cancers. However, methodological problems in these studies make the drawing of rigorous conclusions impossible. The concept of personality characteristics contributing to cancer has not been supported in more recent studies (Kimball, 1978; Surwicz, et al., 1976).

Cancer must be seen in its social and personal dimensions. This disease is feared by many who equate it falsely with certain death. The fight against cancer has become something of a national priority, as has the fight against heart disease. Mounting evidence of environmental causes of cancer, often delayed 20 or more years after exposure, calls for vigorous community based work. And, finally, the increased number of options in cancer treatment (drugs versus radiation versus surgery) challenges the patient to be assertive and to move toward a partnership with the physician. These are all areas of potential social work involvement.

Summary

In this discussion, we have seen that many efforts to correlate specific symptoms with specific personality patterns have not been supported. However, stress is implicated as a risk factor in a range of illnesses, although the link is as yet unspecified. Cultural and personality factors, such as isolation, appear to increase the risk of at least heart diseases. Simplistic explanations of psychophysiologic diseases do injustice to the patient both because they attach blame to people in need of support and treatment and because they discourage efforts to develop optimal therapies. Social workers can help other professionals and the public change their attitudes toward psychosomatic illnesses and can help patients comply with treatments and modify their lifestyles to minimize or eliminate debilitating conditions.

Somatogenic Disease

Somatogenic diseases have been included in the field of psychosomatic illness to accommodate the recent view that every illness has psychological features that influence its course and the individual's adjustment. The illness, like the patient, cannot be split into physical, psychological, and social components without losing a sense of the whole.

Serious illness is a threat to the integrity of the self. Anxiety relating to illness affects the ability of patients and their families to meet obligations and provide mutual support. If the challenge of adult life is to preserve continuity through change, this goal is even more problematic in illness. One's very body may be reshaped and the image of the body assaulted through numerous medical and surgical procedures. The new amputee, the newly diagnosed diabetic, and the new mother all must confront themselves in a novel way.

Adaptation never occurs in a vacuum. Whether the patient emerges from illness diminished, enhanced, or unchanged depends on personality structure, previous coping experiences, and present conditions. The supports available in the family, hospital, and community also influence the adaptive process.

The significance of illness must always be assessed for the individual client. Loss, increased dependence, and impaired self-esteem are common problems in a society that values independence and defines individuals by their work. However, the experience of illness is not always negative: expressions of caring and freedom from daily life stresses often accompany it. Illness is, after all, the major acceptable excuse to avoid work or other obligations. Moreover, illness frequently brings people into contact with others around them and with their own philosophical, emotional, and spiritual beliefs. It may, then, be growth oriented or contain both positive and negative elements.

Greater awareness of these factors and those discussed in the previous sections has increased demand within the medical community and among the public for more social psychological services in health care. Many of these services are provided by social workers.

Social Workers in the Health Field

The social worker has long been a part of the medical field. The first medical social worker was hired in 1905 at the Massachusetts General Hospital in Boston. Dr. Richard C. Cabot initiated the position when he recognized the need to address the nonmedical dimensions of patient care, that is, the influence of the patient's social situation on recovery from or adjustment to illness (Saunders, 1971). As medical social work spread to health settings with broader foci, practice aims were revised to reflect this transition. These aims include understanding the impact of the illness on the patient and initiating appropriate treatment, facilitating relationships with physicians and medical services, preventing problems that create or exacerbate illness, and nurturing factors that enhance health. To accomplish these goals, the social worker must have a thorough knowledge of human development and behavior, particularly under stress. The worker must be able to apply this knowledge to choose the most appropriate interventions for the patient.

Social workers who specialize in the medical field must also be well informed about the processes and consequences of illness. Every disease has a "trajectory," a normal course from beginning to end, with common and uncommon variants (Fagerhaugh & Strauss, 1977). There are certain treatments usually applied to each condition, and these treatments have what might be called "subtrajectories," regular courses associated with particular side effects, benefits, and risks. This sort of information enables the skilled worker to educate the patient and to make informed diagnoses for social work purposes. Pathologic denial, for example, must be separated both from normal denial in the first stages of adjustment to a disease and from euphoria induced by a prescription drug. Male sexual dysfunction is often a symptom of depression or relationship problems, but in cardiac or hypertensive patients it may be a drug reaction (suggesting the need for medical evaluation) and in renal patients it is a common complaint, which may respond to testosterone injections. The social worker must be particularly alert to danger signs that indicate the need for prompt medical intervention and to restrictions that certain patients must follow (e.g., aspirin with ulcers). Understanding the course of medical treatment also helps the social worker support and facilitate the medical regimen that has been prescribed (Turner, 1968).

Social workers in medical settings provide a secondary service. It is important for them to have clear goals, a clear role definition, and professional security. Much of their role is educative. Care providers, administrative staff, and patients often do not know what social work can contribute. Formal and informal group and individual teaching must be part of the social worker's job. In a setting that itself provides medical education, the social worker has an additional responsibility to educate trainees about the importance of social psychological factors in illness and about the necessity of seeing the patient as a whole person.

Social workers have contact with a wide range of illnesses and disabilities and often develop subspecialities. Each disease has unique features. Unfortunately, it is not within the scope of this chapter to explore every disease and disability. Rather, chronic renal failure is used as an example of a complex disease.

A Disease Trajectory: Renal Failure

At the end stage of renal disease, the kidneys are unable to purify the blood. This may be due to diabetes, high blood pressure, intrinsic disease of the urinary tract, or other factors. Renal failure may be the end of a long disease process or a sudden development. This disorder strikes people of all ages, races, and social conditions.

"Uremia," the buildup of toxins usually removed by the kidneys, leads to death if untreated. Symptoms include fatigue, malaise, apathy, and nausea; uremia also causes organic brain impairment (Sheridan, 1977). The patient is placed on a restricted diet and given medication.

Until 1960, renal failure was untreatable. In the sixties, technological developments led to a treatment called "dialysis," in which the work of the kidneys is taken over by a machine that clears toxins from the blood (less commonly, through the peritoneal cavity). As often happens in medicine, technological capability created numerous human problems. In the early days, treatment was experimental, lengthy, and extremely expensive. There were too few machines and centers to serve all who needed dialysis. The difficulty of selecting patients (and thus condemning others to certain death) was addressed by various means, few of them satisfactory. Patients accepted for treatment, their families, and the staff who cared for them suffered from the stress of constant, life-and-death uncertainty.

The transplantation of kidneys in the late sixties also developed as a treatment option. The use of cadaver kidneys and a matching technique analogous to blood typing has a success rate of about 50%; the rate is higher for kidneys from living related donors. However, not all renal failure patients are candidates for such surgery, and, although a well-working transplant is the closest approximation to normal kidney function, there is a constant risk of rejection.

Over the past decade, Medicare has funded dialysis and transplantation, easing the financial strains on patients. Treatment centers have proliferated, so that all who need treatment have an opportunity to receive it. Nevertheless, the stresses remain, and the amount of tax money necessary to maintain these programs has brought them under government scrutiny.

The emotional concomitants of dialysis and transplantation are in part reactions to stress and in part reactions to physiological changes. Mood swings accompany rapid alterations in the body's fluid balance during dialysis. The body image of the patient is altered by the experience of being attached to the dialysis machine on a regular basis or of possessing a surgically implanted kidney.

Adaptation to dialysis moves through stages that are similar to the stages described by Kübler-Ross (1969). In the initial, "honeymoon" period, patients are aware of feeling better but soon realize the disadvantages of the disease. They deny, then generally enter into a superficial adaptation, followed by discouragement and depression when their beginning efforts to normalize life fail. There may be extreme feelings of sadness, abandonment, and inability to cope on the part of both patient and family. Such periods of depression are often accompanied by problems with the "fistula" (the shunt that permits attachment to the machine) and may be accompanied by suicidal ideation or attempts. However, many patients adapt well to treatment and maintain or resume active, meaningful lives.

The social worker needs to be aware of the physiological changes and disease processes associated with dialysis and transplantation, as well as the processes of normal adaptation and the particular danger signals. Note that these stages are conceptual, not linear or literal, and may be experienced in a different order than that described here. Each patient must be assessed and supported individually, and services should also be offered to family members. For the patient with poor adaptation potential, such programs as home dialysis, self-care within the treatment center, or patient education can increase a sense of control over illness and treatment. This is particularly important for men who have difficulty with dependence on technicians; on the other hand, home dialysis has also been associated with a high degree of marital strain.

The social worker carries the responsibility of providing the dialysis or transplantation treatment team with knowledge of the patient as he relates to the family, the community, and the service delivery network. Much of the practice of renal social work takes place within a community network: a series of clinics affiliated with a hospital, referral patterns within the medical community, and relationships with other medical and social service providers who offer financial, transportation, or supportive services. The social worker may also become active in the educational or research programs of the National Kidney Foundation and its Council of Nephrology Social Workers, in state and federal programs that affect kidney patients, and in mass screening programs for the conditions that lead to kidney failure.

Mrs. D was a 55-year-old, markedly obese diabetic in renal failure. The social worker's initial contact was for patient education and evaluation for a dialysis program. She felt that Mrs. D's personality was compatible with the program and that Mrs. D would probably make a good adjustment, but there were immediate practical problems. Mrs. D could walk only a few steps at home because of her weight and her arthritis. She was frightened of falling because of the risk to her feet (which were prone to serious infection due to her diabetes). Before her kidneys failed, she had been living a largely sedentary life at home. Her husband and grown children had been doing the bulk of the housework, and all were satisfied with this arrangement. Now Mrs. D would have to cope with leaving the house three times per week for dialysis since home treatment was not desired by the family.

The medical staff saw Mrs. D as a marginal candidate for dialysis because of her age, fears, and sedentary lifestyle, and the unit turned down her first application for services. The unit suggested that she should learn to walk on crutches, but Mrs. D rejected this because she was afraid of falling and because she feared that a crutch would injure the fistula in her left arm. The social worker had to perform two roles—education and confrontation—before the medical staff understood that mobility was a life-and-death issue, not a luxury, for Mrs. D. The physicians then prevailed upon the unit to accept Mrs. D as a patient. During Mrs. D's stay, the social worker attended the dialysis team conferences, at which she explained that Mrs. D's fears about the fistula were reasonable. In time, Mrs D was fitted with a wheelchair, to which she quickly adjusted. Shortly before Mrs. D's discharge, the social worker made a home visit with the dialysis unit team to assess physical barriers and adaptive equipment necessary for Mrs. D's discharge. Following this visit, the family had a ramp constructed, which allowed Mrs. D to leave the house easily.

Mrs. D made a good adaptation to dialysis, although staff initially found her a difficult patient because she cried during the first few treatments. Staff projected this discomfort, stating that they were afraid other patients would become upset. The social worker assessed both Mrs. D and the other patients and shared with staff her impression that the crying was Mrs. D's personal and cultural means of handling any stress. Shortly thereafter, Mrs. D was transfered from the acute to a chronic treatment center, where she made a good adjustment and continued to receive her care on a regular and satisfactory basis.

In this case, the worker offered services at multiple levels: assessment, casework, and education were offered to the patient; education and confrontation were used with the medical staff, whose experience with dialysis patients had been limited; and the dialysis technicians received information, reassurance, and the security of having the situation assessed by a mental health professional. Finally, the patient was aided in her transition from one care setting to another.

Special Issues in Medical Social Work

A number of issues are important in dealing with illness, whether the worker is located in a hospital or in another setting and wherever the illness is perceived along the psychosomatic continuum.

In a primary setting, such as a family service agency, social workers meet with clients who recognize their problems and have made some commitment to work on them. In a secondary setting such as a hospital, workers often have clients who never would have approached a social agency for services. Accordingly, some clients may need to be convinced of the importance of treatment, and less traditional casework methods may be required.

The Medical Community

In relation to the medical profession, social work is not only an auxiliary profession but also a lower status one. Hospitals are organized around physicians, who are the de facto heads of most treatment teams. Referrals tend to come from physicians, sometimes phrased as they would be to other physicians and sometimes as they would be to assistants. Generally, private patients may not be seen without the permission of the attending physician, no matter how much social need is perceived by the rest of the staff. Most physicians do not oppose social work intervention, but in the medical hierarchy they have the right to do so.

Medical personnel often think of social workers as "nice ladies" who work with the poor but do not have expertise. This view may be communicated to patients or may show up as resistance to more aggressive casework on the part of the social worker. Most of the time, patient education and demonstration of results gradually will change perceptions. However, there are always some individuals who are uncomfortable with the social worker's focus on emotional problems and who will devalue or resist services for this reason. It is worthwhile for the social worker to remember that staff, as well as patients, can be the target of services.

Certain value conflicts arise around medical practice. The medical profession is highly invested in saving lives. Although there is a growing concern for the quality of the life to be saved, serious differences of opinion sometimes arise over a patient's right to refuse treatment. Few of these situations are clear-cut, and they often mobilize strong feelings in everyone involved. In advocating for patients, social workers must also remember that they have an obligation to staff.

Medical personnel as a group have difficulty dealing with limits, their own and others'. The insightful worker will recognize referrals that are made because the physician, usually reluctant to grant the importance of psychological elements in physical disease, has become unusually aware of these elements when the limits of medical intervention have been reached. The worker's response should always be to do whatever can be done and to help everyone come to terms with limits as part of life.

Pain

For many illnesses, pain is the major symptom. It may even be definitional (e.g., headache). Pain is a subjective experience, the perception of which depends on setting and circumstances.

Within the medical community, pain has additional meanings. While pain relief is a usual focus of treatment, sometimes pain infliction is necessary for diagnostic or treatment procedures; pain relief may even have to be postponed because pain is the major diagnostic clue in some disorders. In such instances, there is an unspoken bargain that the infliction of pain or the postponement of relief will be as brief as possible. Pain, like illness, has its trajectory. When staff and patient agree on the expected course of pain and no complications arise, the transactions around the pain are usually satisfactory. When, however, a patient reports "too much" or "too little" pain, social sanctions follow. Staff members have their own interpretations of pain and reactions to it, so that some nurses withhold medications they think are addicting or that the patient does not need. Generally in such transactions, the patient's past experience with pain and medication is discounted and malingering is alleged (Fagerhaugh & Strauss, 1977).

Chronic pain differs from acute pain in that it often has no diagnostic significance—it is simply there. It calls for an adaptation that is different from the adaptation to illness and it challenges the patient's ideas about the meaning of life. Pain medications work relatively well for acute pain of short duration, such as postoperative pain, but have many disadvantages for the chronic patient. Over time, such medications lose their effectiveness, so that larger and larger doses must be taken of stronger and stronger medications. Addiction, though not a real problem in many instances (such as terminal cases), continues to be feared by the medical and lay communities.

Some new techniques have been tried for the alleviation of chronic pain regardless of cause. Relaxation has been used for various diseases with links to stress. Sometimes, these methods are coupled with "positive imaging." Thus, Bresler and Trubo (1979) described an angina sufferer who imagined his pain as a huge elephant on his chest; over time, he put the elephant in a diet until finally its ears grew so large in comparison to its body that it was able to fly away; eventually, the elephant came to serve as a personal advisor to the patient, whose pain had diminished markedly. Note that most reports of these more innovative techniques are anecdotal and that their value remains to be proven.

Death and Dying

Working with patients who are dying can be an enormously challenging and draining experience for a social worker. Nowhere else is it as important to be in touch with one's own reactions and sense of self. Counseling the dying and their families presents special opportunities for satisfaction but makes special demands on the worker for genuineness.

Death, like sex, has only recently come out of the closet. For years, a conspiracy of silence surrounded this subject. Medical personnel and families tried to protect the patient from knowledge that she was dying. Frequently, this meant that the patient suffered even more, believing that death was imminent but unable to talk to anyone about it. Now it is recognized that most dying patients know what is happening to them and give behavioral clues of how they wish the subject of their death to be handled. For the majority, that way is open discussion. The worker's goals may be to facilitate communication and to allow grief to be expressed at the patient's own pace and in his own way.

In this society, contact with the dead and dying is limited to specialized occupational groups, such as medical personnel, clergy, and morticians. Such professionals of necessity develop routinized ways of dealing with stressful situations and of detaching themselves from them. In many ways, death, is mass produced. It is noteworthy in this regard that few professional schools in the helping professions teach skills for dealing with the dying or their families.

An important concept for social work with the dying is the hospice program, developing across the country. In hospices, the main concern is to help the patient live until she dies and to allow the family to participate in this process and to go on living afterward. The hospice emphasizes comfort. Thus, pain medications are dispensed liberally and patients are allowed a degree of control over the medications they receive. Generally, hospices use a team approach, with physician, nurses, chaplain, social worker, and volunteers working with both the patient and the family. Home care may also be provided. The hospice program provides a holistic approach to the dying patient as he faces the inevitable conclusion to his life.

Iatrogenic Problems

Iatrogenic problems are those caused by medical treatment itself. There are many such problems; this section considers two.

Medication side effects are generally not well recognized outside the medical community. Patients often assume that each pill works the same in each person and that results are highly predictiable. This is not so. Medications have a range of effects and dosage must often be adjusted to accommodate patient response. There is no medication that is free from side effects, and the taking of any drug always entails a calculation of risks and benefits.

It is impossible to list all potential side effects, even of commonly prescribed medications. Several professional and popular references are available, and many communities have a drug information service staffed by a clinical pharmacist. While it is not the place of a social worker to modify prescribed regimens, knowledge of what drugs the patient is taking could be an important piece of information for treatment. Birth control pills, for example, have been associated with depression; antihypertensives with lethargy; and steroids occasionally with psychosis. The problems associated with prolonged use of minor tranquilizers have been well publicized.

Advances in medical technology can provide great benefits but may have associated problems. As was seen in the case of renal dialysis, patient selection and access may be a prominent issue. Additionally, it is difficult to refuse to do what medical science has the power to do. It takes great courage for a patient, family, or treatment team to withhold heroic measures for the sake of quality of life (or death). However, the social worker is often called upon to assist in this process.

Patients' Rights and Consumer Oriented Medicine

Recently, there has been growth of the concept that patients have the right to specify some of the conditions under which their medical care is to be received. At its most conservative, the patients' rights movement postulates that patients are entitled to courtesy, privacy, and respect for their wishes. Sometimes, rights are stated as mutual: caregivers, too, have the right to make some demands necessary for the orderly running of the facility.

There is growing recognition that because the patient pays the bill (or has it paid on her behalf), she is in a position of strength. The physician is open to questioning and is obligated to give satisfactory service. This approach obviates much of the fear that patients have of their physician. Knowing that they will not be forced to follow the physician's orders and that there is generally a range of treatments from which to choose helps many patients seek help at the first sign of a problem and not wait for a critical situation to develop. Second opinions perform a similar function. However, this approach calls for patients to take much responsibility for their own medical care. The patient must be active in observing and reporting symptoms, in ratifying treatment decisions, and in following prescribed regimens. Not all patients feel comfortable challenging their physicians, nor do all physicians feel comfortable with assertive patients. Some people would rather leave their health care—and, ultimately, responsibility for their health—in the hands of professionals and family members.

Financing Health Care

The American system of fee-for-service medicine is well entrenched. Most third-party payers do not cover preventive services or those designed to avert more serious conditions. Thus, hysterectomies and spinal fusions are paid without question; PAP smears and therapeutic exercise sessions are not. In other cultures, physicians have been rewarded for keeping patients healthy. The U.S. equivalent of this approach is the "health maintenance organization," in which a patient's total medical care (including preventive services) is covered by fixed monthly premiums. Such plans provide an incentive for the institution to save money through early detection, the use of physician extenders (such as nurse practitioners), and patient education. Although many of these plans have been quite successful, they have not seriously challenged the prevailing system and they are frequently accused (often unjustly) of denying services to patients in order to save money.

The high cost of medical care, much of it financed through welfare and Medicare payments, has become a serious concern. Our society has acted on a belief that no one should do without medical care for lack of ability to pay, although services received by the rich and the poor are by no means equal. Yet the serious question has arisen of whether we can really afford the level of services currently provided or whether the money might better be spent in other directions. To date, attempts to limit costs have been instituted but not attempts to restrict access. Shortened hospital stays, outpatient diagnostic and surgical procedures, and review boards have slowed the rate of cost increase somewhat. However, it does not appear likely that a socialized medical system will be adopted in the near future.

Issues in Social Work Treatment of Psychosomatic Disorders

In treating clients with suspected psychosomatic disorders, it is imperative to assess the extent of medical pathology. Organic problems are not always clear-cut, especially in neurological conditions, and thus a thorough medical evaluation is important while psychological evaluation and treatment proceeds. The importance of coordination of medical and social work efforts cannot be overemphasized. Pankratz and Glaudin (1980) observed that even though negative medical results have been received, the clinician cannot say with certainty that psychological intervention is sufficient and that no medical intervention will prove to be necessary.

A young social worker developed a pain in her right shoulder. On reviewing her life situation, she became aware of her feeling that many people were "on her back" but that her position was "right." Despite this analysis, the pain persisted. Some days later, while working on a research project in the library, she discovered that long hours at the microfilm machine, which called for holding the arm in an unnatural position, were the actual cause of the pain.

Because of the stigma attached to psychosomatic illness, the physician may have difficulty getting the patient into psychological treatment. Furthermore, the patient feels the symptom as physical and may have an unconscious need for the symptom to keep unmanageable emotions in check. Therefore, physician referrals for counseling often go unheeded by patients with psychosomatic disorders. The physician, then, is in the position of trying to appease the patient and may prescribe pain medication or refer the patient to another medical facility or specialist. Consequently, many individuals with psychological components to their illness do not receive appropriate help.

In the initial interview with a patient manifesting psychosomatic illness, the social worker should focus on the frustrations of living with illness and what this means to the individual. The interviewer should be empathetic, not confrontive (Pankrantz & Glaudin, 1980). Watzlawick and associates (1974) put it this way: "In helping the psychosomatic patient cooperate with assessment and treatment, the experienced clinician is ever mindful of the threatening nature of this material, the importance of minimizing defensiveness, and the value of using the patient's own language to promote agreement and subsequent change." It is important to see clients as they see themselves and to deal with the person as a whole rather than as a conglomeration of "real" and "imaginary" symptoms (Hossenlopp & Holland, 1977).

The initial interview lets the worker investigate underlying psychosocial problems. Statements about the frustration and loneliness resulting from illness and questions about the consequences of the illness in relation to other family members and social systems may uncover depression, frustration, and interpersonal difficulties. This information is essential in assessing the individual's situation.

As treatment progresses and the defenses weaken, the interaction between the individual's psychological and social circumstances can be discussed in relation to the illness. The individual can be helped to deal better with stress and to express the emotions relating to stressors in more productive ways. Physical symptoms seldom disappear entirely, but as the relationship of stress to the symptoms comes into conscious awareness, physical symptoms tend to decrease in both frequency and intensity (Hossenlopp & Holland, 1977). However, it is not unusual for the individual with psychogenic symptoms prematurely to terminate treatment if the elicited material is too threatening. Thus, every contact with the individual should be learning, as well as a helping, experience (Sheridan & Kline, 1977).

Social workers most often use the casework method with patients, but groups composed of patients and/or their families have benefited patients in similar situations or with similar illnesses. Such groups may have educational, therapeutic, or combined goals. The social worker can also serve as a consultant concerning individual patients or, in a broader, administrative role, concerning patient care in general. In addition, the social worker has a role in the community in helping to establish more comprehensive resources to assist the ill and the disabled and to improve overall health.

Social workers involved in health care often participate in interdisciplinary teams. Such participation calls for continuous dialogue and cooperation among the members of the team. The effectiveness of the team approach depends in large part on the ability of team members to sort out roles when each may be operating from a different frame of reference. Although the social worker participates as an equal member of the team, her training in communication skills and behavior dynamics makes it appropriate for her to try to facilitate the work of the team as a whole.

For social workers outside the health care setting, effective service to patients who have physical symptoms requires that the worker develop relationships with medical consultants. This may be difficult. It is important for workers not to be defensive about their lack of medical knowledge and to understand that community based physicians are often equally ignorant about social work. Mutually respectful communication is the answer.

Whatever the disease entity or work setting, an approach that stresses the here and now is preferable to one that focuses on blame. With the former approach, workers can focus on whatever seems to be effective in relieving symptoms. Although it is important to know about the pathophysiology of ulcers, etiology becomes academic if relaxation techniques appear to moderate symptoms.

Of course, the practitioner never advises about specific drug regimens but refers such questions to the patient's physician. It is also unprofessional to undermine a patient's relationship with his physician, although at times it is necessary to suggest that patients consider a change. Nor should social workers endorse unproven methods of treatment or attempt treatments that they are not competent to carry out. Finally, while workers may encourage a positive attitude toward illness, stoicism in the face of undiagnosed pain is not appropriate. Painful symptoms *always* call for medical evaluation. Within these broad guidelines, there is great scope for creative therapy.

Conclusion

The focus of study about psychosomatic illness has shifted from origins of disease to the psychological elements associated with the course of illness and recovery or adaptation. The concept of holistic medicine has been revived and steps taken to reunite mind and body. This has led to an expansion of the field of psychosomatic illness to include all illnesses since all diseases have emotional implications for the patient and family.

Current questions for social work researchers relate to the psychological effect of illness on the patient. For instance, do different illnesses create unique psychological difficulties or are there elements common to all illnesses? What is the effect of different treatment modalities on adjustment? What influences do cultural and sociological factors have on the presentation of, or the adjustment to, illness? The social worker has the opportunity and obligation to help answer these questions to contribute to our understanding of psychosomatic illness and the professional social worker's armamentarium.

Much of this research will be conducted by interdisciplinary teams. It is imperative that social workers become familiar with the language and techniques of research so that they can take part in investigations into the psychosocial aspects of disease.

In conclusion, the field of psychosomatic illness is a complex one in which we can describe effects but speak only tentatively about causes. Social workers should look carefully at their theorizing because many times it reveals more about them than about their clients.

References

AMERICAN PSYCHIATRIC ASSOCIATION: *Diagnostic and Statistical Manual of Mental Disorders*, ed 3, Washington, DC, American Psychiatric Association, 1980.

BARCKLEY V: Grief, a part of living. *Ohio's Health* 1968; 20:34–38.

BARTLETT H: *Fifty Years of Social Work in the Medical Field*. New York, National Association of Social Workers 1957.

BRESLER DE, TRUBO R: *Free Yourself from Pain*. New York, Simon & Schuster, 1979.

BUDOFF PW: *No More Menstrual Cramps and Other Good News*. New York, Putman, 1980.

CASSEM NH: Treating the person confronting death, in Armand N (ed): *The Harvard Guide to Modern Psychiatry*. Cambridge, Belknap, 1978, pp. 579–606.

CREER TL: *Asthma Therapy*. New York, Springer, 1979.

FAGERHAUGH SY, STRAUSS A: *Politics of Pain Management: Staff-Patient Interaction*. Addison-Wesley, 1977.

FRIEDMAN M, ROSENMAN RH: *Type A Behavior and Your Heart*. New York, Knopf, 1974.

GOLDBERG RL: The social worker and the family physician. *Soc Casework* 1973; 54: 489–495.

HENRY JP, STEPHENS PM: *Stress, Health, and the Social Environment*. New York, Springer, 1977.

HOSSENLOPP CM, HOLLAND J: Ambulatory patients with medical and psychiatric illness care in a special medical clinic. *Int J Psychiatry Med.* 1977; 8:1–11.

JENKINS CD, TUTHILL RW, TANNENBAUM SI, et al. Social stressors and excess mortality from hypertensive diseases. *J Human Stress* 5:29–40.

KAPLAN HI: History of psychophysiological medicine, in Freedman M, Sadock BJ (eds): *Comprehensive Textbook of Psychiatry.* Baltimore, Williams & Wilkens, 1975, vol 2, pp. 1624–1631.

KIMBALL CP: Diagnosing psychosomatic situations, in Wolman BB (ed): *Clinical Diagnosis of Mental Disorders* New York, Plenum, 1978, pp. 677–708.

KLERMAN GL, IZEN JE: The effects of bereavement and grief on physical health and general well-being. *Adv Psychosom Med* 1977; 9:63–104.

KÜBLER-ROSS E: *On Death and Dying.* New York, Macmillan, 1969.

LYNCH JJ: *The Broken Heart: The Medical Consequences of Loneliness.* New York, Basic Books, 1977.

MECHANIC D: Social psychologic factors affecting the presentation of bodily complaints. *N Engl J Med* 1972; 286:1132–1139.

O'CONNOR KK: Treatment for adults with psychosomatic symptoms. *Health Soc Work* 1977; 2:89–110.

OSTFELD AM, D'ARTRI DA: Rapid sociocultural change and high blood pressure. *Adv Psychosom Med* 1977; 9:20–37.

PANKRATZ LD, GLAUDIN V: Psychosomatic disorders, in Woody RH (ed): *Encyclopedia of Clinical Assessment.* San Francisco, Jossey-Bass, 1980, pp. 148–168.

REES LW: A reappraisal of some psychosomatic concepts. *Psychother Psychosom* 31:1–4, 9–17.

PHILLIPS B: Health services: social workers in, Saunders B (ed): *Encyclopedia of Social Work,* ed 16. New York, National Association of Social Work, 1971, pp. 615–625.

SHERIDAN MS: Renal disease and the social worker: a review. *Health Soc Work* 1977; 2:122–157.

SHERIDAN MS, KLINE K: Psychosomatic illness in children. *Soc Casework* 1978; 59:227–232.

SINGER MT: Psychological dimensions in psychosomatic patients. *Psychother Psychosom* 1977; 28:13–27.

SPANACINO J: The type A behavior pattern: a critical assessment. *J Human Stress* 1979; 5:37–50.

SPITZER RL (chair): Somatoform disorders, in American Psychiatric Association: *Diagnostic and Statistical Manual of Mental Disorders,* ed 3. Washington, DC, American Psychiatric Association, 1980, pp. 241–252.

STERNBACH RA: *Pain Patients.* New York, Academic, 1974.

SUDNOW D: *Passing On: The Social Organization of Dying.* Englewood Cliffs, Prentice-Hall, 1967.

SUROWICZ FG, BRIGHTWELL DR, WEITZEL WD, et al: Cancer, emotions, and mental illness: the present state of understanding. *Am J Psychiatry* 1976; 133:306–309.

TURNER F: Physical handicaps, in Turner F (ed): *Differential Diagnosis and Treatment in Social Work.* New York, Free Press, 1968, pp 353–510.

WATZLAWICK P, WEAKLAND J, FISCH R: *Change: Principles of Formulation and Problem Resolution.* New York, Norton, 1974.

WOLF S (chair): The role of stress in peptic ulcer disease, panel discussion. *J Human Stress* 1979; 5:27–36.

18

Social Work with Retarded Adults

Enola K. Proctor

The major goal of social work in the field of mental retardation is to enable retarded persons to achieve the highest possible degree of self-support and personal and social adequacy (Conley, 1973). Social workers selecting mental retardation as an area of practice recognize that the potential for change in retarded persons is increasing, the means to intervene are improving, and new avenues of service delivery are being developed. Social workers who have not focused on retardation as a specialty will confront issues associated with this disability to an increasing degree. As they attempt to enter the mainstream of society, retarded persons will experience new problems and will request the same services that nonretarded persons receive. Thus, workers in potentially all settings and fields of practice will require knowledge about retardation and interventions appropriate for retarded clients.

Not all social workers are prepared for this challenge. To date, knowledge of and programs for retarded persons have focused on children.

The writing of this chapter was supported in part by a faculty research award from the George Warren Brown School of Social Work, Washington University, St. Louis. I would like to acknowledge the assistance of Mary Howkins in the preparation of this material and the comments of Larry Davis and Clifford Ridenour on an earlier version of the chapter.

The experience of retarded persons over the life span—and the adult years in particular—has not been thoroughly considered. Social work training often has not provided students with sufficient knowledge about retardation. Yet some understanding of the nature, diagnosis, etiology, and manifestations of retardation is essential, along with an awareness of the ways in which sexism, racism, and stereotypes about retardation may affect service delivery. In addition, workers need to be familiar with the problems that retarded persons and their families frequently experience. And, finally, at a time when new approaches to intervention are being identified, social workers need to know the range of professional responses that are available for addressing problems associated with mental retardation.

Definitions and Diagnosis of Retardation

Mental retardation is not a single syndrome but a state of impairment that can be recognized in an individual's behavior. The American Association on Mental Deficiency (AAMD) recently defined "mental retardation" as "significantly subaverage intellectual functioning existing concurrently with deficits in adaptive behavior, and manifested during the developmental period" (Grossman, 1977, p. 5). This definition incorporates two dimensions: intellectual functioning and adaptive behavior. Deficits in either dimension alone constitute an insufficient basis for labeling a person mentally retarded. For a person to be diagnosed mentally retarded, "impairments in intellectual functioning must co-exist with deficits in adaptive behavior" (Grossman, 1977, p. 12). The relationship between intellectual functioning and adaptive behavior is not fully understood. According to the AAMD, levels of function in intellectual behavior and in adaptive behavior generally correlate, although persons of similar intellectual capacity may exhibit widely varying patterns of behavior. In general, individual discrepancies in levels of performance on the two dimensions is most likely when retardation is mild.

Four levels of intellectual impairment are presently recognized by the AAMD: "mild retardation," in which measured intelligence ranges from the low 50s to the upper 60s; "moderate retardation," in which measured intelligence ranges from the upper 30s to the low 50s; "severe retardation," in which intelligence ranges from 20 to the mid-30s; and "profound retardation," in which measured intelligence is below the low 20s.* Like intellectual ability, adaptive behavior is categorized in

---

*A borderline category of retardation was eliminated in 1973 because most persons whose intelligence falls within its boundaries do not exhibit significant impairment in adaptive behavior.

terms of impairment into mild, moderate, severe, and profound. The AAMD Adaptive Behavior Scale describes the highest degree of behavioral performance in various areas of functioning (e.g., independent functioning, physical functioning, communication, and social skills) for each of the four levels of retardation. The deficit in adaptive behavior can be determined by identifying the pattern of an individual's routine functioning. The validity of intelligence and adaptive behavior as criteria for labeling persons mentally retarded has been challenged repeatedly by critics.

Intelligence, or abstract reasoning ability, is but part of a broad range of mental abilities (Mandelbaum 1977), and measured intelligence itself varies over time for any one person. Moreover, the significance of an individual's intelligence is not constant over the life span; society's emphasis on intellectual performance peaks during the middle school years, or at about ages 10–14.

Intelligence must be measured by standardized tests that are individually administered by specifically trained persons. However, a variety of weaknesses remain in diagnostic procedures. Test results are not always comparable because a variety of intelligence tests are employed. Measurement errors may approximate 10 IQ points per individual, according to the AAMD (Grossman, 1977). The problem of cultural bias in intelligence testing is significant. The AAMD (1978) acknowledged that the application of IQ tests across cultures "unless properly standardized, is likely to lead to serious errors in individual diagnosis and the rates of retardation" (page xi).

Adaptive behavior includes intellectual, affective, motivational, social, and motor abilities. Environmental or societal demands for an individual's adaptive behavior vary widely. Whether persons' adaptive behavior will contribute to their being labeled mentally retarded depends upon the degree to which they can meet standards of personal and social responsibility expected for their age and cultural group. As with measured intelligence, the significance of deficit in adaptive behavior is likely to peak at certain ages. During late adolescence and adult life, the deficits many persons exhibit in vocational or social adjustment may contribute to their identification as mentally retarded.

Measurement of adaptive behavior may be fraught with even more problems than assessment of intellectual functioning: "Despite the longevity of the idea in relation to mental retardation, measurement of adaptive behavior has not achieved the sophisticated precision that would be desirable" (Chinn et al., 1979, p. 6). Measurement of adaptive behavior requires information on what a person routinely does, a task that may be difficult. Most assessment scales of adaptive behavior for use with retarded persons were developed primarily from populations of institutionalized persons. Because such scales do not reflect the broad range of behaviors characteristic of mildly retarded persons living in the community (Grossman, 1977), their validity for noninstitutionalized retarded persons has not been established. Although general rating scales can provide a basis for inferring deficits in adaptive behavior, problems of reliability mandate that their use be supplemented by clinical judgment.

Characteristics of Mentally Retarded Adults

Mentally retarded adults are a heterogeneous group. Persons labeled mentally retarded may be nearly totally dependent on others for their care or may function behaviorally and intellectually nearly as well as persons in the mainstream of society. Thus, the label "mentally retarded" may be applied to the working person who is merely "slow," the person with nearly normal IQ whose behavior is maladaptive, and the institutionalized person with extensive brain damage who requires almost total care. In fact, persons who are classified mentally retarded may have little in common beyond this label.

Approximately 59% of the more than 6 million mentally retarded persons in the United States are over the age of 20 (Goodman, 1978). Thus, more than 3.6 million adults are mentally retarded. As the survival rate and longevity of retarded persons improve, the number of adult retarded persons in society is likely to grow. Conley (1973) estimated that of the retarded adults in the 20–64 age group, approximately 80% are mildly retarded, 8% are moderately and severely retarded, and approximately 3% are profoundly retarded. Severe retardation is less frequent among adults than among children because almost 50% of profoundly retarded children die before the age of five (Conley, 1973).

Adults may be less likely than children and adolescents to be identified as mentally retarded. Conley (1973) concluded from nearly available study that the reported prevalence of mental retardation steadily increases with age until the mid-teens. After this age it steadily declines among whites, although at least one study found an increased rate of retardation with age among black persons. During the teenage years, academic and social pressures on individuals peak and the inability of persons to cope with these pressures may result in their being identified as retarded and therefore referred to services. For some persons, attainment of adult status and assumption of adult responsibility may change their own attitudes and the attitude of others, improving their adjustment and rendering their appearance "normal". About 70% of all mentally retarded persons have no physical manifestations of their retardation (Cleland, 1978). However, some aged persons with limited education, physical disabilities, or ethnically identifiable characteristics may be perceived and labeled retarded even when their intellectual functioning is not impaired (Wood & Mueller, 1970).

Retarded persons may have physical or emotional disabilities ranging from the barely noticeable to those that are totally incapacitating. Information about extent of physical disability among noninstitutionalized retarded adults is scant; however, multiple handicaps are probably more prevalent among retarded adults than among retarded children (Conley, 1973), just as they are more common among nonretarded adults than among nonretarded children. Poor health also appears to be a potentially significant problem for retarded adults. Older retarded persons, in particular, are in need of comprehensive identification and treatment of illness and information about community health care resources. When relatives were surveyed, two-thirds reported concern about the poor health of their retarded adult family member (Wood & Mueller, 1970). Mildly retarded adults who are free of physical disability have nearly normal mortality rates. Mortality rates are approximately doubled for moderately retarded persons and three times normal among severely retarded persons (Conley, 1973). Health problems and increased mortality rates among retarded persons quite likely reflect the fact that society traditionally has accepted physical disability and illness among retarded persons and, consequently, health care services have not been provided.

Most retarded adults are poor; it is estimated that more than 75% live in isolated rural areas or urban slums and that almost half have below poverty level incomes (Mandelbaum, 1977; Wood & Mueller, 1970). Although in some cases poverty may cause retardation and in other cases retardation greatly reduces a person's learning potential, the association between poverty and retardation also reflects the fact that society does not insure the provision of economic resources to mentally retarded persons.

Not all mentally retarded adults living in the community are known to or served by social service agencies. Once retarded adolescents leave the domain of formal education, appropriate services may not exist for them and hence they may lose contact with professional services. Even when services are available, retarded adults often are unable to cope with bureaucracies and therefore refrain from seeking services. More severely retarded persons generally remain visible to retardation services, while those with higher capacities for community and/or vocational adjustment become invisible in the community. As a consequence, it is difficult to obtain accurate demographic data about noninstitutionalized retarded adults (Goodman, 1978).

Certain groups of retarded persons are more likely than others to seek or receive services. For example, although men exceed women only slightly in the total adult retarded population, they outnumber women two to one in agency client populations of retarded persons (Conley, 1973). This may indicate that men are more likely to behave in ways that draw the attention of agencies (Conley, 1973), that cultural expectations for vocational and community adjustment are generally higher for men than for women, or that women are less likely than men to receive services that they need.

Race also affects the extent to which retarded clients receive professional attention and services. Tobias (1969) found that although black and Puerto Rican retarded adolescents were more likely than white retarded adolescents to receive special education services while enrolled in public schools, black and Puerto Rican retarded adults were less likely than whites to receive vocational services from the state division of vocational rehabilitation. Seventy percent of Puerto Rican and black retarded adults who had never been employed had had no contact with vocational rehabilitation services. Retarded members of minority groups are also less likely than white persons to be institutionalized in facilities for retarded persons, but as they become older they are more likely to be placed in mental hospitals or imprisoned than are whites (Conley, 1973). Thus, when retarded members of minority groups are placed in residential treatment, the facility is more likely to be inappropriate to their needs. Although it has been suggested that minorities are better able to accept mental retardation in their families and therefore do not require professional services (Conley, 1973), it is likely that this view reflects racism in the delivery of services. That is, public and private agencies may be less accessible to or less concerned about problems of mental retardation in minority group families until problems are severe enough to require institutionalization.

Retarded adults with histories of problems are also more likely to be represented in agency populations, as compared to household populations. Usually, retarded adults do not come into contact with agencies until their behavior becomes problematic (Conley 1973). Moreover, by definition the term "mental retardation" means that deficits in performance arise during the developmental years. Hence, retarded adults whom practitioners see in agencies are likely to have histories of problems in behavior, performance, and adjustment.

In summary, adult retarded clients in social service agencies are likely to be young adult, male, white, and poor and to have a history of problem behavior. However, workers should be aware that certain factors have operated to produce a client group from the total population of adult retarded persons. In particular, clients may be more severely retarded than are persons in the general population of retarded persons and such factors as sex and race may have rendered their behavior particularly unacceptable. Most important, workers should realize that the range of behaviors seen among their clients does not accurately reflect the range of behaviors possible for retarded persons. In addition, agency administrators and workers should realize that excluded from client status are two groups: retarded adults who are doing very well in the community and retarded adults who experience problems but lack access to or attention from agencies.

Etiology of Mental Retardation

Hundreds of complex conditions have been identified as causes of mental retardation. The AAMD grouped these causes as follows:

1. infection and intoxication: maternal and childhood infectious diseases and intoxications that can result in brain damage or malformation include rubella, congenital syphilis, viruses, bacteria, parasites, toxemia of pregnancy, and drugs or poisons ingested during pregnancy
2. trauma or physical injury: labor difficulties due to malposition, disproportion, and knotted cords can result in brain damage
3. metabolic or nutritional disorders: inborn errors in the metabolism of lipids, carbohydrates, or protein can result in mental retardation, e.g., Tay-Sachs disease and phenlyketonuria (PKU); inadequate diet, parasitism, and feeding problems also can lead to delayed development and mental retardataion
4. gross postnatal brain disease: this large group of disorders includes neurofibromatosis, intracranial tumors, and degenerative white matter.
5. factors of unknown prenatal influence: common conditions associated with retardation at birth include microcephaly, macrocephaly, and premature closure of cranial sutures
6. chromosomal abnormality: possible causes of chromosomal abnormality include gene mutation, drugs and chemicals, radiation, aged gametes, and viruses; most notable among chromosomal abnormalities is Down's syndrome, which affects approximately 10% of the retarded institutionalized population
7. gestational disorders: prematurity, postmaturity, or low birth weight can result in mental retardation
8. psychiatric disorders: certain forms of retardation may follow psychosis, particularly when anxieties are so severe that the child's learning and development are retarded; however, only severe and pervasive psychological problems generally result in mental retardation
9. environmental influences: general psychosocial disadvantages resulting from inadequate diet, inadequate medical care, and poor housing can result in retardation

The term "mental retardation" is generally employed when there is no evidence of damage to the central nervous system (CNS). When such pathology is evident, the term "mental deficiency" is frequently employed and the degree of retardation is generally severe. CNS pathology is present in about 25% of cases of retardation. Such retardation is randomly distributed across socioeconomic groups, while retardation without CNS damage is more likely to be concentrated among lower socioeconomic groups.

Although it is sometimes possible to identify the factors responsible for an individual's mental retardation, in most cases either the exact cause of mental retardation is unknown or the manner in which particular biological deficits operate to produce retardation is unknown. For example, although chromosomal abnormalities are linked to Down's syndrome, the relationship between an extra chromosome and the resultant mental retardation is not clearly understood (Grossman, 1977).

Identification of etiology in the traditional sense may serve rather limited purposes in work with retarded clients. Persons whose retardation is of the same etiology may evidence widely varying levels of intellectual functioning and adaptive behavior. Moreover, persons with approximately the same levels of intellectual functioning and adaptive behavior may exhibit widely varying manifestations of retardation and, hence, present very different problems. And, finally, for all persons, mental-retardation is a concept descriptive of current behavior, not of potential. Thus, neither an overall label of retardation, nor an understanding of etiology, nor a determination of degree of retardation necessarily implies prognosis. Instead, prognosis for an individual depends upon conditions associated with the retardation and, most important, the treatment and training opportunities available to the individual.

The primary purpose of diagnostic classification is to furnish statistical data on the incidence, prevalence, and characteristics of various forms of retardation for administrative, programing, or research purposes. Such data can increase knowledge of the nature, prevention, and amelioration of conditions associated with retardation (Grossman, 1977). However, the complexity of factors within diagnostic groups is such that classification cannot be assumed to prescribe specific services or treatments for each individual client within the group. Rather, specific objectives must be determined on an individual basis. It is critical for workers to view a person's status as mentally retarded as potentially dynamic, rather than permanent, and as amenable to change over time as a result of improvements in social functioning, intellectual functioning, or environmental expectations.

Mental Retardation and the Social Work Profession

During the first half of this century, social work's involvement in problems associated with mental retardation was rather tentative. Mentally retarded persons were segregated from others in the population, in general, and from other clients served by social welfare agencies and programs, in particular. Retardation itself was viewed as immutable and social workers tended to reflect the view of the larger society that "retarded persons [are] quite incapable of benefiting from the opportunities and services available to the rest of the population" (Dybwad, 1970, p. 310). Scientific knowledge revealed little understanding of the nature of retardation nor could it suggest appropriate professional interventions. Just as society's general response was segregation of retarded persons, the professional response frequently was institutionalization. Most social workers viewed the problem of retardation as the responsibility of health or mental health professionals.

Perceptions of mental retardation began to change in the early 1950s with the organization of parent advocacy groups. In the early 1960s, the President's Panel to Combat Mental Retardation expressed the view that mental retardation is a national problem to which professional response—including prevention—is both possible and crucial. Subsequent developments in behavior change technologies and their application to problems of retarded persons led to the gradual realization that even severely retarded persons are capable of acquiring a wide range of self-help, vocational, and interpersonal skills. In the 1970s, stimulated in large part by an awareness of advances in other countries, professionals in the United States began to strive for integration of retarded persons into the mainstream of community activity and services. Thus, the principle of "normalization" was proposed, a concept defined by Wolfensberger (1972) as "utilization of means which are as culturally normative as possible, in order to establish and/or maintain personal behaviors and characteristics which are as culturally normative as possible" (p. 28). Since the early 1970s, the goal of enabling retarded persons to function as normally as possible has become more widely advocated.

Unfortunately, development within social work in the 1950s and 1960s continued to be hampered by a "seeming lack of promise of returns" (Beck, 1969, p. 101), with theory and practice focusing on the impact of diagnosis on the family. However, as other professions demonstrated the responsiveness of retarded persons to intervention, social work rechanneled its traditional concern into more innovative service approaches to retarded clients and their families.

Social workers are now involved in a broad range of activities in the field of retardation, including individual counseling with retarded clients, family counseling, future planning with retarded clients and their parents, group work with retarded adolescents and adults, consultation with staff in residential facilities, advocacy on behalf of retarded citizens, and planning and administration of services in the field of retardation. Social workers in a wide range of settings—such as state departments of mental health, departments of vocational rehabilitation, hospitals, public and special schools, and family counseling services—have retarded persons among their clients. Because the range of settings is so extensive, data on the number of social workers who work with retarded clients are not currently available. However, by the late 1970s, 527 MSW social workers and 809 BSW social workers were employed in public residential facilities for retarded persons (Scheerenberger, 1978).

If, as anticipated and desired, retarded persons enter the mainstream of community life, social workers in settings that traditionally have not served retarded persons can expect increasingly to encounter retarded clients. Practice experience now suggests that retarded clients can benefit from the same services and information that nonretarded persons receive. However, social workers sometimes may need to modify their interventive approaches. To the extent that social work can make available to retarded clients the services that nonretarded persons traditionally have used, then the profession will be operationalizing the normalization concept, which has been widely accepted as an ideal.

Common Areas for Social Work Intervention in the Treatment of Mental Retardation

As the discussion of diagnosis and etiology indicated, each mentally retarded adult with whom a social worker comes into contact will present a unique set of needs. Just as manifestations of retardation and abilities vary, so do clients' presenting problems and desired outcomes. The major goal of service in the field of mental retardation is to enable retarded persons to achieve the highest possible degree of self-support and personal and social adequacy (Conley, 1973); many of the specific problems presented by retarded clients reflect their current difficulty in achieving such support and adequacy. While no retarded individual should be presumed to experience problems in all these areas, a number of general problem areas may be common among adult retarded clients. Specific needs and desired outcomes within each of these areas should be determined from individual assessment.

Self-image and Interpersonal Relationships

Retarded persons are frequently assumed, to lack the ability to conceptualize themselves in abstract terms and thus to be unable to develop a self-concept. However, retarded persons do express self-referent perceptions, which, in turn, may affect their relationships with others. These self-references are often negative. Retarded adults frequently describe themselves as slow, lazy, or crazy and often express the desire to be like other people (Nitzberg, 1970).

A number of factors may contribute to such a view of self. Generally, retarded persons are aware that others view them as different or hold negative attitudes toward them. Repeated vocational failures may further diminish self-concept, as work is so highly valued in American society. Many retarded adults have histories of academic failure, have been subject to frequent criticism, and have depended upon permission of parents or teachers to perform even routine actions (Katz, 1970). Sheltered home experience or institutionalization may deny opportunities to learn and practice decisionmaking and action initiation. In fact, helplessness has been identified as a pervasive personality style in the retarded sufficiently meaningful that it discriminates between typical behavior patterns of retarded and nonretarded persons (Floor & Rosen, 1975).

Among retarded children, personality problems frequently are tolerated or ignored (Department of Health, Education, and Welfare, 1978), such that the severity of such problems may increase over the years. Retarded persons are sometimes rejected from adult programs and services because of personality problems, yet they may experience difficulty obtaining adequate treatment for these very problems. Psychiatric professionals often are not willing to work with mentally retarded persons and professionals in the field of mental retardation may not be sensitive to emotional problems. The importance of social work's potential contribution here is evident.

Katz (1970) stressed the importance of the retarded person's developing an appropriate self-image as an adult. This may involve appearance, dress, and gait; assumption of responsibilities; successful performance of adult work roles; and independence in decisionmaking.

The practice literature indicates that retarded adults may have fewer friendships than nonretarded persons and may be more likely to experience difficulties in their relationships with others. The gap between abilities of retarded persons and others may be wider among adults than among children, making retarded persons increasingly isolated as they mature. One study found that more than half of the retarded adults living in the community who were surveyed did not participate in any habilitative programs (Stanfield, 1973). The opportunities for such persons to develop friendships are minimal: "For these young adults graduation from school marked the beginning of a life of relative isolation from peers and segregation from the community at large" (Stanfield, 1973, p. 551).

A variety of specific deficits in social skills and interpersonal behavior may complicate those relationships that retarded adults do enjoy. According to the literature, retarded adults frequently have difficulty displaying or verbalizing affect, perhaps as a result of years of effort to "control bad feeling" (Scanlon, 1978). In addition, they often exhibit lack of self-control, inability to restrain impulses and behavior that might be objectionable to other people, and inability to postpone immediate satisfaction (Corvin, 1970; Gardner & Stamm, 1971; Katz, 1970). According to Gardner and Stamm, this may reflect a "lack of adequate verbal control of non verbal behaviors." That is, among retarded persons, control or functional relationships between verbal control and other classes of behavior represented by verbal content frequently have not been established. Thus, a retarded client may verbally acknowledge that a certain action is inappropriate yet may not refrain from engaging in that very action. Because self-control is best developed early in life, the retarded adult who has not developed a satisfactory level of self-control by adulthood may present a serious problem (Katz, 1970). While general suggestions likely will not be very effective, interventions that set and maintain limits may be successful in increasing desired behaviors (Katz, 1970). In addition, the improvement of such abilities as athletic and artistic skills, the increase of knowledge of current events, and the development of a range of interpersonal skills may help the retarded client become more confident, more likely to be accepted by others, and more satisfied in interpersonal relationships.

Marriage and Sexuality

Although many societies view sexuality and marriage among retarded adults as important to their successful integration into community life (Craft & Craft, 1976), no other issue has been more fraught with fears and stereotypes in this country. This issue presents very immediate concerns for retarded clients and their families. The frequent isolation of retarded adults may make it difficult for them to form relationships and develop the capacity to handle the accompanying emotions and responsibilities. Affirmation of the sexual rights of their adult retarded children may be difficult for parents, requiring them to face their own feelings and values about sexual behavior, their potential discomfort in discussing sex with their children, and the negative image of sexuality among retarded persons dominant in society. Fearful of these issues, parents and professionals frequently have responded in protective rather than facilitative ways. Yet the right of retarded persons to marry is now widely recognized; the President's Panel on Mental Retardation affirmed nearly two decades ago that mental retardation in and of itself should not be a legal disqualification for marriage.

An increasing body of empirical data is now available to help us understand the consequences of sexual behavior, marriage, and parenting among retarded adults. David and associates (1976) reported that most institutionalized mildly and moderately retarded persons experience some kind of sexual activity, although few have adequate knowledge regarding contraception. According to Conley (1973), about three-fourths of the male and three-fifths of the female mildly retarded persons in the United States are married and living with their spouses. Very few adults with IQs of less than 50 marry. Some, but not all, studies have indicated high divorce rates among retarded persons. "Mildly retarded adults appear to have no fewer but probably not significantly more children than the average" (Conley, 1973, p. 263), although when they bear unusually large families, children seem more likely to be retarded probably due to adverse environmental circumstances. Data from a study of marriage among retarded persons in north Wales suggest that the success of marriage depends less on the severity of retardation than on the amount of support available to the couple, such as social services and interested relatives and friends (Craft & Craft, 1976). While the companionship of marriage can overcome loneliness and provide a source of comfort, married retarded persons often experience problems that are caused by divergent expectations, sexual dysfunction, and, for some couples who choose to remain childless, a sense of loss or disappointment. Overall, however, marriage appears to bring enrichment and happiness to the lives of retarded persons.

A number of implications for counseling services are apparent. Sexual counseling for retarded persons should be supportive, recognizing that sexual attraction is natural; interpretive, helping clients clarify their feelings about their relationships; and practical, providing contraceptive information and helping clients find acceptable standards for sexual behavior (Walker, 1977). Because many retarded adults see marriage as emancipation from home and because they may encounter certain problems that nonretarded persons can handle more easily, premarital counseling is important. Walker suggested that such counseling focus on areas like financial management, sexuality, the couple's attraction to each other, their expectations regarding division of labor and decision-making, their desires and plans regarding childbearing, and their expected involvement with extended families.

Paula and Michael met at a dance sponsored by the community association for retarded citizens (ARC). She was 23, lived in a group home, and worked 30 hours per week at a bakery. Twenty-two-year-old Michael lived at home with his parents and took the bus to the sheltered workshop each day. Their attraction to each other developed quickly and, in the four months since their meeting, they spent every Friday evening together at ARC events and talked daily by phone.

At Paula's initiative, the couple sought out the social worker available through her group residence. Paula and Michael wished to get married soon. They came to talk to the worker because Paula's mother was afraid they could not manage on their own. Paula and Michael identified a number of concerns. Where would they live? Would their combined earnings and government support be sufficient to cover their expenses? Should they have children? They expressed determination to "show" their parents they could manage on their own, although they had not yet discussed their plans with Michael's parents, whose objections they anticipated.

The worker assessed the resources and strengths of Paula and Michael. Paula had managed very well with minimal supervision in the group home for five years; she could budget her income. Both Michael and Paula could shop, cook, and do laundry. They shared many leisure activities. They had a sense of humor. They communicated their feelings freely with each other. They were willing and able to seek help when they needed it. And they had strong feelings of attraction for each other. Potential problem areas were also identified. Michael had not lived away from home and therefore was not very independent. Their combined earnings were low. Michael's parents were expected to object. Michael wanted children, although Paula was afraid they could not "raise them right."

Once resources and problem areas had been reviewed, the worker helped the couple prioritize the desired outcomes. The first was to seek the approval of their parents. The worker decided to employ role playing and behavioral rehearsal in order to prepare Paula and Michael for discussions with their families. Paula and Michael decided to invite their parents to a meeting with the worker; although they wanted to do the talking, they would feel more confident in the worker's presence. The couple and worker spent four weeks preparing for the family session. During this time, Michael and Paula grew more confident about their own capabilities, they learned to understand each other's perspective, and they anticipated some real concerns their parents might have.

When the couple shared their plans with their parents, the families and the worker were impressed by how clearly and completely they had considered their problems and how to deal with them. Although immediate parental blessings were not forthcoming, the parents acknowledged heretofore unrecognized strengths in their children and expressed a willingness to "wait and see." Paula and Michael's impatience to marry immediately was replaced by an eagerness thoroughly to anticipate problems and solutions.

Paula and Michael met regularly with the worker for seven months to plan their approach to each potential problem. At the worker's suggestions, they met with a clergyman they wanted to perform the marriage ceremony, consulted with a family planning counselor, obtained an advocate from the ARC, and sought additional financial resources through the housing bureau, food stamps, and Medicaid. The worker helped them parctice budgeting their pooled resources and met with the parents from time to time. In their preparation for marriage, Paula and Michael learned how to solve problems and developed, along with their families, an appreciation of how capable they were. The social worker had created the opportunity for them to achieve greater self-support and independence.

Vocational Issues

Just as employment is a primary objective for nonretarded persons in our society, it should be also for retarded adults. According to Conley (1973), ''gainful work is almost always feasible for persons with IQs above forty, unless precluded by physical or emotional handicaps'' (p. 334). Yet unemployment and underemployment are major problems facing adult retarded persons. Many retarded persons who leave school fail either to find immediate employment or to receive vocational services from agencies and therefore never enter the labor market as adults (Tobias, 1969). Almost 700,000 retarded adults are economically idle (Conley, 1973), the majority of whom are only mildly retarded and could be gainfully employed if appropriate services were available. That vocational success is possible is reflected by the large number of retarded persons working in the community: in 1970, approximately 2.9 million adults in the 20–64 age range and with IQs less than 70 were employed in the community (Conley, 1973).

Many retarded adults work at menial tasks and do not receive wages that are adequate to support themselves. Although very limited data are available for purposes of comparison, the data do suggest that mildly retarded noninstitutionalized adults earn about 86% of the salary of nonretarded workers, while moderately retarded adults earn approximately 20% of the earnings of their counterparts in the general population (Conley, 1973).

A number of factors affect the employment success of retarded persons. Retarded adults are more likely to find work during periods of high labor demand; this group is more subject to fluctuations in the national level of economic activity than are others in the general population (Conley, 1973; McCarver & Craig, 1974). Vocational success also depends upon disability. While few severely or profound retarded persons are employed, intellectual deficiency alone does not cause vocational failure among persons with IQs above 40. However, job discrimination, physical disability, and emotional problems do cause such failure. Many employers are hesitant to hire a person who has both physical and mental disabilities. As most jobs available to retarded persons require physical labor, adults who are both retarded and disabled experience greater difficulty locating employment than do persons who are only disabled or only retarded. Because physical handicaps increase over time, unemployment may be more severe among the retarded aged (Conley, 1973).

The race and sex of retarded persons also affects their employment success. As in the general population, black retarded persons are more likely to be unemployed than are white retarded persons (Conley, 1973). Retarded women are less likely to enter the labor market or, once employed, to sustain their employment (Tobias, 1969). Among the mildly retarded, 87% of men and 33% of women are employed; among the moderately retarded, 45% of men and 12% of women are employed (Conley, 1973). The literature suggests that families may be protective of retarded women and that full-time homemaker roles are frequently encouraged for married women (Conley, 1973; Tobias, 1969). Social workers should be concerned that as a result of sexism or racism, vocational roles and rehabilitation services may not be sufficiently available to women or to blacks.

The practice literature also cites motivation, attitudes, and job related behaviors as potential problems for retarded adults. For example, retarded persons are often characterized as unmotivated to work, frightened of work, unreliable, distractable, hypersensitive to criticism, and aspiring to inappropriate job choices (Nitzberg, 1970). However, Conley (1973) suggested that what appears to be a lack of motivation may instead be a mask for fear or resentment or may reflect lack of opportunity to develop habits necessary for job success. In fact, some retarded persons actually may be too motivated; those who spend too much time on tasks may want to insure that they do not make mistakes. Other workers may resent jobs that appear to be menial. Travel necessary for employment and participation in job interviews may be threatening to retarded clients when they lack the skills necessary for these situations (Grinnell & Lieberman, 1977). Practitioners should recognize that clients presenting these problems probably have not had the opportunity to acquire the habits, attitudes, and behaviors that contribute to vocational success.

Relationships with Parents

Successful independent functioning of retarded adults in the community frequently depends upon the help of relatives, usually spouses or parents (Wood & Mueller, 1970), and most retarded adults who are not institutionalized live at home with their parents (Goodman, 1978; Katz, 1967). Thus, the involvement of parents may be a significant ingredient in any work with retarded adult clients.

Parents of retarded adults have not always received from social service agencies the interest, support, and services that they require. Seventy-six percent of parents of retarded adults interviewed by Stanfield (1973) reported that agencies had not been helpful enough in providing family counseling, social and recreational programs, vocational guidance, and planning for the future. Parents frequently come to agencies for professional help when they feel unable to cope with unacceptable behaviors in their retarded adult child, when siblings complain that the retarded family member interferes with friendships and activities, and when elderly parents fear they cannot continue to care for their retarded family member (Corvin, 1968; Katz, 1970).

The professional literature has often characterized the attitudes and reactions of parents of retarded adults in rather negative terms. Although they provide care and support, parents sometimes are portrayed as obstacles to achievement and independence on the part of their retarded child (Goodman, 1978). They have been described as uninformed about available services, exasperated by and resigned to the perceived burden of continual care, fearful of their children's independence, and over-protective (Corvin, 1970; Goodman, 1978; Katz, 1970; Nitzburg, 1970). Nitzburg characterized them as "hard to reach," difficult to involve in treatment, and reluctant to scrutinize their relationships with their retarded offspring.

Perhaps because they wish to avoid disappointment (Nitzburg, 1970) or perhaps because professionals themselves have fostered low expectations (Proctor, 1974), parents frequently underestimate the capacities of their adult retarded child for such accomplishments as self-care, work, travel, and marriage (Katz, 1970). Thus, they continue to do things that the retarded adult is willing and able to do personally. Overprotection may create roles for both parents and retarded offspring that, though convenient and mutually gratifying, preclude achievement and independence. For example, the unemployed retarded woman may serve as companion or housekeeper to her parents; the young retarded man may serve as child for the family so that parents' needs to nurture and care for him can be fulfilled. Workers are not likely to help families successfully alter such roles unless the satisfactions these roles provide are procured in alternative ways.

The literature about parents of retarded adults rarely includes the retarded client's perspective of the parent–child relationship. Rather, the literature seems to imply that only parents have the capacity to perceive or talk about problems in family relationships and to contribute toward the independence of the retarded adult. In fact, just as the progress of a retarded person toward adult status and an optimum balance of dependence–independence may bring frustration, fear, and fatigue to parents, so it may to the retarded client also. Awareness of how much he requires the support of parents may make the expression of negative feelings and the very desire for independence threatening for the retarded client. Thus, the acceptance of these feelings as normal, the perception of the retarded client as neither child nor normal adult but as an adult with certain limitations, the facilitation of parent–child communcation, and the identification of appropriate expectations for achievement may become important foci for social work intervention. The worker's role may be that of intermediary between parent and retarded client, enabling their mutual participation in the specification of problems and the identification of mutually acceptable and desired outcomes.

Nancy was a 46-year-old woman considered to be moderately retarded. No definite etiology for her retardation had been established, although anoxia at birth was suspected. Since her release from an institutional setting six years earlier as part of the facility's efforts to return residents to community living, Nancy had attended a state funded sheltered workshop. Although she comprehended and followed instructions well, her progress toward independent job functioning had been very slow. Nancy repeatedly asked her supervisor to check her work, performed each task slowly and meticulously, and would not move on to new tasks until the supervisor noticed that Nancy was idle and specifically directed her to the next task. These behaviors were frustrating to the supervisor, who requested the social worker to "talk" to Nancy.

The social worker found Nancy to be verbally fluent, though reluctant to express her own ideas, feelings, or desires. Nancy reported that she liked her job at the sheltered workshop because "someone is always there to help."

When the worker met with Nancy and her parents together, information was obtained about Nancy's role at home. The parents, in their late sixties, were both retired. They reported that Nancy was usually "a big help around the house"—setting the dinner table, folding laundry, and accompanying them to the grocery store. However, they commented that Nancy had become increasingly "hard to understand" and "touchy"; she sometimes had stormy outbursts of temper and spent many evenings alone in her room. Nancy did not select her own clothing or activities and she spent most of her time with her parents.

The worker observed that although Nancy seemed capable, her behavior was usually dependent upon others. Her parents reported that they had made no plans for the time when they could no longer care for her or at the time of their death. They felt the workshop experience was "O.K." in that it gave Nancy something to do but believed that she should not be pushed to an actual job situation because she could not "manage." Moreover, they feared "girls like Nancy might be taken advantage of and shouldn't have to work anyway."

The worker believed Nancy to be capable of much more autonomy than either her workshop experience or her home situation afforded. The stormy outbursts were seen as reflecting Nancy's frustration, which she could not or feared to express. The following factors were seen as contributing to Nancy's situation: the early response to Nancy's retardation had been an expectation of lifelong dependence; Nancy's potential for achievement had not been identified or encouraged in the institution, by her parents, or in the workshop; as a result of sexism, vocational success was not expected by Nancy, her parents, or professionals working with her; her parents were unaware of options for care for Nancy after their death and they responded, out of fear, by ignoring this problem; and, after years of being treated like a child, Nancy could not verbally express her frustration with her current situation or her own fears about the future.

The worker, exploring these issues with Nancy, proposed that they work together to "see what she is capable of." The worker formulated a sequence of desired outcomes, all defined in terms of more independent functioning. The outcomes ranged from selecting her own clothing for the day, to attending a social event sponsored by the community association for retarded citizens, to learning to ride the bus to the workshop. Longer range outcomes included spending a weekend as a guest in a hostel for retarded adults and demonstrating initiative in the assumption of new tasks at the workshop. The interventive approach insured that both the behaviors being reinforced and the reinforcers for those behaviors were linked to independence; thus, Nancy's display of independent behaviors was reinforced with opportunities for even greater independence, such as selecting T.V. programs to watch and planning dinner menus.

In addition, the worker met regularly with Nancy's parents to discuss her progress with them; most important, they were encouraged to attend group meetings of other parents of retarded adults. At some of these meetings, programs were presented to inform parents of new developments in services to retarded persons. For most parents, their attitudes toward and perceptions of their retarded children had not kept pace with revelation of the actual capacities of the latter. Therefore, the group worker sought to increase parents' understanding of the potential for independence in their children. In less structured groups, parents were encouraged to discuss fears and concerns, including fears that their children would fail, would be taken advantage of, and would need care and support after their own deaths.

The worker recognized that Nancy required the opportunity to practice autonomy, support and reinforcement for independent behaviors, and new perceptions of her capabilities by her parents and herself. Most of all, Nancy and her parents needed help in understanding that they could provide and care for her in new ways—by fostering opportunities for her increased self-sufficiency.

Residential Options

Although at one time retardation itself implied institutionalization, presently only about 4% of retarded persons ever reside in institutions (McCarver & Ellis, 1974). Yet institutional facilities remain a significant service setting for mentally retarded person. In his study of 239 public residential facilities, Scheerenberger (1976) reported the average daily population in institutions for retarded persons as 153,584, nearly two-thirds of whom were age 22 and older. He further reported 70% of the resident population to be profoundly or severely retarded; 16%, moderately retarded, and 12%, ·mildly retarded. Almost two-thirds of retarded persons who are institutionalized have multiple handicaps (Sheerenberger, 1976). Retarded persons are generally institutionalized because their behavior is unacceptable to the community, because their family is unable to care for them, or because the resources of the community are inadequate (McCarver & Ellis, 1974). After they reach the age of 40, mentally retarded persons are more likely to be placed in public mental hospitals than in public institutions for retarded persons (Conley, 1973).

Heal and associates (1978) reviewed the literature in an effort to identify the effects of institutionalization, although it is difficult to study institutionalization as a specific intervention because so many elements affect the individual and because institutions vary considerably from one another. They concluded that commitment to an institution often results in a decline in IQ scores unless the preinstitutional environment was extremely impoverished, in which case institutionalization may result in an increased IQ score. Although institutions are frequently characterized as very protective environments in which individuals do not learn decision-making and independence, Heal and associates identified some positive effects. Institutionalization appears to enhance the motivation of residents to interact with other adults. In addition, institutionalized retarded persons are more likely than their community based peers to make their own decisions when free to do so, to set higher aspiration levels for themselves, and to withdraw more quickly from boring tasks. Current standards dictate that the care, treatment, and training provided to residents should be comprehensive and individualized, whatever their degree and range of disability, although critics argue that this ideal is far from reality in many institutional settings. It is further argued that residential placement should be of the shortest possible duration and should be used only when less restrictive alternatives have been exhausted (Scheerenberger, 1976).

In recent years, retarded individuals have been transferred from large, often publicly supported institutions to smaller, sometimes private facilities in the community. The development of residential alternatives to large institutions began along with the parents' movement in the 1950s and momentum increased in the 60s. The number of insitutionalized residents rose steadily until its peak in 1967. Although the total number of public residential facilities has continued to increase, institutions have become smaller in size. Conroy (1977) criticized these trends, noting that although many retarded residents have relocated to newer and smaller institutions, the number of institutionalized residents has changed only slightly in recent years. He called this pattern "interinstitutional transfers" charging that it represents neither normalization nor deinstitutionalization. Readmissions appear to have risen dramatically in number during the same years in which the number of releases increased. Thus, it appears that deinstitutionalization began earlier and has advanced further for the mentally ill than for retarded persons.

Consistent with the values of normalization, deinstitutionalization, and mainstreaming, community residence for retarded adults has been sought by parents, advocates, and professionals. The options for community placement include halfway houses or group residences, which ease the transition from institution to community; foster homes; and the client's own family home (Katz, 1970; McCarver & Ellis, 1974). More permanent residences include hostels for small groups of persons who are able to work or participate in programs during the day; boardinghouses, in which the retarded adult does not need to shop and cook; and individual or group apartments, some of which provide professional staff for referrals to vocational, medical, and social services when necessary (Katz, 1970).

In spite of the support voiced for deinstitutionalization, little is known about the factors that facilitate community adjustment. Neither level of intellectual impairment nor age has beeen shown to influence postinstitutional adjustment. Floor and Rosen (1975) suggested that community adjustment depends upon the retarded client's personality. However, most objective data indicate that the level of available support is the most critical factor. Most persons released from institutions to community residences require extended supervision, and their success often depends on the help of parents, other relatives, or spouses (McCarver & Ellis, 1974; Wood & Mueller, 1970). According to a study of the social adjustment of retarded adults living in the community, retarded persons often have few resources on which to rely in times of crisis (Edgerton & Bercovici, 1976). With marginal job security, few skills, and no reliable network of friends, these persons have only tenuous control over their lives. Moreover, support persons also need community resources to support them in times of crisis or to provide respite from caregiving. Wood and Mueller suggested that contracts be drawn up between families and state and local communities for sharing responsibility for lifetime care of retarded persons.

Community attitudes are another critical factor in the successful community adjustment of retarded persons. Communities frequently hold dual standards of behavior, tolerating less deviation in the behavior of retarded persons than they do in the case of nonretarded persons. The public also continues to harbor fears of retarded persons and misconceptions about retardation (e.g., retardation and mental illness always coexist). Claiming that property values will decline or neighborhood children will be endangered, community groups often oppose the creation of group homes for disabled or mentally retarded persons. Local zoning ordinances are frequently used to block establishment of these homes, and in only 20 states is such use of zoning ordinances illegal. Conroy (1977) concluded that "public pressure to get people out of institutions has far outstripped its essential corollary: pressure to create normalizing community service systems'' (p. 46). Thus, a challenge that remains is to create an atmosphere that enables retarded persons to develop their full potential and to contribute to society (Lippman, 1977).

Interventions and Anticipated Outcomes in the Social Work Treatment of Mental Retardation

In many respects, social work with mentally retarded clients is similar to work with nonretarded persons. As with nonretarded clients, goals generally include development of intellectual, physical, social, and vocational skills; adjustment to tasks of day-to-day working and living; and assistance with crises or problems. Often, retarded clients can utilize the same agencies and services that nonretarded persons use. In other cases, retarded clients require additional or slightly modified services. The following discussion examines key issues in work with retarded clients.

During the past decade, vocational training, procedures for social skill acquisition, and programs for community adjustment have demonstrated the nature and range of effects now possible in the field of retardation. Advances in motor skills, self-help skills, social relationships, and vocational performance are now reasonable expectations for even severely retarded clients. Therefore, social work with retarded clients should be outcome oriented; that is, desired changes in the client's functioning should always be identified and their attainment should be expected.

A number of factors help identify outcomes appropriate for each client. First, outcomes should be linked to a thorough assessment of the client's current functioning and not to such diagnostic factors as etiology or level of retardation. Wolfensberger (1972) distinguished the field of retardation from other fields of practice as one that has nearly overcome a ''fixation'' upon etiology to focus, instead, on reasonable and attainable goals that address client problems. The problem areas reviewed in the preceding section are those in which retarded persons frequently have difficulty; yet no client should be assumed to experience problems in all such areas of functioning. Outcomes should be related to the specific problems of the individual client. It is important to note that retarded adults appear to experience frequent and marked fluctuations in functioning over time and to experience pervasive instability as a consequence of such specific changes as illness, loss of job, or death of relative or advocate (Edgerton & Bercovici, 1976). Therefore, social workers should base their interventions on an assessment sufficiently thorough to identify a range of possible problems and to anticipate the consequences of outcome attainment for the client's more general functioning. For example, moving a client from a sheltered workshop to a job in private industry, while significantly strengthening her financial resources, might be deleterious insofar as it removed her from contact with peers, who provide her only social support.

Various outcomes may differ in their relation to the retardation itself. Many outcomes are related not to impaired intellectual or behavioral functioning itself but rather to the "second-order consequences" of the retardation (Churchill & Glasser, 1965). Examples would include outcomes related to communication skills, adjustment in work, and problems in personal relationships. Attainment of such outcomes would be expected to improve the client's functioning but not to affect the actual level of retardation. In contrast, other outcomes are related to the impaired functioning, in which case intervention is directed toward the aspect of intellectual functioning or adaptive behavior that gave rise to the diagnosis of mental retardation. These outcomes are generally cognitive or behavioral and their attainment might even alter the diagnosis of retardation. Pursuit of this later type of outcome is consistent with current views of retardation as being a state of potentially modifiable behavior. The distinction between different types of outcomes on the basis of their relationship to actual impairment may help practitioners set more realistic goals and to anticipate the consequences of their attainment. In some cases, such as clients with extensive CNS damage, the intervention might produce outcomes related to second-order consequences but not to impaired functioning itself. In other cases, direct treatment aimed at improving intellectual capacity is appropriate and realistic. Workers always should be clear about the aims of their treatment and about the extent to which attainment of outcomes can be reasonably expected.

Professionals working with retarded adults need to recognize the client's capacity to participate in the identification of desired outcomes and to realize that outcomes that professionals assume to be important may not be ones desired by clients. This distinction is evident in the data provided by Edgerton and Bercovici (1976), which indicated that while professionals valued competence and independence, clients attached greater importance to confidence and satisfaction—a subjective sense of well-being—instead. Professionals should be careful to avoid the tendency to assume *for* retarded persons the nature of their needs and wants, a pattern that most adult clients have experienced for many years. Client participation in outcome identification can become a source of growth and maturity and even poor decisions may be preferable to wise decisions imposed by others.

Finally, outcomes should maximize the competence of the retarded client to the fullest possible extent. That is, outcomes should be such that they address and minimize idiosyncracies that might lead others to perceive retarded persons as different. For example, when teaching grooming habits to retarded men and women, workers should encourage them to obtain stylish and flattering haircuts rather than settling for styles that might accentuate physical attributes characteristic of their Down's syndrome. Wolfensberger (1972) pointed out that too often professionals assist retarded clients toward skills that facilitate their physical adaptation but neglect socially normative skills and behaviors.

Worker Attitudes

Professionals should be cautious that the stereotypes and attitudes about retarded persons common in society do not affect their practice. Some of the more detrimental stereotypes include assumptions that all retarded persons are alike except for the degree of their deficiency, that mental retardation is a specific condition of deficient intellect, that mental retardation is irreversible or permanent, and that mentally retarded adults are similar to adolescents or children. Unfortunately, it is not uncommon for professionals to refer to retarded adults in childlike or condescending ways or to employ instructional materials that were originally designed for children. Borenzweig (1970) noted that often treatment groups are composed of individuals whose abilities vary so widely that they have nothing in common beyond their being defined as retarded; in such cases, workers have not taken the time to observe the individuality of their retarded clients. Perhaps responding to their experience or training, professionals often tend to overlook adaptive and normal behaviors to focus on abnormality (Segal, 1970; Willis, 1978; Wolfensberger, 1972). As a result, workers may set unrealistically low goals for clients.

Retarded Adults as Clients

Like everyone else, retarded persons experience distress, are aware of how they feel and interact with others, are willing to attempt new behaviors, and desire the respect of others and themselves. Yet the ways in which mentally retarded adults differ from nonretarded clients in their learning may have implications for intervention. Retarded adults often have limited experience and, as a result, workers may view their productions of personal histories as meager (Nitzberg, 1970). Their previous experiences may lead retarded clients to expect failure in treatment, and lack of experience with and expectations for adult roles may make their collaboration or participation as "co-equals on a treatment team" (Nitzberg, 1970) difficult. Retarded adults often have a poor comprehension of abstractions and a verbal style characterized by repetitions and irrelevant, illogical statements (Nitzberg, 1970). Those who display bizarre mannerisms, seizures, or palsy behavior may make workers uncomfortable. The skills of retarded clients may develop more slowly and less competently than those of the nonretarded, and as adults they are more likely to need supportive—and sometimes lifelong—aid (Conley, 1973). Nitzberg suggested that the retarded client can be difficult for the worker in that retarded clients can "frustrate in us the culturally induced need to be rewarded for our pains and to succeed as quickly as possible" (p. 475). Workers need to counter these problems by focusing on each client's unique strengths and goals.

Special Considerations

The extent to which interventive approaches need to be different for retarded clients depends upon both the client's level of intellectual disability and the outcomes sought. However, workers should always be cognizant of the possibility that their interventive style needs to be modified. This section includes specific suggestions for the overall approach to social work practice with adult retarded clients.

Workers may need to meet with clients in shorter and more frequent sessions. Selan (1976) suggested that workers should not extend sessions beyond the attention span of the client, whether it be 15 minutes, 30 minutes, or an hour. Because repetition may facilitate memory and learning, sessions might be as frequent as three times per week (Department of Health, Education, and Welfare, 1978).

Explanations should be thorough, with repetitions and examples. Although language should not be childish, workers should communicate clearly, employing specific and readily understandable words, facial expressions, and gestures (Corvin, 1968). Sitting with the client on the same side of the desk may be helpful because more direct contact tends to enhance the clarity of what is communicated (Nitzberg, 1970).

The literature also suggests that workers be directive and active, structuring the treatment situation and, at times, teaching the client how to be a client. Explanation of treatment concepts, in particular, may require almost a constant search for simple, clear language. Workers need to be explicit about the roles, purposes, and outcomes of treatment; retarded clients cannot be assumed capable of perceiving subtle cues of workers' expectations (Selan, 1976). Because the display of genuine interest in and affection for the client may be particularly important (Nitzberg, 1970), workers need an adequate range and ease of expression in nonverbal communication. Selan cautioned that retarded persons often interpret silence as hostility or uninterest.

Because the memory of retarded persons may be impaired and because retarded persons tend to view sessions as discrete experiences rather than interconnected events (Nitzberg, 1970), it may be important for each session to consist of complete and coherent learning experiences. Sessions should end with a summary of what has been achieved.

Finally, because the acquisition of new information and skills come more slowly to retarded clients, workers may need to expect longer term treatment relationships. Campbell and Browning (1975) found that the behavior of retarded persons was modified by intervention, although changes that might be expected in a second session with nonretarded clients did not occur until after the ninth session with retarded clients.

Group Work

Groups, community meetings, and task oriented meetings may be helpful forms of intervention with some retarded adults. The literature suggests that group participation seems to enhance the verbal capacity and social adjustment skills of mildly and moderately retarded persons (Borenzweig, 1970; Lee, 1977). Task oriented groups can be helpful for the pursuit of specific goals, such as teaching money management and current events, providing all group members can benefit from the same learning activities. Community meetings, in which all members of a residential or work group meet to share problems and successes, may help overcome feelings of isolation while increasing cohesion.

Certain characteristics of retarded persons may affect group dynamics and, in turn, the success of the group. Some of the elements generally regarded as necessary to group process may be lacking with retarded adults. For example, communication and interaction may be so limited that interdependence among group members does not develop fully. Instead of looking to each other, retarded group members often look to the leader. Group sanctions may not emerge, minimizing the impact of the group upon the attitudes, values, and behaviors of individual members. Varied intellectual and verbal capabilities among members may make group work difficult unless the worker composes the group carefully. Borenzweig (1970) suggested that in groups of retarded adults, the major objective may be membership itself, rather than group interaction, and the worker may remain the central person in the group. Limiting group size to small numbers is generally advised.

Specific Interventions

Much of the traditional literature on social work with retarded adults fails specifically to identify and describe appropriate and effective interventions. Most often, interventions are globally described, such as the "worker–client relationship," "support," and "acceptance." Increasingly, however, it is possible to recommend specific interventions and discuss their application vis-à-vis the attainment of specific outcomes. Greater specificity in descriptions of interventions is typical in behavioral literature.

One important approach to intervention with retarded individuals is "didactic teaching." In a didactic approach, the worker assumes the role of a teacher, instructing and assisting the client to acquire new skills and behaviors. Didactic teaching generally requires the worker to take a directive and active role and assumes that the worker is familiar with principles of learning. Even tasks that might appear simple to the worker should be broken down into specific and small steps to help insure the success of the client's learning. Workers should then focus on only one skill or behavior at a time; component substeps of the learning task should be ordered so that each accomplishment contributes to the next and, finally, to completion of the larger task. This approach is particularly well suited to attainment of self-help outcomes such as bedmaking, shaving, budgeting, and travel by public transportation (Corvin, 1968; Katz, 1970).

Practitioners working with parents can make these didactic skills available to them so that they can deal more effectively with everyday problems. Although social work with parents of the retarded has often focused on such issues as acceptance of the retarded child's limits (Proctor, 1976) or long-range planning, Nitzberg (1970) asserted that "parents have every right to know *what to do*" with their retarded child (p. 489). Equipping parents with skills for didactic teaching can increase their motivation to work with the retarded person in that both the direction and the means for attainment of success are clearly evident. Parents should be taught to identify and order task substeps, to be consistent, to exercise patience, to emphasize practice, and to make frequent use of rewards and praise (Katz, 1970).

Workers may also arrange for, or engage in "modeling" for the client. Modeling is an interventive approach in which someone demonstrates the performance of the desired new skill or behavior to the client. The effectiveness of modeling may be enhanced if another client, or someone similar to the client, serves as model. Modeling is especially appropriate when the desired new response is not already in the behavioral repertoire of the client. Grinnell and Lieberman (1977) demonstrated the effectiveness of modeling for increasing the social skills of retarded adults.

Review, repetition, and rehearsal are other components of intervention important in work with retarded clients. Whether the worker delivers verbal instruction or uses modeling, the review and practice of skills within a session can help clients remember the new skill and enable the worker to check on the extent of learning. Rehearsal may also facilitate the transfer of learning from the treatment setting to the client's everyday environment.

Assumptions about Relationships among Outcomes

In practice with nonretarded persons, it is frequently assumed that changes in various domains of behavior are interrelated and that attainment of certain outcomes will produce, or encourage the attainment of, other outcomes. For example, changes in a client's self-perceptions may be presumed to produce changes in his interpersonal relationships; changes in feelings may be presumed to produce changes in overt actions; and changes in verbal behavior may be presumed to produce changes in motor behaviors. Outcomes whose attainment subsequently lead to attainment of other outcomes were called "instrumental outcomes" by Rosen and Proctor (1981).

Whether the relationship between instrumental and subsequent outcomes that is sometimes assumed to work with nonretarded clients also holds for retarded clients is not known. It frequently appears that changes achieved in the behavior of retarded clients do not generalize across time, to new settings or contexts, or from one area of behavior to another. For example, Gardner and Stamm (1971) observed that producing change in a retarded client's verbal behavior frequently does not lead to change in overt behavior, suggesting that the relationship between instrumental and subsequent outcomes is likely to be tenuous among retarded clients.

Assumptions regarding the relationship among outcomes have a variety of implications for practice, including the type and number of outcomes toward which intervention is directed and the range of interventions that must be employed. Consider the implications suggested by the following case illustration.

Ronald was a moderately retarded 31-year-old man, referred to the social worker by the supervisor at a vocational rehabilitation center. The supervisor complained that Ronald was not fully participating in training sessions that would prepare him for a new job. Ronald was tardy to sessions, did not listen to the supervisor's instructions, and frequently interrupted instructions by joking with other trainees. Ronald complained to the social worker that the supervisor was a "jerk" and that the training sessions were "boring."

Social worker A decided to spend sessions talking to Ronald about the necessity of his participation in the training sessions if he was to get a new job and about the supervisor's desire to be helpful and teach Ronald the skills he needed. Implicitly or explicitly, the treatment outcomes sought were Ronald's verbal acknowledgment that the training was important, Ronald's admission that the supervisor was trying to help him, and Ronald's verbal expression of his willingness to cooperate with the supervisor and participate in training sessions. These outcomes, rather typical of those in talk therapies, reflected the worker's assumption that their attainment would lead to on-the-job behaviors consistent with them—that is, cooperative actions and participation in training. Thus, changes in verbal behaviors were viewed by the worker as instrumental outcomes and the intervention was directed toward their attainment.

Social worker B took a somewhat different approach, although this worker also wanted Ronald to discuss the supervisor and the training in a more positive way. However, this worker did not view a change in Ronald's verbal behavior as *sufficient* for producing change in his job related behavior. This worker assumed that for retarded persons change occurs more slowly and less efficiently and in small increments. Changes in Ronald's actual participation in training were assumed to require specific interventions; therefore, in addition to the talk therapy directed toward change in verbal behavior, modeling and reinforcement were used to attain the desired outcomes in on-the-job behaviors.

Because these workers held different assumptions about the relationship among outcomes in work with retarded clients, their interventive approaches differed. Thus, the number of targeted outcomes and number of interventions employed were different. It should be noted that neither approach is known to be right or wrong. Therefore, workers must observe retarded clients, in general, and each retarded client served, in particular, for indications of outcome attainment. If clients appear to achieve certain outcomes but fail to maintain other—albeit related—outcomes, then additional interventions to be directed toward each desired outcome are needed. Workers who fail to notice the weakness of certain relationships between instrumental outcomes and other outcomes in their retarded clients and who, therefore, fail to provide sufficient intervention for the range of anticipated changes will experience frustration and discouragement in their work. Thus, workers' understanding both of the individual client's behavior and of patterns of behavior change that may be unique among retarded clients is critically important to the effectiveness of their practice.

State of Current Practice Knowledge

Current practice knowledge is inconclusive regarding some additional issues. Borenzweig (1970) characterized as primitive the state of professional knowledge about the behaviors that retarded persons routinely exhibit and those of which they are capable. Thus, workers are frequently unsure of the performance potential they can realistically attribute to their clients and, therefore, cannot select optimum ways for helping clients realize their potential. Professionals may err in two ways: on one hand, expectations may be set so low that retarded clients remain less active, competent, and self-sufficient than they could become (Proctor, 1976); on the other, when inefficiencies in learning among retarded clients are ignored, expectations may be set unrealistically high, thereby overtaxing the client's capacity (Wood & Mueller, 1970) and frustrating the worker. Professionals need to identify areas in which the functioning of retarded clients can be enhanced and these should become foci for intervention. Knowledge of a client's potential is also important in establishing appropriate and realistic outcomes, according to which the effectiveness of intervention can be evaluated.

Knowledge of the effectiveness of specific interventions is also incomplete. Terms such as "education," "counseling," and "psychotherapy" frequently have subsumed a variety of specific methods, including occupational, music, speech, and relationship therapies (Lee, 1977; Sternlicht, 1966). According to Gardner and Stamm (1971), counseling and psychotherapy with mentally retarded clients "remains a vague, ill defined, and suspect form of behavior intervention [because very often] neither salient psychotherapeutic process or outcome variables have been delineated or independently manipulated in order to determine their relative usefulness" (pp. 50–51). Practitioners can make a valuable contribution to social work knowledge if, when reporting cases from their practice, they specify both the interventive process and the outcomes attained.

Areas for Future Social Work Action and Research in the Field of Mental Retardation

A number of directions for future research and professional actions are apparent. Training for social work with retarded persons should assume greater importance. Many professionals are uninformed about retardation and its consequences (Borenzweig, 1970); yet, mentally retarded clients have the right to and will seek social services of the same type and quality as those that nonretarded clients use. As noted earlier, workers employed in schools, family planning, marital and family counseling, public welfare, and health care can expect increasingly to work with mentally retarded clients.

The planning and development of services for retarded persons also requires additional emphasis. Of particular importance are more adequate income maintenance, recruitment of retarded persons into vocational training, and provision of comprehensive support services for retarded clients living in the community. Wood and Mueller (1970) suggested that social workers should advocate for less stringent definitions of social dependence and the guarantee of access to social and rehabilitation services. These efforts should be directed at lessening the stigma of retardation and providing appropriate social work services to retarded clients (Wood & Mueller, 1970).

The efforts of social workers also are needed in the areas of public education and advocacy on behalf of retarded adults. Understanding of retardation can help communities overcome traditional fears and thereby facilitate the integration of retarded persons into community life. Social workers can advocate for protection of the civil rights of retarded adults, such as the right to drive a car if they can do so safely, the right to sue, the right to make decisions involving sterilization, the right to marriage, and the right to make a will (Katz, 1970).

Finally, all social workers should actively work for the prevention of retardation. Support of research on the causes of birth defects and support of social policies in the areas of income maintenance, nutrition, and prenatal and infant health care can contribute to the prevention of medical retardation.

Collaboration with other professions is important in service delivery to retarded adults. Just as the nature of retardation itself is complex, so must be efforts at meeting the needs of retarded persons. As Dybwad (1970) stated, ''The problem of mental retardation is far too pervasive to be conveniently pigeon-holed in any one of the professional compartments'' (p. 311). Medical, job training, educational, psychological, and social services all contribute to the prevention and remediation of retardation. Social workers should be alert to issues that require an interdisciplinary approach, whether their task is service to an individual client, advocacy on behalf of a group of retarded citizens, or development of social policies. Yet the unique contribution of social work may derive from its comprehensive approach to the problems of retarded clients, which is informed by and encompasses the individual client, the client's family and larger social support network, community resources, and national social policies.

References

American Association on Mental Deficiency: Rights of mentally retarded persons: an official statement of the American Association on Mental Deficiency. *Ment Retard* 1973; 11:56–58.

BECK HL: *Social Services to the Mentally Retarded*. Springfield, Thomas, 1969.

BEGAB MJ, RICHARDSON SA (eds): *The Mentally Retarded and Society: A Social Science Perspective*. Baltimore, University Park Press, 1974.

BORENZWEIG H: Social group work in the field of mental retardation: a review of the literature. *Soc Serv Rev* 1970; 44:177–183.

Brown DL: Obstacles to survival for the mentally retarded. *Soc Work* 1972; 17:98–101.

Button WH: Sheltered workshops in the United States: an institutional overview, in *Rehabilitation, Sheltered Workshops, and the Disadvantaged.* Ithaca, Cornell University Press, 1970, pp 3–48.

Campbell DR, Browning PR: Therapist's approach and avoidance responses and the verbal behavior of mentally retarded clients. *J Counsel Psychol* 1975; 2:320–323.

Chinn, PC, Drew CJ, Logan DR: *Mental Retardation: A Life Cycle Approach.* St. Louis, Mosby, 1979.

Churchill SR, Glasser PH: *Small Groups in the Hospital Community: Lecture and Proceedings.* Lansing, Michigan Department of Mental Health, 1965.

Cleland CC: *Mental Retardation: A Development Approach.* Englewood Cliffs, Prentice-Hall, 1978.

Conley RW: *The Economics of Mental Retardation.* Baltimore, Johns Hopkins Press, 1973.

Conroy JW: Trends in deinstitutionalization of the mentally retarded. *Ment Retard* 1977; 15:44–46.

Corvin G: Tell him . . . *Parent–Staff Exchange* 1968; 1:1–6.

Craft A, Craft M: Subnormality in marriage. *Soc Work Today* 1976; 7:98–101.

David HP, Smith JD, Freedman E: Family planning services for persons handicapped by mental retardation. *Am J Public Health* 1976; 66:1053–1057.

Department of Health, Education, and Welfare: *The Nation's Use of Health Resources, 1969.* Government Printing Office, 1980.

Department of Health, Education, and Welfare: *Mental Retardation: The Leading Edge, Service Programs That Work.* Government Printing Office, 1978.

Dybwad G: Income and social services for the mentally retarded: a specialized task in social welfare, in Schreiber M (ed): *Social Work and Mental Retardation.* New York, Day, 1970, pp 309–315.

Edgerton RB: *The Cloak of Competence: Stigma in the Lives of the Mentally Retarded.* Berkeley, University of California Press, 1967.

Edgerton RB, Bercovici SM: The cloak of competence: years later. *Am J Ment Defic* 1976; 80:485–497.

Floor L, Rosen M: Investigating the phenomenon of helplessness in mentally retarded adults. *Am J Ment Defic* 1975; 79:565–572.

Floor L, Rosen M, Baxter D, et al: Socio-sexual problems in mentally handicapped females. *Training School Bull* 1971; 68:106–112.

Gardner WI, Stamm JM: Counseling the mentally retarded: a behavioral approach. *Rehabil Counsel Bull* 1971; 15:46–57.

Goodman DM: Parenting an adult mentally retarded offspring. *Smith Coll Stud Soc Work* 1978; 48:209–234.

Goodman L: The sexual rights of the retarded: a dilemma for parents. *Fam Coordinator* 1973; 22:472–474.

Grinnell RM Jr, Lieberman A: Teaching the mentally retarded job interviewing skills. *J Counsel Psychol* 1977; 24:332–337.

GROSSMAN HJ (ed): *Manual on Terminology and Classification in Mental Retardation.* Washington, DC, American Association on Mental Deficiency, 1977.

HALPERN AS, BROWING PR, BRUMMER ER: Vocational adjustment of the mentally retarded, in Begab MJ, Richardson SA (eds): *The Mentally Retarded and Society: A Social Science Perspective.* Baltimore, University Park Press, 1975, pp 365–376.

HEAL LW, SIGELMAN CK, SWITZKY HN: Research on community residential alternatives for the mentally retarded. *Int Rev Res Ment Retard* 1978; 9:209–249.

HEBER R: A manual on terminology and classification in mental retardation. *Am J Ment Defic* 1954; 64 (suppl 2).

HOLLAND P: Changing social policies on mental retardation. *Soc Serv Rev* 1972; 46:251–262.

KATZ E: A report of an independent living rehabilitation program, in Meyen EL (ed): *Planning Community Services for the Mentally Retarded.* Scranton, International Textbook, 1967, pp 207–213.

KATZ E: *The Retarded Adult at Home: A Guide for Parents.* Seattle, Special Child Publications, 1970.

KURTZ RA: Advocacy for the mentally retarded: the development of a new social role, in Begab MJ, Richardson SA (eds): *The Mentally Retarded and Society: A Social Science Perspective.* Baltimore, University Park Press, 1975, pp 377–394.

LEE DY: Evaluation of a group counseling program designed to enhance social adjustment of mentally retarded adults. *J Counsel Psychol* 1977; 24:318–323.

LIPPMAN L: Normalization and related concepts: words and ambiguities. *J Child Welfare* 1977; 56:301–310.

MANDELBAUM A: Mental health and retardation, in B Saunders (ed): *Encyclopedia of Social Work,* ed 7. Washington, DC, National Association of Social Work, 1977, vol 2, pp. 868–879.

MCCARVER RB, CRAIG EM: Placement of the retarded in the community: prognosis and outcome. *Int Rev Res Ment Retard* 1974; 7:146–207.

MUELLER JB, PORTER R: Placement of adult retardates from state institutions in community care facilities. *Community Ment Health J* 1969; 5:289–294.

NIRJE B: The normalization principle and its human management implications, in Kugel RB, Wolfensberger W (eds): *Changing Patterns in Residential Services for the Mentally Retarded.* Washington, DC, 1969, pp 159–179.

NITZBERG J: Casework with mentally retarded adolescents and young adults and their families. In Schreiber M (ed): *Social Work and Mental Retardation.* New York, Day, 1970, pp 463–481.

PROCTOR EK: New directions for work with parents of retarded children. *Soc Casework* 1976; 57:259–264.

ROSEN A, PROCTOR EK: Distinctions between treatment outcomes and their implications for treatment evaluation. *J Consult Clin Psychol* 1981; 49:418–425.

SCANLON PL: Social work with the mentally retarded client. *Soc Casework* 1978; 59(3):161–166.

SCHEERENBERGER RC: Public residential services for the mentally retarded, in Ellis NE (ed): *International Review of Research in Mental Retardation, Volume 9.* New York, Academic Press, 1978, pp 187–208.

Segal A: Workers' perceptions of mentally disabled clients: effect on service delivery. *Soc Work* 1970; 15(3):39–46.

Selan BH: Psychotherapy with the developmentally disabled. *Health and Soc Work* 1976; 1(1):73–85.

Stanfield JS: Graduation: what happens to the retarded child when he grows up? *Except Child* 1973; 39:548–552.

Sternlicht M: Psychotherapeutic procedures with the retarded. *Int Rev Res Ment Retard* 1966; 2.

Tobias J: Social and ethnic factors related to utilization of rehabilitation services by the mentally retarded. *Rehabil Lit* 1969; 30:226–236.

Walker PW: Premarital counseling for the developmentally disabled. *Soc Casework* 1977; 58:475–479.

Wills TA: Perceptions of clients by professional helpers. *Psychol Bull* 1978; 85:968–1000.

Wolfensberger W: *The Principle of Normalization in Human Services.* Toronto, National Institute on Mental Retardation, 1972.

Wood V, Mueller J: Self-maintenance and community behavior of adult retardates, in Schrieber M (ed): *Social Work and Mental Retardation.* New York, Day, 1970.

19

Senescence

CHARLOTTE KIRSCHNER

The over-65 age group is the fastest growing segment of the U.S. population. In 1978, there were more than 24 million elderly, about 11% of the population; their numbers increased by 18% between 1970 and 1978, while the total population of the United States grew by on 5%. The Census Bureau (1979) projected that 17% of Americans, or approximately 52 million, will be over 65 by the year 2030, with the proportion over 75 increasing at an even faster rate than the 65–75 segment. Chronic disabling conditions become more common with age. The over-75 age group is especially vulnerable to mental disorders. Thus, it will be a continual challenge in the years ahead for mental health professionals to meet the needs of these older adults.

The social work profession is in a position to play an important role in the treatment of aging clients. "Ageism," the prejudices and stereotypes that are applied to older people, discourages interest in them on the part of professionals and pessimism about their treatability (Butler & Lewis, 1977). But the value system that underlies social work leads social workers to be concerned about those in whom this society lacks interest. Believing in the "intrinsic value, the meaning and dignity of being human . . . working with the aged is one of those fields in social work that, by setting forth the issue so clearly, gives the worker a chance to test, temper, and affirm this core value of our profession" (Soyer, 1976, p. 152). Furthermore, since the process of aging involves biological, psychological, social, cultural, and environmental factors, a multifaceted knowledge base and array of skills are necessary to address the mental health needs of the aged. The variety of social work methods and interventions that are entering the repertoire of social work practitioners (Meyer, 1975) makes them uniquely suited to help this client group.

Description of Senescence

"Senescence" is the gradual deterioration of the adult organism—the process of change that occurs after maturity. "Aging" is the process of change that occurs from birth until death. In common usage, however, the terms "senescence" and "aging" and "old" and "elderly" are interchangeable, and this practice is followed here. The onset of senescence will be put at age 65, although this is an arbitrary figure chosen by legislators as the age for receiving social security retirement benefits, first in Germany in 1848, then in England in 1911, and then in the United States in 1935. Whatever the legal retirement age, chronological and biological age are not necessarily the same. Aging, per se, is not a disease and the aged are not a homogeneous group. There are more differences among older persons than there are similarities, and this point must always be kept in mind.

History of Gerontological Social Work

Gerontological social work is a relatively new specialty. Lowy (1979) gave a comprehensive review of the history of social work with the aging in his most recent textbook. A few social work pioneers, most notably Randall (1945), were calling attention to the aged in the 1940s and 1950s. The Gerontological Society of America was founded in 1945. The New York School of Social Work held a conference on social treatment of the older person in 1947. In 1952 Shore wrote about group work with the institutionalized aged, and in 1953 Wickenden pinpointed the needs of older people and showed that these needs were not being met. In 1954 Francis and colleagues described how a family agency served the elderly, and in 1957 Posner pointed to the lag in services to the aged. In 1958 the Council on Social Work Education held a seminar on aging, and in 1961 the National Council on Aging held a seminar on casework with aging clients. Also in 1961 the National Association of Social Workers collaborated with the American Public Welfare Association to arrange a seminar on social group work with older people (National Association of Social Workers,

1963). Treatment issues with older clients were addressed by Milloy (1964), Leach (1964), Blenkner (1965), and Wasser (1966) in the 1960s. Brody (1966, 1967, 1970, 1977, 1979) has made important contributions to practice with the aged, as have Blank (1978), Kosberg (1979), Lowy (1955, 1962a, b, 1963, 1967, 1979), Meyer (1975), Monk (1979, 1981), Pincus (1970), and Silverstone (1976).

Until research, done largely in the 1950s, led to better understanding of the characteristics and needs of the elderly, this group was largely ignored by society; the most severely mentally impaired were relegated to the back wards of state hospitals. The recent trend toward deinstitutionalization has affected old people profoundly: the number of aged in state mental hospitals dropped by 40% between 1969 and 1973 (Butler, 1975). Nursing homes and residential facilities have replaced mental hospitals for the aged who cannot manage in the community. More recently, the increasing costs of nursing home care have stimulated efforts to improve community resources to enable old people to remain in their own homes for as long as possible.

Today, social workers meet their aged clients in a variety of settings, ranging from senior centers and nutrition programs, where the well aged come to socialize and pursue hobbies, to specialized agencies on aging, social security offices, general hospitals, psychiatric hospitals, day hospitals, community mental health centers, family agencies, home care programs, residential facilities, nursing homes, hospices, and private offices. Social work treatment with the elderly may consist entirely of therapeutic services, which the client does not view as psychotherapy and which can be considered preventive inasmuch as such services maintain mental health. At the other end of the continuum, the social worker may be called upon to treat older clients who suffer from severe psychopathology.

Distinctive Features of Gerontological Social Work

Social work treatment of the psychopathology found in senescent clients has some unique features.

Understanding Normal Aging

Symptoms of disease occur in old age, but old age is not a disease. The process of aging in itself probably plays a small role, in the production of psychopathology. Therefore, the social worker must know what constitutes typical and expectable behavior in old age in order to differentiate between normal aging and mental illness.

Need for Worker Self-Awareness in Practice with Older Clients

Self-awareness on the part of the professional, always important in social work, is critical in working with this age group. Social workers in other fields of practice can avoid identification with their clients; "only in gerontological practice are social workers confronted with a person's final destiny and with the true meaning of a person's life" (Monk, 1981, p. 62). Practitioners in this area of practice constantly confront their own final destiny, and any unresolved fears about aging, illness, loneliness, or death will interfere with their ability to help clients.

Relationship Issues with Older Clients

A trusting relationship between social worker and client is a tool that is used to bring about change in any age group. In work with the elderly, the therapeutic relationship can become an end in itself, a substitution for lost family members or friends. Social workers are invariably younger than their clients and they must learn to be comfortable with this situation and even learn to use the age differential therapeutically. Taking on a filial role can overcome the resistance of some clients to professional intervention (Rosengarten, 1980) and, when appropriate, the worker should allow himself to be treated as a beloved son, nephew, or grandchild. This conscious use of the relationship is different from "transference," which is frequently present but is unconscious and represents a displacement onto the therapist of feelings the client has toward figures from the past. Thus, it is possible for a young worker unconsciously to be identified with a parent of the client, although the age difference makes it more likely that she will represent a child (Meerloo, 1978).

"Sociologic transference" has been described in which the young therapist becomes the personification of a rejecting, youth oriented society (Linden, 1978). In this situation, the aged client may react by rejecting the young worker, whose best recourse is to identify what is happening between them and thus counteract negative feelings.

"Negative countertransference," the displacement onto the client of the worker's unresolved experiences with parents, can interfere with the helping process. Being unconscious, these feelings are, by definition, inaccessible, but they can sometimes be uncovered through supervision or consultation.

Elderly clients who do not see themselves as candidates for psychotherapy will often put workers in a social role, thinking of them as friends. Meyer (1981) said that "friendship is hardly sufficient to serve as a professional purpose, although in many ways, without so naming it, social workers serve that vital purpose for their clients'' (p. 72). This is especially true in dealing with lonely old people. It does no harm to accept a cup of tea and socialize a bit as long as every contact is professionally meaningful and workers do not confuse their purpose with the social role they appear to be filling. The social role can include touching, which is an important nonverbal communication with a client group that suffers from impairments of vision and hearing.

Familiarity With Drugs Used by the Elderly

The elderly as a group differ from young or middle-aged people in their responses to drugs. Their rate of drug metabolism is slower and they frequently take many drugs concurrently (Reidenberg, 1980). Lower dosages of drugs should be used to compensate for their more intensive effect and longer duration of action in the elderly. Special attention must be paid to undesirable side effects and to adverse interaction of one drug with another (Zung, 1980). Drug toxicity can present symptoms that may be mistaken for more serious conditions, as will be described subsequently. For these reasons, social workers should become familiar with the general properties of the most common medications that their clients are taking and work closely with their clients' physicians in monitoring drugs.

Team Work with Older Clients

The processes and problems of aging are multidisciplinary. Biological, psychological, social, economic, and political factors are involved. Therefore, a social worker who is a specialist in gerontology must be a generalist in practice:

> A person with a broad view who can look at an entire social situation, analyze the interaction between people in all the resource systems connected to that situation, intervene in those interactions, determine which specialists are needed from a variety of disciplines, and coordinate and mobilize the knowledge and skill of many disciplines. (Minahan & Pincus, 1977, p. 352)

Social workers who help the aged must collaborate with the many other professionals in the fields of health and human services who are involved with their clients. In some settings, this collaboration is achieved through membership on interdisciplinary teams. Where the setting does not automatically provide for such teams (in private practice, for example) social workers must reach out to the other professionals and create their own network for collaborative care. Social workers may sometimes have problems communicating and consulting with physicians, who are perceived to have more status, power, and prestige (Mailick & Ashley, 1981). But work with a client group exhibiting chronic health problems demands such collaboration, and social workers must learn the art of persuading even their resistant medical colleagues to exchange information about their patients. The complexity of the problems of aged individuals means that all professionals have much to learn from each other in the delivery of services to this client group.

Advocacy for the Aged

Social workers in the field of aging face a great challenge in keeping well informed about political issues that affect their clients, services that are available to them, and ways to improve these services by making them more accessible and tailoring them to clients' needs. It is appropriate for social workers to turn their attention to all aspects of the aged person's environment, taking on advocacy positions with respect to the rights of the elderly and even becoming lobbyists for legislation to improve conditions for this group.

Normal Aging

An understanding of the normal and inevitable processes of aging is important to enable the social worker to make the distinction between aging and the problems of the aged. As people age, they often show great individuality, but certain characteristics are virtually universal.

All organ systems suffer a loss of cells with advancing age (Palmore, 1974). Changes in tissue and muscle mass are normal. Loss of height, redistribution of fat, decline in muscle strength, bone and joint changes, wrinkling of skin, graying and loss of hair, loss of auditory and visual acuity, and a general slowing down are all familiar accompaniments to aging (Rossman, 1980).

With diminished prospects for the future, the old tend to reminisce about the past. While there may be a loss in speed of response with age, it has been found that if older persons are given enough time on tests, they demonstrate no decline in intellectual abilities. "Some abilities may, in fact, increase, such as judgment, accuracy, and general knowledge" (Butler & Lewis, 1977, p. 23).

In a society that is youth oriented, work oriented, and future oriented, the aged are devalued, and many suffer from a damaged self-image and a loss of self-esteem. If people live long enough, they inevitably outlive friends, relatives, and even adult children. There is a loss of opportunity for sexuality, especially for women, who usually outlive their husbands and cannot find substitute partners. The incidence of chronic illness and disability rises with advancing age, yet most of the aged are healthy enough to carry on their major activities most of the time (Palmore, 1974). Many people age successfully: they find use for what they have attained in a lifetime of learning and adapting; they conserve strength and resources as necessary; and they adjust creatively to those changes and losses that occur as part of the aging experience (Butler, 1975).

Aunt Tess, age 82, has been widowed for 15 years. A retired school teacher, she has always been an amateur artist. Her oil paintings decorate the walls of her apartment. She now regularly goes to the senior center, where, except for taking time to join the others for lunch, she spends the better part of every day painting. Her only son lives nearby and visits frequently. She worked hard all her life, her marriage had its ups and downs, and she worried a lot about her son, who had difficulty choosing a career. Now her son has settled down and she has stopped worrying about him. She lives modestly on social security benefits, a teacher's pension, and some savings. She has outlived all her siblings, but her nieces and nephews keep in close touch. They have noticed that she is getting frail—her hair is white and she moves more slowly than she used to. She has become more talkative and somewhat repetitive. Yet, she is always fun to be with. She never complains. She is a great family historian. Recently, one of her paintings was chosen for a citywide exhibit of the work of senior citizens. In an interview she said she had mixed feelings about the honor: "I am pleased that my work was chosen, but I would like it to stand on its own merit. I want people to say that it's a good painting, not that it's a good painting for an old lady!"

Aunt Tess, white, middle-class, well educated, and healthy, is aging successfully. Members of minorities and those with fewer social and economic advantages may also age successfully as long as they are not suffering from disease or poverty, although cultural differences will lead to different patterns of aging (Dancy, 1977; Lum et al., 1980; Red Horse, 1980; Salcido, 1979).

Developmental Theory of Aging

The developmental view sees aging as the final stage of the normal life cycle. Erikson (1959) stated that each phase of the life cycle is characterized by a phase-specific developmental task that must be solved; critical psychological conflicts must be resolved at each stage of growth. In the final stage, the healthy personality must achieve "integrity"—acceptance of one's life as one has led it. Monk (1981) called this "morale"—an acceptance of life and aging with fortitude and optimism rather than with resignation and defeat, a feeling of having done something good in life, and a generalized sense of adequacy, peace, and well being" (p. 65). Butler and Lewis (1977) observed that it is imperative that older people continue to be flexible if health is to be promoted and maintained. They noted the potential of the elderly for strength, ''as well as for a richer emotional, spiritual, and even intellectual and social life than may be possible for the young'' (p. 20).

Differential Diagnosis with Aging Clients

Individuals who are not successful in adjusting to the biological, social, and environmental changes that come with aging; who are experiencing stress brought on by age related problems such as widowhood, retirement, chronic illness, and inability to live independently; or who are unable to substitute new relationships and activities for those that have been lost will usually develop symptoms of anxiety and depression that bring them to the attention of mental health professionals. A differential diagnosis must be made between a reaction to a situational crisis and more severe psychopathology. It is also important to distinguish between age related disorders and lifelong dysfunctional patterns of behavior. These problems frequently overlap, adding to the complexity of evaluating the mental health of aged clients. Social workers should become familiar with DSM III (American Psychiatric Association, 1980) in order to speak the language of their medical colleagues (Williams, 1981). The new nomenclature uses a multiaxial system for evaluation that includes five areas of assessment. This approach should lead to a more comprehensive understanding of disorders and to improved treatment of clients.

A complete assessment should be conducted in the client's home whenever this is feasible. The home setting allows for an evaluation of physical and mental health, as well as social, familial, financial, and environmental factors. A history of previous lifestyle and coping patterns and an evaluation of present functioning will help the social worker pinpoint the level of the client's health or psychopathology and choose the intervention that is likely to be most effective in dealing with the problem. Basic needs must be met and clients must be helped to negotiate the maze of community resources and government entitlements in order to gain access to adequate food, clothing, housing, medical care, homemaker services, transportation, and the like. Once their basic needs have been met, aged persons can make use of various psychotherapeutic interventions, depending on the diagnosis of their difficulties.

Situational Crises in Aging

A client who is reacting to a series of age related stresses with mild symptoms of anxiety and depression but who is functioning at a generally high level of emotional maturity will relate well to others, will have adapted well to stressors in the past, will have considerable insight and a fairly strong social support system, and will show many features compatible with a diagnosis of adjustment disorder or transient situational disturbance (Gaitz & Varner, 1980). In social work terminology, the transitional crisis faced by an aged person can be conceptualized as a "problem in living," a temporary dysfunctional transaction between the person and the social and physical environment that requires professional intervention (Gitterman & Germain, 1976).

Mrs. R, an 82-year-old widow, referred herself for counseling because she suffered from insomnia, listlessness, tearfulness, and loss of interest in social activities. She was increasingly isolated, feared leaving her apartment, and worried that she would become a burden to her children, from whom she was hiding her concerns. Her symptoms followed several falls both in the house and on the street; however, her physician found no neurological signs that could account for the accidents. Mrs. R had a history of good mental health, a large circle of friends, many of whom were still living, and warm relationships with two married daughters and their families. However, she had recently lost a sister. She suffered from postural changes due to osteoporosis; had constant arthritic pain in her legs and feet, which made walking difficult; and had increasing difficulty with vision. Two years before, her ophthalmologist had recommended cataract surgery, which she had resisted. She feared hospitalization, having had a stormy convalescence from abdominal surgery many years earlier, and she dreaded the prospect of wearing "those horrible eyeglasses." She thought it possible that her poor vision and difficulty in walking had caused her to fall and her greatest fear was that she would end up in a wheelchair, totally dependent on others.

Treatment of Mrs. R, which lasted six sessions, drew on a mix of theoretical perspectives. The approach was active, crisis oriented, short-term, with a focus on the present problem (Parad, 1965). Mrs. R was helped to do the grief work necessary to come to terms with the loss of her sister (Glick et al., 1974; Lindemann, 1944; Pincus, 1975). She talked about her sister's death and her regret at not having been sufficiently understanding of her during her lifetime. The social worker helped Mrs. R draw on past strengths and previous coping patterns to adapt to her changing situation in life (Hartmann, 1964; Wasserman, 1979). Her wish for continued independence was recognized as a positive attitude stemming from a lifelong pattern that was compatible with the values of society (Berezin, 1978). However, yet it was suggested that she could act as a role model for her adult children by allowing herself to become more dependent upon them when it was appropriate. By accepting her limitations gracefully, she could show them an example of successful aging. At the same time, the social worker educated the client about the advances in lens implants and contact lenses following cataract surgery, and Mrs. R said she would reconsider having the operation in the hope that better vision would enable her to get around more easily. Treatment terminated with Mrs. R reporting a more honest relationship with her daughters, and acceptance of their help when it was appropriate, and a lessening of her symptoms of anxiety and depression.

Age Related Emotional Problems

Sleep Disorders

Many elderly clients complain of insomnia. Chronic, lifelong insomnia is often associated with emotional conflict. The anxiety the elderly experience about poor sleeping habits probably produces more harm than the actual lack of sleep. Therefore, a social worker should be familiar with the normal sleep patterns of the aged not in order to dismiss the complaints but in order to reassure the client that old people take longer to fall asleep, their sleep is lighter, and they have more frequent awakenings than is the case with younger individuals. Clients should be encouraged to pursue simple rituals at bedtime, such as taking a warm bath, having a glass of warm milk, or using eye shields to keep out light. Active sexual activity, including masturbation, can be an excellent sleep inducer (Butler & Lewis, 1977). Regular exercise during the day, if possible (walking is fine), and avoidance of caffeine after late afternoon will also help. If clients have great difficulty falling asleep, they should get out of bed, turn on the light, and read or watch television until they feel drowsy.

Many old people take medication for insomnia, although such medication loses its effectiveness when taken over a long period of time. Chloral hydrate is effective and relatively safe as a sleep medication; doxepin (Sinequan) relieves anxiety and depression and also helps alleviate sleep disorders; barbiturates such as phenobarbital and secobarbital (Seconal) may produce hangover and delirium or may have the paradoxical effect of causing stimulation; flurazepam (Dalmane) has been known to cause confusion and light-headedness in the aged and should be administered in small doses (Butler & Lewis, 1977; Walker & Brodie, 1980). As with any condition requiring medication, collaboration with the attending physician is of paramount importance.

Problems with Sexuality

Probably the most commonplace myth about old people is that they are uninterested in sex. Normal sexual activity continues into old age unless serious illness or the lack of a partner interferes. Indeed, older women have reported having more sexual enjoyment after menopause because they are no longer concerned about pregnancy (Neugarten, 1968). Women who experience a decline in vaginal lubrication as a result of aging can be counseled to use a lubricant. Older men require a longer period of time to achieve erection and may need more tactile stimulation, but they also have greater control of ejaculation. Fear of nonperformance can lead to impotence in the older man and counseling of both partners either jointly or individually can be very reassuring (Butler & Lewis, 1971). Persistent problems in the area of sexuality, as in other disorders, may have to be referred for medical or psychiatric consultation (Glover, 1977).

The attitudes of society toward sexuality in old age can be particularly harmful in institutions that make no provisions for privacy and even have an unspoken conspiracy to prevent sexual contacts. Nevertheless, as staff members on the night shift will report, where there is a will, there is a way, and lounge areas in ambulatory facilities are often crowded with couples!

Death and Dying

> Today, after decades of silence, there is a plethora of books and articles on the subject of death and dying [bringing] a new, burgeoning awareness that dying people are people with needs that can be attended to and that the process of dying presents some problems that can be solved or ameliorated with the help of the social worker. (Pilsecker, 1975, p. 190)

A conspiracy of silence around the subject is usually related to the professional person's discomfort with thoughts of dying and not to any reticence on the part of the patient. Indeed, it has been found that dying people often appreciate the chance to talk openly about their situation and are relieved when given an opportunity to do so (Kübler-Ross, 1970). It is generally agreed that the dying person needs to know the truth, but that it should be tempered with optimism (Weisberg, 1974). Their greatest fear is usually that they will die alone and in pain, and they need reassurance that someone will always be in attendance and that pain will be alleviated. Hospitals and nursing homes are offering staff training to increase sensitivity to the needs of dying patients and to help all professionals deal with their own feelings about death. Hospice beds are being set aside to meet the special needs of these patients.

This is a time when reminiscence and the "life review" are particularly applicable techniques to relieve anxiety (Butler, 1963; Pincus, 1970). This process encourages a reexamination of past experiences with the goal of resolving old conflicts. Some positive results can be a patching up of relationships and a sense of identity and self-esteem in remembering past accomplishments. Discretion is advised, however, in case the review leads to feelings of despair that one's life has not been worthwhile.

Profound religious and philosophical convictions regarding immortality and an afterlife help people accept approaching death with equanimity, and the social worker needs to collaborate with the client's priest, minister, or rabbi in order to take advantage of the therapeutic value of such convictions. At the very least, even if the social worker does not share these beliefs, she should not interfere with them if they are held by the client.

Families can be aided during this period by allowing them to talk about their grief and to experience anticipatory mourning.

Mental Disorders of Aging

Depression

Depression is the most common of all mental disorders and it is particularly prevalent in senescence, a time when the individual suffers multiple losses—loss of friends and family members; loss of role, status, and therefore self-esteem; and loss of health and sensory function, with accompanying damaged self-image. Brief, simple depressive episodes might be regarded as inevitable concomitants of these losses (Zetzel, 1978). Such depression is referred to as "reactive" because it is triggered by external events. On the other hand, depression associated with intropsychic conflict has no apparent precipitating cause. Another classification distinguishes between "neurotic depression" and "psychotic depression" on the basis of the severity of the psychopathology. Psychotic depression is accompanied by serious impairment of reality testing, along with guilt and massive self-reproach, profoundly diminishing the person's capacity to meet the ordinary demands of life. Classification of depression in the aged is complex, with suicide a serious risk (the elderly account for 25% of reported suicides). Therefore, psychiatric consultation is recommended. Drug therapy or electroshock therapy may be indicated in severe cases (Zung, 1980). The social worker should be guided by a functional approach, determining through the client's symptoms and response to therapy whether or not he can be restored to a previous level of adaptation through social work treatment.

Common symptoms of depression are insomnia, with difficulty falling asleep as well as early morning awakening; poor appetite or excessive eating; constipation; crying spells; feelings of hopelessness, helplessness, and worthlessness; and suicidal thoughts. Depression in the aged can be masked by somatic complaints and can be induced by excessive doses of tranquilizing medication such as diazepam (Valium), a popular and much overused drug (Comfort, 1980; Reidenberg, 1980). At low doses, amitriptyline (Elavil), imipramine (Tofranil), and doxepin (Sinequan) have been found to be effective for depression in the aged (Butler & Lewis, 1977).

Mrs. L, age 79, widowed 40 years ago, was referred by her physician for counseling. She had developed numerous somatic complaints for which he could find no physical cause. Evaluation revealed a history of chronic depression, beginning with a brief psychiatric hospitalization following the birth of her first child. After the sudden and untimely death of her husband, Mrs. L, left without funds, opened a small retail business, raised two children, and sent them through college. She immersed herself in work all her life, taking little time off for pleasure. At age 72 she retired, feeling that she deserved some rest, but instead of enjoying retirement she grew increasingly despondent. Most recently, her family had been making plans for a gala eightieth birthday party in her honor. Instead of looking forward to the celebration, Mrs. L was horrified at the prospect and begged that the party be called off. Meanwhile, she developed a variety of aches and pains that required frequent visits to her physician, who was unable to alleviate her symptoms. Exploring her feelings about approaching 80, Mrs. L said she hated growing old and useless and often wished she were dead.

The worker concluded that Mrs. L was experiencing a situational crisis (the approaching birthday) superimposed on a reactive depression (following retirement), possibly aggravated by a lifelong history of depression. Treatment focused on Mrs. L's negative view of herself and other old people as "useless." Basically depressed all her life, Mrs. L had derived whatever self-esteem she possessed from her role as the family provider. When retirement robbed her of this role, she felt useless. Using Beck's (1976) principles of cognitive therapy, the worker showed Mrs. L how her negative thoughts about herself were contributing to her depression. Through the relationship, using persuasion, encouragement, and re-education, the worker influenced Mrs. L to adopt a more positive attitude toward the future (Brussel & Irwin, 1973). She was urged to investigate volunteer work in the community in order to regain mastery over her environment. Through her church, she found work in a nearby hospital once a week. She was soon a familiar sight in the hospital corridors, with staff exclaiming about her remarkable vitality. She had found a substitute role for the one she had lost through retirement. The birthday party was a success; Mrs. L enjoyed it more than she had expected. Therapy, which had lasted six months, was gradually terminated, but Mrs. L and the social worker continued to talk occasionally by telephone.

Hypochondriasis

Hypochondriasis is a condition in which the client expresses an overconcern with matters of health and reports bodily complaints for which there are no apparent physical bases. This condition may be used to ward off anxiety and may also be a means of communicating with others. There is much overlap between depression and hypochondriasis. Anyone who has worked in a medical facility serving the aged is familiar with the long line of regulars waiting each day to see the physician. These people should not be dismissed as having imaginary complaints. They need to be listened to in order to relieve their anxiety (Butler & Lewis, 1977).

Paranoia*

Paranoid states can vary from mild suspiciousness and mistrust of people to severe delusions of persecution. The symptoms can be related to a long-standing personality disorder, or they can be an overreaction to the physical limitations and losses experienced by aged persons. ''The paranoid symptoms represent the patient's attempt to deny his disabilities and to counteract a feeling of loss of control by blaming others, frequently a relative or neighbor'' (Jacobson, 1981, p. 803). In extreme forms of paranoia, especially when associated with schizophrenia or brain disease, drug therapy is indicated. Haloperidol (Haldol) is often used successfully. However, mild paranoid reactions are often amenable to social work treatment (Ross, 1978).

Miss M, an 85-year-old woman who had never married and who lived alone in a middle-income housing development, had applied for an apartment in a residence for the elderly. The residence rejected her application, stating that Miss M needed more assistance than the facility could provide, but she refused to consider the health related facility recommended for her. She was referred to a social worker for help in finding suitable living arrangements. Interviews were conducted in the client's home.

Miss M was furious at having had her application for the residence rejected after having been on a waiting list for over a year. She did not understand how it had been determined, on the basis of one interview, that she was not an appropriate candidate for the facility. She wanted to move from her present apartment because she was convinced that a former housekeeper was breaking in and stealing her things. She had twice changed her locks, but she was still concerned because she thought that this woman had befriended the locksmith and was getting duplicate keys. Miss M was particularly upset about the disappearance of her half-fare card for public transportation. She desperately wanted to move but did not want to live in an institution.

The social worker used Goldfarb's (1969) concept of a therapeutic dependence relationship in treating Miss M's paranoia. According to Goldfarb, the losses of senescence lead to a decreased sense of mastery, feelings of helplessness and fear, and a search for aid. Within the security of a dependent relationship, patients may become relatively self-sufficient. Miss M was experiencing memory loss and had undoubtedly misplaced her half-fare card. The worker carefully avoided taking a position for or against the reality of Miss M's perceptions and concentrated only on gaining her trust and recognizing her feelings. For example, after a breathless account of how the housekeeper had copied the keys, let herself in during Miss M's absence, and stolen the half-fare card, the worker said, ''How upset you are, Miss M!'' She responded, ''You are the first person I have spoken to about this who really understands me.''

* See Chapter 13.

The social worker visited weekly for almost a year, helping Miss M with routine correspondence, with telephone calls about social security and Medicare benefits, and with finding and interviewing a new housekeeper. However, most of the time, she just sat and listened to Miss M's complaints about storekeepers, neighbors, the landlord, and the various clinics she had to attend. Little by little, the idea of moving to a health related facility was introduced as a way of finding a safe place in which to live, a place in which Miss M would be protected from the environment she felt was so hostile and in which she could get medical care when she needed it. Miss M finally hired a taxi, visited the recommended facility, and made an application on her own. The social worker came to her apartment on moving day and visited her several times in the facility after she was settled, intervening only once with the administration when Miss M had a problem with the dining room staff.

Senile Psychosis

Late life schizophrenia, characterized by withdrawal and isolation, with accompanying thought disorder, personality impairment, and sometimes delusions and hallucinations, may be chronic schizophrenia carried into old age or may be associated with brain disease. It is rare to see a newly developed schizophrenic disorder in an older person (Butler & Lewis, 1977). Drug treatment is usually indicated, with chloropromazine (Thorazine) and thioridazine (Mellaril) among those medications most frequently prescribed. These drugs have strong sedative properties but a low incidence of undesirable side effects such as involuntary movement disorders (Walker & Brodie, 1980). Social work treatment should concentrate on environmental intervention for the patient and on helping families cope. Some state mental hospitals, local psychiatric hospitals, and community mental health centers have mobile geriatric teams that make emergency home visits when individuals are unable to take care of themselves and are posing a danger to themselves or to others.

When there is no family, a social agency may have to provide court ordered protective services (Fisher & Solomon, 1974; Wasser, 1971). A social worker acting as a case manager in such a situation becomes involved in an intervention that has not been requested by the client and is carried out only for those who are most disabled and incompetent. This situation may conflict with social work's basic belief in client self-determination and creates stress for the social worker. The task here is to bolster the client's sense of personal integrity and not allow the dependence that accompanies the receipt of protective services to "carry a price tag of moral degradation or infantilization" (Monk, 1981, p. 64). Clients who resist protective services should be approached with gentle persuasion and their self-esteem injured as little as possible.

Age Related Organic Mental Disorders

Organic mental disorders are the most prevalent psychiatric disorders of later life. Surveys have found organic mental disorder in 20% or more of persons over age 80 (Raskind & Storrie, 1980). But many such disorders are treatable, and even in those that are irreversible the client can benefit from environmental supports that make the most of his remaining strengths. The essential feature of the organic mental disorders is transient or permanent brain dysfunction due to a primary brain disease, a systemic disease, or drugs or other toxic substances affecting the brain.

The term "acute reversible brain syndrome," formerly used to describe transient brain dysfunction, has been replaced in DSM III by the term "delirium." "Chronic irreversible brain syndrome," formerly used to describe permanent brain dysfunction, has been replaced with the term "dementia." The older definitions were imprecise and led to confusion, unreliability, and age prejudicial reactions in communicating about the psychopathology of senescence. "Senility" has been and, unfortunately, is still being used as a catchall term to describe any signs of *confusion*, forgetfulness, or *disorientation* in an aged person. Physicians will sometimes write "OBS" (organic brain syndrome) or "OMS" (organic mental syndrome) on hospital charts of aged patients instead of taking the time to make a more valid and reliable diagnosis. The misdiagnosis of dementia has been shown to result in denial of care to the elderly (Glassman, 1980). Social workers have a responsibility to their aged clients to refer them for good diagnostic workups when they show signs of brain dysfunction.

All organ systems suffer cell loss as the body ages, and the loss of brain cells has generally been thought to be responsible for the progressive decline in mental functioning that is seen in many aged clients. However, disease of brain tissue is implicated in many mental disorders and sophisticated neurological examination, including a number of laboratory procedures, is often necessary to pinpoint the cause of brain dysfunction in the aged. Even then, it is not always possible, with the present state of knowledge, to make a definitive diagnosis. The social worker, by skillful interviewing and careful observation, can evaluate memory impairment, disorientation to time, place, or person, lack of judgment, and the presence of delusions as part of a preliminary assessment of the presence and severity of mental impairment in the client.

Dementia

There are two common types of senile dementia: in the condition termed "senile dementia of the Alzheimer type," senile plaques and neurofibrillary tangles are found in the brain; in dementia due to cerebral arteriosclerosis, damage to the blood vessels interferes with blood flow to the brain, causing deterioration of cerebral tissue (Butler & Lewis, 1977). The symptoms of both types are severe memory impairment; confusion; and disorientation first to time, then to place, and finally to person, with the client unable to identify close relatives and, in the last stages of Alzheimer's and related diseases, unable to differentiate between self and others. There is also a lack of judgment, deterioration in self-care, impairment of thought processes, lack of affect, and, finally, helplessness, with bladder and bowel incontinence. Social isolation, environmental stress, and preexisting personality problems can play a part in the development of dementia. During the early stages, the individual is aware of the decline and often uses denial to cope with the attendant anxiety and depression. This can make management difficult, as there is an unwillingness to accept help. Paranoia, agitation, and hostility may be secondary behavioral features of the dementia. These behaviors can usually be controlled with medication if there is someone to administer it regularly. Haldo, Mellaril, Thorazine, Navane, and Stelazine have all been used to decrease agitation and hostility, although there is the danger of side effects such as lethargy, increased confusion, and involuntary movement disorders (Raskind & Storrie, 1980). Since there have been no definitive, controlled studies on the effectiveness of these drugs, physicians follow their personal preferences, based on their own experiences.

Environmental supports that make the most of the client's remaining strengths are extremely important techniques for social work intervention in cases of senile dementia. Some institutions put up bulletin boards indicating the date, including the day of the week, but these, of course, must be kept current to be effective. Color coding has been used to help people find their rooms. Even in the client's home, simple aids can be effective in lessening confusion and disorientation, as long as the setting is basically safe.

Mr. W, age 88, was frequently agitated upon awakening and telephoned his daughter-in-law in a panic almost every morining, worried that he would forget his appointments for the day—a visit to the doctor, dentist, or podiatrist or an occasional luncheon date with a friend. The family consulted a social worker, who made a home visit and found that Mr. W was managing in his hotel apartment in spite of some memory loss and occasional confusion. There was an elevator operator on duty and someone at the switchboard at all times. In addition, a maid came in to straighten up every morning.

In spite of all this protection, Mr. W had difficulty getting started for the day—hence the phone calls. The social worker suggested a consultation with a geriatric psychiatrist, whose diagnosis was cerebral arteriosclerosis. The daughter-in-law was advised to telephone Mr. W in the mornings rather than wait for his call. She matter-of-factly reminded him what day it was and talked calmly about his plans for the day. A large calendar, with a page for each day, was placed on his bedside table, and Mr. W got into the habit of tearing off the top sheet every night upon retiring. If he forgot, the maid made sure that the calendar was up-to-date. A digital clock with large, easy-to-read numbers was provided. These aids lessened Mr. W's early morning confusion, and he was able to manage for many months, until his deteriorating condition required that he have a companion.

The sister and brother-in-law of Miss S, age 72, called a social worker for advice about her symptoms of "senility," which they had noticed six months previously but which had recently grown worse. The social worker made a home visit and noticed rolls of toilet tissue on a chair in the living room and a box of dry cereal on the floor in the bedroom. Engaging Miss S in conversation—asking simple questions about how she spent her time, where she shopped, what day of the week it was—the worker soon realized that Miss S did not know where she was, what day it was, or what her sister was named. The social worker recommended an emergency consultation with a neurologist, who hospitalized Miss S immediately for a diagnostic workup. From the hospital she was placed in a nursing home, where she died in less than a year. The diagnosis was advanced Alzheimer's disease.

Delirium

The symptoms of this reversible brain disorder are similar to those of dementia; thus, a careful history and a complete medical workup are important in order to differentiate between a condition that is fixed and untreatable and one that could respond to treatment. Possible causes of delirium are physical illnesses such as congestive heart failure, malnutrition and anemia, infection, cerebrovascular accidents (commonly called "strokes"), head trauma, alcoholism, drastic environmental changes, sudden bereavement, and drug toxicity (Butler & Lewis, 1977). Any one or a combination of these factors can lead to symptoms resembling dementia in aged persons.

Dementia occurs in a normal state of consciousness, has a gradual onset, and its most prominent symptoms are memory impairment and loss of intellectual capacities. Delirium can also show features of defective reasoning, disorientation, and memory impairment, but it is characterized by a clouded state of consciousness, rapid onset, and a fluctuating course with lucid intervals. A more active therapeutic approach is indicated in delirium. Aged persons with treatable, temporary brain dysfunction must not be written off as senile.

Drug Toxicity

The social worker making a home visit is often in a position to pick up evidence of drug toxicity. There is a great potential for drug abuse among the elderly, as they often collect both over-the-counter and prescription drugs and sometimes take these medications indiscriminately. An examination of a client's medicine cabinet can be alarming. Minor tranquilizers and barbiturates are the most frequently abused: "These patients are particularly at risk for 'doctor hopping' and may be receiving prescriptions for tranquillizers and sedative hypnotics from a number of different sources" (Busse & Blazer, 1980, p. 412). It has been said that the most common cause of sudden, unexplained mental illness in the old is medication, "self administered, doctor administered, or borrowed from neighbors" (Comfort, 1980, p. 3). When drug toxicity is suspected, it should be called to the attention of a physician, whether the client is at home or in an institution. This, of course, will require the client's cooperation. The social worker who has developed a trusting relationship with the client can encourage her to collect all the medicine bottles in a plastic bag and bring them to the next appointment with the physician (Comfort, 1980).

Mrs. G, age 83, slept poorly, could not manage her own affairs, had lost interest in life, and spent most of the day in bed. Very unsteady on her feet, she was unable to walk to the bathroom without assistance. Her physician advised the family to think about nursing homes, and they consulted a social worker, who made a home visit. Mrs. G was fearful of nursing home placement and asked the social worker to help her remain in her own home. The client's speech was slurred, and the worker suspected drug toxicity. Mrs. G was getting various medications from her regular physician, and she also received prescriptions for tranquilizers from an elderly practitioner who had an office in her apartment building. It took a number of home visits to establish a trusting relationship with Mrs. G, who then agreed to a consultation with a geriatric psychiatrist. The worker accompanied Mrs. G to the psychiatrist and convinced her to bring along all the pills she was taking. The psychiatrist confirmed that large doses of sleeping medication in combination with tranquilizers were responsible for Mrs. G's condition. She changed Mrs. G's medication, saw her regularly to monitor for adverse side effects, and, within six weeks, the client was again leading a normal life.

Group Work for Problems in Aging

Group Work with the Aged

Group work has been used successfully with aged clients wherever they gather. The nature of the setting and the needs of the individuals determine the composition and the goals of the group, as well as the role of the professional in relation to the members. Therapy groups in which the goal is to change attitudes and modify behavior are not generally found in settings serving the aged. Task centered groups formed to solve common problems and achieve mutual purposes are more common. Groups are also used for educational, recreational, and socialization purposes; in the sense that they maintain mental health, they can be considered therapeutic.

A group can provide its members with a sense of belonging, can replace lost relationships, and can alleviate the loneliness and isolation that often accompany old age. Older persons involved in a decisionmaking group have an opportunity to achieve control and mastery over some aspect of their lives, thereby contributing to increased self-esteem and counteracting feelings of uselessness that come from being outside the mainstream of society (Lowy, 1962, 1963a; Shore, 1952).

Mr. F, an 80-year-old widower, had been a successful businessman. Now a resident of a nursing home in a large city, he suffered from congestive heart failure, requiring an oxygen tank at his bedside at all times. He had little to do with the other residents, preferring to keep to himself, reading or watching television, and, when he felt well enough, attending an occasional concert in the auditorium. His social worker convinced him to attend a few group meetings in the lounge on his floor, and his intelligence and organizational abilities were immediately noticed by the other residents. He was chosen to represent his section on the resident council and soon was elected chairman. The council became involved in many matters pertaining to the general welfare of the residents of the nursing home: members were instrumental in getting the telephone company to install an additional public telephone in one of the lounges, and a meeting with a representative of the city department of transportation resulted in the resetting of the traffic signal at the corner to give ambulatory residents more time to get across the busy intersection. The council's proudest moment came when, in collaboration with resident councils from other nursing homes in the city, it succeeded through petitioning legislators in changing a federal regulation governing the number of days a Medicaid recipient could be absent from the home to visit family members. Needless to say, everyone benefited from these group experiences, especially Mr. F, who as able to leave his bed more often and who seemed to have less need of the emergency oxygen.

Group Work with Families of the Aged

Group meetings have been helpful to families of the aged. Friends and relatives councils in nursing homes give family members emotional support and a constructive role in the care of their relatives. Family members who are maintaining the elderly at home have opportunities to join self-help groups to discuss common problems and seek solutions. Manuals to help families organize such groups are available from the Family Service Association of America, the Community Service Society of New York, and the Institute of Gerontology of the University of Michigan at Ann Arbor, to name a few. The Alzheimer's Disease and Related Disorders Association holds group meetings at locations all over the United States for relatives of patients suffering from these disorders. Through sharing their problems and collectively devising strategies for practical management, many families have been helped to cope with the severe stress of caring for a mentally disabled relative.

Family Treatment for Problems in Aging

Therapy for Adult Children

One of the myths about the care of the aged is that the nuclear family's increasing isolation has caused a lessening of filial responsibility in the past few generations. On the contrary, adult children have been found to be intensely involved in helping their parents cope with a wide range of problems (Simos, 1973) and have been found to provide extensive assistance to their elders at substantial sacrifice and strain (Monk, 1979). Ackerman (1958), a pioneer in family therapy, pointed out a crisis in the life of one member of a family may have pervasive effects on the mental health of the others. With four- and even five-generation families becoming the norm, problems of the elderly can have a far-reaching impact on families, with even the youngest children reacting emotionally to events in the lives of their grandparents and great-grandparents. Family counseling, therefore, is an important aspect of social work treatment of the psychopathology of senescence. While the parent is coping with the developmental tasks of aging, the family, with a life cycle of its own, is involved in developmental tasks that may not mesh with the needs of the individual members (O'Connell, 1972):

> At a time when the parent needs help adjusting to the aging process, the adult children are facing the problems of menopause, the climacteric, and retirement; grandchildren are experiencing the difficulties of adolescence or new marriages; great grandchildren are being born and are claiming the attention of the family. . . . Struggling with their own developmental tasks, adult family members have little energy left to invest in helping the aging parent. (Kirschner, 1979, p. 209)

Yet the family's help and emotional support are crucial whether the parent is living in an institution or being maintained at home. The mental health of an aged parent is often dependent on good family relationships, and the social worker who shows sensitivity to the needs of family members does a great service to the aged client.

Unresolved conflicts of the past can interfere with the capacity of a family to help a parent cope with the problems of aging. Adult children, regressing to childhood roles, may be unable to act in an appropriately firm manner when a crisis tests their capacity to be depended upon by the parent (Savitsky & Sharkey, 1972). Social work intervention can help adult children achieve the stage of "filial maturity," in which they free themselves of their childhood roles in relation to their parents so that they can be depended upon to assume the responsibilities that the situation demands (Blenkner, 1965). Parents wanting to maintain their independence for as long as possible will sometimes deny their need for help, and adult children unable to deal with everyone's anxiety will then maintain a conspiracy of silence about the parent's changing condition. Bringing the entire family together to talk openly about the problem is usually a relief for all. The social worker should avoid uncovering the past except for the purpose of learning about the parent's previous lifestyle and how he coped with crises. With a therapeutic focus on the present, family communication is made easier and strengths can be found in all the generations to help everyone adapt to the parent's changing needs (Kirschner, 1979). Sometimes it is necessary to work separately with the adult children before arranging a family interview that includes the parent. The children may have been struggling with the problem for months, unsure of how to proceed and when to intervene. Some families infantalize their elders, prematurely taking over decisionmaking for them. Other families wait too long to offer help. Our society gives no guidelines to adult children struggling to find the right formula for helping aged parents without sacrificing their own lives or overlooking the needs of the younger generation. Professional intervention can help families take the steps necessary to resolve a crisis related to an aged parent.

Mrs. A, age 49, married and the mother of two teenagers, consulted a social worker at the suggestion of her physician. She had been suffering from headaches, which he thought were the result of stress she was under regarding her husband's parents. Her father-in-law, age 87, who suffered from senile dementia, had recently been discharged from the hospital after having had emergency prostate surgery. Her mother-in-law, age 77, had a chronic cardiac condition, yet she had roomed in with her husband at the hospital. The elderly man had no memory and poor judgment. His mental condition had deteriorated over the past two years and he needed help in most activities of daily living. For example, he would put his shoes on his bare feet and then try to pull on his socks over his shoes. In the bathroom, he was unable to differentiate between the hot and cold water faucets and tried to urinate in the wash basin. After the surgery, his disorientation increased; yet his wife insisted on caring for him at home and would not let her children hire any help.

The mother-in-law really could not manage, however, and called her daughter-in-law constantly for advice. Mr. A told his wife that his mother had always catered to his father and he did not think she would ever accept any help. Apparently, the son was not aware of how much his wife was involved, and she, on her part, wanted to spare him and did not know whether she should urge him to intervene with his parents. Meanwhile, her headaches got worse.

The social worker suggested that Mrs. A bring her husband to the next interview. She helped them communicate more openly about the problem, and Mr. A admitted that he had been trying to avoid the issue becuase it reminded him of painful situations in the past when he had felt neglected because his mother was so involved with father. He recognized that a more mature attitude was needed, especially since his wife was now being drawn into his parents' problems. An interview was scheduled in the parents' home with the entire family participating. The mother surprised Mr. and Mrs. A by agreeing to hire a part-time attendant for her husband, who appeared to have no objection to the arrangement. The social worker, in a follow-up telephone call, learned that the father was getting along well with the attendant and the mother was telling everyone, "My son insisted that I get help at home," thereby saving face and assuaging and guilt she was feeling about relinquishing some of the caretaking role.

Families in crisis can be helped in a few meaningful sessions if the social worker takes an active approach to relieve tensions (Parad, 1965) and is flexible about home visits, individual and family interviews, and follow-up telephone calls: "The social worker must be genuinely accessible, and should not become involved with an aging family unless . . . prepared to see them through their crisis" (Kirschner, 1979, p. 211).

Therapy for Aged Couples

Aging may bring stress to a previously happily marriage or create new situations that exacerbate old problems. Such factors as the children leaving home, retirement, and chronic illness all contribute to a change of roles and require that the couple adapt to each other's needs in ways they may not have anticipated. Inability to cope with these changes may cause one or both of the partners to seek help. The goals of marital counseling for older couples should be to diminish anxiety and help them accept the realities of their changed circumstances. Couples who have had a satisfactory relationship over many years can generally be helped through a situational crisis. A poor marriage, on the other hand, may not survive the transition to old age, especially if the partners have lifelong personality problems that interfere with adjustment to change. If such a marriage does survive, the partners will probably be locked into their psychopathologic patterns of relating to each other.

Mrs. J, age 63, consulted a social worker for help in changing the direction of her life. Influenced by the women's movement, she wanted to get a job and be self-supporting, although she had not worked since her early twenties. Consultation with her physician uncovered a history of depressive episodes, and evaluation of the interaction in the interview suggested the possibility of a thought disorder. Further exploration revealed that her husband, age 68, wanted to retire and move to another city, a plan that terrified Mrs. J. The desire to pursue a career and be self-supporting at this stage of her life, given her emotional problems, was unrealistic, and the worker suggested joint interviews with the husband with the goal of arriving at a plan for their future that would be acceptable to both partners. Mr. J turned out to be a passive man, who through 38 stormy years of marriage had always deferred to his wife in important decisions. He now suffered from a cardiac condition and had been told by his physician that he should stop working. Mrs. J recognized intellectually that some change in their lifestyle was necessary, and her husband, unable to carry out his plans without her approval, waited for her to make a decision for both of them. During several months of counseling, Mrs. J vacillated constantly while Mr. J remained immobilized. They then broke off treatment, no closer to a solution than when they had started. The marriage remained intact, with no change in the long-standing pathological interaction. Presumably, it would take another crisis to force a shift in their behavior.

Conclusion

The social work treatment of the psychopathology of senescence is varied and complex and no approach to practice can cover every situation. The senescent client cannot be described as a single entity. There are more differences than similarities among people of this age group. Likewise, social work practice differs across settings, depending on the definition of the professional function. For example, the social worker in a senior center may recognize the need for family treatment but may be prevented from carrying it out because of the constraints imposed by the agency.

In general, some treatment principles are applicable to all elderly clients wherever they are found. People who have lived to be 70, 80, or older are *survivors* and they must be presumed to have developed strengths during a lifetime of diversified experiences. The social work task is to draw on these strengths, to remind clients that they have overcome difficulties in the past, and to help them, through an optimistic approach, to make the most of the time they have left.

Jarvik (1976) stated what she considers to be perhaps the most important unanswered question about aging:

> Given [the] biological changes, the rising frequency of somatic illness, physiological decline, physical debilities, malnutrition, overmedication (iatrogenic or self-induced), sensory deficits, reduction in mental agility, economic deprivations, social losses, and the increasing proximity of death, all of which are associated with advancing chronological age, why is not every old person in a profound state of depression?(p. 326)

This is an appropriate question for social work investigation. If we can define the characteristics of the nondepressed elderly, we may have an important new key to treatment approaches. Isolating such variables as early childhood history, family mental health, parental marital history, and sibling relationships may give us a clue to factors that contribute to, or mitigate against, the development of depression in an aging person. The effect of environmental factors on mental health can be a rich source of information. Much research is being conducted in these areas, but more needs to be done. If we can develop a profile of an aging person who is able to cope with losses while maintaining an optimistic view of the future, we may better understand where and how to use our strategies for intervention with those aged individuals who need professional help.

References

ACKERMAN NA: *The Psychodynamics of Family Life.* New York, Basic Books, 1958.

American Psychiatric Association: *Diagnostic and Statistical Manual of Mental Disorders,* ed 3. Washington, DC, American Psychiatric Association, 1980.

BECK AT: *Cognitive Therapy and Emotional Disorders.* New York, International Universities Press, 1976.

BEREZIN MA: Some intrapsychic aspects of aging, in Steury S, Blank ML (eds): *Readings in Psychotherapy with Older People,* US Dept of Health, Education, and Welfare publication no. 78–409. Rockville, National Institute of Mental Health, 1978, pp 30–39.

BLANK ML: Raising the age barrier to psychotherapy, in Steury S, Blank ML (eds): *Readings in Psychotherapy with Older People,* US Dept Health, Education, and Welfare publication no. 78–409. Rockville, National Institute of Mental Health, 1978, pp 62–67.

BLENKNER M: Social work and family relationships in later life, with some thoughts on filial maturity, in Shanas E, Streib G (eds): *Social Structure and the Family.* Englewood Cliffs, Prentice-Hall, 1965, pp. 46–59.

BRODY EM: The aging family. *Gerontologist* 1966; 6:201–206.

BRODY EM: Aging is a family affair. *Public Welfare* 1967; 25:129–133.

BRODY EM: Serving the aged: educational needs as viewed by practice. *Soc Work* 1970; 15:42–51.

BRODY EM: *Long Term Care of Older People: A Practical Guide.* New York, Human Sciences, 1977.

BRODY EM: Long term care of the aged: promises and prospects. *Health and Soc Work* 1979; 4:29–59.

BRODY EM, BRODY S: Decade of decision for the elderly. *Soc Work* 1974; 19:544–554.

BRODY BM, SPARK GM: Institutionalization of the elderly: a family crisis. *Fam Process* 1966; 5:76–90.

BRUSSEL JA, IRWIN T: *Understanding and Overcoming Depression.* New York, Hawthorne, 1973.

BUSSE EW, BLAZER DG: Disorders related to biological functioning, in Busse EW,

Blazer DG (eds): *Handbook of Geriatric Psychiatry.* New York, Van Nostrand Reinhold, 1980, pp 390–414.

Busse EW, Blazer DG (eds): *Handbook of Geriatric Psychiatry.* New York, Van Nostrand Reinhold, 1980.

Butler RN: The life review: an interpretation of reminiscence in the aged. *Psychiatry* 1963; 26:65–76.

Butler RN: *Why Survive? Being Old in America.* New York, Harper & Row, 1975.

Butler RN, Lewis MI: *Sex after Sixty.* New York, Harper & Row, 1971.

Butler RN, Lewis MI: *Aging and Mental Health,* ed 2. St. Louis, Mosby, 1977.

Casework with the aging. *Soc Casework* 1961; 42:219–290. Proceedings of a Seminar held at Arden House, Harriman Campus of Columbia University, October 30–November 4, 1960.

Comfort A: *Practice of Geriatric Psychiatry.* New York, Elsevier, 1980.

Council on Social Work Education: *Toward Better Understanding of the Aging.* Aspen, Council on Social Work Edcuation, 1958.

Dancy J: *The Black Elderly: A Guide for Practitioners.* Ann Arbor, University of Michigan Institute of Gerontology, 1977.

Erikson E: Identity and the life cycle. *Psychol Issues* 1959; 1:18–171.

Fisher LD, Solomon JR: Guardianship: a protective service program for the aged. *Soc Casework* 1974; 55:618–621.

Francis H, Guthartz JC, Preston F, Bienstock IJ: Serving the older person: a multiple approach by the family agency. *Soc Casework* 1954; 35:299–308.

Gaitz CM, Varner RV: Adjustment disorders of late life: stress disorders, in Busse EW, Blazer DG (eds): *Handbook of Geriatric Psychiatry.* New York, Van Nostrand Reinhold, 1980, pp 381–389.

Gitterman, A. & Germain, C. Social work practice: a life model. *Soc Serv Rev* 1976; 50:601–610.

Glassman M: Misdiagnosis of senile dementia: denial of care to the elderly. *Soc Work* 1980; 25:288–292.

Glick IO, Weiss RS, Parkes CM: *The First Year of Bereavement.* New York, Wiley, 1974.

Glover BH: Sex counseling of the elderly. *Hosp Pract* 1977; 12:101–113.

Goldfarb AI: The psychodynamics of dependency and the search for aid, in Kalish RA (ed): *The Dependencies of Old People.* Detroit, Wayne State University Institute of Gerontology, 1969, pp 1–16.

Hartmann H: *Essays on Ego Psychology.* New York, International Universities Press, 1964.

Jacobson SB: Psychiatric treatment of the aged. *NY State J Med* 1981; 81:802–804.

Jarvik LF: Aging and depression: some unanswered questions. *J Gerontol* 1976; 31:324–326.

Kirschner C: The aging family in crisis: a problem in living. *Soc Casework* 1979; 60:209–216.

Kosberg JI (ed): *Working with and for the Aged.* Washington, DC, National Association of Social Workers, 1979.

Kübler-Ross E: *On Death and Dying.* New York, Macmillan, 1970.

Leach JM: The intergenerational approach in casework with the aging. *Soc Casework* 1964; 45:144–149.

Lindemann E: Symptomatology and management of acute grief. *Am J Psychiatry* 1944; 101: 141–148.

Linden ME: Transference in gerontologic group psychotherapy, in Steury S, Blank ML (eds): *Readings in Psychotherapy with Older People,* US Dept of Health, Education, and Welfare publication no. 78–409. Rockville, National Institute of Mental Health, 1978, pp 146–156.

Lowy L: *Adult Education and Group Work.* New York, Whiteside, 1955.

Lowy L: Decision making and group work, in Bernstein S (ed): *Explorations in Group Work.* Boston, Boston University School of Social Work, 1962. (a)

Lowy L: The group in social work with the aged. *Soc Work* 1962; 7:43–50. (b)

Lowy L: Meeting the needs of the aged on a differential basis, in Proceedings of the Seminar *Social Group Work with Older People.* Lake Mohouk , N.Y., June 5–10, 1961. New York, National Association of Social Workers, 1963, pp. 43–67.

Lowy L: Roadblocks in group work practice with older people. *Gerontologist* 1967; 7:109–113.

Lowy L: *Social Work with the Aging.* New York, Harper & Row, 1979.

Lum D, et al The psychosocial needs of the Chinese elderly. *Soc Casework* 1980; 61: 100–106.

Mailick M, Ashley AA: Politics of interprofessional collaboration: challenge to advocacy. *Soc Casework* 1981; 62:131–137.

Meerloo JA: Transference and resistance in geriatric psychotherapy, in Steury S, Blank ML (eds): *Readings in Psychotherapy with Older People,* US Dept of Health, Education, and Welfare publication no. 78–409. Rockville, National Institute of Mental Health, 1978, pp 86–93.

Meyer CH: Social work purpose: status by choice or coercion? *Soc Work* 1981; 26:69–75.

Meyer CH (ed): *Social Work with the Aging.* National Association of Social Workers, Washingtion, 1975.

Milloy M: Casework with the older person and his family. *Soc Casework* 1964; 45:450–456.

Minahan A, Pincus A: Conceptual framework for social work practice. *Soc Work* 1977; 22:347–352.

Monk A: Family supports in old age. *Soc Work* 1979; 24: 533–539.

Monk A: Social work with the aged: principles of practice. *Soc Work* 1981; 26:61–68.

Social Group Work with Older People. National Association of Social Workers, Washington, 1963.

Neugarten BL: *Middle Age and Aging.* Chicago, University of Chicago Press, 1968.

O'Connell P: Family developmental tasks. *Smith Coll Stud Soc Work* 1972; 42:203–210.

PALMORE EB (comp): *Normal Aging: Reports from the Duke University Longitudinal Study.* Durham, Duke University Press, 1970-1974.

PARAD HJ: *Crisis Intervention: Selected Readings.* New York, Family Service Association, 1965.

PILSECKER C: Help for the dying. *Soc Work* 1975; 20:190-194.

PINCUS A: Reminiscence in aging and its implications for social work practice. *Soc Work* 1970; 15:47-53.

PINCUS L: *Death and the Family: The Importance of Mourning.* New York, Pantheon, 1975.

POSNER W: Adapting and sharpening social work knowledge and skills in serving the aged. *Soc Work* 1957; 2:37-42.

RANDALL O: The aged. *Soc Work Yearbook* 1945; 8:36-39.

RASKIND MA, STORRIE MC: The organic mental disorders, in Busse EW, Blazer DG (eds): *Handbook of Geriatric Psychiatry.* New York, Van Nostrand Reinhold, 1980, pp 305-328.

RED HORSE JG: American Indian elders: unifiers of Indian families. *Soc Casework* 1980; 61:490-493.

REIDENBERG MM: Drugs in the elderly. *Bull NY Acad Med* 1980; 56:703-714.

ROSENGARTEN L: Taking on a filial role to care for frail elderly. *Pract Dig* 1980; 3:10-14.

ROSS F: Social work treatment of a paranoid personality in a geriatric institution, in Steury S, Blank ML (eds): *Readings in Psychotherapy with Older People,* US Dept of Health, Education, and Welfare publication no. 78-409. Rockville, National Institute of Mental Health, 1978, pp 102-116.

ROSSMAN I: Bodily changes with aging, in Busse EW, Blazer DG (eds): *Handbook of Geriatric Psychiatry.* New York, Van Nostrand Reinhold, 1980, pp 125-146.

SALCIDO RM: Problems of the Mexican American elderly in an urban society. *Soc Casework* 1979; 60:609-615.

SAVITSKY E, SHARKEY H: The geriatric patient and his family: a study of family interaction in the aged. *J Geriatr Psychiatry* 1972; 5:3-19.

SHORE H: Group work program development in homes for the aged. *Soc Serv Rev* 1952; 26:181-194.

SILVERSTONE B, HYMAN HK: *You and Your Aging Parent,* New York, Pantheon, 1976.

SIMOS BG: Adult children and their aging parents. *Soc Work* 1973; 18:78-85.

SOYER D: Reverie on working with the aged, in Turner FJ (ed): *Differential Diagnosis and Treatment in Social Work,* ed 2. New York, Free Press, 1976, pp 150-155.

U.S. Bureau of the Census: Statistical Abstract of the United States, ed. 100. Washington, D.C. 1979.

WALKER JA, BRODIE HKH: Neuropharmacology of aging, in Busse EW, Blazer DG (eds): *Handbook of Geriatric Psychiatry.* New York, Van Nostrand Reinhold, 1980, pp 120-124.

WASSER E: *Creative Approaches to Casework with the Aging.* New York, Family Service Association, 1966.

WASSER E: Protective practice in serving the mentally impaired aged. *Soc Casework* 1971; 52: 510–522.

WASSERMAN SL: Ego psychology, in Turner FJ (ed): *Social Work Treatment*, ed 2. New York, Free Press, 1979, pp 33–68.

WEISBERG LM: Casework with the terminally ill. *Soc Casework* 1974; 55:337–342.

WICKENDEN E: *The Needs of Older People and Public Welfare Services to Meet Them.* Chicago, American Public Welfare Association, 1953.

WILLIAMS JB: D.S.M. III: a comprehensive approach to diagnosis. *Soc Work* 1981; 26: 101–106.

ZETZEL ER: The dynamics of the metapsychology of the aging process, in *Readings in Psychotherapy with Older People* Rockville, National Institute of Mental Health, 1978, pp 40–44.

ZUNG WWK: Affective disorders, in Busse EW, Blazer DG (eds): *Handbook of Geriatric Psychiatry*. New York, Van Nostrand Reinhold, 1980, pp 338–367.

Index

557